SCIENCE, TECHNOLOGY AND SOCIETY

A Cross-Disciplinary Perspective

THE INTERNATIONAL COUNCIL FOR SCIENCE POLICY STUDIES

OFFICERS

President: Prof. J.-J. Salomon
OECD and *Conservatoire National des Arts et Métiers*
Paris, France

Vice-Presidents: Prof. S. R. Mikulinski   Prof. D. de Solla Price
Academy of Sciences of the USSR *Yale University*
Moscow, USSR   *New Haven, Connecticut, USA*

Dr. A. Rahman
Council of Scientific and Industrial Research
New Delhi, India

Secretary-Treasurer: Prof. I. Spiegel-Rösing
Universität Ulm
Ulm, FRG

EFFECTIVE MEMBERS

Prof. A. Diemer
Universität Düsseldorf
Düsseldorf, FRG

Prof. G. Dobrov
Institute of Cybernetics
Kiev, USSR

Prof S. Encel
The University of New
South Wales
Kensington, Australia

Dr. J. Farkas
Hungarian Academy of Sciences
Budapest, Hungary

Prof. C. Freeman
University of Sussex
Sussex, UK

Dr. N. Jecquier
OECD
Paris, France

Prof. B. Schroeder-Gudehus
University of Montreal
Montreal, Canada

Prof. E. B. Skolnikoff
Massachusetts Institute of Technology
Cambridge, Massachusetts, USA

Prof. G. Kröber
Akademie der Wissenschaften der DDR
Berlin, GDR

Dr. R. MacLeod
University of Sussex
Sussex, UK

Prof. I. Malecki
Université Technique de Varsovie
Warsaw, Poland

Prof. E. Mendelsohn
Harvard University
Cambridge, Massachusetts, USA

Prof. R. Richta
Czechoslovak Academy of Sciences
Prague, Czechoslovakia

Dr. M. Roche
IVIC
Caracas, Venezuela

Dr. N. Stefanov
Academy of Sciences
Sofia, Bulgaria

Dr. B. Walentynowicz
Polish Academy of Sciences
Warsaw, Poland

Dr. A. Zahlan
Arab Projects and Developments
Beirut, Lebanon

SCIENCE, TECHNOLOGY AND SOCIETY

A Cross-Disciplinary Perspective

Edited by
Ina Spiegel-Rösing and **Derek de Solla Price**

under the aegis of the
International Council for Science Policy Studies

SAGE Publications
London and Beverly Hills

For information address

SAGE Publications Ltd
44 Hatton Garden
London EC1N 8ER

SAGE Publications Inc
275 South Beverly Drive
Beverly Hills, California 90212

International Standard Book Number
Cloth O 8O39 9858 9

Library of Congress Catalog Card Number
76-55928

First Printing

CONTENTS

PREFACE

The genesis of this volume is bound up with an important step in the international organization of scholars in several social science disciplines who share an interest in examining the social and policy dimensions of science and technology. The prehistory of this movement goes back many years (See MacLeod, 1974[1]), but the decisive new beginning arose from the formation of the International Council (then Commission) for Science Policy Studies at the XIIIth International Congress of the History of Science in Moscow in the summer of 1971. This group had its first formal meeting at Schloss Reisesburg in South Germany in the following year. The idea of this volume had already come about when the editors met in Amsterdam earlier in 1972. As we discussed our researches and the fact that we come from different disciplines and academic traditions, we uncovered a strong need for some sort of cross-disciplinary mode of access to this entire spectrum of scholarship. At the Reisesburg meeting we diffidently proposed an outline of this desideratum as part of the program for the group. Though difficulties were obvious, the idea proved to be infectious and we were charged with pursuing the project further under the aegis of the Council. By the time of the next meeting we had drafted an extended outline, circulated it widely beyond the membership of the Council, and received useful feedback.[2] At this meeting in

---

[1] R. MacLeod, 'The Historical Context of the International Commission for Science Policy Studies', in J.-J. Salomon and I. Spiegel-Rösing, (Eds.), *Science Policy Studies Contributions,* ICSPS, International Union for the History and Philosophy of Science, Tokyo, 1974, pp. 202-210.

[2] We are grateful for the comments received from J. Annerstedt, S. Blume, R. Bowers, J. Goldhar, J. Knudsen, J. Kreutzkam, Z. Kowalewski, M. Moravcsik, A. Rahman, E. Shils, B. Walentynowicz, R. D. Whitley and P. Weingart.

1

Delhi in 1973 we were able to present the consequently improved and expanded version, and also to report the gratifying news that the Ford Foundation had accepted our proposal for the financial backing necessary to such a project. Work now began on the extremely crucial and difficult task of selecting a team of authors from all the different disciplines and fields we felt had to be incorporated. In the course of this work, the contents and boundaries of the sections had to be specified and negotiated with prospective authors. Our procedure was to send each prospect a statement of the concept of the book and its organization, outlining the contents we proposed for his or her section. Not all bids were successful, but we eventually assembled the team.

In the course of drafting every chapter there were kilos of correspondence back and forth between the editors and the authors, sorting out matters of detail and emphasis, positions to be taken and explained. The next stage, somewhat unusual for any cooperative work but an essential part of our scheme to form a comprehensive yet coordinated exposition, was a four-day conference of all authors in Paris in April 1975. Each author had been sent by the editors a fairly lengthy and detailed critique of their draft. At the conference this was amplified by a full discussion in which all authors joined in the task of providing foundations for the reworking of the draft.

During the next year the completed chapters with all revisions and amplifications were finished and the editors then conferred for six days, reviewing the assembled manuscripts and editing them, often rather heavily, into the complete volume. Many considerable changes were made; the link passages were added in the last process.

Already in the conception of this volume we had seen it must comprise three main sections. In the first section we felt it was necessary to state the contextual values of science and technology in society, particularly the evolving critical attitudes to science and technology and the interplay between the making of science policy and our scholarly understanding of all these processes.

In the second section we had to take each of the scholarly disciplines which constituted the 'social study of science and technology' and combine them. This has been far from the ideal presentation for a set of related topics, but this organization was forced on us by the very fragmentation of this sort of research, by its focus on separate disciplines. It is our hope that this juxtaposition will begin a process of cross-disciplinary accessibility.

Third, we have organized a section around types of issues in science policy (i.e. science policy studies). In this the authors come from a single wide discipline but bring to bear very different modes of attack on their range of topics. Here it is not the disciplinary separation but the intradisciplinary specialization which we have tried to bridge by juxtaposing them to each other and to the previous section.

Thus, the purpose of this volume is primarily to contribute to the intellectual integration of a field, and it is directed mainly toward scholars in the various constituent subfields. We hope it may also serve some purposes in teaching and for science policy makers in the field of science and government, but these can only be secondary and subsequent tasks. Teaching and application are related to particular national systems and these cannot easily be combined with the cross-nationality of scholarship. In particular, we have not therefore surveyed the large literature devoted to the analysis of management of research and development, nor the burgeoning discussion of technical scientific content of specific current technologies.

The cross-nationality of scholarship notwithstanding, we have made no extensive review of the corpus of literature from the socialist world. This is an error, not of omission, but of default. Our original intention had been to have for each chapter a related counter-chapter but this proved to be infinitely more difficult that the interdisciplinary and intradisciplinary bridges we did attempt. Within our framework of resources it could not be done.

In a volume that includes the sociological analysis of scientific collaboration, we cannot escape a comment on the division of editorial tasks. During the entire process a considerably greater part of the work load has been borne by the editor who is first named precisely for that reason.

We have received widespread support and help for this project. The International Council for Science Policy Studies has given us continual reinforcement, encouragement and a forum for discussion. In particular we record our thanks to Günter Kröber and to A. Rahman. The Ford Foundation gave crucial and generous support without which nothing could have been done. The authors gave an unusual amount of detailed and painstaking collaboration. Roy MacLeod, Sanford Lakoff and Georges Ferné were consultants for particular sections, and Jerome Ravetz gave splendid overall advice and criticism. Many others gave important and valuable services which are acknowledged in the individual chapters. In addition to these, our special thanks are due to our secretaries, Marie-Luise Hefuna and Ann Leskowitz, and to our editorial assistant, Catharine Parsons. To all of them our deepest thanks and gratitude.

I. Spiegel-Rösing
D. de Solla Price

1

The Normative and Professional Contexts

I. SPIEGEL-RÖSING
JEAN-JACQUES SALOMON
J. R. RAVETZ

Chapter 1

THE STUDY OF SCIENCE, TECHNOLOGY AND SOCIETY (SSTS): RECENT TRENDS AND FUTURE CHALLENGES

I. Spiegel-Rösing

Universität Ulm

INSTITUTIONAL DEVELOPMENT AND 'REGIONALIZATIONS'

Origins of the field We cannot claim that altruism, curiosity, the search for truth, or any other ulterior motive is the source from which the study of science, technology and society (SSTS) grew. Neither can we state that the disinterested pursuit of knowledge or the practical solutions that this study offers has been the mainspring of its maintenance and expansion.

The study of science, technology and society is, as Jean-Jacques Salomon has put it, born of war (Salomon, 1973, and Chapter 2 of this book).[1] World War II is a crucial turning point in the changed relationship of science to

---

'Studies of science, technology and society' (SSTS) will be used throughout this chapter as the generic term which refers to both 'social studies of science' (SSS) and 'science policy studies' (SPS). No special importance is attached to this particular term; other ones would do equally well.

I gratefully acknowledge the comments which I received on the draft of this chapter from Roy MacLeod, Jean-Jacques Salomon, Jerry Ravetz and Dorothy Nelkin.

[1] This is not to deny a much longer intellectual history of the field. As in all other fields in the process of institutionalization, SSTS researchers are busy writing the histories of their field as part of its 'disciplinary ideology' (Hagstrom, 1965). For some 'Western' historical highlights of the field see Salomon, Chapter 2; for some 'Eastern' accounts see Dobrow, 1974a. There is even some East-West consensus on some of the 'fathers' of the field, such as Ossowska and Ossowski, 1936, and Bernal, 1939. But there is no doubt that the extensive institutional development of the field is a post World War II development.

power, i.e. military, economic and political power. It is this very change which led to the largely dominant political attitude of *laissez faire* toward the development of science, and to massive government support of science; in turn, this trend led to the need for control and direction of science, with the concomitant need for instrumental knowledge of control. There are certainly other aspects of the development of science which have contributed essentially to the development of studies on science and technology, such as the enormous *quantitative* growth of science, its growing capital intensity, its new problems of communication, and the *qualitative* changes in internal (disciplinary and subdisciplinary) and organizational structure (big science institutions, science as a wage work). Most of these conditions, however, can themselves be significantly traced back to the new experience in the scale of use of science and technology in World War II.

If war, economic expediency and political power are essential conditions in the origin and early institutional development of the field of SSTS, then the misdirection of science and technology, the consequent widespread disillusionment about their unconditional usefulness and desirability, are important ingredients of its recent development. There is an imbalance in the development of research fields, with glamorous natural sciences and technological fields by far outweighing the socially relevant 'soft' sciences. Social problems — involving urbanization, traffic, drug abuse, youth criminality — have been eclipsed by the publicity surrounding the Apollo moon shots. There has been political and public apathy and irresponsibility toward the negative side effects of unchecked scientific development, the consequences of which are tragically evident in the ecological degradation of our natural environment. All this has combined to produce a forceful 'anti-science' climate. The inescapable limits of budgetary growth, combined with the need for equal funding for *all* sciences, has led to a new political rhetoric if not an actual reorientation of priorities at the national level toward social goals for the development of science and technology (Freeman *et al.,* 1971). One of the most important documents of this new orientation is the well-known Brooks Report (OÉCD, 1971). The following few paragraphs quoted from this report show the extraordinary spectrum of difficulties that arises from such intended redirection of science priorities. In great part this exerpt outlines the problems for which SSTS research must find solutions:

> The conditions for the success achieved in many space and defence projects are not yet evident in the social sphere. The goals are complex, unclear, and the subject of conflicting interests and a wide diversity of values and preferences among the people affected. The underlying basic knowledge is spotty, fragmented, and often not firmly established in a scientific consensus. Not only is it more difficult to achieve the ends proposed, but also, if not mainly, it is more difficult to determine what the ends themselves should be. In a democratic society, the problem of goal-setting gives rise to an arbitration between conflicts of interests, in a context of imperfect information, ambiguity, negotiation, and divergent pressures. Competing value judgements multiply between budget considerations of economy and political considerations of needs and effectiveness.

Furthermore, even if there is a consensus on the value to be attached to certain social ends, this is not sufficient to determine the programmes that can meet them. Many of our social goals are stated in too generalized terms to be readily translatable into concrete, applied research tasks — at least in the present state of basic understanding. Moreover, we are dealing not with a single, simple goal but with a complex of mutually dependent and interacting goals. If we commit ourselves exclusively to achieving one goal, we may find that we have created entirely new problems or failed on other goals of equal importance. Thus the situation is something like a soft pillow which, when we push it in one place, bulges out in another. These difficulties are particularly great in the case of R & D activities because the state of knowledge is not even sufficient to allow us to specify what we don't know and hence to design the research to find it out, let alone develop the necessary remedies (OECD, 1971, 56).

Research in the field of SSTS has always derived its justification and support by promising solutions to problems of science and technology in view of dominant political goals. In the course of investigating these problems, SSTS researchers have already developed an expanding body of knowledge on the functioning of science and technology within society. This body of knowledge is certainly one — although not the most important — reason for the continued development of SSTS research. What is more important is the professional interest of the people doing the research. There is nothing special about SSTS researchers' professional self-interest; status maintenance strategies are part of the politics of all fields of research (Spiegel-Rösing, 1974), and the absence of such strategies may, as we know from historical examples, lead to the 'death' of a field in spite of its intellectual fruitfulness (Fisher, 1966, 1967). Thus the intellectual content of the field, its relation to what is deemed politically relevant and urgent, combined with the self-perpetuating force of its practitioners, form what we can see today as the institutional make-up of SSTS.

Institutional development While the conditions for the emergence of a special field of investigation into the development and use of science and technology have existed since World War II, and while important although rather technocratically oriented research has been done since that time, the massive institutional development of the field did not begin in most countries until the mid-1960's. Today SSTS exhibits all the signs of an institutional field, such as specialized research institutions and teaching programs, organization at a national and international level, and specialized media of communication.[2]

Specialized research institutions for SSTS have developed in many

---

[2] For a more comprehensive picture of present institutional development within the field, the reader is referred to the growing number of national state-of-the-art reports that have recently been published. For references, see 7 and 8 on page 12. Additional references for institutional development will be given only when available in the journal literature or as books.

countries. In the United States Cornell University has established the 'Program on Science, Technology and Society' and Harvard University, the Program on Public Conceptions of Science'. In Canada there is the 'Institut d'Histoire et de Socio-Politique des Sciences' at the University of Montreal. The USSR boasts the 'Institute for the History of Science and Technology' at the Academy of Sciences, Moscow, and the 'Department of Interdisciplinary Problems of Science Studies and Information Science' in Kiev. In Great Britain Sussex University has a 'Science Policy Research Unit' and Edinburgh University, a 'Science Studies Unit'. In France there are the 'Centre de Recherche Science, Technologie et Société' of the Conservatoire National des Arts et Métiers and the 'Groupe d'Etudes et de Recherche sur la Science' of the Ecole Pratique de Hautes Etudes, both located in Paris. Sweden has the 'Research Policy Program' at Lund University and the 'Institute for Science Theory' at Göteborg University. Finally, in the Federal Republic of Germany, a 'Science Studies Unit' is located at the University of Bielefeld and an 'Institute for Science Policy Studies' at the University of Ulm; while in the German Democratic Republic there is the 'Institute for Theory, History and Organization of Science' at the Academy of Sciences, Berlin. These are but a few examples of a growing trend.[3]

At the national level, SSTS researchers have organized themselves in informal groups or formal sections or societies. Again, a few examples may illustrate this development. In the United States a 'Society for Social Studies of Science' has recently been created with a membership approaching three hundred people after a few months of existence. In Great Britain SSTS researchers meet regularly as the British Sociological Association's 'Sociology of Science Study Group' (See Whitley, 1975), and in France as the 'Club de Gif' (See Bardos, 1973). In Poland there is the 'Committee of the Science of Science' at the Polish Academy of Sciences (See Walentynowicz, 1975), and in the Federal Republic of Germany the German Sociological Association has created a 'Section for Science Studies' (Wissenschaftsforschung). All of these groups meet regularly, organize conferences, exchange research information and edit newsletters and/or reports on their activities.

SSTS has also organized at the international level with the 'Sociology of Science Research Committee' of the International Sociological Association; the 'Parex Group' which, starting with a Paris-Sussex cooperation, is developing into a kind of European federation of SSTS researchers; and the 'International Council for Science Policy Studies', which is a section in the Division of History of the International Union for the History and Philosophy of

---

[3] For most of these institutions regular reports are available; for a more complete list of institutions, see the country reports mentioned in footnote 7 on page 12. Short portraits of SSTS research institutions in many countries appear in Baitsch *et al.*, 1974.

Science.[4]

Research in the field is financed by many sources, but there are also some special public programs for the promotion of research in the field, such as those in Science Resources and policy studies at the National Science Foundation in the United States; the Action Thématique Programmée (ATP) Recherche sur la Recherche, at the CNRS in France; and the priority area Science Studies (Wissenschaftsforschung) of the Volkswagen Foundation in the Federal Republic of Germany.

With the expanding research in SSTS, specialized media of communication, such as journals, publication series, newsletters and information bulletins, have increased. Thus in the USSR there are several special journals for this field, such as *Naukovedonie i Informatika*. In Poland the Committee of the Science of Science publishes very actively in the journal *Zagadnienia Naukoznawstwa* and the annual or biannual review *Problems of the Science of Science*. In several countries journals that have first been special information organs for their sponsoring science policy bodies have increasingly moved toward including professional articles in the field. Thus in France the DGRST has developed the journal *Progrès Scientifique* under the editorship of J.-P. Bardos; and in the Federal Republic of Germany the Stifterverband für die Deutsche Wissenschaft publishes *Wirtschaft und Wissenschaft (Economy and Science)*. Several international journals have also been created for the field; among the more important ones are *Social Studies of Science (An International Review of Research in the Social Dimensions of Science and Technology)*, *Research Policy (A Journal Devoted to Research Policy, Research Management and Planning)*, and *Minerva (A Review of Science, Learning and Policy)*.

There are some SSTS research institutions which have created their own regular media of publication: as for instance the two series *Studies and Research Reports* and *Science and Society* (Akademie-Verlag) of the German Democratic Republic's Institute for Theory, History and Organization of Science; or the series *Science Studies Reports* of the Science Studies Unit of the Federal Republic of Germany's University of Bielefeld. In addition to journals and special series of publications, there is an increasing number of news and information letters in the field which report on institutional developments, on new research programs, on publications, positions, conferences and workshops. Examples of these are the *SSSS Newsletter* (published by the Society for the Social Study of Science), the *Stopnews: Interdisciplinary Newsletter on Science, Technology, Public Policy and Sociology* (published by the Science, Technology, Public Policy and Sociology

---

[4] For reports available in journals and as books on the work of the International Council for Science Policy Studies, see Rahman (1972), Skolnikoff (1973), Schroeder-Gudehus (1974), MacLeod (1974), Salomon and Spiegel-Rösing (1974) and Spiegel-Rösing and MacLeod (1976).

Program of Purdue University), and the *Newsletter* (published by the Harvard University Program on Public Conceptions of Science).

With the expansion of the field an increasing need has developed for secondary information sources. Dictionaries of terms have therefore been published,[5] as have regular bibliographies,[6] country reports[7] and international reviews of the institutional development of the field.[8] In addition to this, an interchange of experience is increasingly being organized in the teaching area. Thus the journal *Social Studies of Science* publishes regular course bibliographies in related fields,[9] and the SISCON group is preparing special teaching material.[10] Finally, review articles on teaching efforts in various countries are now beginning to appear.[11]

With all this rather vigorous institutional development, a tentative professional identity has been developed in the field. Gradually, discussion on the definition of the field, its internal structure, its boundaries, its disciplinary status, its relationship to other fields, has subsided.[12] There is much research work to be done, from many perspectives, and matters of definition and subdivision have been seen as increasingly irrelevant to this effort. However, at least two kinds of subdivision, or 'regionalization', as I prefer to call it, are usually distinguished and should be mentioned. These regionalizations are reflected in the cognitive and institutional development of the field; the first is sociopolitical and the second is cognitive or intellectual.

Sociopolitical regionalization   In a very preliminary way, at least two sociopolitical regions can be identified in the study of science and technology and society; for purposes of brevity let me call these East (socialist) and West (bourgeois). Though the emphasis of the present volume is explicitly on the Western part of the field, I would like to point out at least a few similarities

---

[5] See *Science Policy: A Working Glossary*, Third Edition 1976.

[6] Such as the monthly bibliography *Current Literature on Science of Science*, edited by A. Rahman of the Council of Scientific and Industrial Research, New Delhi; and the quarterly *Bibliography on Science Policy Studies and Notes on Institutional Development*, edited by I. Spiegel-Rösing of the Institute of Science Policy Studies, University of Ulm. In addition, many of the journals and newsletters of the field publish regular bibliographies.

[7] USA: Teaching and Research (1973), Heitowit and Epstein (1975). USSR: Mirsky (1972), Rabkine (1974). Poland: Walentynowicz (1975). GDR: Altner (1971), Spiegel-Rösing (1973a). FRG: Baitsch *et al.* (1974). France: Recherche sur la Recherche (1973).

[8] Such as Baitsch *et al.* (1974).

[9] Easlea (1973), Nelkin *et al.* (1974), Jamison and Elzinga (1975) and Bloor (1975).

[10] For a list of SISCON publications: Dr. W. F. Williams, Physics Administration Building, University of Leeds.

[11] Lowe and Worboys (1975); Rip and Boeker (1975).

[12] This has, perhaps, been most consciously debated in the socialist countries. See Mirsky (1972), Rabkine (1974), Kröber and Laitko (1972, 1975).

and differences between them and to note some sources for further study.

At a superficial glance East and West look very similar with respect to their research emphasis (See Figure 1). Their 'interest profiles', based on self-reported research emphasis of individual SSTS research within socialist[13] and nonsocialist[14] countries, are significantly correlated for the following sixteen areas of research:[15]

1. Philosophy (including methodology and logics) of science and theory of science.
2. Ethics of science.
3. Sociology of science.
4. Classification of scientific fields and disciplines.
5. Creativity and psychology of researchers.
6. History of organization of science and of scientific communities.
7. Organization, administration and management of R & D (including information and communication).
8. Economics, productivity, efficacy, financing, etc., of R & D.
9. Statistics of science and technology.
10. Planning of R & D, planning of human resources in science and technology, public policy for science and technology (including relations with education, economy, foreign affairs, industry, health, agriculture, environment, etc.).
11. Technological forecasting, futurology.
12. International science policies, international cooperation in science and technology, comparative study of national science policies.
13. Legislation of science and technology.
14. Transfer of technology.
15. Assessment of technology.
16. Science and society; popularization of science.

The similarities in research emphasis between socialist and nonsocialist countries which are apparent in Figure 1 are, of course, a reflection of the data base of the UNESCO (1971) survey on which I have based this analysis. They may also significantly reflect the time period at which the original UNESCO data were collected (1970-1971). But other observers of the de-

---

[13] The socialist countries include Bulgaria, Czechoslovakia, Hungary, Poland, Rumania, the Ukraine, the USSR and Yugoslavia.

[14] The nonsocialist countries include Austria, Belgium, Denmark, France, Federal Republic of Germany, Iceland, Ireland, Italy, the Netherlands, Norway, Spain, Sweden, Switzerland, Turkey and the United Kingdom, as well as the United States and Canada.

[15] I have based this analysis on UNESCO (1971). For more detail, see I. Spiegel-Rösing, 'A Note on Activity and Interest Profiles of Science Policy Study Units in Europe and North America', in *Science and Society,* Poland, in press (summary in Baitsch *et al.,* 1974, 87-93).

Figure 1:

Science Policy Interest Profiles of European and
North American UNESCO Member States (UNESCO, 1971)

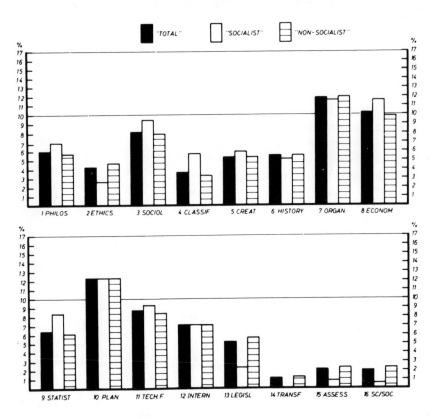

velopment of the field have also pointed to the important first-glance similarities in research emphasis between East and West (Rabkine, 1974). These
superficial quantitative similarities do, however, blur some of the important
and indeed fruitful qualitative differences between socialist and nonsocialist
approaches to the study of science, technology and society.

A first difference is the apparently closer relationship in the socialist
countries between SSTS research and political legitimation. I have already
tried to show this in a preliminary way for the USSR[16] and in a more
thorough analysis for the German Democratic Republic (Spiegel-Rösing,
1973a). A second difference seems to me to be a stronger, basically technocratic orientation in the socialist countries on questions of organization and

---

[16] See my chapter on the development of science policy studies in the USSR in
Baitsch *et al.*, (1974, 169-179).

management of science and technology, and particularly on efficiency of research. This is, for instance, reflected in some socialist definitions of the field:

> Science of science is the integrated investigation of experiences on the functioning of scientific systems; its goal is the working out of methods in order to increase – by way of organization – the resources of science and the effectivity of research.[17]

Or in Rabkine's words (1974, 47):

> Assurément, les contextes idéologiques et politiques sont différents; mais on ne peut qu'être frappé par la similitude des préoccupations et des attentes. Cependant, il y a des frontières très nettes comme celle que trace l'aspiration en U.R.S.S. à une 'gestion scientifique' de la science, liée a l'essor de la cybernétique, de l'informatique et de la prévision technologique: c'est là une aspiration dont seuls témoignent en Occident les scientifiques positivistes et parfois les technocrates.

Whether one follows this last polemic or not, a stronger socialist orientation to problems of efficiency of science and technology, their planning, prediction and control, accords well with the socialist premise that a 'socialist society can only be built to plan, according to scientific principles, and in accordance with the laws of development of society as recognized by Marxism-Leninism' (Kröber and Laitko, 1972, 17). Quantitatively as I have shown in Figure 1, there seemed to be no difference in 1971 between socialist and nonsocialist countries with respect to those areas of research relevant to questions of efficiency, planning and prognosis (Nos. 7-11 on the list shown earlier and in Figure 1). It may well be that because of the basic socialist premise of the necessity of a planned and systematic development of society, certain recent developments which have seemed in the West to lead away from such orientation have not occured in the socialist countries. But this is a hypothesis which needs much more careful comparative analysis.

A third difference, somewhat opposed to the one just mentioned, is a much stronger preoccupation in socialist countries with the basic underlying conceptual and ideological problems of the development of science, technology and society. This is perhaps best illustrated by the research program of the GDR Institute for Theory, History and Organization of Science, which has a strong position within the SSTS efforts of COMENCON countries.[18] The development of a comprehensive, complex, basic theory of science is seen as the precondition for progress in the field:

> Science is a societal phenomenon. Its real position in the socialist society, its function as a weapon in class struggle, as an instrument in the direction of societal processes of

---

[17] See Dobrow (1974a, 21) for more detail and for the research program based on this definition. See also Dobrow 1970a, 1970b, 1971a, 1971b, 1971c, 1974b.

[18] See the volume on the COMENCON symposium on 'Science and Research in Socialism', in Kröber *et al.*, 1974.

development as a productive force, its role as a sphere of development of socialist personalities, as well as its contribution to the societal reproduction process, require an exact theoretical formulation of the essence of science and of its developmental regularities in order to be able, on this basis, to direct, plan and organize the real processes of science efficiently (Kröber and Laitko, 1972, 17).

... A theory is necessary which is able to give a coherent theoretical representation of socialist science as a basis of its conscious development . . . . It is incontestable that research on science needs a complex theoretical center. For this we prefer . . . the term Marxist-Leninist Theory of Science . . . . The presently most important epistemological task in the development of science of science is, therefore, its theoretical synthesis . . . . We think that the transition of science of science from the stage of an interdisciplinary federation to the status of a new discipline is characterized by the development of the Marxist-Leninist Theory of Science (Kröber and Laitko, 1975, 153-155).

Whether we choose to emphasize these and other differences between a socialist and a bourgeois approach to the study of science, technology and society rather than their similarities is, of course, a matter of personal taste and ideological position.[19] I think that much insight can be gained by examining the differences and asking how they came about. There are very few systematic descriptions and analyses of these differences (one of the few being a very stimulating comparative analysis of the bourgeois sociology of science in the Federal Republic of Germany and the socialist sociology of science in the German Democratic Republic; see Rilling, 1975), even though the investigation of the social, economic, political and cultural conditions which influence the content and direction of research is one of the most important research tasks of the field. Whether or not there are different types of science, such as socialist, bourgeois and capitalist science, one certainly cannot avoid asking whether there is a socialist and a bourgeois study of science. The increasing contribution of Third World countries to the study of science, technology and society — with India being presently particularly active[20] — opens up the additional question of whether there is an indigenous science and a third sociopolitical region of SSTS research. This, of course, is still an open question.

Cognitive regionalization and the place of 'scientometrics'   East and West agree in distinguishing two different intellectual regions in the field of the study of science, technology and society. These are: social studies of science (SSS) and science policy studies (SPS). It is not necessary to go into much

---

[19] Marxist-Leninist SSTS researchers would certainly insist on a basic difference: 'today science does not exist as a homogeneous world-wide system, but in the form of two systems of science, socialist and capitalist, which are contrary with respect to their socio-economic content' (Kröber and Laitko, 1972, 13).

[20] See, for instance, the review volume edited by Rahman and Sharma (1974); see also Rahman 1972 and 1973.

detail here about the differences between the two because this regionalization is also reflected in the structure and content of the present volume. I will only briefly mention four major differences and will then raise the question of the place of 'scientometrics' in these fields. SSS and SPS differ with respect to 1) their disciplinary origin, 2) their major sources of research questions, 3) the consequent emphasis on cognitive or operational problems and 4) their focus on science or technology.

The social studies of science – sociology, psychology, history, philosophy, etc., of science (See Part II of this volume) – are well-articulated subfields of different mother disciplines with very widely differing intellectual traditions. With the exception of the economics of science and, obviously, the history of technology, they all focus primarily on science; the social studies of science have greatly neglected technology. By doing so they have only reinforced the tendency to neglect the wider socio-political context of science – a tendency which is often criticized by reviewers of the field (e.g. Blume, 1975; Spiegel-Rösing, 1973b). This relative neglect of the wider social and political context is in part caused by the fact that many of the research questions with which they deal are generated intra-scientifically, that is, through anomalies in the research process, inconsistent results, new models, transfer of concepts from other research areas, etc. (This fact is the source of many research problems in the field.) Although they are to a considerable degree intra-scientifically determined, these research questions do not lack socio-political overtones; at the same time however, 'real world issues' are seldom the beginning of a new research program in the social studies of science. Consequently, what they try to solve in most cases are cognitive problems (to know how science functions), rather than operational problems (to know how science can be governed or directed). There are some modest signs that this intra-scientific or 'centripetal' orientation, as Blume (1974) has called it, is beginning to be overcome: there are beginnings of a political sociology of science (Blume, 1974); an increasingly self-conscious social history of science (See MacLeod, Chapter 5); a greater emphasis on a social history of technology (See Layton, Chapter 6); a philosophy of science that has started to discover models of science as a productive force (the neglect of which is, of course, exclusively 'bourgeois'; see Böhme, Chapter 9); and an economics of science that returns to the broader and more integrative political economy approach (See Freeman, Chapter 7).

Science policy studies (See Part III of this volume), on the other hand, draw primarily from a political science background. Thus they are not as fragmented as the social studies of science with respect to their disciplinary composition. Their fragmentation is along issues and national orientations. This is precisely because a much greater part of their research problems is generated extra-scientifically, i.e. in the 'real world' of science and technology; consequently they are much more oriented to operational problems in the development, direction and control of science and technology than to 'intellectual' problems in their functioning. As technology is a greater issue and problem raiser than science in the field of policy, it is precisely technology on which science policy studies largely focus. Most of them, being issue-oriented, tend to be unhistorical in approach, a fact about the field which is often criticized (See Schroeder-Gudehus, Chapter 13). In mirror image to the neglect of the socio-political sphere which often characterizes the social studies of science, there is in science policy studies a relative neglect of the internal social and cognitive functioning of science and technology, however important this may be for their control and direction. Thus we may say that science policy studies are too 'centrifugal' in their orientation (Blume, 1974).

There are several areas of research that are apt to mediate across this cognitive regionalization, and several of these are explored by the authors of this volume. At this point I would like to discuss briefly one field of research which cannot be exclusively subsumed under either one of the two cognitive regions. This field is 'scientometrics', the quantitative mathematical study of science and technology.[21] Scientometrics is not characterized by its focus on particular problem areas but by its methodology, that is to say the use of quantitative indicators of the structure and development of science in order to decide the basic regularities of their functioning and direction. The research area investigated in the scientometric tradition covers a very wide range of topics:[22] the quantitative growth of science (e.g. Derek Price, 1963; Menard, 1971); the speciality substructure in science (e.g. Small and Griffith, 1974; Griffith *et al.*, 1974; Kranze, 1972); the development of disciplines (e.g. Goffman, 1971; Meadows and O'Connor, 1971); the relationship of science and technology (e.g. Derek Price, 1965a, 1968); the 'half-life' of scientific contributions (e.g. Derek Price, 1956; Meadows, 1974, Chapter 5); the communication structure in science and in technology (Derek Price, 1971b; Crane, 1969; Zuckerman, 1970; Cole and Cole, 1973); the conditions and measurement of productivity and creativity of scientists (e.g. Derek Price, 1963; Zuckerman, 1967; Menard, 1971, Chapter 5); the relationship between scientific development and economic growth (e.g. Derek Price, 1969b); the structure and development of scientific manpower (Menard, 1971, Chapter 4; Spiegel-Rösing, 1972); and the criteria for investment in science (e.g. Derek

---

[21] This term has been coined by Derek de Solla Price, who initiated this field of research (See particularly Derek Price, 1963) and who is seen in both the East (e.g. Mirsky, 1972; Dobrow, 1974a) and the West (e.g. Wynne, 1974) as one of its most outstanding representatives. We have no special chapter on this approach in the present volume for two reasons. First, most of the chapters draw on the work of scientometrics, which is thus partly reviewed; second, Derek Price is presently preparing an integrative book on this field to be entitled *Analytical Theory of Science*.

[22] Almost the whole range of topics is perfectly illustrated by the work of Derek Price (See the selected bibliography which follows).

Price, 1971a).[23]

This incomplete list does make sufficiently clear the fact that, topically, scientometrics covers traditional research areas of both social studies of science and of science policy studies, and the fact that the data produced by scientometrics are therefore relevant to both fields. At least in this sense scientometrics can be said to mediate between the social studies of science and science policy studies. And it does not only cut across this cognitive regionalization of the field but also across its socio-political regionalization; by its very research premises and methodology it is less affected by the socio-political differences in the field. Even though I cannot subscribe to the claim that it is 'value-free', it can be maintained that socialist scientometrics[24] and bourgeois scientometrics are less different than either socialist or bourgeois social studies of science and science policy studies. Whether scientometrics, beyond its topical linkage across the socio-political regionalization, is apt to integrate these subdivisions of the field at the fundamental theoretical level is still a debated question. This may well depend on the tendencies and developments that social studies of science and science policy studies take.

TENDENCIES AND DEFICIENCIES

Some recent research tendencies in the field   Research in the field of science, technology and society has progressed through notable changes since about the beginning of the Seventies. This present section sets out to identify some of these recent tendencies. Their diagnosis is based on the contents of the present volume and on other work in the field which I happen to know; it is, therefore, a Western or bourgeois account. I cannot judge whether these tendencies do equally apply to SSTS research developments in socialist countries. Moreover, this account is speculative, subjective and normative: it represents those changes which have inspired me the most and those changes which, in my view, should be integrated into the study of science, technology and society. Thus, what I identify as tendencies in the development of research in this field may be seen as heuristic dimensions one could lay on the field, and as some possible and desirable avenues of future development.

I see five interdependent and related research tendencies emerging in the recent development of social studies of science and of science policy studies. I

---

[23] A good overall view of the field can be obtained in the following four books: Derek Price, 1963; Menard, 1971; Cole and Cole, 1973; and Meadows, 1974. For a critical review of part of scientometrics, see Gilbert and Woolgar, 1974.

[24] For the study of scientometrics in socialist countries, see Mirsky (1972), Rabkine (1976) and the bibliography of Dobrow at the end of this chapter.

would like to call these tendencies: 1) humanistic, 2) relativistic, 3) reflexive, 4) desimplifying and 5) normative. Some of these tendencies (e.g. those of desimplification) have been primarily generated 'intra-scientifically', that is to say through attempts to overcome deficiencies in the research programs themselves; others (e.g. the normative tendencies) have arisen primarily from the changed relationship of science and technology, the effects of which we are increasingly and inescapably witnessing. Coming from these different sources, these tendencies have not been equally absorbed by both social studies of science and by science policy studies since, as I have pointed out, these fields characteristically have a different major source of research questions. I shall illustrate these tendencies from research fields where they seem to emerge most visibly.

Humanistic tendencies   In the study of science, technology and society, these tendencies refer to the attempt to get the 'actor' back into the picture: the actor not as an abstract unit of analysis or a positivistic robot, but as a human being who has emotions, conflicts, inconsistencies, and who does not live in a social vacuum but rather mediates between the wider socio-political and cultural context and the kind of science which results from it. To investigate science from such a humanistic vantage point opens up at least three important broader perspectives of research in the field. First, the image of the scientist and the scientific process is subjectivized. Second, there is a shift in investigation away from preconceived concepts toward research that starts from the concepts as perceived by the actor in his specific situation – thus making new methodologies and new disciplines relevant to the study of science, technology and society. And third, we note a movement away from the technocratic perspective in investigating research management as well as science, technology and public policy making. The subjective, emotional, irregular, unpredictable and changing is coming to the foreground – certainly in part as a reflection of the wider counterculture climate.

If the image of the scientist up until now has been that of an objective, dispassionate, truth-seeking fellow, then he has certainly been dethroned. Within the sociology of science, dogmatism, resistance to innovation, the fighting of new ideas and the stubborn clinging to old ones are no longer treated as exotic exceptions to be explained away, but as important phenomena of the development of science (See Mulkay, Chapter 4). In addition, there are in the recent psychology of science, which for a long time has been paradoxically 'unhumanized' (See large sections of the review by Fisch, Chapter 8), signs which indicate that the 'subjective side of science' is being brought back into the picture, and that an important line of significant research which was initiated by Kubie (1954, 1961, 1962) is finally being investigated (See also Maslow's insistence on demechanized science; 1966). Mitroff's work (1974) is a good example of this new trend; he focuses on the affective side of scientific work: how preconceptions, emotional hang-ups, stresses and frustrations affect the scientific process. It is a significant contribution toward the balancing of the pure 'story-book image' of the scientist, as Mitroff calls it, with that of a human actor. Holton's work (1973) is equally important in this respect because of his emphasis on a 'Z-axis' in the analysis of the scientific process, on its thematic, imaginative, even illogical content, on the subjective and motivating part of scientific thinking. He has shown in several of his fascinating studies that all these ingredients are essential in allegedly hard physics.

Another aspect of this humanistic tendency is to approach phenomena not as predefined by the investigator but from the vantage point of the actor, from his perception, his definition of the situation. Significant examples can be seen in the history and sociology of science. In the program which MacLeod outlines (See Chapter 5) for a new social history of science, it is not prefixed concepts which are investigated but 'concepts devised by men and women in specific historical times'. With such a perspective, the long controversy over internal and external histories of science loses its polarization. There are other signs within the social studies of science of this return to the humanistic perspective: the growing emphasis on the ethno-methodological approach to the sociology of science (Law, 1974); the trend toward a much stronger relationship with social anthropology (Wynne, 1974) and toward anthropological field research to investigate the interest and perceptions of the people affected by science and technology. Nelkin outlines this last movement (See Chapter 11) in her proposed program for a wider perspective in the science, technology and public policy field.

There is a last tendency in SSTS research which I would also tend to subsume under the humanistic heading. It is the movement away from the technocratic optimism which has for considerable time prevailed in the operational part of science policy studies. This optimism implied that by devising techniques — PBBS and the like — the policy decision-making processes and the management of science could be rationalized; that is to say, the human element of it could be discarded. Biting critiques on the fallacy of such science policy myths have now begun to appear (e.g. Salomon, 1973). If decision making in science and technology is bound up with 'conflicting values, ambivalent attitudes and diverse interests' (See Nelkin, Chapter 11), then it cannot be mechanized; nor can measurement of some of the basic data for science policy decision making and research management, such as measurement of R & D and of technological growth (See Freeman, Chapter 7; Layton, Chapter 6). In addition, we can see in the field of science and development a movement away from simple recipes to a much broader perspective (e.g. Cooper, 1972). This movement includes an analysis of what developmental 'help' and technology transfer mean to the people of the developing country concerned, people with their indigenous culture and social and political tradition. Sardar and Rosser-Owen (Chapter 15) present a forceful example of this particular perspective on science, technology and development (even though it may be perhaps for some economics of science a bit one-sided).

Relativistic tendencies   These aspects of humanization are closely linked to and, indeed, imply a second tendency I would like to call 'relativistic'. Much of the movement away from conceptualizing the functioning of science and technology in absolute terms has come about by a process of 'historization': the observer conceptualizes phenomena, not as valid for all times, but as relative to a specific period of time. Other relativistic tendencies which have gained emphasis in SSTS refer to the cultural context, the socio-economic conditions, the particular discipline or research field, the organizational context, etc. Examples of such relativistic tendencies can be seen in both cognitive regions of the field, in both social studies of science and science policy studies.

In the philosophy of science there is a growing awareness of the epochal changes in the very parameters which support the development of science and of the historical relativity of scientific concepts. This is shown, for instance, in the growing assimilation into Anglo-American and German philosophies of science, of French epistemologists such as Foucault (See Böhme, Chapter 9). In the sociology of science, the Mertonian norms — seen for a long time as valid for science in absolute terms — are now being replaced by concepts such as cognitive and technical standards which are relative to particular fields of research (See Mulkay, Chapter 4) and relative to the wider social norms which depend on the socio-economic context and the time period involved (e.g. Rilling, 1975). With this development many traditional concepts of the sociology of science lose their absolute ring. In the older exchange framework, reward in science could be described as exchanged for 'information' or an 'original contribution', that is to say, a fixed kind of achievement. Mulkay (Chapter 4) shows that reward is now seen as conditional: relative to the prevailing cognitive framework of a research area in a particular period of time. It is this changing cognitive framework which is linked to the acceptance or rejection of ideas. In addition, there is in the economics of science an increasing tendency to take into account the epochal changes in the role of R & D in industrial innovation and in the locus of innovation in industry (See Freeman, Chapter 7). Finally, and perhaps most importantly, some of the most heatedly discussed concepts in the history of science, namely external and internal conditions in the development of science, lose their absolute meaning. What is internal and external to science cannot be defined for all times; it depends on the specific circumstances of science in different periods. Barnes (1974) has most significantly contributed to this fruitful process of relativization. MacLeod (Chapter 5) gives many further examples of the pitfalls of an 'extrapolation backwards of routine modern concepts'.

Reflexive tendencies   If we adopt the view that in investigating science and technology we must start from the perception of the actor in a specific situation and time, then we can hardly escape applying this perspective not only to science as the object of investigation, but also to the scientific researcher as the subject of investigation. The SSTS researcher is obviously also affected by his cultural and socio-economic context in the kinds of questions he raises, the methods he uses and the kind of results he deems relevant and important. He has social and personal preconceptions and preferences, and it is, of course, important to ask how these are reflected in his research. I term this increasing readiness for a critical self-analysis of research in the field a reflexive tendency. Such a reflexive attitude to research in the field raises important questions: In what way does the ideology in science and the ideology for science (Bhaskar, 1975) reflect back on the research on science? Is there, as I have asked before, a socialist and a bourgeois approach to science and technology with respect to the kinds of question that can be raised and — more importantly — that cannot? There are, I think, some definite signs of an increasing reflexive analysis of research in the field, in terms of its social, cultural, economic and political pre-conceptions.

We can in part see the recent wave of country reports as a sign of such a reflexive attitude. This view particularly applies to such studies that do indeed attempt to analyze the political and economic context in relation to the kind of research that has been done. Some attempts of this kind can be found in Rabkine (1974) for the USSR, in Spiegel-Rösing (1973a) for the GDR, and in Rip and Boeker (1975) for The Netherlands. More closely at the research level, this volume testifies in many parts to the growing reflexive tendency, perhaps most explicitly in the chapter by MacLeod, who shows that

> the hermeneutical problems inherent in any reconstruction of the pursuit of natural knowledge must involve a recognition of the historian's own traditions, beliefs and objectives . . . . A reflexive historiography . . . must accept from the knowledge of the discipline itself that the reasons why we are interested in science will affect what we say about science, the periods we choose to examine, and the view of science we take.

This is an insight which surely does not apply to the history of science alone. The sociology of science is manifesting an increasing need 'to account for itself' (Bloor, 1973); this is exemplified by Mulkay's analysis of extra-scientific factors involving the ideology of science in the preservation of some models of the development of science (such as functionalism).

In the editorial instructions which we gave the contributors to the present volume, we asked for this reflexive analysis to become an integral part of their essays. The results show that such reflexive attitudes tend to come more easily in the area of social studies of science than in that of science policy studies. This is precisely because this kind of reflexivity has mostly arisen intra-scientifically and can therefore be assimilated more easily by those research areas that do, for a significant part, generate their research problems from within.

De-simplifying tendencies There is a clearly discernable tendency in research on science, technology and society to de-simplify its approach methodologically as well as conceptually. This tendency shows itself in at least three distinguishable ways: 1) a movement away from 'black-boxism', 2) a strongly felt need for rapprochement of hitherto separate approaches, and 3) a discontent with linear, one-factor, polarized models of explanation.

By the expression 'black-boxism' we mean analysis in terms of input-output relations with no concern about what happens in between. (The 'box', after all, remains 'black' − one cannot see what is happening in there.) All varieties of black-boxism have increasingly come under attack in the study of science, technology and society. The movement away from such a simplified approach is perhaps best illustrated by recent developments in the sociology of science concerning the investigation of the conditions of scientific innovation and the reward system of science (Mulkay, Chapter 4). A similar movement has been clearly demonstrated in the study of the conditions of technological development. Layton (Chapter 6) criticizes all black-box approaches in the history of technology and suggests that technology and technological sciences be studied 'as bodies of knowledge and social systems of interaction'. In addition, there is in the economics of science a clear movement away from conceptualizing science and economic growth, on the one side, in terms of investment, and, on the other, in terms of results. Instead, economists are investigating the interacting conditions that are responsible for different input-output results (See Freeman, Chapter 7). In research concerned with the relation of science and technology to development, technology transfer has long been the big input, and economic growth, the output. Recently, however, there has been much preoccupation with examining the kind of technology in relation to the kind of social system, on the theory that these two variables are the essential conditions of whatever development results (Cooper, 1972). Sardar and Rosser-Owen (Chapter 15) clearly illustrate this de-simplifying tendency by emphasizing such concepts as alternative technology and intermediate technology, alternative education system, indigenous culture and domestication.

Another sign of this de-simplification is the emerging need for rapprochement between hitherto separate approaches and traditionally fragmented divisions of labor. There is hardly a chapter in this book which does not point out this need for integration. Böhme (Chapter 9) sees a solution to the major conceptual deficiencies in the philosophy of science only in a joint and integrated approach involving the sociology, history and philosophy of science. MacLeod (Chapter 5) points out that in a more encompassing social history of science, the study of science as part of the wider cultural context is essentially dependent on interdisciplinary collaboration. Mulkay (Chapter 4) tells us that in the field of sociology of science, the cry for an integration of separate disciplinary approaches has become a standard phrase. Fisch (Chapter 8) asks for a closer collaboration with sociologists of science in order to tackle the wider problems raised by the deficiencies of present research. Layton (Chapter 6) states that there must be an intra-disciplinary as well as an inter-disciplinary integration if the history of technology is to become fruitful; he also points out a strong need to overcome national differences in the study of technology. Freeman (Chapter 7) also demands cross-national and inter-disciplinary bridges in the area of the economics of science; indeed, he views the need to contribute to such cross-disciplinary communication as one of the major justifications for his contribution to this book. In the section of this book devoted to science policy studies there is no chapter that does not point out the dilemmas which have arisen from contradiction between the diffuse, complicated, far-reaching and intertwined issues of science and technology policy – and the fragmented approaches which various slices of disciplinary traditions have accorded them. If policy issues are interacting in myriads of ways with social, political and economic conditions (Skolnikoff, Chapter 14), how can a piecemeal approach uncover their essential dimensions?

In this context we note that a dual process is modifying the two areas of SSTS research. There is in those fields that have hitherto concentrated mainly on the social aspects of science development an increasing interest in the study of scientists' cognitive processes. This is clearly discernible, for instance, in the sociology of science (Mulkay, Chapter 4; see also Novotny, 1973). Similarly, we note in the psychology of science a growing emphasis on what scientists think, i.e. on their thought processes rather than their actions and outputs (see Fisch, Chapter 8). This trend is illustrated, for instance, by Singer's program (1971) for a psychological epistemology of science. At the same time there is a parallel process of what, somewhat unhappily, we might term 'socialization', that is to say increasing awareness of social conditions in the development of science and technology, in those fields which have hitherto concentrated almost exclusively on their cognitive aspects. This is clearly the case in the history of sciency (See MacLeod, Chapter 5). Layton (Chapter 6) points to similar tendencies in the history of technology.

A further aspect of the de-simplifying tendency in SSTS research can be seen in the burgeoning discontent with all kinds of linear models, one-factor explanations, pure descriptions, one-way models and polarized concepts. Linear models of innovation are certainly in disrepute today (See Layton, Chapter 6), as are linear concepts of technology transfer (See Freeman, Chapter 7) or development (Sardar and Rosser-Owen, Chapter 15). For Sardar and Rosser-Owen, development is not just linear economic growth but a multidimensional process, a 'strategic blend of private and collective actions with their intended and unintended consequences through which a society moves from one state of organization, one system of ideas, beliefs and traditions, and one stock of equipment to another'.

Normative tendencies   By normative tendencies I mean the increasing readiness to take the normative aspects of science and technology into account. These normative aspects involve the criticism of science and the changing public conceptions of science and technology, the ethical dimensions of the conduct and use of science and technology, the social responsibility of scientists and technologists. Again, almost every chapter in this volume exemplifies this new awareness. Thus Ravetz (Chapter 3) as well as Salomon (Chapter 2) analyze changing approaches to research on science and technology in the context of the changing role of science and technology in society; they point to the fact that the criticism of science moved 'into' science and, by doing so, into research on science as well. For Ravetz in particular, the problems that scientific and technological development raises in society and the concomitant new role of scientists are key problems of SSTS research. The need for scientists publicly to take responsibility for the consequences of their work is for him one of the central contradictions of present thinking on science and technology; he considers it to be an open question whether this contradiction will prove constructive or crippling. Salomon raises an equally fundamental question, one which research on science has curiously ignored for too long: What are science and technology for? Indeed, what kind of society is it that we want? Socialist SSTS researchers seem to have a much easier time in both posing and answering that question (See Kröber and Laitko, 1972, 1974, on socialist science studies). As there is no simple answer to this question in a pluralist society, decision making in science and technology policy cannot be a completely rationalized process. SSTS research recognizes this and recently has put more normative emphasis on the conceptualizing of decision making (See particularly Nelkin, Chapter 11; and Lakoff, Chapter 10) and on increasing analysis of the decision making process.

   This new awareness is also emerging in the social studies of science. Böhme (Chapter 9) forcefully raises the question of the relevance of the philosophy of science in order to investigate the possibility of using science more directly for social purposes. Mulkay (Chapter 9) reflects on the potential sociological problems raised by the new, expanding role of scientists and by the social demands of society. MacLeod (Chapter 5) states that the essential contribution of a social history of science to science policy is normative: 'whether the goals set by science policies and mediated by the scientific elite are serving the public interest — to that question the history of science may have much to say.'

Deficiencies   The humanistic, relativistic, reflexive, de-simplifying and normative tendencies which I have just described appear to draw a very positive and optimistic picture of the trends in the development of SSTS research fields. I have emphasized before that this account is subjective, speculative and normative. But to say this does not suffice; it is necessary that I point out some of the less happy characteristics of present-day research on science, technology and society. It is these characteristics which are, I am afraid, somewhat less subjective, speculative and normative.

I see four major and fairly obvious deficiencies in the SSTS research area, and again, the essays in this book testify to these deficiencies. The first of them I would like to call somewhat perniciously the 'rhetoric pathos' of the field. The second I would term its still very widespread fragmentation. The third, closely related to fragmentation, would be its very important lack of comparative research; and the last, its 'bigness and hardness bias'.

Rhetoric pathos   We cannot really separate the five positive tendencies I described earlier from the rhetoric in which they are couched. In their writings scholars certainly manifest a growing awareness of problems in the field, but their rhetoric carries with it few detailed solutions for these problems. This is perhaps most obvious in respect to what I have termed the normative tendency. There can be no doubt that scholars demonstrate through their choice of topics and their choice of words an increasing sensitivity to the value dimensions of science and technology; there can be no doubt that they recognize the need for the modern scientist to take a stand, to assume his share of social responsibility. Salomon (Chapter 2) for example, certainly raises the essential questions: What is science for? What kind of society do we want, anyway? But he cannot really formulate answers to these questions, nor help us to formulate our own answers. Similarly, Ravetz (Chapter 3) asks whether the intrusion of social responsibility into science will in the long run prove crippling or constructive to scientific progress, but he cannot tell us how research might contribute to the elucidation of that issue. Nelkin (Chapter 11), on the other hand, presents an excellent catalogue of research which would be exactly relevant to these questions – but her presentation does not hide the fact that these are proposed programs and not achievements which she could report in the summary of her chapter.

If the new role of the socially responsible scientist and technologist is as essential as Layton (Chapter 6) and Lakoff (Chapter 10) claim, where is the psychology and sociology of science that would tackle this new role concept? Where is the research project which would investigate the extent to which science has learned to assimilate the new social concerns and goals? Böhme (Chapter 9) asks under which socio-economic, cognitive and organizational conditions it would be possible to redirect the scientific effort. There are simply no responses, to this question and to all the other questions, as of yet.

'How to perceive the ethics of a savant in the new disenchanted age, is a problem . . . left to the reader', says Ravetz (Chapter 3) in criticism of

Salomon (1973), and yet this is a criticism which applies equally well to his own writing and to much of the rhetoric which permeates the field. It should be added that much of the criticism of science which is raised 'from within' — including that which stems from research on science — does not raise the obviously implied critique of society. Although there are some fruitful suggestions for actual research directions (e.g. Holton, 1975) and some beginnings of research activity itself.,[25] the concept of 'social responsibility in science and technology' is still largely a value confession which researchers in the field unanimously espouse but rarely incorporate into actual research.

Of course, this criticism is itself rhetoric. I cannot myself offer a coherent concept of a new ethics of science and technology which would be embedded in a normative concept of society. I can only point to some of the research questions relevant to its development and emphasize the need to lift the normative rhetoric to normative research.

Fragmentation   In spite of much rhetoric concerning the widely felt need to integrate (See the section on de-simplification), we are far from reaching this goal. The disciplines which constitute the social studies of science still march more or less separately, each with its own traditions, methodologies and concepts. And certainly within each of these disciplines, research is characterized by fragmented and separate efforts. There is no integration in the philosophy of science, for instance, as Böhme (Chapter 9) points out: the lines of research which investigate recurrent partial progress of scientific developments do not merge with those which focus on epochal changes in the processes themselves; there is no contact between theories of the logical reconstruction of science and theories of science as a productive force. In the history of science MacLeod (Chapter 5) notes the lack of consensus between separate methodological and conceptual approaches, as does Layton (Chapter 6) in the history of technology. Fisch (Chapter 8) tells us that the psychology of science is largely characterized by single, one-variable studies that do not combine to form any coherent picture. The situation is no different for the disciplines of science policy studies; only the lines of separation are different along issues and nations. Thus Skolnikoff (Chapter 14) criticizes the dominance of 'segments of issue-oriented research' over integrative attempts to conceptualize problems across issue areas. Schroeder-Gudehus (Chapter 13), Lakoff (Chapter 10) and Nelkin (Chapter 11), among others, point out the 'national fragmentation'.

Finally, in addition to the fragmentation which exists within each region of SSTS there is, of course, the large gap between the two regions. There is hardly any cross-reference between the social studies of science and science

---

[25] See particularly the efforts of the Harvard University Program on Public Conceptions of Science, and the activities of the Institute of Society, Ethics and Life Sciences, which is sponsored by the Hastings Center.

policy studies. Much of what researchers in the first region investigate seems to be irrelevant to researchers in the second, and vice versa. Böhme (Chapter 9), Mulkay (Chapter 4) and Lakoff (Chapter 10), among others, point out some areas of contact, but on a broader level the challenge of cross-regional communication is unmet.

Lack of comparative research   The lack of systematic comparative research is one of the most obvious deficiencies in both the social studies of science and science policy studies. In the first region there are many useful and exciting case studies on the conditions surrounding the development of science (See Mulkay, Chapter 4), but much of this work is in the form of one-shot exercises. The various disciplines undertake very little comparative research; by this I mean to say that they attempt very few comparisons of scientific and nonscientific processes, of science and technology, of scientific efforts in different socio-economic contexts. The reason for this lack of comparisons is obvious. All comparative research is beset with extraordinary methodological problems. In order to carry out sociological research on the comparative development of disciplines for example, the researcher would need cross-disciplinary indicators for cognitive and institutional development: indicators for coherence, precision, articulation, consensus, plurality, etc. Some useful conceptual beginnings have been made in that direction (e.g. Whitley, 1974), but they are too general for use in research. Those attempts which have been made to operationalize these criteria (e.g. Spiegel-Rösing, 1976) are hardly applicable across many disciplines.

In the region of science policy studies the comparative research which we most need is that which would investigate the differences between successes and failures: in science and technology policies, in management of innovation, and in organization and administration of research. It is, of course, extremely difficult to find units of analysis that are structurally similar enough to permit such comparisons. Project SAPPHO (Achilladelis *et al.*, 1971), which compares successes and failures in industrial innovation, illustrates the methodological possibilities and difficulties of such research. It is difficult to see how in many areas of SSTS research a conclusion that is valid for more than one institution, one research area, one sample of scientists or technologists, is to emerge if the researchers do not tackle the methodological and substantive tasks inherent in comparative research.

The bigness and hardness bias   The 'bigness bias' refers to the preference, among SSTS researchers, for investigating the top structures of science and technology. Psychologists of science want to study genius (See Fisch, Chapter 8), and sociologists of science want to study scientific elites (See Mulkay, Chapter 4). Historians of technology want to study heroic inventions (See Layton, Chapter 6), and researchers within the various disciplines of science policy studies want to study big nations across all areas of research. (There are frequent complaints in this volume about United States bias in research.)

There are certainly some good research reasons for the priority of these 'big objects' of study. For instance, researchers study the elites of the scientific community because of their mediating role between external goals and internal research processes (See Mulkay, Chapter 4). Yet this bigness bias disregards some very important phenomena in science: the non-Nobel-Prize-winning scientist worker and his alienation from his work; the mediocre daily tasks in science that add up to 'progress'; the small technological increments that contribute to new technology, etc. We cannot deny that with its bigness bias SSTS tends to reinforce the well-known elitist element in the ideology of science which is at the base of much of the present 'anti-science' feeling.

The 'hardness bias' in SSTS research refers to the preference for investigating 'hard' sciences, particularly physics, to the relative neglect of the biological sciences, of medicine, agriculture and — mostly — the social sciences. This bias is perhaps most extreme in the sociology of science (See Mulkay, Chapter 4), but it is also characteristic for other SSS and SPS research areas. This brings us to a very important problem. Many countries today are undergoing changes in science policy which result in stronger emphasis on social goals (See Salomon, Chapter 3). There is no doubt that both science and the public support the necessity of this orientation, and that within the studies of science and technology the rhetoric is close to unanimously in favor of it. Yet there is still very little investigative research involving the 'soft' sciences, which are precisely the fields most likely to make a significant contribution to the implementation of the new social goals. Thus, because of the exclusivity of its objects of investigation, SSTS research certainly seems to be moving in partial contradiction to its avowed subscription to these goals.

Future research I have tried to outline some of the more positive tendencies in research on science, technology and society, and to summarize some of its more widely recognized deficiencies. It is tempting to speculate on future developments which would relieve research in this area of its rhetoric and direct it into more fruitful channels. It is also important, in the light of the positive and negative aspects I have mentioned, once more to inquire about the role of scientometrics in the study of science, technology and society.

Because of the broad and diverse field of research which SSTS encompasses, I find it impossible to list specific priorities for the field. Many of the authors of this volume have done this for their own research area, indicating some of the desirable directions which emerge from the critical analysis of the state of research in their field. I can, however, indicate a few examples of the kind of research which — taking the positive and the negative aspects into account — might be of value in the future.

We can expect that future research will concentrate increasingly on problems which transcend the fragmentations and regionalizations which characterize the field today. Research will particularly focus on topics that mediate between the cognitive and the social, the internal and the external. This work will by necessity be comparative. Examples of such comparative and mediating research may lie in the study of such issues as government policies toward industrial technological innovation across the socialist-nonsocialist borderline, or the new roles and advisory functions of scientists and technologists in the 'disenchanted age', or the clash that arises between the demands of science and the demands of society (See Lakoff, Chapter 10; Ravetz, Chapter 3; Nelkin, Chapter 11). The scientific community, where external demands are translated into the practice of science, can be expected to have a continued important role in mediating research (See Mulkay, Chapter 4).

Perhaps the practitioners of the psychology of science will investigate the socialization of scientists, a topic which has so far received only superficial attention. If they do so we will at last have some data on how the changing societal situation of science is absorbed, transformed and integrated into science, and how diverse cultural contexts and societal demands affect scientific and technological development (See MacLeod, Chapter 5, and Sardar and Rosser-Owen, Chapter 15).

In order to cross the national boundaries reflected in science policy studies we will need, not only comparative research on government policies, but also investigations of the implications of science and technology for the international scene. As Skolnikoff (Chapter 14) points out, this may even become 'one of the organizing themes of science policy studies'.

Finally, the crucial public position of science and technology in society may become an important area of empirical research. This would be especially meaningful if it were investigated across the socio-political boundaries I have mentioned. In this context it would be particularly fruitful to investigate the 'legitimacy' of science and technology, and the epochal reasons for an increasing legitimation deficit. (This is already an organizing theme in some present political sociologies, e.g. Offe, 1971, Habermas, 1973, 1974). If I could single out any particular content area of SSTS for future study, then I certainly would say that the social sciences have to be investigated with respect to all the mediating and comparative themes mentioned.

At a very global and abstract level, the kind of research I feel would be most desirable can be characterized briefly. It is research that cuts across the cognitive and socio-political regionalizations of the field. It must compare the situation of science and technology in diverse socio-economic and cultural conditions. It must reflect the historicity of the phenomena investigated, including the historicity of its own approach. Finally, it must abandon rhetoric and focus directly on the problems, conflicts and contradictions that arise from the new goals of science.

If we now look at scientometrics we note, at a very general level, that it does not incorporate most of the positive and negative aspects of current

SSTS research. Scientometrics attempts to discover objective indicators of the development of science and to focus on universal laws of science, on its fundamental structure and functioning. In so doing it tends to avoid some of the major lines of fragmentation of both the social studies of science and science policy studies. Methodologically, as I have mentioned before, these lines of fragmentation cut across the socio-political regionalization of the field; topically, they cut across its cognitive rationalization. The particular rhetoric which characterizes this fragmentation is conspicuously absent from scientometrics. Because it focuses on 'objective' and 'universal' laws, scientometrics purposely ignores all aspects of what I have called the humanistic tendencies: the subjectivisation of the scientist, the view of science from the perspective of the actor, etc. It also disregards the relativistic and normative tendencies, and whether this is to its advantage is a debated question. With this methodological attitude, what scientometrics furnishes is basic data which cannot be ignored by either the social studies of science or science policy studies.

SSTS: ITS AUDIENCES, CRITICS, TASKS

In an age of questioning the role of science and technology in society, it is certainly not enough to reflect upon research developments and internal tendencies of the SSTS field. It is necessary to ask what functions this research has, what relevance to the rest of science, to potential users outside science, and to the public. Keeping these questions in mind, I think we can distinguish three main task-areas for SSTS research.

Knowledge production and its impurities A first task for SSTS is obviously the production of knowledge. It is not the first task in the sense of being the most important; by itself knowledge production is only relevant to a small circle. But it is first in the sense that it underlies other tasks as an essential precondition. In this case the primary audience for knowledge production is, of course, the SSTS research community, but it is hard to conceive of knowledge production in this field as a pure research activity with no wider scientific community, no potential user, no public in mind. This is so, first of all, because much of the research on science and technology is publicly financed, sometimes directly, through research grants and sometimes indirectly, through the use of university facilities and teaching positions. Second — and this is what makes SSTS different from other fields of research — because the knowledge produced in studies on science and technology, quite simply, is going to affect science and technology. This is not merely true in the simple sense that other research fields may have to take into account results from this field in their own theory building or data production; this is a desirable and unproblematic kind of influence. What is less obvious and certainly more problematic is the potential influence of SSTS research on the criteria of the scientific research process itself, and on the ideology of science.

There is no evidence so far that theories and data produced by SSTS research have indeed substantially influenced the research processes in other fields — but it is certainly not absurd to raise the question. How, for example, do models of the development of science, devised by the social study of science, influence the way that science actually develops? We need only think of the enormous influence that Kuhn's model of the development of science (Kuhn, 1970, see Böhme, Chapter 9) had on the social sciences, opening as it did a flood of preoccupations with paradigmatic maturity or immaturity. SSTS may also affect science by challenging some of its cherished underlying assumptions, such as that of the non-directibility of basic research and the basic corollary of this assumption, the need for scientific autonomy. The social studies of science are far from capable of showing how the content of science can be directed to external goals. If, however, they could, it would affect quite dramatically the attitude and position which science could take toward the government and the public. With respect to the wider scientific community in particular, pure knowledge production in the field is thus clearly contaminated.

The third reason why it is hard to conceptualize basic knowledge production in SSTS as a pure activity is that such studies are affected by their environment. They share some of the ideologies of science; they are conducted on the same underlying assumptions; they are, like the rest of science, dependent on public legitimation, but they are also subject to more general political and cultural forces. Much of this book underlines this last fact.

If knowledge production in SSTS is recognized as being dependent on public legitimation, as being a potential influence on the rest of science and as being susceptible to the scientific and nonscientific context in which it is conducted, then I see two important requirements for SSTS research. The first is that SSTS reflect upon and investigate how research on science affects the development of science. So far very little thought or research has been directed to this problem. The second is that it investigates how research done on science and technology is itself affected by its scientific as well as its wider social, economic, political and cultural contexts. Both of these requirements stem from the need for what I have called reflexivity. Reflexivity is much enhanced by outside criticism. Science policy studies are an important source of criticism for the social studies of science and vice versa. More important, the same is true of socialist and bourgeois SSTS. Such cross-regional discussion and argument should be considered carefully in future SSTS institution building (i.e. in compositions of international bodies, editorial boards, etc.). Finally, scientists from other fields are important critics of SSTS. They are often in a better position to see the implications of SSTS for their fields than the SSTS researcher is. Clearly research on science often requires close collaboration with scientists from the fields being investigated; but such collaboration is also necessary in order for the SSTS to foster its own critical pattern.

If by 'pure' research we mean that which responds only to internally generated questions and uncontaminated curiosity, then there is no such thing as pure research. If pure research in SSTS is not to be blind research, it must proceed reflexively and in close contact with all of its potential critics.

Application and its impracticabilities   A second main task for SSTS, closely related to the first, is application. Application is obviously of primary importance to the potential users of SSTS research results (science and technology policy makers, research managers and university administrators). All potential users want recipes and solutions, but producing solutions to user problems is obviously too narrow a view of application. It is too narrow because in most cases SSTS cannot deliver recipes or solutions; it may never be able to. Such a view is too narrow because it also neglects other important functions of the field that may become relevant to users, although the field may not always simplify or solve their problems.

There are three important considerations involved in relating SSTS to the user audience which needs its research results. The most basic consideration is the description of phenomena and the collection of data. Description is, of course, never a simple objective process. Total descriptions are impossible. What aspects are selected? What is the criterion for selection? The user interest? The SSTS researcher's preconceptions and ideology? And what is the effect of selection? The aspects selected are also the ones most likely to be changed; even description and data collection cannot proceed without reflexivity.

A second consideration is that one must see SSTS as contributing to the solution of practical policy problems. There are large areas of SSTS research not explored with respect to their applicability: the relevant data are unused. Few SSTS researchers actually reflect upon the practical implications of their research; but then, there are few policy makers who are ready to listen. It is both the fault of the researchers and the fault of the policy makers that the two groups communicate so poorly. Researchers make some of their results unintelligible to policy makers, but policy makers are overly concerned with quick and simple solutions and the legitimation of their policies. It is important for the user audience value of SSTS that it investigate the conditions under which its research results could be transferred to the policy making process. There are some important beginnings, such as the investigations of the use of the social sciences in the policy-making process conducted by the OECD, but there is not enough coherent research effort focusing on such a crucial problem. There may well be a need for a new subfield of SSTS: praxeology, as it is called in socialist countries.

Besides data collection and description, and contributions to the solution of policy problems, there is a third consideration for the user audience, one which, unfortunately, complicates the situation. This kind of contribution is understandably less popular among decision makers in research administration and science policy who already must deal with party politics, legitimation and schedules. Nonetheless, it is crucial that SSTS continue to point out problems and question solutions. The social studies of science contribute significantly to this annoying task: philosophy, history and sociology of science all point to the limitation of a purely allocative model of science government. Historians of science question sweeping generalizations about science policies and strategies of research support (See MacLeod, Chapter 5). Psychologists of science point to the 'unpractical' fact of the value-laden nature of all measurements of productivity and creativity in science (See Fisch, Chapter 8). Sociologists of science raise questions about the potential contradictions between external demands on science and the role of the scientific community in monitoring the quality of research (See Mulkay, Chapter 4). Economists of science disillusion the technique-oriented managers of innovation by showing that 'muddling through' remains the realistic slogan of the day. Economists of science also help to discard all the simple, linear models of technological innovation that would make the allocation of R & D resources so much easier (See Freeman, Chapter 7). Such 'impractical' – that is to say, problematizing – contributions from the field of science policy studies demonstrate that the global impacts of technology cannot be handled within the traditional, national politics of governments (See Skolnikoff, 1972 and Chapter 14). They also demonstrate that scientific advice to policy makers has important normative elements and cannot, therefore, be used in any simple way to solve public policy controversies (See Lakoff, Chapter 10: Nelkin, Chapter 11).

This important user-oriented function of the social studies of science and of science policy studies is, of course, in danger of remaining pure muckraking if it does not also point out alternatives. Alternatives come easier to the researcher who reflects upon his own research presuppositions and on the dangers and challenges of the public position of his field. This is all the more essential since SSTS, like all other sciences, is dependent on user support – from governments, industry, public and private foundations – and they must legitimate what they do. It is not easy to question the user interest and, at the same time, avoid undermining the financial support for one's own research.

Ethics of science and technology in society   The third task of SSTS is the most elusive, complicated and controversial. It must criticize the role of science in society. Can the social studies of science and science policy studies contribute to a new ethic and identity for science that includes public as well as scientific values? Can they contribute to strengthening the social responsibility which scientists feel for the consequences of their research? Can they contribute through teaching to an increase in the number of scientists and technologists who do research with an awareness of social values? Can they contribute to the mediation between the legitimacy of public demands on science and the necessity of internal scientific functioning? Can they develop a criticism of science and technology while working on the foundations of its public legitimacy? These questions are certainly open. This third task is aided by careful and critical analysis of the teaching activities in the field (for some promising signs see MacLeod, 1976; Lowe and Worboys, 1975), by the participation of SSTS researchers in organizations explicitly directed to the communication between a responsible science and a critical public (such as the various national Societies for Responsibility in Science) and, by conducting research on the questions raised by a new ethics of science.

   Looking at the broad range of current studies on science, technology and society – with all their promising tendencies, unremedied deficiencies and challenging tasks – it is difficult to escape the impression that an almost unmanageably broad area of research and analysis is opening up. The tasks ahead are extraordinary. I hope that this volume will illuminate some of the goals which are yet to be achieved.

BIBLIOGRAPHY

Achilladelis *et al.*, 1971   Achilladelis, B. *et al.*, *Project SAPPHO: A Study of Success and Failure in Innovation*, Brighton, Science Policy Research Unit, University of Sussex, 1971.

Altner, 1971   Altner, P., 'The Development of the Science of Science in the German Democratic Republic', in Polish Academy of Sciences, *Problems of the Science of Science*, Warsaw, 1971, pp. 150-154.

Baitsch *et al.*, 1973   Baitsch, H., Fliedner, T. M., Kreutzkam, J. B. and Spiegel-Rösing, I. S., *Memorandum zur Förderung der Wissenschaftsforschung in der Bundesrepublik Deutschland (On the Promotion of Science Policy Studies in the FRG: A Memorandum)*, Essen, Stifterverband für die Deutsche Wissenschaft, 1973.

Bardos, 1973   Bardos, J. P., 'Recherche sur la recherche en France: Le club de Gif', *Le Progrès Scientifique*, No. 167, 1973, pp. 3-9.

Barnes, 1974   Barnes, B., *Scientific Knowledge and Sociological Theory*, London and Boston, Routledge and Kegan Paul, 1974.

Bernal, 1939-1967

Bhaskar, 1975

Bloor, 1973

Bloor, 1975

Blume, 1974

Blume, 1975

Cole and Cole, 1973

Cooper, 1972

Crane, 1969

Crane, 1971

Dobrow, 1970a

Dobrow, 1970b

Dobrow, 1971a

Dobrow, 1971b

Dobrow, 1971c

Dobrow, 1974a

Dobrow, 1974b

Easlea, 1973

Bernal, J. D., *The Social Functions of Science,* Cambridge, MIT Press, 1967.

Bhaskar, R., 'Feyerabend and Bachélard: Two Philosophies of Science', *New Left Review,* No. 94, 1975, pp. 31-44.

Bloor, D., 'Wittgenstein and Mannheim on the Sociology of Mathematics', *Studies of History and Philosophy of Science* 4, No. 2, 1973, pp. 173-191.

Bloor, D., 'A Philosophical Approach to Science (Course Bibliography)', *Social Studies of Science* 5, No. 4, 1975, pp. 507-517.

Blume, S. S., *Toward a Political Sociology of Science,* New York and London, The Free Press, Macmillan/Collier Macmillan, 1974.

Blume, S. S., *Science Policy Research: Its Current State and Future Priorities,* unpublished report to the Social Science Research Council, Sussex University, February, 1975.

Cole, J. R. and Cole, S., *Social Stratification in Science,* Chicago, University of Chicago Press, 1973.

Cooper, C., 'Science, Technology and Production in the Underdeveloped Countries: An Introduction', *The Journal of Development Studies* 9, No. 1, 1972, pp. 1-18.

Crane, D., 'Social Structure in a Group of Scientists: A Test of the "Invisible College" Hypothesis', *American Sociological Review,* 34, 1969, pp. 335-352.

Crane, D., 'Transnational Networks in Basic Science', *International Organization* 25, No. 3, 1971, pp. 585-601.

Dobrow, G. M., *Wissenschaftswissenschaft (Science of Science),* Berlin (East), Akademie-Verlag, 1970.

Dobrow, G. M., *Aktuelle Probleme der Wissenschaftswissenschaft (Current Problems of Science of Science),* Berlin (East), Dietz Verlag, 1970.

Dobrow, G. M., *Potential der Wissenschaft (The Potential of Science),* Berlin (East), Akademie-Verlag, 1971.

Dobrow, G. M., *Wissenschaftsorganisation und Effektivität (Science Organization and Efficiency),* Berlin (East), Akademie-Verlag, 1971.

Dobrow, G. M., *Prognostik in Wissenschaft und Technik (Prognosis in Science and Technology),* Berlin (East), Dietz Verlag, 1971.

Dobrow, G. M., *Wissenschaft: ihre Analyse und Prognose (Science: Its Analysis and Prognosis),* Stuttgart, Deutsche Verlags Anstalt, 1974.

Dobrow, G. M. , *Leitung der Wissenschaft (Management of Science),* Berlin (East), Akademie-Verlag, 1974.

Easlea, B., 'An Introduction to the History and Social Studies of Science: A Seminar Course for First-Year Science Students', *Science Studies* 3, No. 2, 1973, pp. 185-209.

Fisher, 1966   Fisher, C. S., 'The Death of A Mathematical Theory:
                                A Study in the Sociology of Knowledge', *Archives for
                                History of Exact Sciences* 3, 1966, pp. 137-159.

Fisher, 1967   Fisher, C. S., 'The Last Invariant Theorists: A Socio-
                                logical Study of the Collective Biographies of Mathe-
                                matical Specialists', *European Journal of Sociology* 8,
                                1967, pp. 216-244.

Freeman *et al.*, 1971   Freeman, C. *et al.*, 'The Goals of R & D in the 1970's',
                                Science Studies 1, 1971, pp. 357-406.

Gilbert and Woolgar, 1974   Gilbert, G. N. and Woolgar, S., 'The Quantitative
                                Study of Science: An Examination of the Literature',
                                Science Studies 4, No. 3, 1974, pp. 279-294.

Goffman, 1971   Goffman, W., 'A Mathematical Method for Analyzing
                                the Growth of a Scientific Discipline', *Journal of the
                                Association for Computing Machinery* 18, 1971, pp.
                                173-185.

Griffith, *et al.*, 1974   Griffith, B. C., Small, H. G., Stonehill, J. A., and Dey,
                                S., 'The Structure of Scientific Literatures II: Toward
                                a Macro- and Microstructure for Science', *Science
                                Studies* 4, No. 4, 1974, pp. 339-365.

Habermas, 1973   Habermas, J., *Legitimationsprobleme im Spätkapital-
                                ismus (Problems of Legitimation in the Late Capi-
                                talism)*, Frankfurt am Main, Suhrkamp, 1973.

Habermas, 1974   Habermas, J., 'Können komplexe Gesellschaften eine
                                vernünftige Identität ausbilden? (Can Complex
                                Societies Develop a Reasonable Identity?)', in *Zwei
                                Reden aus Anlass des Hegel-Preises (Two Addresses on
                                the Occasion of the 'Hegel-Preis' Award)*, Frankfurt
                                am Main, Suhrkamp, 1974, pp. 23-84.

Hagstrom, 1965   Hagstrom, W. O., *The Scientific Community*, New
                                York and London, Basic Books, 1965.

Heitowit and Epstein, 1975   Heitowit, E. and Epstein, J., *List of Formal Teaching
                                and Research Programs in the General Area of Science,
                                Technology and Society at (or Affiliated with) U.S.
                                Colleges and Universities*, Program on Science, Tech-
                                nology and Society, Cornell University, unpublished
                                manuscript, 1975.

Holton, 1975   Holton, G., 'Scientific Optimism and Societal Con-
                                cerns', *Hastings Center Report* 5, No. 6, 1975, pp.
                                39-47.

Jamison and Elzinga, 1975   Jamison, A. and Elzinga, A., 'Science: Its Theory and
                                Practice. An Introduction for Doctoral Students (Bib-
                                liography)', *Social Studies of Science* 5, No. 2, 1975,
                                pp. 223-234.

Krauze, 1972   Krauze, T. K., 'Social and Intellectual Structures of
                                Science: A Mathematical Analysis', *Science Studies* 2,
                                1972, pp. 369-378.

Kröber and Laitko, 1972   Kröber, G. and Laitko, H., *Sozialismus und Wissen-
                                schaft (Socialism and Science)*, Berlin (East), Deut-
                                scher Verlag der Wissenschaften, 1972.

Kröber and Laitko, 1975   Kröber, G. and Laitko, H. (Eds.), *Wissenschaft: Ihre
                                Stellung, Funktion und Organisation in der entwickel-
                                ten sozialistischen Gesellschaft (Science: Its Position,*

Kröber *et al.*, 1974

Kubie, 1954

Kubie, 1961

Kubie, 1962

Kuhn, 1970

Law, 1974

Lowe and Worboys, 1975

MacLeod, 1974

MacLeod, 1976

Maslow, 1966

Meadows, 1974

Meadows and O'Connor, 1971

Menard, 1971

Mirsky, 1972

Mitroff, 1974

Function and Organisation in the Developed Socialist Society), Berlin, Dietz Verlag, 1975.
Kröber, G., Laitko, H. and Steiner, H. (Eds.), *Wissenschaft und Forschung im Sozialismus. Probleme ihrer Entwicklung, Gestaltung und Analyse (Science and Research in Socialism. Problems of Their Development, Shaping and Analysis)*, Material of the COMEN-CON Symposium on Questions of the Marxist-Leninist Theory of Science, Berlin, (East), Akademie-Verlag, 1974.
Kubie, L. S., 'Some Unsolved Problems of the Scientific Career', *American Scientist* 42, 1954, pp. 104-112.
Kubie, L. S., *Neurotic Distortion of the Creative Process*, Lawrence, Kansas, University of Kansas Press, 1961.
Kubie, L. S., 'The Fostering of Creative Scientific Productivity', *Daedalus* 91, 1962, pp. 294-309.
Kuhn, T. S., *The Structure of Scientific Revolutions*, 2nd Edition, Chicago, University of Chicago Press, 1970.
Law, J., 'Theories and Methods in the Sociology of Science: An Interpretive Approach', *Social Science Information* 13, No. 4/5, 1974, pp. 163-172.
Lowe, P. D. and Worboys, M., 'The Teaching of the Social Studies of Science and Technology in British Polytechnics', *Social Studies of Science* 5, No. 2, 1975, pp. 177-192.
MacLeod, R., 'The Historical Context of the International Commission for Science Policy Studies', in Salomon, J. J. and Spiegel-Rösing, I. (Eds.), *Science Policy Studies Contributions*, Tokyo, IUHPS, 1974, pp. 202-210. See also *Archives Internationales d'Histoire des Sciences* 25, No. 97, 1975, pp. 314-323.
MacLeod, R., *Cultural, Social and Political Influences on Science Policy Studies: Reflections on Science Policy Studies in British Universities 1966-766*, Lecture given at the Second Formal Meeting of the International Council for Science Policy Studies, Paris, April 1976.
Maslow, A. H., *The Psychology of Science*, New York, Harper and Row, 1966.
Meadows, A. J., *Communication in Science*, London, Butterworth, 1974.
Meadows, A. J. and O'Connor, J. G., 'Bibliographical Statistics as a Guide to Growth Points in Science', *Science Studies* 1, 1971, pp. 95-99.
Menard, H. W., *Science: Growth and Change*, Cambridge, Harvard University Press, 1971.
Mirsky, E. M., 'Science Studies in the USSR (History, Problems, Prospects)', *Social Studies* 2, 1972, pp. 281-294.
Mitroff, K. K., *The Subjective Side of Science*, Amsterdam, Elsevier, 1974.

Nelkin *et al.*, 1974

Novotny, 1973

OECD, 1971

Offe, 1972

Ossowska and Ossowski, 1936

Derek Price, 1963

Derek Price, 1965a

Derek Price, 1965b

Derek Price, 1968

Derek Price, 1969a

Derek Price, 1969b

Derek Price, 1970

Derek Price, 1971a

Derek Price, 1971b

Rabkine, 1974

Rabkine, 1976

Rahman, 1972

Rahman, 1973

Nelkin, D., Hershey, C. and Mueller, D., 'The Impact and Control of Technological Change', *Science Studies* 4, No. 1, 1974, pp. 97-103.

Novotny, H., 'On the Feasibility of a Cognitive Approach to the Study of Science', *Zeitschrift für Soziologie* 2, No. 3, 1973, pp. 282-296.

OECD, *Science, Growth and Society: A New Perspective*, Paris, OECD, 1971.

Offe, C., *Strukturprobleme des kapitalistischen Staates (Structural Problems of the Capitalist State)*, Frankfurt am Main, Suhrkamp, 1972.

Ossowska, M. and Ossowski, S., 'The Science of Science', *Organon*, 1, 1936, pp. 1-12. See also *Minerva* 3, 1964, pp. 72-82.

Price, Derek de Solla, *Little Science, Big Science,* New York and London, Columbia University Press, 1963.

Price, Derek de Solla, 'Is Technology Historically Independent of Science? A Study in Statistical Historiography', *Technology and Culture* 6, 1965, pp. 553-568.

Price, Derek de Solla, 'Networks of Scientific Papers', *Science* 149, 1965, pp. 510-515.

Price, Derek de Solla, *The Difference between Science and Technology,* Detroit, Michigan, Thomas Alva Edison Foundation, 1968, pp. 1-16.

Price, Derek de Solla, 'The Structures of Publication in Science and Technology', in Gruber, W. H. and Marquis, D. G. (Eds.), *Factors in the Transfer of Technology,* Cambridge, MIT Press, 1969, pp. 91-104.

Price, Derek de Solla, 'Measuring the Size of Science', *Proceedings of the Israel Academy of Sciences and Humanities* 4, No. 6, 1969, pp. 98-111.

Price, Derek de Solla, 'Citation Measures of Hard Science, Soft Science, Technology and Nonscience', in Nelson, C. E. and Pollock, D. K. (Eds.), *Communicating Among Scientists and Engineers,* Lexington, Mass., Heath, 1970, pp. 3-22.

Price, Derek de Solla, 'Principles for Projecting Funding of Academic Science in the 1970's', *Science Studies* 1, 1971, pp. 85-99.

Price, Derek de Solla, 'Some Remarks on Elitism in Information and the Invisible College Phenomenon in Science', *Journal of the American Society for Information Science* 22, 1971, pp. 74-75.

Rabkine, Y. M., 'Origines et développements de la recherche sur la recherche en Union Soviétique', *Le Progrès Scientifique,* No. 170, 1974, pp. 39-51.

Rabkine, Y. M., 'Scientometric Studies in Chemistry', *Social Studies of Science* 6, No. 1, 1976, pp. 128-132.

Rahman, A., 'International Commission for Science Policy Studies: First Meeting', *Journal of Scientific and Industrial Research* 31, 1972, pp. 407-408.

Rahman, A., *Anatomy of Science,* New Delhi,

National Publishing, 1972.

Rahman *et al.*, 1973 — Rahman, A., Bhargava, R. N., Qureshi, M. A. and Sudarshan, P., *Science and Technology in India*, New Delhi, Indian Council for Cultural Relations, 1973.

Rahman and Sharma, 1974 — Rahman, A. and Sharma, K. D. (Eds.), *Science Policy Studies*, Bombay and New Delhi, Somaiya Publications, 1974.

'Recherche sur la recherche', 1973 — 'Recherche sur la recherche en France: Le Club de Gif', *Le Progrès Scientifique*, Whole No. 167, 1973.

Rilling, 1975 — Rilling, R., *Theories und Soziologie der Wissenschaft. Zur Entwicklung in der BRD und DDR (Theory and Sociology of Science. Its Development in the FRG and GDR)*, Frankfurt am Main, Fischer Taschenbuchverlag, 1975.

Rip and Boeker, 1975 — Rip, A. and Boeker, E., 'Scientists and Social Responsibility in the Netherlands', *Social Studies of Science* 5, No. 4, 1975, pp. 457-484.

Salomon, 1973 — Salomon, J.-J., *Science and Politics*, London, Macmillan Press, 1973.

Salomon and Spiegel-Rösing, 1974 — Salomon, J.-J. and Spiegel-Rösing, I. (Eds.), *Science Policy Studies Contributions*, Tokyo, International Commission for Science Policy Studies, 1974.

Schroeder-Gudehus, 1974 — Schroeder-Gudehus, B., 'International Commission for Science Policy Studies: New Delhi Meeting', *Science Studies* 4, No. 1, 1974, pp. 105-107.

Science Policy: A Working Glossary, 1976 — *Science Policy: A Working Glossary*, Third Edition, Washington, D.C., U.S. Government Printing Office, 1976.

Singer, 1971 — Singer, B. G., 'Toward a Psychology of Science', *American Psychologist* 26, 1971, pp. 1010-1015.

Skolnikoff, 1972 — Skolnikoff, E. B., *The International Imperatives of Technology*, Research Series No. 16, Berkeley, California, Institute of International Studies, University of California, 1972.

Skolnikoff, 1973 — Skolnikoff, E. B., *International Commission for Science Policy Studies* 3, 1973, pp. 89-90.

Small and Griffith, 1974 — Small, H. and Griffith, B. C., 'The Structure of Scientific Literatures I: Identifying and Graphing Specialties', *Science Studies* 4, No. 1, 1974, pp. 17-40.

Spiegel-Rösing, 1972 — Spiegel-Rösing, I., 'Journal Authors as an Indicator of Scientific Manpower: A Methodological Study Using Data for the Two Germanies and Europe', *Science Studies* 2, 1972, pp. 337-359.

Spiegel-Rösing, 1973a — Spiegel-Rösing, I., 'Science Policy Studies in a Political Context: Conceptual and Institutional Development of Science Policy Studies in the German Democratic Republic', *Science Studies* 3, 1973, pp. 390-410.

Spiegel-Rösing, 1973b — Spiegel-Rösing, I., *Wissenschaftsentwicklung und Wissenschaftssteuerung (Development and Control of Science)*, Frankfurt am Main, Athenäum-Verlag, 1973.

Spiegel-Rösing, 1974 — Spiegel-Rösing, I., 'Disziplinäre Strategien der Statussicherung (Disciplinary Strategies of Status Maintenance)', *Homo* 25, No. 1, 1974, pp. 11-37.

Spiegel-Rösing, 1976

Spiegel-Rösing, I., *The Cognitive and Institutional Structures of Two Disciplinary Approaches in Attitude Research. An Empirical Investigation*, unpublished research report, 1976.

Spiegel-Rösing and MacLeod, 1976

Spiegel-Rösing, I. and MacLeod, R., 'The International Council for Science Policy Studies', *Social Studies of Science* 6, No. 1, 1976, pp. 133-135.

Teaching and Research in the Field of Science Policy, 1973

Teaching and Research in the Field of Science Policy — A Survey, Staff Study for the Subcommittee on Science, Research and Development of the Committee on Science and Astronautics, U.S. House of Representatives, Ninety Second Congress, Second Session, Serial CC, Washington, D.C., U.S. Government Printing Office, 1973.

UNESCO, 1971

UNESCO, *Science Policy Research and Teaching Units*, Science Policy Studies and Documents, No. 28, Paris, 1971.

Walentynowicz, 1975

Walentynowicz, B., 'The Science of Science in Poland: Present State and Prospects of Development', *Social Studies of Science* 5, No. 2, 1975, pp. 213-222.

Whitley, 1974

Whitley, R., 'Cognitive and Social Institutionalization of Scientific Specialties and Research Areas', in Whitley, R. (Ed.), *Social Processes of Scientific Development*, London and Boston, Routledge and Kegan Paul, 1974, pp. 69-95.

Whitley, 1975

Whitley, R. D., 'The British Sociological Association's Sociology of Science Group', *Social Studies of Science* 5, No. 4, 1975, pp. 485-488.

Wynne, 1974

Wynne, B., *Sociology of Science* (Teacher Text to Unit 1, 2 and 3), SISCON, 1974.

Zuckerman, 1967

Zuckerman, H., 'Nobel Laureates in Science: Patterns of Productivity, Collaboration and Authorship', *American Sociological Review* 32, 1967, pp. 391-403.

Zuckerman, 1970

Zuckerman, H., 'Stratification in American Science', *Sociological Inquiry* 40, 1970, pp. 235-257.

Chapter 2

SCIENCE POLICY STUDIES AND THE DEVELOPMENT OF SCIENCE POLICY

Jean-Jacques Salomon

OECD and *CNAM, Paris*

INTRODUCTION

Even without a complete understanding of the factors underlying the almost universal rise of science policy immediately after World War II, we are aware of the general truth that events precede reflection: 'Minerva's bird,' said Hegel, 'rises at dusk, when the die is cast.' But there are few areas in the field of political action which show better the gap between history as it is made, through empirical decisions imposed by circumstances, and history as the object of academic research and theoretical analysis. The studies devoted to science policy have developed alongside the growth of this new field of government responsibility – new in the sense that it was only just after World War II that this field was given institutional recognition through bodies, mechanisms, procedures and a bureaucratic and political staff specifically concerned with these questions.

It is now commonplace to point out that the Manhattan Project and the development of the first atomic bombs marked an irreversible turning-point in the relations between science and the state: the establishment of science as a 'national asset', the direct intervention of governments in the direction and range of research activities, the recruiting of researchers (See Lakoff, Chapter 10). The change in scale showed by research activities (100,000 researchers in the world – scientists, engineers, and technicians – in 1940; ten times this number twenty years later; Freeman and Young, 1965) goes hand in hand with technological developments which had a direct effect on the relations between nations. The perfecting of nuclear weapons, rockets and computers altered the most traditional law of the balance of power: it was no longer enough to avoid being at the mercy of the enemy, one now had to forestall him. In this new kind of international competition, scientific and technical research constituted a powerful strategic and diplomatic resource (See Chapters 12, 13, 14): each gain achieved by one camp called for a greater effort in the other, for a higher degree of investment, greater means and manpower to be set up, and technological objectives to be attained. Thus started the process of technological escalation, the most spectacular feature of which was the strategic weapons system, which in point of fact affected all areas of scientific and technological research.

Science policy developed in this context of strategic competition as a consequence of the impossibility of establishing real peace at the end of World War II. In this sense science policy is obviously only one feature of an overall policy determined by rivalry, struggles and clashes between nations; and the directions it has followed have constantly reflected and echoed the vicissitudes of international tensions. There is an obvious link between the emergence of international crises (Berlin, Korea, Cuba, Vietnam) and the increase in expenditure on R & D (from 1940 to 1960 the total extent of the United States federal expenditure devoted to R & D for each five-year period was practically double what it had been in the preceding period (OECD, 1967). But in another sense the growing influence exercised by technological and scientific affairs on politics in general could be regarded as a cause as well as an effect of the international climate of insecurity: the 'balance of fear' was measured according to the progress of technology; and the proliferation of technical innovations, first in the military sector, but also in the civil sector, caused the nations or groups of nations which were at odds on a political and ideological plane to live in the constant fear – real or imaginary – of being surpassed on a technological level by their opponents (Chayes and Wiesner, 1969).

No other sector of policy better demonstrates the degree of autonomy which technological development can reach in highly industrialized societies, and the extent to which this can influence political, national and international decisions, rather than be influenced by them. As Senghaas (1972) has shown, the technological escalation of the armament system can no longer be regarded as an 'action-reaction' phenomenon with an external impetus (each power pursuing research according to the technological proficiency of its potential opponent). We are dealing here with a process which is now firmly established within each of the great powers (the threat to each nation being assessed according to the level of development reached by its own armament system). Thus there is an internal dynamic process in technological development, the planning of which is not influenced by any new political or even strategic decisions. This does not mean, of course, that this internal dynamic process is politically neutral: the 'tyranny of armament technology' has to go through a 'scientific-industrial-military-administrative complex' which is far from being mythical (Senghaas, 1972).

In fact the problem posed by atomic weapons was so new and crucial that for a long time it obscured all other problems. The first studies on science policy were made following the arguments on nuclear weapons, by members of the scientific community who had taken part in the Manhattan Project (mostly in the *Bulletin of Atomic Scientists*). If the policy itself was the work of administrative bodies, the studies underlying that policy were the work of scientists (physicists for the most part) who were connected with it. It is hardly surprising, therefore, if the literature of the first few post-war years was based first on articles and reports. And it was again the arguments on nuclear weapons which caused the new role played by scientists in relation to political power to be questioned (Snow, 1960; Gilpin, 1962; Gilpin and Wright, 1964).

The same process affected the studies concerning science policy proper; certain decisions were taken in the context of a discussion which was confined to the 'corridors of power', the administrative and political spheres; academic studies followed long afterwards, so that there exists a real gap between decision making and the studies devoted to science policy. And it is significant that this gap should exist both in the East and in the West (Richta *et al.*, 1967). In order to understand the meaning of this it is necessary to follow the evolution of science policy studies in relation to the development of science policy — i.e. the different periods it went through from 1940 or 1945 to the present day. It will be seen that each of these periods corresponded, with a certain lapse of time, to a specific period in science policy studies.

THE PREHISTORY OF SCIENCE POLICY

Among the different areas of government intervention by the state, science policy seems a newcomer, but the historian of science will find it easy to show that neither the idea nor the thing itself were really absent from the development of science as an institution before World War II. In short, it is all a question of definition and historical perspective. In fact, the arguments on the definition of science policy have been as fruitless as those at an academic level concerning the range of science policy studies. Before the second half of the Twentieth Century there had, in fact, been various interventions on the part of the state, which had acted as protector, patron, director or client of science. It was, however, only from World War II onwards that these interventions took on a decided, organized and institutionalized form. What, then, was 'lacking' before?

By science policy we mean here the collective measures taken by a government in order, *on the one hand,* to encourage the development of scientific and technical research and, *on the other,* to exploit the results of this research for general political objectives. Today these two aspects are complementary: policy *for* science (the provision of an environment fostering research activities), and policy *through* science (the exploitation of discoveries and innovations in various sectors of government concern) are on a par in the sense that scientific and technological factors affect political decisions and at the same time condition the development of various fields (defense, economy, social life, etc.) which are not in themselves scientific or technical. Thus science policy is determined by the idea of a deliberate integration of scientific and technological activities into the fabric of political, military, economic and social decisions. Policy *for* and *through* science: this complementary system became possible in the aftermath of World War II (OECD, 1963).

For even if these two aspects did exist beforehand, they rarely did so *simultaneously* — and in any case only for short periods at a time. From the time of the Scientific Revolution in the Seventeenth Century, research activities have needed the recognition and support of the state (hence academic institutions) and this support was given in view not only of the progress of knowledge *per se,* but also in view of making use of the results of research for practical ends, in the context already of 'national objectives'. Such was the case with the calculation of longitude, which was essential if one was to have command of the oceans (Merton, 1938 and 1957). Just as the progress of knowledge has depended on the support of political power, so the interest of the state has had to rely on the advice of scientists and the exploitation of their work (Salomon, 1970). Academic institutions are especially affected by this political overtone because of that double function which was explicit from the start (Hahn, 1971). Until the Nineteenth Century, however, it was only during exceptional periods, marked by the interest of the state in the military exploitation of the results of scientific research, that this double function was really implemented, in particular during the French Revolution (Fayet, 1960).

Before the Nineteenth Century — i.e. before the industrialization era — science made more promises than it could keep (the beginning of the Industrial Revolution was due more to technological development than to science proper). And the cost of research was not such as to necessitate heavy public investment. In that sense it may be said that for the whole of that period, unlike the present day, theoretical studies preceded practical knowledge, and these studies were mostly of an utopian nature. In Bacon's *New Atlantis,* Condorcet's *Fragment sur l'Atlantide,* Babbage's *Reflections on the Decline of Science* and Renan's *L'Avenir de la Science,* the need for support, on the part of the state, of research activities was advocated because of the promise of science and the potential use of its results. Nevertheless, in the relations between science and state, the doctrine of *laissez-faire* prevailed, all the more naturally because the lapse of time between scientific research and its application remained long, and consequently the involvement of the state in scientific matters remained limited to sectors which could guarantee relatively quick results.

What characterizes modern science as opposed to ancient science is its very power to manipulate, since mathematical formulation and experimentation make it possible for action to be applied to natural phenomena in order to transform them. In this sense the link with political power was present from the beginning of the scientific revolution as implied by the new horizon in which lay its theoretical approach (Lakoff, 1966; Salomon, 1970). But that link was all the less effective, institutionalized and systematic because science had little influence on economic, military and technical development, and at the same time, because the state intervened little in its affairs. The age of institutionalized science policy only really started when scientific activities began to have a direct effect on the course of world affairs, thereby causing the state to become aware of a field of responsibility which it now could not evade.

In the West the examples of a closer link between science and the state provided by World War I and the post-war period were only a rough sketch of a process which was to be accelerated and firmly established by the time of World War II. Institutions were then created to coordinate scientific research in the context of the war effort, but they were abandoned after the war. In particular, even though the crisis of the Thirties caused some people to become aware of the role which science could play in economic and social development, this awareness did not go so far as to provide the state with the means to orient the direction of scientific research, or even to organize it in a more coherent manner (Dupree, 1964). France alone among the democratic powers endeavored to recognize the jurisdiction of politics over scientific affairs by setting up, in the context of the Popular Front, the post of Under-Secretary of State, which was first given to Irène Joliot-Curie, then to Jean Perrin. The fact that these two Nobel Prize winners occupied a ministerial post, and the establishment of the Centre National de la Recherche Scientifique — an institution concerned with the promotion of basic research — are the first signs in the West of the recognition on the part of the state, both of the role played by science in economic and social affairs and of the political concern that it should be integrated into the general fabric of government decisions.

This case, unique in the West, was inspired in part by Soviet experience. For it was indeed in Russia that the closest link ever to be wrought between science and politics was established by the triumph of the revolution. The progress from ideology to action presents here a model of organization inasmuch as it attempted to integrate science — recognized as national capital and proclaimed as a public service — into the social system as a productive force among other productive forces. Certainly at that time in the USSR, scientific activities enjoyed a status and a support which had no equivalent in other countries before World War II; research was considered inseparable from the political system of which it was both the means and the end. Nevertheless, heavily as political factors might have weighed on the development of science as an institution, it is not certain that the model set forth by the Soviet regime gave rise then to a real science policy (Graham, 1967; Zaleski *et al.*, 1969).

It was at any rate that model which served as reference to Bernal when he wrote his book *The Social Function of Science* (1939), a pioneer work heralding the enormous changes which were soon to affect the relations between science and the state. No other work has done more to ensure the recognition of scientific activities as a social institution which both affects and is affected by the development of the social system as a whole. If, in many respects, Bernal's analysis shows an utopian approach directly inspired by the hopes which the Age of Enlightenment and Nineteenth-Century positivism had placed in the politically liberating and inevitably beneficent character of science, he is nevertheless the first to have perceived and analyzed — even though with a certain bias — all the aspects which could bring scientific and technological research activities themselves into objects of empirical research. The contents page of *The Social Function of Science* contains the basic themes which were to provide the ground for science policy studies when, in the aftermath of World War II, according to Bernal's own words in the preface of the new edition of his book, 'the scientific revolution entered a new phase — it became aware of itself' (Bernal, 1967).

THE RISE OF SCIENCE POLICY

The nature of the scientific research undertaken during World War II and, above all, the strategic importance of its results, have had consequences beyond anything Bernal might have foreseen. Until then military research had been content with adapting civil technology to the needs of war: the tank of the 1914-1918 war was indeed nothing but a cannon placed in an armored car, and even the use of gases on the battlefield was only a military version of the progress achieved by chemical research in civil life. During and immediately after World War II scientific and technical research, conceived with military ends in mind, became the source of newly-discovered forms of technology which were to be applied on a vast scale in civil life: atomic energy, radar, jet planes, DDT, computers, etc. From then on it became impossible for political power to leave science to its own devices and, at the end of the war, the demobilization of researchers, far from signalling the end of 'mobilized' science as such, gave rise, on the contrary, to systematic efforts to take advantage of research activities in the context of 'national and international objectives'.

The most significant document on this change of affairs was the report made, at the request of President Roosevelt, by Vannevar Bush, who was, during the war, director of the United States Office of Scientific Research and Development. Besides recommending the setting up of a National Research Foundation whose function it would be to support and encourage basic research and science education (which was to lead, in 1950, to the setting up of the National Science Foundation), *Science, the Endless Frontier*, also advocated the development of a national policy specifically concerned with scientific affairs (Bush, 1945). This model of institutionalized science policy was little by little to influence the governments of most industrialized countries. But it was only from 1957 — date of the first Sputnik — that organizations really concerned with science policy were set up.

Whatever the institutional arrangements, the organizations concerned with science policy, wherever they were, all fulfilled at least three functions: information, consultation, coordination. Science policy of any kind had to be prepared by administrative services, clarified by the advice of experts, discussed by interministerial committees at the highest level, and finally, of course, decided upon and implemented. National traditions and structures provided a framework for these functions and, within that framework, specific bodies: according to whether the system adopted was centralized or pluralistic, science policy was developed in various institutions and linked more or less closely with bodies concerned with economic planning. But the functions of these institutions were to draw the inventory of researchers and laboratories, orient research, allocate resources to sectors considered to have priority; in short, to direct and set, if not actually plan, the research programs.

The arguments which followed, on an institutional and political plane, the proposals for the setting up of these administrative bodies specifically concerned with scientific affairs, were centered straight away on two problems; in truth no final solution was found and the answers given varied according to circumstances, that is according to the importance given to decisions which were considered the most urgent, or to sectors of scientific activity considered the most important in the context of the international political climate. The first problem was to ascertain to what extent a centralized system was more efficient than a pluralistic one. In the case of a centralized system, the allocation of resources to research and development benefitting from public support was controlled, if not actually directed, by a single body (as in France or Belgium). In the case of a pluralistic system, the level of resources allocated to each R & D sector which concerned government policy (defense, health, agriculture, etc.), was determined by being set against all the other types of expenditure which affected this sector (as in the United States).

In the first instance, science policy was made up of all R & D activities affecting all sectors; in the second it consisted of the various policies established independently for each sector. The advantage of the first model was that it facilitated the formulation of a collective and long-term policy; but this very fact meant that it paid less attention to the operational needs of the different sectors. The advantage of the second model was that it allowed for a better distribution of R & D activities according to the needs of each sector; but its disadvantage was that it sacrificed long-term needs to the immediate needs of each sector, all of which were assessed independently from one another. Of course no national system of science policy was ever able to adopt in its ideal form either the pluralistic or the centralized system; it was rather a mixture of the two systems, readjusted every now and then, which was finally used by the various national institutions (OECD, 1971).

In fact – and this is the second problem which has never been dealt with properly by the development of science policy – the functions brought about by the elaboration and implementation of science policy did not stop at science proper, but affected also applied research and technology, and thus covered such a vast field (industry, universities, government laboratories) that they were bound to develop a 'horizontal' character, and thus became all the more difficult to fulfill. To what extent could science policy be at the same time policy for science *and* technology? To what extent did it more concern those ministries traditionally responsible for education and higher education than those responsible for industry? If indeed science policy was characterized by the priority given to strategic and prestige research (atomic power, space, defense), to what extent did this policy impinge on the other sectors?

The impossibility of giving a definitive answer to these questions shows that the instutitional development of science policy has reflected topical political and economic concerns rather than stable and unchanging models. Thus the functions exercised by the ministries responsible for scientific affairs have often changed titles, not only from one country to the next, but also within each particular country; sometimes embracing both science and technology, sometimes going from higher education to industrial research and sometimes keeping all these fields separate. Thus the issue of how to coordinate the various sectors affected by R & D activities has never stopped raising problems of competence between the various administrative bodies.

Nevertheless, in all cases new institutions were set up with the purpose of associating the advice of scientists to political decisions; the President's Science Advisory Committee in the United States, or the Comité Consultatif de la Recherche Scientifique et Technique in France, for example. These consultative organizations, wherever they were, were run by a more or less important secretariat (Office of Science and Technology in the United States and Délégation Générale à la Recherche Scientifique et Technique in France) and headed by a distinguished scientist (Special Assistant to the President for Science and Technology in the United States, and Délégué Général in France). In addition, a political post of minister in charge of scientific affairs was created in several countries to allow both for the introduction of the scientific point of view in government machinery and for political intervention in research activities. The consequences of this new relationship between science and power have been widely studied in the United States, particularly by Don K. Price (1965) and Harvey Brooks (1968).

During this period of the 'infancy' of science policy (1945-1957) the problems raised by its existence have been the subject of reports published by the various administrations, and of a vast number of articles published in magazines or specialized journals (*Bulletin of the Atomic Scientists, Science, Scientific American, Nature,* etc.) rather than of books specifically concerned with an effort of synthesis. The situation was summed up in certain collections of published articles, of which the most important was Norman Kaplan's *Science and Society* (1965). It is rather within the framework of specific fields such as the sociology of science (Barber, 1952) and the economics of research and development (See Freeman, Chapter 7) that the problems of science policy have been approached, and not as a field in itself which is not dependent on other subjects. It was only much later that Derek de Solla Price conceived the idea of applying to the study of science as a social institution the same methods of research normally applied to the subject matter of the natural sciences. The notion of this quantitative analysis of scientific data and productivity was to lead him to talk of a 'science of science' as the source of a more comprehensive approach to the phenomena and institutions which are part of science policy (Derek Price, 1963).

It is clear that in the period when science policy as an institution was only just starting, the initiative came from political spheres and administrations influenced mostly by scientists, particularly by physicists who had taken part in the atomic program of World War II. Academic studies on that initiative and its implications had at that time an influence, albeit marginal, on the development of the structures and processes of science policy. It was a starting period which corresponded to a period of euphoria concerning research activities: the prestige lent by scientists, the weight of the progress of atomic research and the faith of the general public in the capacity of science to resolve post-war problems, fostered the establishment of new institutions and the setting up of policies which were considered all the more natural because the climate of international tension and competition engendered by the cold war conferred on them a kind of legitimacy (Meynaud and Schroeder-Gudehus, 1962). The age of utopia was succeeded by the age of pragmatism: it was not until the late Sixties that there came about a period of questioning, partly based on critical thinking linked with science policy studies, but even more directly brought about by historical events.

THE AGE OF PRAGMATISM

When in 1963 the First Ministerial Meeting on Science took place at the

OECD, the Ministers specifically in charge of scientific affairs could still be counted on the fingers of one hand (Mesthene, 1965). Three years later they made up the majority; as a field of government competence, science and technology was no longer considered merely to follow in the wake of educational or cultural policies.

The age of pragmatism can be roughly divided, from 1955 to 1967, into two periods which in any case can hardly be viewed separately. First came a period marked above all by strategic concerns, and in which military (and prestige) objectives prevailed over all others; then came a second period, more specifically determined by the concern of seeing R & D efforts produce economic pay-off. The whole of this period is characterized by a considerable increase in research budgets according to a growth rate which, in many cases, was higher than that of the gross national product.

The cry of alarm raised by the first Sputnik led most industrialized countries to set up institutions concerned with science policy and to increase their scientific and technological budgets. It was a huge and hurried effort of financing but the effort was concentrated only on a small number of objectives; for since science policy had to give priority to the 'competitive struggle' between the two blocs, three quarters of the public funds went towards military, nuclear and space research. Most European countries wished above all to make up for the time lost by the war and the immediate post-war period in matters of manpower, equipment and structures. And Europe — once the birthplace of the Scientific Revolution and the very heart of the international system — discovered at the same time that from now on it stood on the outskirts of that system and that no country in it was capable any longer of undertaking individually and on the same scale the R & D programs undertaken by the super-powers. From that moment, the European countries, even those who were members of the 'Atomic Club' and who allocated the same proportion of their resources as the United States or the USSR to the three priority sectors of military, nuclear and space research, were compelled to go through the process of cooperation in order to achieve their scientific or technical objectives in a more rapid or economic manner (Salomon, 1965).

This need for cooperation, if only to speed up the exchange of information and experience between countries, explains partly why the OECD was able to play a catalytic role in the growing awareness of a certain number of problems peculiar to the newly-founded science policy, and to develop science policy studies which were to become reference works.[1] First of all, the effort to standardize statistical data in matters of R & D (OECD, 1967), secondly, country reviews (OECD, 1966-1973), and thirdly, reports dealing more specifically with certain problems such as the allocation of resources,

---

[1] The position of the author as Head of the Science Policy Division of OECD notwithstanding, we feel the pride of place reasonably justified! (Eds.)

technological innovation or the application of systems analysis techniques to scientific decisions (OECD, 1966 and 1972), generally contributed to make available certain concerns, themes and methods which academic research – at least in Europe – was only to deal with later.

In point of fact, in the United States institutions were created at a governmental level (Rand Corporation) or at an academic level (Columbia University Council for Atomic Studies, Harvard Seminar on Science and Public Policy, Harvard Program on Technology and Society, etc.), which fostered the development of studies on various aspects of science policy. This type of institution was very scarce in Europe until the Seventies (Lund, Sussex), and most of the work undertaken in that field was done under the auspices of OECD. Even though science policy chairs were created very early on in the United States (Harvard, Cornell, MIT), it was not until the Seventies that a small number of academic institutions in Europe started to recognize this field as a specific subject for teaching and research (Sussex, Ulm, Starnberg, Bielefeld, CNAM in Paris).

In that age of pragmatism, the second period opens in 1965 with a discussion on 'technological gaps', which shows the general awareness of the role played by scientific and technological research in international economic competition: rivalry through innovation follows rivalry founded on the production of raw materials and traditional manufactured goods. Research activities were undertaken by ten times more people than before World War II; all industrialized countries increased considerably their scientific and technical investments. But the general picture of national research work cannot hide the gaps existing between work undertaken on the one hand by the United States and the USSR and on the other by the European countries which, far from joining forces in this matter, competed among themselves and often set themselves against one another.

This is the period when Europe feared the threat of the 'brain drain', because it had no overall effort similar to that of the United States and because it had access only as a minor partner to the fruit of scientific discovery and technological innovation. Certain facts showed that the situation was unhealthy. American investments in Europe had shown a sharp increase; European industries were bought up or found themselves in a difficult, if not impossible, state of competition with their American counterparts; and academic institutions were proving inadequate to the demands of modern scientific research even though the student population was constantly on the increase. In fact, these differences were more disturbing from the point of view of statistics (especially R & D inputs), and then only according to sectors: in the field of computers, for instance, an important gap started to widen between the United States and Europe from the years 1959-1960. But if the United States led the way by far from the very start in the sector of semi-conductors and that of advanced electronic systems, there was no great difference between the two shores of the Atlantic in the field of pharmaceutical products or plastics (OECD, 1968-1969). Europe's weak point in both the industrial and the academic field lay not only in the resources it allocated to research activities or even in the structures it displayed; it lay also in its aptitude for innovation, that is, in its aptitude for exploiting the results of research (Ben-David, 1967).

Thus the period of euphoria was followed by a period of questioning and challenge, which does not mean that the general attitude towards science and technology was any less favorable than before. More concern was displayed for the rentability of R & D investments in the civil sector, but these investments continued to grow according to a rhythm which in itself seemed to guarantee a certain coherence if not effectiveness. The age of abundance lasted until 1968, with each industrial country trying to increase the percentage of its gross national product allocated to R & D in order to come as near as possible to the almost magical ratio of 3% which was then exceeded by the United States. At that time there developed two trends in the field of science policy studies: on the administrative level theoretical studies were made in order to ensure a better management of research systems (Jantsch, 1967 and 1971); and on the academic level there were critical studies on the means adopted towards the achievement of the objectives which the countries had set for themselves (Gilpin in the case of France, 1968; Skolnikoff on American foreign policy, 1967). But if these theoretical and critical studies questioned the priorities pursued until then by science policy, science policy studies developed in the wake of a policy the goals of which were not questioned so much as its administrative procedures, its institutional means or the tensions which affected the scientific community, which had now become just another 'pressure group' among others (Greenberg, 1967).

At the same time, in the communist countries, the notion of science policy as evidenced by the West's success in management and technological innovation was taken into account in the reform which led to the establishment of the State Committees for Science and Technology. Science policy studies in a Marxist perspective endeavored to draw the consequences of the changes determining the 'new scientific revolution' (Richta *et al.*, 1967), or concentrated on the study of application of scientific methods to management problems of research activities (Dobrov, 1971). Thus in the USSR and East-European countries, institutes were set up where work was devoted to the theoretical and empirical study of research. There followed a discussion on the subject of whether the budding 'science of science' was part of philosophy or economics or the managerial sciences, and whether it was an autonomous subject rather than the sum of several unconnected subjects (Dobrov, 1966; Mikulinski, 1966; Mirsky, 1972; Spiegel-Rösing, 1973; Rabkine, 1974).

It was at the very time that communist countries were influenced by subjects and methods from the West, that the Western countries began to wonder about the goals of a policy based on these subjects and methods. In

Western countries the tendency to substitute analytical instruments for political ones, such as PPBS or PERT, was questioned, as the application of these instruments to the planning of research proved to be limited (OECD, 1972) or misleading (Sapolsky, 1972), whereas in the Soviet World it was to bring about a large number of theoretical studies which were expected to cause science and technology, from the management of research institutes to the general planning of research work, to be more closely integrated in the process of economic and social development (Kröber *et al.*, 1972 and 1974). But in the West the challenging of the effectiveness of these methods coincided with the emergence of critical thinking on the objectives pursued until then by science policy in the context of economic growth, conceived as an aim in itself. The late Sixties mark the end of science policy as the management of vast technological programs which were supposed to have an almost automatic effect upon the economy. Failures and insufficiencies were here revealed all the more clearly because doubt was cast on the very validity of economic growth exclusively defined by its quantitative aspects.

In the Sixties, the support of basic research and, by degrees, of all scientific activities had all the more credit in political circles because the resources which R & D as a whole enjoyed were plentiful and increasing, if not at an exponential rate, at least at a much faster pace than that of national income. The cause which representatives of the scientific community presented to the public was not a difficult one to plead; it was bound to be successful. In the wake of the post-war technological achievements — nuclear reactors, computers, rockets — anything which seemed technologically possible deserved support in order to be achieved all the sooner. The then predominant role played by physicists in all the national advisory committees on science policy contributed to present science — through the natural sciences only — as a model of reference and even, in terms of publicity, as a prestige-laden image which should serve as an example for the representatives of other subjects to plead their own causes before the public powers. Any appeal to the public powers, whichever the field of research, was in duty bound to point out the economic, social, military or political advantages which society would derive if it were to increase its investments. Even subjects basically far removed from any application were included in this game: high energy physics for instance — when it was a question of building large new cyclotrons — was presented sometimes as a great boon to industry, sometimes as full of promises for long-term applications, even in the field of medicine.

The combination of world events and the change in attitudes toward science and economic growth which started to manifest themselves from 1968 on, made this type of reasoning more and more suspect. The idea that the progress of basic science was bound to guarantee future innovations ceased to be an article of faith, all the more so since future innovation itself ceased to appear altogether as a socially or politically desirable objective simply because it was feasible. An example of this change in attitude is given

by the criticism engendered by the positivist conception of the Harvard
Program on Technology and Society in the United States: the reports published by that Institute were discussed in an article by John McDermot
(1969) which describes technology as the 'new opium' of intellectuals and
managers. The end of the *laissez-faire* period in the relations between science
and politics did not give rise to a questioning of the validity of the goals which
science, now reduced to the state of mere technique, made possible; it in fact
led, according to McDermot's view, to a *laissez-innover*, the cost of which
threatened to be much higher than that of a policy of economic *laissez-faire*,
if one considered the global and planetary character of new technologies and
the consequences which they might have upon man and his environment.

THE AGE OF QUESTIONING

The 'golden age' of science policy — which corresponded to a period of
tension, cold war or strategic competition and economic development careless
of the social or environmental costs it engendered — came to an end in
1968-1969 in the aftermath of the detente, the students' revolt, the growing
awareness of the limits to economic growth, and the American fiasco in
Vietnam, where indeed the systematic application of the methods and products of scientific and technological research proved to be incapable of
controlling a war of popular resistance. On another front, NASA succeeded in
its objectives and a man was able to walk on the moon a year before the
deadline which President John F. Kennedy had set. An American man walked
on the moon. Man's first stride on the moon marked, by reason of its very
success, a turning point: the great options which had fed science policy for an
entire decade now ceased to be taken as articles of faith and the disenchantment affecting the space venture spread to other sectors of research and
development which had only recently been considered priority sectors.

Because of its link with the atomic threat, with war, with the deterioration
of the natural and social environment, and with the quantitative demands of
economic growth, science was suddenly attacked from all sides, jointly by the
conservative and radical points of view; the extreme right wing denounced it
as the costly pastime of high professionals who could not care less about
economic rentability and industrial development, and the extreme left denounced it as an instrument of military and economic domination disregarding society's real needs and all the more dangerous in that it helped to
satisfy imaginary or ostentatious needs.

It is particularly significant that this movement of challenge and rebellion
developed within the scientific community itself, where researchers gathered
not only to challenge the scientific establishment but also to commit themselves politically under the banner of the social responsibility of the scientist.

It was the first time in the history of science — which from the start has been so closely linked with the development of Western societies — that the positivism induced by the methods and achievements of science was questioned by scientists themselves. The movement of Science for the People, in the United States, was the first of a series of militant associations which were to proliferate, with more or less political overtones, in most Western countries.

This disenchantment was first felt in the United States, as a counter-reaction to the success of the great technological programs: the general malaise felt in the universities, the students' revolt, the denouncement of the 'military-industrial complex', were all signs heralding the emergence of a movement which is still spreading and which, by challenging the methods of science policy, has finally also challenged its objectives. The space budget, first by reaching its highest ceiling, then by showing a sharp downturn, was the first to suffer from this turn of events. But other, not less significant, events followed: first the adoption of the 'Mansfield Amendment' forbidding the American Defense Department to subsidize basic research not directly linked with its declared objectives; second, the Congress attack on the SST — rival of the Concorde — because supersonic flights might cause pollution and because methods of ground transportation might be improved if the investments for the SST could be transferred to them; finally, the dismantlement, in the last year of the Nixon administration, of the Office of Science and Technology and the advisory bodies linked to it.

In Europe this malaise was expressed in less acute terms for the very reason that priority options, even though they might be identical to those of the Americans, had nevertheless not brought about the same degree of osmosis between the government and the academic or industrial systems, nor had they lent the same weight to the 'military-industrial complex'. It was felt nevertheless in the effort made by all countries to redirect their research activities towards economic and social ends, or in the readjustments undertaken by countries, such as the United Kingdom and France, who had allocated most of their resources to atomic energy, aeronautics, space and electronic development. The Rothschild 'client-contractor' principle offers the model of a new concept of relations between science and the state in the terms of which the support given to research activities is examined only in relation to their application to ends which concern such or such an administrative body. The Rothschild doctrine, which was adopted in the United Kingdom, shows a tendency which can be seen in most industrialized countries: on the one hand, even though basic research is at the origin of technological changes, it is no longer conceived as a necessary condition for the process which engenders innovations; on the other hand the state is from now on to pay more attention to applied research in relation to specific sectors, and especially those concerned with solving social problems.

As far as science policy studies are concerned, this period of questioning is marked by a series of works, the common denominator of which is that they take the critical analysis of science policy problems as the starting point of a wider study of the relation between science and society – and beyond this, of the legitimacy of the options sought by society as a whole. By challenging the ideology of science (Habermas, 1969) as a technique among others which does away with any pretentions to political neutrality on the part of scientists (Salomon, 1970), as an industrialized enterprise the intellectual and moral standards of which belong to the past (Ravetz, 1971; see also Chapter 3), this wider study includes not only the consequences for science as an institution closely linked with politics, but also the implications for society in general of its own dependence – no less strong – on the scientific and technical phenomenon.

Thus 'Science and Society' becomes the theme of numerous books (Rose, 1969; Schatzman, 1971; Jaubert and Levy-Leblond, 1973), which show the contraditions which the scientific community and institution face in the context of society's options as a whole. Most of these works challenge 'the irrationality of the institution which embodies most brilliantly the rationality of the West' (Salomon, 1970), and put forward, in order for this irrationality to be overcome, the proposal of a new 'critical science' (Ravetz, 1971). However, the emerging social phenomenon of the counterculture deals the most radical blow by far on this subject. The counterculture has contacted an experience outside the pressure and traps of the scientific language and the 'technocratic' procedures in which it is embodied; its radical criticism shows a tendency to confuse the evils of a social practice of science which submits to the demands of industrial systems and competition, with an evil inherent in the very nature of the scientific venture (Roszak, 1969). After questioning the manner in which science as an institution became the object, the stake and the victim of politics, people are questioning the scientific language and method as source, cause and instrument of the disadvantages of progress.

THE NEW SOCIAL OBJECTIVES

Between a paradise lost because of science and an uncertain future to be built with the help of a new science, this critical approach to science policy studies coincided for the first time with the efforts of administrators and decision-makers to reformulate and redirect science policies. It would indeed be too easy to treat as an operation of recuperation on the part of the establishment the balance sheet of science policy presented by the Brooks Report, and the new perspectives which this opened up (OECD, 1971). The stake was obviously more important: the problems existed; they were pressing and could not be avoided. The priorities of the last decade were being re-examined critically, and re-ordered in a manner which, it was felt, would be more concerned with social well-being than with technological progress. On a deeper level, the Brooks Report is the first of a long series of works which no longer questioned merely the nature or the rate of economic growth, but the limits it might encounter and the consequences which it might entail for the international economic situation. Thus, the Meadows Report (1972) and the arguments raised by the Club of Rome and the counter-reports this engendered (Freeman *et al.*, 1973) correspond to a period of readjustment and uncertainty the object of which was far beyond that of science policy.

Once again it was in the United States that this movement first arose, with concerns linked to technology assessment. The problems posed by the deterioration in living standards, the chaotic state of urban development, the difficulties of transportation, pollution, and the threat to the ecology, all this called for control of the course of technical progress. The industrial and technological dynamism of the United States, which only recently had been an object of envy in Europe, made these problems more obvious and sensitive to public opinion, and at an earlier time than anywhere else. Hence the idea, for what it is worth, of technology assessment, a new function of science policy, which would enable possible undesired effects to be foreseen or the real costs of new forms of technology to be assessed in relation to obvious or disregarded social needs (But see Nelkin, Chapter 11).

Beyond the technical problems raised by the introduction and diffusion of technology, this function was aimed at understanding their social implications and after that, at distinguishing the advantages and disadvantages of alternative solutions (Hetman, 1974). It was not an easy function to fulfill since it endeavored to combine a climate of innovation and competition with a system of control of the effects of technological change. In point of fact it was only in the United States that this function was turned into an institution by the creation of the Office of Technology Assessment within Congress itself; it was confirmed by the adoption of legislative measures which guaranteed political control over the various administrative bodies in matters of technological innovation (Derian-Staropoli, 1975).

If this subject fills part of the argument of the Brooks Report, the balance sheet it draws and the perspectives it opens up go beyond technological problems as such and determine new directions for research, pointing out, in particular, the necessity for a close link between the social and natural sciences. The notion of the social sciences as part of science policy has been recognized as such by Western governments which have in fact decided to devote a new program of cooperation to these problems (OECD, 1975). But if the Brooks Report outlines the possible new orientations of science policy, it also points out — and not without reason — the difficulties which these new directions will cause in terms of research programs.

When strategic and prestige objectives predominated, the choices were all the easier because it was relatively easy to perceive the way to achieve them: the setting up of an armament system, the building of an aircraft or a rocket, constituted a specific objective for which the kind of skills, equipment and scientific institutions which would be needed in order to define and maintain a schedule were known from the start. As long as the cost was met in terms of manpower, laboratories and supplies, technological objectives such as the landing on the moon or the development of a nuclear reactor were based from the start on a fund of knowledge, techniques and practical know-how which posed no problems to either the decision makers or the researchers. On the other hand, social objectives refer to research programs the means of which are all the less clear because these objectives themselves are diffuse, fluid and given to partial and progressive solutions.

By going from stable objectives to 'mobile targets' (Salomon *et al.,* 1974), science policy came upon the difficulty of identifying *simultaneously* the ends and the means: urban development, protection from pollution, living standards in general, were 'mobile targets' which could be improved by constant progress but could not be hit 'once and for all'. Besides, these objectives brought into play all sorts of social, economic and political forces which made the technical solutions which had to be found even more difficult to determine: even a problem so closely linked with technological progress as the energy problem had to be approached in the context of collective goals, divergent interests and economic and political constraints; this was all the more true in the case of environmental problems, where technical solutions were linked with compromises between totally different groups and interests, or could at any time be re-examined critically in order for economic constraints or new collective objectives to be taken into account. (This is the case, for instance, of pollution criteria, which are always prone to being increased or decreased.) From this point on the research programs engendered by the new objectives were compelled, as though by nature, to develop in successive stages of adaptation to various conditions determined not only by the progress of skills and techniques but also by the understanding of problems and changes which intervened in the balance of political, social and economic forces (For all this, see Nelkin, Chapter 11).

But until now the proposals for new objectives have brought, in academic institutions as in government laboratories, only very limited or localized changes. At university level the dogma of free research may also lead to self-indulgence: resistance to a more rigorous research may allow one to deal with problems which sometimes may not even have a scientific component. It is very rare to find examples of institutional innovations such as the 'buffer institution', where there is an attempt to integrate interdisciplinary research into a perspective which combines the solution of practical problems with the progress of basic knowledge. It is fair to recognize that these adaptation problems of institutions both in the academic and in the public sector call for a policy of scientific manpower with long-term solutions and means for retraining and reconversion rather than for improvising measures for the reduction of manpower.

But if governments seek a new policy, do scientists seek a new vocation?

In putting forward social objectives as the reasons for which the public powers must support basic research, it is not certain that the scientists will be able to fulfill what they promise. A good part of basic research has obviously nothing to offer towards the solution of the problems engendered by these objectives, and only through a misuse similar to that of 'lobbies' in military or space research, which promise a civil pay-off in order to finance bombs, rockets and moon-walks, would it be possible to claim, for example, that physics and chemistry have more to offer in this field than biology or the social sciences.

One may in fact go further: whatever the contribution of natural sciences and technology to the solution of social problems, it is not evident that this solution is dependent on an increase in R & D investments, rather than on economic and political measures acting directly on production structures, social transfers and the distribution of incomes. For example, does the solution of certain problems from which underdeveloped countries suffer (overpopulation, food, health) really depend on an increased effort in research rather than on differently organized international exchanges? In this context it is no longer enough to state that all basic research is useful in the long term in order for the public powers to feel obliged to increase its credits, rather than those allocated to applied research or, in fact, those of any other sector but science and technology.

The reversal of opinion with regard to the 'social rentability' of scientific investment — counterbalance of the very success which R & D's monumental efforts achieved on the technological level in the last twenty five years — can only be understood in relation to the changes which have effected international relations and the process, if not the actual conception, of economic growth. As the Brooks Report points out, 'science policy is in disarray because society itself is in disarray, partly because the power of modern science has enabled society to reach goals that formerly were only vague aspirations, but whose achievement has revealed their shallowness or has created expectations that outrun even the possibilities of modern technology or the economic resources available from growth' (OECD, 1971). But if the scientific crisis reflects the crisis taking place in society, it nevertheless remains that the changes advocated by the Brooks Report are still within the context of the objectives of economic growth, even if they are adjusted by more 'qualitative' demands. And if another use of science and technology was advocated there, it was on condition that nevertheless the resources allocated to them continue to increase. But these resources in fact were to decrease as a result of the economic difficulties precipitated by the oil crisis of 1973, and the very consequences of that crisis on the energy level were to reduce the scope of those barely attempted efforts to re-direct research activities the solution of social problems.

THE DEATH AND RESURRECTION
OF SCIENCE POLICY

It seems today as if the late Sixties marked the end of science policy as conceived of by industrial countries. This could justly be taken as the penalty of its often brilliant achievements. In each country a long-term effort has enabled the scientific and technical potential to increase considerably. For those who wished it, the great technological enterprises led, in other respects, to undoubted achievements shown, for instance, by the variety of armament systems, the exploration of space, the achievements made in the exploitation of nuclear energy and the new developments in aeronautics and electronics.

Besides the malaise which these priorities may have engendered, it was probably inevitable that a policy concentrated on these vast enterprises would slow down at the end of their venture. All the more so because their scope became more limited as time went by: the decrease of tension on the international plane and economic and social development have had the effect of reducing, in public opinion, the importance of even the most brilliant technological achievements. In countries with a dynamic sector capable of founding its expansion on the exploitation of the possibilities offered by scientific and technical progress, it was discovered that industrial innovation alone did not necessarily mean happiness. Contrary to early hopes, the great strategic objectives did not have a direct effect on the industrial sector as a whole. The balance sheet of aid policy for industrial development looks sometimes so disappointing that certain countries prefer to support other production or trade activities. The unrestricted financing of scientific research does not necessarily bring about innovation or even very important scientific information. Increased production on the part of scientists and engineers — as much as it can be stimulated — is not enough to ensure the broadening of national programs of research and development.

In particular, military and space research have not brought about the 'spin-off' which public relations services and scientists attached to space and military agencies over-optimistically (and often with an excess of propaganda) thought they would. One may well say that the technological products and processes which resulted from this would probably not have come about, or at least not as quickly, without the impetus lent by military and prestige considerations, but it is difficult to say that they would ever have come about ~~ ~~out the disregard for economic profitability which went hand in hand considerations (OECD, 1971).

~~ ~~nly accept the fact that science policy ceased to have a ~~ ~~ the last decade because it had to take account of a ~~ ~~undertaken by public and private executive ~~ ~~respective responsibilities? In this perspec- ~~ ~~e enough to ensure the coordination and control of certain activities. Yet the problems are still there, and if past science policy has not been able to achieve all that was expected of it, it is rather for lack of long-term means of persuasion, and long-term perspectives, than because its function has not been defined. The present phase is marked by a renewed awareness of problems which can only be dealt with properly at the highest government level; it should therefore not be expected that their solution should come from executive bodies working independently of one another.

In fact there is more than ever an essential place to be filled by a political body which would ensure coordination and which might at the same time influence research structure as such and its administrative, academic and economic environment; preserve the overall balance of scientific and technological research activities and direct research programs according to present and future needs. It is all the more important to understand, in order to master it, the diversity of factors intervening in the comprehensive approach to certain sectors (energy, natural resources, raw materials, food), and in which science and technology will always have an essential role to play.

From this point of view, whatever the methodological limits of systems analysis and other techniques specific to 'world models', the fact remains that these instruments could be developed to serve as bases of reference for decision-making. One must, however, be aware of the limits of their application. In the decade 1970-1980 these instruments should not exert the same fascination and raise the same hopes among the technocrats as those raised by the technological forecasts of the Sixties. The fact that the Cassandras of technological forecasting have been succeeded by the Malthuses of systems analysis is far from being a guarantee that a solution will be found for complex problems.

Today, just as yesterday, and tomorrow all the more, these remain only instrumental means which cannot be substituted for decisions and, therefore, can only be used if social structures and the needs and aspirations of man — and thus of politics — are taken into account. The models set by *World Dynamics* (Forrester, 1971) and *The Limits to Growth* have had the merit of attracting attention to world problems, before which decision makers had only too great a tendency to shut their eyes. But, as Marie Jahoda has pointed out, the solution to these problems does not lie solely in the technocratic application of instruments which would reduce history to its physical constraints (Freeman *et al.*, 1973). It was not 'Malthus revisited' by Forrester or Meadows which in 1973-1974 provoked the energy crisis, but the oil-producing Arab countries.

Another aspect to be taken into account by science policy underlines even better the limitations of quantitative methods applied to decision making: namely the issue of public participation on which decision making is more and more dependent. The need to associate the public more closely with decision making can only be understood in the context of the changes which have affected the image of science in the eyes of society and also in the eyes of researchers themselves. As André Malraux has said, 'Until the Twentieth Century the balance sheet of science was totally positive; since the use of gases in 1914-1918 and of the atomic bomb in 1945, this balance sheet also shows some negative aspects.' In this matter science and technology and, more important, the political decisions which concern them, can no longer be confined to the 'corridors of power'. It is not by chance that the last Conference of Science Ministers at the OECD (1975) recognized that the public must be increasingly involved in decisions affecting, among other things, science and technology.

The exaggerated tendency in the Nineteenth Century to see everything in scientific terms caused scientific and technical activity to be considered as a decisive factor in human progress. It was hoped that the social concerns, combined with the system of development peculiar to science, would lead to the progressive establishment of a better social structure. An even more exact technology, leading to the control of social relations and of the relations between society and nature, was to ensure the continuity of progress. At the present time we are witnessing a challenge to this conception of progress: the change brought about by scientific and technological development is not necessarily a factor of 'progress' when it engenders a series of ruptures within societies which are unsettled by the rapid pace of technological development. An object of hope and fear, science appears more and more as the reflection of the great problems of society.

Science has opened itself to social conflicts and has become one of their hostages. Already society is forgetting what it owes science and thinks only of the threats and difficulties it engenders. The piling up of social problems might lead one to expect a great deal from the combined contributions of natural sciences, engineering and social sciences. But the balance sheet of the tentative experiments in that field is disappointing, the returns on techno-logical efforts in the past few decades are not always valid in new situations. Inversely, there is an attempt to develop 'alternative technologies' which might be able, if not to resolve the needs of the industrialized world, at least to foster the development of Third-World countries (Dickson, 1974). Thus, between positivism and Utopia, modern societies are seeking new formulas to make their relation with the products of scientific knowledge more human.

Must we not, in a new social context, adopt different criteria for the appraisal of scientific structures and the exploitation of scientific results? Is it not necessary better to measure the social implications of scientific and technological efforts? Scientists and engineers are the first to be able to attract the attention of the public to the implications of their work. The scientist's social responsibility is here to a real measure in opposition to the traditional concept of scientific responsibility: to alert society at the pre-liminary stage of research is indeed going beyond strict scientific objectivity, and could amount to interpreting preliminary results in the light of hypo-theses which have not been confirmed. Is there not the risk of being unnecessarily alarmist in case of error? Keeping silent, however, might be more reprehensible: the scientist would merely be refusing to draw the public's attention to a possibility. It is not his place to pre-empt decisions which remain basically political decisions. Already various scientific organizations have been concerning themselves with these problems, or have been set up for this purpose (for example, the Council for Science and Society in Great Britain). The new scientific ethos which is at the moment trying to define itself will perhaps facilitate the setting up of a system of public discussion necessary if society is to resolve the problems brought about by the discoveries and application of science (See Chapters 3, 10 and 11).

All this suggests that a new form of exchange will have to be set up between society and technology, one that will take into consideration the aspirations of man in a complex society rather than the 'autonomous' tendencies of science and technology. The basic question is this: toward what ends are science and technology directed? In other words, toward what kind of society? Have we not lost sight of this end because the scientists, the decision makers just like the public at large, believed firmly that technology represented a good thing in itself and was the result of autonomous development?

The Brooks Report has made a valid distinction between two kinds of choices: *tactical* choices, which deal with scientific problems and projects within a given field and are basically dependent on internal scientific criteria; and *strategic* choices which concern areas of great priority and must be guided by objectives external to the scientific community (OECD, 1971).

As soon as these strategic choices are determined by objectives of a social nature, the formulation and elaboration of research programs can no longer fall within the competence of the representatives of a single field or even of connected fields: it is necessary, at the very least, that the specialists of natural sciences and those of social sciences learn to work together. But this in itself would not be enough to encourage public opinion and, through it, the public powers, to foster basic research: at that level of decision making the participation of the future users' representatives (trade unions, consumers, local authorities) is no less useful than that of the representatives of administration and industry.

What is meant by technology assessment is not only the apparently objective advice of technical expertise which might allay the disadvantages of progress, but first the association with technical expertise, of all the social partners which are primarily exposed to these disadvantages. In this sense research activities are not and can no longer be the exclusive business of researchers or of the bodies which subsidize them. If the consumers, the trade unions, the local authorities are directly concerned with the effects — positive or negative — of technical change, is it not normal to recognize that they have a right to have a say in the direction given to technical change through research activities?

The effectiveness of science policy depends on a more obvious and greater role played by science as an institution within society. This is plain from the fears provoked by the establishment of nuclear power stations: for lack of a closer participation of the public in decision making, technological development appears more as a threat than as a solution. But nuclear power stations are just an example among others of certain forms of technology, the large-scale dissemination of which causes public opinion to wonder about the 'negative' consequences of technical change and ever-increasing groups to be formed in order to challenge them. Airports, dams, motorways, jet planes, pesticides (Nelkin, 1971, 1973, 1974; see also Chapter 11) – the list is endless. Nuclear energy adds a further dimension to the supposed or real disadvantages of technical progress – that of the fear of atomic matter. Nothing probably will ever allay that fear, even if in reality the risks presented by atomic power stations have little to do with the real dangers of the atomic weapons system to which public opinion is less sensitive. The 'original sin' which, according to Oppenheimer's phrase, attended the control of fission and caused it to be used to destroy, will always be a part of the argument.

But at least one can see the extent to which the pace, nature and the scale of technological changes impose a double duty on industrial societies: to be more careful in the dissemination of innovations in order to avoid disasters; and to take public opinion more into account in order to avoid being forced to a standstill. Since, in any case, decisions must be taken, the only way to implement them is to get them accepted by informing the public openly, allowing it to take part as much as possible, giving it access to technical data and above all choosing to present these for what they are – details in a file which are valid not because they are technical but because they are part of a political choice.

These matters are never purely technical since a consensus has to be found, not on the way to achieve a program, but rather on the way to adjust strategic objectives to the concerns of individuals and groups. In this sense we should be pleased that public opinion should claim (and obtain more and more) the right to counter-expertise: before the real and imaginary threats posed by technology, the end of the myth of the Expert is, for our science-conditioned societies, a proof of democratic functioning. With all these problems, science policy studies have obviously a great deal to do by way of new fields to clear and exploit, and because of their technical character they will probably always find it more difficult to get rid of their ethical, if not political overtones. The development in the United States of policy research is an indication of this, as is the increase everywhere of studies and meetings on the social and political repercussions of the scientific institution and scientific progress (for instance the risks of manipulating genetic inheritance by the application of discoveries in the field of molecular biology). Just as we have not seen the end – nor shall we ever – of science and technology, we have not seen the end – nor shall we ever – of the systematic analysis on a deeper and ever-renewed level, of the social functions of science and their irreversibly political dimensions.

BIBLIOGRAPHY

General Works:

Caldwell, L. K., *Science, Technology and Public Policy: A Selected and Annotated Bibliography*, Vol. I, 1968; Vol. II, 1969; Vol. III, 1972, Indiana University, Bloomington.

Hewlet, R. G. and Anderson, O. E., *The New World – A History of the United States Atomic Energy Commission*, Vol. I, 1962, and Hewlet, R. G., and Duncan, F., *Atomic Shield* 1947-1952, Vol. II, Pennsylvania State University Press, 1969.

Science, Conflict and Society, Readings from Scientific American, Introduction by Garrett Hardin, Freeman and Company, San Francisco, 1969.

Spiegel-Rösing, I., *Wissenschaftsentwicklung und Wissenschaftssteuerung, Einfuhrung und Material Zur Wissenschaftsforschung,* Athenaum Verlag, Frankfurt, 1973.

To which may be added the bibliography given by Norman Kaplan in *Science and Society,* Rand McNally and Co., Chicago, 1965; the bibliography given at the end of *Problems of Science Policy,* OECD, Paris, 1968, and, of course, those given at the end of some of the books mentioned in this paper.

Specific Works:

Barber, 1952	Barber, B., *Science and the Social Order,* The Free Press, New York, 1952.
Bell, 1960	Bell, D., *The End of Ideology,* The Free Press, New York, 1960.
Ben-David, 1967	Ben-David, J., *Fundamental Research and the Universities,* OECD, Paris, 1967.
Ben-David, 1971	Ben-David, J., *The Scientist's Role in Society: A Comparative Study,* Prentice-Hall, New Jersey, 1971.
Bernal, 1967	Bernal, J. D., *The Social Function of Science,* London, 1939, reissued by MIT Press, Cambridge, Mass, 1967.
Brewer, 1973	Brewer, G., *Politicians, Bureaucrats and the Consultant,* Basic Book, New York, 1973.
Brooks, 1968	Brooks, H., *The Government of Science,* MIT Press, Cambridge, Mass, 1968.
Bush, 1960	Bush, V., *Science, the Endless Frontier; A Report to the President on a Program for Postwar Scientific Research,* 1945, reissued by the NSF, Washington, 1960.
Chayes and Wiesner, 1969	Chayes, A., and Wiesner, J. B., *ABM: An Evaluation of the Decision to Deploy an Antiballistic System,* New American Library, New York, 1969.

Derian and Staropoli, 1975	Derian, J., and Staropoli, *La technologie incontrolée? Une présentation du Technology Assessment*, PUF, Paris, 1975.
Dickson, 1974	Dickson, D., *Alternative Technology and the Politics of Technical Change*, Fontana, London, 1974.
Dobrov, 1966	Dobrov, G. M., *Nauka o Nauka (The Science of Science)*, Naukova Dumka, Kiev, 1966.
Dupree, 1964	Dupree, H. A., *Science in the Federal Government*, Mayer Harper Textbook, New York, 1964.
Fayet, 1960	Fayet, J., *La Révolution française et la science*, Rivière Press, 1960.
Freeman *et al.*, 1973	Freeman, C., *et al.*, *Thinking about the Future*, Sussex University Press, Brighton, 1973.
Freeman and Young, 1965	Freeman, C., and Young, A., *The Research and Development Effort in Western Europe, North America and the Soviet Union*, OECD, Paris, 1965.
Gilpin, 1962	Gilpin, R., *American Scientists and Nuclear Weapons Policy*, Princeton University Press, New Jersey, 1962.
Gilpin, 1968	Gilpin, R., *France in the Age of the Scientific State*, Princeton University Press, 1968.
Gilpin and Wright, 1964	Gilpin, R., and Wright, C., *Scientists and National Policy-Making*, Columbia University Press, New York, 1964.
Graham, 1967	Graham, L. A., *The Soviet Academy of Sciences and the Communist Party*, Princeton University Press, 1967.
Greenberg, 1969	Greenberg, D. S., *The Politics of Pure Science*, New American Library, 1967, published in England as *The Politics of American Science*, Penguin, 1969.
Hahn, 1971	Hahn, R., *The Anatomy of a Scientific Institution – The Paris Academy of Sciences, 1666-1803*, University of California Press, Berkeley, 1971.
Hetman, 1973	Hetman, F., *Society and the Assessment of Technology*, OECD, Paris, 1973.
Jantsch, 1967	Jantsch, E., *Technological Forecasting in Perspective*, OECD, Paris, 1967.
Jantsch, 1968	Jantsch, E., *Perspectives of Planning*, OECD, Paris, 1968.
Jaubert and Levy-Leblond, 1973	Jaubert, A., and Levy-Leblond, J., *(Auto) Critique de la Science*, Seuil, Paris, 1973.
Kaplan, 1965	Kaplan, N., *Science and Society*, Rand McNally and Co., Chicago, 1965.
Kröber *et al.*, 1972	Kröber, G. *et al.*, *Wissenschaftliche Entdeckungen*, Akademie Verlag, Berlin, 1972.
Kröber *et al.*, 1974	Kröber, G. *et al.*, *Wissenschaftliches Schöpfertum*, Akademie Verlag, Berlin, 1974.
Kröber *et al.*, 1974	Kröber, G. *et al.*, *Wissenschaft und Forschung im Sozialismus, Probleme ihrer Entwicklung, Gestaltung und Analyse*, Akademie Verlag, Berlin 1974.
Lakoff, 1966	Lakoff, S. A., *Knowledge and Power*, The Free Press, New York, 1966.
McDermot, 1969	McDermot, J., article in *New York Review of Books*, Vol. XIII, No. 2, 31 July 1969.

Meadows *et al.*, 1972	Meadows, D. *et al., The Limits to Growth,* Wright-Allen Press, Cambridge, Mass, 1972.
Merton, 1957	Merton, R. K., *Social Theory and Social Structure,* The Free Press, New York, 1957.
Merton, 1970	Merton, R. K., *Science, Technology and Society in Seventeenth-Century England,* Bruges, 1938, reissued by Harper Textbooks, New York, 1970.
Mesthene, 1965	Mesthene, E. G., *Ministers Talk about Science,* OECD, Paris, 1965.
Meynaud and Schroeder-Gudehus, 1962	Meynaud, J., and Schroeder-Gudehus, B., *Les Savants dans la vie internationale,* Etudes de Science Politique, Lausanne, 1962.
Mikulinski, 1966	Mikulinski, S. R., *Science as an Object of Specialised Research: Problems of Philosophy* (in Russian), Moscow, 1966.
Mirsky, 1972	Mirsky, E. M., 'Science Studies in the USSR', *Science Studies,* 1972, No. 2, pp. 281-294.
Nelkin, 1971	Nelkin, D., *Nuclear Power and its Critics: The Cayuga Lake Controversy,* Cornell University Press, 1971.
Nelkin, 1973	Nelkin, D., *Methadone Maintenance, A 'Technological Fix',* Cornell University Press, 1973.
Nelkin, 1974	Nelkin, D., *Jetport: The Boston Airport Controversy,* Transaction Book, New Jersey, 1974.
OECD, 1963	OECD, *Science and the Policies of Governments – The Implications of Science and Technology for National and International Affairs,* Paris, 1963.
OECD, 1966	OECD, *Government and Allocation of Resources to Science,* Paris, 1966.
OECD, 1966	OECD, *Government and Technical Innovation,* Paris, 1966.
OECD, 1967 and 1968	OECD, *International Statistical Year for Research and Development,* Vol. I, *The Overall Level and Structure of R and D Efforts in OECD Member Countries,* 1967, Vol. II, *Statistical Tables and Notes,* 1968.
OECD, 1966-73	OECD, *Reviews of National Science Policy: Belgium,* 1966; *France,* 1967; *United Kingdom/Germany,* 1967; *Japan,* 1967; *United States,* 1968; *Italy,* 1969; *Canada,* 1969; *Norway,* 1971; *Austria,* 1971; *Spain,* 1971; *Switzerland,* 1972; *Iceland,* 1973; *Netherlands,* 1973.
OECD, 1968-70	OECD, *Gaps in Technology, General Report,* 1968; *Analytical Report,* 1970; *Sectors Reports: Scientific Instruments,* 1968; *Electronic Components,* 1969; *Plastics,* 1969; *Pharmaceuticals,* 1969; *Non-Ferrous Metals,* 1970; *Electronic Computers,* 1970.
OECD, 1971	OECD, *Science, Growth and Society – A New Perspective* ('Brooks Report'), 1971.
OECD, 1972	OECD, *Analytical Methods in Government Science Policy* – An Evaluation, 1972.
OECD, 1975-76	OECD, *Social Science Policy:* France, 1975; Norway, 1976, and Japan to be published in 1977.
Derek Price, 1963	Price, Derek de Solla, *Little Science, Big Science,* Columbia University Press, New York, 1963.

Don K. Price, 1965   Price, Don K., *The Scientific Estate*, The Belknap Press of Harvard University, Cambridge, Mass, 1965.

Rabkine, 1974   Rabkine, Yakov M., 'Origines et développements de la recherche sur la recherche en Union Soviétique', Le Progrès Scientifique, 170, May-June 1974, DGRST, Paris, pp; 39-51.

Ravetz, 1971   Ravetz, J. R., *Scientific Knowledge and its Social Problems*, Clarendon Press, Oxford, 1971.

Richta *et al.*, 1967   Richta, R., *et al.*, *Civilisation at the Crossroad*, Prague, 1967 (English translation).

Rose and Rose, 1970   Rose, H., and Rose, S., *Science and Society*, Penguin Books, London, 1970.

Roszak, 1969   Roszak, T., *The Making of a Counter Culture*, Doubleday and Co., New York, 1969.

Salomon, 1965-66   Salomon, J.-J., *International Scientific Organisations*, OECD, Paris, 1965; *Supplement*, 1966.

Salomon, 1973   Salomon, J.-J., *Science and Politics*, Paris, 1970, reissued by Macmillan, London, and MIT Press, Cambridge, Mass, 1973.

Salomon *et al.*, 1972-74   Salomon, J.-J. et al., *The Research System, A Comparative Study of the Organisation and Financing of Fundamental Research*, Vol. I, *Germany, France, United Kingdom*, OECD, Paris, 1972; Vol. II, *Belgium, Netherlands, Norway, Sweden, Switzerland*, 1973; Vol. III, *Canada, United States, General Conclusions*, 1974.

Sapolsky, 1972   Sapolsky, H. M., *Creating the Invulnerable Deterrent – Programmatic and Bureaucratic Success in the Polaris System Development*, Harvard University Press, Cambridge, Mass, 1972.

Schatzman, 1971   Schatzman, E., *Science et Société*, Laffont, Paris, 1971.

Senghaas, 1972   Senghaas, D., *Rüstung und Militarismus*, Suhrkamp, 1972.

Shils, 1966   Shils, E., *Criteria for Scientific Development: Public Policy and National Goals*, MIT Press, Cambridge, Mass, 1966.

Skolnikoff, 1967   Skolnikoff, E. B., *Science, Technology and American Foreign Policy*, MIT Press, Cambridge, Mass, 1967.

Snow, 1962   Snow, C. P., *Science and Government*, 1960, republished by Mentor Books, New York, 1962.

Spiegel-Rösing, 1973   Spiegel-Rösing, I., 'Science Policy Studies in a Political Context: The Conceptual and Institutional Development of Science Policy Studies in the German Democratic Republic', *Science Studies* 3, 1973, pp. 393-413.

Weinberg, 1967   Weinberg, A. M., *Reflections on Big Science*, MIT Press, Cambridge, Mass, 1967.

Zaleski *et al.*,   Zaleski, et al., *Science Policy in the USSR*, OECD, Paris, 1969.

Chapter 3

CRITICISMS OF SCIENCE

J. R. Ravetz

University of Leeds

AN EXAMPLE FROM CLASSICAL CIVILIZATION

Although we shall soon see that the "science" that was the object of criticism has been a complex and varied entity, the oldest example of detailed criticism known to me has a surprisingly modern tone. This is the comedy of Aristophanes, *The Clouds*, of around 420 BC. I shall discuss it at some length because of its usefulness in illustrating many of our concerns. A brief quotation will indicate the general style:

Student: What would you say then if you heard another,
        Our master's own?
Strepsiades: Oh, come, do tell me that.
Student: Why, Chaerophon was asking him in turn,
        Which theory did he sanction; that the gnats
        Hummed through their mouth, or backwards, through their tails?
Strepsiades: Aye, and what said your master of the gnat?
Student: He answered thus: the entrail of the gnat
        Is small: and through the narrow pipe the wind
        Rushes with violence straight towards the tail;
        There, close against the pipe, the hollow rump
        Receives the wind, and whistles to the blast.
Strepsiades: So then the rump is trumpet to the gnats!
        O happy, happy in your entrail learning!
        Full surely need he fear nor debts nor duns
        Who knows about the entrails of the gnats.

At one level we can see in the character of Strepsiades a precursor of those

71

modern legislators who occasionally regale their colleagues with lists of ridiculous titles of research projects on which the taxpayer's money is being spent. Certainly the problem of justifying research whose only goal is 'positive' factual knowledge, is one that defies easy solution. It is clear from the dialogue as well as from the context that mere 'positive' knowledge of fleas is only ancillary to other goals. Strepsiades is a rustic who has come to Athens to learn how to argue with the 'wrong logic' in the law courts, and thereby escape the debts that his wastrel son has incurred. He has been directed to this school of 'Socrates' as a likely source of instruction. He is willing to put up with all these irrelevant facts as the price he must pay for mastering the techniques that will enable him to solve his practical problems. For the students and 'Socrates', however, such facts are serious business; they lead to the philosophical study of nature, and the achievement of wisdom. The discipline illustrated in the main body of the play is meteorology; the Gods are not abolished but the phenomena of thunder and rain are 'explained' by coarse jokes about digestive functions.

Thus Aristophanes blended the voices of the Sophists, who hired themselves out to teach debating skills, with those of the 'physiologues', who produced 'disenchanted' explanations of natural phenomena; then he named their representative 'Socrates'. It is likely that this was both inaccurate and unfair, but then Aristophanes was a writer of critical comedies, and in this one the moral is plain. The end comes when the son of Strepsiades displays a superior mastery of the 'wrong logic', to the extent that he is justified in beating up his father; the latter then burns down the school with its inhabitants. The chorus approves, as 'Socrates' and his group have blasphemed the gods. In this little drama the 'positive' facts derive all their significance from their ideological function; and this is seen as clearly by the 'scientists' as by their enemies. Only later do we find spokesmen for science claiming that embattled scientists (such as Galileo) should have both the privileges of an ideological combatant on the right side, and also the immunities of an encapsulated scholar.

The circumstances producing this early criticism of 'science' are worth mentioning. Athens was embroiled in the serious Peloponesian War, having been led by Pericles through a cycle of patriotism, interstate cooperation and ultimately imperialism. The essence of the free Athenian policy, immortalized in Pericles' late oration, might well have been corrupted and destroyed before anyone noticed it was there. At the court of Pericles were 'freethinkers', including the philosopher Anaxagoras, who was eventually tried for impiety. Certainly there was plausibility in Aristophanes' implicit accusation that the 'demythologizing' of nature and of the city had led to a corruption of the people. The relation of the historical Socrates to all this is beyond my present concerns (Ferguson, 1971).

We gain some idea of the rapidity of the change of cosmology in Fifth Century Athens when we consider the tragedy *Prometheus Bound,* by

Aeschylus, only a half-century earlier. There Prometheus lists all his gifts to mankind: they are all techniques, with no 'pure' or philosophical science to be seen. What is startling to a modern reader, and perhaps embarrassing to some, is that the really advanced 'sciences' were those of prognostication by magical means. From our modern viewpoint we can perhaps imagine the intellectual and spiritual disturbance which the denigration and destruction of the old cosmology must have caused more easily than could our predecessors in scholarship. In his classic work on Aeschylus, George Thomson (1941) omits the major part of Prometheus' speech which deals with magic; then he comments on 'the bold naturalism of the account'.

There is also a criticism of 'science' built into the Prometheus legend: the gods are jealous of man's powers. Whether this is simply one of the less enlightened responses of the Greek deities, or whether this reflects a deep fear of uncontrolled knowledge, like the Garden of Eden story, is a matter for speculation. Of the prehistory of this sort of 'science criticism' I can offer only one fragment: for the early Hebrews, iron was an unclean substance and not to be brought into a holy place, because of its associations. Thus a loathing of the evil effects of natural knowledge applied to technical problems can be traced back very far indeed.

CRITICISM IN THE SCIENTIFIC REVOLUTION

Although 'science' is an essentially complicated and confused term, I am here concerned with the cluster of activities and styles that are dominant at the present time. For brevity I can omit descriptions of debates over occult arts and scholasticism from the Medieval and Renaissance periods. However, the Scientific Revolution of the Seventeenth Century is so directly ancestral to our own situation, that a review of debates then can be helpful for perspective on ourselves.

The prophets of the Scientific Revolution had a commitment to a positive dream for a reformed natural knowledge; but not surprisingly, they were more articulate in their criticisms of the existing science and learning. From the criticisms which each of them made we may gain some insights into what he considered to be central to his own program. Bacon's critique was the most broad-ranging, and also the most related to practice. He considered all the different sorts of men claiming to advance knowledge, and found them all wanting in their methods, attitudes and ethics. Although the professed men of knowledge were guilty of just about every one of the seven deadly sins, it was, in my opinion, pride that Bacon found most monstrous. There is little doubt that he saw himself as the inaugurator of a brotherhood of pure reformers of knowledge and then of mankind; the millenarian connotations of *Et Augebitur Scientia* would not have been lost on his readers (Ravetz, 1971). Descartes probably also entertained some ambitions of a messianic character, and his interest in the shadow brotherhood of Rosicrucians is difficult to deny (Arnold, 1958). But his lasting impulse to reform came from his experiences as an adolescent schoolboy. Having believed that books could reveal the Good and True, he turned in his disillusion on the entire syllabus, reserving special scorn for philosophy and theology, and allowing only mathematics a partial exception (Descartes, 1638). By contrast to these two, Galileo seems to have been concerned mainly with natural philosophy, and his brief, disconnected, critical analyses were made mainly in the context of polemical debate.

It is now generally recognized that there were three, not two, sides in the philosophical struggles of the early Seventeenth Century; against the 'mechanists' were arrayed Aristotelians with an 'organic' world view, and 'alchemists' with a 'magic' world view. Of course, there were factions and conflicts within each camp, and each exerted an influence on the other two (Kearney, 1971). The debate between the two 'losing' sides is not well chronicled; van Helmont's sufferings at the hands of the Inquisition are nearly forgotten (Bonelli and Shea, 1975). Nor do we have editions of counter-criticisms by Aristotelians (of the various sorts) to the 'atomists'. Fortunately, we do possess published documents from a great debate on the other front: between Paracelsians and Galileans, roughly speaking, in Civil War England. The occasion was an attempt by more radical educational reformers to include universities in their plans. The attack was led by John Webster, and in a war of pamphlets the defense was made by Seth Ward and John Wilkins. Webster denounced the universities for their supposed conservatism; in their reply the academics cast reflections on his competence, and denounced his alchemical recommendations as antithetical to all Bacon's precepts. But they had to admit that Bacon did advocate experiments as a way to learning, and that they refrained from forcing such things on their students, since the universities were still essentially elite finishing schools rather than centers for advancement of learning or diffusion of useful arts (Webster, 1976).

With the decay into insignificance of its two rivals – outside Germany, at least – the school of the 'mechanical' philosophy of nature came to complete dominance by the end of the Seventeenth Century. But it had lost the prophetic zeal of its earliest proponents, and indeed in England, at least, experimental philosophy came to be regarded as a gentleman's eccentricity, at a time when manners and morals were the prime concern of the cultivated classes. In spite of – or perhaps because of – the near deification of Newton in early Eighteenth Century England, there was no corps of really talented men to continue his work. A savage satire of scientific academicians and industrial innovators was at the heart of the story of Gulliver's voyage to Laputa as told by Jonathan Swift. An equally pungent sociological analysis of scientific dogmatism was made by the philosopher George Berkeley in the course of his debate over the concealed obscurities at the foundation of the calculus (Ravetz, 1971, pp. 219-223). But systematic and socially effective criticism of the dominant styles of science was by this time becoming exceedingly difficult, as 'reason' became the touchstone for all decisions in polite European society.

THE ROMANTIC CHALLENGE AND
ITS DESCENDANTS

It is useful to remember how deeply split was the Enlightenment movement on the question of science. All factions agreed on the necessity of doing away with the corrupt tyranny of the Church. But not all shared the faith of d'Alembert and Condorcet that a Newtonian type of science, both natural and social, would itself bring reason and justice to human affairs. In particular, Rousseau and his followers, combining Arcadian, romantic and populist elements, raised a significant challenge to orthodox science during the revolution, appearing as forerunners of the cultural revolutionaries of recent times (Clagett, 1959).

The flourishing of romantic poetry in England also had its scientific aspects. Blake's contempt for atomism and 'single vision' is well known to today's counterculture, and Coleridge's enthusiastic study of *Naturphilosophie* (Knight, 1972) was more plausible than we now realize, given the exciting and chaotic state of chemistry and biology at the time. But the movement was short-lived; and the English combination of utility and inductivism kept their science rather more practical and less speculative and sensitive, than in Germany.

Germany was, of course, the home and source of romanticism, particularly in science. Swedenborg, the engineer-turned-psychic, provided elements of continuity with earlier enchanted philosophies of nature. To the acute embarrassment of German men of science for a century afterwards, the great poet Goethe considered his work on optics as important as any other he did. Romanticism, in *Naturphilosophie,* had an ontological basis of opposition to the hard experimental science that was to replace it, a commitment to some sort of existence 'beyond reductionism'. Future historical studies may find a surprising number of people of such tendencies among known critical or eccentric scientists. Thus G. T. Fechner, the founder of psychophysics, was led to his classic empirical studies by the need to corroborate his panpsychical philosophy, as exemplified in 'Nanna, or the Soul Life of Plants' (Jaynes, 1972). Also we now find that A. R. Wallace broke with the Darwinian theory of the descent of man from apes because of the intensity of his spiritualist experiences (Kottler, 1974). A direct link to the present-day counterculture is provided by Rudolf Steiner, who combined Goethe with theosophy; and in spite of the apparent isolation of his established followers in 'anthroposophy', he indirectly provided inspiration and insights for the romantics of today.

A link to another contemporary focus of criticism can be found in Max Scheler, the brilliant though eccentric German philosopher of the earlier Twentieth Century. He did not merely mourn the passing of the 'organic' *Gemeinschaft* world in the well-known German style; he also examined modern science as the characteristic production of a peculiar, alienated consciousness (Staude, 1967). Much of the later 'cultural' historical materialism — as, for example, the neglected essay by Christopher Caudwell, *Crisis in Physics* (1939) — seems to contain echoes of Scheler's analysis, though of course without his particular judgment on the phenomenon.

The ontological criticism of modern materialistic scientism has flourished throughout the century, though until quite recently, at least, kept on the sidelines. The biological sciences have produced descendants of vitalism in 'holism'; this developed into the concept of 'levels of organization', as characterized in Whitehead's 'organismic' philosophy, with continuous extensions to mysticism in Bergson — gloriously misunderstood by Bertrand Russell in his essay *Mysticism and Logic* — and in Teilhard de Chardin. From physics came a more 'spiritualist' tendency, most notably seen in Crookes and Oliver Lodge; later Eddington, Jeans and Milne continued the criticism of materialistic science from a more Platonic point of view. E. A. Burtt was the first to analyze Seventeenth Century science as the product of a metaphysical shift; his classic book (1924, 1932) opens with a contrast between Dante's hymn to the Divine Light and the schoolboy Epicurean heroics of Bertrand Russell's 'A Free Man's Worship'. It was to be nearly half a century before professional historians of science could become sufficiently critical of science to appreciate this work.

MODERN RADICAL CRITICISMS OF SCIENCE

Although social criticisms of science on behalf of the non-elite classes were made in earlier centuries, they have gained coherence only recently. The course of Marxist criticism of science may indicate some reasons for this delay. To a large extent, Marxists have wanted only to inherit and purify bourgeois culture, rather than to transform it.

Lenin's vigorous book on philosophy of science (1909) accepted the facts and values of science as unproblematic; indeed, his version of materialism involved commitment to an impersonal, external world and cohered well with a scientism just a shade above the vulgar. It appears that the German Marxists of the 1920's, the first generation of Marxists who really enjoyed a collectivity of educated and academically employed scholars, were rather involved in debates with Kant, Weber and Freud. Marcuse and Mannheim reflected these concerns. Attacks on 'rational' science itself were then the property of a mystical, pre-Nazi Right (Forman, 1971). Hence it was only in the 1930's that Marxist criticisms of science, mainly in England, emerged with intellectual force. This important movement has been studied by Werskey (1975) from several approaches, generally more social than doctrinal. There seems to be a common theme in all the criticisms, namely that science could produce peace and plenty for all – as well as culturally valuable knowledge from pure research – were it not for the 'fetters' imposed by a corrupt and destructive capitalist system. The most eloquent statement of this faith was in J. D. Bernal's *The Social Function of Science* (1939). The mixture of humanitarian, technocratic and reductionist-Faustian motives in Bernal's thought has not yet been fully explored, although B. Easlea (1973) has given some preliminary hints. The use of the Soviet Union as a shining example of the future became increasingly difficult as Stalin's regime became more oppressive; but it was only after the war that a major scientific scandal, the Lysenko episode, really upset the Marxist scientific community and provoked defections on a scientific issue.

In spite of a now lengthy experience of criticism in the West and practice in the East, the Marxist socialist criticism of science has not yet succeeded in articulating a coherent positive alternative. Although the slogan of 'socialist science' has been raised several times in the Soviet Union, it has usually been so entangled with crude and opportunistic campaigns within science as to gain no genuine credibility. The disillusion of J. D. Bernal with Soviet science, though only to be inferred from hints in his writings (Ravetz, 1972), is likely to have been as severe as that of Max Born (Thompson, 1953) or Kapitsa (Roszak, 1969 and 1972) with non-political 'industrialized' science. Indeed, the very possibility of a distinctively 'socialist' science now seems to be an open question for those who have the greatest personal commitment to the idea. Thus the avowedly radical British Society for Social Responsibility in Science recently organized a conference to inquire: 'Is there a socialist science? ' The outcome was far from conclusive.

A different dimension of radical criticism of modern science and technology can be traced back to the ethical and aesthetic writings of Victorians such as John Ruskin and William Morris. Though their ideas were neither stable nor always internally cohesive, they gave a reminder that the industrial system does more than exploit, it blights. Neither aspect is purely derivative of the other. A literary expression of this view was developed by D. H. Lawrence; the critical school of F. R. Leavis developed it further, and this at least as much as Marxism served as a basis for the political radicalization of a generation of English intellectuals (Thompson, 1953). On the more overtly political side, the Ruskin influence – mixed with communitarian ideals and the studies of Kropotkin in social philosophy – has worked through many channels including that of Ghandi to the 'intermediate technology' of Schumacher (1975). Based on 'Buddhist economics', it invokes the increasingly powerful slogan, 'Small is Beautiful'.

Although the 'ethical' approach does not involve an enriched cosmology or enhanced experience for its criticism of science, its themes are shared by many approaches which do. The novelist Aldous Huxley emerged as an important critic of science with his *Brave New World* (1952), which described a science-based utopia where happiness was enforced, and civilization was trivialized and debased. In the Thirties he became a pacifist communitarian consciousness-enhancing prophet; and by the Fifties his experiences with Eastern religion had prepared him for psychedelics. He then became a link to the Leary group, and thereby helped form the synthesis of the 'Politics of Ecstasy' which was so important for a brief period in the Sixties. This movement, identified and named by Theodore Roszak as 'the counterculture' (1972), made cosmology and inner experience the 'base' in reality, and the political-technical complex, the superstructure, rotten in our own time. A more anti-Marxist radicalism would be hard to imagine. Perhaps it was inevitable that the attempt to unite Marxism with a variety of romanticisms dating from the Freudian Revolution of the Twenties, inspired by Marcuse's *One Dimensional Man* (1964), should have had such a brief, though intense, career.

This review of radical critiques of science from the outside would be incomplete without one embarrassing example. Liberal intellectuals tend to assume that all radical popular criticisms of science, as of other elite social institutions, must be from the Left. Philosophically reactionary populism is, if not a contradiction in terms, then at least an anomaly to be explained away. Yet the strength and persistence of the Biblical fundamentalist attack on the teaching of Darwinian evolution in the United States should be a warning against scientific complacency (Garbiner, 1974). Those responsible for this movement feel themselves excluded from a fair share of intellectual influence, just as do Marxist radicals. The more sophisticated defenders of Biblical 'literalism' can argue in a very Lakatosian way about administrative suppression of their research program when it only *seemed* to be undergoing a degenerate phase; certainly neither side of the debate can rigorously prove the truth of its assumptions. Heavy-handed political tactics by scientist-politicians against 'creationist' propaganda have proved counterproductive, just as in the Velikovsky affair (which, although more bizarre in details, has not involved an overt challenge on the principles of scientific evidence). The issues of *Pensee*, published for a time by students in Portland, Oregon, showed a reasonable debate on scientific problems between Velikovsky and his critics (See also Gillette, 1974). Even if the 'reactionary' criticisms of science are of a character with occasional chauvinistic denials by oppressed ethnic and cultural minorities of the originality or value of Western science, these criticisms should serve as a reminder that the dominant style in science, however great its intellectual power and social benefits, can yet be a tool of cultural oppression in many directions.

SCIENCE POLICY STUDIES: FROM PUBLICITY TO POLITICS

A noteworthy feature of the present period is that sharply critical analyses of the scientific endeavor are made by established scholars, whose general radicalism may be mild or even non-existent. This respectable, 'inside' criticism of science reflects the new self-awareness of science, and the loss of its earlier assurance. Looking back on pronouncements of earlier spokesmen of science, we are impressed by their propagandist character. The 'man of science' was, for such as T. H. Huxley (1894), von Helmholtz (1893) or Karl Pearson (1892), a paragon of the best intellectual and moral virtues. One finds this presupposed in the earlier writings of Robert K. Merton – although not in his mature work – and the influence of 'Mertonism' has been so strong that scholarly studies in recent years have been devoted to refuting it (See Barnes, 1972; and Mitroff, 1974). Indeed, such diverse figures as Polanyi, Popper, Bernal and Vannevar Bush could all agree that what science mainly needed was: more latitude for doing its own thing. In itself, science was so innately good that there were no inherent problems of government that might endanger its progress. From earlier centuries through the post-war decade, science policy studies were in essence little more than science publicity pronouncements. The only critical voices from within established science were those of eccentrics like Leo Szilard (1961) and Norbert Wiener (1964).

Science policy analysis as such can therefore be said to begin with two studies whose limited, descriptive appearance belies their fundamental significance. Derek Price's fantastic straight-line, semi-log graph of growth (1963) did more than show a continuity with the past: it tolled a bell for the future. Those commentators who predicted that eventually we would need to give Ph.D.'s to dogs and cats were only partly ridiculous. For Price showed that a situation of unequal growth-rates in scientific demand and societal supply could persist unchanged for only a limited length of time. If the supply of resources could not increase beyond all expectation, the demands of science would need to moderate. In his rigorous, boldly quantitative way, Price exposed one of the fundamental contradictions of 'big' science: that quantitative growth, previously so necessary for vitality, must stop soon. Indeed, one could define 'big' science as that whose claim on resources is so large as to be politically significant, and which is thereby constrained by general social priorities.

A neat contrast to Price's study was that of Alvin Weinberg on 'Criteria of

Scientific Choice' (1967). Instead of impersonal statistics on quantitative growth, we have wise reflections on qualitative choice. For the affluent, post-war, big-science Americans, it was bad enough to remind the world that choices – and rejections – are necessary. But by challenging the absolute value of 'pure science', by including social concerns as legitimate components of any decision on investment in science, he seemed to be betraying the autonomy of the scientific endeavor. Emotive pleading aside, Weinberg's study did prepare for the exposure of an even more basic contradiction in 'big' science: the total confusion of the disparate goals of scientific research and of the appropriate social roles of scientists. We shall return to this later.

My own contribution to science policy studies began shortly after; in late 1964 my article on the Mohole scandal appeared. In it I tried to define corruption in science, importing the norms of social behavior appropriate to politics, business enterprise, or speculative technology. This led to the floating of a publicity stunt that quickly became a gigantic project, with inadequate study of goals, feasibility or costs. Around the same time I began to work up the ideas embodied in my book of 1971; and a problem posed by Derek Price's study became crucial at that early stage. What, after all, is the difference between 'little science' and 'big science' as social activities? All the indicators are continuous; how – in terms of Marxist dialectic – does quantity pass into quality? I recall that the question, phrased without the Marxist terminology, of course, was put by Jack Morrell. The answer to this question was suggested by another part of Marxism: a change in the capital-intensity of scientific research. The old craftsmen-producers who offered their finished products on a market of quality assessment are replaced by managers who must convince an investing agency to provide heavy capital for a future project. Much else follows from this, and is made coherent by it; thus I came to the idea of the 'industrialization of science', and passed on from Marxism to other sources of insight.

Around the same time, Jean-Jacques Salomon saw the present period as one of techno-positivism, of the *savant* or aristocratic scholar being replaced by the *scientifique* or scientific worker (1973). In this insight he had been anticipated in 1960 by John Ziman, who had used the English cricket class distinction between amateur 'gentlemen' and paid 'players'; that is to say, between a 'vocation' and a 'career'. But Ziman still preferred to concentrate on problems internal to traditional science for the basis of his social analysis of knowledge (1968). In his book, Salomon went on to identify the most cruel contradiction of all: that the noble ideals of the traditional scientific endeavor had rested on an illusion of innocence. Science, for so long the destroyer of ideologies, was revealed as a variety of false consciousness. How to preserve the ethics of a *savant* in the new disenchanted age, is a problem Salomon left to the reader.

For the first really consistent, many-sided, Marxist analysis and criticism of science in this present period, we are indebted to Hilary and Steven Rose.

After exploring the historical background in their book (1969), they moved to the attack in 1970 with their essay on the myth of the neutrality of science (Fuller, 1971). With a host of suggestive examples, they showed how both scientific *choice* and scientific *concepts* are ideologically and politically influenced in various degrees. The political lessons of this may seem straight-forward, but the Roses saw some tricky ethical problems, such as: Was Einstein guilty of the bomb? To save something of the functions of the discredited theory of the neutrality of science, they distinguished between a Kuhnian paradigm, subject to ethical judgments, and puzzle solving within it, the last preserve of ethical neutrality. Whether this analysis would hold indefinitely may be doubted. Subsequently they have extended their analysis to describe the 'incorporation' of science in the bourgeois (and also the Soviet) state, wherein science functions as a means both of material pro-duction and of social control, while itself experiencing the social and political stratification and alienation of any techno-bureaucratic enterprise. The 'myth' of 'pure' science has been maintained only by a concentration of attention on the exploits of the academic elite; but this is now weakening, and the various titles implying some separation or opposition between 'science' and 'society' are themselves mystifying and obsolete (Rose, forth-coming). Although their analysis provokes queries and criticisms at many points, the Roses have had considerable success in their sustained endeavor to achieve a Marxist critique of modern science, all the time preserving the standards of civilized debate.

Although the formal sociology of science has been remarkably free of the taint of criticism of its object, some sociologists concerned with policy have contributed useful insights. Stuart Blume studied power in the scientific establishment, and found that it is but imperfectly correlated with scientific attainment (1971). Rather, power — realized through the equivalent of patronage, or the allocation of research funds — derives to a strong degree from contacts in the bureaucracies that feed science. This arrangement is, of course, self-reinforcing.

By the mid-Seventies the stream of 'critical policy' studies became a flood. We now face the problem of having too many approaches to the phenomenon and no inclusive theory for them all. Complementary to my theory of 'industrialization' is Harvey Wheeler's description of the 'bureaucratization' of science (1975). Where I saw the corruptions of 'entrepreneurial' science, he sees the onset of mediocrity and trivialization of research, parallelling the tendencies of high-technology consumer industries like pharmaceuticals and automobiles. Though this too had been anticipated by Leo Szilard long ago, it was then only an inspired guess (1961). Wheeler relates the present process to the current deceleration of growth, and anticipates a rapid ossification of the scientific enterprise. One solution, though more directed at the 'Andromeda Strain' problems of plasmid research, is external political control through the 'constitutionalization of science'.

Jean-Jacques Salomon (See Chapter 2) has dealt with the cycle of 'science policy' as a concern of governments. Now the politically perceived problems are directly technological, such as food, material resources and energy; the role for 'science' is becoming simply to produce industrial results on order. Niceties of allocation of resources between sectors of science are being forgotten in the present harsh climate. All this brings politics directly into science; it is hard to believe that a mere five years ago the British Society for Social Responsibility in Science shocked respectable scientific opinion with its slogan, 'Science is not Neutral'.

We can hardly expect the proposed critical alternatives to established science to be more coherent than the parallel movements in politics. But it is significant that in the realm of ideas, science lacks strong and confident defenses against these attacks. An idea which Dean Harvey Brooks proposed in 1975 indicates the state of ideology of established science; he suggested that American science could be rejuvenated by our making it the focus of another great national endeavor, providing a unifying purpose for the nation! Though this might well come to pass some time in the future, it is, in the wake of the moonrace and Vietnam, a forlorn hope. More symptomatic of the current atmosphere here is a volume of essays produced at the University of Michigan in connection with the quincentenary of the birth of Copernicus. The title is *Science and Society: Past, Present and Future* (Steneck, 1975). In it the social and human relevance of science is exemplified by a quote from the mother of an American black child; a visiting scientist met her on an educational aid project. She said: 'But you never show your white faces around here. You never say "I'm sorry. I'm sorry for what's happening. I'm sorry that we got our white folks walking on the moon while you black folks are falling on your beds sick with hunger and your stomachs rotting. I'm sorry that your boy is an epileptic. . ." Everything in the name of science. But any way you cut it, you're the master, we're the dogs, and I just got to wait and see whether a seizure some day will take my boy away from me. . .' (p. 227).

DOUBTS AMONG THE SCHOLARS

The ideological motivations and functions of the various scholarly disciplines that study natural sciences have long been plain, frequently even to their practitioners. The glorification or defense of science in general, or loyal praise for the founding fathers of some particular specialty, were quite legitimate concerns of the (usually amateur) philosophers and historians of science of the past. Only now, given the combination of professional self-consciousness among some scholars, notably historians of science, with the current mood of disenchantment, can truly critical analysis of the past and present be achieved.

The present era in the philosophy of science was inaugurated by Karl Popper. He was of precisely the right age, situation and talent to seize on the revolutionary significance of Einstein's theory of general relativity: on a very basic point of scientific principle Newton and all who followed him had been wrong. The possibility of honest, competent error in science, the spector of falsehood resulting from the application of scientific method, had not previously been confronted. The various falsifications of established theories in the previous century had each been explained away through a myth of the failings of the side proven wrong. Thus the phlogistonists had 'ignored' the negative weight problem; the calorists had 'ignored' Rumford's experiment; and so on. Incomplete knowledge was never a sufficient cause for scientific error; otherwise our own incomplete knowledge could be leading us astray. Popper broke through this whole tissue of rationalizations, and yet he could retain his faith in science by changing its essence from truth to morality. Popper's genuine scientist does not induce from phenomena or verify hypotheses; for that way lie pseudo-science and the self-deceptions of the astrologer, the Freudian and the Marxist. No, like Einstein, the real scientist proposes a hypothesis and joins in the *criticism* of it. Intellectual honesty, not factology, is the defining characteristic of science (Popper, 1963).

Popper's burning commitment to the liberal intellectual virtues, a quality which informed equally his work on politics and on history, carried him through the severe difficulties of formalizing and refining his ideas, and relating them to actual traditions of thought among scientists and philosophers. One is tempted to compare him to the literary scholar F. R. Leavis, who found moral strength in another great tradition. Though their detailed conclusions were likely to be contrary on the rare points where they overlapped, these two men stirred the consciences – and the imaginations – of intellectuals of a generation now at its peak of influence.

Why the philosophy of science has now no successor to further Popper's prophetic zeal, is an unanswerable question. Perhaps the simple verities are now just too implausible when applied to science. Perhaps it is the ill fortune that Popper's greatest disciple, Imre Lakatos, had a bare fifteen years of philosophical work. Lakatos shared Popper's commitment and had witnessed the systematic prostitution of intellect at really close quarters in a People's Democracy. Moreover, he was subtle, capable of great philosophical originality and in his stronger periods fully sensitive to the complexities of real life. His earlier work was related to the radical side of Popper's insight; he showed that each existing mathematical concept is the product of a historical evolution achieved through a dialectic of 'proofs and refutations' (Lakatos, 1963-1964). He thereby set himself in opposition to the ruling, dogmatic, Euclidean style of teachers and philosophers of mathematics. But every philosophical synthesis rests on an ideological razor's edge; in his later years Lakatos was concerned with establishing the necessity of any given successful program in science, so as to ward off 'externalism', with its openings to political influences and standards in science. But the efforts required for this would be heroic in the extreme. Even with Lakatos (partly under the challenge from Kuhn) the philosophy of science had shifted its attention from the establishing of facts to the making of decisions; and the crucial data were to be found, not in the past, but in the future. The retention of any of the old certainties, even Popper's, would henceforth be problematic.

In startling contrast to all this, Thomas S. Kuhn was not concerned with ideology at all. It seems to me that he was simply bored and irritated by the blinkered puzzle solving of 'normal' science, and strove to understand how it related to the science of great revolutionaries like Copernicus and Einstein. In working out his idea of 'paradigm' and explaining scientific revolutions, he casually jettisoned truth and progress (Kuhn, 1962; see also Böhme, Chapter 9). He probably did not realize the damage this would do to the received ideology of science, and how it would open up the way to a suspicion of arbitrariness in the choice of problems for research and of topics for teaching. Lakatos recognized a threat to 'scientific rationality', and tried to produce a model of scientific debate which accommodated both the idealism of Popper and the realism of Kuhn (Lakatos and Musgrave, 1970). His many difficulties were compounded by his friend, Paul Feyerabend, who in the service of his own 'Dada-anarchist' philosophy of science mercilessly exposed the inconsistencies in Lakatos' account (Feyerabend, 1975). But Kuhn did not escape Feyerabend's critical attentions either. In the course of the great debate, Feyerabend raised the paradox: Since organized crime is, like science, an effort of puzzle solving within a paradigm and, again like science, experiences revolutions, what then does Kuhn's theory tell us of the difference between scientists and gangsters? (Lakatos and Musgrave, 1970, pp. 199-201). I myself gave an indirect answer to this question in a discussion of morale and quality control in 1971.

The historians of science are now sharing the general spirit of rebellion. Whiggery (referring to the 'Whig Interpretation of History') is now nearly a term of abuse among the more sophisticated professionals; they know that the events of the past were quite other than the brave precursors of the glorious present. One historian has argued, though on dubious evidence, that Newton 'fudged' his data on several crucial occasions (Westfall, 1975). Also, the ideological sensitivity of genuine history, breaking the propaganda image of the Good Scientist and the teaching image of Cumulating Facts, has been advanced in a paper entitled 'Should the History of Science be X-Rated?' (Brush, 1974). Indeed, the history of science is now reaching the point of maturity, where it need not stay at the level of muckraking or demystifying exercises. A deeper study of the self-consciousness of science, including its points of contact with reality, along with delusion, could now usefully be attempted.

PERSONAL INTERPRETATION

We have lived long enough with the new atmosphere of criticism of science to be able to grow out of our emotional reactions to it, and to begin to appreciate its meaning for the future of science. We all know that science is intimately linked to society, that science cannot be perfect in an imperfect society, and yet the future of science cannot simply be reduced to that of society. But we still lack a unifying theme to encompass the ongoing technical, social and ideological changes in science. I would like to make a tentative offering in that direction.

The clue to a deep problem is the ambiguities in the term 'science'. Does it mean 'pure' or 'basic', or 'applied' or 'mission-oriented', or even 'R & D', or a bit of all of them in varying proportions at various times and places? The different names refer to very different activities, each with their own internal and external goals and ideologies. To let 'science' cover the whole lot, invoking only the technical puzzle solving common to them all, leaves out some of the most important elements of science of the past and present. To distinguish among the various sorts of science, producing species of hyphenated scientists, might seem more conducive to clarity. But then we find that the categories blend into each other at so many points, that paragraphs of explanation would be needed to establish each demarcation. So we can make a first conclusion: the complex multiplicity of roles and the consequent ambiguity of self-consciousness are now essential structural features of science.

Other social institutions doubtless have the same property; whether science suffers to an exceptional degree could be explored in a disciplined study. But, another feature of the situation of science aggravates its tensions and contradictions. Considering the many roles performed by scientists, we notice that one is almost always absent: that of the consultant professional, who acts on behalf of a client and takes personal responsibility for his decisions. The scientist may produce internally motivated results like a *savant* or scholar; or he may solve technically motivated problems in a corporate enterprise as a *scientifique* or research worker. Only rarely can he do what an independent engineer or physician does as a routine: solve problems and take decisions whose quality is soon tested by the welfare of a client. Now we know that the learned professions have plenty of problems of their own. But to a great extent these arise from a failure to honor a public trust that is embodied in a multitude of particular cases. The scientific community cannot even claim to have such a problem. There are no institutions for qualifying a scientist as a professional or – more significant – for disqualifying him or her.

In this feature of the social structure of science, we can see the sources of the strongly enforced alienation of scientists: from society; from the fruits of their work; from any effective sense of responsibility. Individually cut off from social decisions and their consequences, either by personal remoteness (such as academics) or subservience (such as research employees), they have neither the experience nor the opportunity to do anything to control the engine of total change that they are still fabricating. Even the engineer who insists that it's his duty only to follow orders, is at a higher level of awareness, for he at least sees the problem, and can choose a policy. The community of science is then in a position of creating great power while being deprived of the responsibility for its use. This is a new twist on the old formula for corruption. It may help to explain the essential confusion, in practice and ideology, which has been revealed by the recent critical studies of science.

Clearly this is not a healthy situation. Yet it is built into the style of research, as is evidenced both by the necessary autonomy of some (not easily defined) portions of it, and by its externally directed applications, without which science would receive only small social support. Considered as a problem, it is one that cannot be solved like a puzzle in social administration or education. Indeed, considered as a threatening challenge, it might well be classed as a 'contradiction'. Will it be a driving contradiction, forcing a restructuring of goals, ideas and institutions? Or will it be a crippling contradiction, where established interests cling to their bits of power and security, preventing any change before catastrophe strikes? Only time will tell. But I hope that we have here a useful element in the enormous task of understanding, criticism and action which will accompany the formulation of new science policy studies.

BIBLIOGRAPHY

Aristophanes, 1916	Aristophanes, The Clouds, 423 BC, translated by Benjamin Bickley Rogers, London, Bell, 1916.
Arnold, 1958	Arnold, P., *Histoire des Rose-Croix*, Paris, 1958.
Barnes, 1972	Barnes, B. (Ed.), *Sociology of Science: Selected Readings,* Penguin, 1972, pp. 188-205.
Bernal, 1939	Bernal, J. D., *The Social Function of Science,* London, 1939.
Blume, 1974	Blume, S. S., *Towards a Political Sociology of Science,* The Free Press, New York, 1974.
Bonelli and Shea, 1975	Bonelli, M. R., and Shea, W. R. (Eds.), *Reason, Experiment and Mysticism in the Scientific Revolution,* Science History Publications, New York, 1975, pp. 19-47.
Brooks, 1975	Brooks, H., 'Can Science Be Re-Directed? ', CNAM, Paris, December 1975.
Brush, 1974	Brush, S. G., 'Should the History of Science Be X-

	Rated? ', *Science* 183, 1974, pp. 1164-1182.
Burtt, 1924, 1932	Burtt, E. A., *The Metaphysical Foundation of Modern Physical Science,* 1924, 1932.
Debus, 1971	Debus, A. (Ed.), *Science, Medicine and Society in the Renaissance,* Science History Publications, New York, 1971.
Descartes, 1638	Descartes, R., *Discours de la Méthode* (Deuxième Partie), 1638.
Easlea, 1973	Easlea, B., *Liberation and the Aims of Science,* Chatto and Windus, London, 1973, pp. 325-327.
Ferguson, 1971	Ferguson, J., for the Arts Course Team, *Socrates,* Milton Keynes, The Open University, 1971.
Feyerabend, 1975	Feyerabend, P., *Against Method,* New Left Books, London, 1975.
Forman, 1971	Forman, P., 'Weimar Culture, Causality and Quantum Theory 1918-1923; Adaptation in German Physicists and Mathematicians to a Hostile Intellectual Environment', *Historical Studies in the Physical Sciences* 3, 1971, pp. 1-116.
Fuller, 1971	Fuller, W. (Ed.), *The Social Impact of Modern Biology,* Routledge, London, 1971, pp. 215-224.
Gillette, 1974	Gillette, R., 'Velikowsky: AAAS Forum for a Mild Collision', *Science* 183, 1974, pp. 1059-1062.
Gillispie, 1959	Gillispie, C. C., 'The *Encyclopedia* and the Jacobin Philosophy of Science: A Study in Ideas and Consequences', in Clagget, M. (Ed.), *Critical Problems in the History of Science,* University of Wisconsin Press, 1959, pp. 255-289.
Grabiner and Miller, 1974	Grabiner, J. V. and Miller, P. D., 'Effects of the Scopes Trial', *Science* 185, 1974, pp. 832-837.
Helmholtz, 1893	Helmholtz, H. von, 'On the Relation of Natural Science to Science in General', *Popular Lectures on Scientific Subjects,* 1893, pp. 1-28.
Huxley, 1894	Huxley, T. H., 'On the Advisableness of Improving Natural Knowledge', *Methods and Results,* 1894, pp. 40-41.
Jaynes, 1972	Jaynes, J., 'Fechner, Gustav Theodor', *Dictionary of Scientific Biography,* Vol. IV, Scribner, New York, 1972, pp. 556-559.
Kearney, 1971	Kearney, H., *Science and Change, 1500-1800,* Weidenfeld, London, 1971, Ch. 1.
Knight, 1972	Knight, D., 'Chemistry, Physiology and Materialism in the Romantic Period', *Durham University Journal* 64, 1972, pp. 139-145.
Kottler, 1974	Kottler, M. J., 'Alfred Russel Wallace, The Origin of Man and Spiritualism', *ISIS* 65, 1974, pp. 145-192.
Kuhn, 1962	Kuhn, T. S., *The Structure of Scientific Revolutions,* University of Chicago Press, 1962, pp. 169-172.
Lakatos and Musgrave, 1970	Lakatos, I., and Musgrave, A. (Eds.), *Criticism and the Growth of Knowledge,* Cambridge University Press, 1970, pp. 91-196.
Lakatos, 1963-64	Lakatos, I., 'Proofs and Refutations', *British Journal for the Philosophy of Science* 14, 1963-64, pp. 1-25, 120-39, 221-43, 296-342.

Lenin, 1909	Lenin, V. I., *Materialism and Empiro-Criticism,* 1909.
Mitroff, 1974	Mitroff, I., *The Subjective Side of Science: A Philosophical Inquiry into the Psychology of the Apollo Moon Scientists,* Elzevier, Amsterdam, 1974.
Pearson, 1892, 1900	Pearson, K., *The Grammar of Science,* 1892, 1900, Ch. 1.
Popper, 1963	Popper, K. R., *Conjectures and Refutations,* Routledge, London, 1963, pp. 192-3.
Derek Price, 1963	Price, Derek de Solla, *Little Science, Big Science,* Columbia University Press, 1963.
Ravetz, 1964	Ravetz, J. R., 'The Mohole Scandal', *The Guardian,* 27 October 1964.
Ravetz, 1971	Ravetz, J. R., *Scientific Knowledge and Its Social Problems,* Oxford University Press, 1971.
Ravetz, 1972	Ravetz, J. R., review of *Science in History, Technology and Culture* 13, 1972, pp. 664-666.
Rose and Rose, 1969	Rose, H., and Rose, S., *Science and Society,* Allen Lane, 1969.
Rose and Rose, 1976	Rose, H. and Rose, S., 'The Incorporation of Science', in *The Political Economy of Science,* Macmillan, London, 1976.
Roszak, 1969	Roszak, T., *The Making of a Counter-Culture,* Doubleday and Co., New York, 1969.
Roszak, 1972	Roszak, T., *Where the Wasteland Ends,* Doubleday and Co., New York, 1972.
Salomon, 1973	Salomon, J., *Science and Politics,* Macmillan, London, 1973.
Schumacher, 1975	Schumacher, E. F., *Small Is Beautiful,* Abacus, London, 1975.
Staude, 1967	Staude, J. R., *Max Scheler, An Intellectual Portrait,* The Free Press, New York, 1967.
Steneck, 1975	Steneck, H. H. (Ed.), *Science and Society: Past, Present and Future,* University of Michigan Press, 1975.
Szilard, 1961	Szilard, L., *The Voice of the Dolphins and Other Stories,* New York, 1961.
Thompson, 1953	Thompson, D., *Science in Perspective: Passages of Contemporary Writing,* John Murray, 1953.
Thomson, 1941	Thomson, G., *Aeschylus and Athens,* London, 1941, p. 326.
Webster, 1976	Webster, C., *The Great Instauration: Science, Medicine and Reform,* 1626-1660, Duckworth, London, 1976.
Weinberg, 1967	Weinberg, A. M., 'Criteria of Scientific Choice', *Reflections on Big Science,* Pergamon, 1967.
Werskey, 1975	Werskey, G., 'Making Socialists of Scientists: Whose Side is History On?', *Radical Science Journal* 2/3, London, 1975, pp. 13-50.
Westfall, 1973	Westfall, S., 'Newton and the Fudge Factor', *Science* 179, 1973, pp. 751-758.
Wheeler, 1975	Wheeler, H., 'Science's Slippery Slope', *The Center Magazine,* January/February 1975, pp. 64-72.
Wiener, 1964	Wiener, N., *God and Golem, Inc.,* MIT Press, Cambridge, Mass, 1964.

Ziman, 1960   Ziman, J., 'Scientists: Gentlemen or Players?', *The Listener* 68, 1960, pp. 599-607.

Ziman, 1968   Ziman, J., *Public Knowledge,* Cambridge University Press, 1968.

2

Social Studies of Science: The Disciplinary Perspectives

M. J. MULKAY
ROY MACLEOD
E. LAYTON
C. FREEMAN
R. FISCH
GERNOT BÖHME

Chapter 4

SOCIOLOGY OF THE
SCIENTIFIC RESEARCH COMMUNITY

M. J. Mulkay

University of York

INTRODUCTION: PURE AND
APPLIED RESEARCH

The scientific research community is composed of those persons who, as a central part of their professional activities, are directly engaged in extending systematic knowledge of natural phenomena.[1] For some purposes it is appropriate to regard all such persons, perhaps within a particular society, as constituting a single social unit. This approach can be useful if, for example, our goal is to estimate the overall economic return from research in relation to the total expenditure needed to sustain the research community. But such a broad, aggregate conception of the research community has been little used by sociologists who, in attempting to understand the social life of research scientists and the connections between social and intellectual processes in science, have focussed on various smaller social groupings or collectivities. One social division within the research community has been seen as particularly important, namely, that between those engaged in 'pure re-

---

[1] What is defined as a 'natural' phenomenon tends to vary over time and from one social grouping to another. We must be careful, therefore, about making simple distinctions between, say, physical sciences and social sciences. Nevertheless, I have drawn my evidence in this chapter almost entirely from studies of physics, chemistry, biology, astronomy and closely related disciplines. The extent to which, and the conditions under which, the findings discussed in this chapter can be extrapolated to other fields of intellectual inquiry must be regarded at present as an open question.

search'[2] and those engaged in 'applied research'. However, there has been some debate over the utility of this distinction (e.g. Chabbal, 1973). It is necessary, therefore, to clarify what these terms mean when they are used in the course of sociological analysis.

The distinction between applied research and pure or basic research has been challenged on several grounds. In the first place, it has been suggested that the distinction often depends on questionable assumptions about the motives of research scientists (Reagan, 1967). Thus pure research is seen as research which is undertaken by scientists who have no interest in the ultimate applicability of the results; while in the case of applied research the researchers' objectives are assumed to be entirely or primarily utilitarian. But, it is pointed out, it is extremely difficult to gather reliable evidence about scientists' motives. Moreover, human motivation is highly complex and there is unlikely to be a simple, direct relationship between participants' motives and the kind of research results forthcoming (Kidd, 1959). In addition, the same research project may be defined quite differently by different social groupings. For instance, research which those scientists actively involved see as 'pure' will often be regarded as 'applied' by the officials providing the funds[3] and by researchers at work in other areas (Barber, 1952).

In view of these difficulties, it has been suggested that we should base our definitions on the *substance* of the research. But this approach also fails to provide a clear demarcation between pure and applied research (Kidd, 1959). For instance, pure research is often thought of as the pursuit of problems which appear to have no immediate practical implications. But there are cases where research into problems of this kind has in fact led to important practical developments (Byatt and Cohen, 1969); as well as instances where attempts to achieve highly specific practical ends have contributed to an extensive reorganization of scientific knowledge (e.g. Mulkay and Edge, 1973). Difficulties of this kind have led some writers to regard the distinction between applied and pure research as inherently ambiguous; and certainly this conclusion is well-founded if our objective is to provide a statistical basis for public decision making (Reagan, 1967; see also the discussion of the Frascati definitions, etc., in Freeman, Chapter 7). But for purposes of sociological analysis a distinction along these lines can be helpful in drawing attention to genuine social divisions within the research community (Sklair, 1973). It is important to understand, however, that from a sociological perspective the

---

[2] I have used the term 'pure research' in preference to 'fundamental research' or 'basic research' because the latter phrases seem to imply, *quite misleadingly*, that scientific knowledge necessarily moves in one direction, that is, from basic to applied research. It cannot be denied, however, that the term 'pure research' does carry an unfortunate connotation of intellectual superiority.

[3] Most of the discussion in the literature has been concerned with the practical problems of providing clear criteria whereby government funds may be distributed between pure and applied research.

distinction is *not* between types of science or between types of motive, but between the social contexts in which research is undertaken (Shepard, 1956). The major characteristics of the social context of pure research are as follows: participants are expected, indeed, they are constrained, to pursue research topics on the basis of their scientific significance. The audience for results consists of other researchers who are working upon the same or related problems and who judge the adequacy of the results by means of scientific criteria (Cole and Cole, 1967). This audience exerts control over the research activities of individual members, not by the exercise of formal authority, but by informal pressures which are legitimated by reference to scientific standards. The context of 'applied research' is significantly different in that participants are expected to produce results which have useful practical consequences. Furthermore, the main audience for these results is composed of non-researchers and this audience determines the activities of researchers by the exercise of formal, bureaucratic authority and by direct control over rewards such as salary and promotion (Marcson, 1960).

Applied research, then, is undertaken on behalf of 'laymen', that is, persons not actively engaged in research of any kind, and communicated to 'laymen', to be used by the latter for purposes other than the further extension of scientific knowledge. In contrast, the results of pure research are intended for and communicated to other researchers, to be used by them in their own pursuit of scientific knowledge. The *intellectual* procedures adopted in pure and applied research are frequently indistinguishable and the scientific results often identical. This means that the findings of practical research are sometimes deemed by those who produce them to be of interest on purely scientific grounds and attempts are made to pass them on to the pure research community. Similarly, information sometimes moves in the opposite direction. But when scientific results are passed in this way from one sector of the research community to the other, researchers enter a social context which is significantly different (Nagi and Corwin, 1972). They are required to use a different means of communication to reach a new audience; an audience which judges their work by different criteria of significance and adequacy, offers different rewards, and so on (Storer, 1966). It is these social variations which are indicated by the sociological distinction between pure and applied research. Even those commentators who have stressed the difficulties of using the distinction between pure and applied research as a basis for public policy, have recognized the existence of these distinct research settings (e.g. Brooks, 1968; Sklair, 1973).

In the West, the social conditions characteristic of pure research *tend* to be found in the universities and those of applied research in industrial and governmental organizations.[4] But the situation is far from simple (OECD,

---

[4] Particularly in France, much fundamental research is done outside universities, with the Centre National de la Recherche Scientifique playing a prominent role (Gilpin, 1968). Similarly, in many Eastern European countries, universities are not the main locus of basic research.

1970; Marcson, 1972). For example, industrial scientists are frequently allowed to engage in some research which is unlikely to have direct practical application and to make their less profitable findings generally available to other scientists (Kornhauser, 1962). Similarly, industrial scientists sometimes acquire and use information published in academic journals or made available through academic contacts. At the same time, highly directed research is regularly contracted by government and industrial agencies to members of universities and to research institutes attached to universities (Orlans, 1968). Some areas of research are so exceptionally fertile as sources of technically useful information that funds are made generally available for their academic exploration, on the assumption that practical benefits will inevitably ensue (Polanyi, 1956).

The situation is also complicated by the fact that scientists may undertake a research project with several audiences in mind and convey their results, in various forms, to both academic and non-academic audiences (Mulkay and Williams, 1971); and by the fact that some researchers are able to move regularly between industrial and university laboratories, retaining a semi-permanent position in each. In addition, there has been in the last few decades an appreciable increase in the extent to which pure research has come to depend on a large supporting technical staff, associated with the use of complex and expensive equipment. Such forms of large-scale, team research tend to heighten the extent of bureaucratic control within the pure research setting and to increase dependence on outside sources of support (Swatez, 1970). Some authors have argued that such 'highly visible big-science activities are only the most obvious manifestations of an escalation in the scale of effort of pure science which is taking place all along the line' (Brooks, 1967, 194). Others, however, have maintained that these changes in the organization of pure research tend to be restricted to a small number of rather prominent fields; that dependence on outside sources for the provision of very large sums of money is by no means incompatible with the pursuit of scientifically defined goals; and that the audience for the results of team research can still be composed primarily of fellow researchers (Hagstrom, 1964).

Despite these complications, sociologists have tended to assume that there is a rough correspondence between, on the one hand, the pure research context and the university community, and on the other hand, the applied context and the non-academic research community. This is adequate as a first approximation, but there has been for a long time a need for more rigorous techniques of identification. It is possible that a move in this direction has been made fairly recently (Derek Price, 1965, 1969). This possibility arises from the observation that the pattern of publication in technological areas appears to be quite different from that found in areas of pure research. In due course, therefore, it may be possible to distinguish between different kinds of research activities by means of bibliographic techniques. However, most sociological studies of the relationships between pure and applied research have used fairly loose operational definitions of these areas or have concentrated on the more easily observed connections between research inside and research outside the universities.

On the whole, the results of these studies have drawn attention to the discontinuities between these two main sectors of the research community. In the first place, little clear evidence has been found of direct and regular connections between academic discoveries and practical developments in industry and government (Sherwin and Isenson, 1967; Langrish *et al.,* 1972; but see also Greenberg, 1967). Secondly, the direct connections which do exist between pure research and practical application depend heavily on personal contact among members of largely, although not entirely, separate social groupings (Gruber and Marquis; see also Layton, Chapter 6). Thirdly, there is a long series of studies showing that scientists who enter industry and government, after having been trained in the university, tend to experience some difficulty in adapting to the social context of applied research (Marcson, 1960; Kornhauser, 1962; Hower and Orth, 1963). However in recent years it has been increasingly argued that the difficulties experienced by scientists in moving from an academic to a non-academic context have been somewhat exaggerated (Cotgrove and Box, 1970; Ellis, 1969).

Although I shall return briefly to these important issues toward the end of this chapter, the focus here is primarily on certain aspects of the pure research community.[5]

THE NORMS OF PURE RESEARCH

Sociological investigation of the modern scientific research community began during the 1940's and 1950's, that is, at a time when most sociologists had adopted a functionalist perspective. One of the central assumptions of this perspective is that the social integration of distinct social groupings depends greatly on some form of normative or moral consensus. Accordingly, one of the first tasks taken up by sociologists of science was that of identifying the social norms which distinguish the scientific community, and in particular the pure research community, from other social groupings. The first systematic exposition of the supposed norms was made by Merton (1942), on the basis of evidence taken mainly from statements by scientists about science.

Merton argued that the continuous extension of certified scientific knowledge is possible only in a community where there is widespread conformity

---

[5] Useful collections and reviews of the sociology of science literature can be found in Barber, 1956; Barber and Hirsch, 1962; Kaplan, 1965; Sills, 1968; Barnes, 1972; Spiegel-Rösing, 1973; Weingart, 1974; and Whitley, 1974.

to four 'institutional imperatives'. The first of these is *universalism*, which requires that information presented to the scientific community be assessed independently of the personal characteristics of the source of the information. The second norm, that of *communality*, defines property rights to scientific knowledge. It requires that scientific knowledge be held in common; it asserts that scientific information belongs to the scientific profession and not to those who were responsible for its discovery. Thirdly, there is the norm of *disinterestedness*, which requires researchers to pursue scientific knowledge without considering their career or their reputation. Finally scientists are exhorted, by the norm of *organized skepticism*, never to take results on trust. This norm requires scientists to be consistently critical of knowledge claims put forward both by other researchers and by themselves.

This analysis (which is discussed again by Fisch in Chapter 8), provided a preliminary account of the way in which social factors within the pure research community could be seen to contribute to the rapid and cumulative growth of 'objective' knowledge. During the 1950's Merton's schema became widely accepted by sociologists as laying the foundation for the interpretation of the internal social processes of scientific development. A number of slight conceptual extensions were, of course, proposed over the years. Thus Merton himself added the norms of *originality* (1957) and *humility* (1963); while others working within the same tradition drew attention to the importance in science of norms of *rationality* and *individualism* (Barber, 1952). But the overall view of the nature of the research community remained essentially unchanged until the late 1960's.

The central contention of this kind of analysis is that science is an activity which depends on its practitioners being open-minded, impartial and self-critical. Scientific knowledge is seen to be, in principle, socially neutral (King, 1971); and the norms of science are seen as preventing scientists from interfering witn this neutrality. On the assumption that there is general conformity to the norms among scientists, it follows that science will grow rapidly because intellectual prejudice and resistance to new ideas will be kept to a minimum; and it follows that scientific knowledge will be peculiarly effective in practical terms because the 'objective' nature of the physical world will be revealed without distortion. Underlying this whole perspective is the idea that the rapid growth of reliable knowledge can occur only within 'open' communities and that, as science has undoubtedly developed much more quickly (Derek Price, 1963) and with more evident practical success than other intellectual movements, so the scientific community must be, internally, more open, uncommitted and self-critical than other social groupings.

This line of reasoning seems also to imply that intervention from outside the scientific community is likely to impede its intellectual progress. For, when outsiders try to influence the course of scientific advance, they tend to introduce into the research community self-interest, intellectual prejudice and secrecy. Thus it appears to follow from this argument that science is most likely to flourish in 'democratic' societies; partly because the values of science are seen as being democratic and partly because democracies are thought to be least likely to exert direct pressure on the pure research community (Merton, 1942).

As we shall see later, this view of the normative structure of science has, in recent years, come under considerable criticism (See also Fisch, Chapter 8). But throughout the 1950's and most of the 1960's it was, in general, accepted uncritically. There are several reasons which can be put forward to explain why this view of the research community was dominant for such a long time, particularly among American sociologists. It should be noted, however, that there is little independent evidence to support the first two of the suggestions which now follow. In the first place, it may be that Merton's formulation simply made explicit certain assumptions about the nature of science which were already widely held among sociologists, and perhaps more widely held among academics and the population at large. In other words, it may be that Merton was making explicit a widespread 'commonsense' account of science. A second factor may have been that Merton's analysis was accepted readily because it was consistent with the political ideology of American academics (see King, 1971 and Friedrichs, 1970).

A third, and more direct, factor may have been that Merton was the only eminent sociologist actively interested in the sociology of science during those years.[6] As a consequence, the few sociologists of science trained in this period were students of Merton and, naturally, they tended to adopt his perspective. Finally, there is the fact that, once the Mertonian account of the ethos of pure science was accepted, attention was drawn to certain associated issues which were becoming amenable to sociological investigation owing to the development of new research techniques. In particular, the analysis of the normative structure of science could not be regarded as complete until it had been shown that rewards were allocated so as to produce general conformity to the norms previously identified. As a result, through the 1960's, there were numerous studies of the distribution of rewards within the pure research community.

THE DISTRIBUTION OF PROFESSIONAL REWARDS

Throughout the 1960's evidence gradually accumulated that, for most

---

[6] For discussion of Merton's part in creating the sociology of science, see Kaplan, 1965, Preface; Barnes, 1972; Downey, 1971; Merton, 1970, Preface; Spiegel-Rösing, 1973; and Coser, 1975.

scientists, recognition of the quality of their work by other competent researchers was an important incentive and a valued reward. It might be thought that this conclusion is almost self-evident; for the research community has little else with which to reward its members other than professional recognition. However, scientists themselves frequently maintain that the pursuit of knowledge is its own reward; and that they require no gratification except that of solving a significant problem (Hagstrom, 1965; Waterman, 1966). One difficulty with this claim is that what is to count as a 'significant problem' and what is to be regarded as a 'solution', depend on the criteria adopted within the relevant grouping (Kuhn, 1970; Law, 1973). Consequently, the response of competent colleagues plays a crucial part in enabling scientists to decide whether or not their problem is significant; whether or not they have produced valid results; and whether or not their results constitute a solution to the problem. Given scientists' strong commitment to cognitive consensus, researchers can, in a very real sense, know that they have made a discovery only after this has been confirmed by competent colleagues (Ziman, 1968; Watson, 1968). Furthermore, there is considerable evidence to show that scientists do, in practice, attribute significance to and seek out professional recognition.

In the first place, there is the fact that scientists have devised a great variety of ways of bestowing recognition; from the award of a multitude of graded prizes and medals, through honorific practices such as eponymy, to the routine procedure of citing that work which has influenced one's own research (Merton, 1957). Secondly, there is the great frequency of priority disputes in science. Priority disputes are arguments to determine, in situations where there is an element of doubt, who should be credited with a specific discovery (Merton, 1957 and 1961). Such disputes occur because the recognition of having made the discovery is usually granted only to the scientist who first communicates the particular finding to the research community. The award of priority to one scientist in no way lessens the quality of the work of those who independently, but subsequently, arrived at the same result. Nor does it reduce the satisfaction they can be presumed to have derived from solving a significant scientific problem. The central issue is that of which scientist is to receive the recognition. The fact that bitter and prolonged disputes over priority have occured throughout the history of modern science indicates clearly that professional recognition plays an important part in the reward system of the scientific community.[7]

Further evidence is provided by the prevalence among researchers of

---

[7] Merton treats disputes over priority as separate from controversies over the validity of results. King (1971) points out that this is an oversimplification and that disagreements about priority are often associated with divergent interpretations of research findings. King's argument does not invalidate, however, the inference that recognition is experienced as an important reward.

anxiety over the possibility of being anticipated in presenting results. 'Scientists are concerned about being anticipated because they hope the solutions to their problems will interest other scientists, and given this hope, it is only reasonable to expect other scientists to approach the same problems . . . . The concern over being anticipated arises because the scientist is . . . oriented toward achieving recognition and is afraid of not receiving it for work he has actually done' (Hagstrom, 1965, 72). It also appears that this concern over receiving proper recognition lies behind the tendency for scientists, particularly in new and competitive fields, to publish as quickly as possible. Sometimes this pressure is so great that scientists abandon normal standards of scientific evidence and research procedures (Reif, 1961; Reif and Strauss, 1965).

Finally, we have the more subtle evidence of the importance of recognition which is furnished by studies such as that which Zuckerman made of the patterns of name ordering among authors of joint research papers (1967 and 1968). Zuckerman compared the publications of a number of Nobel Prize winners with those of a matched sample of less eminent men. Having given some grounds for assuming that in cases of collaboration most credit will tend to accrue to the author whose name comes first, she compared the two groups. She found that Nobel Prize winners tended to be first authors more often than the controls during their early career when they were striving to establish a reputation, but significantly less often than the controls once they had received the highest accolade of science and, as seems likely, further small increments of recognition had come to seem comparatively less important.

Once it had become widely, although not universally (Storer, 1966), accepted by sociologists that recognition by competent colleagues was the basic reward within the research community, there followed a series of studies designed to explore how scientific recognition is actually distributed. These studies made great use of the bibliographic techniques which had already been applied in the history of science (Derek Price, 1962 and 1963) and which have been greatly facilitated by the creation of the *Science Citation Index* (Bayer and Folger, 1966; Garfield, 1964; for reviews of the validity of indicators derived from the SCI, see Cole and Cole, 1973; and Spiegel-Rösing *et al.* 1975).

One widely used indicator of the recognition awarded to a scientist or to a particular paper is the number of references in the research literature to his work in the paper. Citation counts have also come to be used as indicators of the 'quality' or 'worth' of contributions to science (Clark, 1957; Menard, 1971). This use of the number of citations as an indicator of several variables which are thought to be empirically related can raise difficulties of interpretation (Kaplan, 1965; Moravcsik and Murugesan, 1975). For instance, if we use some form of citation count as evidence both of quality and of recognition, we are certain to find a strong association between the two variables solely because the indicators are similar. But this association may be no more than a methodological artifact. Similarly, in some studies the indicators for different variables, although operationally separate, appear to be interchangeable. In other words, the evidence given of variations in quality could equally well be used as evidence of variations in recognition, and vice versa (Cole and Cole, 1967). This does not mean that studies using biblio-graphical techniques are *ipso facto* unreliable. Rather it means that the results must be judged carefully in relation to the specific ways in which the techniques are applied.

The findings available on the distribution of professional recognition in science do, in fact, present a fairly coherent picture. In the first place, recognition probably operates as an incentive (Glaser, 1964a and b). The more recognition a scientist receives, the more productive he is subsequently likely to become (Cole and Cole, 1967). A strong overall relationship exists between various measures of recognition and both quantity and quality of research. This has been found to be the case, for example, for American physicists (Cole and Cole, 1967), for British chemists (Blume and Sinclair, 1973), and for British high energy physicists (Gaston, 1970). Quality of research, measured in various ways, appears to be the most important single determinant of the receiving of recognition. In other words, professional rewards seem to be distributed, at least in physics and chemistry, partly in response to the amount of information participants supply to the research community, but more significantly on the basis of the perceived value of this information. It is also clear that the highest rewards are confined to a relatively small group of highly productive scientists (Derek Price, 1963; Cole and Cole 1973). In the United States, highly productive and eminent scientists tend to be concentrated at the major universities. Furthermore, affiliation with a major university significantly improves a scientist's chances of gaining recognition both in America and Britain[8] (Crane, 1965; Blume and Sinclair, 1973; Halsey and Trow, 1971). Selective recruitment, it appears, is specially important in bringing together the more productive and eminent scientists and the most able students within these elite universities (Knapp and Greenbaum, 1953; Holland, 1957; Crane, 1965).

The extent to which scientists obtain recognition appears to be influenced by their 'visibility'; this variable is measured by the percentage of respondents who said that they were familiar with the work of a particular scientist. The most important single factor affecting the visibility of American physicists is the quality of their research (Cole and Cole, 1968). However, rank of department and prestige of highest award each contribute to a scientist's visibility. In addition to variations among individual physicists in visibility and reputation, there is (i.e. in the mid 1960's) a distinct hierarchy of specialists, with high energy physicists, for instance, being highly visible and

---

[8] Gaston does not find this in his study of British high energy physicists (1970). However, in the light of the work by Blume and Sinclair (1973) and by Halsey and Trow (1971), it seems likely that there are special factors operating in this case.

solid state physicists being much less visible (Cole and Cole, 1968). These results are supported by the findings of another study in which, on the basis of less direct evidence, it is suggested that scientific disciplines, specialties and individuals are placed in hierarchies of scientific prestige (Hagstrom, 1965).

It appears that specialties and research areas which are well known and prestigious find it relatively easy to attract resources and students (Hagstrom, 1965). Similar processes also occur *within* particular areas of research. Thus it has been shown that, in the case of British radio astronomy, an explicit policy was evolved of concentrating resources within the two major and prestigious groups. This, of course, had the effect of making it difficult for new research groups to enter the field (Mulkay and Edge, 1973). It may well be that such a situation develops almost inevitably where the existence of a complex and expensive research technology is combined with a centralized formulation of research policy and a centralized distribution of funds (Ben-David, 1960a). It appears therefore that, both for the specialty and for the research group, receiving recognition becomes self-reinforcing; that is, it leads to receiving more funds, more talented researchers and, hence, to attaining further results deemed to be significant. A process similar to this seems to operate in the careers of individual scientists (Allison and Stewart, 1974). The more eminent a scientist becomes the more visible he appears to his colleagues and the greater the credit he receives for his research contributions. This can be seen through the study of collaboration and multiple discovery; for those who have already established a reputation tend to be given appreciably more credit than their less well known collaborators and to receive greater acclaim for discoveries which were also made independently and simultaneously by scientists of lesser repute (Merton, 1961 and 1968).

Two clear conclusions emerge from these studies of the reward system of science. The first is that rewards are distributed by a social process of exchange, whereby valued information is made available to the research community in return for professional recognition (Hagstrom, 1965; Storer, 1966). The second is that this exchange process generates a self-reinforcing elite structure (Zuckerman, 1970; Cole and Cole, 1973). Certain reservations must, however, be made. Firstly, most of these studies are American and there is a tendency among investigators to concentrate on the discipline of physics. Thus we do not know whether recognition and quality of research are closely linked in biological fields (see, however, Shanin-Cohen, 1974). Nor can we be entirely sure that other national scientific communities have an elite structure like that found in the United States (Ben-David, 1968 and 1971). We have no detailed data to allow us to compare these findings for Western societies with the situation in Socialist countries or with that in the economically underdeveloped nations.[9] Furthermore, there are unresolved

---

[9] This does not mean, of course, that there is *no* literature on science in non-Western societies. See, for example, Amann, 1970, and Gould, 1961. It means only that there is no directly *comparable* literature.

methodological problems. In particular, there is the difficulty already mentioned of establishing measures of scientific quality or significance which are distinct from those of recognition. Until such methodological uncertainties are removed, we must treat the results summarized above with some caution.

Nevertheless, in one respect in particular, these studies of the elite structure of American science are encouraging. They hold a promise of enabling us to establish a link between the analysis of the internal and the external processes influencing the development of the research community. This is so because the visibility of the scientific elite extends in all probability beyond the research community into the domains where political and economic policy are formulated (Don K. Price, 1954; Wood, 1964). Consequently, a crucial area for future study is that of the exchanges which take place in various kinds of society between the members of the scientific elite and the leaders in political and economic life (Lapp, 1965; Blume 1973; but see the complex findings presented in Mullins, 1972b).

SOCIAL EXCHANGE AND SOCIAL CONTROL

In the light of the studies of the reward system which have been outlined above, the view began to develop that in pure science social control, that is the maintenance of social conformity, is effected by a process of social exchange. Whatever a particular scientist's motives are for engaging in research, it appears that they can only be satisfied to the extent to which he establishes a good professional reputation (Merton, 1957; Reif and Strauss, 1965). And the recognition necessary for such a reputation depends on his meeting the social and intellectual requirements of the research community and especially on his producing information regarded as valuable. In other words, receiving recognition and associated rewards is seen to be conditional on conformity to prescribed ways of thinking and behaving.

There are, of course, difficulties with such a view. In the first place the units of exchange are difficult to specify clearly. However, this may not be simply a result of our failure to conceptualize social exchange adequately in the sociology of science. For it may be that social, as opposed to economic, exchange is such that the obligations created in the course of exchange are largely unspecified and that the rate of exchange varies from one transaction to another (Blau, 1964). In addition to conceptual uncertainties of this kind, there are several relevant empirical issues to which little attention has so far been paid. For instance, very little is known about the ways in which recognition awarded by members of a geographically dispersed research network (see below) is 'converted' into other rewards, such as promotion and improved access to funds, which are distributed by social groupings other than research networks themselves (but see Ravetz, 1971). Similarly, although it has been suggested that disputes over priority have become less frequent (Merton, 1961), little is known about long term changes in the availability of and competition for recognition. Finally, little study has been made of exchange processes within the pure research community other than that involving information and *recognition*. There is, however, an indication that purely technical exchanges, that is, of information for *information*, may also be important determinants of social relations in science (Mulkay and Edge, 1973; Collins, 1974).

These are some of the problems which arise out of an awareness of exchange processes in science, but which have so far received little study. One crucial problem, however, which has been pursued is that of the connection between the distribution of professional rewards and the Mertonian norms. The conclusion that there is no institutionalized link between conformity to these norms and the receiving of recognition appears to receive considerable support (Weingart, 1974).[10] The evidence for this is of several kinds. Firstly, there are questionnaire studies designed to measure researchers' commitment to the putative values of science by eliciting responses to verbal formulations of these values. Although there have been only a few such studies and although the numbers of respondents have been small, the results have been uniformly negative (West, 1960; Blissett, 1972). It seems, therefore, that there is no evidence showing any large measure of support among those engaged in pure research for statements intended to embody the supposed scientific ethos.

A second kind of evidence is that, even when scientists express verbal support for a norm such as organized skepticism, they do not necessarily act in accordance with it. Thus in one study it was found that, although every member of a particular university physics department stated that researchers should be highly critical, not one of them could name a scientist who had actually published or submitted critical comments on the poor quality work which, they stressed, filled the journals in their particular field (Mulkay and Williams, 1971; see also Yates, 1968). The reason for their failure to act in accordance with the ideal of organized skepticism appears to have been that such conformity would have brought no recognition. The publication of critical comments was not linked to the reward system. It seems, therefore, that although organized skepticism may operate as part of the *rhetoric* of science, it is not firmly institutionalized in such a way that general conformity is maintained.

A third problem with the Mertonian norms is that they are formulated at such a general level that they appear to be common to the whole academic community. They are, therefore, open to a great variety of specific interpreta-

---

[10] For a different interpretation of the evidence, see the Introduction by N. W. Storer to Merton, 1973.

tions. This may be one reason why there is so little uniformity of response in questionnaire studies. Insofar as they do operate in science, it seems likely that they receive specific content in relation to the theories and techniques current within particular research groupings (Barnes and Dolby, 1970; Mitroff, 1974a and b). In other words, the meaning in a particular research area of values such as 'universalism' is derived from the cognitive and technical commitments of those working in the area. Once that is accepted, there is no incompatibility between studies such as that of Merton and Zuckerman (1971), which shows that referees perform their task without evident *social* bias (i.e. they perform in apparent accordance with the norm of universalism), and those which show that referees discriminate between submissions on the basis of methodological and theoretical criteria (Whitley, 1970; Crane, 1967). The situation can best be conceived, I suggest, not as one where scientists conform in any active way to highly general *social* rules like that of universalism, but rather as one in which researchers are strongly committed to specific *scientific* criteria (King, 1971). It is these scientific standards which exert the greatest influence on their professional activities.

This view is supported by further evidence of several kinds. If, for example, the Mertonian norms are effectively institutionalized in science, it becomes difficult to account for the frequency of intellectual resistance. If the scientific ethos is genuinely impartial, open-minded and self-critical, then intellectual resistance must be explained largely by the intrusion into science of extraneous factors (Barber, 1961). It is not easy, however, to reconcile this inference with the growing body of evidence that intellectual resistance is recurrent in science and is, indeed, an inescapable feature of the growth of scientific knowledge (Kuhn, 1970; Taton, 1962). Moreover, studies of the scientific reward system, and other studies, indicate that receiving recognition depends on conformity to current cognitive and technical standards (Hagstrom, 1965; Polanyi, 1963). Similarly, it appears that the influence of the scientific elite contributes to confining the range of acceptable information within relatively narrow limits (Zuckerman, 1970).

By the late 1960's a revised view of the nature of social control in science was beginning to develop, in response to considerations and evidence of this kind. The crux of the argument was that originality is not rewarded unconditionally in science. Under normal circumstances, originality is rewarded only in so far as it remains within the limits of the existing scientific and technical consensus. Thus undue intellectual deviation is discouraged and the process of social exchange operates, not to maintain conformity to the Mertonian norms, but to foster commitment to the prevailing cognitive framework (Hagstrom, 1965; Lemaine and Matalon, 1969; Mulkay, 1969; Barnes and Dolby, 1970; King, 1971). It has already been shown that the use made of scientific statements can change from one social context to another. Depending on the circumstances, the same proposition can be used as a contingent proposition, as a formally analytic statement, as a rule, as a recommendation, as a prescription, and as a standard for judging the acceptability of other propositions (Hanson, 1965). Sociologists were now emphasizing these latter aspects of scientific knowledge. They were stressing that membership in a scientific research community entails acceptance of the intellectual standards defining what kinds of problems and solutions are legitimate, and that only research which is generally regarded as meeting those standards is rewarded with professional recognition.

At the same time that these changes were taking place in the views of many sociologists of science, a parallel account was being developed by Ravetz (1971) of what he terms 'quality control' in science. In contrast to industrial production, in relation to which quality control is most frequently discussed, the quality of scientific work is maintained without there being a formal hierarchy of decision and control. The basic reasons for this, argues Ravetz, are that scientific research depends so greatly on tacit knowledge and craft skills; and that this knowledge and these skills vary considerably from one field to another. Consequently, the techniques whereby the quality of research is maintained 'are so subtle, the appropriate criteria of adequacy and value so specialized, and the materials so rapidly changing, that any fixed and formalized categories would be a blunt and obsolete instrument as soon as it were brought into use' (Ravetz, 1971, 274).

Consequently, trustworthy assessments of the quality of a given piece of work can only be made by those who are working on the same or similar problems and who are known to be capable of producing results of at least the same level of quality. Thus there can be no separate, formal hierarchy of control in scientific research. All participants, as they use, modify or disregard the results communicated to them, are continually engaged in judging the adequacy and value of their colleagues' work. As a result of these judgments, recognition is allocated and reputations are created; not only for individual researchers, but also for research groups, university departments and research journals. Because judgments of the highest quality can only be made by men who are already eminent, those at the top of the various informal scientific hierarchies exercise great influence over the standards operative within their fields. And those scientists who wish to advance their careers and to produce results which are accepted as significant contributions to knowledge must comply with the standards set by these leaders.

The processes of control, however, are not confined within particular fields of inquiry. For all areas of scientific investigation overlap with, depend upon and compete with their intellectual neighbors. Accordingly the leaders of each field, as they seek to maintain their own repute and that of their special subject in the eyes of the wider research community, and as they strive to ensure that adequate funds and facilities are made available for its further development, are obliged to satisfy the expectations of other eminent men. In this way, the system of quality control ramifies throughout the whole of science.

From this new perspective, what was originally treated by Merton as the central normative component of science, comes to be seen more as an ideology; in other words, as a set of verbal formulations which, without providing an accurate account of scientific activity, furnishes a plausible descriptive rhetoric for use in appropriate circumstances.[11] Although there have been few detailed studies of the emergence of the ideology of science as such, there is some indication that it was created by scientists, particularly in the Nineteenth Century, as they were forced on the one hand to justify their conceptions to antagonistic lay groups and, on the other hand, to protect their autonomy against the threat of political control (Metzger, 1955; Ben-David and Zloczower, 1962; Daniels, 1967; Ravetz, 1971).

The move away from explaining the intellectual development of pure science by reference to a distinctive set of social norms was, of course, greatly influenced by the work of Kuhn (1962), which will be discussed in more detail by Böhme in Chapter 9. For Kuhn had stressed that the central normative element in the scientific community is provided by the current body of knowledge and technique.[12] But this line of thought, whether in Kuhn's original formulation or in its more sociological variants, raises further problems. For example, are there several levels at which intellectual consensus is maintained in science (Kuhn, 1970; Ravetz, 1971)? If there are several levels, what degree of conformity is required at each level (Martins, 1971)? By what processes of social interaction is scientific consensus established (Law and French, 1974)? If intellectual conformity is generally maintained in science – if, in other words, science is an intellectually closed rather than an open community – how can we account for the undeniable capacity of that community to generate major intellectual innovations (Barber, 1961)? Does the degree of conformity and the effectiveness of control vary from one field of research to another and within the same field over time? Which social groupings actually regulate, presumably in part by apportioning the receiving of professional recognition, the extent of intellectual control? No completely satisfactory answer has yet been given to any of these questions. But their pursuit has contributed to increasingly detailed and informative study of the social relationships of pure research and of the development of research areas. Tentative answers to some of these questions will appear in the sections which follow.

----

[11]   Interesting results relevant to this issue are provided by Mitroff (1974a and b) in his analysis of 'Norms and Counternorms' in science. Mitroff suggests that norms of objectivity and emotional neutrality coexist in science with opposing norms prescribing strong personal commitment. He goes on to state that his respondents 'indicated that the only people who took the idea of the purely objective scientist literally and seriously were the general public or beginning science students'.

[12]   This aspect of Kuhn's work is discussed more fully later on, in the section on 'Intellectual Resistance'.

THE FORMAL AND INFORMAL
ORGANIZATION OF PURE RESEARCH

In most Western countries, the majority of those engaged in pure research are located in universities and are dispersed to meet the requirements of the university system.[13] (Marcson, 1972; Cardwell, 1972). Within the universities the main social and intellectual boundaries are those between scientific disciplines, such as physics, chemistry and astronomy. Each discipline passes on its distinctive corpus of knowledge and technique to a fairly distinct body of students; and these separate channels of recruitment are reflected in the existence of separate disciplinary societies, research journals and other means of conveying scientific information and of distributing professional rewards. The emergence of distinct disciplinary organizations and the creation of well-defined intellectual boundaries occured mainly in the Nineteenth Century (Taylor, 1973).

During the present century the connections between the formal organization of disciplines and the actual social groupings which are responsible for the extension of scientific knowledge have become increasingly tenuous (Polanyi, 1962; Mullins, 1968). This is due to two main factors. Firstly, there has been a great increase in interdisciplinary research, brought about by the emergence of problem areas overlapping several major disciplines (Brooks, 1967). In addition, each discipline has itself expanded exponentially, leading to a marked internal proliferation of sub-fields (Derek Price, 1963). Thus each discipline or interdisciplinary area is now composed of a large number of fairly distinct specialties; for instance, physics is divided into solid state physics, nuclear physics, atomic physics, astrophysics, thermodynamics, and so on (Anthony, East and Slater, 1969).

As the scientific community has grown in size, so these specialties have also become large social units. Thus a survey of the American physics communtiy in 1966 found that the biggest specialty, solid state physics, had over 3,000 members; while nuclear physics and optics each had around 2,000 members and acoustics in the region of 1,000, and so on (Anthony, East and Slater, 1969). These figures refer to the United States alone. For the full international physics community, we note that the United States produces about one third of the world's physics literature (Anthony, East and Slater, 1969); if we assume that American physicists produce at the same rate as those of other countries, then, by multiplying the figures above by three, we get very rough estimates of the overall size of these specialties.

---

[13] There has, of course, been a complex interplay between the development of scientific disciplines and the expansion of national university systems (see Zloczower, 1966; Parsons and Platt, 1968). Furthermore, in countries such as France and the USSR, the link between pure research and the universities is much weaker than is suggested in the text above (see Ben-David and Zloczower, 1962).

Scientific specialties, as well as being large, are always widespread geographically. This is not only because their membership is international but
also because, within any one country, there is a tendency for each university
department to try to ensure that the full range of major areas is represented
among its staff (Marcson, 1962). At the same time, specialties are further
fragmented internally by the existence of numerous specialized research
areas. Thus in 1967 a group of solid state physicists in Canada divided their
specialty into twenty seven relatively distinct fields of investigation[14]
(*Physics in Canada*, 1967). In response to their growth in size, their geographical diffusion and their internal scientific differentiation, specialties have
evolved some of the formal characteristics of disciplines. They have formed
their own scientific societies, arranged regular conferences, established
specialized journals, set up study groups on future development, held summer
schools, and so on (Hagstrom, 1965; Mullins, 1972). But despite such developments, specialties have become too big and their scientific scope too
broad to provide their members with a coherent intellectual and social focus
for their research. This focus is provided by much smaller networks of
researchers, numbering at most around two hundred members (Price and
Beaver, 1966; Garvey and Griffith, 1966), and concerned with a fairly narrow
range of closely related problems (Law, 1973).

The importance of these comparatively small social groupings in science is
due to several factors. Firstly, the intensive investigation required in most
fields means that scientists' research activity is highly specialized. Secondly,
there is a limit to the amount of time and effort that researchers can devote
to gathering and absorbing technical information. Thirdly, researchers choose,
on the whole, to communicate with those who are pursuing problems similar
in some way to their own. These factors together lead to a clustering of
communication choices and to the formation of a multitude of loose research
networks (Griffith and Small, 1974a and b). The membership and the
problems of the various research networks tend to overlap in a complex
manner. And the personnel involved in any one network tends to change
rapidly, often being drawn from a number of different specialties and disciplines (Mullins, 1972a). It is these problem networks which appear to be the
basic agents of innovation and of social control in science (Mulkay, 1972a;
Crane, 1972).

---

[14] It is assumed here that participants' categories represent fairly accurately the
social divisions within the specialty. However, there has been no study of the ways in
which participants actually devise and use such categories. It may be, therefore, that at
least in certain circumstances, participants' categories are misleading.

PROBLEM NETWORKS AND PROCESSES
OF COMMUNICATION

Research results become certified knowledge only after they have been communicated to and endorsed by those scientists competent to assess them; that is, in the first instance, the members of small-scale problem networks. Consequently, technical communication plays a central part in the processes which lead to the attainment of scientific consensus and, thereby, the creation of scientific knowledge (Ziman, 1968). The precise nature of scientific communication is problematic for several reasons. In the first place, the audience for any given unit of information, say a research paper, is diffuse and difficult to identify (Mullins, 1968). Secondly, there is often more information potentially available on a given problem than one or even a small group of researchers can collect (Garvey and Griffith, 1970). Thirdly, information can be conveyed in a great variety of ways. For example, it has been suggested that there are approximately fifty important 'channels of exchange of scientific information' in present-day psychology (Garvey and Griffith, 1967, 1011). Finally, there is the fact that access to the various channels of communication is socially structured (Garvey and Griffith, 1967; Gaston, 1972). In general, the studies made so far of communication in science, taking up these problems, serve to confirm and supplement the findings on the reward structure and the nature of scientific elites.

The main institutionalized form of communication in scientific research is by means of the professional journal. In many fields, however, journals enter the process of communication at a relatively late stage and a large proportion of results are widely communicated informally before publication. In such fields, therefore, the journals appear to have become more a means of bestowing a minimal level of formal recognition than a means of communicating new findings of those centrally engaged in the area (Derek Price, 1963; Gaston, 1972). It seems likely that this widespread recourse to informal channels of communication is a response to such factors as the sheer size of the literature, the diverse location of relevant material and the desire to establish a regular, quick and flexible exchange of information with those known to be working on closely related problems (Menzel, 1967; Brittain, 1970; Hagstrom, 1970). Informal communication is also used in particular to pass on the kind of information about techniques which is often left implicit in formal papers presenting research findings (Menzel, 1966). It is likely to be specially prevalent, therefore, in fields where substantive results depend greatly on esoteric technical expertise or where the field is primarily concerned with technical developments (Collins, 1974).

There seems to be a tendency in many fields for intensive informal communication links to develop among the most productive and influential scientists (Price and Beaver, 1966; Garvey and Griffith, 1967; Crane 1972). Derek Price has called such groupings 'invisible colleges' and has argued that they are an inevitable product of the remarkably rapid exponential growth in the numbers of scientists and in the size of the literature[15] (1963; Storer, 1966). Given the connection between scientific output and the receiving of recognition, it seems clear that the elite groupings identified in the course of communication studies are equivalent to those found in the course of studies of the reward system.

The crucial part which these elites play in the operation of the research community has been shown in a number of investigations. Thus, elite members tend to be leaders of research groups or to be linked to a number of less eminent people (Price and Beaver, 1966). Consequently, the informal communication between elite members provides an indirect link between their groups of researchers (Crane, 1972). At the same time, it follows that those less productive researchers who are not associated in this manner with the scientific elite of their field find it difficult to keep in touch with the more important current developments. Thus Garvey and Griffith suggest that in psychology it is precisely those who have greatest need of preprints, etc. – that is, 'young scientists, workers at small institutions and researchers in less developed countries' (1967, 1014) – who are least in touch with the informal network. Nevertheless, despite this apparent inefficiency in the operation of the elite system, elite scientists are key figures in helping to bring together the potentially disparate elements of diffuse and rapidly changing research networks (Ravetz, 1971). In addition, members of these elite groupings probably make an important contribution to the transfer of information, ideas and techniques from one research area to another. This is so, firstly, because they tend to be key members of several overlapping networks and, secondly, because they tend to be carriers of crucial information (Menzel, 1966). They therefore contribute significantly to the unplanned 'cross-fertilization of ideas' which is so important a source of scientific innovation (Koestler, 1964; Mulkay, 1969).

This last conclusion leads us back towards a consideration of the ways in which social processes contribute to the development of scientific knowledge. On the whole, those engaged in studying communication in science have not been concerned with this kind of problem. They have been more interested in examining how the rapid growth of science has affected the procedures whereby information is communicated, than in investigating the processes responsible for scientific growth. In many cases, they have been concerned primarily with identifying and suggesting practical solutions to what are seen

---

[15] Although the term has a good historical pedigree (the members of the early Royal Society were distinguishing themselves from those of the visible Gresham College), it is slightly misleading to call these groupings of elite scientists 'invisible colleges'. This is so, firstly, because their members are in fact likely to be highly visible within their own research network, and secondly, because they are likely to play a prominent part in representing their field in the wider research community and in establishing its scientific repute (Cole and Cole, 1968).

to be 'problems of communication' in science (Garvey and Griffith, 1970). The literature on scientific communication has been criticized, therefore, for failing to consider the content of scientific messages, and for failing to examine the way in which scientific thought changes over time (Hagstrom, 1970). Despite these limitations, these studies, when supplemented with other data, can be used to build up a preliminary account of how social and intellectual factors combine in the course of scientific development. It should perhaps be stressed, however, that in the literature at present available, and in the account which follows, the analysis of intellectual factors is less adequate and less complete than that of social factors. It should also be noted that the next section is a provisional attempt to integrate a complex body of findings which is far from complete and, in many particular instances, far from conclusive.

THE DEVELOPMENT OF RESEARCH NETWORKS

Research networks are amorphous social groupings which, partly due to migration (McGinnis and Singh, 1972; Garvey and Tomita, 1972), and partly due to overlapping membership (Polanyi, 1962), are in a state of constant flux. At any one time the research community as a whole, as well as particular disciplines and specialties within it, is composed of numerous networks at various stages of formation, growth and decline (Crane, 1972). The onset of growth in a new 'area' tends to follow from the perception, by scientists already at work in one or more existing areas, of unsolved problems, unexpected observations or unusual technical developments, the pursuit of which lies outside their current field. Thus the exploration of a new area is usually set in motion by a process of scientific migration (Holton, 1962; Barber, 1968).

Scientific migration is not a random process, for the scientists moving into a new area tend to come from other networks which have specifiable characteristics. In particular, they come from networks which have experienced a pronounced decline in the significance of current results (Mullins, 1972a); from networks whose members have few or no avenues of research easily available (Krantz, 1965); from networks whose members have special competence in or knowledge of techniques which have given some indication of being more widely applicable (Mulkay and Edge, 1973); and from networks which have been disrupted, often by events originating outside the research community, and whose members have consequently no firm commitment to an established research area (Fleming and Bailyn, 1969).

The origins of research networks can usually be identified only retrospectively (but see Meadows and O'Connor, 1971), because even the participants do not realize during the very early stages, that a new area is forming. At the earliest stage researchers at different locations in various countries take up the same or closely related problems often unaware of similar work proceeding elsewhere (Merton, 1961). The lack of communication and the concern with relatively crude exploration of fairly obvious problems leads to multiple discovery, anticipation of results and open competition and dispute (Reif and Strauss, 1965; Mulkay and Edge, 1973). Competition and dispute occur particularly at this stage because most participants are pursuing the same few problems; because informal communication is not yet efficient enough to keep researchers informed of others' research intentions and recent results and, thereby, to enable them to avoid research overlap; and because clear criteria of scientific adequacy and significance are not firmly established within the emerging network.

An early lead in the competition for results tends to be taken by those with best access to such resources as suitable techniques, graduate students, research funds, publication outlets and the legitimacy conferred by the approval of eminent scientists. Consequently, a crucial factor in this early phase is the sponsorship of scientists of high repute who often guide their protegees into new and promising areas, while themselves remaining on the periphery (Barber, 1968; Mulkay, 1972b). The initial results tend to be scattered among various disciplinary journals and in general-purpose journals (Gillmor and Terman, 1973). As a result of these first publications, some of those working independently on similar problems become aware of their common interests and establish informal contact. Such contact is also promoted through the links between existing 'invisible colleges'. Where informal communication is not established, growth appears to be seriously impeded (McGrath and Altman, 1966).

During the early stages of exploration, research problems tend to be loosely defined and results are often given widely differing interpretations. Gradually, however, as a result of continual debate informally and through the journals, general agreement emerges about such issues as the relative significance of different problems, the proper definition of variables and the correct use of techniques. At present, the ways in which scientific consensus is created are little understood and much more detailed investigation is required of this complex topic. Nevertheless, there is evidence that growing consensus is accompanied by associated changes in intellectual and social processes within the network. For example, publications appear in an increasingly narrow range of journals. Similarly, the proportion of references to papers by authors not centrally engaged in the field declines markedly (Crane, 1972). At the same time, a small number of fairly early contributions come to be recognized as particularly important and to be cited regularly. As these central contributions become known to workers in other areas and to potential graduate students, the rate of recruitment into what is coming to be regarded as a 'new and interesting' field increases rapidly. As a result, in many cases, the number of researchers active in the area and the amount of published material grow exponentially.

As the network increases in size, research teams and clusters of collaborators form; they recruit new entrants to the field and train them from the perspective of the increasingly firm scientific consensus (Griffith and Mullins, 1972). Both research groups and individual scientists take up specialist lines of inquiry, which are chosen so as to minimize overlap and, consequently, the likelihood of competition (Gaston, 1971). This process ensures that a relatively wide range of issues is explored (Hagstrom, 1965). Research teams and groupings of collaborators tend to be led by highly productive scientists who exert an important influence on the direction of intellectual development, not only because they are responsible for many of the basic advances, but also because, as we have noted above, they play a major part in the informal dissemination of information within the network.

Research areas tend to develop in response to major innovations which appear early in the sequence of growth. Subsequent work tends to consist primarily of elaborations upon these central contributions. Consequently, in many cases a major proportion of the innovative work is completed before the field has begun to acquire a significant proportion of its eventual membership (Holton, 1962; Crane, 1972). This means that opportunities for making a notable scientific contribution and the chances of receiving an unusual amount of professional recognition decline very quickly after the very earliest period. As this becomes evident to participants and, more slowly, to potential entrants, growth becomes linear instead of exponential. This stage in the development of the network, characterized by linear growth, scientific consensus and predictability of results, resembles what Kuhn (1962) has called 'normal science'. However, this term appears to be misleading. This kind of research *is* normal in the sense that it tends to occur, for a while, in the evolution of most research networks. It is nevertheless always a temporary phase, preceded by a period of uncertain exploration and followed by a period, often equally uncertain, of decline. Thus at the research front scientific consensus is neither a normal feature nor a sociologically unproblematic feature. It is rather something which is being continually abandoned as well as continually created as part of an ongoing social process.

In some areas, the decline of interesting and/or solvable problems, accompanied by a scarcity of professional recognition, may be followed by a breakdown of social control, a rejection of the existing consensus, and its replacement with a new and fertile research framework (Kuhn, 1962). But there is little evidence that this occurs at all frequently. The central feature of the more typical sequence is that the pursuit of the problems with which the network was originally concerned either generates a number of new problems and unexpected observations or it produces results which are seen to have implications for work in other areas. In such cases, growth turns imperceptibly into decline as recruitment falls away and as established members of the network move elsewhere into problem areas in the process of formation. However, research areas which have become well established often take a long time to disappear completely. There is usually *some* work not entirely trivial, which can still be done. In many fields, therefore, a small number of researchers carry on the research tradition long after the focus of interest has shifted elsewhere (Fisher, 1967).

The analysis presented above is couched in terms of the growth and decline of small scale research networks. Very similar processes operate, however, in the emergence of new specialties and new disciplinary areas (Hagstrom, 1965; Ben-David and Collins, 1966; Zloczower, 1966). The major difference is that in the latter case the first period of exploration produces a rapid efflorescence of loosely related avenues of investigation. In such instances the sequence of preliminary exploration, exponential growth and levelling off, can be clearly observed at the level of the specialty or discipline (Mullins, 1972a; Mulkay and Edge, 1973). This account of the social and, less adequately, the intellectual processes of scientific development emphasizes the way in which science grows through the branching of new lines of research. It is, therefore particularly consistent with, and receives support from, those quantitative studies in which the cumulative increase in numbers of research papers, separate journals, scientific abstracts, specialist societies, etc., has been described (Derek Price, 1963; Anthony, East and Slater, 1969; Menard, 1971; Gilbert and Woolgar, 1974). Indeed the literature summarized in this section begins to give us an idea of the kinds of social processes responsible for the distinctive pattern of growth and internal differentiation of the research community.

Concern with the emergence and growth of research networks has led to a recent increase in the number of case studies of particular networks (Crane, 1969; Mullins, 1972a; Law, 1973; Collins, 1974). There is still, however, a lack of detailed evidence in this area. Accordingly the account given in this section of the dynamics of research networks has been compiled from various pieces of evidence taken from quite disparate fields of scientific activity. It must, therefore, be regarded as highly tentative and will undoubtedly need much revision in the light of further study. There are two problems which need particular attention. It has been suggested that in some fields there occurs a move away from pure towards applied research (Menzel, 1967). Such a development would entail a change from a relatively closed, scientific audience, to an external audience; as well as corresponding changes in the reward system, the nature of social control and institutional location. We have little direct evidence at present, however, about this kind of social sequence in science. Secondly, it seems likely that many eminent scientists are socially visible outside as well as inside the research community. Furthermore, it is these men who have most control over the resources of the research community (Lemaine, Lecuyer *et al*, 1972). There can be little doubt, therefore, that influences originating outside the research community upon the direction taken by pure research are mediated through the various scientific elites. Accordingly, as has been suggested already in the discussion of the distribution of professional rewards, much closer study is needed of these elites.

COMPETITION AND SECRECY

In the account given so far of the research community, little attention has been paid to factors likely to disrupt the continuity of social or intellectual development. It should not be thought, however, that the evolution of the research community or the pursuit of scientific knowledge proceeds entirely smoothly. One disruptive phenomenon which has already been mentioned is that of competition for recognition. Such competition occurs, as we have seen, because scientists wish to be rewarded for their efforts and for their results. It also occurs because researchers with similar scientific backgrounds tend to perceive the same problems as significant (Kuhn, 1970; Merton, 1961). Accordingly, it has been suggested that competition is likely to be particularly prevalent in certain parts of physics, where highly developed theories and precise experimental techniques focus participants' attention on a limited range of unambiguous problems (Hagstrom, 1965). Competition occurs, in addition, because decisions to pursue specific problems are taken independently by researchers who have only partial knowledge of others' research intentions. Consequently, competition tends to be most noticeable during the earliest stage in the formation of particular networks, before participants are aware of who else is working in the emergent area and before efficient channels of informal communication have been established. It also seems clear that the prevalence and severity of competition are affected, not only by the cognitive structure of research areas and by the stage of development of research networks, but also by the wider academic context in which research is undertaken (Ben-David, 1965). There is some evidence to show, for example, that the university system in the United Kingdom, because it is highly centralized and because it operates through a relatively cohesive network of sponsorship, is generally less competitive than that in the United States (Gaston, 1973; Ben-David, 1968).

Competition in science has several consequences. As was noted above, it can lead to accelerated publication as researchers strive to make sure that their results are not anticipated (Reif and Strauss, 1965). This, in turn, often means that researchers allow themselves insufficient time to ensure, as far as possible, that their findings are reliable and valid; and it becomes difficult for them to present unified, elaborate and reasonably complete analyses of results (Hagstrom, 1965).

The pressure to publish quickly is likely to be particularly great during the onset of growth in a given area, for it is at this stage that the most significant results are available. And indeed it is at this early stage that researchers make the most use of those journals with the shortest delay between submission and publication (Meadows and O'Connor, 1971). During this first exploratory phase the scientific and technical standards for assessing the quality of results will still be uncertain and work which subsequently would be regarded as slipshod will be allowed into print (Reif, 1961). It seems, therefore, that competitive pressures contribute to a certain amount of poor quality publication. To this extent, competition hinders the extension of certified knowledge. In addition, the threat of competition gives rise to secrecy.

Secrecy in science is a product of two conflicting pressures. On the one hand, researchers want to produce results of high scientific quality. They are, therefore, reluctant to publish their findings until they are quite sure of their reliability and significance. On the other hand, researchers are unwilling to jeopardize their priority in the pursuit of scientific excellence. If they delay publication, yet discuss their research freely, others may make use of their work and publish first. When faced with this dilemma, scientists frequently decide that the threat to their priority can best be avoided, without lowering the quality of their work, by keeping results from potential competitors (Gaston, 1973). This practice of limiting the extent of informal communication has, of course, further consequences. It leads to an avoidable duplication of effort. It also prevents scientists from enjoying the full benefit of technical discussion with those most able to help them improve their current research. Furthermore, it appears that there are no clear rules governing the informal dissemination of scientific information. Consequently, what one group or individual may regard as legitimate restriction of access, may be seen by others as unjustifiable secrecy. Particularly when important discoveries are involved, these divergent interpretations by participants can lead to serious misunderstanding and resentment (Mulkay and Edge, 1973). This may, of course, further reduce the level of effective communication. In short, secrecy appears to some extent to interfere with the system of informal quality control in science and perhaps, thereby, to lower the standard of research. Yet by exercising close control over the flow of information, researchers may be better able to present reliable results which provide a firm foundation for further investigation. Moreover, once results are made public, and usually the delay is very short, all those interested are able to make full use of them. It seems unlikely, therefore, that researchers, by regulating the time at which their findings are published, exert any lasting influence on the direction in which research proceeds.

So far in this discussion of competition, the emphasis has been on its negative consequences for the development of scientific knowledge. There are, however, consequences of a more positive kind (Hagstrom, 1965). In the first place, because professional recognition is scarce and is allocated in accordance with the perceived scientific value of results, the problems which are regarded as highly significant by those competent to judge are certain to be pursued. Secondly, because scientists are in a competitive situation, they tend to choose and to be encouraged to select problems for which their skills and their level of ability are suited (Lemaine, Lecuyer *et al*, 1972). Thus graduate students, who naturally find it difficult to compete with mature scientists, are often given research topics which are somewhat peripheral and which are, therefore, unlikely to attract the attention of older and more experienced researchers. Selection of problems which are far from central is not confined to graduate students, however, and many scientists adopt a strategy of choosing problems which they regard as interesting, yet not sufficiently interesting to generate an uncomfortable amount of competition (Mulkay and Williams, 1971). In addition competition seems, to some extent, to encourage risk taking; that is to say, it encourages some scientists, usually those whose reputation and academic position are secure, to choose topics where reliable results are especially significant but also particularly difficult to obtain (Hagstrom, 1965; Lemaine, 1974).

These competitive pressures, of course, affect research groups as well as individual researchers. Indeed pressures are usually even more severe for research groups because such groups are often forced to make a costly and frequently irreversible investment in large scale research technology. Consequently, research groups tend to avoid competition by concentrating, as far as possible, on techniques and problems which are not the main focus of interest elsewhere (Gaston, 1973). Once one group has achieved a clear lead in a particular field, other groups will tend to choose different areas rather than face duplication of effort and open competition (Mulkay and Edge, 1973). In situations where they depend upon the same funding agency, they may also develop explicit policies of supplementary, rather than competitive, research. In these ways, then, competitive pressures in the research community help to ensure that new and promising areas are explored energetically and that, in most scientific domains, a wide range of techniques is employed and a wide range of problems investigated. This is least likely to happen in areas where techniques are exceptionally costly and where a few groups have established a research oligopoly (see Gaston, 1973; Swatez, 1966).

INTELLECTUAL RESISTANCE

There is one further phenomenon which appears to recur in science and which seems to disrupt its smooth evolution — namely, resistance to innovation (Barber, 1963). This phenomenon could perhaps be regarded as unproblematic, as arising simply from the inadequacies of the proposed innovations, were it not for the fact that many of the scientific developments which were either ignored or resisted most strenuously at their inception have in time entered the domain of firmly established scientific knowledge (Taton, 1962; Feyerabend, 1965). Let me mention just three examples. The legendary long neglect of Mendel's work (see however Garfield, 1969) illustrates how scientists are sometimes unable to perceive the significance of techniques and results which are based upon assumptions different from those generally accepted in the field (Glass, 1953; see also Barber and Fox, 1958). In the case of Pasteur we find a situation where radical departures from current conceptions were not ignored but, instead, received with bitter hostility, even though they were proposed by a scientist of considerable repute (Mulkay, 1972a). Velikowsky's case differs most obviously from the two preceeding ones in that he was clearly not a member of the research community. However, when he published a book which challenged many of the central presumptions of astronomers, geologists and historical biologists, it was greeted by professional members of the relevant fields with violent denunciation and with attempts at suppression. Many of those most critical of the book refused even to read it. It violated, so they were informed, so many fundamental scientific canons that it was not worthy of serious consideration (deGrazia, 1966; Polanyi, 1966-1967).

Despite many dissimilarities, these cases have in common the fact that scientists of their era were unreceptive to new results, new techniques and new ideas, largely because these innovations appeared to be inconsistent with widely held intellectual convictions. Several writers, in the light of such instances of intellectual resistance, have argued that science is characterized by the creation of strong intellectual orthodoxies; and that such orthodoxies are essential to science because they allow researchers to take their interpretative framework for granted and to concentrate on the detailed resolution of issues which appear equally problematic to all those who share that framework (Cohen, 1952). Polanyi, after reviewing the way in which the research community had initially rejected his 'potential theory of adsorption', only to accept it many years later, concludes that: 'There must be at all times a predominantly accepted scientific view of the nature of things, in the light of which research is jointly conducted by members of the community of scientists. A strong presumption that any evidence which contradicts this view is invalid must prevail' (Polanyi, 1969, 92; also 1958).

This interpretation of the nature of scientific inquiry has been developed in a sociological direction by Kuhn (1962; 1970), who has attempted to reconcile the notion of 'scientific orthodoxy' with the frequent occurence of dramatic advances or changes in scientific knowledge by introducing the idea of 'scientific revolution'. As Kuhn's work has already been discussed in this chapter and will be further discussed by Böhme in Chapter 9, let me merely highlight those facets of his analysis which are especially relevant to the present topic. Kuhn argues that research scientists are socialized in such a way that they acquire an exceptionally strong commitment to existing cognitive frameworks (1962). These frameworks are precise and in many cases expressed in quantitative form (1963). Consequently, research proposals and results which are inconsistent with the existing framework are easily perceived and usually opposed, particularly by those older and often more eminent scientists who are more attached to existing conceptions. The findings of 'normal science' are, therefore, highly predictable and, because they are expected, they are easily absorbed.

> Perhaps the most striking feature of normal research problems is how little they aim to produce major novelties, conceptual or phenomenal. Sometimes everything but the most esoteric detail of the result is known in advance, and the typical latitude of expectation is only somewhat wider ... the range of anticipated, and thus of assimilable, results is always small compared with the range that the imagination can conceive (Kuhn, 1962 and 1970, 35).

Radical changes of outlook, it is argued, almost always involve bitter dispute and generate strong opposition. Nevertheless, such changes do occur regularly, partly because any given framework in due course generates less and less solvable problems and more and more anomalies, and also because in established areas there is a continuous recruitment of young researchers who are relatively uncommitted to the existing framework and more likely to see the potential fertility of any new approach. Thus at all levels of social organization in science there occurs an irregular but recurrent alternation between 'normal' and 'revolutionary' science.

Such an account of scientific development depends on several assertions which appear doubtful, especially in the light of some of the information summarized above on the nature of the scientific community. It is far from certain, for example, that scientific research is *typically* conducted within extremely rigid analytical frameworks or that research results can normally be predicted in advance in precise detail (Lakatos and Musgrave, 1970). Even in relatively 'advanced' fields, such as high energy physics (Gaston, 1973) and radio astronomy (Mulkay and Edge, 1973), there is often considerable cognitive ambiguity; and totally unexpected results often occur and are often accepted with little opposition. These characteristics are likely to be even more evident in less highly quantified areas. Yet once we accept that, in many parts of science, research is governed by relatively loose cognitive structures, the likelihood of gradual alterations of perspective increases and that of intellectual resistance and revolutionary development diminishes.

A second assumption central to Kuhn's thesis is that major scientific advances typically involve a change of gestalt; that is to say, they require a reconceptualization, within existing areas. However, the most obvious characteristic of the overall growth of science has been the continuous creation of entirely new areas (Derek Price, 1963). To the extent that this is so, the evolution of science can be seen to depend less on the conceptual reorganization of existing areas, than on the discovery and exploration of 'new areas of ignorance' (Holton, 1962). Because new areas have, by definition, not been conceptualized before, their discovery will not normally generate intellectual resistance, nor will it entail revolutionary upheaval (Mulkay, 1972a). Finally, Kuhn's argument involves the assumption that the membership of research groupings remains fairly stable. For only if membership is relatively stable will marked changes of perspective necessarily require that a large proportion of participants *rethink* their scientific commitments. Yet, as we have noted earlier, research networks tend to be in a state of constant flux, with their membership undergoing continuous replacement by researchers from other areas, as well as by new entrants to research. Accordingly, it may well be that this process of scientific migration contributes to a continuous movement of ideas and techniques between areas and, thereby, to a process of gradual, non-revolutionary development (Mulkay, 1974).

In the light of these considerations it seems probable that, although uncompromising intellectual resistance does occur under certain conditions in science, it is by no means as pervasive as Kuhn suggests. In areas characterized by precise and coherent scientific frameworks, it seems likely that social control will be effective (Hagstrom, 1965) and that resistance to new developments will tend to be relatively inflexible. However, this is an empirical proposition and should not be assumed. In order to put it to the test, we need to devise ways of assessing reliably the degree of cognitive precision and coherence within specific fields, so that systematic comparisons can be made between highly coherent and less coherent areas (Griffith and Mullins, 1972). Furthermore, there are other significant factors involved. For example, rigid intellectual control may be more likely in networks with a stable elite, the members of which can effectively limit access to research facilities and regulate the passage of information through the formal organs of communication. In addition, the creation of a closed orthodoxy may be more probable in research networks which are socially and intellectually distinct, and in situations where there is little exchange of personnel with neighboring networks, perhaps owing to the highly specialized character of the research skills required.

It might well be argued, however, that the conditions favoring the maintenance of scientific orthodoxies and resistance to new ideas are less prevalent now than in the past.[16] Thus in present day science there is a multitude of avenues of communication, so that unconventional ideas can in all probability get published somewhere. Moreover, traditional agencies of control, such as scientific societies, are probably less influential today. Yet, on the other hand, scientific conformity can be maintained to a considerable extent by the informal processes of social exchange described above. Furthermore, the formation of large-scale research teams creates opportunities for formal

---

[16] Ben-David (1963-64) points out that few of Kuhn's examples are taken from Twentieth Century science.

control by scientific leaders which did not exist in past eras. Clearly there is insufficient evidence to decide these issues at present. Consequently, the question of to what extent and in what circumstances the social processes of science actually prevent scientific innovation must remain open for the moment.

THE FUTURE OF THE PURE
RESEARCH COMMUNITY

Throughout most of its history the pure research community has been relatively autonomous and has experienced rapid, cumulative growth. This statement, of course, simplifies the full complexity of the situation. The overall growth rate, for instance, is produced by a multitude of smaller groupings at various stages of growth and decline. Similarly, the degree of autonomy varies over time and from one field to another (Ravetz, 1971). Nevertheless, the statement is accurate as a broad generalization. Its significance lies in the possibility that the organization and dynamics of the research community, as they have been described earlier, depend to a considerable extent on the maintenance of relative autonomy and rapid growth. These latter features are, in turn, products of a specific set of social relations between the research community and the wider society. There are evident signs today that these relations are beginning to undergo a pronounced change which will, by limiting its growth and its autonomy, alter the nature of the research community and the character of the scientific endeavor.

The rapid expansion of scientific research has been made possible by a number of related factors. One of the most important is that, during the last century, science came to be widely regarded as the major source of reliable and valid knowledge about the natural world. Consequently, other fields of inquiry came to appear less worthwhile (Plumb, 1964) and, gradually, science achieved a dominant position within the expanding educational system (Ben-David and Zloczower, 1962). The creation of a firmly established academic science had several further consequences. It provided secure scientific careers. It fostered the development of specialized, disciplinary training. And it led to the recruitment of trained scientists into industry and government (Cardwell, 1972). This cluster of developments meant that science was able to attract an increasing proportion of younger people and, thereby, to expand numerically both inside and outside the universities.

Although much of the social support which made possible the rapid growth of science was based on the premise that its practical applications were overwhelmingly beneficial, little attempt was made by governments until well into the present century to ensure that academic science evolved in a direction that would generate practical benefits. It was generally accepted, not only that scientific knowledge was valid, but also that there was no way in which laymen, or perhaps even scientists, could control its development. In many cases, leading scientists actively promoted these assumptions (Daniels, 1968). In addition, pure research was comparatively cheap. The technical equipment and other facilities involved were on a small scale and most academic researchers were directly paid only for their teaching. Accordingly, until the 1930's at least, there seemed to be no need for governments to try to regulate directly the advance of scientific knowledge (Kaplan, 1962). Thus academic scientists remained fairly autonomous and the continuing influx of new researchers was diverted into new fields of investigation in accordance with the largely internal logic of scientific development[17] (Rose and Rose, 1969).

In recent years there have been increasingly clear signs that scientific growth is likely to slacken and that the autonomy of the pure research community is being appreciably curtailed. Derek Price (1963) has argued, for example, that exponential growth, which has characterized scientific development for a very long period, always becomes logistic and that, if we look closely at the curve of scientific growth, we can see that it is likely to level off in the near future. It may well be that the details of Price's prediction are not entirely accurate (Gilbert and Woolgar, 1974). Nevertheless, it seems inevitable that in the next few decades the number of people engaged in pure research will become much more stable (Rose and Rose, 1969). One sign that growth limiting processes have already begun to operate is the recent fall in recruitment, measured by the number of students who choose to study science at university and to continue into research careers (The Dainton Report, 1968; The Swann Report, 1968). This decline has been noted in Western Europe and the United States, as well as in Britain (Rose and Rose, 1969).

If this trend continues, it may well have a major impact on the internal dynamics of the research community. In the first place, there will be fewer new entrants available to help in the exploration of new lines of inquiry. Secondly, the levels of competition will probably diminish considerably, thereby reducing the likelihood of risk taking and the professional incentive for mature researchers to move into new and, therefore, unpredictable fields. A reduction in the number of new entrants into science will not only reduce the number of researchers available for given areas, it will also weaken one of the crucial social mechanisms fostering scientific innovation.

This conclusion, however, may be too strong. As we have already noted, major innovations tend to be produced by a small band of highly productive scientists. It may be that these highly talented and motivated people, whose

---

[17] Marxist scholars have, of course, argued differently. They have maintained that modern science has developed, despite its *laissez-faire* organization, more or less in direct response to the economic requirements of the ruling class (Hessen, 1931; Bernal, 1939).

interest in science appears often to begin in childhood (see Fisch, Chapter 8), will still enter science even in a period of declining recruitment. If scientific research continues to attract such people, and if their productivity is unaffected by the falling off of routine research (Cole and Cole, 1973), then the level of innovation may change much less dramatically than I have suggested above.

The falling rate of recruitment into science is not an isolated phenomenon. It appears, rather, to be but one aspect of a decline in social support for science, deriving from a changed perception of its beneficence. (These changes and their political consequences are discussed by Salomon in Chapter 2, Ravetz in Chapter 3, and Lakoff in Chapter 10.)[18] Since World War II, a much more critical view of science has gathered weight. From this new perspective, science is seen as being inseparable from such unwelcome developments as pollution, the hydrogen bomb and a runaway technology (Ellul, 1965). One version of this 'anti-science' view is expressed by Marcuse when he states that: 'The traditional distinction between science and technology becomes questionable. When the most abstract achievements of mathematics and theoretical physics satisfy so adequately the needs of IBM and the Atomic Energy Commission it is time to ask whether such applicability is not inherent in the concepts of science itself' (1962). Thus in recent years the scientist's freedom to pursue knowledge subject only to the technical judgments of his colleagues has been increasingly challenged. The activity of the research scientist is more and more regarded, not as a morally neutral search for the truth, but as a narrow, and in some respects irresponsible, moral posture.

These views are by no means confined to laymen. Many of the leaders of the scientific community appear to have become aware of the difficulty of the moral problems facing them (Ravetz, 1971). In addition, there are signs of more widely based movements of opinion within the scientific community. For instance, the American Society for Social Responsibility in Science and its British counterpart have considered the possibility of requiring an ethical statement of principle from their members and have attempted to increase public awareness of the likely effects of developments in basic and applied research (Rose and Rose, 1969). Similarly, a number of schools of 'critical science' have developed recently, in which the aims are both political and scientific; namely, to investigate and understand the various kinds of damage produced by modern science and technology and then to ensure that these abuses are abolished or controlled (Commoner, 1966; Ravetz, 1971; see also Nelkin, Chapter 11).

The demands made by those critical of science are paralleled by changes in

---

[18] For the alternative view that this decline and the loss of social support may be due to an inevitable saturation of exponential growth in the most developed nations, see Derek Price, 1961.

the relationship between science and government (Salomon, 1970 and Chapter 2; see also Lakoff, Chapter 10). In the past, governments appear to have accepted the argument that outside intervention would only disrupt pure research and that those engaged in this activity, if left alone, would inevitably but unpredictably generate practically useful knowledge (Ravetz, 1971). In recent decades, however, the support of pure research has become increasingly costly. As a result, governments, which provide most of the funds for pure research (Glass, 1970), have come to require some tangible return for their support (Storer, 1966). Increasingly, therefore, attempts have been made to assess the benefits of research in relation to economic growth, welfare, armaments and national prestige (Byatt and Cohen, 1969; Rose and Rose, 1969). Furthermore, governments have become increasingly committed to a 'policy for science' which reflects social, economic and political, as well as scientific, priorities (Brooks, 1971; Blume, 1973; Salomon, 1970, 1973 and Chapter 2). Thus, as research has come to absorb a significant proportion of our GNP, it has come to be seen as competing with other areas of governmental policy for scarce resources. Accordingly the view has formed that, despite the internal logic of scientific development and the undeniable element of unpredictability in scientific advance, a policy can be formulated which will influence appreciably the direction in which science evolves.

On the whole, governments have not been critical of science or of scientists. They have been more concerned to ensure that 'the maximum social benefit' is extracted from scientific knowledge, now and in the future. Nevertheless, the policy of present day governments toward science resembles that of those critical of science in several important respects. Both policies advocate a decrease in the autonomy of the research community and an increase in the responsiveness of scientists to audiences other than their immediate colleagues; and both policies advocate that scientists' activities be judged by social and moral criteria as well as by technical standards.

If those trends continue, we can expect to see the emergence of a fairly stable pure research community, characterized by a steady rate of recruitment and, perhaps, by a somewhat lower level of innovation than at present. Not only will this community be dependent on the state for financial support, as it is now, but it will also be noticeably more responsive to the demands of governmental agencies (Ravetz, 1971; Williams, 1973). It is difficult to envisage, however, any way in which *detailed* control over the direction of scientific research can be exercised by those who are not active members of the research community. It seems likely, therefore, that some form of consultation will persist between eminent scientists and government representatives, in the course of which official policy will be translated into decisions to support specific research projects (Blume, 1973).

It is at this point in the political process that scientists will be able to retain some degree of self-determination. The exact nature of this consultative process, and therefore the degree of effective scientific autonomy, will vary from one country to another. In situations where non-scientists exercise great control and where major rewards, such as research facilities, funds and promotion, do not depend on meeting the expectations of a technically competent audience, it seems probable that conformity to scientific-technical standards will decline (Greenberg, 1969). In other words, the system of quality control in pure research will be disrupted[19] (Ravetz, 1971). At the same time, it appears likely that certain groups, both inside and outside the research community, will persist in criticizing the nature of science, the uses to which it is put, and its strong links with the state; and that they will continue to devise and implement new forms of social organization for research. Whether a modified version of the existing system evolves or whether an entirely new structure develops will depend primarily upon changes in the wider social context from which scientific research derives its support.

It seems probable, then, that the social organization of pure research will come increasingly to resemble that which is at present characteristic of applied research. It may be possible, therefore, to gain some insight into the likely effects of the extension of lay control over pure research by examining the results of studies of scientists in applied contexts. Accordingly, let me conclude this review with a brief section on applied research. It should be noted that there is a very large literature on scientists in industry and government at which I can do no more than hint in the few remaining pages.

SOCIAL CHARACTERISTICS OF APPLIED RESEARCH

From the beginning, the sociological analysis of science has been based on the assumption that the social context of applied research is different from that of pure research (Barber, 1953; Marcson, 1972). Much attention has, therefore, been devoted to studying these differences and to examining the consequences of employing scientists, supposedly trained in the 'pure science ethos' of the universities, to produce practically useful results in industry and government (Hower and Orth, 1963; Walters and Cotgrove, 1967). In this connection great emphasis has been placed on differences between pure and applied research with respect to the audiences for scientific information, the system of rewards and the structures of authority.

---

[19] This does *not* mean that the existing system of quality control in science must be regarded as ideal. It may well be absolutely essential that we interfere with the internal processes of the research community in order to make science more receptive to the wider social context. It does mean, however, that if we are able to devise an effective policy for science, we must seek to understand as accurately as possible the present character and dynamics of the scientific community.

In the pure research community the scientist produces information initially for other scientists who are competent to judge his work and who have the same professional objective, namely, the extension of certified knowledge. In applied science, the scientist undertakes research on behalf of an industrial corporation or some similar agency. Consequently, he is expected to pass on his results to other members of the corporation, who in many cases are incompetent to judge the scientific merit of his work and who assess it, primarily, as a potential source of economic profit for their own organization (Marcson, 1960). In this situation, it seems that scientists can adopt either of two primary responses (Merton, 1957; Glaser, 1963; Goldberg, 1965). One is to identify with the local organization and to concentrate on meeting its requirements. But this response, it is argued, tends to separate researchers from their professional reference group, to reduce their access to certified scientific knowledge, to lower their productivity, and, thereby, to lessen their contribution to the employing organization (Shepard, 1956). The second response is to remain primarily identified with the wider research community. But this response often leads to frustration and disillusionment because the researcher's professional aspirations almost inevitably conflict with his organizational responsibilities (Kornhauser, 1962).

The basic sources of frustration for the 'cosmopolitan' applied scientist are the restriction of his freedom to choose his own projects and of his freedom to communicate his findings to professional colleagues. Applied scientists in industry, for example, are employed to provide their organization with information which can be converted into economic profit. But once this information is made generally available, the economic advantage to the employing organization is lost. Thus all commercial organizations limit the extent to which their scientists are allowed to communicate with outside colleagues (Hill, 1964). Similar restrictions are applied even more stringently to those engaged in military research (see Sapolsky, Chapter 12). As a result, applied researchers tend to be deprived of full participation in the research community and to be unable to receive in full the important incentive of professional recognition (Glaser, 1964b).

For those scientists who adopt a local, organizational orientation, the difficulties of research in an applied context seem to be different, although still considerable. These difficulties stem mostly from the nature of the authority structure and the related system of promotions (Shephard, 1958). Those actively engaged in applied research tend to work within highly specialized and internally integrated groups, which exist to deal exclusively with technical problems (Livingston and Milberg, 1957). In contrast, organizational policy is formulated at higher levels of management by persons who, on the whole, have little technical background and who are concerned with issues in which technical considerations often play a minor part. Consequently, applied researchers are often required to abandon, at the behest of non-technical superiors, what they themselves regard as promising lines of inquiry (Marcson, 1960).

This organizational cleavage between scientists and management has further effects. On the one hand, because research units tend to develop a strong solidarity based upon their members' conception of themselves as 'technical personnel', they are frequently reluctant to fill positions within non-technical management (Duncan, 1972). On the other hand, because the top organizational positions lie outside the research hierarchy, those scientists who are most strongly committed to the organization are forced to leave research if they are to achieve the highest levels of rewards (Allison, 1969). At the same time, some studies have shown that when scientists do try to enter higher management they are seen as a threat by non-technical personnel, who tend to oppose their policies and who seek to minimize their impact on organizational affairs (Burns and Stalker, 1961).

So far in this section I have described some aspects of the main tradition of sociological investigation into applied research. The central conclusions reached in this literature are as follows: applied research depends on the employment of scientists trained by those engaged primarily in pure science. Many scientists consequently retain a strong commitment to pure research and find it difficult to adapt to the demands of a different social setting. The social structure of the organizations in which applied research is carried out limits the full participation of applied scientists. As a result, applied researchers experience considerable dissatisfaction and fail to contribute as productively as possible to organizational objectives.

In recent years, a number of studies have been completed in which the prior emphasis on the maladjustment of scientists in applied research has been challenged. In these studies no support is found for the simple view that potential applied scientists acquire, during their university education, attitudes and values which are unsuitable for industrial research. Instead it is stressed, on the basis of data on science students as well as on those employed in research, that complex processes of differential selection and adaptation ensure that those least committed to pure science are most likely to enter applied research.

Evidence has been presented which suggests that prospective scientists who perform well in the academic context and who express strong interest in communicating significant findings to other scientists, tend disproportionately to enter pure science (Cotgrove and Box, 1970). Those with weaker academic interests are, in contrast, more likely to go into applied research. At the same time, many of those who have academic inclinations but who are unable to reach the level of educational attainment necessary for university research, enter industry or government and accept realistically the limitations imposed there (Cotgrove and Box, 1970; Barnes, 1971). Barnes' longitudinal study is important here because it indicates that the commitment by young scientists to the ideals of pure science is, on the whole, no more than nominal and that, within a few months of entering industry, they have altered their view of research in accordance with the demands of the industrial setting. It must be stressed that this is merely one study, based upon a rather small sample. Nevertheless, there are other recent findings which are consistent with its line of argument. In some studies, for instance, scientists in industry fail to report any major dissatisfactions (Ellis, 1969). Furthermore, the dissatisfaction which does exist appears to be connected in no obvious way with commitment to an academic ethos, but to arise from career difficulties from concern over salaries, and from underemployment of technical expertise (Ellis, 1969; Cotgrove and Box, 1971; Duncan, 1972).

Although some of those who have carried out these recent studies have been highly critical of their forerunners, their analyses represent a change of emphasis rather than a major departure from the main tradition. For instance, the more recent studies are still centrally concerned with questions of adjustment and productivity; and all existing studies of applied research recognize that there are *some* scientists who appear to be frustrated by their exclusion from pure science. In addition, it should be noted that the findings of each study are based on a limited population, with special characteristics which may well restrict the generality of the conclusions reached. Thus studies of scientists in the electronics industry, a field in which scientists have become extensively employed comparatively recently, tend to emphasize conflict and dissatisfaction (Marcson, 1960; Burns and Stalker, 1961). In contrast, studies of the chemical industry, where scientists have made an important contribution since the last century, have depicted a more integrated situation (Cotgrove and Box, 1971). It may be, therefore, that broad conclusions about dissatisfaction, productivity and integration among applied scientists are unhelpful, because these factors vary from one setting to another. Whether or not this is so, can only be resolved by means of comparative studies of research in different applied contexts. Finally, it must also be borne in mind that there may be long term changes in the nature of academic science. If academic research is moving toward that form of organization already found in applied science, we can reasonably expect not only that any social discontinuities between the two spheres will be on the decline but also that, if there *have* been problems peculiarly characteristic in the past of applied science, they will tend to appear increasingly in the future within the academic setting.

SUMMARY

Scientific research is undertaken in a variety of social contexts. For analytical purposes, a distinction can be made between the context of pure research and that of applied research. In the case of applied research, scientists produce information for an audience composed mainly of non-researchers. The members of this audience judge the results of research primarily in relation to non-scientific criteria and provide those who furnish valuable findings with such bureaucratic rewards as promotion and increases in salary. In the case of pure research, scientists pursue topics largely on the basis of their scientific significance. Their results are communicated in the first instance to fellow researchers, who respond with informal rewards which are allocated in accordance with scientific standards of adequacy and value. As a result of these and other disparities in organization, the social dynamics of the two kinds of research setting are appreciably different; and it appears that neither information nor research personnel move without difficulty across the boundary between pure and applied research.

Sociological analysis of the pure research community began with an examination of its normative structure. It was suggested, initially, that this community was characterized by a distinctive set of social norms which ensured that its members were, in the course of their professional activities, exceptionally self-critical, impartial and open-minded. Although there was little direct evidence for this view of the scientific ethos, it persisted with only minor modification throughout the 1950's and 1960's. However, the analysis could not be regarded as complete until a satisfactory account had been given of the way in which general conformity to the supposed social norms of science was maintained within the research community. Consequently, a number of studies were undertaken during the 1960's into the distribution of rewards in science.

Examination of priority disputes, of anxiety among researchers about being anticipated in presenting results, of patterns of name ordering in collaborative papers, and so on, led to the conclusion that the central professional reward in science is recognition by competent colleagues. Recognition is awarded partly in response to the amount of information that researchers supply but, more significantly, in response to the perceived scientific value of this information. In most fields there exists a relatively small number of scientists who are responsible for work which is deemed to be of the highest quality. These scientists receive a disproportionate amount of professional recognition, as a result of which they become highly visible in their own field and in neighboring areas. Membership of these elite groupings tends to be self-reinforcing. For it enables elite scientists to acquire more research facilities and it leads to their receiving greater recognition than less eminent men for a given contribution. The formation of self-maintaining elites appears to be repeated at the level of the research group, the specialty and the discipline. Thus the research community can be seen, from this perspective, as a complex series of overlapping informal hierarchies based upon scientific repute.

The series of studies of the reward system of science carried out during the last decade or so has not only revealed the hierarchical structure of the research community, but has also clarified the nature of social control in science. It appears that researchers are led to conform to the expectations of their colleagues, at least partly because the receiving of recognition is contingent upon such conformity. However, there is no clear evidence that the award of recognition is institutionally linked to conformity to the values of universalism, disinterestedness, etc. Rather, recognition is furnished in response to the provision of information which is judged to be valuable in the light of currently accepted cognitive and technical standards. In other words, the reward system operates primarily to maintain conformity to established conceptions and techniques. Such conformity is engendered informally as scientists respond to the findings and research proposals of their colleagues, discouraging certain kinds of work and approving others. Although there is no separate, formal hierarchy of control, eminent scientists exercise great influence over the standards operative in their fields. At the same time, the leaders of any given field compete with those of other fields for scientific preeminence and for access to scarce resources. They are consequently obliged, to some extent, to meet the scientific expectations of their peers. In this way, the processes working to maintain conformity to scientific standards extend throughout the research community.

The pure research community is formally divided into a number of disciplines and disciplinary areas. Each of these is, in turn, further divided into specialties and sub-specialties. Many of these intellectual and social boundaries are firmly institutionalized within the university system and have, therefore, a considerable influence on the organization of scientific education and research. Nevertheless, the intellectual scope of disciplines and specialties is too great to provide their members with a specific focus for their research. This is supplied by much smaller research networks, whose members share a concern with a narrow range of related problems. These networks are of fundamental importance in science because research findings can become certified knowledge only after they have been communicated to, and recognized as valid by, those most competent to judge them; that is, in the first instance, the members of such a network.

The research community is composed of a multitude of overlapping problem networks, each of which is undergoing a similar sequence of intellectual and social development. The formation of new networks and the creation of new research areas usually begins with a movement of scientists out of declining areas in pursuit of topics which are both more significant and more likely to confer professional recognition than those available in their existing fields. During the first, exploratory phase, communication between those involved in a new area is often inefficient. As a result, there tends to be considerable duplication of effort, divergence in the interpretation of results, and a relatively high level of outright competition. In many cases, however, a number of important contributions are produced and recognized quite quickly. These contributions serve to define the scope of the field and their acceptance signifies an increasing scientific consensus.

Growing consensus is associated with an increasingly cohesive network, with the emergence of a band of elite members, with a rapid influx of new entrants and with a cumulative growth of research findings. Because major innovations tend to occur at a fairly early stage, a large proportion of the most significant work is usually completed before the field reaches its maximum size. Consequently, the growth of the network is accompanied by a rapid decline in the availability of interesting findings and in opportunities for obtaining recognition. As this becomes known to researchers outside the area, recruitment falls away and a period of stable development follows. The decline of interesting and solvable problems is likely to continue, however, and as it does so, opportunities in neighboring fields come to appear more attractive. Gradually, therefore, the network breaks up and its members move elsewhere to contribute to the exploration of entirely new areas. In many cases, the problems pursued in these new areas are unexpected offshoots of the declining field of investigation.

Science grows, then, through the continual formation, dissolution and reformation of research networks – and through the continual creation of limited areas of intellectual consensus, followed by an expansion into unexplored realms of inquiry. That scientists have been remarkably successful both in establishing intellectual agreement and in revealing new areas for investigation, is shown by the way in which the scientific community and the range of scientific knowledge have expanded cumulatively over a long period of time. Nevertheless, neither the evolution of the research community nor the creation of scientific consensus proceeds entirely without discord or disruption. One source of difficulty is that the relationships among research scientists involve a delicate balance between cooperation in the pursuit of shared problems and competition for the recognition associated with the solution of these problems. Thus competition occurs throughout science, becoming particularly noticeable in the early stages of new areas. Competition, in turn, leads to 'unnecessary' publication, to the hasty presentation of results and, thereby, to a lowering of scientific standards.

Because researchers are frequently in a potentially or actively competitive situation, they often keep secret their research intentions and preliminary results, in order to prevent others from using their information to publish first. However, scientists can receive no reward for their work until it has been made public. Indeed, results must be subjected to the scrutiny of competent colleagues before they can join the corpus of certified knowledge. It seems likely, therefore, that secrecy in modern, professional science is usually of short duration. Furthermore, the consequences of secrecy and competition are by no means wholly negative. For instance, by controlling other scientists' access to their findings, researchers may be able to devote more time and effort to improving the quality of their work. This stratagem is, of course, only necessary in a competitive situation. But competition also encourages scientists to choose problems for which their skills and resources are most appropriate, to develop a specialized expertise which ensures that their work is not exactly duplicated elsewhere, and to take up new problems in the study of which potential competitors have been unable to establish a commanding lead. In short, competition helps to ensure that a wide range of topics is investigated in any given field and that new and promising areas are explored vigorously.

One of the most notable features of the scientific research community is the way in which its members are able to negotiate areas of intellectual consensus. Once established, these agreed scientific frameworks make possible detailed and cumulative investigation of a limited range of phenomena. At the same time, they sometimes become intellectual orthodoxies which are highly resistant to change. Accordingly, it has been argued that scientific development at all levels alternates between periods of predictable, orthodox research and periods of revolutionary change of perspective. In the light of this analysis, scientific evolution is seen as being characterized by major intellectual and social discontinuities. However, although scientific research does undoubtedly create intellectual orthodoxies, these do not give rise inevitably to recurrent scientific revolutions. One reason for this is that cognitive structures are in many cases sufficiently imprecise to allow a continuous and gradual modification. Secondly, many scientific orthodoxies are never revised by the research community but are simply abandoned, as the research front moves into new fields of inquiry. Thus it seems probable that rigid intellectual resistance is not uniformly present in science, but that it occurs under specifiable conditions and at particular points in the development of a research area. Although there is no conclusive evidence on this topic, there are grounds for expecting intellectual resistance to occur when a research area has entered its phase of decline, and especially in areas with a precise cognitive framework, with a strong and stable elite, and with low rates of migration.

For much of its history the pure research community has been relatively free from direct outside intervention. It has also been widely regarded as the main source of reliable knowledge and has experienced little difficulty in attracting new members. In recent years, however, all this has changed. There has been a fall in recruitment. Many scientists and laymen have come to regard certain aspects of the scientific endeavor as pernicious. And there has been a pronounced move towards regulating scientific development in accordance with non-scientific criteria. If these trends continue they will undoubtedly alter the nature of the research community. A slower rate of recruitment is likely to weaken competitive pressures inside the community and, possibly, to reduce the rate of innovation. It will also mean that there are simply fewer new entrants free to move into emergent fields. At the same time, there will be strong pressure from audiences outside the research community for scientists to concentrate on those research areas which appear most relevant to economic and political objectives. In the years to come, therefore, it seems that the boundaries between the social contexts of pure and applied research will become less and less distinct.

EVALUATION

I have tried in this chapter to base the presentation on a wide range of empirical evidence and to use this evidence to provide a coherent account of what is currently known about the modern scientific research community. It is, of course, impossible in a review of this kind to examine in detail the adequacy of the research methods used in each of the studies which are cited as furnishing acceptable evidence. Neither is it possible to explore fully the whole range of plausible interpretations in relation to every issue discussed, nor to identify all those avenues of inquiry which appear to be important yet which have so far been largely ignored. Accordingly, in the main body of the chapter I have had no choice but to restrict myself to occasional asides about such crucial issues as the adequacy and completeness of the available evidence and about the existence of topics requiring further investigation. Let me conclude, therefore, by making a few remarks of a general nature on these subjects.

In the first place, there is no doubt that the basic stratum of evidence is in many respects incomplete. A great deal of the evidence, for example, about the distribution of rewards and the exchange of information for recognition comes from studies of physicists. It is difficult to judge, therefore, how far these findings can be generalized to the biological or to the social sciences. There is an indication in a recent study (Allison and Stewart, 1974) that the reward system in biology works in a significantly different manner from that of physics, chemistry or mathematics. But these differences have yet to be investigated in detail. When they are understood more fully, they will undoubtedly lead us to modify the initial approximate analysis put forward in the course of this chapter. Moreover, although many of the studies of scientific rewards and social exchange in science are precise and quantitative, they depend on methodological assumptions, in particular about the nature of scientific citations, which have not been firmly established or even carefully explored (see, however, Shanin-Cohen, 1974; Moravcsik and Murugesan, 1975). Consequently, not only do we need more substantive studies of the allocation of rewards, and so on, in fields of scientific endeavor for which documentation is at present lacking, but we also need further investigation into the research techniques upon which new findings will depend.

The shortage of reliable evidence is not confined to the topics of inquiry mentioned in the previous paragraph. Thus the lack of direct data on commitment to the 'social norms of pure research' is astonishing, given that these norms were first formulated over thirty years ago and given the frequency with which they have been mentioned in the literature. Similarly, there is simply insufficient evidence to enable us either to estimate the varying incidence of intellectual resistance, innovation, secrecy or competition as between different disciplines or specialties (although, see Hagstrom, 1965), or to judge the overall rates of secular change in these phenomena. Once again, comprehensive studies of phenomena of this kind will be valuable, indeed possible, only to the extent to which methodological difficulties, in this case those of devising valid cross-disciplinary measures of, say, innovation, can be resolved (Przeworski and Teune, 1970).

The same lack of data and a similar need to resolve conceptual and methodological problems are evident in relation to other aspects of the scientific community; such as the nature of the connection between social factors within that community and its cognitive development, and the relationship between the research community and external agencies. Although this latter topic was, once again, first explored from a sociological perspective several decades ago (Merton, 1939 and 1942), it has since received only sporadic attention (e.g. Hirsch, 1961). Accordingly, no systematic body of sociological information has accrued. Political scientists have, of course, examined the political actions of natural scientists (See subsequent chapters) and there has been increasing interest in the economic and technological impact of academic research (See Freeman, Chapter 7). But few attempts have been made by sociologists either to conceptualize or to document the interplay between internal and external processes in a systematic fashion (For moves in this direction, see Böhme *et al.*, 1973; Spiegel-Rösing, 1974; MacLeod *et al.*, 1976).

An explicit concern with analyzing the links between social processes and cognitive development within science is of fairly recent origin, stemming from the work of Kuhn (1962) in particular and becoming clearly evident among sociologists only since the late 1960's (Mulkay, 1969; Whitley, 1972). Although there have already been several useful empirical studies bearing on this theme, as well as some conceptual discussion as I have noted earlier, the great bulk of work remains to be done (Law and French, 1974). One of the central conceptual difficulties in this field arises from the fact that any specific realm of scientific inquiry, or any particular body of scientific knowledge, is to a considerable degree culturally unique. Consequently, we cannot establish general conclusions about the relationship between scientific knowledge and social processes until we have identified relevant dimensions of scientific knowledge which are common to a range of research areas.

Until now, attention has focused on the normative dimension of scientific knowledge as, for example, in Law's (1973) distinction between permissible, preferred and impermissible problems; and upon the degree of cognitive consensus achieved and maintained in research areas. But clearly, although these facets of scientific knowledge are important and in need of more study, we must go much further if we are to understand the fine detail of the social production of scientific knowledge. We need to know much more, for example, about the ways in which scientists define problems as 'interesting' and as worthy of sustained research (Davis, 1971), and we need to know much more clearly whether differences in social processes are associated with cognitive variations, such as variations in the degree of quantification of research results, in the extent of experimental control, in the level of research technology and so on. If we are to succeed in developing a systematic and generalized analysis of the linked processes of cognitive and social change in science, we must have reliable information on a wide-ranging and comparable set of issues for a considerable variety of scientific fields. One way of moving toward this objective is by means of a series of case studies of scientific development. But such studies, if they are to have a cumulative effect, must be undertaken from a sociological perspective which is held in common, at least to the extent that the scholars involved attempt to answer a similar range of questions. Case studies of this kind are, of course, extremely difficult to complete, if only because they require sociologists to understand highly esoteric and 'technical' cultures. Nevertheless, such studies are now being undertaken and brought to fruition, and the special methodological problems are, at least, coming to be recognized, if not solved (Zuckerman, 1972; Mulkay, 1974; Law, 1975).

BIBLIOGRAPHY

Allison, 1969	Allison, D. (Ed.), *The R and D Game*, Cambridge, Mass., The MIT Press, 1969.
Allison and Stewart, 1974	Allison, P. D. and Stewart, J. A., 'Productivity Differences Among Scientists: Evidence for Cumulative Advantage', *American Sociological Review* 39, 1974, pp. 596-606.
Anthony and Slater, 1969	Anthony, L. J. and Slater, M. J., 'The Growth of the Literature of Physics', *Rep. Proq. Phys.* 32, 1969, pp. 709-767.
Barber, 1952	Barber, B., *Science and the Social Order*, New York, The Free Press, 1952.
Barber, 1961	Barber, B., 'Resistance by Scientists to Scientific Discovery', *Science* 134, 1961, pp. 596-602.
Barber, 1968	Barber, B., 'The Functions and Dysfunctions of "Fashion" in Science', *Mens en Maatschappij* 43(No. 6), 1968, pp. 501-514.
Barber and Fox, 1958	Barber, B. and Fox, C., 'The Case of the Floppy-Eared Rabbits: An Instance of Serendipity Gained and Serendipity Lost', *American Journal of Sociology* 64, 1958, pp. 128-136.

Barber and Hirsch, 1963   Barber, B. and Hirsch, W. (Eds.), *The Sociology of Science,* New York, The Free Press of Glencoe, 1963.

Barnes, 1971   Barnes, B. 'Making Out in Industrial Research', *Science Studies* 1, 1971, pp. 157-75.

Barnes, 1972   Barnes, B., *Sociology of Science: Selected Readings,* London and Baltimore, Penguin Books, 1972.

Barnes and Dolby, 1970   Barnes, S. B. and Dolby, R. G. A., 'The Scientific Ethos: A Deviant Viewpoint', *European Journal of Sociology* II, 1970, pp. 3-25.

Bayer and Folger, 1966   Bayer, A. E. and Folger, J., 'Some Correlates of a Citation Measure in Science', *Sociology of Education* 39, 1966, pp. 381-390.

Ben-David, 1960a   Ben-David, J., 'Scientific Productivity and Academic Organization in Nineteenth Century Medicine', *American Sociological Review* 25, 1960, pp. 828-843.

Ben-David, 1960b   Ben-David, J., 'Roles and Innovations in Medicine', *American Journal of Sociology* 65, 1960, pp. 557-568.

Ben-David, 1963-4   Ben-David, J., 'Scientific Growth: A Sociological View', *Minerva,* 2, 1963-4, pp. 455-476.

Ben-David, 1965   Ben-David, J., 'Scientific Productivity and Academic Organization in Nineteenth Century Medicine', in Kaplan, J. (Ed.), *Science and Society,* Chicago, Rand McNally, 1965.

Ben-David, 1968   Ben-David, J., *Fundamental Research and the Universities,* Paris, OECD, 1968.

Ben-David, 1971   Ben-David, J., *The Scientist's Role in Society,* Englewood Cliffs, N.J., Prentice-Hall, 1971.

Ben-David and Collins, 1966 Ben-David, J. and Collins, R., 'Social Factors in the Origins of a New Science: The Case of Psychology', *American Sociological Review* 31, 1966, pp. 451-465.

Ben-David and Zloczower, 1962 Ben-David, J. and Zloczower, A., 'Universities and Academic Systems in Modern Societies', *European Journal of Sociology* 3, 1962, pp. 45-85.

Bernal, 1939   Bernal, J. D., *The Social Function of Science,* London, Routledge, 1939.

Blau, 1964   Blau, P., *Exchange and Power in Social Life,* New York, Wiley, 1964.

Blissett, 1972   Blissett, M., *Politics in Science,* Boston, Little, Brown and Co., 1972.

Blume, 1973   Blume, S., *Toward a Political Sociology of Science,* London, Collier Macmillan, 1973.

Blume and Sinclair, 1973   Blume, S. S. and Sinclair, R., 'Chemists in British Universities: A Study of the Reward System in Science', *American Sociological Review* 38, 1973, pp. 126-138.

Böhme *et al.,* 1973   Böhme, G., van den Daele, W., and Krohn, W., 'Die Finalisierung der Wissenschaft', *Zeitschrift für Soziologie* 2, 1973, pp. 128-144.

Brittain, 1970   Brittain, J. M., *Information and Its Users,* Bath University Press, 1970.

Brooks, 1967   Brooks, H., 'Science and the Allocation of Resources', *American Psychologist* 22, pp. 187-201.

Brooks, 1971   Brooks, H., *Science, Growth and Society,* Paris, OECD, 1971.

Burns and Stalker, 1961   Burns, T. and Stalker, G. M., *The Management of Innovation*, London, Tavistock, 1961.

Byatt and Cohen, 1969   Byatt, I. C. R. and Cohen, C. V., *An Attempt to Quantify the Economic Benefits of Scientific Research* London, HMSO, Science Policy Studies No. 4, 1969.

Cardwell, 1972   Cardwell, D. C., *The Organization of Science in England*, London, Heinemann, 1972.

Chabbal, 1973   Chabbal, R., 'Rapport du groupe de travail sur les sciences pour l'ingénieur', *Le Courrier du CNRS* No. 9, 1973, pp. 3-6.

Clark, 1957   Clark, K., *America's Psychologists*, Washington, D. C., Psychological Association, 1957.

Cohen, 1952   Cohen, I. B., 'Orthodoxy and Scientific Progress', *Proceedings of the American Philosophical Society* 96, 1952, pp. 505-512.

Cole and Cole, 1967   Cole, S. and Cole, J. R., 'Scientific Output and Recognition', *American Sociological Review* 32 (June), 1967, pp. 377-390.

Cole and Cole, 1968   Cole, S. and Cole, J., 'Visibility and the Structural Bases of Awareness of Scientific Research', *American Sociological Review* 33, 1968, pp. 397-412.

Cole and Cole, 1973   Cole, J. R. and Cole, S., *Social Stratification in Science*, Chicago and London, University of Chicago Press, 1973.

Collins, 1974   Collins, H. M., 'The TEA Set: Tacit Knowledge and Scientific Networks', *Science Studies* 4, 1974, pp. 165-186.

Commoner, 1966   Commoner, B., *Science and Survival*, London, Gollancz, 1966.

Coser, 1975   Coser, L. A. (Ed.), *The Idea of Social Structure: Papers in Honor of Robert K. Merton*, London, Harcourt, Brace, Jovanovich, 1975.

Cotgrove and Box, 1970   Cotgrove, S. and Box, S., *Science, Industry and Society*, London, Allen and Unwin, 1970.

Crane, 1965   Crane, D., 'Scientists at Major and Minor Universities', *American Sociological Review* 30, 1965, pp. 699-714.

Crane, 1967   Crane, D., 'The Gatekeepers of Science: Some Factors Affecting the Selection of Articles for Scientific Journals', *American Sociologist* 2, 1967, pp. 195-201.

Crane, 1969   Crane, D., 'Social Structure in a Group of Scientists', *American Sociological Review,* 36, 1969, pp. 335-352.

Crane, 1972   Crane, D., *Invisible Colleges,* Chicago, Chicago University Press, 1972.

The Dainton Report, 1968   Dainton Report, The, *Enquiry into the Flow of Candidates in Science and Technology into Higher Education*, HMSO, Cmnd 3541, 1968.

Daniels, 1967   Daniels, G. H., 'The Pure-Science Ideal and Democratic Culture', *Science* 156, 1967, pp. 1699-1705.

Daniels, 1968   Daniels, G. H., *American Science in the Age of Jackson,* New York and London, Columbia University Press, 1968.

Davis, 1971   Davis, M. S., 'That's Interesting! Towards a Phenomenology of Sociology and a Sociology of Phenomenology', *Philosophy of Social Science* 1, 1971, pp. 309-344.

Downey, 1971 — Downey, R. J., 'Sociology and the Modern Scientific Revolution', *Sociological Quarterly* 8, 1971, pp. 239-254.

Duncan, 1972 — Duncan, P., 'Scientists as Managers', in Halms, P. (Ed.), *Sociology of Science,* Sociological Review Monograph No. 18, University of Keele, 1972.

Ellis, 1969 — Ellis, N. D., 'The Occupation of Science',, *Technology and Society* 5, No. 1, 1969, pp. 33-41.

Ellul, 1965 — Ellul, J., *The Technological Society,* London, Cape, 1965.

Feyerabend, 1965 — Feyerabend, P. K., 'Problems of Empiricism', in Colodny, R. G. (Ed.), *Beyond the Edge of Certainty,* New Jersey, Prentice-Hall, 1965.

Fisher, 1967 — Fisher, C. S., 'The Last Invariant Theorists', *Archives of European Sociology* 8, 1967, pp. 216-244.

Fleming and Bailyn, 1969 — Fleming, D. and Bailyn, B. (Eds.), *The Intellectual Migration: Europe and America, 1930-60,* Cambridge, Mass., Harvard University Press, 1969.

Friedrichs, 1970 — Friedrichs, R., *A Sociology of Sociology,* New York, The Free Press, 1970.

Garfield, 1964 — Garfield, E., 'Science Citation Index – A New Dimension in Indexing', *Science* 144, 1964, pp. 649-654.

Garfield, 1969 — Garfield, E., 'Would Mendel's Work Have Been Ignored if the Science Citation Index Was Available 100 Years Ago? ', *Current Contents* 47, November 1969, pp. 5-6.

Garvey and Griffith, 1966 — Garvey, W. D. and Griffith, B. C., 'Scientific Information Exchange in Psychology', *Science* 146, 1966, pp. 1955-1959.

Garvey and Griffith, 1967 — Garvey, W. D. and Griffith, B. C., 'Scientific Communication as a Social System', *Science* 157, 1967, pp. 1011-1016.

Garvey and Griffith, 1970 — Garvey, W. D. and Griffith, B. C., 'Scientific Communication: Its Role in the Conduct of Research and Creation of Knowledge', *American Psychologist* 25, 1970, pp. 349-362.

Garvey and Tomita, 1972 — Garvey, W. D. and Tomita, K., 'Continuity of Productivity by Scientists in the Years 1969-1971', *Science Studies* 2, 1972, pp. 379-383.

Gaston, 1970 — Gaston, J., 'The Reward System in British Science', *American Sociological Review* 35, No. 4, 1970, pp. 718-732.

Gaston, 1972 — Gaston, J., 'Communication and Reward System of Science', *Sociological Review Monograph No. 18,* University of Keele, 1972.

Gaston, 1973 — Gaston, J., *Originality and Competition in Science,* Chicago and London, University of Chicago Press, 1973.

Gilbert and Woolgar, 1974 — Gilbert, G. N. and Woolgar, S., 'The Quantitative Study of Science: An Examination of the Literature', *Science Studies* 4, No. 3, 1974, pp. 279-294.

Gillmor and Terman, 1973 — Gillmor, C. S. and Terman, C. J., 'Communication

Modes of Geophysics: The Case of Ionospheric Physics', *Eos* 54, No. 10, 1973, pp. 900-908.

Gilpin, 1968 — Gilpin, R., *France in the Age of the Scientific State,* Princeton, Princeton University Press, 1968.

Glaser, 1964a — Glaser, B., 'Comparative Failure in Science', *Science* 143, 1964, pp. 1012-1014.

Glaser, 1964b — Glaser, B., *Organizational Scientists: Their Professional Careers,* Indianapolis, Bobbs-Merill, 1964.

Glass, 1960 — Glass, B., 'The Academic Scientist, 1940-1960', *Science* 132, 1960.

Goldberg, 1965 — Goldberg, C. C., 'Local-Cosmopolitain: Undimensional or Multidimensional? ', *American Journal of Sociology* 70, 1965, pp. 704-710.

Gould, 1961 — Gould, S. (Ed.), *Sciences in Communist China,* Washington, D. C., AAAS, No. 68, 1961.

Grazia, 1966 — Grazia, A. de, *The Velikowsky Affair,* New York University Press, 1966.

Greenberg, 1967 — Greenberg, D. S., *The Politics of Pure Science,* New York, New American Library, 1967.

Griffith and Mullins, 1972 — Griffith, B. C. and Mullins, N. C., 'Coherent Social Groups in Scientific Change', *Science* 177, 1972, pp. 959-964.

Griffith and Small, *et al.,* 1974a — Griffith, B. C. and Small, H. G. *et al.,* 'The Structure of Scientific Literatures I: Identifying and Graphing Specialties', *Science Studies* 4, No. 1, 1974, pp. 17-40.

Griffith and Small, *et al.,* 1974b — Griffith, B. C. and Small, H. G. *et al.,* 'The Structure of Scientific Literatures II: Toward a Macro- and Microstructure for Science', *Science Studies* 4, No. 4, 1974, pp. 339-365.

Gruber and Marquis, 1969 — Gruber, W. H. and Marquis, D. G. (Eds.), *Factors in the Transfer of Technology,* Cambridge, Mass., MIT Press, 1969.

Hagstrom, 1964 — Hagstrom, W. O., 'Traditional and Modern Forms of Scientific Teamwork', *Administrative Science Quarterly* 9, 1964, pp. 241-263.

Hagstrom, 1965 — Hagstrom, W. O., *The Scientific Community,* New York, Basic Books, 1965.

Hagstrom, 1970 — Hagstrom, W. O., 'Factors Related to the Use of Different Modes of Publishing Research in Four Scientific Fields', in Nelson, C. and Pollock, D. (Eds.), *Communication among Scientists and Engineers,* Lexington, Mass., D. C. Heath, 1970.

Halsey and Trow, 1971 — Halsey, A. H. and Trow, M., *The British Academics,* London, Faber and Faber, 1971.

Hanson, 1965 — Hanson, N. R., *Patterns of Discovery,* Cambridge, Cambridge University Press, 1965.

Hessen, 1931 — Hessen, B. 'The Social and Economic Roots of Newton's "Principia" ', in *Science at the Crossroads,* London, 1931, reprinted by F. Cass, 1971, with an introduction by Wersky, P. G.

Hill, 1964 — Hill, K. (Ed.), *The Management of Scientists,* Beacon Press, 1964.

Hirsch, 1961 — Hirsch, W., 'The Autonomy of Science in Totalitarian

Societies', *Social Forces* 40, 1961, pp. 15-22.

Holland, 1957 — Holland, J. L., 'Undergraduate Origins of American Scientists', *Science* 126, 1957, pp. 433-437.

Holton, 1962 — Holton, G., 'Models for Understanding the Growth and Excellence of Scientific Research', in Graubard, S. R. and Holton, G. (Eds.), *Excellence and Leadership in a Democracy*, New York, Columbia University Press, 1962.

Hower and Orth, 1963 — Hower, R. M. and Orth, D. C., *Managers and Scientists*, Cambridge, Mass., Harvard University Press, 1963.

Kaplan, 1962 — Kaplan, N., 'The Western European Scientific Establishment in Transition', *The American Behavioral Scientist* 6, 1962, No. 4, pp. 17-21.

Kaplan, 1965a — Kaplan, N., 'The Norms of Citation Behavior', *American Documentation* 16, No. 3, 1965, pp. 179-184.

Kaplan, 1965b — Kaplan, N. (Ed.), *Science and Society*, Chicago, Rand McNally, 1965.

Kidd, 1959 — Kidd, C. V., 'Basic Research — Description vs. Definition', *Science* 129, 1959, pp. 368-371.

King, 1971 — King, M. D., 'Reason, Tradition and the Progressiveness of Science', *History and Theory* 10, 1971, pp. 3-32.

Knapp and Greenbaum, 1953 — Knapp, R. H. and Greenbaum, J. J., *The Younger American Scholar: His Collegiate Origins*, Chicago, University of Chicago Press, 1953.

Koestler, 1964 — Koestler, A., *The Act of Creation*, London, Hutchinson, 1964.

Kornhauser, 1962 — Kornhauser, W., *Scientists in Industry*, Berkeley, University of California Press, 1962.

Krantz, 1965 — Krantz, D. L., 'Research Activity in "Normal" and "Anomalous" Areas', *Journal of the History of the Behavioral Sciences* 1, pp. 39-42.

Kuhn, 1962 — Kuhn, T. S., *The Structure of Scientific Revolutions*, Chicago, Chicago University Press, first edition 1962.

Kuhn, 1963a — Kuhn, T. S., 'The Essential Tension: Tradition and Innovation in Scientific Research', in Taylor, C. and Barron, F. (Eds.), *Scientific Creativity*, John Wiley and Sons, 1963.

Kuhn, 1963b — Kuhn, T. S., 'The Function of Measurement in Modern Physical Science', in Crombie, A. C. (Ed.), *Symposium on the History of Science*, London, Heinemann, 1963, pp. 31-60.

Kuhn, 1970 — Kuhn, T. S., *The Structure of Scientific Revolutions*, Chicago, Chicago University Press, enlarged edition, 1970.

Lapp, 1965 — Lapp, R., *The New Priesthood — The Scientific Elite and the Uses of Power*, New York, Harper and Row, 1965.

Langrish et al., 1972 — Langrish, J. et al., *Wealth from Knowledge*, London, MacMillan, 1972.

Law, 1973 — Law, J., 'The Development of Specialties in Science: The Case of x-Ray Protein Crystallography', *Science*

Studies 3, No. 3, 1973, pp. 275-303.

Law, 1975 — Law, J., 'Theories and Methods in the Sociology of Science', *Social Science Information* 14, 1975.

Law and French, 1974 — Law, J. and French, D., 'Normative and Interpretive Sociologies of Science', *The Sociological Review* 22, 1974, pp. 581-595.

Lemaine, 1974 — Lemaine, G., 'Social Differentiation and Social Originality', *Europ. J. Soc. Psychol.* 4, No. 1, 1974, pp. 17-52.

Lemaine, Lécuyer et al., 1972 — Lemaine, G., Lécuyer, B.-P., Gomis, A. and Barthélémy, C., *Les Voies du Succes: sur quelques facteurs de la réussite des laboratoires de recherche fondamentale en France,* Paris, CNRS, 1972 (offset).

Lemaine and Matalon, 1969 — Lemaine, G. and Matalon, B. 'La Lutte pour la vie dans la cité scientifique', *Revue Française de Sociologie* 10, 1969, pp. 139-165.

Livingston and Milberg, 1957 — Livingston, R. T. and Milberg, S. H. (Eds.), *Human Relations in Industrial Research Management,* New York, Columbia University Press, 1957.

MacLeod, Lemaine et al., 1976 — MacLeod, R., Lemaine, G. et al., *New Perspectives on the Emergence of Scientific Disciplines,* Mouton, Autumn 1976.

Marcson, 1960 — Marcson, S., *The Scientist in American Industry,* New York, Harper and Row, 1960.

Marcson, 1962 — Marcson, S., 'Decision Making in a University Physics Department', *The American Behavioral Scientist,* December 1962, pp. 37-8.

Marcson, 1972 — Marcson, S., 'Research Settings', in Nagi, S. Z. and Corwin, R. G. (Eds.), *The Social Contexts of Research,* New York Wiley-Interscience, 1972.

Marcuse, 1962 — Marcuse, H., *One Dimensional Man,* London, Routledge and Kegan Paul, 1962.

Martins, 1971 — Martins, H., 'The Kuhnian "Revolution" and its Implications for Sociology', in Hanson, A. H., Nossiter, T. and Rokkan, S. (Eds.), *Imagination and Precision in Political Analysis,* London, Faber, 1971.

McGinnis and Singh, 1972 — McGinnis, R. and Singh, V. P., 'Mobility Patterns in Three Scientific Disciplines', paper presented to ASA, New Orleans, Louisiana, August, 1972.

McGrath and Altman, 1966 — McGrath, J. E. and Altman, I., *Small Group Research: A Synthesis and Critique of the Field,* New York, Rinehart and Winston, 1966.

Meadows and O'Connor, 1971 — Meadows, A. J. and O'Connor, J. G., 'Bibliographic Statistics as a Guide to Growth Points in Science', *Science Studies* 1, No. 1, 1971, pp. 95-99.

Menard, 1971 — Menard, H. W., *Science: Growth and Change,* Cambridge, Mass., Harvard University Press, 1971.

Menzel, 1966 — Menzel, H., 'Scientific Communication: Five Sociological Themes', *American Psychologist* 21, 1966, pp. 999-1005.

Menzel, 1967 — Menzel, H., 'Planning the Consequences of Unplanned Action in Scientific Communications', in de Rueck, A.

	and Knight, J. (Eds.), *Communication in Science,* London, Churchill, 1957.
Merton, 1942	Merton, R. K., 'Science and Democratic Social Structure', in Merton, R. K., *Social Theory and Social Structure,* New York, The Free Press, 1949.
Merton, 1957	Merton, R. K., 'Priorities in Scientific Discovery', *American Sociological Review* 22, No. 6, 1957, pp. 635-659.
Merton, 1961	Merton, R. K., 'Singletons and Multiples in Scientific Discovery', *Proceedings of the American Philosophical Society* 105, No. 5, 1961, pp. 470-486.
Merton, 1963	Merton, R. K., 'The Ambivalence of Scientists', *European Journal of Sociology* 4, 1963, pp. 250-282.
Merton, 1968	Merton, R. K., 'The Matthew Effect in Science', *Science* 159, 1968, pp. 56-63.
Merton, 1970	Merton, R. K., *Science, Technology and Society in Seventeenth-Century England,* New York, Harper Torchbooks, 1970.
Merton, 1973	Merton, R. K., *The Sociology of Science,* Chicago and London, Chicago University Press, 1973.
Metzger, 1955	Metzger, W. P., *Academic Freedom in the Age of the University,* New York, Columbia University Press, 1955.
Mitroff, 1974a	Mitroff, I. I., 'Norms and Counter-Norms in a Select Group of the Apollo Moon Scientists', *American Sociological Review* 39, 1974, pp. 579-595.
Mitroff, 1974b	Mitroff, I. I., *The Subjective Side of Science,* Amsterdam, Elsevier, 1974.
Moravcsik and Murugesan, 1975	Moravcsik, M. J. and Murugesan, P., 'Some Results on the Function and Quality of Citations', *Social Studies of Science* 5, 1975, pp. 86-92.
Mulkay, 1969	Mulkay, M. J., 'Some Aspects of Growth in the Natural Sciences', *Social Research* 36, No. 1, 1969, pp. 22-52.
Mulkay, 1972a	Mulkay, M. J., *The Social Process of Innovation: A Study in the Sociology of Science,* London, Macmillan, 1972.
Mulkay, 1972b	Mulkay, M. J., 'Conformity and Innovation in Science', in Halmos, P. (Ed.), *Sociological Review Monograph* No. 18, University of Keele, 1972.
Mulkay, 1974a	Mulkay, M. J. 'Conceptual Displacement and Migration in Science: A Prefatory Paper', *Science Studies* 4, 1974, No. 3, pp. 205-234.
Mulkay, 1974b	Mulkay, M. J., 'Methodology in the Sociology of Science: Some Reflections on the Study of Radio Astronomy', *Social Science Information* 13, No. 2, 1974, pp. 107-119.
Mulkay and Edge, 1973	Mulkay, M. J. and Edge, D. O., 'Cognitive, Technical and Social Factors in the Growth of Radio Astronomy' *Social Science Information* 12, No. 6, 1973, pp. 25-61.
Mulkay and Turner, 1971	Mulkay, M. J. and Turner, B. S., 'Over-production of Personnel and Innovation in Three Social Settings',

	Sociology 5, No. 1, 1971, pp. 47-61.
Mulkay and Williams, 1971	Mulkay, M. J. and Williams, A. T., 'A Sociological Study of a Physics Department', *British Journal of Sociology* 22, No. 1, 1971, pp. 68-82.
Mullins, 1968	Mullins, N. C., 'Informal Communications Networks among Biological Scientists', *American Sociological Review* 33, 1968, pp. 786-797.
Mullins, 1972a	Mullins, N. C., 'The Development of a Scientific Specialty: The Phage Group and the Origins of Molecular Biology', *Minerva* 10, No. 1, 1972, pp. 51-82.
Mullins, 1972b	Mullins, N., 'The Structure of an Elite: The Advisory Structure of the U.S. Public Health Service', *Science Studies* 2, No. 1, 1972, pp. 3-29.
Nagi and Corwin, 1972	Nagi, S. Z. and Corwin, R. G. (Eds.), *The Social Contexts of Research*, New York, Wiley-Interscience, 1972.
OECD, 1970	OECD, *The Measurement of Scientific and Technical Activities* (Frascati Manual), Paris, 1970.
Orlans, 1968	Orlans, H. (Ed.), *Science Policy and the University*, Washington, D.C., The Brookings Institution, 1968.
Parsons, 1968	Parsons, T. and Platt, G. M. 'Considerations on the American Academic System', *Minerva* 6, No. 4, 1968, pp. 497-523.
Physics in Canada, 1967	*Physics in Canada*, Ottawa, Science Secretariat, Special Study No. 2, May 1967.
Plumb, 1964	Plumb, J. H., *Crisis in the Humanities*, Harmondsworth, Penguin Books, 1964.
Polanyi, 1956	Polanyi, M., 'Pure and Applied Science and their Appropriate Forms of Organization', *Dialectica* 10, No. 3, 1956, pp. 231-242.
Polanyi, 1958	Polanyi, M., *Personal Knowledge*, London, Routledge and Kegan Paul, 1958.
Polanyi, 1962	Polanyi, M., 'The Republic of Science', *Minerva* 1, No. 1, 1962, pp. 54-72.
Polanyi, 1963	Polanyi, M., 'The Potential Theory of Adsorption', in *Knowing and Being*, London, Routledge, 1963.
Polanyi, 1966-7	Polanyi, M., 'The Growth of Science in Society', *Minerva* 5, 1966-7, pp. 533-545.
Derek Price, 1962	Price, Derek de Solla, *Science since Babylon*, Yale University Press, 1962.
Derek Price, 1963	Price, Derek de Solla, *Little Science, Big Science*, New York, University Press, 1963.
Derek Price, 1965	Price, Derek de Solla, 'Is Technology Historically Independent of Science?', *Technology and Culture* 6, No. 4, 1965, pp. 553-568.
Derek Price, 1969	Price, Derek de Solla, 'The Structures of Publication in Science and Technology', in Gruber, W. H. and Marquis, D. G. (Eds.), *Factors in the Transfer of Technology*, Cambridge, Mass., MIT Press, 1969.
Derek Price, 1971	Price, Derek de Solla, 'Is There a Decline in Big Science Countries and in Big Science Subjects?', XIIIth International Congress for the History of Science, Moscow and Leningrad, 18-28 August 1971.

Summary of paper (with contributions by Kedrov and Mikulinsky) in *Literaturnaya Gazeta* 35 (USSR), 25 August 1971, p. 13.

Price and Beaver, 1966   Price, Derek de Solla and Beaver, D., 'Collaboration in an Invisible College', *American Psychologist* 21, 1966, pp. 1011-1018.

Don K. Price, 1954   Price, D. K., *Government and Science*, New York, University Press, 1954.

Przeworski and Teune, 1970   Przeworski, A. and Teune, H., *The Logic of Comparative Inquiry*, New York, Wiley Inter-Science, 1970.

Ravetz, 1971   Ravetz, J. R., *Scientific Knowledge and Its Social Problems*, Oxford, Clarendon Press, 1971.

Reagan, 1967   Reagan, M. D., 'Basic and Applied Research: A Meaningful Distinction?', *Science* 155, 1967, pp. 1383-1386.

Reif, 1961   Reif, F., 'The Competitive World of the Pure Scientist', *Science* 134, 1961, pp. 1957-1962.

Reif and Strauss, 1965   Reif, F. and Strauss, A., 'The Impact of Rapid Discovery upon the Scientist's Career', *Social Problems* 12, No. 5, 1965, pp. 297-311.

Rose and Rose, 1969   Rose, H. and Rose, S., *Science and Society*, Harmondsworth, Penguin Books, 1969.

Salomon, 1970   Salomon, J.-J., *Science et Politique*, Paris Editions du Seuil, 1970. Published in English as *Science and Politics*, London, Macmillan, 1973.

Shanin-Cohen, 1974   Shanin-Cohen, N., 'Innovation and Citation', unpublished paper, Department of Sociology, Hebrew University of Jerusalem.

Shepard, 1956   Shepard, H. A., 'Basic Research and the Social System of Pure Science', *Philosophy of Science* 23, 1956, pp. 48-57.

Shepard, 1958   Shepard, H. A., 'The Dual Hierarchy in Research Management', *Research Management* 1, 1958, pp. 177-187.

Sherwin and Isenson, 1967   Sherwin, C. W. and Isenson, R. S., 'Project Hindsight: A Defense Department Study of the Utility of Research', *Science* 156, 1967, pp. 1571-1577.

Sills, 1968   Sills, D. L. (Ed.), *International Encyclopedia of the Social Sciences*, New York and London, Macmillan and Company, The Free Press, 1968, Vol. 14, pp. 92-117.

Sklair, 1973   Sklair, L., *Organized Knowledge*, London, Hart-Davis, McGibbon, 1973.

Spiegel-Rösing, 1973   Spiegel-Rösing, I., *Wissenschaftsentwicklung und Wissenschaftssteuerung*, Frankfurt am Main, Athenaum, 1973.

Spiegel-Rösing, 1974   Spiegel-Rösing, I., 'Disziplinäre Strategien der Statussicherung', *Homo* 25, 1974, pp. 11-17. For an English version, see Salomon, J.-J. and Spiegel-Rösing, I. (Eds.), *Science Policy Studies Contributions*, Tokyo, ICSPS, 1974, pp. 105-145.

Spiegel-Rösing, Fauser and Baitsch, 1975   Spiegel-Rösing, I., Fauser, P., Baitsch, H.,, *Messung von Forschungsleitung. Institutionen, Gruppen, Ein-*

zelpersonen, Bonn, Bundesministerium für Bildung und Wissenschaft, 1975.

Storer, 1966   Storer, N. W., *The Social System of Science,* New York, Holt, Rinehart and Winston, 1966.

The Swann Report, 1968   Swann Report, The, *The Flow into Employment of Scientists, Engineers and Technologists,* HMSO, Cmnd 3760, 1958.

Swatez, 1970   Swatez, G. M., 'The Social Organization of a University Laboratory', *Minerva* 8, No. 1, 1970, pp. 36-58.

Taton, 1962   Taton, R., *Reason and Chance in Scientific Discovery,* New York, Science Editions Inc., 1962.

Taylor, 1973   Taylor, Sir J., *The Scientific Community,* Oxford, Oxford University Press, 1973.

Walters and Cotgrove, 1967   Walters, G. and Cotgrove, S. (Eds.), *Scientists in British Industry,* Bath, Bath University Press, 1967.

Waterman, 1966   Waterman, A. T. 'Social Influences and Scientists', *Science* 151, 1966, pp. 61-64.

Watson, 1968   Watson, J. D., *The Double Helix,* New York, Athenaum Publishers, 1968.

Weingart, 1974   Weingart, P. (Ed.), *Wissenschaftssoziologie 2: Determinanten wissenschaftlicher Entwicklung,* Frankfurt am Main, Athenaum Fischer Taschenbuch Verlag, 1974.

West, 1960   West, S. S., 'The Ideology of Academic Scientists', *IRE Transactions of Engineering Management* EM-7, 1960, pp. 54-62.

Whitley, 1970   Whitley, R. D., 'The Operation of Science Journals: Two Case Studies in British Social Science', *Sociological Review* 18, 1970, pp. 241-258.

Whitley, 1972   Whitley, R., 'Black-Boxism and the Sociology of Science', in Halmos, P. (Ed.), *The Sociology of Science,* Sociological Review Monograph, No. 18, University of Keele, 1972, pp. 61-92.

Whitley, 1974   Whitley, R. (Ed.), *Social Processes of Scientific Development,* London and Boston, Routledge and Kegan Paul, 1974.

Williams, 1973   Williams, R., 'Some Political Aspects of the Rothschild Affair', *Science Studies* 3, No. 1, 1973, pp. 31-46.

Wood, 1964   Wood, R. C., 'Science and Politics: The Rise of an Apolitical Elite', in Gilpin, R. and Wright, C., *Scientists and National Policy Making,* New York and London, Columbia University Press, 1964.

Yates, 1968   Yates, F., 'Theory and Practice in Statistics', *Journal of the Royal Statistical Society, Series A (General)* 131, 1968, pp. 463-474.

Ziman, 1968   Ziman, J., *Public Knowledge: The Social Dimension of Science,* Cambridge, Cambridge University Press, 1968.

Zloczower, 1966   Zloczower, A., *Career Opportunities and the Growth of Scientific Discovery in 19th Century Germany, with Special Reference to Physiology,* The Eliezer Kaplan School of Economics and Social Sciences,

Hebrew University of Jerusalem, 1966, unpublished thesis.

Zuckerman, 1967   Zuckerman, H. A., 'Nobel Laureates in Science' Patterns of Productivity, Collaboration and Authorship', *American Sociological Review* 32, 1967, pp. 391-403.

Zuckerman, 1968   Zuckerman, H. A., 'Patterns of Name Ordering among Authors of Scientific Papers', *American Journal of Sociology* 73, 1968, pp. 276-291.

Zuckerman, 1970   Zuckerman, H. A., 'Stratification in American Science', *Sociological Inquiry,* 40, 1970, pp. 235-257.

Zuckerman, 1972   Zuckerman, H. A., 'Interviewing an Ultra-Elite', *The Public Opinion Quarterly,* 36, 1972, pp. 159-175.

Zuckerman and Merton, 1971   Zuckerman, H. A. and Merton, R. K., 'Patterns of Evaluation in Science: Institutionalisation, Structure and Functions of the Referee System', *Minerva* 9, No. 1, 1971, pp. 66-100.

Chapter 5

CHANGING PERSPECTIVES IN THE SOCIAL HISTORY OF SCIENCE

Roy MacLeod

University of Sussex

INTRODUCTION

History, J. H. Hexter has written, is the way men give shape to their experience. For nearly a century, the history of science has borne the task of shaping our understanding of the dynamic which underlies the growth of scientific ideas. Yet until this generation there have been few significant scholarly attempts (Merz, 1904-1912) to consider that dynamic as itself problematic — problematic in relation both to the mentalities of different cultures in different periods, and to the development of different structures of knowledge in the modern world. For less than a decade there has been a movement among people and institutions toward a general recognition that the hermeneutical problems inherent in any reconstruction of the pursuit of natural knowledge must involve a recognition of the historian's own traditions, beliefs and objectives. Today it is a truism that historiography reflects contemporary concerns. Within the last five years, prompted by considerations of size, cost, instrumental power, the political justification of science and the logic of dominion embedded in scientific method, historians have sought in new and more searching ways to define cultural sources and conditions of scientific creativity, and the nature and consequences of that activity. Looking beyond appearances, historians of science have set out to find the statue in the marble, and have asked how and why scientific attitudes, techniques and concepts have acquired the particular status they enjoy.

Within these five years, however, the search for causes and conditions has revealed several new characteristics. Problems once defined as primarily philosophical, sociological or historical are now seen to require intellectual cross-referencing and subtle contextual definition. The dense theology of causality, rationality and objectivity has required new interpretation in the light of categories devised by men and women acting in historical time to categorize, explain and generalize regularities evident in nature. The study of science, long an exemplar in philosophy, is achieving a *locus standi* in general history (Hillinger, 1973, Gowing, 1975). As the accompanying bibliography amply reveals, the logical reconstruction of science is acquiring a human dimension.

Some small part of this recent effort has appeared in print. Much more is still gestating within doctoral theses or research programs begun since the mid-1960's. At different levels, important difficulties are arising. Some of these difficulties derive from ill-starred attempts to project contemporary definitions into inappropriate historical contexts; others are caused by overly zealous borrowing from other models and vocabularies; still others arise from long-standing epistemological debates about the contingency of knowledge. These debates are, according to taste, either impenetrable or irrelevant, but in either case they divide many scholars in the field. Within many fields in the history of science there is today no discernable consensus, either as to methodological demarcations or to conceptual definitions (cf. Agassi, 1963; Barnes, 1974). On the contrary, there is a plurality of beliefs, methods and, implicitly, ideologies among historians of science. There are positions, and there are 'schools'; more interesting, there are approaches which have not yet become formally defined.

Some of these approaches (Ravetz, 1971) have furnished the background for discussions on the generation of policies for science. In looking to history, however, the student of science policy has now to confront a bewildering set of conjectures about the pursuit of knowledge, its social functions and its place in the social fabric of western culture. Among these conjectures there are few compelling generalizations (Geoffrey Price, 1976), and they have many limitations. And very few of these conjectures (though Needham counts as many as ten) have applied themselves to understanding why traditions other than those we speak of as 'Western' and 'scientific' defend and operate apparently 'unreasonable' systems of belief and knowledge.

From this debate and concern over the past decade has emerged an increasing interest in what has been called externalist history or the social history of science. This activity, once given the status of a specialty, has since come to generate much important work in the history of science. As a means of organizing knowledge, it presents valuable perspectives to the study of science policy. However, its emergence has not come about unopposed. Some people have felt that emphasis on the social activity of science has diminished the primacy of internal explanations, which are based on the close study of experiments, observations and theories (Hesse, 1970, 1973). They have categorized the information derived from the study of science as a social activity as secondary, incidental and derivative (Lakatos, 1973). There are important professional and epistemological issues still unresolved, and there are questions of method still undefined. The prospect of a social historiography of science is, however, receiving increased attention, and this chapter will attempt to place its problems and possibilities in context. As a unifying principle, the following pages will focus on the so-called internalist/externalist debate, and some of the changing directions in the field. The essay will conclude by outlining some possible goals of a social historiography of science, and some of the difficulties it must surmount.

THE SOCIAL HISTORY OF SCIENCE AND THE INTERNALIST/EXTERNALIST DEBATE

In 1968 the *International Encyclopedia of the Social Sciences* devoted an introductory article to the history of science. In that article, T. S. Kuhn observed:

> ... there seem at times to be two distinct sorts of history of science, occasionally appearing between the same covers but rarely making firm or fruitful contact. The still dominant form, often called the 'internal approach', is concerned with the substance of science as knowledge. Its newer rival, often called the 'externalist approach', is concerned with the activity of scientists as a social group within a larger culture. Putting the two together is perhaps the greatest challenge now faced by the profession, and there are increasing signs of a response (Kuhn, 1968; 76).

The same year, George Basalla's pioneering volume of edited essays appeared under the title *The Rise of Modern Science: External or Internal Factors?* After discussing several selections, intended to reveal different explanations for the remarkable events we consider to form part of our scientific culture, Basalla concluded:

> The internalists have been given the last word because their interpretation of the rise of modern science is acceptable to most historians of science today. Perhaps some future proponents of an externalist interpretation will offer strong proof that the intellect is decisively conditioned by external forces (Basalla, 1968, xiv).

Indeed, Basalla added, until that time, 'the organization and conceptual growth of science will best be studied as a part of man's intellectual heritage'.

Eight years later, in 1976, S. G. Kohlstedt remarked that the history of science, as a field, has become 'increasingly interested in questions often noted as "external", i.e. the study of science in relation to a particular social setting'. Believing this to indicate a step away from the tracing of developments in a specific discipline, Ms. Kohlstedt continued:

> Externalists investigate the nature of the community of scientists, the impetus for

pursuing particular lines of research, and the importance of public interest and support, both moral and financial. By implication they argue that the environment of science affects its effort and product. Together with sociologists of science, historians of science now frequently consider the nature of scientific communities, comparing them over time and across national boundaries (Kohlstedt, 1976; 173).

Assuming that these two positions are representative, and that Kuhn's prediction is accurate, what has occurred in the last decade to encourage such a development?

During the 1920's — a period of rapid institutional development in the history of sciences[1] — three intellectual approaches pervaded and oriented historical writing in the field. First there was the considerable legacy of Comtian positivism, which characterized the story of science from remote antiquity, but especially from the Renaissance and the 'Scientific Revolution' of the Seventeenth Century, as one of steady accomplishment, a march of the intellect, achieving victories over myth and supersition by a lengthy process of observation, trial, error and eventually the codification of laws and theories. This tradition, epitomized by Paul Tannery in France and George Sarton, first in Europe and then in America, aspired to an exhaustive 'histoire générale des sciences', which would embody the progressive development of the human mind. The second approach arose from the contributions of the history of philosophy, as reflected in the work of E. A. Burtt and Ernst Cassirer. This approach bestowed special rewards on the achievements of rational and objective knowledge, and on the establishing of normative and universal standards of scientific truth. A third tradition, particularly powerful in France, derived from the work of Pierre Duhem, who took up a critique of Nineteenth Century mechanistic determinism and attempted to provide an alternative explanation of the progress of scientific ideas in physical theory as systems of mathematical propositions, deduced from principles representing experimental laws. In trying to establish the historical genesis of modern physics, Duhem turned to medieval explanations of bodies in motion. Only by understanding and working through this tradition, he believed, could one find a basis for understanding the implications of the mathematization of nature in the Renaissance and in the 'new philosophy' of the Seventeenth Century.

In Europe this historiographical framework had enormous influence on E. J. Dijksterhuis and Alexandre Koyré, both of whom remained untranslated into English until after World War II. Koyré adopted a neo-Kantian epistemology, presumably through L. Brunschvicg and E. Meyerson (who together also had a formulative influence on the early Bachelard), which became of enormous cultural importance. It was important not least because it acted as a rational bulwark against conflicting philosophical tendencies toward anti-

---

[1] See A. Thackray, and R. Merton, 'On Discipline Building: The Paradoxes of George Sarton', *Isis,* IXIII, 1972, pp. 473-495.

positivism, anti-intellectualism, Bergsonism (and ultimately existentialism) which flourished in French and German philosophical and political thought after World War I. But this framework also provided, in the 1930's and after, a set of conventions fundamental to a new historical theory of science. In Koyré this theory of science had its basis in a philosophical realism, predicated on the conviction that mathematics is the historical key to our understanding of nature. Accordingly, the leading feature of the history of scientific thought has been the mathematization of nature, a process which does not occur in linear steps, but which requires discontinuous philosophical leaps, which appear to us now as 'mutations' in the history of ideas. Koyrés idealist philosophy, while it did not hesitate to ascribe an essential cultural role to nontheoretical extrascientific ideas, could not be reduced to the determination of philosophical leaps in response to such influences. For Koyré, positivist methodology, formal logic and historical and philosophical relativism were all equally anathema.[2]

In the years following World War II (cf. Koyré, 1956), it was Koyré's influence which was destined to have a leading impact upon scholarship in the history of science. This impact was chiefly felt in the United States, where the professional and intellectual climate proved highly receptive. This was not completely fortuitous. America, and to a lesser extent, Britain, had far greater institutional possibilities for the diffusion of particular collective mentalities, while at the same time, no equally powerful intellectual system to provide an alternative form of historiographical coherence. Koyré's history of philosophy appealed equally to historians and to philosophers, who were in any case persuaded of the singular importance of understanding, within realist conventions, the place of scientific ideas in the history of ideas generally. It is a remarkable irony that the epistemology of Gaston Bachelard, appearing in France about the same time as that of Koyré and ultimately wielding an enormous influence over generations of French historians and philosophers, was not seen to be important to the development of the history or philosophy of science in America and Britain. Only within the last four years, and even then largely through the mediations of political theorists, has this influence become visibly relevant.

During the late 1920's and early 1930's, while these three influences were at work, a line of argument developed which sought to emphasize the role of social and economic factors in scientific development. This approach, which had complex roots in German social philosophy and Russian Marxist ideology, achieved a rivetting relevance in the depths of economic and industrial depression. It received particular prominence in the Second International Congress of the History of Science, held in London in 1931. At that meeting,

---

[2] Thus, 'it is not by giving up the apparently unattainable goal of knowledge of the real but by pursuing it bravely that science progresses along the road to truth'. (A. Koyré, *Les Origines de la science moderne,* Paris, 1956, p. 25).

the surprise appearance of a Soviet delegation, and the publication of its papers in a volume entitled *Science at the Crossroads* (1931), profoundly affected a small group of British scientists, including J. D. Bernal, J. Needham, Lancelot Hogben and the science journalist J. G. Crowther (Crowther, 1941). This group, quite outside the intellectual or institutional mainstream, such as it was, in the history of science, constituted an important echelon in the 'social relations of science movement' in Britain in the late 1930's. Through Bernal's *Social Function of Science* (1939), this tradition has had an important influence on public discussion of political and economic planning ever since (Werskey, 1971, 1974).

It was characteristic of this Marxist contribution that, while it gloried in the name of science (particularly applied science and technology), it placed little emphasis on the intellectual traditions which nourished or retarded the pursuit of science. Hessen's congress essay on the social and economic roots of Newton's *Principia* appeared to some as 'vulgar Marxism', and as simplistic economic determinism (Clark, 1949), an outlook which Soviet scholars today cordially disavow (Mikulinski, 1975). In fact, the message of Hessen, read again today, is far more penetrating than his critics would then admit (Werskey, 1971). But in the meantime, another, far more subtle, form of socio-economic interpretation soon followed in the form of R. K. Merton's classic study of science and technology in Seventeenth Century England (1938, 1970). There were two leading arguments in Merton's study: that, following Weber, puritanism had impelling consequences for the pursuit of natural knowledge and that, following the guidelines of Bacon, social and economic necessities exerted a significant 'pull' on invention and experiment. These arguments proved to be the starting point of a long and, as yet, unended debate on religion, capitalism and science (Hill, 1965); the second, as Merton later remarked, has until recently (Webster, 1974) been generally ignored, or rather dismissed, as either trivially true (in the case of specific technologies) or historically untestable (in the case of specific theories which transcend immediate political necessities). At the same time, Merton's emphasis on the importance of manual work, systematic technology and direct confrontation with nature became *dépassé* among historians of ideas, who believed that the important transformations in world outlook of the Sixteenth and Seventeenth Centuries, whether in optics, astronomy or mechanics, owed little of importance to new instruments, or to the social milieu. On the contrary, they argued that contemporaries of Galileo, Descartes, Harvey and Newton interpreted well-known phenomena in new ways because of pervasive and diverse intellectual influences such as Renaissance neo-Platonism, a revived mechanicalism and a rekindled interest in alchemy and the *corpus Hermeticum,* and because of a generalized reaction against the sterility of Aristotelian scholasticism (Kearney, 1971; Yates, 1964).

With few exceptions (e.g. Lilly, 1948, 1949), the historiographical approaches in the history of science in America and Britain after the Second World War had little affinity with either this socio-economic debate or with Merton's influence. Indeed, Merton's influence was felt far more by American empirical sociologists, who through the 1950's and early 1960's fashioned an activity of their own. This 'sociology of science' was, and is, predominantly quantitative, and generally concerned with issues such as communication, mobility and reward, issues which are part of the public management of science today (Storer, 1966, Crane, 1972, Gaston, 1973). Sociologists working during this period were not above using historical materials, and they certainly conceded the importance of the historical context (e.g. Ben-David's pioneering work, 1960, and with Zloczower, 1962; Barber, 1952, Barber and Hirsch, 1962). A few historians, among them Derek de Solla Price, endeavored to provide this context, stressing the role of technology and instrumentation in generating scientific problems and in framing results. Price's work forced attention to the fact that claims for the sufficiency of broad social factors in understanding scientific development were themselves insufficient; that the history of scientific ideas everywhere gives evidence of internal constraints, and that the study of techniques and their development can, in a sociological perspective, bring fresh insight to bear upon both 'internal' and 'external' traditions. But for the most part, and often in neglect of Merton's historical judgment, the sociology of science proceeded in directions which led away from the history of science. This fragmented the area further (See Cole and Cole, 1973). At the same time, historians of science had generated a new self-confidence (See Clagett, 1962) that the history of science could, and should, be analytically separate from general history (which did not distinguish sufficiently between primary and secondary factors in the development of ideas), from philosophy (which dealt in linguistic formalisms unrelated to the real world), from sociology (which had as its chief focus the study of scientists, not science), and from the history of technology (which was, in any case, antifactual). Throughout the 1950's and the early 1960's work of enormous importance appeared in the internal history of science, work which created high standards of definition and proof for debate about the relative roles of experimentation, personality and philosophical preparation (Cf. Clagett, 1959, Cohen, 1956; Guerlac, 1961; Hesse, 1963). However, to some, it appeared that these sets of problems were more than matters of emphasis; that they were, in fact, different and separable historiographic enterprises. A demarcation of this kind, which to all intents made no value judgments either way, was given by C. C. Gillispie in 1959, and, significantly, reprinted in Barber and Hirsch's first 'textbook' in the sociology of science (1962):

> Science presents itself to history under two aspects: first in its own evolution and secondly in its accommodation by culture. Which is the more important is a question of perspective, and which the more interesting a matter of taste. The evaluation of scientific ideas related the progress of science to nature, and is the more elegant and

precise a subject. But its cultural history related it to society, and it is that to which we are asked to address ourselves. I think it obvious that science, which is about nature, cannot be determined in its content by the social relations of scientists. At most it may be touched in style and pace and – within limits imposed by the logical interdependence of the sciences – in order of development. (Gillispie in Barber and Hirsch, 1962; 89).

Gillispie went on to say that, in his paper, he used the term 'French science' in the sense of scientific culture. The following year A. Rupert Hall made explicit this more or less procedural separation between internal and external domains in his important essay, 'Merton Revisited' (1963). Hall's essay, unlike Gillispie's, did make value judgments. Hall claimed that:

In its crudest forms at any rate the socio-economic interpretation of the scientific revolution as an offshoot of rising capitalism and mercantile militarism has perished without comment. Its unilluminating conclusions rested on defective logic and improbable psychology; .... the true situation is far too complicated to yield such simple generalisations .... (Hall, 1963; 9).

In Hall's view, social and economic explanations tell us something about scientific movements, but not about science as a system of knowledge about nature. As there is, and must be, a demarcation between these domains, so there must be a demarcation between historians who study the one and the other.

It was widely felt in the mid-1960's, that Hall's intellectual critique revealed important anxieties about the necessity of preserving the rational, objective status of science, and of avoiding the historical treatment of scientists as 'puppets', as regimented figures dancing to the invisible drums of determinist economic forces. Ironically, however, Hall's essay was important because it raised in the collective consciousness of a new generation of historians the memory of Merton's early work. Indeed, the forcefulness with which Hall criticized Mertonian historiography served to make some curious to know more about it. Among historians in the late 1960's a new tide was rising, and one could sense the groundswell. Paradoxically, this tide was not principally composed of the older pioneers of institutional history or the history of technology or economic development, but of scholars such as P. M. Rattansi (1963), and A. Debus (1965), who were coming to the history of science from other disciplines, or who, like R. Horton (1967), were looking at science from other perspectives. In 1967 A. R. Hall observed a dropping off of interest in social explanations of science, as evidenced by the contents of *Isis* and *Annals of Science* between 1953-1963. Yet soon thereafter, the picture began to change. For example, the colloquium on 'Critical Problems' organized in 1957 by Marshall Clagett (1962) was devoted chiefly to intellectual problems in the history of the physical sciences.[3] By 1961 A. C.

---

[3] This included, incidentally, A. R. Hall's well-known demarcation between the 'scholar' and the 'craftsman', in which he took up a position similar to that of Koyré. See A. Koyré, 'Les philosophes et la machine', in *Études d'histoire et de la pensée scientifique*, Paris, 1966, pp. 279-309.

Crombie admitted in his Oxford Conference on *Scientific Change* (1963) that there existed at least the possibility of seeing physical problems in a broader cultural, biographical and technical dimension; indeed, this meeting provided a forum for the discussion of T. S. Kuhn's early conclusions on dogma as a factor in scientific explanation. And by 1969 D. H. Roller's volume of *Perspectives* (1971) presaged a remarkable turnabout, presenting an enormous variety of puzzles and interpretations. By the date of M. Teich and R. M. Young's *Festschrift* for Needham (1972), historiographic debate on the status of objectivity and rationality and on the relations between scientific ideas and social structures was well underway. The tide had definitely turned.

No social indicator is without its limitations, and it would be difficult to put a date to the origins of this new interest. It could be argued that the single most important impetus in the direction of a new social historiography of science has come as a result of T. S. Kuhn's *Structure of Scientific Revolutions* (1962, 1970).[4] Kuhn's model for the explanation of scientific development (See Böhme, Chapter 9) did not have an immediate impact on historians of science; indeed, its influence was acknowledged far more quickly in other fields notably including economics, psychology and anthropology. Kuhn's book expressly excluded the consideration of external factors from its account of scientific development and did not stimulate fresh historical work of a kind familiar to the socio-economic externalists of a generation earlier. On the contrary, Kuhn was careful to distinguish between the study of concepts and problem structures, and the study of factors external to these, which affect timing and direction. The effect was to limit the influence of external factors (including the rise of technology and technological needs) to the creation of contexts where cross-fertilization between different specialties can occur (Kuhn, 1968, 81).

Despite these self-imposed limitations, Kuhn's book and its critics opened the way to a contagious acceptance of a powerful (if imprecise) analytical vocabulary, which in turn quickened fresh historical interest in the wide range of factors which (in Kuhn's terms) may have affected 'normal science', which have shaped 'paradigms', or which have precipitated 'crises states' and 'revolutions' in the realm of ideas. Indirectly, and partly through ensuing debates with Karl Popper, Imre Lakatos and Stephen Toulmin, questions of enormous epistemological importance have arisen from this discussion. One result has been to expose again the problematic roots of assumptions concerning the nature of continuity and discontinuity in science (Toulmin, 1972). Another result has been an increasing interest in the day-to-day preoccupations of the scientific community and in the 'industrialization' of scientific methods (cf. Ravetz, 1971). A further result has come with renewed interest in a

---

[4] It would be tempting, but more difficult, to trace a comparable line of development from James Watson's revealing account in *The Double Helix* (London: Weidenfeld and Nicholson, 1968).

historically-based sociology of scientific knowledge (Barnes, 1974; Bloor, 1976).

Among the far-reaching consequences of Kuhn's work has been the recognition that it is not easy to disengage internal from external questions. In 1970, Michael King proposed an 'epistemological agnosticism' in the sociology of science, on the grounds that it was impossible to do sociological research if one felt threatened at every turn by the fearsome task of making Kantian decisions about whether reality is socially constructed, and knowledge totally culture bound. Increasingly among philosophers and sociologists, this self-denying ordinance no longer applies (Martins, 1972; Crane, 1972). Few historians, however, have as yet felt the necessity of meeting such problems head-on. Instead, there appears to be only a very gradual movement in this direction, and even then, only towards asking questions which explore, rather than provoke, epistemological debate. However, that this movement is significant, and spreading, there can be no doubt. Several historians — including Kargon, Thackray, Fox and Forman — have begun to occupy territory somewhere between more traditional 'internalist' and 'externalist' positions. New journals, such as *Social Studies of Science* (formerly *Science Studies*) have specifically encouraged this development; some older journals, such as *Technology and Culture* have opened their pages to more interdisciplinary material; and others have changed their format and orientation to allow wider coverage of problems and methods. (Consider *Chymia''s* transformation into *Historical Studies in the Physical Sciences* in 1969 and recent changes in the editorial policies of *Annals of Science* and *History of Science*). It is indicative, perhaps, that the report of the United States delegation to the XIIIth Congress of the History of Science in Tokyo in 1974 should choose to refer to

> a trend in these conferences toward more general problems, questions of professionalization, the transmission of science and technology to 'non-initiating' countries, and ecological and environmental problems deriving from industrialization.[5]

Increasingly we are beginning to realize that, as Kuhn observed, 'although the internal and external approaches to the history of science have a sort of natural autonomy, they are in fact, complementary concerns'. Moreover, we are beginning to accept that:—

> Until they are practised as such, each drawing from the other, important aspects of the scientific development are unlikely to be understood (1968; 81).

Within certain directions and with definite limitations, this note of inquiry has begun to bear fruit.

---

[5] R. Multhauf in *Isis*, 66, 1975, p. 481.

THE CHANGING SCOPE OF THE SOCIAL HISTORY OF SCIENCE

Since the mid-1970's, after a decade of hard battle on shifting fronts in which speed, mobility and tactical enterprise seem to have been more in evidence that strategic planning, a steady flow of work in the social history of science has begun to emerge. To paraphrase Churchill's words concerning El Alamein: before about 1968 there were few victories; after then, despite qualifications, there have been few defeats. Happily the metaphor is not exact, as nearly everyone working in the history of science has profited from this fresh stimulus. In its wake, has come growing confidence among social historians of science and a growing willingness to remove barriers between the dominant historical traditions.

This willingness to remove barriers and to seek a more integrated historical perspective does not, however, reflect merely a weak ecumenicity. In December 1975, George Basalla, commenting on the first fifty years of the History of Science Society, criticized externalists for limiting themselves to a social history of science defined by internalists. 'Consequently', he wrote

> the externalists became convinced they were writing the social history of science when they told us something about the family background of the Royal Society, or called our attention to the emergence of yet another scientific discipline as a recognised profession. The externalists, in the very act of opposing the internalists, aped them by staying as close as possible to the scientific figures and communities being studied in strictly internalistic ways (Basalla, 1975, 468).

Basalla appealed for a social history of science which would be more than an 'appendage' to the 'conceptualist approach'.

To date, the onus of proof has rested on the externalists. In the words of Mark Blaug:

> To be convincing, 'externalists' must produce instances of (i) internally consistent, well corroborated, fruitful and powerful scientific ideas which were rejected at specific dates in the history of science because of external factors; or else instances of (ii) incoherent, poorly corroborated, weak scientific ideas which were in fact accepted for external reasons.[6]

It is, of course, difficult to find unambiguous examples of either case. Paul Forman's work (1971) foreshadows the possibility of finding examples relevant to the first case, while the history of Soviet genetics offers unhappy reminders relevant to the second. But one might easily argue that it is a

---

[6] This argument, applied to a different sphere, is formulated in M. Blaug, 'Kuhn *versus* Lakatos, or Paradigms *versus* Research Programmes in the History of Economics', (delivered to a Conference on the History of Economic Thought, London, 1974), p. 37. I am indebted to Professor Blaug for his formulation.

weakness of the social history of science that, outside the Marxist framework of the 1930's and the functionalist framework of the 1950's, it has failed to produce theoretical explanations which yield unambiguously generalizable results. One might equally well argue, however, that this is its strength. The social history of science has so far avoided theoretical generalizations.

However, this search for proof positive, based on certain assumptions of historical causality, did after all, concede internalist ground rules. In 1954, Needham singled out, as the root of the problem, the internalist's concern with establishing causes:

> scenting economic determinism under every formulation . . . [the internalists] insist that the Scientific Revolution, as primarily a revolution of unscientific ideas, cannot have been 'derivative' from some other social movement such as the Reformation or the rise of capitalism . . . they do not like to admit that scientists have bodies, eat and drink and live social lives among their fellow men whose practical problems cannot remain known to them; nor are the internalists willing to credit their scientific subjects with subconscious minds.

If one applies different definitions of argument, if one agrees with Marc Bloch, that history is composed of 'multiple wave-trains', and necessarily lends itself to argument by inference and ascription – it is not clear who is finally to decide that the *onus probandi* of historical respectability rests on the findings of social historians. Before this issue is resolved, however, there is clearly greater need for mutual comprehension. As Popper remarked, 'genuine philosophical problems are always rooted in problems outside philosophy'. As Popper's illuminating autobiography (1976), *Unended Quest*, amply reveals, to inquire deeply into the reasons underlying the defensive posture of the internalist position is inevitably to inquire deeply into personal and sometimes political experience, and into the sources of given intellectual commitment; into deepseated fears of epistemological relativism, dating in some cases from the 1920's; and into reasons for holding intricate and well-supported beliefs in the primacy of natural causes and in the logical sequences of conceptual development.

Whatever their personal tastes or commitments, it would serve historians well not to quickly dismiss these factors, nor to leave their opponents' arguments unread. It is by no means a simple matter of clear polarities. The internal traditions of Tannery and Duhem are rich in critical reflections on the inadequacy of attempts to identify logical certainty with natural reality; they also acknowledge the centrality of intuition, common sense and epistemological continuity in scientific theory. Social historians would also be unwise to forget that Koyré and Bachelard, among others, sought for a world of relations in which to imbed the mutations or epistemological obstacles which, to them, comprised the real thrust of scientific change. Their attitude reflected in the 1930's the epistemological skepticism of the Vienna circle. The history of their position – a history of reaction against intuitionism and a struggle toward philosophical realism and a redefined theory of culture — forms the tangled bank of philosophical assumptions underlying our own intellectual heritage.

No rapprochement between internalism and externalism is possible which does not take into account the history of these philosophies of science. Indeed, when we turn to Koyré, who exerted such a great influence on Anglo-Saxon, particularly American, historians, we discover a philosophical legacy which has seldom been examined by the English-speaking world. For Bachelard, for whom the lineage of ideas reaches from Althusserian Marxism to structuralism to the whole tapestry of contemporary French epistemology, our picture is even more complex, involving the understanding of the cultural necessity for making judgments on the nature of truth among competing ideas, and for endorsing the cognitive superiority of the rational sciences. For both Koyré and Bachelard, for definably historical reasons, the status of scientific knowledge is supreme. For the same reasons it has been understood as socially unproblematic. Science has become, as Pietro Redondi has put it (1975), 'epistemologically privileged', conferring cultural superiority on the ideas and on the representatives of the rational elite. The internal history of science has had as its object the defense of that privilege.

It is clear that historians today must pay their intellectual debts to the history of philosophy. But it also follows that the philosophical preoccupations of an earlier generation should not be allowed to override or constrain the historiographical premises we find important today. Fortunately, there are hopeful signs that historians can reject an exclusively internalist historiography without, as Koyré feared, falling into the traps of Bergsonian intuitionism, Hessenian determinism, Bernalian necessity, or whatever other pitfalls await the philosophically unwary.

Here one must be prepared to let commitment guide, explicitly, one's choice of problems or research techniques. There is an implied condescension in Lakatos' candid dismissal of the social studies of science as being at best redundant, at worst pernicious. This attitude has prompted more outrage than argument. But within the last five years, outrage has given way to endeavor. Drawing in some cases on work done two decades ago, the material basis for a new social history of science is acquiring a recognizable shape. It is difficult to avoid doing injury to it by imposing arbitrary categories, but for ease of reference perhaps one can describe this new work in terms of (1) its emphasis upon scientific institutions (including societies and universities), (2) the scientific professions, (3) scientific disciplines, specialities and research programmes, and (4) studies of science in relation to wider social developments.

As Roger Hahn has observed (1971)

> . . . the scientific institution is the anvil on which the often conflicting values of science and society are shaped into a viable form. The institution's success is in large part determined by its ability to make the peculiar enterprise of science palatable to

society while at the same time maintaining the advancement of the discipline itself.
(Hahn, 1971; x).

From the Seventeenth Century onwards, the scientific institution develops
the sense of community and, ultimately, of prestige and reward. For institutional historians the important questions are largely of objectives and structures, set within definable contexts. It is the special virtue of the institution
that it does lend insights into the changing social, economic and intellectual
ecology of science. This is especially evident in studies of national scientific
traditions and their influence on national prestige. France has been well
served by C. C. Gillispie (1959), H. Guerlac (1961), and in more recent years
by R. Fox (1973, 1974) and H. Paul (1971, 1972). The history of Scottish
science has had as its advocate J. B. Morrell (1974); the USSR has become
better known through L. Graham (1967); while Germany is more clearly
understood in the work of R. McCormmach (1974) and Frank Pfetsch (1970,
1974). The United States, which for years weighed against the virtues of
'Yankee practicality', the overwhelming contribution of recent European
immigrants to American scientific prestige (Fleming, 1968; Weiner, 1968),
has recently found good reason for (retrospective) self-confidence (Daniels,
1972; and especially Reingold, 1972a), and fresh reason to dispute the
summary judgment of de Tocqueville. Needless to say, the current bicen-
tennial celebrations have done nothing to undermine this sentiment.[7] At the
same time, the work of Ann Moyal on Austrialia has amplified the discussion
of colonial science and the diffusion of science across national boundaries
(1976), a discussion which was stimulated a decade ago by Fleming (1964)
and Basalla (1967). Eastern European countries are no less notable for their
concern with the history of national science, but few of these studies have yet
reached an English-reading audience.

It is perhaps in the relations of science and politics that studies of
scientific institutions have had the most to offer, although recent work is
giving the notion of 'political context' an even wider definition. A genus of
institutional studies in the relations of science and statecraft is appearing in
the work of Brigitte Schroeder-Gudehus (1966, 1973), who has examined
internationalism in science and its enemies in the period of 1919-1939. P. G.
Werskey's long-awaited study of 'scientists for socialism' in the same period
will say a great deal about the hidden agenda underlying the radical and
reformist positions in Britain and, in turn, 'science and society' movements
abroad.[8] Interest in the history of scientific societies, which languished
slowly after Ornstein and Stimson's pioneering work in the 1940's, has begun

---

[7] Cf. the current American Academy of Arts and Sciences project on *Knowledge in
American Society 1860-1970.*
[8] Cf. R. MacLeod, 'The Historical Context of the International Council on Science
Policy Studies', *Archives internationales d'histoire des sciences*, 25, 1975, pp. 314-328.

to gather momentum. To date, French sources have been most extensively treated, following Crosland's study of the Society of Arcueil (1967) and then Hahn's volume on the Académie des Sciences (1971). In Britain, Schofield's classic study of the Lunar Society (1963), Shapin's study of the Royal Society of Edinburgh (1971) and of provincial scientific institutions in England (1972), and Morris Berman's analysis of the Royal Institution (1972) together reveal close interpenetration of political sympathies, personal ideas and philosophical assumptions in scientific research, a phenomenon further supported by very tangible interests of class and social status. One now sees the vicissitudes of the early Royal Institution in a totally new light, knowing that the early managers and proprietors considered investment in science to be a means not only of exploiting natural resources, but also of improving rural incomes, diminishing the burden of the poor and containing the possibilities of a popular revolution which could be sparked off by invasion from France!

In America, Reingold's studies (1972 *et seq.*) have told us how the need for communication helped to forge a perceived partnership with the larger intellectual community of Europe. The histories of Associations for the Advancement of Science convey the same driving zeal to cultivate an identity for the pursuit of science, but on a basis which often reveals the provincial roots of scientific enterprise; we see this clearly in the writings of A. D. Orange for England (1971) and in the work of Sally Kohlstedt for the United States (1976). These Associations, as D. M. Knight has reminded us (1975), were important from their beginnings among the *Naturforscher* of post-Napoleonic Germany in both political and scientific terms. In the absence of a cultural center like Paris or London, German scholars needed to move more freely from place to place, stimulating discourse and creating the opportunity for ideas. The concept found a warm reception in other countries, including Britain and France, where the provinces resented metropolitan arrogance, and in countries including the United States and Sweden, where there was no single metropolitan center. It is likely that studies of both metropolitan and provincial societies will tell us much more about the processes which encourage and legitimate scientific knowledge and its social ideology. Incidentally, these studies will also tell us more about the expectations and advantages which members actually derived from science – whether in terms of shared expertise, stimulation of ideas, social advancement or professional prestige. It has not been long since the letters FRS were widely construed to mean 'Fees Raised Since' by a literate public doubtful of metaphysics and critical of intellectual pretension.

From the history of societies to the history of universities is not, in time, a narrow bridge. Although they have often had no more than a casual acquaintance with science, by the turn of the century the relationship of scientific research to institutionalized learning was, at least in Great Britain and the United States, a sealed partnership. As Loren Graham (1967) has shown, the distinction between academic institutions and universities continues in Eastern Europe to have ideological as well as scientific importance. But to Western eyes it is chiefly the university which ultimately gives the firm base line to the production of knowledge. J. B. Morrell (1974) has shown how difficult it was to build that base in Scotland, while Spitzer (1970) and Sviedrys (1970) have explored the problematic relation between support and results in research at Cambridge. Perhaps, however, it is the German university – the source of the seminar, the Ph.D., the laboratory in the form we know it – that attracts greatest interest, and here the field is still very open.

Pfetsch's statistical survey (1970) has provided a framework for asking the kinds of questions which distinguish between Turner's (1971) study of the Prussian professoriat and McCormach's (1974) and Pyenson's (1976) works on Wilhelmian physicists. Both essays invite the reader to ask how the social structure affects the cultural preference for different scientific ideas, and how particular structures affect the rate and direction of research. Implicitly, W. V. Farrar's study (1975) makes similarly important remarks on rate and direction of research. Farrar reminds us that close relations, dating from the Middle Ages, have existed between German universities and the German guild system. Both had their origins in urban life, in commerce (whether of objects or ideas); both instituted a technical language (Latin, in the universities); both required a masterpiece (for which read 'thesis'); both frequently involved a *Wanderjahr* in which an apprentice (student) would acquire the skills of different craftspersons (professors). It is plausible that the chief, but not only, assumption underlying this system was that it would produce good scholarly results. However, Farrar argues, this was not necessarily true in every case (as every university dean must know from personal experience); indeed, it follows from the guild comparison that, at least until 1850, the system of 'levelling' did not foster intellectual likeness or innovation. If this is so, what can be said about the extent of competitive scholarship in which Ben-David and Zloczower (1962) found a clue to Germany's intellectual leadership in the Nineteenth Century? (And *a fortiori* what must be said in vindication of other pluralistic systems of university organization?) Political changes within Germany after Bismarck's unification probably form part of the answer to these questions, but answers must also be sought in changes in the style of professional research, and, most significant, in the 'timeliness and promise' of research problems in different fields.

The success of Liebig and Giessen – strikingly contrasted with the failure of Thomson at Edinburgh (Morrell, 1972) – was perhaps a matter of charisma, personal leadership, access to students and controlled channels of publication. But it also owed much to the intellectual character of Liebig's science. As Farrar (1975) points out:

> chemistry had reached that interesting point in its development where only a small stock of theoretical ideas had to be mastered before embarking on fruitful, practical work. (Farrar, 1975; 185).

Given an accessible body of theory, and access to necessary techniques, the 'Giessen system' quickly became a model for other universities. It does not seem to have worked in areas governed by different philosophical conditions; or where different tactical goals were considered more important. Different sets of conditions which affect the success of laboratories (whether in universities, academies or government departments) and the criteria by which the success can be measured, are still openly problematic and await careful study. But within its context the 'Giessen system' turned German chemistry into a towering edifice.

Turning from the study of scientific institutions, one finds growing attention to the professionalization of science, and to the historical context of what Ben-David calls the 'scientific role'. In the historical literature, Mendelsohn's valuable introduction (1964) has not been replaced; but Daniels (1967) has elaborated upon it considerably; and important qualifications have been made by for example, Hufbauer's (1970) work on German chemistry and by historians working at Sussex University in England, and the École Pratique de Hautes Études en Sciences Sociales in Paris.

Indeed, the social position of the 'man of knowledge' is being revealed in far greater depth and with far greater subtlety. As Kuhn demonstrated in his critique of Ben-David (1972), it is doubtful that the idea of a unifying 'scientific role' has much explanatory power when applied earlier than the late Nineteenth Century, and it clear that professional science as such is a very recent formulation. The use of social and contextual factors which have connotations for the intellectual development of science cannot be loosely generalized. In certain cases, considerable injury to evidence can result from the overly ambitious projection of sociological judgments onto quite different periods, over three centuries (although there is a strong temptation, apparently supported by quantifiable data, to do so). It is equally injurious to assume that the idea of a special role, with its powerful normative connotations, has operated for a very long time as a unifying, organizing element in Western science. The danger of such temptations is well borne out for the Seventeenth Century in the work of Middleton (1971), and even more so in that of Debus (1965), Rattansi (1971), Yates (1972) and Webster (1975). The distinction between the Renaissance 'Magus' and the 'man of science' involves more than a change in nomenclature and a complex series of religious and political reorientations. In the Eighteenth Century, as Hahn (1975) has shown, the role of science was not at all transparent, and well into the Nineteenth Century the meaning attached to that role was not by any means universally established. One might well argue that it took three generations of scientific institution building, and possibly the 1914-1918 war, to elevate to general acceptance the idea of a scientist. Within the last century this process has owed as much, if not more, to social and economic pressures as to the definition of an internally generated intellectual code.

The contextual self-image of the scientist and the factors affecting his role have significant effects on the state of scientific research in a given period, on the problems chosen for study and, indirectly, on the cultural styles which influence the conduct and reorganization of science. As Hahn (1975) points out, it was the special institutional conditions of French intellectual life which dispersed the efforts of Frenchmen into part-time work, ultimately making it 'impossible for the French to meet the German and English challenge in the course of the Nineteenth Century'. The issue, as it affects the choice of problems, the generation of research programs and the lives of people working in these programs, is not without interest today. Is it not curious that:

> Because of the career patterns forged [in France] in the eighteenth century, the advancement of science remained a part-time activity well into our own century even for those who were trained by the most progressive educational system in the world (Hahn, 1975, 136).

It is likely that future historians of professionalization will reach far more revealing – and worrying – insights than these. In industrialized societies, where the roles and expectations of professions are closely wedded to the purpose of the state, the relations of professionalization and bureaucracy acquire special importance. It is surprising that so few historians of science have as yet pursued them.

Summarizing so far, we can say that the historical study of institutions, universities and pressures towards professionalization are increasingly thought to help explain why given problems are chosen, and why scientists choose particular ways of justifying and legitimating their claims to knowledge. But the study of professions has still far to go, and if current sociological assumptions have not given us greater understanding, they have, at least, stimulated historical concern.

At the same time, this discussion raises another more strategic question. In what direction can historians, examining both contextual and internal issues, find an easy forum for discussion? Possibly the study of individual scientific disciplines will provide a convenient focus. Certainly, it is already a highly popular domain. Ben-David's careful and provocative paper of 1960, which for many years had no rival, now finds itself a middling tree in a growing forest. There are several reasons for this. As Russell McCormmach has observed (1971), there are strong internal justifications:

> the historian of science who is disssatisfied with the traditional disjunction of his specialty – social vs. intellectual history, external vs. internal history – will find the discipline a natural unit of study for relating the scientific to the non-scientific world; the prevailing institutions and culture affect the scientist's thought and career largely through the mediation of the discipline. (McCormach, 1971; x).

There are also practical justifications, as research students today find in the study of new disciplines an almost inexhaustible supply of Ph.D. material.

Since Hagstrom's early work (1965) the idea of the scientific discipline (and the related concepts of 'specialities' and 'problem-areas') have provided convenient access to professional and conceptual norms to several sociologists (Mullins, 1972, Mulkay, 1972; Law, 1973; Bourdieu, 1976; see also Mulkay, Chapter 4); and recently, several theses on new disciplines and specialities have appeared (cf. Symes, 1975).

Some attempts are now being made to systematize what is known about disciplines, the social pressures which affect them, and their consequences on the development of new ideas, techniques and concepts (Lemaine *et al.*, 1976; Stehr, 1975; Edge and Mulkay, 1975). These attempts do provide an excellent analytical focus for specific questions concerning the effect of external factors on the rate, direction and content of science in given periods. Moreover, within the social unit of the discipline, the research program becomes a natural focus. The works of Elkana on Helmholtz (1970, 1974), of Trenn (1971), and Badash (1966) on Rutherford and Soddy, of Frankel on Fresnel and corpuscular optics (1976), and of Fisher on invariant theory (1966) are prompting a growing concensus that what is considered to be the validity of scientific knowledge, by itself, hardly accounts for the success or failure of a research program. Far more weighty are the interplays between shared knowledge and rewards. As an organizing principle, the research program, moving beyond Lakatos' original definition (1970), presents today not so much a general model of the growth of science (See Böhme, Chapter 9), as a historical network for locating particular problem shifts, metaphors, analogies and legitimations for the exploration of explanations gained and serendipity lost. As such it serves as a kind of fulcrum, in relation to both intellectual or technical problems (whether determining the relation of spectral lines or the origin of meteorites) and to the people involved in their solution. In 1859, in a letter to Principal Forbes written during Forbes' priority dispute with Tyndall concerning the explanation of glacial motion, William Whewell observed:

> You see that your discoveries have passed from the stage when people say that they are not true, to the next stage when people say that they are not new, and the truth of your theory is allowed . . . .[9]

The research program discloses the public side of science, with all the intrigue and fanfare one finds on the path to the double helix. At the same time, it incorporates the internal processes by which beliefs are transformed into knowledge.

Recently, to the armory of concepts surrounding research programs, Gerald Holton has added the notion of thematic analysis (1973); Holton has

---

[9] Quoted in George Forbes, 'Introduction to Le Chanoine Rendu', *Theory of the Glaciers of Savoy*, translated by Alfred Wills, London, Macmillan, 1874, p. 11.

set himself the task of discovering the reasons which underlie intellectual preferences for certain kinds of concepts, methods and evidence, and the factors which predispose one toward certain kinds of explanations. Holton's intention seems to be less to provide a rational system to replace the logic of discovery or the logic of justification, than to say something about what actually happens to a scientist in dealing with others. In Great Britain and Europe this approach has only begun to attract interest. (Cf. Bloor 1976). But it may become a useful source of insight if it helps historians focus upon cases where scientists 'give away' reasons, redesign experiments, change their minds, move from one puzzle to another, select certain research students and not others, reorganize their laboratories, or give particular kinds of advice to government. Questions of intellectual style and motivation are, after all, not incidental to the scientific enterprise. (Cf. Wynne, 1976).

This becomes all the more apparent when we assume a cultural perspective outside the disciplinary matrices which scientists construct or the research programs they devise. The analytical apparatus which historians focus on these structures must be located in known terrain. Largely owing to the work of Yates (1964), Rattansi (1973) and McGuire (1973), we have been forced to revise our views about the enormous importance of Hermeticism, alchemy and the iconography of naturalistic belief in the tumult of late Sixteenth Century Europe. Whether we are dealing with the Scientific Revolution or any period since, we cannot ignore what Thackray has called the cultural geography of natural knowledge. In mapping this terrain, several methods have come into use. One still highly contentious approach is that of 'proso-pography', or the study of collective biographies, usually of elites and often of particular members of institutions or societies. Drawing upon methods used in political history and following a tradition familiar to students of Braudel and the historiography of *Annales,* the two contexts which have generated the most interest to historians of science are the revolution of science in the Seventeenth Century (Merton, 1938, 1970), and the Industrial Revolution of the period 1780-1830 (cf. Mathias, 1972; Musson and Robinson, 1969; Shapin and Thackray, 1974). This is not accidental; it is clearly important to locate and define what constitutes the size and spirit of cultural entrepreneurship and intellectual ambition during periods of enor-mous intellectual economic and political transformation. By counting, sorting, stratifying and cross-referencing over time and place, one hopes to reveal stages in the cognitive development of self-selecting social groups of natural philosophers, as well as social influences on what Rudwick has called the 'thought-worlds of individual scientists'. Using the prosopographical method, historians are looking behind and within disciplines and research programs to identify the source of the amateur tradition (Kohlstedt, 1976; Morrell, 1971), the relationship among rational entertainment, polite learning and natural theology, and the collective contradictions involved in becoming, in Descartes' phrase, the 'masters and possessors of nature'. Looking at groups of men in interaction, Charles Webster has begun to clean the cobwebbed tapestry of the Baconian philosophy, revealing gilded threads which bound proposals for educational reform and intellectual revolution into visions of the *felicitas ultimi saeculi.* Looking two centuries later, Arnold Thackray's collective biographies of Manchester men have turned attention to the value-transcending, socially cohesive utility of natural science in the earthly world of industrial England.

For growing numbers of historians the study of science, not uninteresting in itself, becomes gripping when seen as a key ingredient in a deep transformation of thought, society and culture. More and more we realize that the perspectives carried from the laboratory are far from sufficient to account for the history of science itself. For example, the frequency with which the 'displacement of concepts', as Schon (1963) has put it, has been recognized – it is now generally accepted in Darwin's use of Malthus (Young, 1969) and in Scrope's use of political economy (Cf. Rudwick, 1974), to name two instances – has alerted historians to the necessity of writing social or cultural history in which science plays a central but by no means isolated role. The possibility of a cultural history of scientific knowledge is already being explored in several ways. Three approaches seem especially interesting.

First, a particular body of knowledge with immediate social dimensions can be studied to disclose its cultural assumptions. Robert Darnton has ably demonstrated this in relation to mesmerism (1968), as have Farrall (1969), MacKenzie (1976), MacKenzie and Barnes (1975), Rosenberg (1966, 1967, 1974) and Allen (1976) in relation to eugenics. That social ideologies can adopt those parts of scientific knowledge which are acceptable to the interests of a class, or a system of other social beliefs, is no longer in doubt. Precisely what importance ideology does have for the 'scientificity' of those beliefs, however, is still closely and rightly debated (See Shapin, 1975, and Cantor, 1975, on phrenology). The debate will undoubtedly continue, because the study of the cultural permeation of science by ideological interest, and of particular concepts as relayed through popular science literature and popular institutions, requires us to revise our assumptions about the traditional 'great chain of being'. In the course of studying the sociology of class and the sociology of education, scholars in Great Britain and France are discovering historical examples, too frequent to be trivial, of economic and 'scientific' assumptions which govern the uses of scientific knowledge by different social interests (Jurdant, 1971). The social historian of science cannot ignore these relationships.

There are two further approaches to the cultural history of science. The first of these requires that historians explore the social function of scientific ideas as they filter into larger social ideologies. This diffusion of ideas has been noted in the general intellectual development of Nineteenth Century America (Lurie, 1965, 1974) and in the political reverberations of German romanticism (Culotta, 1974); in the philosophical defense of national interests in Japan and Germany (Watanabe, 1964; Burchardt, 1970); in the rejection of scientific modes of thought in Seventeenth Century India (Rahman, 1973), and in the support of modernization theories in Twentieth Century China and Russia (Buck, 1975; Lewis, 1972).

A second related approach directs historians to cases where there are apparent compatibilities between dominant conceptions in political affairs and dominant themes in science. Mendelsohn (1974) has suggested that this possibility applies to the events of 1848; Weiner (1968) and Salomon-Bayet (1975) feel that political accommodations to circumstances have a direct effect on 'the life of concepts within the civil order' (Salomon-Bayet, 1975, 1039). Both of these approaches will give the social history of science itself a new character. Proponents of both approaches accept the fact that 'instrumental rationality' and 'the scientific world view' have become widely identified with the vocabulary of 'efficiency' and 'scientific management' — whether with capitalist or socialist connotations, it has made little difference. They also accept that this is not an accident, but a consequence of the legacy of Bacon and Descartes.

Such redefinitions as these are already having enormous effect on the way in which we see science, and what we regard as problematic about its development. The area of debate has moved rapidly from history to sociology and political science. But this progress has left several important conceptual issues quite unresolved. Over the last five years, as the foregoing sketch has illustrated, the social history of science has exhibited a remarkable vigor. Recently, it is especially remarkable that social historians are beginning to inform their work with an increasing concern for philosophical rigor We have reached a stage where it is considered wise to combine cautious historical generalizations with a careful revision of traditional philosophical assumptions. This is undoubtedly a sign of healthy development. Unfortunately, we have not yet come very far toward reshaping our vision of what, a generation ago, Derek de Solla Price (1961) hinted might become a new humanities of science. It is likely that in the normal course of events considerable time will pass before, in many graduate departments of the history of science, the human reconstruction of science will form an acceptable focus for the historian's craft. For this delay there are several reasons; and among these, several bear upon our understanding of what questions we can legitimately regard as internal or external to science. To move the discussion forward, we need to establish a consensus on several matters of definition, and on questions of fundamental epistemological importance. To some of these questions, and their consequences, we will now turn.

EPISTEMOLOGICAL OBSTACLES AND EXTERNALIST GOALS

As the preceding summary has suggested, what is particularly interesting, historiographically, about much of this new work over the last five years is its increasingly evident refusal to fall into any neat classification of internal or external. Nonetheless, the internalist/externalist dichotomy, however sterile it may be, is not yet abandoned. On the contrary, in view of the frequency with which historians mention it, reports of its death, to paraphrase Mark Twain, seem widely exaggerated.

That scientific knowledge has a social role is widely accepted; at the same time, there seems to be no lack of debate on the changing relationship between this acceptance and the actual work of historians of science (see Basalla, 1975). There cannot but be debate, one reflects, as long as the *Isis* 'Critical Bibliography' devotes a separate category to 'Science and Its History from Special Points of View', and thus demarcates four 'externalist' from the remaining thirty five 'internalist' sections which make up the bibliography. There is equally debate (now admittedly, more often apparent than real) implicit in the titles of several new university departments which in the last five years have styled themselves in terms of the 'History and Sociology of Science', the 'History and Social Aspects of Science', or the 'History, Philosophy and Social Relations of Science'. God, having never countenanced the division of nature into departments, is now asked to contemplate the natural history of knowledge fragmented into rival camps. Even these rival camps are themselves, divided. If there is a vigorous methodological plurality among internalists (Agassi, 1963; Geoffrey Price, 1976), there is an even greater lack of conceptual unanimity among 'externalists'.

Some historians would define externalism in Marxist terms, admitting several levels and possibilities of interpretation; others would give it simply institutional or administrative connotations. It is not clear that conceptual unanimity needs to be the first goal of a new historiography, or that, if it existed, it would satisfy the doubts of skeptics. It is clear, however, and perhaps worrying, that in an important sense the historical perspective outlined above is not widely understood as constituting a totality, and, as such, a valuable departure. This uncertainty underlies the reasonable fear that the enterprise may draw perilously near to 'territory somewhere between history, which it tends to ignore, and bad, or at least dull, sociology', a territory inhabited by people who generate 'dreamy, unimaginative defenses of the *status quo* in government, science and society' (Basalla, 1975).

There is, admittedly, no consensus of opinion on the definition of externalism in the history of science. Bearing in mind the different studies surveyed earlier in this chapter, we may outline a preliminary definition in three dimensions, according to 1) methods of research, 2) domains of research and 3) categories of questions. Following this preliminary definition, it may be useful to dwell briefly upon the problems they expose.

The *research methods* of the externalist historian are those of social, economic, political and cultural historians. Their choice of evidence, their choice of periods and problems, their use of archives, reflect a particular interest in the contextual developments which had had a bearing on science or on our present conception of it. The *domains* which externalist historians occupy can vary considerably, and few among them would welcome the restrictive title which 'externalist' implies. However, as we have seen, they have concentrated most of their recent work in the following areas:

1) The history of scientific institutions, including the development of teaching and research within scientific societies, professional associations, clubs, academies, institutions, laboratories, etc., and the relationship between these departments and the administrative, political or personal objectives of governments and elites. This does not exclude, of course, the relevance of technical reason, or of a scientific *Weltbild,* to the assumptions underlying such developments. However, this form of history may not be concerned with scientific ideas, particularly or at all, but rather with the factors impelling innovation in bureaucracies or in social systems generally (cf. Orange, 1971; Paul, 1971; Mulkay, 1972).

2) The history of the consequences of scientific activity, including the outcome of scientific endeavor in terms of specific technologies, treatments, legislation and public policies (cf. Manning, 1967; Mathias, 1972).

3) The cultural history of science and scientific ideas, including the relationship between science and other belief systems (Horton and Finnegan, 1973), the context of scientific beliefs (Bell, 1975) and values within larger political and intellectual developments (Yates, 1972; Wright, 1975; Weiner, 1968), and the contribution of scientific ideas to scientific world views (Turner, 1974; Wilson, 1974).

The *categories of questions* which can be termed externalist also cover a considerable range. Again, there is no agreed agenda. However, we may assume that most questions which interest social historians relate to sets of influences upon the rate, direction and, perhaps, the content of scientific activity.[10] Some of these questions concern external intellectual factors and their transmission in the development of scientific ideas, as in cases where concepts and techniques generated by practical work are conveyed to those involved in fundamental research. Thus, practical knowledge of plant breeding was steadily incorporated into biological research on the dynamics of heredity. Similarly, the solution of industrial problems, as in the history of steam technology, became of major importance to the study of heat, energy and thermodynamics. (Cardwell, 1971).

---

[10] The arguement of this section owes much to continuing discussion with my colleagues in Project PAREX and is developed in detail in our collective volume (Lemaine *et al,* 1976).

Other questions concern the effects of different institutional contexts on scientific development. It is apparent that the history of universities, new departments or key personalities is relevant to the development of, for example, atomic physics (Gowing, 1974), genetics, (Rosenberg, 1967), psychology (Ben-David, 1960), and physiology (Zloczower, 1966, Geison, 1972). Social historians have not yet agreed upon precisely what these effects have been and what generalizations can be drawn from them, but leading lines of historical research are now clearly drawn.

Third, there are questions which concern the effects, both direct and indirect, of political or economic factors on scientific development. Thus, historians have long considered particular imperatives to be of special import-ance in the promotion of certain specific fields (such as the development of genetics as a by-product of the American government's policy toward agri-culture; or the development of bacteriology as a response to Pasteur's work with the brewing and silk industries). In this domain connections are often most easily established in the medical and biological sciences, where social and economic demands become associated with scientific efforts to meet those demands and with subsequent generation of research programs (as in such fields as entomology, ecology, parasitology and immunology).

Fourth, there are questions which concern the effects of wider, more diffuse social influences on scientific development. Here, economic historians continue to debate the consequences for science arising from political move-ments (Forman, 1973), of demographic change, and the imperatives of imperialism and profit seeking (Berman, 1972). This domain offers much scope, and, predictably proves the area of greatest contention. In this area are, perhaps, the greatest number of unresolved questions and the most pressing need for conceptual clarity.

In this brief outline, proponents of externalist history use specific research methods, move within specific domains and ask questions broadly concerning the influence on the rate, direction and content of research; they have an intelligible set of goals. But it is easier to outline the task than it is to pursue the problems it raises, as externalist historians and even their critics have discovered. Compounded partly of method and definition and partly of explanation, these difficulties are fundamentally philosophical. Although few historians have attempted to articulate these difficulties, and fewer still to pose solutions for them, at one level, they involve a question which is easily put, and, at least superficially, widely discussed: How does one measure the *rate,* define the *direction* and specify the *content* of science? The question of *rate* — the speed with which new knowledge grows within a field — has become a special study in its own right, with elaborate analytical devices of quantitative measurement (Derek Price, 1963). *Direction* implies that know-ledge proceeds along specifiable paths, affecting and being affected by the rate at which it was prompted or resisted. Merton's earliest work formulated the questions implied by associating social influences with rate and direction;

these questions have been fundamental to subsequent work on rewards, stratification and mobility in science and to work on creativity and innovation. While historians have varied widely in the emphasis they give to different definitions, they leave no doubt that the rate and direction of scientific development are in fact influenced by contextual and intellectual factors which operate in a complex interaction.

It has been by no means clear, however, that social or contextual factors can influence the content of science. On this point the greatest difficulty emerges, and here the battle lines have been drawn (See Ben-David, 1970). Paul Forman (1971), in defining the task of the externalist historian, has put the proposition forcefully:

> ... the historian cannot rest content with vague and equivocal expressions like 'prepared the intellectual climate for' or 'prepared, so to speak, the philosophical background for', but must insist upon a *causal* analysis (my italics), showing the circumstances under which, and the interactions through which, scientific men are swept up by intellectual currents. (Forman, 1971, 3).

To date, few historians would claim to have demonstrated unequivocally the causal influence of social factors of the kind described above on the intellectual currents and conceptual contents of science as they are traditionally understood. Indeed, using traditional definitions it is unlikely that clear-cut proofs are possible either way. In suggesting a pragmatic 'agnosticism', King (1971) attempted to get round the philosophical barrier thus posed. Put in its simplest terms, the question of causal influence, if not unanswerable, is at least generally unresponsive to investigation; in any case, it could be argued, much can be discovered about the social dimensions of science without establishing a strong and necessary relationship between context and content.

Within the last three years, however, there have been calls to end this moratorium. In order to do so, historians will have to redefine the vocabulary of the debate, and in particular to redefine what we mean by the content of science, in relation to a wider epistemological and sociological framework (Bloor, 1973, 1976). In this process, what we take to comprise the content of science — its methods and formulae, concepts and conventions, laws and theories, analogies and metaphors — becomes an expression of the views of people involved at different times in the pursuit of knowledge about the natural world. This process of re-definition has suggested a new line of attack upon the central problem of the sociology of knowledge. In turn, this has opened to historians a valuable, moderate route of inquiry which leads somewhere between total commitment to the logical necessity of scientific development, and total abandonment to historical relativism.

However, this path will not be an easy one. The sociology of scientific knowledge is to all accounts made easier if, by science, we can mean that changing set of institutional and instrumental activities which helps the scientist: 1) elaborate or codify by experiment or observation the conceptual 'language' we use to explain anomalies or regularities in nature; 2) devise new forms of instrumentation or techniques of assessment to interpose between ourselves and nature; and 3) generate the particular skills, through education and research, which are necessary to the pursuit of natural knowledge. But to demonstrate the efficacy of this definition, to prove whether it actually tells us something about the pursuit of natural knowledge, we must translate this philosophical position, and its sociological redefinition, into historical time. We must be able to show that, at many different levels, scientific activity can be influenced by contextual factors operating through and upon the scientific investigator. At several levels social historians are reasonably agreed upon the plausibility of this. It is, for example, unconvincing to explain the genesis of the Linnaean system of classification without describing, first of all, the social, economic and intellectual pressures which naturalists throughout Europe felt to classify and explain plant and animal life, and, second, the community of scholars within Europe — and more specifically, within Sweden — which contributed to or resisted that system. The fact that the historian must dwell on the ideas, qualifications and constraints of living people compels his attention to social realities. But, given these realities, what follows? He must find historical evidence to support the contention that redefining scientific activity sociologically can have important positive consequences for its explanation, historically. If we accept that we cannot assume the nature of science to be a fixed, Platonic ideal, then it already follows that what is internal or external to a given form of scientific activity also depends on the definition given by the historical 'actors' involved (Barnes, 1974).

Barnes (1974) has recently and intriguingly proposed that we envisage scientific investigators as working within a moving time frame, one which changes relative to both the self-image of science and its conceptual content. In an attempt to dislodge the philosophical debate from its encrusted moorings, he has defined four elements which operate within science:

1) Elements peculiar to the subculture of the particular actors employed in scientific activity in given historical contexts.

2) Elements essential to that subculture, and defined by it.

3) General elements accepted by the subculture but not part of it.

4) Elements explicitly not part of this given subculture (that is to say, those peculiar to other subcultures).

To be consistent, these distinctions are themselves variable both in time and in place. But it is clearly the third category which allows discussion about boundaries between internal and contextual factors. The boundaries will be defined differently at different times by different cultures in different institutional and conceptual settings. Barnes cites three different studies, in descending order of 'boundary definition', to support his case: that of Paul Forman on causality and Weimar physics in the 1920's (1971); that of R. M. Young on Darwin's uniformitarianism in the 1850's (1972); and that of Alexandre

Koyré on the mathematization of nature in the Seventeenth Century (1956, 1961). In each case, what counts as external to science depends entirely on what boundaries were seen to exist, at the time, and by the 'actors' themselves, between the contents of science and its cultural context.

The definition of boundaries, their permeability, and the limitations of external influences at a given time, can be guided by the study of institutions which make explicit at least some assumptions about motivation and intent. It follows that if one takes the self-approved mandate of the early Royal Society to guard its Fellows from the 'contrary imaginations' of civil war (See Webster, 1975), one needs to know as much about the social and political context which required that kind of declaration, as about the consequences, if any, of the 'exclusion principle' actually applied. In this way ideas, shaped by context, are seen to suit purposes; questions arising from either similar or different subcultures provoke and influence the generation of scientific concepts. The shared values and normative goals of a given time can, with time, fade from view as explicit ideas which are part of the common culture, and become part of the received wisdom of the scientific field. In this event, external factors become internalized.

This approach does not, of course, wholly dispose of the epistemological barrier to strong externalist explanations. Indeed, it reinforces the idea that there is something quintessentially 'internal' about science which still requires explanation. However, it does two other things. First, it provides a powerful deterrent to the 'backwards extrapolation' of routine modern concepts, whether cognitive (as implied in our use of the word 'science') or analytical (as implied by the phrase 'scientific role').[11] More important, it provides a way to avoid the necessity of a simple internal/external dichotomy. There may well be matters of content which are remote from external influence, but these are matters for discovery and discussion, not for assertion; they are work for the historian, who rejects the anachronistic use of contemporary standards in judging what belongs within science and what does not. From now on, historical judgments about the content of science, hence about the effect of external factors on that content, must take into account different definitions of that content.

It follows that we cannot usefully dispute the causal influence of external factors on the content of science, nor can we make claims that broad changes have affected the course of science in any simple, direct or uniform fashion, precisely because the content of science itself is changing. We must consider the *modus operandi* involved in the pursuit and exposition of natural knowledge, clearly allowing, as we do so, for many possible external factors (whether immediate or diffuse) which have come to inform and redefine its internal development (whether pedagogical, psychological or technical). By asking prior questions about the historical values and meanings of science, we

---

[11] See Kuhn on Ben-David, 1972.

defer the causal imperative of Forman's self-denying ordinance, and possibly diminish its relevance. More immediately, we avoid a 'vulgar Marxism' by making no claim for the economic determination of scientific development; we replace a static base/superstructure analogy with a highly heuristic set of possible mediations.

This discussion, interpreting and amplifying Barnes' views, (see Barnes, 1977) does not solve all the epistemological problems of externalist history. Far from it. But it does offer an escape from the more obvious dangers of historical and epistemological relativism because it makes no claim for the complete social reconstruction of reality, or for complete cultural variation in standards of knowledge. (Cf. Bloor, 1976). At the same time, it avoids an over-simplifying idealism because it implies that the proposition 'science is universalistic' is itself problematic. It also avoids what Lakatos has called 'historiographical positivism' because it insists on relational contexts, and disposes of easy generalizations about scientific progress or the caliber of 'the rise of modern science'. The discussion is not closed, but opened; 'Whig' interpretations are made redundant; scientific hagiography is put at a discount; and the social historiography of science is given, at least, a working philosophical basis.

Looking to the future, it is not unlikely to suppose that the social historiography of science will become philosophically more reflexive, because it will become sociologically self-conscious. The use of evidence and interpretations will be governed by two limiting conditions. First, as Kohlstedt (1976) has concisely put it, we must accept that the reasons why historians are interested in science will affect what they say about science, the periods they choose to examine, and the view of science they take. Second, we must recognize that interpretations of scientific development which are founded upon categories of uniquely validated knowledge, free from causal relations other than those imposed by logic, will not be refuted merely by argument. Our understanding of science will reflect our own presuppositions, and many questions will remain a matter of belief and of ideology. The potential danger of this approach – of being left totally without bearings, lost in a relativistic sea – is one which need not immediately materialize. For the present, over-arching theories of historical explanation are suspect; at the same time, there is enormous scope for what Merton has modestly called 'second-order generalizations'. We practice today within a perspective of modest approximations and working hypotheses.

The social history of science will require a new set of conventions and shared meanings, partly sociological, partly institutional and partly cognitive. We must not, however, suspend philosophical judgments on these conventions, because to do so will lead merely to the construction of sociological categories which ignore or distort historical perspectives. The social historiography of science is founded, above all, upon the relations between thought and action, and focused upon the reasons why people believe as they do, the ways they present and use their beliefs, and the consequences of these beliefs for that which becomes accepted as knowledge. Quite conceivably, the historian's concern for factors which affect the rate, the direction and the content of scientific development will be enriched by prosopography and the study of individual disciplines, specialities and institutions; it will be informed by the grammar of anthropology, linguistics and critical sociology. For the historian, the analytical limitations of conventionalism in philosophy, of functionalism in sociology, and of institutional archetypes in political science, have now become abundantly clear (Geoffrey Price, 1976; Sheppard and Johnston, 1975). He needs a new vocabulary with a much more finely structured set of analytical distinctions, and a new theory of mediations. As the foregoing outline has suggested, there is no lack of volunteers willing to attempt the tasks involved.

The resolution or redefinition of epistemological relations, using sociological insights in historical time, will almost certainly continue to be the hallmark of important new work in the social history of science. But, for working historians, it is tedious to let discussion degenerate into a list of desiderata. Indeed, as Martin Rudwick (1975) has put it, 'theoretical discussions in this area tend to float rather free from concrete examples'. There is clearly a case for moving back to primary sources, to the historical fabric, to the study of specific scientific ideals, techniques and instruments. Within the texture of a new social history of science, conventional questions may be recast in a perspective which focuses not upon the explication of science, but upon the structures and mentalities of a given period; on the relations of knowledge and tradition, of institutional structures, theories of patronage, endowment, aristocracy, bureaucracy, industrialization, social space and class mobility, demographic change, and military and economic imperialism.

Recent discussions (Basalla, 1975) suggest that social historians of science must attempt to define a social historiography of science which will be more than an appendage to the conceptualist approaches of the past. If there is any consensus in the field, it is in support of the proposition that historians must work with philosophers and sociologists to fashion an enterprise which sees historical differences between knowledge and belief as problematic questions of conjectural and contextual emphasis, rather than as *a priori* demarcations (Allen, 1976; Lemaine *et al*, 1976), and which has as its purpose the explanation of 'changes in intellectual aim, social purpose and institutional structure of natural knowledge within defined temporal and geographic limits' (Thackray, 1970). A synthesis of approaches seems to be widely favored (Allen, 1976).

There are historians, however, of very different persuasions who argue otherwise. Hall (1963) could envisage no synthesis, only demarcation. Lakatosians may never convert to a research program in which human reconstruction holds a status equivalent to logical reconstruction. Mikulinski (1975) believes that a synthesis between internalism and externalism would be as inadmissable as a compromise between vitalism and mechanism. Indeed, Mikulinski resolves the problem by proposing, not unexpectedly, a Marxist analysis, a third theory, by which public needs (as evident in the material conditions of social life) define a problem which is caught and formulated by science and transformed into an internal problem.

However, these difficulties seem today to be more semantic than real. It would not be easy in 1976, to defend a distinction, as Hall attempted to do in 1963, between our understanding of the scientific movement and our understanding of science as a system of knowledge of nature (Hall, 1963, 13). Even Mikulinski's dichotomy is ultimately resolvable into a question of mediation. It is in the structure of thinking that he sees an intermediate link between socio-economic conditions and the research programs of science — whether these be in classificatory Eighteenth Century systems designed to make sense of new botanical discoveries, or in principles of natural selection designed to bring order to the empirical experience of animal breeding. Since at least the Seventeenth Century, science has been and continues to be a complex series of socially organized attempts to define and solve problems concerning the operations of nature. The organization of that inquiry, the definition of its aims and the legitimacy of its achievements rest upon negotiated conventions which are culturally ambiguous, resistant to oversimplification, and to varying degrees accessible to sensitive study. The study of these conventions and their mediation is perhaps the chief objective of the social history of science today.

Does this make historical understanding irrelevant to those changing constellations of questions within the universe of science policy? The answer is partly yes and partly no. We might argue that the enormous growth of scholarship in the history of science over the last fifty years gives us a guide to the conduct of science in the future. In considering science, as in studying economics, we can no longer agree with Marshall that 'explanation is prediction written backwards'. We cannot assume that scientific activity today is simply the result of two hundred and fifty years of progressive development. We cannot assume that the contexts of discovery and justification have always been the same, and we cannot expect confidently to apply lessons from historical experience. In historical terms, we know too little of revolutions in political affairs to predict their occurrence, or to prejudge their consequences. Similarly, it is no exaggeration to say that we know too little about the effects of different influences on science during different periods to trust the applied use of our analytical conventions.

Nonetheless, just as our historical experience can and does enrich our perception of the present, so our knowledge of similarities and differences, continuities and discontinuities, in the scientific effort should deepen our resistance to accepting sweeping generalizations about the role of science policies, and to making facile assumptions about the nature and consequences of scientific research. The social historian can introduce a degree of realism into public affairs which sets the functions of science in perspective.

The history of science, as Dixon Long has observed, 'seems to provide an ambivalent framework for the examination of science policy making' (1971). In a sense, this is as it should be. At a time when science policies are in search of new directions; when the external verities of the independent scientific tradition seem to be in disrepair; and when the purposes of higher learning require vigorous public defense, the different uses of historical argument become visibly relevant. Governments and economic interests may believe that policies designed to affect the conduct and usefulness of scientific activity may not require historical criticism or justification. But such policies presuppose that convincing answers have been found to a much more fundamental question – whether the goals which are set by science policies and mediated by political and economic processes are serving the larger public interest. On that question, history and historians will have much to say.

BIBLIOGRAPHY

Agassi, 1963   Agassi, J., 'Towards an Historiography of Science',
                          History and Theory 2, 1963.
Agassi, 1975   Agassi, J., 'Science in Flux', in Cohen, R. S. and
                          Wartofsky, M. W. (Eds.), *Boston Studies in the Philo-
                          sophy of Science,* Dordrecht, D. Reidel, 1975.
Allen, 1976   Allen, G., 'Genetics, Eugenics and Society: Internalists
                          and Externalists in Contemporary History of Science',
                          Social Studies of Science 6, No. 1, 1976, pp. 105-122.
Artz, 1966   Artz, F. B., *The Development of Technical Education
                          in France, 1500-1850,* Cambridge, MIT Press, 1966.
Bachelard, 1934   Bachelard, G., *Le Nouvel esprit scientifique,* Paris,
                          Félix Alcan, 1934.
Bachelard, 1949   Bachelard, G., *Le Rationalisme appliqué,* Paris, 1949.
Badash, 1966   Badash, L., 'How the "Newer" Alchemy was Re-
                          ceived', *Scientific American, 215,* 1966, No. 2.
Barber, 1952   Barber, B., *Science and the Social Order,* New York,
                          Macmillan, 1952.
Barber, 1968   Barber, B., 'The Sociology of Science', *International
                          Encyclopedia of Social Sciences,* 1968, pp. 92-99.
Barber and Hirsch, 1962   Barber, B. and Hirsch, W. (Eds.), *The Sociology of
                          Science,* New York, The Free Press, 1962.
Barnes, 1972   Barnes, B., 'Sociological Explanation and Natural
                          Science: A Kuhnian Reappraisal', *Arch. Europ. Sociol.*
                          XIII, 1972, pp. 373-391.
Barnes, 1974   Barnes, B., *Scientific Knowledge and Sociological
                          Theory,* London, Routledge and Kegan Paul, 1974.
Barnes, 1977   Barnes, B., *Knowledge and Social Interests,* London,
                          Routledge, 1977.

Basalla, 1963	Basalla, G., *Science and Government in England, 1800-1870*, unpublished Ph.D. thesis, Harvard University, 1963.
Basalla, 1967	Basalla, G., 'The Spread of Western Science', *Science* 156, 1967, pp. 611-622.
Basalla, 1968	Basalla, G. (Ed.), *The Rise of Modern Science: Internal or External Factors?* Lexington, Mass., D. C. Heath, 1968.
Basalla, 1975	Basalla, G., 'Observations on the Present Status of History of Science in the United States', *Isis* 66, 1975, pp. 467-470.
Bell, 1975	Bell, C., 'Beliefs, Knowledge and Science', *Futures* 7, August 1975, pp. 341-347.
Ben-David, 1960	Ben-David, J., 'Scientific Productivity and Academic Organization in Nineteenth Century Medicine', *Amer. Soc. Rev.* 25, 1960, pp. 828-843.
Ben-David, 1970	Ben-David, J., 'Introduction to "Sociology of Science" ', *International Social Science Journal* XXII, 1970, pp. 7-27.
Ben-David, 1971	Ben-David, J., *The Scientist's Role in Society*, Englewood Cliffs, New Jersey, Prentice-Hall, 1971.
Ben-David and Zloczower, 1963	Ben-David, J. and Zloczower, A., 'Universities and Academic Systems in Modern Societies', *Eur. J. Sociol.* 3, 1963, pp. 45-84.
Berman, 1971	Berman, M., *Social Change and Scientific Organization: The Royal Institution 1799-1810*, unpublished Ph.D. dissertation, Johns Hopkins University, 1971.
Berman, 1972	Berman, M., 'The Early Years of the Royal Institution 1749-1810: A Re-Evaluation', *Science Studies* 2, No. 3, 1972, pp. 205-240.
Berman, 1975	Berman, M., 'Hegemony and the Amateur Tradition in British Science', *J. Social History*, Winter 1975, pp. 30-50.
Bernal, 1939	Bernal, J. D., *The Social Function of Science*, London, Routledge and Kegan Paul, 1939.
Bernal, 1953	Bernal, J. D., *Science and Industry in the Nineteenth Century*, London, Routledge and Kegan Paul, 1953.
Bernal, 1954	Bernal, J. D., *Science in History*, London, C. A. Watts, 1954.
Bloor, 1971	Bloor, D., 'Two Paradigms for Scientific Knowledge?' *Science Studies* 1, 1971, pp. 101-115.
Bloor, 1973	Bloor, D., 'Wittgenstein and Mannheim on the Sociology of Mathematics', *Stud. Hist. Phil. Sci.* 4, 1973, pp. 173-191.
Bloor, 1976	Bloor, D., *Knowledge and Social Imagery*, London, Routledge, 1976.
Bourdieu, 1976	Bourdieu, P., 'The Specificity of the Scientific Field and the Social Conditions of the Progress of Reason', *Social Science Information* 14, No. 6, 1976, pp. 19-47.
Brush, 1974	Brush, S. G., 'Should the History of Science Be Rated X?' *Science* 183, 22 March, 1974, pp. 1164-1172.
Buchdahl, 1965	Buchdahl, G., 'A Revolution in Historiography of

	Science', *History of Science* 4, 1965, pp. 55-69.
Buck, 1975	Buck, P., 'Order and Control: The Scientific Method in China and the United States', *Social Studies of Science* 5, No. 3, 1975, pp. 237-269.
Burchardt, 1970	Burchardt, L., 'Wissenschaftspolitik und Reform-diskussion im Wilhelminischen Deutschland', *Konstanzer Blatter für Hochschulfragen* 8, 1970, pp. 71-84.
Canguilhem, 1968a	Canguilhem, G., *Etudes d'histoire et de philosophie des sciences*, Paris, 1968.
Canguilhem, 1968b	Canguilhem, G., 'L'Object de l'histoire des sciences', in *Etudes d'histoire et de philosophie des sciences*, Paris, 1968.
Cantor, 1975a	Cantor, G. N., 'Phrenology in Early Nineteenth Century Edinburgh: An Historiographical Discussion', *Annals of Science* 32, 1975, pp. 195-208.
Cantor, 1975b	Cantor, G. N., 'A Critique of Shapin's Social Interpretation of the Edinburgh Phrenology Debate', *Annals of Science* 33, 1975, pp. 245-256.
Cardwell, 1957	Cardwell, D. S. L., *The Organization of Science in England*, London, Heinemann, reprinted, 1972.
Cardwell, 1971	Cardwell, D. S. L., *From Watt to Clausius*, London, Heinemann, 1971.
Christie, 1975	Christie, J. R. R., 'The Rise and Fall of Scottish Science', in Crosland, M. (Ed.), *The Emergence of Science in Western Europe*, London, Macmillan, 1975.
Clagett, 1962	Clagett, M. (Ed.), *Critical Problems in the History of Science*, Madison, University of Wisconsin Press, 1962.
Clark, 1949	Clark, G. N., *Science and Social Welfare in the Age of Newton*, Oxford, Oxford University Press, 1949.
Cohen, 1948	Cohen, I. B., *Science, Servant of Man*, Boston, Little Brown and Co., 1948.
Cohen, 1952	Cohen, I. B., 'Orthodoxy and Scientific Progress', *Proc. Amer. Phil. Soc.* 96, 1952, pp. 505-512.
Cohen, 1956	Cohen, I. B., *Franklin and Newton*, Philadelphia, American Philosophical Society, 1956.
Cohen, 1961	Cohen, R. S., 'Alternative Interpretations of the History of Science', in Frank, P. G. (Ed.), *The Validation of Scientific Theories*, New York, Collier Books, 1961.
Cole and Cole, 1973	Cole, J. and Cole, S., *Social Stratification in Science*, Chicago, University of Chicago Press, 1973.
Cowan, 1972	Cowan, R. S., 'Francis Galton's Statistical Ideas: The Influence of Eugenics', *Isis* 63, 1972, pp. 509-528.
Crane, 1972	Crane, D., *Invisible Colleges: Diffusion of Scientific Knowledge in Scientific Communities*, Chicago, University of Chicago Press, 1972.
Crombie, 1963	Crombie, A. C. (Ed.), *Scientific Change*, London, Heinemann, 1963.
Crosland, 1967	Crosland, M., *The Society of Arcueil: A View of French Science at the Time of Napoleon I*, London, Heinemann, 1967.
Crosland, 1975	Crosland, M. (Ed.), *The Emergence of Science in*

	Western Europe, London, Macmillan, 1975.
Crowther, 1941	Crowther, J. G., *The Social Relations of Science*, London, Macmillan, 1941.
Crowther, 1974	Crowther, J. G., *The Cavendish Laboratory, 1874-1974*, London, Macmillan, 1974.
Culotta, 1974	Culotta, C. A., 'German Biophysics, Objective Knowledge and Romanticism', in McCormach, R. (Ed.), *Historical Studies in the Physical Sciences* 4, 1974, pp. 3-18.
Daniels, 1967	Daniels, G., 'The Progress of Professionalization in American Science: The Emergent Period, 1840-1860', *Isis* 58, 1967, pp. 151-160.
Daniels, 1972	Daniels, G. H. (Ed.), *Nineteenth Century American Science: A Reappraisal*, Evanston, Illinois, Northwestern University Press, 1972.
Darnton, 1968	Darnton, R., *Mesmerism and the End of Enlightenment in France*, Cambridge, Harvard University Press, 1968.
Debus, 1965	Debus, A. G., *The English Paracelsians*, London, Oldbourne, 1965.
Edge and Mulkay, 1975	Edge, D., and Mulkay, M., 'Case Studies of Scientific Specialties', in Stehr, Nico (Ed.), *Wissenschaftssoziologie – Studien und Materialen*, Opladen, Westdeutscher Verlag, 1975.
Elias, 1971	Elias, N., 'Sociology of Knowledge: New Perspectives', *Sociology* 5, No. 2, 1971, pp. 194, 368.
Elkana, 1970	Elkana, Y., 'Helmholtz' "Kraft": An Illustration of Concepts in Flux', *Hist. Stud. in the Phys. Sciences* 2, 1970, pp. 263-298.
Elkana, 1974	Elkana, Y., 'Boltzmann's Scientific Research Programme and its Alternatives', in Elkana, Y. (Ed.), *The Interaction between Science and Philosophy*, Atlantic Highlands, New Jersey, Humanities Press, 1974.
Farley and Geison, 1974	Farley, J. and Geison, G., 'Science, Politics and Spontaneous Generation in Nineteenth Century France: The Pasteur-Pouchet Debate', *Bull. Hist. Med.* 48, 1974, pp. 161-198.
Farrall, 1969	Farrall, L. A., *Origins and Growth of the English Eugenics Movement, 1865-1975* (Unpublished doctoral dissertation, Indiana University, 1969).
Farrall, 1975	Farrall, L., 'Controversy and Conflict in Science: A Case Study in the English Biometric School and Mendel's Laws', *Social Studies of Science* 5, No. 3, 1975, pp. 269-302.
Farrar, 1975	Farrar, W. V., 'Science and the German University System, 1790-1850', in Crosland, M. (Ed.), *The Emergence of Science in Western Europe*, London, MacMillan, 1975.
Fellows, 1961	Fellows, E. W., 'Social and Cultural Influences in the Development of Science', *Synthèse* 13, No. 2, 1961, pp. 154-172.
Feuer, 1971	Feuer, L. S., 'The Social Roots of Einstein's Theory of Relativity', *Annals of Science* 27, 1971, pp. 277-298, 313-344.

Feuer, 1974   Feuer, L. S., *Einstein and the Generations of Science*,
                       New York, Basic Books, 1974.
Fisher, 1966   Fisher, C. G., 'The Death of a Mathematical Theory: A
                       Study in the Sociology of Knowledge', *Arch. Hist. of
                       Exact Sciences* 3, 1966, pp. 137-159.
Fisher, 1968   Fisher, C. G., 'The Last Invariant Theorists: A Social
                       Study of the Collective Biographies of Mathematical
                       Specialists', *Europ. J. Sociol.* 8, 1968, pp. 216-244.
Fleming, 1950   Fleming, D., *John William Draper and the Religion of
                       Science*, Philadelphia, University of Pennsylvania,
                       1950.
Fleming, 1964   Fleming, D., 'Science in Austrialia, Canada, and the
                       United States: Some Comparative Remarks', *Proc. Xth
                       International Congress of the History of Science* 1,
                       Ithaca, 1964, pp. 179-196.
Fleming, 1968   Fleming, D., 'Emigré Physicists and the Biological Re-
                       volution', *Perspectives in American History* 2, 1968,
                       pp. 152-189.
Forman, 1968   Forman, P., 'The Doublet Riddle and Atomic Physics
                       circa 1924', *Isis* 59, 1968, pp. 156-174.
Forman, 1971   Forman, P., 'Weimar Culture, Causality and Quantum
                       Theory, 1918-1927', in McCormmach R. (Ed.),
                       Historical Studies in the Physical Sciences Vol. 3,
                       Philadelphia, University of Pennsylvania Press, 1971,
                       pp. 1-115.
Forman, in press   Forman, P., 'The Helmholtz-Gesellschaft: Support of
                       Academic Physical Research by German Industry after
                       the First World War', in press.
Forman, 1973   Forman, P., 'Scientific Internationalism and the Wei-
                       mar Physicists: The Ideology and Its Manipulation in
                       Germany after World War I', *Isis* 64, 1973, pp.
                       151-180.
Forman, 1974   Forman, P., 'The Financial Support and Political
                       Alignment of Physicists in Weimar Germany', *Minerva*
                       XII, 1974, pp. 39-66.
Forman *et al.*, 1975 Forman, P., 'Physics circa 1900: Personnel, Funding
                       and Productivity of the Academic Establishment', in
                       McCormach, R. (Ed.), *Historical Studies in the
                       Physical Sciences* 5, 1975.
Fox, 1973   Fox, R., 'Scientific Enterprise and the Patronage of
                       Research in France, 1800-1870', *Minerva* 11, 1973,
                       pp. 442-473.
Fox, 1974   Fox, R., 'The Rise and Fall of Laplacian Physics', in
                       McCormach, R. (Ed.), *Historical Studies in the
                       Physical Sciences* 4, 1974, pp. 89-136.
Frankel, 1976   Frankel, E., 'Corpuscular Optics and the Wave Theory
                       of Light: The Science and Politics of a Revolution in
                       Physics', *Social Studies of Science* 6, 1976, in press.
Gaston, 1973   Gaston, J., *Originality and Competition in Science: A
                       Study of the British High Energy Physics Community*,
                       Chicago, University of Chicago Press, 1973.
Geison, 1970   Geison, G. L., *Sir Michael Foster and the Rise of the
                       Cambridge School of Physiology, 1870-1900*, un-

published Ph.D. dissertation, Yale University, 1970.

Gillispie, 1959 — Gillispie, C. C., 'Science in the French Revolution', *Behavioral Science* 4, No. 1, 1959, pp. 67-101; reprinted in Barber, B. and Hirsch, W. (Eds.), *The Sociology of Science*, The Free Press of Glencoe, 1962, pp. 89-97.

Gizycki, 1973 — Gizycki, R. von., 'Centre and Periphery in the International and Scientific Community: Germany, France and Great Britain in the Nineteenth Century', *Minerva* 11, 1973, pp. 474-494.

Gowing, 1964 — Gowing, M., *Britain and Atomic Energy, 1939-1945*, London, 1964.

Gowing, 1975 — Gowing, M., 'What's Science to History, or History to Science?' Inaugural Lecture, University of Oxford, 22 May 1975 (Oxford, Clarendon Press, 1975).

Graham, 1967 — Graham, L., *The Soviet Academy of Science and the Communist Party, 1927-1932*, Princeton, Princeton University Press, 1967.

Graham, 1975 — Graham, L., 'The Formation of Soviet Research Institutes: A Combination of Revolutionary Innovation and International Borrowing', *Social Studies of Science* 5, 1975, pp. 303-330.

Guerlac, 1961 — Guerlac, H., *Lavoisier – The Crucial Year*, London, Oxford University Press, 1961.

Hagstrom, 1965 — Hagstrom, W. O., *The Scientific Community*, New York, Basic Books, 1965.

Hahn, 1971 — Hahn, R., *The Anatomy of a Scientific Institution: The Paris Academy of Sciences, 1666-1903*, Berkeley, University of California Press, 1971.

Hahn, 1975 — Hahn, R., 'Scientific Careers in Eighteenth-Century France', in M. Crosland (Ed.), *The Emergence of Science in Western Europe*, London, Macmillan, 1975, 127-138.

Haines, 1969 — Haines, G., *Essays on German Influence upon English Education and Science, 1850-1919*, Connecticut College Monograph No. 9, Newlands, Connecticut College, 1969.

Hall, 1962 — Hall, A. R., 'The Scholar and the Craftsman in the Scientific Revolution', in Clagett, M. (Ed.), *Critical Problems in the History of Science*, Madison, University of Wisconsin, 1962, pp. 3-23.

Hall, 1963 — Hall, A. R., 'Merton Revisited', *History of Science* 2, 1963, pp. 1-16.

Hall, 1969 — Hall, A. R., 'Can the History of Science Be History?' *British J. Hist. Sci.* 4, 1969, pp. 207-220.

Heilbron, 1974 — Heilbron, J. L., *H. G. J. Moseley. The Life and Letters of an English Physicist, 1887-1915*, Berkeley, University of California, 1974.

Hesse, 1963 — Hesse, M., *Models and Analogies in Science*, London, Sheed and Ward, 1963.

Hesse, 1970 — Hesse, M., 'Hermeticism and Historiography: An Apology for the Internal History of Science', in Stuewer, R. H. (Ed.), *Historical and Philosophical Perspectives of Science*, Minneapolis, University of Minnesota Press, 1970.

Hesse, 1973

Hesse, M., 'Reasons and Evaluations in the History of Science', in Teich, M. and Young, R. M. (Eds.), *Changing Perspectives in the History of Science*, London, Heinemann, 1973.

Hesse, 1971

Hesse, M., *Forces and Fields*, London, Nelson, 1971.

Hessen, 1971

Hessen, B., 'The Social and Economic Roots of Newton's *Principia*', in Bukharin, N. *et al.*, *Science at the Crossroads*, London, Kniga, 1931 reprinted by Cass, 1971.

Hill, 1965

Hill, C., *Intellectual Origins of the English Revolution*, Oxford, Clarendon Press, 1965.

Hillinger, 1973

Hillinger, D. A. 'T. S. Kuhn's Theory of Science and Its Implications for History', *American Historical Review* 78, No. 2, 1973, pp. 370-393.

Holton, 1973a

Holton, G., 'The Thematic Component in Scientific Thought: Origins of Relativity Theory and Other Essays', *The Graduate Journal* IX, supplement, 1973.

Holton, 1973b

Holton, G., *Thematic Origins of Scientific Thought: Kepler to Einstein*, Cambridge, Harvard University Press, 1973.

Holton, 1974a

Holton, G., 'Striking Gold in Science: Fermi's Group and the Recapture of Italy's Place in Physics', *Minerva* XII, 1974, pp. 159-198.

Holton, 1974b

Holton, G., 'Finding Favour with the Angel of the Lord: Notes Towards the Psychobiographical Study of Scientific Genius', in Elkana, Y. (Ed.), *The Interaction between Science and Philosophy*, Atlantic Highlands, New Jersey, Humanities Press, 1974.

Holton, 1975

Holton, G., 'On the Role of Themata in Scientific Thought', *Science* 188, 25 April 1975, pp. 328-338.

Horton, 1967

Horton, R., 'African Traditional Thought and Western Science', *Africa* 37, 1967, pp. 50-71, 155-187; reprinted in Marwick, M. (Ed.), *Witchcraft and Sorcery*, Harmondsworth, Penguin Books, 1970.

Horton and Finnegan, 1973

Horton, R. and Finnegan, R., *Modes of Thought*, London, Faber, 1973.

Hufbauer, 1970

Hufbauer, K., *The Formation of the German Chemical Community*, unpublished Ph.D. dissertation, University of California, Berkeley, 1970.

Hufbauer, 1971

Hufbauer, K., 'Social Support for Chemistry in Germany during the Eighteenth Century: How and Why Did It Change?' in McCormach, R., *Historical Studies in the Physical Sciences* 3, 1971, pp. 205-232.

Hunter, 1966

Hunter, D. A., 'The History of American Science – A Field Finds Itself', *Amer. Hist. Rev.* LXXI, 1966, pp. 863-874.

Jacob and Lockwood, 1972

Jacob, M. C. and Lockwood, W. A., 'Political Millenarianism and Burnet's *Sacred Theory*', *Science Studies* 2, No. 3, 1972, pp. 265-280.

Jurdant, 1973

Jurdant, B., *Les Problèmes théoriques de la vulgarisation scientifique*, thèse de doctorat de troisième cycle,

Université Louis Pasteur, Strasbourg, 1973.

Kargon, 1966 — Kargon, R. H., *Atomism in England from Heriot to Newton*, London, Oxford University Press, 1966.

Kargon, 1974 — Kargon, R. H. (Ed.), *The Maturing of American Science*, Washington, American Association for the Advancement of Science, 1974.

Kearney, 1971 — Kearney, H., *Science and Change 1500-1700*, London, Weidenfeld and Nicolson, 1971.

Kevles, 1971 — Kevles, D., 'Into Hostile Political Camps: The Reorganization of International Science in World War I', *Isis* 62, 1971, pp. 47-60.

King, 1971 — King, M. O., 'Reason, Tradition and the Progressiveness of Science', *History and Theory* 10, 1971, pp. 3-32.

Knight, 1975 — Knight, D. M., 'German Science in the Romantic Period', in Crosland, M. (Ed.), *The Emergence of Science in Western Europe*, London, Macmillan, 1975, pp. 161-178.

Knorr *et al.*, 1976 — Knorr, K. D., *Determinants and Controls of Scientific Disciplines*, Dordrecht, Reidel, 1976.

Kohlstedt, 1976 — Kohlstedt, S. G., 'The Nineteenth Century Amateur Tradition: The Case of the Boston Society of Natural History', in Holton, G. and Blanpied, W. A. (Eds.), *Science and Its Public: The Changing Relationship*, and in Cohen, R. S. and Wartofsky, M. W. (Eds.), *Boston Studies in the Philosophy of Science* XXXIII, Dordrecht, D. Reidel, 1976.

Koyré, 1939 — Koyré, A., *Etudes Galiléennes*, Paris, Hermann, 1939.

Koyré, 1956 — Koyré, A., 'The Origins of Modern Science: A New Interpretation', *Diogenes*, No. 16, 1956.

Koyré, 1961 — Koyré, A., 'Influence of Philosophical Trends on the Formulation of Scientific Theories', in Frank, P. G. (Ed.), *The Validation of Scientific Theories*, New York, Collier Books, 1961.

Koyré, 1965 — Koyré, A., *Newtonian Studies*, Cambridge, Harvard University Press, 1965.

Kuhn, 1961 — Kuhn, T. S., 'The Function of Dogma in Scientific Research', in Crombie, A. C. (Ed.), *Scientific Change*, London, Heinemann, 1961, pp. 347-369.

Kuhn, 1962 — Kuhn, T. S., *The Structure of Scientific Revolutions*, Chicago, University of Chicago Press, 1962.

Kuhn, 1968 — Kuhn, T. S., 'The History of Science', *International Encyclopedia of the Social Sciences* 14, 1968, pp. 74-83.

Kuhn, 1971 — Kuhn, T. S., 'The Relations between History and the History of Science', *Daedalus* 100, 1971, pp. 271-304.

Kuhn, 1972 — Kuhn, T. S., 'Scientific Growth: Reflections on Ben-David's "Scientific Role"', *Minerva* 10, 1972, pp. 166-178.

Kuhn, 1975 — Kuhn, T. S., 'Tradition mathémathique et tradition expérimentale dans le développement de la physique', *Annales* 30, 1975, pp. 975-998.

Lakatos, 1970 — Lakatos, I., 'Falsification and the Methodology of

Scientific Research Programmes', in Lakatos, I. and Musgrave, A. (Eds.), *Criticism and the Growth of Knowledge,* Cambridge, Cambridge University Press, 1970.

Lakatos, 1973   Lakatos, I., 'History of Science and its Rational Reconstructions', in Buck, R. C. and Cohen, R. S. (Eds.), *Boston Studies in the Philosophy of Science,* Vol. 3, Dordrecht, D. Reidel, 1973, pp. 91-136.

Lakatos, 1974   Lakatos, E., 'History of Science and its Rational Reconstructions', in Elkana, Y. (Ed.), *The Interaction between Science and Philosophy,* Atlantic Highlands, New Jersey, Humanities Press, 1974.

Law, 1973   Law, J., 'The Development of Specialties in Science: The Case of X-Ray Protein Crystallography', *Science Studies* 3, No. 3, 1973, pp. 275-304.

Lemaine, *et al.,* 1976   Lemaine, G. *et al., Perspectives in the Study of Scientific Disciplines,* The Hague, Mouton, 1976.

Lenzen, 1959   Lenzen, V. P., 'Science and Social Context', in *Civilization,* Berkeley, 23, 1943, 3-26.

Levere, forthcoming   Levere, T., *Coleridge and the Scientific Imagination,* forthcoming.

Lewis, 1972   Lewis, R. A., 'Some Aspects of Research and Development Effort of the Soviet Union, 1924-35', *Science Studies* 2, No. 2, 1972, pp. 153-180.

Lilley, 1949   Lilley, S., 'Social Aspects of the History of Science', *Archives internationales d'histoire des sciences* II, No. 6, 1949, pp. 376-443.

Lilley, 1953   Lilley, S., 'Cause and Effect in the History of Science', *Centaurus* III, Nos. 1 and 2, 1953, pp. 58-72.

Long, 1971   Long, D., 'The Government of Science: A Comparative Approach', *Science Studies,* I, 1971, 263-286.

Luke, 1972   Luke, E., 'The History of Science in America: Development and New Directions', in Daniels, G. (Ed.), *Nineteenth Century American Science,* Evanston, Northwestern University Press, 1972, pp. 3-21.

Lukes, 1973   Lukes, S., 'On the Social Determination of Truth', in Horton, R. and Finnegan, R. (Eds.), *Modes of Thought,* London, Faber, 1973.

Lukes, 1974   Lukes, S., 'Relativism: Cognitive and Moral', *Proc. Artist. Soc.* XLVII, 1974, pp. 165-189.

Lurie, 1965   Lurie, E., 'Science in American Thought', *J. World History* VIII, No. 4, 1965, pp. 638-665.

Lurie, 1974   Lurie, E., *Nature and the American Mind: Louis Agassiz and the Culture of Science,* New York, Science History Publications, 1974.

MacKenzie and Barnes, 1975   MacKenzie, D. A. and Barnes, S. B., 'Biometrician *versus* Mendelian: A Controversy and Its Explanation', in Stehr, N. (Ed.), *Wissenschaftssoziologie – Studien und Materialen,* Opladen, Westdeutscher Verlag, 1975.

MacKenzie, 1976   MacKenzie, D. A., 'Eugenics in Britain', *Social Studies of Science,* 6, 1976, pp. 499-532.

Manning, 1967   Manning, T. G., *Government in Science: The U.S. Geological Survey, 1867-1894,* University of Kentucky Press, 1967.

Martins, 1972   Martins, H., 'The Kuhnian "Revolution" and its Implications for Sociology', in Nossiter, T. S. *et al, Imagination and Precision in the Social Sciences: Essays in Memory of Peter Nettl*, London, Faber and Faber, 1972.

Mathias, 1972   Mathias, P. (Ed.), *Science and Society 1600-1900*, Cambridge, Cambridge University Press, 1972.

McCormmach, 1971   McCormmach, R. (Ed.), 'Foreword' to *Historical Studies in the Physical Sciences*, 3, 1971, ix-xxiv.

McCormmach, 1974   McCormmach, R., 'On Academic Scientists in Wilhelmian Germany', *Daedalus* 103, 1974, pp. 157-172.

McGuire, 1973   McGuire, J. E., 'Newton and the Demonic Furies: Some Current Problems and Approaches in History of Science', *History of Science* XI, 1973, pp. 21-48.

McMullen, 1970   McMullen, E., 'The History and Philosophy of Science: A Taxonomy', in Stuewer, R. H. (Ed.), *Historical and Philosophical Perspectives of Science*, Minneapolis, University of Minnesota Press, 1970.

Meadows, 1974   Meadows, A. J., *Communication in Science*, London, Butterworth, 1974.

Mendelsohn, 1964   Mendelsohn, E., 'The Emergence of Science as a Profession in Nineteenth Century Europe', in Hill, K. (Ed.), *The Management of Scientists*, Boston, Beacon Press, 1964.

Mendelsohn, 1974   Mendelsohn, E., 'Revolution and Reduction: The Sociology of Methodological and Philosophical Concerns in Nineteenth Century Biology', in Elkana Y. (Ed.), *The Interaction between Science and Philosophy*, Atlantic Highlands, New Jersey, Humanities Press, 1974.

Merton, 1938   Merton, R. K., 'Science, Technology and Society In Seventeenth Century England', *Osiris* IV, No. 2, 1938; reprinted with new introduction, New York, Harper and Row, 1970.

Merton, 1975   Merton, R. K., 'Thematic Analysis in Science: Notes on Holton's Concept', *Science* 188, 25 April 1975.

Merz, 1904-1912   Merz, J. T., *A History of European Thought in the Nineteenth Century*, London, William Blackwood, 1904-1912 (4 Vols.).

Middleton, 1971   Middleton, W. E. K., *The Experimenters: A Study of the Accademia del Cimento*, Baltimore, Johns Hopkins Press, 1971.

Mikulinsky, 1975   Mikulinsky, S. R., 'The Methodological Problems of the History of Science', *Scientia* 110, 1975, pp. 83-97.

Miller, 1970   Miller, H. S., *Dollars for Research: Science and Its Patrons in Nineteenth Century America*, Seattle, University of Washington Press, 1970.

Morrell, 1969   Morrell, J. B., 'Thomas Thomson: Professor of Chemistry and University Reformer', *Brit. J. Hist. Sci.* 4, 1969, pp. 245-265.

Morrell, 1971   Morrell, J. B., 'Individualism and the Structure of British Science in 1830', in McCormach, R. (Ed.), *Historical Studies in the Physical Sciences* 3, 1971, pp. 183-204.

Morrell, 1972	Morrell, J. B., 'The Chemist Breeders: The Research Schools of Liebig and Thomas Thomson', *Ambix* XIX, 1972, pp. 1-46.
Morrell, 1974	Morrell, J. B., 'Reflections on the History of Scottish Science', *History of Science* XII, 1974, pp. 81-94.
Moyal, 1976	Moyal, A. M., *Scientists in Nineteenth Century Australia: A Documentary History,* Melbourne, Australia, Cassell, 1976.
Mulkay, 1972	Mulkay, M., *The Social Process of Innovation,* London, Macmillan, 1972.
Mullins, 1972	Mullins, M. C., 'A Model for the Development of a Scientific Specialty: The Phage Group and the Origins of Molecular Biology', *Minerva* 10, 1972, pp. 51-82.
Musson and Robinson, 1969	Musson, A. E. and Robinson, E., *Science and Technology in the Industrial Revolution,* Manchester, Manchester University Press, 1969.
Nakayama *et al.*, 1974	Nakayama, S. *et al., Science and Society in Modern Japan,* Tokyo, University of Tokyo Press, 1974.
Nandy, 1972	Nandy, A., 'Defiance and Conformity in Science: The Identity of Jagadis Chandra Bose', *Scientific Studies* 2, No. 1, 1972, pp. 31-86.
Needham, 1954	Needham, J., *Science and Civilization in China,* Vol. III, Cambridge, Cambridge University Press, 1954.
Needham, 1956	Needham, J., 'Mathematics and Science in China and the West', *Science and Society* 20, 1956, pp. 320-343; reprinted in Barnes, B. (Ed.), *Sociology of Science,* Harmondsworth, Penguin, 1972.
Nef, 1952	Nef, J. U., 'The Genesis of Industrialism and of Modern Science, 1540-1640' in Downs, N. (Ed.), *Essays in Honour of Conyers Read,* Chicago, Chicago University Press, 1952.
Olby, 1974	Olby, R., *The Path to the Double Helix,* London, Macmillan, 1974.
Olson, 1975	Olson, R., *Scottish Philosophy and British Physics, 1750-1880: A Study in the Foundations of the Victorian Scientific Style,* Princeton, Princeton University Press, 1975.
Ornstein, 1938	Ornstein, M., *The Role of Scientific Societies in the Seventeenth Century,* Chicago, 1938.
Orange, 1971	Orange, A. D., 'The British Association for the Advancement of Science: The Provincial Background', *Science Studies* I, Nos. 3 and 4, 1971, pp. 315-330.
Paul, 1971	Paul, H. W., 'Science and the Catholic Institutes in Nineteenth Century France', *Societies* 1, No. 4, 1971, pp. 271-282.
Paul, 1972	Paul, H. W., *The Sorcerer's Apprentice: The French Scientist's Image of German Science, 1840-1919,* University of Florida Social Sciences Monograph 44, 1972.
Paul, 1974	Paul, H., 'La science française de la seconde partie du XIXe siècle vue par les auteurs anglais et américains', *Rev. d'Hist. des Sciences* XXVII, No. 2, 1974, pp. 147-163.

Pfetsch, 1970 — Pfetsch, F., 'Scientific Organization and Science Policy in Imperial Germany, 1871-1914: The Foundations of the Imperial Institute of Physics and Technology', *Minerva*, 8, 1970, pp. 557-580.

Pfetsch, 1971 — Pfetsch, F., 'Determinaten des Wachstums wissenschaftlichen Organisationen in Deutschland', *Kölner Zeitschrift für Soziologie und Sozial-Psychologie* 23, 1971, pp. 704-726.

Pfetsch, 1974 — Pfetsch, F., *Zur Entwicklung der Wissenschaftspolitik in Deutschland,* Berlin, Duncker und Humblot, 1974.

Phillips, 1974 — Phillips, D. L., 'Epistemology and the Sociology of Knowledge: The Contributions of Mannheim, Mills and Merton', *Theory and Society* 1, 1974, pp. 59-88.

Polanyi, 1958 — Polanyi, M., *Personal Knowledge,* London, Routledge and Kegan Paul, 1958.

Popper, 1970 — Popper, K., 'Reason or Revolution?' *Arch. Europ. Soc.* XI, 1970, pp. 252-262.

Derek Price, 1961 — Price, Derek de Solla, *Science since Babylon,* New Haven, Yale University Press, 1961.

Derek Price, 1963 — Price, Derek de Solla, *Little Science, Big Science,* New York, Columbia University Press, 1963.

Derek Price, 1965 — Price, Derek de Solla, 'Is Technology Historically Independent of Science? A Study in Statistical Historiography', *Technology and Culture* 6, 1965, pp. 553-568.

Derek Price, 1975 — Price, Derek de Solla, 'Comment on the Observations, by George Basalla, on the Present Status of History of Science in the United States', *Isis* 66, 1975, pp. 470-472.

Geoffrey Price, 1976 — Price, Geoffrey, *The Politics of Planning and the Problems of Science Policy,* Leeds, SISCON, 1976.

Pyenson and Skopp, 1976 — Pyenson, L. and Skopp, D., 'Educating Physicists in Germany *circa* 1900', unpublished manuscript, 1976.

Rahman, 1973 — Rahman, A., 'Sixteenth and Seventeenth Century Science and India and Some Problems of Comparative Studies', in Teich, M. and Young, R. M., *Changing Perspectives in the History of Science,* London, Heinemann, 1973.

Rattansi, 1963 — Rattansi, P. M., 'Paracelsus and the Puritan Tradition', *Ambix,* XI (1963), 24-32.

Rattansi, 1971 — Rattansi, P. M., 'Science and the Glory of God', *New York Review of Books,* 6 May 1971, pp. 34-35.

Rattansi, 1973 — Rattansi, P. M., 'Some Evaluations of Reason in Sixteenth and Seventeenth Century Natural Philosophy', in Teich, M. and Young, R. M. (Eds.), *Changing Perspectives in the History of Science,* London, Heinemann, 1973.

Ravetz, 1971 — Ravetz, J., *Scientific Knowledge and Its Social Problems,* London, Oxford University Press, 1971.

Redondi, 1975 — Redondi, P., 'Introductory Notes on Epistemology and the History of Science in France, *Scientia* 110, 1975, pp. 171-196.

Reingold, 1972a — Reingold, N., 'American Indifference to Basic Research: A Reappraisal', in Daniels, G. (Ed.), *Nineteenth Century American Science: A Reappraisal*, Evanston, Illinois, Northwestern University Press, 1972, pp. 36-62.

Reingold, 1972b   Reingold, N., *The Papers of Joseph Henry*, Washington, The Smithsonian Institution, Vol. 1: 1972, Vol. 2: 1975.

Roberts, 1973   Roberts, G. K., *The Royal College of Chemistry (1845-1853): A Social History of Chemistry in Early Victorian England*, unpublished Ph.D. dissertation, Johns Hopkins University, 1973.

Roller, 1971   Roller, D. H. D. (Ed.), *Perspectives in the History of Science and Technology*, Norman, University of Oklahoma Press, 1971.

Rosenberg, 1966   Rosenberg, C., 'Science and American Social Thought', in van Tassel, D. and Hall, M. G. (Eds.), *Science and Society in the United States*, New York, Dorsey, 1966.

Rosenberg, 1967   Rosenberg, C., 'Factors in the Development of Genetics in the United States', *J. Hist. Med.* XXII, 1967, pp. 27-46.

Rosenberg, 1974   Rosenberg, C., 'Science and Social Values in 19th Century America: A Case Study in the Growth of Scientific Institutions', in Thackray, A. and Mendelsohn, E. (Eds.), *Science and Values*, New York, Humanities Press, 1974.

Rudwick, 1963   Rudwick, M. J. S., 'The Foundations of the Geological Society of London: Its Scheme for Cooperative Research and Its Struggle for Independence', *Brit. J. Hist. Sci.* I, 1963, pp. 325-355.

Rudwick, 1974   Rudwick, M. J. S., 'Poullett Scrope on the Volcanoes of Auvergne: Lyellian Time and Political Economy', *Brit. J. Hist. Science*, 7, 1974, 205-242.

Rudwick, 1975   Rudwick, M. J. S., 'The History of the Natural Sciences as Cultural History', Inaugural Lecture, Free University, Amsterdam, 1975.

Salomon, 1970   Salomon, J.-J., 'Histoire de la science et politique de la science', *Organon* 7, 1970, pp. 51-60.

Salomon, 1974   Salomon, J.-J., *Science and Politics*, London, Macmillan, 1974.

Salomon-Bayet, 1975   Salomon-Bayet, C., 'L'Institution de la science', *Annales* 30, 1975, pp. 1028-1044.

Sanderson, 1972   Sanderson, M., *The Universities and British Industry 1850-1970*, London, Routledge and Kegan Paul, 1972.

Schofield, 1963   Schofield, R. E., *The Lunar Society of Birmingham*, Oxford, The Clarendon Press, 1963.

Schon, 1963   Schon, D., *Displacement of Concepts*, London, Tavistock.

Schroeder-Gudehus, 1966a   Schroeder-Gudehus, B., *Deutsche Wissenschaft und Internationale Zusammenarbeit, 1914-1928*, Geneva, Dumaret and Golay, 1966.

Schroeder-Gudehus, 1966b   Schroeder-Gudehus, B., 'Charactéristiques des relations scientifiques internationales, 1870-1914', *J.*

	World History 10, 1966, pp. 161-177.
Schroeder-Gudehus, 1973	Schroeder-Gudehus, B., 'Challenge to Transnational Loyalties: International Scientific Organizations after the First World War', *Science Studies* 3, No. 2, 1973, pp. 93-118.
Shapin, 1971	Shapin, S., *The Royal Society of Edinburgh: A Study of the Social Context of Hanoverian Science*, unpublished Ph.D. dissertation, University of Pennsylvania, 1971.
Shapin, 1972	Shapin, S., 'The Pottery Philosophical Society 1819-35: An Examination of the Cultural Uses of Provincial Science', *Science Studies* 2, No. 4, 1972, pp. 311-336.
Shapin, 1975	Shapin, S., 'Phrenological Knowledge and the Social Structure of Early Nineteenth Century Edinburgh', *Annals of Science* 32, 1975, pp. 219-243.
Shapin and Barnes, 1977	Shapin, S. and Barnes, B., 'Science, Nature and Control: Interpreting Mechanics Institutes', *Social Studies of Science* 7, 1977, pp. 31-74.
Shapin and Thackray, 1974	Shapin, S. and Thackray, A., 'Prosopography as a Research Tool in the History of Science: The British Scientific Community, 1700-1900', *History of Science* XII, 1974, pp. 1-28.
Sheppard and Johnston, 1975	Sheppard, J. and Johnston, R., *Science and Rationality*, Leeds, SISCON, 1975.
Shils, 1973	Shils, E., 'The Academic Calling in Imperial Germany', *Minerva*, 1973, pp. 571-632.
Spitzer, 1970	Spitzer, P. G., *Joseph John Thomson: An Unfinished Social and Intellectual Biography*, unpublished Ph.D. dissertation, Johns Hopkins University, 1970.
Stehr, 1975	Stehr, N. (Ed.), *Wissenschaftssoziologie – Studien und Materialen*, Opladen, Westdeutscher Verlag, 1975.
Stimson, 1948	Stimson, D., *Scientists and Amateurs*, New York, Henry Schuman, 1948.
Storer, 1966	Storer, N., *The Social System of Science*, New York, Holt, Rinehart and Winston, 1966.
Sviedrys, 1970	Sviedrys, R., 'The Rise of Physical Sciences at Victorian Cambridge,' in R. McCormmach (Ed.), *Historical Studies in the Physical Sciences*, 2, Princeton University Press, 1970.
Symes, 1975	Symes, J. M. D., 'Instruments Progress and Policy in Science: The Cases of IR and N MR Spectroscopy in Chemistry', unpublished M.Phil. thesis, University of Sussex, 1975.
Thackray, 1970	Thackray, A., Review of Basalla (Ed.), *The Rise of Modern Science: Internal or External Factors*, *Isis*, 61, 1970, 398.
Thackray, 1970a	Thackray, A., 'Science and Technology in the Industrial Revolution', *History of Science* 9, 1970, pp. 76-89.
Thackray, 1970b	Thackray, A., 'Science: Has Its Present Past – A Future?' in Stuewer, R. H. (Ed.), *Historical and Philosophical Perspectives of Science*, Minneapolis, 1970, pp. 112-127.

Thackray, 1974a   Thackray, A., 'Natural Knowledge in Cultural Con-
                         text: The Manchester Model', *Amer. Hist. Rev.*
                         IXXIX, 1974, pp. 672-709.

Thackray, 1974b   Thackray, A., 'The Industrial Revolution and the
                         Image of Science', in Thackray, A. and Mendelsohn, E.
                         (Eds.), *Science and Values*, New York, Humanities
                         Press, 1974.

Toulmin, 1971   Toulmin, S., 'Rediscovering History', *Encounter,*
                         January 1971, pp. 53-64.

Toulmin, 1972   Toulmin, S., *Human Understanding*, Vol. 1, Oxford,
                         Clarendon Press, 1972.

Trenn, 1971   Trenn, T., 'Rutherford and Soddy: From a Search for
                         Radioactive Constituents to the Disintegration Theory
                         of Radioactivity', *Rete* I, 1971, pp. 51-70.

Turner, 1974   Turner, F. M., *Between Science and Religion: The
                         Reaction to Scientific Naturalism in Late Victorian
                         England*, New Haven, Yale University Press, 1974.

Turner, 1971   Turner, R. S., 'The Growth of Professorial Research in
                         Prussia, 1818-1848 — Causes and Context', in
                         McCormmach, R. (Ed.), *Historical Studies in the
                         Physical Sciences* 3, 1971, pp. 137-182.

Watanabe, 1964   Watanabe, M., 'The Early Influence of American
                         Science on Japan', *Actes du congrès international
                         d'histoire des sciences X,* 1962, pp. 197-208.

Webster, 1974   Webster, C. (Ed.), *The Intellectual Revolution of the
                         Seventeenth Century*, London, Routledge and Kegan
                         Paul, 1974.

Webster, 1975   Webster, C., *The Great Instauration: Science, Medicine
                         and Reform, 1626-1660,* London, Duckworth, 1975.

Weiner, 1968   Weiner, C., 'A New Site for the Seminar: The Refugees
                         and American Physics in the Thirties', *Perspectives in
                         American History* II, 1968, pp. 190-234.

Weiner, 1968   Weiner, D. P., *Raspail: Scientist and Reformer*, New
                         York, Columbia University Press, 1968.

Weiner and Noland, 1957 Weiner, P. and Noland, A. (Ed.), *The Roots of Scienti-
                         fic Thought,* New York, Basic Books, 1957.

Werskey, 1971   Weiner, P. G., 'British Scientists and "Outsider" Poli-
                         tics, 1931-1945', *Science Studies* 1, No. 1, 1971, pp
                         67-84.

Werskey, 1975   Werskey, P. G., 'Making Socialists of Scientists: Whose
                         Side is History On?' *Radical Science Journal* 2/3
                         1975, pp. 13-50.

Wilson, 1974   Wilson, D., 'Kelvin's Scientific Realism: The Theo
                         logical Context', *The Philosophical Journal* (trans. R
                         Philos. Soc. Glasgow), 11, No. 2, 1974, pp. 41-60.

Wright, 1975   Wright, P., 'Astrology and Science in Seventeenth
                         Century England', *Social Studies of Science,* 5, No. 4
                         1975, pp. 399-422.

Wynne, 1976   Wynne, B., 'C. G. Barkla and the J. Phenomenon: A
                         Case Study in the Treatment of Deviance in Physics'
                         Social Studies of Science, 6, 1976, pp. 307-347.

Yates, 1964   Yates, F., *Giordano Bruno and the Hermetic Tradi
                         tion,* London, Routledge and Kegan Paul, 1964, 1971

Yates, 1972   Yates, F., *The Rosicrucian Enlightenment,* London, Routledge and Kegan Paul, 1972.

Young, 1969   Young, R. M., 'Malthus and the Evolutionists', *Past and Present,* 43, 1969, 109-45.

Young, 1971   Young, R. M., 'Evolutionary Biology and Ideology – Then and Now', *Science Studies* 1, No. 2, 1971, pp. 177-206; reprinted in Fuller, W. (Ed.), *The Social Impact of Modern Biology,* London, Routledge and Kegan Paul, 1971.

Young, 1972   Young, R. M., 'The Historiographic and Ideological Contexts of the Nineteenth Century Debate on Man's Place in Nature', in Teich, M. and Young R. M. (Eds.), *Changing Perspectives in the History of Science,* London, Heinemann, 1972.

Zilsel, 1942   Zilsel, E., 'The Sociological Roots of Science', *Amer. J. Sociology* XLVII, No. 4, 1941-42, pp. 544-562.

Zloczower, 1966   Zloczower, A., *Career Opportunities and the Growth of Scientific Discovery in Nineteenth Century Germany,* Jerusalem, Hebrew University, 1966.

Chapter 6

CONDITIONS OF TECHNOLOGICAL DEVELOPMENT

E. Layton

University of Minnesota

INTRODUCTION: SCIENCE POLICY AND TECHNOLOGY

Technology is a fundamental component of science policy. Technological and economic development are not, of course, the only goals of science policy, but they are certainly among the foremost. In this connection we may define three areas of concern: the rate of economic growth, its direction, and its qualitative social effects. Technological development is the most important source of growth in per capita income, and all nations are interested in increasing their standard of living. But growth has a direction. Science policy is one of the means by which nations link scientific and technological activities to national goals. These are not all economic. Specific policies may increase food production, advance national defense, improve a nation's position in foreign trade, or contribute to public health. Inevitably this involves priorities; certain economic, technological and scientific sectors will be emphasized and not others. Policy formulation is complicated by the fact that programs influence one another. Military expenditures will influence the civilian economy, for example. Scientific and technological activities also influence the quality of life. Environmental pollution and social dislocation are among the less happy consequences of technological activities, and they have become of increasing concern to all nations in recent years.

Though the need for understanding how technology works is clear, our present knowledge is far from satisfactory. The entire field of technological studies is characterized by divergent research traditions, with only minimal contacts with each other. Scholars from the fields of economics, sociology, anthropology, psychology, history and policy studies are in radical disagreement with each other on basic assumptions and methodology. Thus, it is difficult to compare the results obtained within one discipline with those from another. At present no discipline is more than tangentially committed to the study of technology. All too often the results involve attempts to see technology as something else, frequently as a special case of economics or of science. What is needed is an understanding of technology from inside, both as a body of knowledge and as a social system. Instead, technology is often treated as a 'black box' whose contents and behavior may be assumed to be common knowledge.

Another source of bias, one which the present study cannot claim to have avoided, is related to the fact that most of the studies of technological development have been done in the United States. There is no *a priori* reason to assume that the American model in technology or science is universal. A critical need of the entire field, therefore, is interdisciplinary and international synthesis.

Definitions of terms   Nothing better indicates the underdeveloped state of technological studies than the basic disagreements over such fundamental terms as invention, innovation and diffusion. It will be useful to characterize each and to note a few of the differences.

1. Invention may mean any particular stage in the process of technological development, from the first idea to the final product, or it can be applied to the entire process. In this study we will use it to mean that stage of development at which an idea has been developed sufficiently to draw up plans, construct a working model, or in some fashion establish technical feasibility; this is the stage at which inventions are normally patentable (this is the definition used by Freeman in Chapter 7).

2. Innovation consists of carrying the process from invention to practical use, usually involving an extended period of development, additional research, and production and tooling problems. In economic literature the emphasis is upon innovation as an economic act, the marketing of a product. This is a necessary assumption if innovation is to be assimilated within an economic theory based upon the market system. But it is too restrictive, since many important technological innovations are not marketed in the usual sense, as is the case, for example, with the work of non-profit organizations (for Freeman, Chapter 7, innovation is simply the introduction of a new technique). There are two basic types of innovation, product innovations and process innovations. The first, as the name suggests, involves new products. The second represents changes in the method of production.

3. Diffusion involves the spread of an innovation among potential users. Diffusion is treated differently by different disciplines. Anthropologists and sociologists are concerned with the earliest stage in technological development: that is, with the general ideas which initiate the process (Rogers, 1962;

Barnett, 1953). They are concerned with diffusion as a social process. Economists are interested in the final stage of technological development, innovation. They see diffusion as an economic process (Mansfield, 1968a, 1968b).

Technology and technique Another source of confusion lies in the ambiguous use of the term 'technology'. Originally, technology meant systematic knowledge of the industrial arts. This knowledge was then implemented by means of techniques. In modern usage, particularly in English, this distinction has become blurred. Technology is often taken to comprise both the knowledge and the means of its utilization (but see Freeman, Chapter 7). In this chapter, 'technology' will be used mostly in its original and narrower sense, as knowledge.

MEASUREMENT OF THE GROWTH OF TECHNOLOGY AND TECHNIQUE

There are, unfortunately, no direct ways of measuring the growth of technology and technique. And while a number of indices have been developed, almost all are subject to debate; and cross-comparisons of data generated by one method with those generated by another are dubious and difficult. The best data are probably the statistical compilations of the deployment of personnel and money in science and technology which are produced by governments and international agencies. But even here, there are difficulties in comparing materials from different countries and agencies (Freeman and Young, 1965).

Production functions Perhaps the largest literature on technical development has been produced by economists. For the more advanced countries, there are reasonably good statistical series for basic economic variables, such as employment, output and the like. From these it is possible to construct indices to productivity and economic growth in a fairly straightforward manner (Kendrick, 1961; Domar *et al.*, 1964).

Robert Solow in 1957 showed how one might separate the influence of technology from that of capital, labor and other inputs in order to construct an aggregate production function for the entire economy over time (Solow, 1957 and 1959). To do this he had to introduce a number of simplifying assumptions about the behavior of the economy. On this basis Solow found that over eighty seven per cent of the increased per capita consumption in the United States between 1909 and 1949 was due to technical change, and only a little over twelve per cent was due to capital investment. A number of other models have been devised by Solow and others, and the economists are still debating their value and validity (Brown, 1966; Gold, 1973a and 1973b).

Aggregate production functions provide, at best, a rather crude index of technical growth. Quite apart from their economic limitations, the thing measured — 'technical change' — is a residual category. It comprises all growth not directly attributed to capital and labor inputs. Thus, it lumps technology with techniques and nontechnical factors. But aggregate production functions do provide policy makers with useful, if imperfect, information about the total economic benefits derived from technical change, as well as a measure of the growth of techniques that is independent of short-run market fluctuations.

Patent statistics   The analysis of patent statistics is another of the crude but useful tools developed by economists. As with the aggregate production function, the methodological difficulties are enormous. Jacob Schmookler has shown how patents may be used to give comparisons of the rate of patenting in a given industrial area and short-range fluctuations in market conditions (Schmookler, 1966). He was able to show clear correlations between the number of patents and fluctuations in demand. However, Schmookler himself has pointed out the limitations of his data. Patents are claims to property. They are not innovations and the great majority are never used. The meaning of patents changes over time in response to institutional and political changes. Thus, patents do not provide a reliable index to long-range trends. In the United States, for example, the number of patents granted annually increased two and a half times between 1880 and 1955, but other indicators of technological activity, such as research manpower and money, indicate a much larger increase. Similarly, patent laws differ from country to country, some having examining systems and other having no prior search, so that data obtained from patents are not well suited to international comparisons. In a sense, the use of patents complements the use of an aggregate production function; the latter is an index of long-range trends in techniques, the former an index of short-range fluctuations in technology (Schmookler, 1962).

The same economic indices used to measure the rate of technical growth also allow estimates of its direction. Here, too, the basic reliance is on standard economic indices, such as inputs and outputs, but broken down by industrial sectors, institutions and agencies. The specific role of techniques in each subcompartment can be estimated, again by the use of various assumptions which allow the separation of these effects from those due to other nontechnical factors. Production functions may be constructed for separate industries, often with greater assurance than for the total economy. These methods also allow comparisons among nations — for example, those of Western Europe and the United States — not merely in aggregate growth, but for specific economic sectors (Denison, 1967). Comparisons of this sort can be used to help isolate gaps in technological development and to lay the groundwork for policies which might close them (OECD, 1968).

Indirect social costs and benefits of technological change   The effects of scientific and technological activities upon the quality of life are much more difficult to measure than their rate and direction. Economic indices do not account for the social costs of congestion, pollution, noise, and social dislocation, which cannot be accurately or fully measured in terms of money or resources. Obviously, nations need not wait for precise measurement to formulate policies; but fuller and more precise knowledge permits better policies. Here social changes and environmental changes must both be measured. In both cases there are considerable difficulties. The basic sciences involved, ecology and the social sciences, are not sufficiently developed to provide any adequate guide to policy. Both involve problems of data gathering and observation. Social and ecological systems are very dynamic, and the effects of technology are usually much smaller than the natural fluctuations which take place. It is, therefore, very difficult to isolate the effects in which one is interested with any degree of assurance. The further to complicate matters, both fields involve value judgements in their application. Just how much unemployment or how much change in an ecological system is 'acceptable' (Nisbet, 1973)?

While the social costs of scientific and technological activity have received much attention in recent years, there are also indirect benefits which should not be ignored. It is rather a commonplace that both science and technology may produce unexpected economic and social benefits. Thus, the invention of transistors led to better, more compact hearing aids for the deaf, an unplanned social benefit. Such happy accidents are variously referred to as 'spillover' (in economics), 'spinoff' (in technology), and 'serendipity' (in science). Some effort has been made to measure the amount of technological spinoff from the United States military and space programs, but these results are still rather preliminary and inconclusive (Operations Research Office, 1959; Denver Research Institute, 1963; and Sapolsky, Chapter 12).

Economic analyses suggest that in many sectors the indirect social benefits warrant a larger investment in R & D. The level of R & D of a private firm is determined by its own return; but the returns of the firm from its R & D are influenced by many institutional factors: the size of the productive units, the competitiveness of the market, the effectiveness of patent laws and so on (Nordhaus, 1969). The net social and economic benefit, however, may be much higher and warrant a higher level of expenditure in R & D. A classic case is agriculture. There the average productive unit is very small and it is economically and socially impractical to expect them to support a significant level of R & D. On the other hand, the benefits of research, both to farmers and to the nation, are very great. In this case, therefore, agricultural R & D has been taken over by government and non-profit agencies in virtually every country.

But if agriculture is an extreme case, it is not unique. In many industries the level of R & D is well below the social optimum. Econometric models have been devised to describe this situation, and empirical data have been gathered (for example, on the returns of R & D in various industries). While much of this research is still preliminary, it has led to several proposals for national policies of selective governmental support for industrial R & D, especially in those cases where the economic and social benefits would justify a considerably higher level of R & D than the industry maintains (Mansfield, 1968b; Nelson *et al.*, 1967).

The study of innovations   A more direct measure of technological development is the study of innovations.[1] Particular historical case studies can be very illuminating, but overall evaluations of national performance of R & D or comparisons between scientific and technological contributions to the innovative process require large-scale collaborative works. Several have been sponsored by government agencies. The OECD's study of one hundred ten significant innovations developed since 1945 was intended to pinpoint gaps in the development of technology within member countries (1970). But it also provided a useful sample against which to measure each nation's research performance. This study brought out strengths and weaknesses within the process of innovation. In comparative terms, the figures suggest that United States firms had a significant advantage in turning inventions into innovations but little or no advantage in the inventive process itself.

In the OECD study, technical experts identified significant innovations, but a detailed analysis of the innovations themselves was not attempted. A typical procedure is to attempt to analyze innovations into basic units, specifically isolating research events which were important to the innovation. These events are much more numerous than the innovations, and they can be categorized and subjected to statistical analysis. One of the most recent and most sophisticated uses of this technique was a study of fifty one successful British innovations (Langrish *et al.*, 1972). The innovations approach can also be used to study innovations that failed: such studies tend to show the dominance of market factors (*On the Shelf*, 1971).

The use of statistical studies of innovation has run into perplexing difficulties. The results are often contradictory. Part of the difficulty lies in sampling. It is not simply that the samples may be skewed, but without a good grasp of the technological system, it is impossible to determine what a balanced or representative sample would look like. Perhaps on a deeper level, innovations are themselves rather arbitrary entities, which may be useful for some purposes but not all. Innovations are not uniform, atomistic units. One innovation may represent only a minor modification of another. Nor is there

---

[1] For an extensive analysis of this literature, with bibliographies, see Keith Pavitt's work, OECD, 1971.

any uniformity in the determination of what constitues a research event:
these, too, may vary in magnitude. This limitation has been only partially
eased by recent efforts to distinguish larger and smaller 'events' (Battelle,
1973). There is no assurance that different investigators examining the same
innovations would not come up with different numbers of research events for
the same innovation. Innovation itself is tied rather closely to economics, its
most common definition being in terms of the marketing of a new product.
But in this case the number of innovations then depends on the structure of
the industry in question. In large integrated firms, as in computers, a large
number of incremental advances in technology would be aggregated into a
single innovation.

The flow of information   There is one method of measurement which has
not yet been given an extensive test in technology, but which has been used
with considerable effect in the study of science. This is the method which
analyzes the journal literature, a method developed by Derek Price and others
(Derek Price, 1965; Garfield, 1964a). The growth in the number of journals
and journal articles is an index of the growth of knowledge. An analysis of
the citations provides insights concerning the flow of information within the
scientific system. The patterns revealed in the growth and flow of information mirror social organization and functions, thus allowing generalizations
about the scientific system. Changes in the structure and behavior of technology permit the same type analysis to be applied there. All of the more
professional engineering and technical journals have organized themselves
along scientific lines, and the technologists have adopted conventions in
citation, authorship and the like which are very similar to those in basic
science. Technological journals constitute a very substantial part of the
Science Citation Index, so a mass of statistical material is available. So far
only the barest beginning has been made in using this material on technology,
but the results are quite promising.[2] In one study, for example, a particular
medical journal was shown to be an important link between medical science
and clinical medicine (Garfield, 1974). A study of technology by these means
would be particularly promising for analyzing the interaction of science and
technology; engineering journals do cite basic science journals with a fair
degree of frequency (Waldhart, 1974).

Embodiment of science in technology   Most methods of measuring technology suffer from a serious problem, which we can call 'embodiment'. To be

---

[2] A problem with this approach is that the output of technology is no longer the
private property of invention, but a public property of a special sort of technological
knowledge which is closely allied to the international knowledge system of science. How
then is one to treat technological invention and the subsequent technical innovation?
(Eds.)

used at all in technology, scientific knowledge must somehow be related to a technical invention. The invention of the transistor was in some sense a consequence of scientific activity, and it should be possible to evaluate the role and importance of particular kinds of research activities in the initial invention.[3] But transistors were then embodied in a host of electronic devices, many of which would be evaluated as new inventions. But a study of inventions might not make the embodied knowledge manifest; it would be rated as part of the existing 'state of the art'.

There are some ways of allowing for embodiment. The National Science Foundation's study of innovation, Project TRACES, employed a graphical technique called the 'histogram' (IIT, 1968) which shows the embodiment of science in technology. But the lines drawn between 'events' can be quite arbitrary and they may beg the question as to the actual interactions taking place. Network analysis offers an attractive alternative. The relationships among references in scientific and technological papers can be put into graphical form. The patterns revealed in this manner are objective, and they can be used to isolate the pivotal papers which have served to incorporate important scientific advances in technology (Garfield, 1964b).

THE SOURCES OF TECHNICAL DEVELOPMENT: LINEAR-SEQUENTIAL MODELS

Studies of innovation have produced a variety of models intended to explain technical development. Behind the many disagreements and differences of interpretation there are certain broad uniformities. As Langrish and others have recently pointed out, all of these models postulate linear-sequential models of the innovative process (Langrish *et al.*, 1972). That is, the models assume that the events leading to innovation can be arranged in a linear sequence of cause and effect and that the first events cause or account for the remainder. These models fall into two broad categories: 'discovery-push' and 'demand-pull'. Each of these types then falls into subcategories. The demand might come from customers or others external to the firm, or it might be based on management's assessment of its own or others' prospective needs. Discovery-push models stress variously the role of science in producing invention, or the dependence of inventions on prior discoveries in technology. Another issue is the degree to which technological discoveries come either from large R & D laboratories or from private inventors and small firms (See Freeman, Chapter 5).

---

[3] The case of the transistor is currently under dispute. Compare Nelson (1962) with Gibbons *et al.* (1970).

Linear-sequential models of the inventive and innovative processes in effect define the structure and functioning of a technological social system. In this connection, it should be noted that these models are all based on *a priori* assumptions, rather than on investigation of how technology, in fact, really does work. Jevons and associates question all linear-sequential models. They found that the fifty one innovations they investigated did not, in fact, fit any linear model. Linearization is a way of simplifying data in order to manipulate it statistically. In almost all cases the investigations have been done by engineers, scientists or economists without training in the historical method or knowledge of the history of technology. In-depth, historical case studies often reveal overlapping and interactions between social and technical events and between science and technology. It might be truer, from this point of view, to see the development of technology not as a simple linear sequence, but as a flow which includes both social and technical events, and an important amount of interaction between the various categories of events. Within a complicated, branching network of interacting events, the adoption of a point of view or a criterion of selection which relates certain categories of events to other categories of events in a linear fashion must always be arbitrary and idiosyncratic. This is the basis for a number of well-known historical fallacies.

Necessary and sufficient conditions of technological change   The advance of technology requires both social and technical events. Technical capability is a necessary condition for successful innovation. There has long been a recognized need for a cure for cancer, but none has yet appeared. 'Throwing money at problems' is notoriously wasteful; if the end is not technically feasible, the program will fail. But technology does not exist for its own sake; technological activities are initiated and funded because they are assumed to meet technical and social needs. The recognition of a need is sufficient condition for technological development, just as technical feasibility is the necessary condition (Layton, 1970). Both conditions must be met for successful technological development (See Nelkin, Chapter 11).

Several studies of innovation credit need-pull with stimulating from two-thirds to three-quarters of all innovations (for a summary, see OECD, 1971). This is not incorrect; the importance of social needs is not in question. But a one-sided emphasis can lead to oversimplification. Many of the studies stressing need-pull used the firm as the basic unit of study, and many relied upon information about innovations provided by managerial personnel.

Since innovations do not have any single point of origin, it is certainly pointless to speak of a 'gap' between discovery and application, nor to speculate about whether this gap is getting longer or shorter. Unfortunately, precisely such a tradition entered early into technology policy literature and is almost impossible to exorcise. It is on the other hand quite useful to study the process of innovation in order to see what factors delay and what factors facilitate successful technological development. Though there may be much data available, there are alas no systematic studies which deal with the timing specifically.

Conflicts among innovation studies   Given the fact that innovations do not have a single point of origin, it is not surprising that the most controversial and conflicting studies are those which do attempt to assign credit either to science or to technology for particular innovations. The problems may be illustrated by several studies made under the auspices of the United States government: Project Hindsight (Sherwin and Isenson, 1966 and 1967), TRACES (IIT, 1968), and the results of the Charpie Panel (see p. 214). They present radically different pictures of the sources of technological development. Project Hindsight attributed technological growth to mission-oriented, engineering R & D; TRACES found the mainspring of technological progress in basic scientific research; the Charpie Panel of the Department of Commerce stressed the continuing importance of the individual inventor and the small firm. It is not surprising that these studies led to opposing conclusions on government policy toward technology.

The cases of Projects Hindsight and TRACES are particularly illuminating because the root of much of the difficulty is ideological. In the early Nineteenth Century science changed from an amateur avocation to a mass profession. Like most professions, science developed an ideology, a philosophical viewpoint, which reflected its own values and interests. Scientists like Joseph Henry insisted that every mechanical device was based upon prior advances in theoretical science (Henry, 1886, 323-351). Indeed, since Francis Bacon this had been a fundamental tenet for the social license of basic science. By the Twentieth Century, it had become a truism among physical scientists that major advances in technology were dependent upon basic research in science. These assumptions were built into the science policy legislation enacted after 1945. Vannevar Bush, one of the principal architects of American science policy, held that

> basic research leads to new knowledge . . . . It creates the fund from which the practical applications of knowledge must be drawn. New products and new processes do not appear full-grown. They are founded on new principles and new conceptions, which in turn are painstakingly developed by research in the purest realms of science (Bush, 1945, 13-14).

Similarly, a recent British governmental publication maintained that the justification for basic research was 'that this constitutes the fount of all new knowledge, without which the opportunities for further technical progress must eventually become exhausted' (Central Advisory Council, 1968, 4).

The American Department of Defense accepted these assumptions uncritically. It provided massive aid to basic research after 1945, and some of its personnel were important in the establishment of the National Science

Foundation. In all, the Department of Defense spent about ten billion on scientific research between 1945 and 1966, of which about twenty five per cent went for undirected or basic research. Project Hindsight raised doubts about the validity of the assumptions underlying this massive expenditure (Sherwin and Isenson, 1966 and 1967). Project Hindsight took eight years and consumed some forty man-years of time on the part of thirteen teams of scientists and engineers. Unfortunately, none of them had the benefit of any professional training in the history of science or the history of technology. They analyzed twenty weapon systems thought to be critical to the nation's defense, and they isolated some seven hundred research 'events' which had made these systems possible. Each event was classified as being either technological or scientific. If it fell under the latter category, it was further classified as mission-oriented science or as non-mission-oriented science. Of all the events, ninety one per cent were classified as technological; only nine per cent were classified as scientific, and of these only 0.3 per cent — representing two events — fell into the non-mission-oriented or basic science category (Sherwin and Isenson, 1967).

Since Project Hindsight challenged the mission of another agency, the National Science Foundation (the NSF) commissioned its own study, Project TRACES (IIT, 1968). At first confined to five innovations, a recent follow-up, 'Interaction of Science and Technology in the Innovative Process, Some Case Studies', has expanded the analysis to ten innovations (Battelle, 1973). A total of five hundred thirty three events were isolated of which thirty four per cent were non-mission-oriented research; thirty eight per cent were mission-oriented research; and twenty six per cent were classed as development. The general result was to confirm the traditional model; in these ten cases technological innovation appeared to depend on prior basic research. Innovation seemed to move in an orderly sequence from basic research to applied research to development.

Both Hindsight and TRACES invite suspension of scholarly judgment. There is more than a suspicion that the interests of sponsoring agencies influenced the results (Kreilkamp, 1971). But the problem lies more in the arbitrary assumptions which are implicit in the models than in the details of the methodology. Discovery-push models tend greatly to exaggerate the role of one factor, either science or technology, and to underestimate the others; many histories of technology, for example, are still records of great inventions and engineering achievements, and they give little hint that science played any role at all in technological development. Here again linear models select out one type of event from a complex stream. The choice of events is always arbitrary, but the really critical questions are those concerned with the nature of the actual interactions.

THE ROLE OF SCIENCE IN
HISTORICAL PERSPECTIVE

The history of technology   To understand the present relationships between science and technology, it is necessary to understand their historical
development. The history of technology is of fundamental importance to this
as well as to studies of innovation and diffusion. The history of technology is
a rapidly emerging field, although much of the output so far is frankly
antiquarian and without historical explication; many existing histories display
nationalistic biases and place emphasis upon heroic inventors and 'firsts'.[4]
There has been a shift away from hero worship and nationalism toward the
study of design traditions and research fronts.[5] While socio-cultural and
scientific factors in the development of technology were neglected in the
past, this situation is now beginning to change. Recent scholarship is not only
more critical, but it draws upon a broader basis of social and economic
history and sociology, etc., for its research and it is gradually evolving new
methods. Increasingly, historians are going beyond the artifacts to treat
technology as a social phenomenon with intellectual and philosophical dimensions (Rurup, 1974; Mitcham and Mackey, 1973; Layton, 1974). A
beginning has been made, particularly for the United States, in the study of
the professional and social development of technology (See Calhoun, 1960;
Calvert, 1967; Layton, 1971). These tendencies, along with cognate developments in the history of science, have raised serious doubts about the traditional views of the relationship of science and technology; a new interpretation is emerging, even though consensus on its details is still far away.
(For examples, see Derek Price, 1965; Gillispie, 1957; and Smith, 1961).

Interactions of science and technology   Science and technology, which
had been historically separate, came into close interaction during the Nineteenth Century. Prior to the Nineteenth Century, few inventions were based
upon science; Franklin's lightning rod is one of the rare exceptions. On the
other hand, it is easy to find inventions that were based almost wholly on the
empirical insights of craftsmen, with no discernible scientific input. But by
the latter half of the Nineteenth Century science stimulated many inventions
leading to the growth of science-based industries, as in electricity and chemistry.

The fact of science's increasing impact on technology led to the idea that

---

[4] On the emergence of the history of technology, see Multhauf (1974). Ferguson
(1968) provides a very useful bibliography.

[5] On the decline of the 'heroic' theory, see Layton (1973). Examples of the study of
design traditions are provided by Derek Price (1959), Gille (1967), Reti (1969), Cardwell
(1971), and Mayr (1970).

technology was applied science. But, rather paradoxically, when attempts have been made to apply this model of science-technology relations to historical case studies, they have frequently failed. Historians of technology have virtually abandoned this model, since it is seldom helpful in understanding technological development. Thus, the invention of the transistor, though it involved science in rather fundamental ways, cannot be explained simply as an application of preceding advances in basic science (Gibbons and Johnson, 1970).

The difficulties of the applied science model may be illustrated by a pioneering study of innovations conducted in 1966 by the Materials Advisory Board of the United States National Academy of Sciences. On the request of the Department of Defense, the Materials Advisory Board did a series of historical case studies of important recent innovations in materials in order to detect uniformities which might enhance research effectiveness. The Board constructed a seven-stage model which assumed an orderly sequence from basic science to engineering application. But the results did not fit the model. The editors could reach no agreement, and left it to each author to evaluate his own results. The source of the disagreement is quite clear from the report. In none of the historical case studies examined could the innovation be explained by prior advances in basic science. In most cases, the innovation derived from technological activity (Materials Advisory Board, 1966). This fact was doubtless an important starting place for the Department of Defense's next study, Project Hindsight. But perhaps a more correct deduction from the data would be that science and technology were so intermixed that a sharp separation would not be possible. The transistor again provides an example. The work on it was done by an interdisciplinary team which included both physicists and engineers. Attempting to divide the credit for this innovation between two neat compartments is just not possible if one knows enough of the actual circumstances.

The source of confusion is quite simple. The divisions between science and technology are not between the abstract functions of knowing and doing. Rather, they are social; they are between communities that value knowing and doing, respectively. Differences in value and social need lead to further differences in institutional setting. Thus, technologists in the Nineteenth Century absorbed not merely the results of science, but more fundamentally, its methods and institutions. Engineers, for example, adapted the experimental and theoretical methods of physics to their own use. To do this they needed new institutions which were analogous to those in physics: the scientific professional society, the research journal, and the research laboratory. By these means they could generate the specific knowledge needed by their community. Engineers might borrow the results of physics; the new institutional framework made this relatively easy. But in the normal case technological communities met their own needs. In short, technology became itself scientific and a generator of the scientific knowledge most closely associated with practice (Layton, 1971b).

The technological 'sciences'   Technology has always incorporated elements of systematic knowledge. This is one of the original meanings of 'science': the knowledge associated with an art. But under the impact of modern science, the very structure of technological knowledge was transformed in the Nineteenth Century. The most obvious result of this was the growth and proliferation of technological sciences. Thus, in engineering there are some twenty distinct sciences, ranging from the strength of materials to theories of control, plasticity and combustion (Potter, 1967; Rapp, 1974). In medicine there are distinctive sciences such as pathology, anatomy and physiology. In agriculture there are sciences such as those of soils and plant pathology. But besides these more or less formal sciences, there are bodies of scientific knowledge associated with design (in engineering), clinical medicine and, in general, technological practice. These are less abstract, less idealized. Thus, the theory of structures is less abstract than physics, for example, in incorporating idealized versions of manmade devices. But in turn, structural design, which has become scientific in some respects, is much less abstract than structural theory. That is, the designer must take into account a more complex reality. The theorist may assume that the materials are uniform, but the designer must be aware of nonuniformities in his materials and make due allowances for them.

The effect of the rather heterogeneous nature of the science in technology, ranging from systematic scientific disciplines to rules in engineering handbooks, is to provide an avenue by which knowledge can move readily from basic science to technology, and also in the reverse direction. Unfortunately, the precise nature of the flow of information and the social interactions is unknown, both for the behavior of total systems and also for specific innovations or discoveries. But the existence and importance of the interactions made possible by the new technology are beyond doubt. The fruitfulness of the modern, interdisciplinary research laboratory lies in its ability to bring together technologists representing every level of technological activity with persons trained in the basic sciences.

Science and technology have become intermixed. Modern technology involves scientists who 'do' technology and technologists who function as scientists. An engineer who makes a contribution to the theory of thin shells (a branch of structural theory) is doing science; if he is at a university and is not responding to a practical demand, his work is 'pure' science, though the results would normally be published in an engineering journal. Similarly, physicists may be employed in technological problems of production and quality control. The old view that the basic sciences generate all the knowledge which technologists then apply will simply not help in understanding contemporary technology.

Since it has been customary to think of science and technology as different things, the assimilation of a rather substantial portion of all science within technology can create paradox and confusion in our thinking. The technological sciences are a vital part of technological communities, since in this way it is possible to ensure that these sciences are responsive to the needs of practice. But this means that there are two quite different ways to think about 'science'. If we think of community membership we get one count, but if we think of function and the different nature of the 'sciences' (Rapp, 1974), we get a quite different one. Those engaged in fundamental research include many who, by community membership, are technologists such as engineers, physicians and agronomists. Similarly, the number of those engaged in doing technology include many persons trained in the basic sciences (See Mulkay, Chapter 4).

THE INSTITUTIONALIZATION OF APPLIED SCIENCE

The interdisciplinary research laboratory   The interdisciplinary research laboratory has been the most significant institution for modern technological development. It is characterized by collaborative research undertaken by teams of scientists and technologists. It cuts across the sharp distinctions which used to prevail between science and technology. Multidisciplinary team research is as characteristic of basic research in 'big science' as it is in industrial research. Nor is there a sharp distinction in functions; industrial research laboratories do some basic research and basic science laboratories are sometimes associated with advances in technology. Today it is better to think in terms of a complex research system which includes both basic and applied research, the differences consisting mainly in the values and particular institutional settings. Similarly, multidisciplinary research laboratories take on a variety of forms and may be funded by private corporations, governments or international agencies (OECD, 1972, 1973).

It is probably fruitless to attempt to assign a specific point of origin for the modern industrial R & D laboratory. The idea is rather clearly sketched in Bacon's *New Atlantis*, and there were many attempts to direct scientific research to technological ends over the centuries. But two sources were particularly significant for modern developments, though neither represented a wholly new beginning. The German dye industry in the Nineteenth Century systematically applied chemical research to the development of new products (Beer, 1958, 1959). The rise of interdisciplinary research is sometimes associated with the founding of the General Electric Research Laboratory in 1906 (Birr, 1957). The growth of R & D laboratories has been spectacular. By 1927 there were one thousand industrial research laboratories in the United States, and by 1960 there were over five thousand; but the bulk of the research was concentrated in the three hundred largest of these (Nelson, 1967; OECD, 1970).

While the interdisciplinary R & D laboratory has been spectacularly successful, it has its limitations. Bureaucratic research organizations are rigid in structure and tend to follow their own bent, a phenomenon which has been termed 'technological momentum' (Hughes, 1969). Much of the success of the modern R & D laboratory has hinged upon effective efforts to overcome the natural barriers of bureaucratic inertia. Studies of innovation have stressed the role of two types of individuals whose activities have been shown to be critical in several important developments: 'gatekeepers' are technical people who are especially important in communicating new ideas within the organization, while 'champions' are managerial personnel who defend new ideas and promote their development. The R & D manager has been critical to success. The most effective R & D managers have often been both 'gatekeepers' and 'champions'; that is, they have been persons with the ability to recognize the potential value of new knowledge from outside the firm and with the willingness to raise funds and otherwise support the development of knowledge.[6]

Rigidity does not come simply from within the laboratory. In large firms, the operating divisions concerned with manufacturing existing products often resist innovations developed by the R & D laboratory.[7] At General Electric, for example, it was found necessary to place management of the laboratory directly under top management, since the operating divisions, when they had a share in its control, used to resist change in their own fields. Even so, the R & D manager needs to develop the entrepreneurial ability to persuade top management figures to accept innovations, which must then frequently be imposed upon operating divisions against their will (Birr, 1957).

Convergence in research   Effective R & D management is not simply the breaking down of barriers, but also the effective relating of research to the goals of the firm. This has been expressed as 'convergence' rather than 'divergence' in research (Mees, 1950). The problems of achieving convergence center around the fact that the manager must focus on issues of specific interest without missing fortuitous discoveries which may lead in promising new directions.

This plus the demands for economy and efficiency reflected in the overwhelming stress placed upon short-term projects is an inherent limitation

---

[6]   One of the first studies to recognize these managerial types was that of the Materials Advisory Board (1966). They have been systematically studied by Allen and Cohen (1969).

[7]   This is part of the continuing war between staff and line bureaucracies. Some remarkable case studies of 'live' resistance to innovation are provided by E. E. Morison (1966). A systematic study of resistance can be found in the work of Bright (1964).

upon the large R & D laboratory (Baker, 1967). These laboratories are not 'invention factories'. They do not produce large numbers of 'way out' inventions, since such ideas tend to be stopped very early if they are out of the main lines of interest as defined by a convergent policy. For novel, risky inventions in totally new areas, the private inventor and small firm still have a vital role to play. For the private sector, the size of the industry and of its markets must be such that a large R & D enterprise is economic. These conditions are most easily met in a science-based industry which serves a large market, so that the average firm size is large. Even so, large-scale R & D will only be beneficial if products change rather frequently as a result of techno-logical innovation, as is the case with industries which serve military as well as civilian markets.

Aerospace, electronics and chemicals are by far the most research-intensive industries. In the United States these industries absorb more than three quarters of all R & D in manufacturing industries. The figures are comparable if slightly lower in Western Europe, ranging from 43.3 per cent in Norway in 1963 to 72.6 per cent in France in 1964. Military and other governmental needs tend to inflate the figures for the leading nations, of course; in the United States the government finances about sixty per cent of all industrial R & D. The bulk of industrial R & D is done in a comparatively small number of rather large firms in the United States. European analysts have held that their nations were handicapped by a larger number of smaller firms, so that the size of R & D units in the research-intensive industries is below optimum. Consolidation and rationalization have, however, been retarded both by national rivalries and by the structure of the markets in question. Even where collaboration has been obtained, Europeans complain that the numerous committees and groups which must be consulted delay decision and give the advantage to the more centralized American competitor (OECD, 1970).

Government R & D   Government R & D institutions are similar in many respects to those in industry. That is, governments do research for specific industries or missions, such as in agriculture and medicine. But governments also attempt to set policies which link R & D to national goals. Since more R & D is done in the private sector in Western nations, this poses inherent limitations on government policy. A primary problem is that of getting good information upon which to base policy. This involves more than statistics, since they, too, can be used for special pleading. Informal contacts between the policy makers and the R & D agencies and users are required if a true picture is to be obtained. The measurement of research effectiveness is notoriously difficult, and governmental laboratories are particularly susceptible to technological momentum which can lead to their losing effec-tive contact with the ultimate users of their technology. For this reason, there has been a tendency in Western nations to transfer R & D functions to the private sector whenever practicable (OECD, 1971).

But private R & D is no panacea. Many economic studies suggest that its advantages lie in the pressure of the market system and competition, which ensures that managers are very vigilant about costs and the effectiveness of programs. But these mechanisms do not apply with equal force to government research contracts, and firms may delay programs and run up costs. At any rate, the United States' shift from the arsenal system of in-house R & D in military areas to extramural research has been something less than an unqualified success, as the concern for large cost overruns in military projects demonstrates. It can be argued that the United States' greatest contribution to technology has not been in manufacturing but in agriculture, where the government made a massive, continuing commitment in the 1860's. The result of more than a century's effort has been to convert American agriculture into a science-based and moderately research-intensive industry (Harding, 1947). The phenomenal productivity has sometimes been an embarrassment, but it is also a national and world asset in an impending age of overpopulation and food scarcity.

Industrial R & D   Not least among the areas of governmental concern with technology is that of the encouragement of invention. Patent policies and direct rewards in the form of pensions or bounties have been standard means employed by governments to promote technology since the Renaissance. But changing socio-economic conditions have lessened the effectiveness of these traditional policies, while the rise of the large R & D laboratory has in many ways made the problem all the more acute and important. For big, collaborative R & D institutions are not always the best means of producing inventions, but they do develop them from invention to innovation. A few inventions, of course, have received great publicity, such as nylon and the transistor; there are some reasons for believing that these inventions may be atypical (Mansfield, 1968b).

Empirical studies, mostly dealing with American experience, suggest that the more fundamental inventions are not usually made in the large R & D laboratory. A pioneering study by Jewkes and associates was the first to challenge the assumption that most modern inventions were produced by collaborative research in large institutions (Jewkes *et al.*, 1958). These results appeared to indicate the continued vitality of the individual inventor. They were utilized by the Charpie Panel of the United States Department of Commerce to support its claim that public policy should stimulate individual inventors and small firms.[8] While these results were criticized on several counts, more detailed studies of particular industries have served to confirm

---

[8] The term 'Charpie Panel' is an informal one. Its official report is the United States Department of Commerce, *Technological Innovation: Its Environment and Management,* Washington, D.C., pub. no. 0-242-736 (1967).

the main conclusions (Myers and Marquis, 1969). In the case of DuPont, one of the most research-intensive of all chemical firms, it turns out that nylon was the exception. A study of the twenty five inventions that were most important in producing innovations showed that only ten of them had been invented at DuPont; and of these ten only three were commercially important. In most cases the basic invention had been purchased and then subsequently developed. The inventors were, in many cases, individual inventors and small firms (Mueller, 1962). A study of the aluminum industry from 1946 to 1957 revealed that of seven major inventions only one had originated with large, primary producers (Peck, 1962). A study of thirteen major innovations in the American steel industry from 1940 to 1955 indicated that none were invented by major American steel producers (Hamburg, 1963).

Despite the existence of large R & D laboratories, individual inventors and small firms are particularly important in the research intensive industries. The proliferation of small electronics firms circling the Boston-Cambridge area is well known; these firms are often referred to simply as 'Route 128', the name of the road on which they are situated. In the special cold war situation where military procurement provided unusual capital availability for this special entrepreneurial role, individual inventors and small firms were freer to exploit novel possibilities, whereas large firms tended to be tied to an existing field or product.

Technological sophistication and social need   The rapid growth and the scientific glamour of research-intensive industries tend to obscure the fact that most industries are not research-intensive, and that much technological work is relatively unsophisticated. But there is no correlation between the economic and social impact of an innovation and the degree of its technical refinement. Inventions are not solely based on technical profundity; insight into social need is equally important. Indeed, a major portion of modern industry is quite unrelated to the science-technology complex and, therefore, to any science policy. The first design in a new field of industry may be quite crude and totally outside science. R. G. LeTourneau, the inventor of the bulldozer, quite typically was a practical mechanic without formal technical education. The prototype machine was assembled from known components using an acetylene torch (Selby, 1970). In such cases, the design may be greatly refined by systematic R & D when the basic product has already proved itself and larger firms enter the field.

The large R & D laboratory is strongest in producing product innovations; it is weaker on process innovations. Samuel Hollander studied the DuPont rayon mills. He found that the largest number of process innovations came from production personnel rather than from the R & D laboratory, and the former innovations had the largest economic impact (Hollander, 1965). Unfortunately, Hollander did not specify the occupations of the production people involved. But there is fragmentary evidence that workers continue to be an important source of inventions and other improvement in technology. Charles R. Walker for example, studied the effects on the workers of an automated plant for the manufacture of steel pipe. He discovered that the workers had invented a way of running the new machinery which considerably increased its output (Walker, 1957). Except for the accident of an industrial-relations study, this technological advance would have been unreported, or credited to management. There is a need for better information on this type of invention. Most plants have some mechanism for fostering the inventiveness of the workers, but it is seldom much above the level of a suggestion box. There are no national policies on this subject in the West, though the Soviet Union has placed great emphasis upon workers' inventions as a matter of principle.

There is no question that inventions taking place outside the large, bureaucratic R & D organizations are important, nor has it ever been doubted that they should be significant concerns of public policy intended to foster technological development. Several conditions are important. First, significant inventions are usually made by people with at least some education in science and technology, often self-education. This suggests that technical education is not a matter simply for specialists; the wide diffusion of technical information and know-how is also important. But, beyond this, governments need to encourage individuals who have bright ideas. Revisions in the patent system have been suggested, but other factors seem to be more influential. The number of patents granted to private individuals has declined dramatically in the Twentieth Century; most patents are assigned to firms. This means that the private inventor is compelled to assume an entrepreneurial role; many of the firms receiving patents are quite small. But, this being the case, there is a need for mechanisms to encourage such activity. A number of policies were formulated by the Charpie Panel (U.S. Department of Commerce, 1967). There is also a need for a better understanding of the role of workers in technological improvements, and a systematic review of the mechanisms which encourage or discourage their active participation in technological development.

CHANGING CONCEPTIONS OF TECHNOLOGY

In the spirit of the new criticism of science (See Salomon, Chapter 2, and Ravetz, Chapter 3), and of the new relations between science and society (See Lakoff, Chapter 10, and Nelkin, Chapter 11), technological developments which were once politically neutral — such as power plants, highways or weapons — now lead to rancorous debate. Some critics argue that growth itself is harmful (Meadows *et al.*, 1972).

The new emphasis is upon making technology serve human needs. Of course, technology by its very nature fulfills goals which are set by some section of society. Economic factors, variously defined, have been the principal means of linking technology to social needs; but a purely economic calculus is too narrow. Most of the issues of current concern are noneconomic and do not show up on a balance sheet (Rosenberg, 1971).

Governments have responded by two types of activities. The first is regulatory and planning agencies (such as those discussed by Nelkin in Chapter 11). But *ad hoc* programs may conflict; measures to lessen pollution may worsen the energy problem. So there is also need for coordination and overall planning. Planning in an area of intangibles is difficult. Ways of measuring social health would provide a more objective basis for action. Efforts are underway to devise systems of statistical social indicators which might serve social and technological policy formulation in the same way that economic indices assist in the making of economic policy (Bauer, 1966). Creating a technology that is truly responsive to social needs requires not only new mechanisms for directing technology; it requires, rather, a sweeping transformation of technology itself. In the case of automobile emissions, some sort of control can be achieved by 'bolt on' devices, but this approach is expensive and inefficient. A redesign of the present engine would be more effective, but an optimal solution might well involve a totally new design. Designers usually have some range of choice in the basic technology with which they are dealing, and aside from piston engines, there are other possible options in the form of turbines, steam engines, electric batteries and fuel cells. The choice of the piston engine was not made on the basis of minimizing emissions; this has never been a significant consideration in the evolution of automotive engines. Adding at this late date a new factor of fundamental importance to the engineering problem may destroy the optimal solution.

The implications of a more socially responsive technology go far beyond merely adding specific bits of technical knowledge to those which already exist. 'Bolt-on' knowledge will probably prove to be as unsatisfactory as 'bolt-on' gadgets. A change in the inner structure of technology will be necessary; this change will be as profound as that which transformed pre-industrial technology into its present form.

From all this it is transparently clear that our present knowledge of the historiography and social studies of technology are inadequate to satisfy the needs of policy-making theories. Current ideas are often naive and contradictory even in such basic theoretical infrastructures as 'technology and technique', 'invention and innovation' and, above all, in the still mystical relationship between science and technology. What we need is knowledge from other social science disciplines to provide a means of relating to the social environment all that we presently understand about the substantive developmental changes in technical practice.

BIBLIOGRAPHY

Allen and Cohen, 1969   Allen, T. J. and Cohen, S. I., 'Information Flow in Research and Development Laboratories', *Administrative Science Quarterly* 14, March 1969, pp. 12-19.

Baker, 1967   Baker, N., "The Effects of Perceived Needs and Means on the Generation of Ideas for Industrial Research and Development Projects', Institute of Electrical and Electronic Engineers, *Transactions on Engineering Management* EM-14, December 1967, pp. 156-163.

Barnett, 1953   Barnett, H. G., *Innovation, The Basis of Cultural Change,* New York, McGraw-Hill, 1953.

Battelle, 1973   Battelle, Columbus Laboratories, *Interactions of Science and Technology in the Innovative Process: Some Case Studies,* National Science Foundation contract NSF-C667, Columbus, Ohio, Battelle Memorial Institute, 1973.

Bauer, 1966   Bauer, R. E. (Ed.), *Social Indicators,* Cambridge, Mass., MIT Press, 1966.

Beer, 1958   Beer, J. J., 'Coal-Tar Dye Manufacture and the Origins of the Modern Research Laboratory', *ISIS* 49, June 1958, pp. 123-131.

Beer, 1959   Beer, J. J., *The Emergence of the German Dye Industry,* Urbana, Illinois, University of Illinois Press, 1959.

Birr, 1957   Birr, K. A., *Pioneering in Industrial Research,* Washington, D.C., Public Affairs Press, 1957.

Bright, 1964   Bright, J. R., *Research, Development and Technological Innovation,* Homewood, Illinois, Irwin, 1964.

Brown, 1966   Brown, N., *On the Theory and Measurement of Technological Change,* Cambridge, Cambridge University Press, 1966.

Bush, 1945   Bush, V., *Science, The Endless Frontier: A Report to the President,* Washington, D.C., U.S. Government Printing Office, 1945.

Calhoun, 1960   Calhoun, D. H., *The American Civil Engineer: Origins and Conflict,* Cambridge, Mass., Harvard University Press, 1960.

Calvert, 1967   Calvert, M. A., *The Mechanical Engineer in America, 1830-1910,* Baltimore, Johns Hopkins Press, 1967.

Cardwell, 1971   Cardwell, D. S. L., *From Watt to Clausius,* Ithaca, New York, Cornell University Press, 1971.

Central Advisory Council for Science and Technology, 1968   Central Advisory Council for Science and Technology, *Technological Innovation in Britain,* London, HMSO, 1968.

Denison, 1967   Denison, E. F., *Why Growth Rates Differ,* Washington, D.C., Brookings Institution, 1967.

Denver Research Institute, 1963   Denver Research Institute, *The Commercial Application of Missile/Space Technology,* Denver, Colorado, University of Denver, 1963.

Domar *et al.*, 1964   Domar, E. *et al.*, 'Economic Growth and Productivity in the United States, Canada, United Kingdom, Germany and Japan in the Postwar Period', *Review of*

	Economics and Statistics 46, February 1964, pp. 33-40.
Ferguson, 1968	Ferguson, E. S., *Bibliography of the History of Technology,* Cambridge, Mass., MIT Press, 1968.
Freeman and Young, 1965	Freeman, C. and Young, A., *The Research and Development Effort in Western Europe, North America and the Soviet Union,* Paris, OECD, 1965.
Garfield, 1964a	Garfield, E., 'Science Citation Index', *Science* 144, 8 May 1964, pp. 649-654.
Garfield, 1964b	Garfield, E., *The Use of Citation Data in Writing the History of Science,* Philadelphia, Institute for Scientific Information, 1964.
Garfield, 1974	Garfield, E., 'Journal Citation Studies VI, Journal of Clinical Investigation,' *Current Contents* 14, January 1974, pp. 5-8.
Gibbons and Johnson, 1970	Gibbons, M. and Johnson, C., 'Relationship between Science and Technology', *Nature* 227, 11 July 1970, p. 125.
Gille, 1967	Gille, B., *Engineers of the Renaissance,* Cambridge, Mass., MIT Press, 1967.
Gillispie, 1951	Gillispie, C. C., 'The Natural History of Industry', *ISIS* 48, December 1951, pp. 398-399.
Gold, 1973a	Gold, B., 'Technology, Productivity and Economic Analysis', *Omega* 1, No. 1, 1973, pp. 5-24.
Gold, 1973b	Gold, B., 'The Impact of Technological Innovation – Concepts and Measurement', *Omega* 1, No. 2, 1973, pp. 181-191.
Hamberg, 1963	Hamberg, D., 'Invention in the Industrial Research Laboratory', *Journal of Political Economy* 71, 1963, pp. 95-115.
Harding, 1947	Harding, T. S., *Two Blades of Grass: A History of Scientific Development in the United States Department of Agriculture,* Norman, Oklahoma, University of Oklahoma Press, 1947.
Henry, 1886	Henry, J., *Scientific Writings of Joseph Henry,* 2 vols., Washington, D.C., Smithsonian, 1886.
Hollander, 1965	Hollander, S., *The Sources of Increased Efficiency: A Study of DuPont Rayon Plants,* Cambridge, Mass., MIT Press, 1965.
Hughes, 1969	Hughes, T. P., 'Technological Momentum in History: Hydrogenation in Germany, 1898-1933', *Past and Present* 44, August 1969, pp. 106-131.
IIT, 1968	IIT Research Institute, *Technology in Retrospect and Critical Events in Science* (TRACES), National Science Foundation contract NSF-C535, 2 vols., Chicago, IIT Research Institute, 1968.
Jewkes *et al.,* 1958	Jewkes, J. *et al., The Sources of Invention,* London, MacMillan, 1958.
Kendrick, 1961	Kendrick, J., *Productivity Trends in the United States,* Princeton, New Jersey, Princeton University Press, 1961.
Kreilkamp, 1971	Kreilkamp, K., 'Hindsight and the Real World of Science Policy', *Science Studies* 1, January 1971, pp. 43-66.

Langrish *et al.*, 1972   Langrish, J., Gibbons, M., Evans, W. G. and Jevons, F. R., *Wealth from Knowledge,* London, MacMillan, 1972.

Layton, 1970   Layton, E. T., 'The Interaction of Technology and Society', *Technology and Culture* 11, January 1970, pp. 27-31.

Layton, 1971a   Layton, E. T., *The Revolt of the Engineers: Social Responsibility and the American Engineering Profession,* Cleveland, Ohio, Press of Case Western Reserve University, 1971.

Layton, 1971b   Layton, E. T., 'Mirror Image Twins: The Communities of Science and Technology in Nineteenth Century America', *Technology and Culture* 12, October 1971, pp. 562-580.

Layton, 1973   Layton, E. T. (Ed.), *Technology and Social Change in America,* New York, Harper, 1973.

Layton, 1974   Layton, E. T., 'Technology as Knowledge', *Technology and Culture* 15, January 1974, pp. 31-41.

Mansfield, 1968a   Mansfield, E., *Industrial Research and Technological Innovation,* New York, Norton, 1968.

Mansfield, 1968b   Mansfield, E., *The Economics of Technological Change,* New York, Norton, 1968.

Materials Advisory   Materials Advisory Board, *Report of the Ad Hoc
Board, 1966   Committee on Principles of Research-Engineering Interaction,* Washington, D.C., National Academy of Sciences, 1966.

Mayr, 1970   Mayr, O., *The Origins of Feedback Control,* Cambridge Mass., MIT Press, 1970.

Meadows *et al.*, 1972   Meadows, D. H. *et al., The Limits to Growth,* New York, New American Library, 1972.

Mees, 1950   Mees, C. E. K., *The Organization of Industrial Scientific Research,* New York, McGraw-Hill, 1950.

Mitcham and Mackey, 1973   Mitcham, C. and Mackey, R., 'Bibliography of the Philosophy of Technology', *Technology and Culture* 14, Part 2, April 1973, pp. 1-205.

Morison, 1966   Morison, E. E., *Men, Machines and Modern Times,* Cambridge, Mass., MIT Press, 1966.

Mueller, 1962   Mueller, W. F., 'The Origins of the Basic Inventions Underlying DuPont's Major Product and Process Innovations, 1920-1950', in *The Rate and Direction of Inventive Activity,* Princeton, New Jersey, Princeton University Press, 1962, pp. 323-358.

Multhauf, 1974   Multhauf, R. P., 'Some Observations on the State of the History of Technology', *Technology and Culture* 15, January 1974, pp. 1-12.

Myers and Marquis, 1969   Myers, S. and Marquis, D. G., *Successful Industrial Innovations,* Washington, D.C., National Science Foundation, NSF 69-17, 1969.

Nelson, 1962   Nelson, R., 'The Link Between Science and Invention: The Case of the Transistor', in *The Rate and Direction of Inventive Activity,* Princeton, New Jersey, Princeton University Press, 1962.

Nelson *et al.*, 1967   Nelson, R., Peck, M. J. and Kalachek, E., *Technology,*

	Economic Growth and Public Policy, Washington, D.C., Brookings Institution, 1967.
Nisbet, 1973	Nisbet, I. C. T., 'Ecology: Hard Push on a 'Soft' Science', *Technology Review* 76, October-November 1973, pp. 16-17.
Nordhaus, 1969	Nordhaus, W. D., *Invention, Growth and Welfare: A Theoretical Treatment of Technological Change,* Cambridge, Mass., MIT Press, 1969.
OECD, 1968	OECD, *Gaps in Technology: General Report,* Paris, OECD, 1968.
OECD, 1970	OECD, *Gaps in Technology: Analytical Report,* Paris, OECD, 1970.
OECD, 1971	OECD, *The Conditions for Success in Technological Innovation,* Paris, OECD, 1971.
OECD, 1972	OECD, *The Research System,* Vol. I (France, Germany, United Kingdom), Paris, OECD, 1972.
OECD, 1973	OECD, *The Research System,* Vol. II (Belgium, Netherlands, Norway, Sweden, Switzerland), Paris, OECD, 1973.
On the Shelf, 1971	*On the Shelf,* London, Center for the Study of Industrial Innovation, 1971.
Operations Research Office, 1959	Operations Research Office, Johns Hopkins University, *Defense Spending and the U.S. Economy,* Baltimore, Maryland, Johns Hopkins, 1959.
Peck, 1962	Peck, M. J. 'Innovations in the Postwar American Aluminum Industry', in *The Rate and Direction of Inventive Activity,* Princeton, New Jersey, Princeton University Press, 1962, pp. 279-298.
Potter, 1967	Potter, J. H., *Handbook of the Engineering Sciences,* 2 Vols., Princeton, New Jersey, Princeton University Press, 1967.
Derek Price, 1959	Price, Derek de Solla, 'On the Origin of Clockwork, Perpetual Motion Devices and the Compass', U.S. National Museum *Bulletin* 218, 1959, pp. 81-112.
Derek Price, 1965	Price, Derek de Solla, 'Is Technology Historically Independent of Science? Study in Statistical Historiography', *Technology and Culture* 6, Fall 1965, pp. 553-568.
Derek Price, 1965	Price, Derek de Solla, 'Statistical Studies of Networks of Scientific Papers', *Science* 149, 30 July 1965, pp. 510-515.
Rapp, 1974	Rapp, F., *Contributions to a Philosophy of Technology: Studies in the Structure and Thinking in the Technological Sciences,* Dordrecht, Boston, D. Reidel, 1974.
Reti, 1969	Reti, L., 'Leonardo Da Vinci the Technologist", in Reti, L. and Dibner, B., *Leonardo Da Vinci Technologist,* Norwalk, Conn., Burndy Library, 1969.
Rogers, 1962	Rogers, E. M., *Diffusion of Innovations,* New York, The Free Press, 1962.
Rosenberg, 1971	Rosenberg, N., 'Technology and the Environment: An Economic Exploration', *Technology and Culture* 12, October 1971, pp. 543-561.

Rurup, 1974   Rurup, R., 'Historians and Modern Technology', *Technology and Culture* 15, April 1974, pp. 161-193.

Schmookler, 1962   Schmookler, J., 'Comment', in *The Rate and Direction of Inventive Activity*, Princeton, New Jersey, Princeton University Press, 1962, pp. 78-83.

Schmookler, 1966   Schmookler, J., *Invention and Economic Growth*, Cambridge, Mass., Harvard University Press, 1966.

Selby, 1970   Selby, R. H., *Earthmovers in World War II: R. G. LeTourneau and his Machines*, unpublished Ph.D. dissertation, Cleveland, Ohio, Case Western Reserve University, 1970.

Sherwin and Isenson, 1966 Sherwin, C. W. and Isenson, R. S., *First Interim Report on Project Hindsight: Summary*, Washington, D.C., Office of Director of Defense Research and Engineering, AD 642-200, 1966.

Sherwin and Isenson, 1967 Sherwin, C. W. and Isenson, R. S., 'Project Hindsight', *Science* 156, 23 June 1967, pp. 1571-1577.

Smith, 1961   Smith, C. S., 'The Interaction of Science and Practice in the History of Metallurgy', *Technology and Culture* 2, Fall 1961, pp. 357-367.

Solow, 1957   Solow, R. M., 'Technical Change and the Aggregate Production Function', *Review of Economics and Statistics* 39, August 1957, pp. 312-320.

Solow, 1959   Solow, R., 'Investment and Technical Progress', in Arrow, K. *et al.*, *Mathematical Models in the Social Sciences*, Stanford, California, Stanford University Press, 1959, pp. 89-104.

U.S. Department of Commerce, U.S. Department of Commerce, *Technological Innova-*
1967   *tion: Its Environment and Management*, Washington, D.C., pub. no. 0-242-736, 1967.

Waldhart, 1974   Waldhart, T. J., 'Utility of Scientific Research: The Engineer's Use of the Products of Science', *IEEE Transactions on Professional Communication* 17, June 1974, pp. 33-35.

Walker, 1957   Walker, C. R., *Toward the Automatic Factory: A Case Study of Men and Machines*, New Haven, Conn., Yale University Press, 1957.

Chapter 7

ECONOMICS OF RESEARCH AND DEVELOPMENT

C. Freeman

University of Sussex

INTRODUCTION

The economics of research and development may be interpreted either in a broad or in a narrow sense. In the broad sense it is concerned with the influence of research and development on the economy as a whole, as well as on the performance of individual enterprises and industries. In the narrow sense it can be taken as referring simply to the internal economics of the R & D system itself, i.e. the efficient use of resources within R & D laboratories.

This chapter is concerned almost entirely with R & D in the broad sense. One reason for this is that economists have actually made very little contribution to the study of the internal economics of R & D, but the main reason is that the most interesting science policy problems are concerned with the role of R & D in society. Moreover, the effectiveness of any R & D project, program or laboratory can often only be measured in terms of its social and economic consequences, as direct measures of R & D 'output' are mostly very unsatisfactory. Particularly in industry, the objectives of R & D are often primarily 'economic' in the sense that they are directed to savings of energy, materials, labor or capital or to other ways of improving economic performance.

Many science policy problems have an economic aspect, as there are usually a number of possible solutions and one consideration is usually comparative cost. Economics differs from accountancy in attempting to consider not just money expenditures, but the 'real' use of resources, and opportunity costs — that is, the alternatives which are foregone if a particular course is adopted.

As we shall see, schools of economic thought differ considerably in the extent to which they are interested in the very wide issues of 'social cost' and 'social benefit'. But in principle economics is certainly concerned with these issues and in practice this concern is growing. So too is the interest in long-term problems. It is important to make the point at the beginning, because the scientist's image of the economist is often that of a Scrooge-type figure concerned only with saving money over the short term. Engineers and scientists often have this image because economists have sometimes been skeptical about expensive technical developments. But in fact economists have provided a fairly sophisticated type of justification for substantial expenditures on fundamental research, despite the absence of any demonstrable short-term profit or benefit in the accountancy sense (Nelson, 1959), and all schools of economic thought have actually had a very respectful attitude to science and invention.

The contribution which any individual discipline may make to the understanding and resolution of policy problems depends on a complex combination of circumstances. Among these are the relevance and intelligibility of its analytical framework, and the extent to which various affected interest groups and decision makers find it expedient to make use of these ideas for their own purposes.

Problems of communication also affect the extent to which other research disciplines may take up ideas and theories from the economics literature and the extent to which a trans-disciplinary synthesis of some problems may be attained. The fragmentation of disciplines and subdisciplines does not correspond to the real world behavior of social systems, or to the requirements of policy making for science and technology. It is therefore essential for those who are interested in developing policy studies to try to improve the communication between disciplines, and where possible to supersede the uni-disciplinary approach. This however, cannot be attained by neglecting the findings of other disciplines, but only by thoroughly understanding them. That is the justification for a chapter specifically concerned with economic aspects of science policy. Although economists have recently concentrated some attention on the 'economics of R & D', they have usually been aware that this was only part of the wider problems of technical change and social development (See Layton, Chapter 6, and Sardar and Rosser-Owen, Chapter 15).

This chapter therefore sets out to do three things: first, to clarify the definitions and conceptual framework commonly used in the economics literature and to relate these to those used elsewhere; second, after this preliminary ground clearing, to review historically the approach of the main schools of thought among economists to problems of research, development and technical innovation; and third, to discuss some of the most recent empirical research findings in order to assess how far they may be held to confirm or refute the speculations and judgments of these various schools.

DEFINITIONS AND CONCEPTUAL FRAMEWORK

Economics is still far from consistent in its use of terminology, but it is probably more consistent than many science policy studies. Because of the inconsistencies between disciplines and within disciplines it is very difficult to get a generally accepted set of definitions in transdisciplinary policy studies. But this is more likely to be attained if the conceptual framework used within each discipline is fairly explicit. The problem is further complicated by intercountry and interideological differences, which create problems in standardization of definitions and statistics; but some progress has been made and the following comments on terminology would probably rate fairly high agreement among economists.

a) **Technology** This is one of the expressions which suffers from immense confusion in its use. Sometimes it is used exclusively in the original meaning of the word: a body of knowledge about techniques. At other times it is used to describe the actual physical hardware used for production. Quite frequently it is now used exclusively for very modern glamorous techniques of production, as though the older craft techniques did not really count.

Economists differ to some extent from other disciplines in making what may at first appear to be a somewhat pedantic distinction between techniques and technology. Actually, however, this distinction is important and in my view science policy studies would benefit from adoption of the economics usage in this case. The essence of the matter has been well put by Mansfield (1968, 10-11):

> Technology is society's pool of knowledge regarding the industrial arts. It consists of knowledge used by industry regarding the principles of physical and social phenomena (such as the properties of fluids and the laws of motion), knowledge regarding the application of these principles to production (such as the application of genetic theory to the breeding of new plants), and knowledge regarding day-to-day operations of production (such as the rules of thumb of the craftsman). Technological change is the advance of technology, such advance often taking the form of new methods of producing existing products, new designs which enable the production of products with important new characteristics, and new techniques of organization, marketing and management. . . . It is important to distinguish between a technological change and a change in technique. A technique is a utilized method of production. Thus, whereas a technological change is an advance in knowledge, a change in technique is an alteration in the character of the equipment, products and organization which are actually being used. For a technological change to be used, much more is required than the existence of the information. The proper people must possess the information and must be part of an organization which can make effective use of the information.

This brings out the extremely important distinction between the generation and dissemination of new technology, and the application of this knowledge in operating systems. This application is *technical innovation.* Industrial research and development activity is mainly concerned with generating advances in technology. In principle, therefore, it is quite possible to spend heavily on R & D with very little effect on the actual techniques used by industry and no change at all in industrial productivity. Insofar as the objective of the R & D was improvement in industrial efficiency, this would be wasted, unproductive expenditure. Much of the literature on management of R & D in industry and government is concerned with the avoidance of such waste, which is clearly related to the separation of specialization of the R & D function, the production function and the marketing function in contemporary industrial societies. Sociologists such as Burns and Stalker (1961) and communications specialists such as Tom Allen (1966) have contributed more than economists to the understanding of this phenomenon. Socialist economies have also become acutely aware of the problem and much of the science policy discussions in the Soviet Union in the 1960's were concerned with measures to improve the coupling between industry and specialist research organizations (Amann, Perry and Davies, 1969). Similar problems have arisen in the case of the big space programs and other R & D in government laboratories.

An even more acute problem exists in many developing countries, where technological dependence on foreign countries and multinational corporations creates exceptionally severe science policy problems. Among these problems are the mismatch between the knowledge output of the R & D system (usually much more R than D) and the actual needs of the agricultural, industrial and social system (Some aspects of these problems are taken up by Sardar and Rosser-Owen in Chapter 15).

Another extremely important reason for emphasizing the distinction between 'technique' and 'technology' is that empirical research in industrialized countries has shown that firms in the same industry may vary enormously in the extent to which they use the most up-to-date technology, and that these differences account in large measure for the very wide variation in interfirm productivity. Thus the concept of a 'technological frontier' is a useful one. The cost of making improvements in the case of firms which are at or close to the frontier may be very considerable, as they may have to create new technology themselves by research and development. But for those who are far from the frontier of technology, technical progress may be extremely rapid either simply through imitation or through the purchase of licenses and know-how. This 'catching up' phenomenon is obviously one reason why countries with rather low R & D expenditures, such as Italy, were nevertheless able to achieve very high rates of productivity increase in the post-war period (Williams, 1967).

b) **Technical change**   The emphasis in economics on the distinction between technological change and change in technique is also important in relation to the role of capital investment. If a much better technique can be adopted at very low cost, clearly there would be a great economic advantage in this form of technical change. An example of such a change might be the reorganization of an accounting system to dispense with much of the paper work, or a new managerial system. Where such changes involve no new capital investment in equipment they are described by economists as *disembodied* technical change. But Kaldor (1961), Salter (1966) and other economists have argued that most important technical change *does* involve new investment in plant and equipment – i.e. it is *embodied* technical change. If they are right, then this is extremely relevant to the theory of economic growth and to economic policy and technology policy, for it would mean that a high rate of economic growth can only be attained by a high rate of capital investment in new plant and equipment and the rapid replacement of old vintages of capital equipment by new generations embodying more advanced technology. Such concepts lie behind many postwar taxation changes and economic policies designed to subsidize private capital investment and accelerate scrapping of old machinery.

A rather specialized problem in definition of 'technical change' in the economics literature relates to the concept of a shift *along* a production function, as opposed to a shift in the production function itself. At any given state of technology there are in principle a variety of different but equally efficient ways in which a commodity may be produced or a service provided. For example, a road may be built using a large amount of manual labor, picks and shovels and wheelbarrows; at the other extreme it may be built using bulldozers, excavators and other machinery with scarcely any manual labor. For the economist the 'advanced' capital-intensive technique is not necessarily the most efficient one; which one is to be preferred will depend on the relative availability of and the relative price of labor and of capital in the particular society. Where labor is abundant, unemployed and cheap, and capital is scarce, a very labor-intensive technique may be just as 'efficient' as a capital-intensive one where labor is dear. Thus, in principle, with no actual change in technology, a different technique may be adopted in a particular industry or country, simply because of a change in relative factor prices. A 'production function' is a representation of the spectrum of available techniques. Historically, as real wages rise, industrialized countries tend increasingly to exploit labor-saving technology, which may already have been in existence, but was not economic to use previously because labor was so cheap. Thus some 'changes in technique' are simply a shift along a production function, while others involve a shift in the production function itself. Economists are not always consistent on this point. In practice it is often very hard to separate a movement along a function from a shift in the function, but the distinction is nevertheless important in some of the theoretical debates.

A question which has preoccupied many economists is the question of the relative extent of *labor-saving* technical change versus *capital-saving* technical change (Fellner, 1961, 1962). The example shown in Table 1 (Enos, 1961) is a good example of technical change which saved a great deal of labor, materials, energy and capital per unit of output. This process of change was *embodied* and it involved new technology; i.e. it involved investment in new generations of oil refineries which used the fluid-bed catalytic cracking process instead of the older techniques. But although it involved heavy capital investment, the increase in productivity was so great that there was a saving of over eighty per cent in the amount of capital investment *per unit of output*. The improvement in labor productivity, however, was even more dramatic: a ninety eight per cent reduction in input of man-hours per unit of output. Thus, although the technical change saved both labor and capital, the overall bias was in the direction of labor saving. If this were characteristic of technical change in general then there would be a tendency in the economy for the capital/labor ratio (K/L) to grow; i.e. there would be a rise in the capital employed per man. Some economists have argued that as this tendency has occurred historically, there has been pressure on the capital-intensive technologies to seek more capital-saving inventions and 'induce' innovations, thereby rendering technical change more 'neutral', and preserving a fairly constant capital-output ratio (K/O) in the industrialized countries with a steadily falling labor-output (L/O). But in the aggregate the question is a very complex one, since it involves not only the relative prices of labor and capital and the elasticity of substitution of one for the other, but also the extent to which new labor-intensive service and manufacturing industries may grow up at the same time as other branches of the economy are becoming more capital-intensive (Blaug, 1963).

Table 1: Productivity Comparison of the Burton Fluid Catalytic Cracking Processes

Production Inputs	Inputs per 100 Gallons of Gasoline Produced		
	Burton Process:	Fluid Process: Original Installations	Fluid Process: Later Installations
Raw Materials (Gallons)	396.0	238.0	170.0
Capital ($, 1939 Prices)	3.6	0.82	0.52
Process Labor (Man Hours)	1.61	0.09	0.02
Energy (Millions of BTU's)	8.4	3.2	1.1

Source: Enos, 1962a, p. 224.

Another possible consequence of a strong persistent labor-saving bias in technical change could be the generation of so-called 'technological unemployment'. This was a cause of considerable concern in the industrialized countries in the 1930's, but more recently the debate has been particularly intense in relation to the employment problems of developing countries (Cooper, 1972, 1973).

It has been argued that there is considerable merit in the economist's distinction between changes in technology and changes in technique, since this brings out the crucial role of capital investment embodying new knowledge, and of information systems, communication and education in diffusing new knowledge to potential users. However, it must be admitted that the more specialized use of the expression 'technical change' is more controversial when it comes to the so-called 'residual factor' in aggregate production function models. We shall return to this later.

c) **Inventions, innovations and diffusion**   All schools of economists have recognized that the process of technological change involves a continuing stream of inventions. Whether, like the neoclassical school, they tended to regard these as exogenous to the system, or, like the Marxists and Galbraith, they put them at the center, they are all agreed that the generation and application of inventions is essential for economic progress in general.

The concept of *invention* as used by economists corresponds very closely to that used by most Patent Offices, although of course millions of inventions are never patented, and what can be patented varies to some extent according to particular national patent laws. An invention is a novel idea, sketch or model for a new or improved product, process or system. It may never actually be used outside the laboratory or the inventor's workshop or proverbial attic. It need not necessarily imply any empirical test of feasibility, but as Jewkes (1958, 17) suggests, it normally does convey the first confidence that something should work and the first rough test that it will in fact work.

The more rigorous testing which usually follows for those inventions selected for further experimental development leads to the majority of them falling by the wayside. Even of those of the more promising inventions which are submitted to Patent Offices, the majority are never actually applied. Thus only a small minority of the total universe of inventions ever makes the grade and reaches the point of application in an operating system outside the inventor's workshop.

The rather specialized meaning generally given to the term *innovation* in economics is by no means generally appreciated in other disciplines, nor does it correspond precisely to the everyday meaning. Schumpeter (1939) argued that there is no necessary connection between invention and innovation, and following Schumpeter, most economists now use the term innovation to describe any changes in technology introduced for the first time. Schumpeter was thinking primarily in terms of commercial application, whether in products, processes or systems of organization, but the term is used for all types of novel methods and products, including, for example, medical or military innovations. Although this usage is widely accepted, there is still an element of ambiguity arising from the fact that the expression is used both to describe the whole process of development and launch of a new product or process (as in 'management of an innovation'), and to pinpoint the precise time of introduction of such a new product or process. (By the 'date' of an innovation, economists usually mean the date of the first commercial launch.)

Innovation in new systems or processes may embody a large number of inventions in components, materials and subsystems, or none at all in the case of organizational or incremental changes. Indeed, some economists and sociologists have queried the realism of attempting to distinguish and measure discrete units of technological and technical change. Gilfillan (1935) argued that in the case of shipbuilding, and in other industries too, technical change was the result of an infinite number of very small improvements and adaptations, rather than the result of big steps by heroic 'inventors' or 'innovators'. Some economists, such as Schmookler (1966), have used patent statistics to measure a large number of small inventions. Schmookler, too, has argued that they are more representative of technological change than 'major' inventions. Gilfillan may be right, at least for the first few thousand years of shipbuilding, but it would be difficult to deny that such inventions as Xerography or the atomic absorption spectrometer did represent imaginative leaps. Both types of change are important, but the work of Gilfillan (1935), Schmookler (1966), and Hollander (1965) is valuable in drawing attention to the fact that anonymous, nonpatented, incremental improvements in technique, as well as minor patented inventions, have very great cumulative consequences. So, too, does the 'learning curve', an expression coined to describe the improvement in skill and productivity associated with repetitive experience in such industries as aircraft production (Arrow, 1962; Sturmey, 1964).

Probably the most comprehensive attempt to classify inventions and to distinguish them from 'acts of skill' was made by Usher (1955):

> The distinction between acts of skill and inventions is suggestively drawn by Gestalt psychology. Novelty is to be found in the more complex acts of skill, but it is of a lower order than at the level of invention. As long as action remains within the limits of an act of skill, the insight required is within the capacity of a trained individual and can be performed at will at any time. At the level of invention, however, the act of insight can be achieved only by superior persons under special constellations of circumstances. Such acts of insight frequently emerge in the course of performing acts of skill, though characteristically the act of insight is induced by the conscious perception of an unsatisfactory gap in knowledge or mode of action.

Although they might not be happy with Usher's concept of 'superior persons', most economists would probably go along with some such distinction between 'acts of skill' and 'acts of insight', and certainly with Usher's insistence that the process of technical change does not consist exclusively of a small number of acts of genius. It is partly for this reason that economics has contributed more to studies of overall productivity change than to case studies of major innovations or the diffusion of innovations.

The concept of *diffusion* of an innovation in economics is essentially similar to that in the other social sciences; it is normally used to describe the spread process of discrete identifiable technical changes by successive waves of adopters. The expression 'adoption' is used almost interchangeably with 'diffusion' to describe this process, and economics has taken over from sociology the classification of adopter populations into 'early', 'middle', and 'late' adopters (Rogers, 1962). The pioneering studies in this field were mainly by rural sociologists on the adoption of agricultural innovations and on the adoption of medical and educational innovations. In 1962 it was still possible for Rogers to complain that there were very few studies of diffusion in manufacturing industry and scarcely any contribution from economists. Since that time, however, Mansfield (1961, 1968) has contributed substantially to the understanding of the economics of the diffusion process concentrating on the investment aspect, and a number of other valuable empirical studies have been made by economists (Metcalfe, 1970; Fisher, 1973; Ray and Nabseth, 1974; Scott, 1975).

Economists have also made a major contribution to the understanding of the international process of diffusion of technical change; but the focus of attention in these studies is usually the 'transfer of technology' (Cooper and Sercovich, 1971). The adoption of new techniques by developing countries has proved a particularly fruitful and important field of research (Cooper, 1972, 1973, 1976). It is important to recognize here again the important distinction between the 'transfer of technology' (strictly speaking the transfer of knowledge about techniques) and the 'diffusion of innovation' (the adoption of new techniques). The distinction is not a purely pedantic one, for reasons which have already been discussed, and it is one which is frequently blurred in 'technology transfer' studies. In the context of the developing country there is an important difference between simply importing a new machine or 'turn-key' plant with very little understanding of its technology and development, and importing a particular machine or process with a local understanding of the new technology behind it – and the concomitant capacity to maintain, modify or change it. The transfer of technology is a much wider problem than the simple 'diffusion' of new machines embodying a new technique, though such diffusion is obviously an extremely important vehicle of technology transfer.

With the rapid development of this field of empirical research (technology transfer, diffusion, adoption), there is clearly some danger of an excessively schematic approach. Rosenberg (1975) has warned against the dangers of an overly rigid adherence to Schumpeter's distinctions between inventions, innovations and diffusion. The 'adoption' process for a new technique usually involves many further inventions and innovations both by 'early' and by 'late' adopters as well as by the original innovators. An oversimplified schematic approach may obscure the real complexity of a many-sided continuous process of technical and technological change. Katz (1971, 1972) has demonstrated the very great potential importance of modifications to new techniques by subsidiaries of multinational corporations, while Bell (Bell and Hill, 1974; Bell *et al.*, 1976) had demonstrated the dangers of import of foriegn techniques in the absence of an adequate capacity to modify, adapt, select and change these techniques. For these reasons the seminal paper by Cooper and Sercovich (1971) is particularly important; it emphasizes the variety and the interdependence of a large number of mechanisms of transfer of technology, such as the import of capital goods, licensing, know-how agreements, training and education, imitation, information systems and so on. The development of an indigenous capacity to generate and assimilate new technologies is an extremely important aspect of overall development policies. Such technology policies embrace the simple 'adoption' and 'diffusion' processes, but they must be much more ambitious if they are to satisfy most developmental goals, and if they are to avoid total technological dependence.

d) **Research and experimental development**   So far the emphasis in this discussion of technology, technique, invention, innovation and diffusion has been a conceptual framework which could be applied almost equally well to a Nineteenth Century economy or a Twentieth Century economy, and the reader may reasonably be asking: what about the economics of research and development? It was essential to give a fairly full background before taking up this question, because mainstream economics scarcely concerned itself with R & D at all before the 1950's, and even now, although the importance of R & D is fully recognized, it is still not really integrated into teaching and research. Moreover, as has been indicated, there is considerable uncertainty as to the relationship between the R & D system, and the earlier, more familiar concepts of invention, innovation and technical change.

Definitions of 'R & D' were generally established only in the 1950's, and they still present some problems of reconciliation with the older concepts. Broadly speaking, however, economists have accepted the standard international definitions embodied in the 'Frascati' Manual (OECD, 1970) and make increasing use of the R & D statistics based on these definitions. Several economists have attempted to represent schematically the relationships between the formal R & D system and the activities of industry. One of the most useful such representations is that of Ames (1961), reproduced here as Table 2.

One of the valuable features of this representation is that it emphasizes the interdependence of the whole R & D system, and the role of 'feedback' inputs throughout. Like most others who have used R & D statistics, economists are well aware of the difficulties of making a sharp boundary dividing 'basic' from 'applied' research (Mulkay, Chapter 4). There are similar prob-

Table 2: Inputs and Outputs of the R & D System

Stage	Illustrative Inputs		Illustrative Outputs	
	Feedback Inputs from:	Other Inputs:	Feedback Output:	Other Outputs:
Basic research	Orders from entrepreneurs Basic research Inventive work Development work 'Bugs'*	Scientists Laboratories Nonspecific labor Materials: power, fuel	New scientific problems Laboratory results	Hypotheses and theories Research papers: formulas
Inventive work and applied research	Orders from entrepreneurs Basic research Development work 'Bugs'	Output of basic research Scientists Engineers Laboratories Nonspecific labor Materials: power, fuel	New scientific problems Laboratory results Unexplainable successes and failures	Patents Nonpatentable inventions: memoranda, working models, sketches Research papers
Experimental development work	Orders from entrepreneurs Development work 'Bugs'	Inventive output Engineers Draftsmen Other labor	New scientific problems Need for inventions Unexplainable successes and failures	Blueprints Specifications Samples Pilot plants Prototypes Patents Manuals
New-type plant construction	Orders from Entrepreneurs 'Bugs'*	Development output Resources of an ordinary construction firm	'Bugs'	New-type factory

*Bugs, or persistent, irritating obstacles to the completion of units of information contracted for, may have unexpected but important consequences. The observation that pitch-blende spoiled photographic plates led one scientist to keep the two apart (a 'bug') and another to discover radioactivity. The point is important enough to mention here but too diffuse to treat in detail.

Source: Ames (1961), with minor modifications.

lems in separating 'experimental development' from 'new-type plant construction' or from trial production in an existing plant. Ames' table differs from
the Frascati Manual in representing 'new-type plant construction' as part of
the R & D system. This would apply only to experimental pilot plants in the
Frascati system.

The introduction of the adjective 'experimental' into the expression 'research and experimental development' was a useful amendment adopted at
the 1970 Frascati meeting. It adds precision to the use of the word 'development', which has many other meanings, including some quite different ones
in economics. It also clarifies the most essential feature of this type of
scientific and technological activity, and distinguishes it from such activities
as routine design, using established techniques, or feasibility studies for
engineering projects.

Layton in Chapter 6 has discussed thoroughly the limitations of 'linear'
innovation models, and many economists (Williams, 1967) have criticized the
oversimplified schematic representation of the industrial innovation system,
according to which projects pass in a clearly defined sequence from the basic
stage through the applied stage and development into production. This of
course, never did correspond to real life and, to be fair to those who
developed the definitions of R & D, none of them imagined that it did. Very
often it is the other way around – a problem arising in production generates
demands for experimental modification to a machine or process, which in
turn raises some applied research, and which ultimately may even stimulate a
new line of basic research. Ames' table brings out these interdependencies
particularly well by his emphasis on feedback and on 'bugs'.

Perhaps the main difficulty experienced by economists in using the stan-
dardized R & D definitions and statistics is in locating 'inventive activity'.
Because their interest had been concentrated on industrial production, the
earlier conceptual framework of economists was based on the invention-
innovation relationship. Increasingly, it was recognized that inventions often
required 'development' before innovations could be launched, so that before
'R & D' appeared on the scene, economists had grown accustomed to
thinking in terms of 'Invention-Development-Innovation'. Some of them saw
'scientific research' as lurking somewhere in the background and bearing some
vague relationship to invention. In the chemical and electronic industries it
became increasingly apparent that 'research' and 'inventions' were rather
closely interrelated, but in such industries as mechanical engineering it still
appeared that 'inventions' bore little or no relationship to scientific research
and were more the result of mechanical igenuity. Economists were therefore
sometimes slightly puzzled as to where to locate 'invention' in the framework
of R & D definitions. Both Ames and Machlup (1962) linked 'applied
research' and 'invention', but although historically one can see the reasons for
this, there seems to be no point in trying to force 'invention' into one part of
the R & D rubric. Inventions, in fact, may occur anywhere in the R & D

system, and still to a large extent outside the formal R & D system altogether. Schmookler (1966) has shown that a large number of patents in the United States were still generated outside R & D, and many are generated during experimental development work.

It therefore seems essential to preserve the 'invention-innovation' conceptual scheme alongside the formal R & D concepts and measures. The sources of technological change in industry and elsewhere remain pluralistic; the R & D statistics give us a measure of the extent of professionalization of experimental scientific and technical activities. But economics has made an important contribution to science policy studies by emphasizing that, important though industrial R & D now is, it is not responsible for all inventions, is not the only source of 'technological change', and by itself does not necessarily lead to a flow of useful innovations.

It has frequently been pointed out that the number of patents increased much more slowly than the expenditures on R & D since 1939. It seems far more probable that this reflects a change in the *locus* and professionalization of R & D than a decline in the rate of technological change or R & D productivity.

Economics is therefore in the position of using simultaneously three main sets of concepts in its research on problems related to science policy: 1) technology, technique, technological and technical change; 2) invention, innovation, and diffusion; 3) research and experimental development. As we have seen, one of the most important questions which is now being debated among economists is the extent to which the formal professional R & D system is now the main source of: a) technological change, b) inventions and c) innovations. Clearly this is a fundamental problem for all science policy, so that nothing could be gained by attempting to scrap any one set of these concepts.

e) **Summary of definitions**   *Technology* is a body of knowledge about techniques. Technological change is new knowledge of such techniques. *Techniques* are the methods employed to produce and distribute commodities and services. *Changes in technique* do not necessarily imply new technology; they may simply represent imitation and *diffusion* of existing techniques and factor substitution. *Technical change* is the adoption of different techniques. *Inventions* are identifiable discrete contributions to technological change, but they are not the only way in which technology changes nor are they the only source of innovation in the economy. Inventions which are introduced into the regular system of production and provision of services are *technical innovations*. The process of *innovation* is the first introduction of new techniques, which may often be followed by a spread process of diffusion. Technical change involves both the first-ever innovation and the *diffusion* or *adoption* of innovations by others. *Applied research and development* is systematic activity directed to the advance of technology. *Basic research* is the search for new knowledge which does not necessarily have a technological objective, but which ultimately may very well influence technology. If decision makers think it is likely to do so, but do not quite know how, they may call it 'background' or 'oriented basic research'. *Research and development* constitutes an important but not unique source of *technological* change.

A HISTORICAL REVIEW OF ECONOMIC THOUGHT ON TECHNICAL CHANGE

a) **Adam Smith and the classical economists**   Smith, Malthus, Ricardo, James Mill and John Stuart Mill attempted to analyze and explain the long-run tendencies of the economic system as a whole. Smith's 'Wealth of Nations' (1776) is frequently regarded as the starting point of political economy, although this view does less than justice to Stuart, the French physiocrats and other forerunners of the classical school. However, Adam Smith's book was certainly the most widely read of any economic text of the Eighteenth Century, and almost certainly the most influential, both in terms of government policies and the development of economic theory, including attitudes toward science and invention.

Many of the leading ideas of 'The Wealth of Nations' became the conventional wisdom of economic theory. The Marxist school, too, owed a great deal to the classical heritage, although it established its own independent conceptual framework. The central idea, for which Adam Smith is justly famous, is expressed in the metaphor of the 'invisible hand' and its corollary (to use the expression coined by Lassalle), the 'night-watchman state'. This basic concept, according to which the satisfaction of consumer needs can best be attained by a 'laissez-faire' economic policy, permitting competitive enterprises to pursue their own advantage, was elaborated by the neoclassical economists to provide an elaborate rationalization of the ideal behavior of a capitalist economy.

Adam Smith himself was never in danger of confusing the model with reality. He was extremely realistic about the dangers of monopoly, and even the most enthusiastic trust-buster could not better his formulation of the dangers of businessmen in the same line of business forming a conspiracy against the public interest. He recognized that the 'night-watchman' state would inevitably have some social responsibilities which went well beyond holding the ring and protecting property. Such responsibilities he classified as those which, although not to the private advantage of any single individual to provide, would bring a general advantage to the community. Thus Adam Smith not only established antimonopoly attitudes and policies as an enduring characteristic of classicial and neoclassical economics; he also provided the loophole for Pigou and the whole 'welfare' school of economics to develop the idea of 'social benefit' and 'social cost', and thereby to undermine the pure 'free enterprise' tradition. Although this qualification is important in relation to the further development of economic thought, there can be no doubt that the main thrust of Adam Smith's polemic was against the many forms of central and local governments' petty interference with business in his own day, and that it favored unleashing the profit-motivated entrepreneurial initiative of businessmen and traders.

This background is necessary to an understanding of Adam Smith's treatment of invention and technical change, which is our central concern. Like so much that he did, it set the tone for classical political economy. He was remarkably perceptive in his comments on science and invention, as the following often quoted passage shows (Smith, 1776, 8):

> All the improvements in machinery, however, have by no means been the inventions of those who had occasion to use the machines. Many improvements have been made by the ingenuity of the makers of the machines, when to make them became the business of a peculiar trade; and some by that of those who are called philosophers or men of speculation, whose trade is not to do anything but to observe everything; and who upon that account are often capable of combining together the powers of the most distant and dissimilar objects. In the progress of society, philosophy or speculation becomes like every other employment the principal or sole trade and occupation of a particular class of citizens. Like every other employment, too, it is sub-divided into a great number of different branches, each of which affords occupation to a peculiar tribe or class of philosophers; and this sub-division of employment in philosophy as well as in every other business, improves dexterity and saves time. Each individual becomes more expert in his own peculiar branch, more work is done on the whole, and the quantity of science is considerably increased by it.

In this passage there is the clear recognition that technical change is influenced both by 'science' outside the particular productive process and by the inventiveness of those who operate the process and make the machines. There is also the application of one of Adam Smith's most characteristic ideas — the division of labor — to science itself, and even to the subdivisions of science. In this he largely anticipated the rise of professionalized R & D and the many subdisciplines of contemporary science and technology. He also anticipated much of the contemporary discussion among economists on the sources of invention.

It is notable also that Adam Smith introduces science and invention at the very beginning of his book, when he is embarking on his discussion of the causes of improvements in productivity, and hence of increase in the 'wealth of nations'. Although the thrust of the argument is related to the enormous productivity advances which are facilitated by division of labor and specialization in the productive process, characteristically he is thoroughly aware of the complementarities in the process of socio-economic change, and relates the division of labor both to science and invention (in the previous passage) and to the enlargement of the market and the removal of barriers to trade.

Although his theory of the division of labor recently came in for some sharp criticism (Robinson and Eatwell, 1973), Adam Smith contributed to economics much that has remained typical since then: the emphasis on productivity and the interest in technical change as a source of productivity improvement; respect for science and education and a recognition that it was in the public interest for government to promote education and remove impediments to the diffusion of knowledge; condemnation of monopolies *inter alia* because they would frustrate the technical dynamism of competitive capitalism. Each of these topics has remained a major theme of subsequent economic theory and research, and the final section of this paper comments briefly on the findings of recent empirical research in all three areas.

This is not the place to enlarge on the contribution which each of the classical economists made to political economy in relation to the understanding of science and technical change. It is in any case doubtful whether any of them made much advance on Adam Smith's formulations. Here it is possible only to comment briefly on one major controversy which continues to reverberate around the world, and which is still of central importance for contemporary science policy and economic policy: the Malthusian theory of population.

b) **Malthus**   By and large the emphasis of Adam Smith was optimistic: he saw great possibilities of improving living standards and increasing the wealth of nations, provided the barriers to trade and industry were removed. Economics had not yet attained its status as 'the dismal science'. It achieved this special position partly as a result of the famous 'Essay on Population' (1798) by the Reverend Thomas Malthus. Both directly and indirectly this had a very considerable influence on the development of economic thought, as well as on government social and economic policies. It owed part of its shock effect to a technique of presentation which has since become all too common in economic advocacy: the use of an oversimplified and rather dramatic mathematical model to represent tendencies in the real world. There is, of course, no objection to the use of mathematical models in science, but there is very great danger in forgetting the importance of empirical verification of the mathematical assumptions and in basing policies on the assumption that an untested model *does* represent the real world's behavior.

To be fair to Malthus he was aware of these dangers, and in subsequent editions of his 'Essay' he endeavored to present some of the empirical evidence. The collection and review of the evidence led him to modify his argument considerably, but the message which reached the public continues to this day to be essentially the unequivocal statement of the first Essay: whereas human population tends to grow by geometrical progression if unchecked by famine, war and disease, the means of subsistence can increase at best by arithmetic progression. The conclusion is obvious: the hopes of improving the lot of the laboring poor are slender or non-existent, since such a policy will tend to be self-defeating by encouraging families to have children which neither they nor society can afford to maintain. This simple but seminal idea was important not only for its influence on economic thought but even more for its influence on policy – for example, in the reform of the English Poor Law and attitudes to the Irish famine. The idea was also important for its influence on the formulation of the Darwinian theory of biological evolution and on much subsequent discussion of 'survival of the fittest' in eugenics.

It must be remembered that, as in some developing countries today, the circumstances in England at the time of the Napoleonic wars made the basic theorem fairly plausible. This was a time of rapidly growing population, of food shortages and substantial local unemployment. It was before the opening up of vast new lands in North and South America and the growth of large-scale international trade in grain. The plausibility of the basic concept is further born out by its continuing appeal to this day, although its influence now is far greater among ecologists than among economists.

The interest of the Malthusian controversy for the purposes of this chapter lies in its direct relevance to the concept of technical progress in economic theory. The basic Malthusian idea could prove wrong if either or both of two things occurred: if human beings learned to regulate population growth and to stabilize it by means other than vice, disease, famine and war; or if improvements in agricultural technology and their application in world agriculture permitted productivity to rise fast enough to keep up with the increase in demand for food. Malthus himself discussed these two possibilities, but since he regarded the second alternative as inconceivable, he put the main emphasis on the first. Because he was somewhat prudish about birth control, this led him to a rather impractical moralizing advocacy of 'prudential restraint' in relation to sexual behavior. It is therefore hardly surprising that he remained somewhat pessimistic about the chances of success. Birth control technology has in fact already made an enormous difference in the possibilities of voluntary regulation of family size, although Malthusians are entitled to point out that the most effective techniques are not yet available to most of the world's population. The nightmare of Bangladesh appears to give substance still to the validity of the Malthusian model, at least on a local level.

Here, however, our central concern is with the first issue raised by the Malthusian controversy: technical progress in agriculture. Curiously enough it was not the mainstream economists who took issue with Malthus on this crucial point, but Karl Marx.

c) Marx   His bitter and substained onslaught on Malthusian ideas (Meek, 1953) is remarkable for several reasons. Whereas he treated Adam Smith and Ricardo with considerable respect (in the case of Ricardo, almost reverence), he treated Malthus with withering contempt, regarding him as an apologist for reaction, and also as a plagiarist. The bitterness of his sarcastic polemics is surpassed only by the contemporary attack of the neo-Marxists on the neo-Malthusians.

More important than the tone of the course is the content of the Marxist critique, and here the argument rests fundamentally on the issue of science and technical progress. The young Engels already in 1844 set out the basic points to which he and Marx frequently returned (Meek, 1953, 63):

> Where has it been proved that the productivity of the land increases in arithmetical progression? The area of the land is limited – that is perfectly true. But the labour power to be employed on this area increases together with the population; and even if we assume that the increase of output associated with increase of labour is not always proportionate to the latter, there still remains a third element – which the economists, however, never consider as important – namely, science, the progress of which is just as limitless and at least as rapid as that of population. For what great advances is the agriculture of this century obliged to chemistry alone – and indeed to two men alone, Sir Humphrey Davy and Justus Liebig? But science increases at least as fast as population; the latter increases in proportion to the size of the previous generation, and science increases in proportion to the body of knowledge passed down to it by the previous generation, that is, in the most normal conditions it also grows in geometrical progression – and what is impossible for science?

This passage is remarkable for its almost boundless faith in science and technical progress, and this faith remained a characteristic feature of mainstream Marxist economics. Engels, of course, had no more empirical foundation for his assumption about the exponential growth of science than Malthus had for his more pessimistic assumption about the slow growth of agricultural productivity. Whether there are now, or are likely to be in the future, diminishing returns to investment in scientific research, remains an open and extremely important question for science policy and economic research. But in any event, the combination of the opening up of the new lands in the American continent, Victorian colonialism and improvements in agricultural productivity temporarily banished the Malthusian specter, so that for at least a century the Marxists appeared to have the better of the argument. Whether they still do is a matter of world-wide debate (Meadows, 1972; Cole *et al.*, 1973). At least so far as economists are concerned, the Marxist position has been generally accepted by almost all schools of thought, including the neoclassical – although until recently without much attention to the conditions necessary to sustain continuity of technical progress. Paradoxically, it was again Marx who produced the fullest explanation of technical change in a capitalist economy and paid the greatest tribute to its achievements (Marx and Engels, 1848):

> The bourgeoisie, during its rule of scarce one hundred years, has created more massive and more colossal productive forces than have all the preceding generations together.

At the center of the Marxist explanation of the immense technical dynamism of capitalism was the concept of competitive pressure on each capitalist firm to improve its process of production in order to resist the tendency to a falling rate of profit (Marx and Engels, 1848):

> The bourgeoisie cannot exist without constantly revolutionising the means of production, and thereby the relations of production, and with them the whole relations of society. . . . Constant revolutionising of production, uninterrupted disturbance of all social conditions, everlasting uncertainty and agitation distinguish the bourgeois epoch from all earlier ones.

In the first volume of *Capital* (1867) Marx traced in great detail the historical transformation of productive techniques in the development of capitalist society. Although he placed the main emphasis on process innovations induced by competitive pressure, he also recognized the role of product innovations and of scientific discoveries generating new products. His discussion of the enlargement of the world market has an extraordinarily modern ring, although it echoes Adam Smith's discussion and Ricardo's theory of international trade (1817):

> The bourgeoisie has through its exploitation of the world market given a cosmopolitan character to production and consumption in every country. To the great chagrin of reactionaries, it has drawn from under the feet of industry, the national ground on which it stood. All old-established national industries have been destroyed or are daily being destroyed. They are dislodged by new industries, whose introduction becomes a life and death question for all civilised nations, by industries that no longer work up indigenous raw material, but raw material drawn from the remotest zones; industries whose products are consumed, not only at home, but in every quarter of the globe. In place of the old wants, satisfied by the production of the country, we find new wants, requiring for their satisfaction the products of distant lands and climes. In place of the old local and national seclusion and self-sufficiency we have intercourse in every direction, universal interdependence of nations. And as in material, so also in intellectual production (Marx and Engels, 1848).

Like the great classical economists, Marx was interested in the long-range tendencies of development of the economic system; and whereas he was extraordinarily optimistic about the potential of science and technology, he believed that the social relations of capitalist production would increasingly become a barrier to the continued growth of the productive forces. He interpreted the periodic cyclical crisis of 'overproduction' as symptomatic of the long-range incompatibility of the increasingly concentrated and socialized production process and the private ownership and control of capital. Whereas the neoclassical economists stressed the beneficial optimizing effects of the 'invisible hand' of perfect competition, Marx stressed the growth of monopolies arising from the very process of competition itself; the instability of investment and technical change; the growing severity of crises and the growth of class conflict. These processes, he predicted, would lead to the replacement of the capitalist economic system by a socialist system, or to the common ruin of the contending classes. Since his day, economics, like the other social sciences, has been an ideological battleground for Marxists and non-Marxists, and increasingly now for many varieties of Marxist.

Although probably all Marxists would still agree about the importance of technical change in a competitive capitalist economy, there has been some difference of emphasis on the effects of monopoly on technical change. Following Lenin (1915), Marxist economists in the interwar period tended to stress the tendency toward stagnation and retardation of technical change under monopoly. Since World War II, however, it has been difficult to deny that even monopoly capitalism has shown considerable technical dynamism. Most Marxists would stress the influence of military demands upon the economy, but the growth of the civil sector has also been very much more rapid and sustained than was commonly assumed to be likely in Marxist discussions of the 1930's and 1940's (Varga, 1935 and 1947). But whereas this question has been a subsidiary one in Marxist economics it has been one of the central issues in the development of non-Marxist theory to which we now return.

d) Neoclassical economics   This is the description generally applied by historians of economic thought to the dominant school of economics in Western Europe and the United States from the 1870's to the Keynesian 'revolution' of the 1930's (Roll, 1934). Although there were important variations of emphasis between the leading exponents (Walras, Menger, Pareto and Jevons), there were also important common assumptions and emphases.

For our purposes the important assumption was the continuity of technical change but its exclusion from the center of the stage. The emphasis was on the mathematical refinement of the classical *laissez-faire* perfect competition model. The neoclassical school was particularly successful in developing marginal analysis of consumers' behavior and of firms' behavior in relation to fluctuations in prices and demand. Simplifying assumptions were made of rationality in economic choice, 'perfect' mobility of factors of production, 'perfect' information available to decision makers, and equal access to technology. Of course it was realized that the world was a good deal more untidy than the assumptions of the perfect competition model; but on the one hand the neoclassicals argued that the approximation was close enough to give a good working model of many market situations for everyday short-term purposes; and on the other hand they tended to argue that the real world *ought* to be like the model. Marxist critics and some other heretics rejected both these arguments, but 'welfare' economics and Keynesian economics both started as tendencies within the neoclassical framework, which had a mathematical elegance not at that time approached by other social science disciplines.

Like the classical economists, the neoclassicals retained a high regard for science and technology and recognized in principle that technical change was the main source of economic progress, but they tended to take it for granted as a relatively gradual and painless process, not seriously disturbing the tendency toward long-range equilibrium. In this respect they were much more optimistic than Malthus and Ricardo. When policy issues came up, such as public provision for education or abolition of the patent system, economists usually took up a position of strong support for measures to ensure the widest and most rapid access to knowledge, and particularly to technology. This meant that the economics profession until quite recently favored the abolition of the patent system as a form of monopoly and a restriction on access to new technology.[1] But in practice they paid very little attention or none at all to the ways in which the system actually worked, or to the ways in which inventions were made and used.

The emphasis of the neoclassical school on self-adjusting market mechanisms and the almost automatic tendency to 'equilibrium' received a severe shock during the 1929-1933 world depression. Apart from strengthening of Marxist tendencies and a revival of interest in other heretical schools, the main effect of this shock was to spawn the Keynesian revision of the neoclassical doctrine. Although this was of the greatest importance for many branches of economic theory and policy, and especially for the theory of employment and investment, it is actually of little interest from the narrower standpoint of this discussion. For Keynes remained typical of the neoclassical school in believing that the power of 'science and compound interest' could lead to an age of prosperity, while disregarding all the detailed problems of the advance of science and invention, and their influence on the behavior of the firm and society.

This highly abstract approach of the main neoclassical school and the Keynesian revisionists continued into the 1950's and still found expression in the attempts to develop long-term growth models based on the so-called 'aggregate production function'. The Keynesian revolution at least had the effect of stimulating a revival of interest in the old preoccupation of classical political economy with the long-range tendencies of the economic system. As we have already seen, among the interesting problems facing economic historians and economists are such questions as the long-term growth of capital stock and its influence on economic progress, the tendency to substitute capital for labor as the relative prices of factors of production change, the influence of technical change on economic growth, and the sources of technical change.

A very considerable effort in the 1950's and 1960's, particularly in the United States, went into the development of economic models based on long-range historical time series and designed to measure the respective

---

[1] Characteristically, Adam Smith was an exception, exempting patents for invention from his general onslaught on monopoly.

contribution of labor, capital and other factors to economic growth. In practice the other factors boiled down to a residual 'third factor', which was usually described as 'technical change', although it was a rag-bag for all social, managerial, structural, educational, political, psychological and technological changes other than the purely quantitative increase in the volume of labor (usually measured in man-hours) or the volume of capital (measured in various controversial ways). Some economists, particularly Denison (1962 and 1967) attempted to go further by disaggregating the 'technical change' residual into various components, and estimating the statistical 'contribution' of each to measured growth.

Initially most of the early studies (Solow, 1957; Abramovitz, 1956) showed that 'technical change' supposedly made a very large contribution to growth. But critics pointed out that the long-range time series which were used, particularly for the measurement of capital, were conceptually unsound and of dubious accuracy, and that quite different results could be obtained even with the data and assumptions commonly accepted in the work (Kennedy and Thirlwall, 1972, for a review of the whole controversy; Griliches and Jorgensen, 1966; Jorgensen and Griliches, 1967). More radical critics (OECD, 1967) argued that the whole line of research was misdirected, and usually based on unrealistic neoclassical assumptions about factor incomes, perfect competition and marginal productivity.

Although some enthusiasts continue to advocate the use of the aggregate production function approach, most economists now seem more skeptical about the feasibility of this method, and increasingly, about the theoretical assumptions underlying the work (Lave, 1966; Kennedy and Thirlwall, 1972). Studies based on this method may be particularly criticized for their failure to recognize the importance of complementarities in social and technical change, for their neglect of all other social science disciplines, for their lack of historical sense, and for their reductionism in relation to technical change. The use of the concept of 'technical change' in aggregate production function work departs so far from the concept in all other disciplines, and especially in the natural sciences and engineering, that it is unlikely to gain any general acceptance outside economics. Even within economics it is a source of confusion, and it would probably be better if the growth modelers simply called their third factor a residual, as Domar suggested (1961).

The growth models of the 1950's and the 1960's did at least have the merit of attempting to escape from the blind alley of static equilibrium analysis, but like the rest of neoclassical economics they suffered from a failure to get to grips with the actual process of science, invention, innovation and technical change.

e) **Schumpeter** Whereas mainstream neoclassical and Keynesian economics largely neglected innovation and technical change, this was not at all true of Schumpeter, who restored it to a central position in his theory of economic development. Moreover, he attacked head-on the limitations of the neoclassical approach to static equilibrium analysis even before the world crisis of 1929-1933 (1928, 377):

> What we unscientifically, call economic progress means essentially putting productive resources to uses *hitherto untried in practice,* and withdrawing them from the uses they have served so far. This is what we call 'innovation'. What matters for the subject of this study is merely the essentially discontinuous character of this process, which does not lend itself to description in terms of a theory of equilibrium. . . . Innovation, unless it consists in producing and forcing upon the public a new commodity, means producing at smaller cost per unit, breaking off the old 'supply schedule' and starting a new one. It is quite immaterial whether this is done by making use of a new invention or not; for on the one hand, there has never been any time when the store of scientific knowledge has yielded all it could in the way of industrial improvement, and, on the other hand, it is not the knowledge that matters, but the successful solution of the task *sui generis* of putting an untried method into practice − there may be, and often is, no scientific novelty involved at all, and even if it be involved, this does not make any difference to the nature of the process.

Schumpeter was prepared to accept that the neoclassical form of perfect competition was an approximate description of some types of market over the short term, but he emphasized increasingly that the other kind of competition, based on innovation, was the really important kind.

> In capitalist reality as distinguished from its textbook picture, it is not that kind of competition which counts [competition, that is, within a rigid pattern of invariant conditions of production] but the competition from the new commodity, the new technology, the new source of supply, the new type of organisation,. . .competition which strikes not at the margins of the profits, and the outputs of existing firms, but at their very lives. This kind of competition is as much more effective than the other as a bombardment is in comparison with forcing a door, and so much more important that it becomes a matter of comparative indifference whether competition in the ordinary sense functions more or less properly.

Thirty years later, competition based on new technology is more widely recognized as being of greater importance, but the textbooks are still very largely based on the old paradigm.

Schumpeter's interest in innovation not only led him to criticize the 'received' theory of equilibrium (he seems to have been the first to use this expression about neoclassical economics), but also to criticize the theory of monopoly and the theory of entrepreneurship. Both classical and neoclassical economists had generally taken it for granted that competition stimulated technical change and that monopoly retarded it. Like many other propositions in the neoclassical paradigm it was rarely subjected to empirical tests, but it seemed plausible enough and individual instances could be cited. Indeed, Marxist economics also largely accepted the general view and Lenin cited the example of the electric lamp cartel as evidence, while Rosa Luxembourg stressed that technical innovations were usually launched by small new firms rather than by large monopolistic ones.

Schumpeter certainly did not deny that important innovations were made by small new firms, and indeed, he pointed repeatedly to the creative leaps made by entrepreneurs establishing new branches of industry from very small beginnings (1928, 384):

> for a firm of comparatively small size, which is no power on the money market and cannot afford scientific departments or experimental production and so on, innovation in commercial or technical practice is an extremely risky and difficult thing, requiring supernormal energy and courage to embark upon. But as soon as the success is before everyone's eyes, everything is made very much easier by this very fact. It can now, with much-diminished difficulty, be copied, even improved upon, and a whole crowd invariably does copy it – which accounts for the leaps and bounds of progress as well as the setbacks.

Indeed, one of Schumpeter's criticisms of the neoclassical paradigm was that it converted the entrepreneur into a kind of competent bureaucrat, as the assumptions of rationality, perfect information and equal technology deprived entrepreneurial activity of risk and individuality. Schumpeter believed that this was remote from reality and stressed the unique importance of the entrepreneur in the development of capitalism (1928, 379):

> Successful innovation is . . . a feat not of intellect but of will. It is a special case of the social phenomenon of leadership. Its difficulty consisting in the resistances and uncertainties incident to doing what has not been done before; it is accessible for, and appeals to, only a distinct type which is rare. Whilst differences in aptitude for the routine work of 'static' management only result in differences of success in doing what everyone does, differences in this particular aptitude result in only some being able to do this particular thing at all. To overcome these difficulties incident to change of practice is the function characteristic of the entrepreneur.

f) The economics of oligopoly and Galbraith   However, although more than any other economist of his period Schumpeter stressed the creative role of entrepreneurship, he also recognized that the nature of the innovative process was changing with the rise of the giant corporations. Economists of all schools were of course aware of the process of concentration which was proceeding in many branches of industry and commerce. There was intense debate both within the profession and outside it on the theoretical and policy problems arising from this process of concentration, cartelization and monopolization. The neoclassical school mainly clung to the traditional view and strongly advocated antitrust policies to restore competitive markets. But as the feeling spread that giant firms were here to stay, a new interest grew up in studying the behavior of firms in highly concentrated branches of industry: the economics of 'imperfect competition' and the economics of 'oligopoly'. It was recognized that the formal models of firm behavior in conditions of perfect competition (where no single firm could influence prices) could not be used to explain oligopoly situations, and neither could the models of pure monopoly. The situation was more akin to one of bargaining between nation states with temporary alliances and tacit price understandings, alternating with periods of instability and open warfare. Economists such as Joan Robinson (1934) attempted to formulate models which would explain firm behavior in these situations, but it was generally recognized that price could not be predicted. It was, however, agreed that under conditions of oligopoly, firms would prefer to avoid price competition altogether and rely on such weapons as advertising and product differentiation.

Intense controversy surrounded (and still surrounds) the question of technical change in these conditions of oligopoly. While traditional neo-classical economists still took the view that both oligopoly and monopoly would slow down technical change, an increasing number of economists began to argue the opposite view. They did so for a variety of reasons, but one of the principal arguments they gave related to the cost of innovation. It was widely accepted that technical economies of scale were extremely important in such industries as steel and cement, giving an overwhelming advantage to large firms in these branches. Some economists began to argue that scale advantages applied to process and product innovations and to the cost of running R & D departments. They also pointed out that large firms could afford to take bigger risks, because they would not be ruined by a single failure. This line of reasoning culminated with Galbraith's much-quoted and much-disputed statement in his 'American Capitalism' (1952, 91):

> A benign providence . . . has made the modern industry of a few large firms an almost perfect instrument for inducing technical change. . . . There is no more pleasant fiction than that technical change is the product of the matchless ingenuity of the small man forced by competition to employ his wits to better his neighbor. Unhappily it is a fiction. Technical development has long since become the preserve of the scientist and the engineer. Most of the cheap and simple inventions have, to put it bluntly, been made.

Already in 1928 Schumpeter had anticipated some of the consequences of the emergence of trusts and large corporations for the process of technical change (1928, 384):

> All this is different in 'trustified' capitalism. Innovation is, in this case, not any more embodied *typically* in new forms, but goes on, within the big units now existing, largely independently of individual persons. It meets with much less friction, as failure in any particular case loses its dangers, and tends to be carried out as a matter of course on the advice of specialists. Conscious policy towards demand and taking a long term view towards investment becomes possible. . . . Progress becomes 'automatised', increasingly impersonal and decreasingly a matter of leadership and individual initiative. This amounts to a fundamental change in many respects, some of which reach far out of the sphere of things economic.

We have here the basic elements of Galbraith's 'technostructure' which he outlined in his 'American Capitalism' and developed more fully in his 'New

Industrial State' (1968). But whereas there were only glimmerings in Schumpeter's writings of the role of professionalized 'captive' industrial R & D departments (Solo, 1951), in Galbraith's work there is the full recognition that the 'long-term view towards investment' now normally implies a deliberate long-term strategy for the firm's own R & D.

In Galbraith's 'New Industrial State' there is also an extremely witty elaboration of several other ideas which were only embryonic in Schumpeter's formulations, particularly 'conscious policy toward demand', which has become Galbraith's theory of producer sovereignty and manipulation of the consumer; and the 'automatization of progress' which has become Galbraith's corporate management 'technostructure', planning and launching new products and processes, and increasingly linked to government through the military-industrial complex.

In important respects there is some convergence between Galbraith's theory of state managerial capitalism and the Marxist-Leninist concept of state monopoly capitalism. Both stress the role of the military-industrial complex; the influence of large corporations on the state; the role of state expenditures, investment and promotion of R & D; and demand manipulation. However, there are also important differences. Galbraith stresses the 'countervailing power' of consumers and the possibility of exerting this power through democratic political process, with the implication that the state power need not necessarily be subordinate to the military-industrial complex. Most (but not all) Marxists tend to argue in line with the traditional Leninist theory of the state, that this concept is illusory and that large-scale military expenditures have now become essential to the attempt to avert economic crisis under capitalism (Barna, 1957). They also tend to argue that Galbraith overestimates the degree of stability and planning attained by the new industrial state.

The work of Galbraith and Schumpeter represents a return to the classical tradition of political economy in its broad approach to innovation and the long-term development of the capitalist system. But their ideas remain highly controversial, although increasingly influential among economists. There are, of course, purely ideological and political reasons for the continuation of such debate, but it may prove possible to resolve some of the issues by an appeal to the empirical evidence. The final section of this chapter reviews some of the recent results of applied economic research and the extent to which they confirm or refute the hypotheses and opinions of the various schools. The field is so vast that it is inevitably highly selective. The issues which are briefly taken up are: the sources of inventions, the role of the large corporation, the management of innovation and uncertainty in innovation, and the goals of R & D. As we have seen from a brief review of some of the main schools of economic thought, all of these have been major issues in the development of economics; all of them are controversial; and all of them are relevant to science policy.

SOME RECENT EMPIRICAL RESEARCH

a) **R & D statistics and technological change**   In one of the best known postwar studies of invention, Jewkes and his colleagues (1958) start off by asking the question which has possibly occurred to the reader several times during the previous brief review of economic thought, and particularly during that of the neoclassical school: Why did economics confine itself to such broad generalizations about technical change and why were empirical studies of the actual process so neglected (Jewkes *et al.*, 1958, 3)?

> Future historians of economic thought will doubtless find it remarkable that so little systematic attention was given in the first half of this century to the causes and the consequences of industrial innovation. Material progress, it had long been taken for granted, was bound up with technical advance and technical advance, in turn, with change, variety and novelty; but whence this novelty, how closely it was related to rising standards of living, whether and how it might be stimulated or stifled; all this ground remained largely untrodden by the economic historian or the economic theorist. The comparative disregard of one, if not the main, spring of economic progress is not altogether mysterious. The subject is not one to which economic analysis is easily applied; it may yet prove impossible to apply it so. And the descriptive economist finds his way blocked by the complexity of the subject: the growing specialisation in science and technology presents to the outside observer a barrier even to the simplest understanding of what is occuring there.
>
> A more important reason is simply that economists have been occupied in other ways where it seemed easier to reach results or where the immediate and practical value of their ideas seemed to be greater.

Jewkes goes on to observe that the situation in the 1950's was changing and that economists were taking a much greater interest in problems of innovation and growth. However, he pointed out that one of the difficulties which they encountered as they attempted to overcome their past neglect and to enter this difficult field, was the lack of any usable statistics such as they were accustomed to work with in other fields. But even as he wrote, this situation too began to change. He was able to make a little use of the very first official British survey of United Kingdom research and development expenditures. Since that time, these statistics have become fairly regular (although not annual) and more detail has become available. Most European countries, the United States and Japan now publish regular R & D manpower and expenditure statistics, so that international comparisons are becoming increasingly possible as a result of the work of OECD (1963, 1967, 1970, 1971, 1974). A small number of firms now also publish a very limited amount of information on R & D.

However, the fact that most of the presently available statistics deal with R & D may give an undesirable bias to the emphasis of empirical research. For example, a number of writers (Charpie, 1967) have suggested that R & D is a low proportion of the total costs of launching a new product or a new process, and have pointed to the importance of the other costs which are incurred by the innovating firm, such as tooling, detail design, and sales promotion. One-sided emphasis on R & D could also lead to a neglect of those types of technological change which do not arise from the firm's own R & D, but from other sources within and outside the firm. One of the few thorough quantitative studies which has been made (Hollander, 1965) suggested that in DuPont rayon plants most productivity improvements did not arise from the firm's own central R & D laboratories. Again, Muller's study (1962) of DuPont's product innovations showed that most of them originated from outside the firm.

However, as against this, the fact that in the face of competitive pressures almost all large firms and some small ones operate R & D laboratories, suggests that they frequently derive a clear economic and technical advantage from these activities, unless we postulate completely irrational behavior. Several empirical studies have shown some relationship between 'research intensity' of firms and of industries (measured as a ratio of R & D expenditures to net output or sales) and the growth of productivity or output (Mansfield, 1968; Minasian, 1962; Katz, 1972; Freeman, 1962). The relationship is a complex one because of the degree of uncertainty in R & D decision making, inter-industry relationships and other factors influencing productivity growth, and because of non-R & D contributions to technical change. Nevertheless, both these empirical results and numerous case studies of individual innovations suggest that R & D expenditures represent a very significant proportion of the total effort directed toward the generation and introduction of new technology. There is also a question of real historical changes in society. The growth of professional full-time R & D laboratories in industry and in the government sector is almost entirely a Twentieth Century phenomenon. The catch phrase 'Research Revolution', although like all such expressions a crude oversimplification, does capture an important aspect of social change in this century. Even if numerous inventions and innovations were made in the Eighteenth and Nineteenth Centuries without professional and specialized R & D laboratories, while many contemporary inventions come from precisely such laboratories, this fact in itself is worthy of explanation and discussion.

b) **The sources of invention and innovation**   The extent and the significance of this shift in the locus of inventive and innovative activities in industry is one of the main problems debated by economists since Jewkes and his colleagues published their classic study (1958). On the basis of about sixty case studies of important Twentieth Century inventions they maintain that the importance of the new professional R & D laboratories has been greatly exaggerated. In their view the creative independent inventor, frustrated but persistent, remains today as in the past the principal source of important industrial inventions. The large corporate R & D environment may often inhibit rather than stimulate the work of such individuals, but they frequently flourish in the more tolerant university atmosphere or in small new firms.

The arguments of Jewkes and his colleagues have been supported by the empirical findings of Hamberg (1966) and others. But they have also been criticized on the grounds that the samples may be unrepresentative, and that they exaggerate the role of the inventor' in the complex social process of innovation. Freeman (1967) pointed out that the expenditure on corporate R & D was very small in the early part of this century but has been far bigger since World War II. One would therefore expect a change in pattern during the Twentieth Century, and in his view Jewkes' own sample bears out this interpretation, as also do the patent statistics.

Moreover, the few empirical studies which have been made do not support the folklore on the share of R & D in total innovation costs. Whereas it was often stated that R & D accounted typically for only about ten to fifteen per cent of the costs of launching a new product or process (Charpie, 1967). Mansfield's work (1971) and Canadian data (Stead, 1974) show that R & D costs were typically between twenty five and sixty per cent of total innovation costs.

The view that company-based R & D is now playing a key role in industrial invention and innovation is not inconsistent with the many empirical findings which demonstrate the importance of pluralism in sources of new technology (Carter and Williams, 1957, 1958 and 1959; National Science Foundation, 1969 and 1973; Science Policy Research Unit, 1972). To introduce a new product or process the firm must often obtain knowledge from many different sources: from customers, suppliers, universities, public laboratories, competitors, licensers and so forth. But all of this knowledge must be used, modified and synthesized in such a way that it meets the specific requirements of the individual firm for innovation. Sometimes this will be quite possible without formal R & D activity, particularly in minor modifications to existing products and processes, such as those described in Hollander's study (1965). But major new steps typically require formal R & D activity, even if the original creative ideas and many other ideas come from sources outside the firm. Jewkes' own case studies (1958), as he himself emphasizes, bear out the importance of systematic and often prolonged development work in taking inventions to the point of commercial launch.

They also confirm the great importance of inter-industry differences. Research intensity varies enormously and the so-called 'traditional' industries (of low research intensity) often rely on the R & D performed by the suppliers of machinery and materials. In a typical traditional industry – pottery, for example – empirical work has shown the extent to which technical change has been influenced by scientific work on materials performed largely outside the industry (Machlin, 1973). In such cases of 'technological dependence', in-house R & D is less significant in particular firms or branches of industry but still very important for the economy as a whole. Agriculture is the best example of an industry where R & D is performed intensively, but almost entirely by government, industrial and university laboratories. However, Katz (1971 and 1972) found a strong association between the performance of 'adaptive R & D' and growth of sales and profitability in subsidiaries of foreign firms in Argentinian manufacturing industry. He argues that autonomous and deliberate technological effort by the local branch enterprise is extremely important to modify technology which is imported directly from the parent company. He adopts a definition of 'adaptive R & D' which includes some technical and engineering activities directed to productivity improvement but excluded from the OECD definitions of R & D. These activities were also shown to be important sources of technical change in Hollander's study (1965), and this emphasizes the need to measure other scientific and technological activities as well as R & D itself.

Economists are probably now largely in agreement that there has been an important shift in the source of inventions in the Twentieth Century, a shift which has made technological advance based on R & D a much more deliberate part of the strategy of firms. Nevertheless, an important area of debate and controversy remains; it turns largely on the question of the relative importance and difficulty of the most radical and original inventions and their source by comparison with the many minor improvements and secondary inventions. In the second edition of their book (1969) Jewkes and his colleagues cite new evidence in support of their thesis that major original inventions continue to emerge from sources other than the large corporate R & D laboratory.

Much more could be done, both with patent statistics and with other representative samples and lists of inventions, to test alternative interpretations of the trends in sources of invention. But most of the recent empirical work has shifted away from the emphasis on inventions to more comprehensive measures of technological change and of innovations. The reason for this shift of interest appears to be mainly the acceptance of the view that inventions are only one element, although an important one, in a wider process. Consequently much of this literature is based on enumeration of 'information inputs' or 'technical and scientific events'. It must be admitted that this method presents very considerable difficulties of deciding what is an 'event' or a 'piece of information', and of weighting their relative importance. But so too, of course, does the earlier analysis based on listing inventions or patents.

One major advantage of a broader approach to the sources of technological change lies in elucidation of the relationship between science and technology. The output of scientific research can seldom be patented, nor is it usually susceptible to analysis in terms of 'inventions'. Nevertheless it has undoubtedly influenced the nature and direction of technical change. The point at issue has been: how much and through which mechanisms? This question is an important one from a policy point of view, insofar as public support for expenditure on fundamental research or industrial support of basic research laboratories may or may not be justified by the supposed contribution to economic efficiency (Byatt and Cohen, 1969). An American Defense Department study, Project Hindsight (Sherwin and Isensen, 1966) stimulated a considerable debate when it found that only a very small proportion of the knowledge needed for incorporation in major American weapon systems came from fundamental research. Many academic scientists pointed out that a lot depended on the time period of the analysis and on the scientific knowledge 'embodied' in technologists and scientists through their education and training. The development of this controversy is discussed by Layton in Chapter 6 and is not pursued further here.

Several British empirical studies have followed up this American work, and have attempted to establish in greater detail the nature and extent of the interaction between science and technology (Langrish, 1972; Gibbons and Johnston, 1974; Rothwell and Townsend, 1973). As in the American studies, differences in sample, approach, measurement methods, and bias of the investigators obviously affect the results and their interpretation. Langrish (1972) tends to belittle the relevance of university-based research for industry, while Gibbons and Johnston (1974) stress the large amount of formal and informal contact between technologists and university or government-based scientists. The studies agree on the importance of transfer of embodied scientific knowledge in the form of new scientific instruments developed in the course of basic scientific research.

Obviously, a great deal depends on the branches of industry which are examined. In electronics, pharmaceuticals and scientific instruments, much of the technology can legitimately be described as 'science-based' as well as 'science-related'. In these industries there is a very strong interaction between science and technology; this intereaction is also evident from the study of the technology publications pattern (Derek Price, 1965). But in some other 'traditional' industries there is often little or no interaction, as was shown for example in a Dutch study of materials handling (Pavitt and Walker, 1974).

A strong relationship between 'science' and 'technology' does not necessarily imply an institutional interaction between universities and industry, or between government laboratories and industry. Another factor to take into account is the strength of the scientific research which is carried out in-house by captive R & D laboratories within industry itself. During the Nineteenth Century the German chemical industry made considerable use of the findings of university chemistry departments and a tradition of strong interchange and extramural financial support was established. But as the research laboratories within industry became better endowed and stronger in scientific terms, they were less dependent on external sources and more capable of generating their own science and technology. Langrish (1974) showed that the sources of scientific and technological abstracts believed to be relevant for the chemistry industry changed dramatically between 1884 and 1952. Whereas in 1884 only thirty per cent of the abstracts originated in industry, by 1952 this had risen to eighty seven per cent. Langrish himself emphasizes that industry still needs contact with the universities because some of the most important developments in science still start in the universities. In the case of semi-conductors, Bell Laboratories were usually ahead of the universities, so that the American telecommunications industry virtually had its own university (Nelson, 1962). Freeman (1974) has argued that the professional R & D department represents the main point of entry by which science influences technology within the firm, rather than the machine, as Marx had suggested. As Layton points out in Chapter 6, it is the place where mixed teams of scientists and technologists are the norm.

c) **Research, innovation and size of firm**   Difficulties of definition and measurement still leave many questions unresolved in relation to the sources of invention, the interaction between science and technology, and the relative significance of formal R & D in the overall process of technological change. But there are other areas where R & D statistics and empirical investigations enable us to answer some questions with more precision. One such area is the degree of concentration in industrial R & D activities, the relative research intensity in different branches of industry and the relationship between firm size and source of innovation.

The OECD statistics (1967 and 1971) show conclusively that the performance of R & D is highly concentrated in large firms in all the industrialized capitalist countries. The extreme case is that of the Netherlands where only five firms account for over sixty per cent of all industrial R & D. The surveys also show that the vast majority of the smallest firms do not perform any R & D at all. However, care is needed in the interpretation of these statistical results. Several economists (Hamberg, 1964; Turner and Williamson, 1969) have pointed out that despite the concentration, there is no clear-cut association between research intensity and size of firm. A few small firms have a very high research intensity while some large firms have a low one. Morand (1968 and 1970) has even argued that at least in France, there is evidence of an inverse correlation, but there are problems here relating to the statistics on research associations.

Turner and Williamson (1969) and Freeman (1974) point out that some types of R & D can only be undertaken with very large resources (nuclear reactor development, prototypes of large aircraft, etc.). These are necessarily the prerogative of the large firm. But in other branches of technology advances may still be made with very limited resources or by individual inventor-entrepreneurs. Small firms may enjoy some competitive advantages in industries such as scientific instruments and machinery because of lower overhead costs, better communications and stronger motivation. They may also take half-developed products from large laboratories and bring them more swiftly to the point of launch, through the mobility of individual inventors (Shimshoni, 1970). Sometimes, of course, they will be established for the sole purpose of exploiting an invention. This has been particularly important in the case of scientific instruments.

This interpretation was supported by an empirical survey on the sources of over a thousand postwar British innovations (Freeman, 1972). This showed that eighty per cent of the innovations were launched by firms with an employment of one thousand or more, and sixty per cent by firms employing more than ten thousand. The share of small firms (employing fewer than two hundred employees) was only about ten per cent. This was much less than their share of total output, but greater than their share of R & D expenditures.

Thus, the empirical data on numbers of innovations and on R & D expenditures on the whole support the view of Galbraith on the concentration of innovative activities in capitalist industry. But they also show that enough important innovations are still made by new firms and by very small firms to justify policy measures designed to facilitate the entry of newcomers into monopolized industries.

Although some economists (Hamberg, 1964 and 1966; Scherer, 1965 and 1973) have argued that among the largest firms there is some tendency for research intensity to fall, and although many economists have argued that monopoly may induce stagnation, the empirical evidence does not give very strong support to these views. The NSF statistics show that in half the American industries, research intensity was actually higher than in the four largest firms. A higher research intensity does not mean that there may not be tendencies to withhold research results, to delay applications and to prevent diffusion through patents and other devices. It is naturally difficult to establish such tendencies through empirical investigations, but they exist on a scale sufficient to justify both safeguards on the patent system (compulsory licensing, etc.) and deliberate antitrust policies. Despite the obvious difficulties, this is an important neglected field for joint research by economists, technologists and patent lawyers. A general weakness of this whole line of research has been the failure to relate statistical measures of concentration and research intensity to the detailed market structure and competitive situation in each product line, and to study the phenomenon of product differentiation in depth. One major empirical study (Sciberras, 1975) suggested that in one highly concentrated industry, that of semi-conductors, there was little or no evidence of delay in application, because profit maximization strategies pursued by firms indicated the need for early exploitation rather than delay.

In general, the evidence does not appear to justify the view that present-day capitalism has ceased to be technically dynamic because of the prevalence of oligopoly and the high degree of concentration in research and innovation. It is the original Marxist view of the tendencies in capitalist society which is supported by the empirical findings on innovation, rather than the neo-Marxist and neoclassical stagnationist hypotheses of the 1930's. Capitalism remains a system characterized by a high rate of technical change and by a constant restless uncertainty. Although innovation has become bureaucratized and concentrated in very large firms, the overall rate of technological change has not diminished; rather, the reverse is true. As Marx foresaw, technological competition has been one of the main factors leading to industrial concentration, but this has not eliminated uncertainty and instability.

d) **Uncertainty, management of innovation, and theory of the firm**   Empirical studies of innovation and of R & D decision making provide us with good explanations of this continuing instability and uncertainty. Schumpeter (1928) had expected greater stability from the bureaucratization of innovation, and Galbraith, too, suggests that the combination of 'producer sovereignty' and planning by large corporations implies greater stability (1968).

Both overlook the evidence on the actual difficulties of 'planning' innovation. A whole number of empirical studies in several different countries have established three points fairly conclusively. First, rather few firms employ sophisticated techniques of R & D project evaluation, forecasting or programming (Baker and Pound, 1964; FBI, 1961; Naslund and Sellstedt, 1973; Olin, 1972; Clark, 1974; Roberts, 1968). Second, large errors with respect to both cost and time are characteristic of R & D evaluation, even in firms with considerable experience (Mansfield, 1971; Thomas, 1971; Olin, 1972). Third, market uncertainty is much greater than technical uncertainty, although both are very important. Almost all case studies of important innovations show how bad the forecasts were, and how much the unexpected influenced the outcome, even where very sophisticated management techniques were used – as, for example, in the case of DuPont's synthetic leather material 'Corfam' (Jewkes, 1958; Freeman, 1974). However, it must be remembered that most of these studies refer to large technical advances. Many minor 'incremental' innovations are much less uncertain in their outcome and much more easily managed and planned.

Nevertheless, the important conclusion remains that the bureaucratization of innovation, new management techniques and the concentration of R & D activities in large firms have not necessarily reduced the uncertainty associated with innovation in capitalist markets. The evidence from socialist countries also suggests considerable margins of error in R & D estimates (Amann *et al.*, 1969), but the empirical literature on innovation in socialist economies is not discussed here.

The continuing high degree of uncertainty associated with many innovative activities is consistent with the findings of industrial economists on 'higgledy-piggledy' growth (Downie, 1958; Marris, 1964) and with theories of 'muddling through' (Lindblom, 1959). It has long been obvious from the behavior of the Stock Market that prediction of future performance of industrial companies is akin to backing horses. There are many reasons for this, but among the more important is the difficulty of estimating the consequences of launching any major new product.

At one time it was thought that this uncertainty applied mainly to the military field because of the peculiar pressures prevailing there and the availability of large amounts of money from government sources to private firms (Marshall and Meckling, 1962). However, civil aircraft projects are vulnerable to the same problems, and the importance of Mansfield's work (1971) is his demonstration that civil projects in quite a different industry − that of pharmaceuticals − also suffered from very large cost overruns and other errors in forecasting.

One major empirical study on industrial innovation, Project SAPPHO (Science Policy Research Unit, 1972; Rothwell, 1974) set out to measure systematically the characteristics of successful and unsuccessful attempts to innovate by a series of paired comparisons. This technique presupposes that failures are as common as successes, and the investigators found no difficulty in discovering plenty of failures in the two industries which they investigated (chemicals and scientific instruments). The study did find that there were a number of features which clearly distinguished the pattern of success from the pattern of failure. For example, successful attempts were almost always characterized by a better understanding of user needs, acquired in a great variety of different ways. They also showed better communication with outside sources of science, greater thoroughness in eliminating 'bugs' at the experimental development stage (rather than greater speed in launching), and generally a larger team employed on development (although not a larger R & D department). But although these differences emerge from *ex post* analysis, they are difficult to plan for in advance, since they are relative and not easily amenable to management control. Consequently, from this and other recent surveys of innovation (Langrish, 1972; Mansfield, 1971; Allen, 1967) it seems reasonable to conclude that the management of innovation will continue to be a process of muddling through rather than one of planned and rational optimization.

However, it must be remembered that just because of the high risks of the radical innovations, much of the R & D activity and other technological activities of firms are not devoted to the major new product or process but to relatively minor changes and modifications. For some time now, economists have assumed largely on the basis of indirect and descriptive evidence that by far the greater part of industrial R & D expenditures went for development projects with: a) low risk of technical failure, b) short project life, c) quick pay-back on application (Mansfield, 1968; Nelson, Peck and Kalachek, 1967). This general view has now been explicitly confirmed by a useful piece of empirical survey research (Schott, 1975). This showed that for a representative sample of United Kingdom manufacturing firms, sixty per cent of all applied R & D expenditures were on projects which lasted less than two years, and only eleven per cent on projects which lasted more than four years. It has been known for some time that expenditures on fundamental research by industrial firms were less than five per cent of total industrial R & D expenditures.

Schott's sample did not include aircraft firms where development projects often take much longer, and where government extramural R & D expenditure in industry has also been very important. But her results do confirm the view that a large part of industrial R & D is devoted to product and process improvements and product differentiation, rather than to radical innovation or fundamental advances in technology. The risks are often much smaller in product differentiation, and it is possible to make some changes in technique with a high degree of confidence in the outcome. This applies also to late adopters of innovations already proven elsewhere in industry and in many cases to licensees of established processes. But the recent major international diffusion study (Ray, 1974) and Fisher's work on process control computers (1973) indicate that it is still often difficult for early adopters to make an accurate estimate of the costs and benefits of adoption, even when they attempt such evaluation.

The presence of uncertainty in relation to many types of R & D and technical change does not of course mean that decision making becomes completely irrational. Industrial R & D is a special type of investment behavior but part of the same spectrum. As with gambling behavior, the very high extra rewards which accrue to some successful innovators (true entrepreneurial profits in Schumpeter's sense) justify firms in taking considerable risks. (They also justify a 'portfolio' type of approach to R & D budgeting.) The empirical findings of innovation studies restore in some measure the true importance of entrepreneurship. They show that even in very large firms the 'business innovator' is the key individual who has to link new technological possibilities with the market.

All of this has major implications for the theory of the firm, which is only just beginning to penetrate the economics literature. Nordhaus (1969) has attempted to modify the traditional theory to accommodate empirical findings within an essentially neoclassical framework, but a Hungarian study (Kornai, 1972) uses the empirical findings of the innovation literature to argue that equilibrium theories are no longer tenable. Other economists who have been attempting to develop an alternative behavioral theory of the firm (Cyert and March, 1963; Marris, 1964; Lamberton 1965 and 1971; Gold, 1971) recognized that the *costs* of acquiring new technology are an extremely important aspect of firm behavior, and that the assumptions of 'perfect information' and equal access to technology are so unrealistic that they must be discarded, except in the case of a few industries. One possible approach to the classification of alternative firm strategies in relation to the acquisition of new technology has been put forward by Freeman (1974). But it is the work of Nelson (1971) and Nelson and Winter (1973) which appears to offer the greatest possibility for a new theory of the firm, which could be reconciled with the findings of applied economics in relation to innovation and with much of the previous achievements of economic theory. Kaldor (1972) and Hahn (1973) have pursued this debate on the irrelevance (Kaldor) or importance (Hahn) of the concept of equilibrium for the development of economic theory.

e) **Project evaluation, cost benefit, programming and technology assessment** The 'R & D industry' differs from all other industries conventionally studied by economists in the nature of its activity and in the form of its organization. While, like other industries, it has some inputs of materials and energy, these are relatively unimportant in understanding its performance. While again it may build prototypes of pilot plants, it does this only in order to generate new information and to contribute to technology. Very few of its units operate as independent, profit-making enterprises. Most of them are either the 'captive' laboratories of industrial enterprises, or government institutions, or parts of higher educational institutions. As such they may often have no separate accounts.

Although it is quite unique in its structure and its mode of operation, the R & D industry resembles all other industries in having economic problems. Clearly it is possible to use resources more or less efficiently in research and development, and it is possible to organize the work in many different ways to achieve better results. Problems of project evaluation, programming and budgeting continuously arise in the management of R & D at all levels, including central government.

In practice economists have contributed relatively little to the 'managerial' literature on R & D, perhaps because of the daunting problems of 'output' measurement. A glance at the 'output' columns in Table 2 shows how difficult it is to reduce this type of output to any comparable units of value or other measures. Some of the basic problems have been discussed by Machlup (1962) and by Freeman (UNESCO, 1969), but there are few solutions. None of the methods proposed are satisfactory. They range from peer group assessment, which raises all the problems described by Mulkay in Chapter 4, to counts of numbers of inventions, of patents and of innovations. Schmookler (1966) used patent statistics to analyse the long-term trends in four industries in the United States. He came to the extremely important (although still debatable) conclusion that inventive activity *followed* demand and investment, rather than stimulated it; but he did not attempt to relate his patent numbers to the *input* of research or inventive work in the industries concerned. Reekie (1973) and Freeman (1965) have shown that patent statistics are also useful in international comparisons and in comparing the inventive output of firms and individuals.

The methods most widely used in practice are probably indirect rather than direct. This means putting R & D back in its social context and attempting to assess its performance by measuring the 'output' indirectly in terms of some perceived contribution to wider social purposes. Thus, for example, the performance of military R & D systems may be assessed by various 'improvements' in weapons systems; the performance of medical R & D systems by reductions in mortality or duration of illness; and the performance of industrial R & D systems by improvements in processes and products or by various measures of productivity growth and of returns to investment in innovation. As we have seen, these techniques may often be unsatisfactory because of the difficulty of disentangling the specific 'contribution' of R & D from other sources of technical improvement and innovative performance. These problems vary in their severity, and there seems to be little alternative to some such approach, combined with the use of partial indicators and peer group assessment techniques. This means that the measurement of R & D performance must often be largely a politico-sociological process to which economists may make a modest contribution.

At the very least it should be possible for economists to assist in setting up 'output-budgeting' procedures and in improving project estimation techniques and programming. Output budgeting simply means relating R & D expenditures to the declared – or concealed – objectives of the organization, or of the government in the case of national R & D expenditures. This is a very elementary procedure, but it is surprising how frequently it is ignored, and how much resistance there is to its implementation. One of the greatest benefits of the national collection and publication of R & D expenditure and manpower statistics was that it permitted simple output budgeting for national R & D expenditures for the first time, and thereby a firm basis for national debates on science policy priorities. At the microlevel, a good budgeting and appraisal system similarly permits a well-structured debate on the firm's objectives and priorities in its R & D policies.

The OECD comparative statistics showed, for example, the extremely high proportion of total scientific and technical resources devoted to military objectives and to 'prestige' areas such as space exploration. By contrast they showed the relative neglect of environmental research and of many other types of research concerned with improving the quality of life (OECD, 1971). Even without knowing much about the relative 'efficiency' of military or space research by comparison with medical, environmental or agricultural research, this forms a starting point for a serious political and social debate about national and international priorities for R & D in the narrow sense, and for science and technology in general (Cooper *et al.*, 1971). It also enables attention to be concentrated on the opportunity costs of major projects and programs.

In the past the unwillingness to look at these opportunity costs stemmed from a reluctance to accept that there are *national* issues of resource allocation for science and technology. Economists who have long been accustomed to believing in the neoclassical tradition that decentralized investment decision making yields better results than centralized decision making do not readily accept that there are any global resource allocation problems. For different reasons many politicians and scientists adopt a similar view, and argue that policy for science and technology is purely a departmental microproblem (See also Salomon, Chapter 2). This philosophy has found explicit formulation in the British Rothschild Report (1971), but it is widely held among government policy makers in the United States, too. It has been reinforced by the failure to formulate a satisfactory theory of the total investment in R & D related to national goals. It has not proved possible to develop such a measure of the 'optimal' total expenditure on R & D, even for that fraction of R & D devoted to economic objectives. Although percentage of GNP is a widely used rough indicator, its association with long-term growth rates is highly problematical for many reasons (Williams, 1967). Among the most important of these are international transfers of technology, the complementarity of factors affecting economic growth and resources of technical change other than R & D. Although Schott (1975) has made a valiant attempt to make progress with her measures of the stock of knowledge, she has not resolved any of these problems.

Although it is not possible to prescribe precise targets for levels of R & D investment related to goals of economic growth, this does not mean to say that economists have not been able to make some contribution to the debate on scale and direction of R & D investment related to national goals (for example, Cooper *et al.*, 1971; Matthews, 1970; Quinn, 1968; Cairncross, 1972; Nelson, Peck and Kalachek, 1967; National Science Foundation, 1971; Lithwick, 1969). Economists in the socialist countries have not been able to resolve the fundamental theoretical problems either, but in the socialist countries the responsibility of central government for strategic priorities in allocation of resources is unequivocally accepted, and many developing countries also attempt such long-term strategic planning. In all countries considerations of military security and attitudes of secrecy surrounding major programs effectively prevent or limit open discussion and appraisal of strategic priorities and the opportunity costs of various alternatives.

It was frequently argued by advocates of high levels of military expenditure that the indirect spin-off benefits to the civil economy were so great as to provide a sufficient justification for these expenditures, even without taking into account the military 'benefits'. The logic of these arguments was always suspect and the empirical studies have generally shown a rather low return from 'spin-off' (A. D. Little, 1963). However, this does not mean that the very high levels of government military R & D expenditures during and since World War II have been without important social and economic consequences. The development of a military-industrial complex in the United States (Galbraith, 1967; Sapolsky, Chapter 12) is clearly a sociological development of the greatest importance, and several empirical studies have shown the economic importance of military procurement and development finance in those industries in which these expenditures are concentrated, e.g. in the United States electronic industries (Golding, 1972; Tilton, 1971; Little, 1963). R & D statistics have also served to demonstrate the crucial role played by the governments of Western mixed economies in financing civil R & D activities. In the industrialized countries, they usually finance nearly all academic and prestige R & D, most agricultural and health R & D, and – in some countries – significant amounts of civilian industrial R & D (Pavitt and Worboys, 1974; Gilpin, 1975; OECD, 1974). As in other areas of national resource allocation, economists have inevitably become involved in debates and analyses as to what the government's role in financing such R & D activities ought to be (Pavitt, 1975; Salomon, Chapter 2). The primary role of government in basic research, and in other 'public goods' areas such as health and environment, is widely accepted by economists, governments and the scientific community in all Western countries. Nelson (1959) has argued in terms of welfare economics that government support for basic research can be justified on economic grounds, given that any resulting application tends to happen after long time periods and in unexpected places. For these and other reasons, the basic research community has organized itself so that the basic knowledge is published and freely available. But this means that industrial firms will tend to under-invest in basic research, since they cannot fully appropriate the benefits that result from it; this underinvestment will be all the more marked if industrial firms are averse to longer-term and more risky activities. Although this view has been partly challenged by Hirschleifer (1971), it remains the dominant view.

However, there is much more intense debate about the degree to which governments should become involved in funding civilian, industrial R & D (See again Salomon, Chapter 2). Galbraith (1968) has argued that, given what he considers to be the growing scale imperative of modern technology, they will increasingly and inevitably be drawn into subsidizing industrial R & D in order to cover ever more costly risks. On the other hand, Pavitt and Worboys (1974) have argued that the R & D statistics show no clear-cut tendency toward increasing government involvement over time; neither do they show any tendency toward uniformly high levels of government involvement either across country or across industry. Eads and Nelson (1971) and Jewkes (1972) have questioned the economic reasons advanced to justify government support if the market is likely to make them commercially viable, as is shown by the private development of the IBM 360 series, of the Boeing 747, and by the huge expenditures on North Sea oil. They also question the existence of the external economic benefits for such projects in terms of technological 'spin-off', contributions to the balance of payments, etc. Moreover, they fear that government-financed projects will always be difficult to stop once they have been started. Eads and Nelson argue that, instead of *supplementing* the private market by financing a few, very expensive commercial development projects, governments should *complement* the private market by financing many more smaller-scale applied research and exploratory development projects in sectors of longer-term social and economic importance.

However, the skepticism of economists about the benefits of large-scale government-funded development projects has not had any noticeable effects in reducing expenditures on them. For example, in an influential and widely read book on the British economy, Peck (1968) argued that far too many resources were being devoted to the aircraft industry; in 1974, the level of investment remains more or less the same. Why is this the case? Clearly the answer to this question lies in the area of *political* economy, where the economist has to take account of the work of political scientists like Dörfer (1973), Nieburg (1966), and Sapolsky (1972 and Chapter 12 of this book) who have analyzed the lobbies, pressure groups and power struggles surrounding large-scale R & D projects.[2]

The work of political scientists and sociologists has shown the way in which formal techniques of project evaluation may be manipulated by interest groups, and that apparently sophisticated methods of management and control are often not quite what they seem (See Nelkin, Chapter 11). Sapolsky's work (1972) on the use of PERT in the Polaris Project is a particularly good example of this.

No formal technique of project evaluation or technology assessment can be divorced from the subjective judgments, bias, and values of the estimators and decision makers. Thomas (1971) has shown that the tendency of engineers to underestimate development costs is deliberate and has in part at least a sociological explanation. However, the underestimation of development costs, although a very serious problem, is probably a less difficult one to resolve than the estimation of benefits. Indeed, the whole experience of cost-benefit analysis is full of examples of the pitfalls and limitations of this mode of assessment (Prest and Turvey, 1967; Page, 1975). The most difficult questions are probably those of the so-called 'intangible benefits', such as enhancement or degradation of amenity, but even the apparently more straightforward estimates can be a source of very great confusion and error as well as deliberate exaggeration.

A highly pertinent example of this is the estimate of the rate of return to research on hybrid corn in the United States by Griliches (1958). This has been repeatedly cited in the economics literature as one of the very few examples of an attempt to measure and compare the costs and benefits of a particular piece of agricultural research. It was particularly welcome to

---

[2] We should also recognize the important contributions made in the tradition of 'muckraking' (now called 'investigative') journalism to our understanding of science and technology lobbies: for example, D. Greenberg's analysis of the United States basic research lobby, (1969).

advocates of higher levels of R & D expenditures as it supposedly demonstrated an extraordinarily high rate of return to this type of research. But in
fact, as Wise (1975) has forcefully pointed out, alternative and more plausible
methods of calculation give very different results and a much lower rate of
return. In particular, the additional 'innovation' and 'diffusion' investment
necessary to derive the benefits from the original research was ignored in the
calculations. The net benefits are still important in this case but far less than
estimated. Similar criticisms can be made of many other applications of
cost-benefit and rate-of-return calculations. The best that can be said for all
these formal techniques is not that they give any precise answers, but that
they provide a framework for structuring what is essentially a policy debate.
The more recent fashion for 'technology assessment' is not discussed here as
it is the subject of a separate chapter by Dorothy Nelkin (Chapter 11), but
her analysis is consistent with this conclusion.

If this is firmly kept in mind then it is obviously at least as important to
ensure adequate participation of affected groups in the debate as it is to use
any particular technique. The problem is political and managerial, as well as
technological and economic. The general conclusion which emerges, therefore, is that the most critical problems of allocation are political and strategic
(See also Salomon, Chapter 2). This is confirmed by many empirical studies
of national policies for science and technology; for example, Gilpin (1968,
1970) has shown how government policies toward science and technology in
de Gaulle's France were heavily bound up with foreign policy objectives, and
how science and technology strategies have been conditioned by national
perceptions of international 'challenges'. Pavitt (1972) has shown how, during
attempts at European technological cooperation in the 1950's and 1960's,
there was always a fundamental conflict between the political objectives of
the participating countries, on the one hand, and the requirements of managerial and economic efficiency, on the other. (See also Chapters 13 and 14
by Schroeder-Gudehus and Skolnikoff.) Effective cooperation at least among
economists, political scientists and sociologists is essential for a better understanding of these aspects of science and technology politics. This points to a
more general conclusion of this entire survey, discussed in the final section.

f) **Conclusions and future research**   In this short survey it has not been
possible to cover many important fields of economic research which are
increasingly concerned with problems of science and technology. One such
field is international trade, which has been revolutionized in the past twenty
years as a result of a series of empirical studies relating product innovation
and technological change to export performance. This line of investigation
was initiated by Leontief's demonstration (1956) that the commodity composition of United States exports could not be adequately explained by the
traditional theory of comparative advantage, which postulated that the
United States comparative advantage should be in capital-intensive products.

Posner (1961) and Vernon (1966) developed a theory of 'technological gap' trade based on leadership in innovation in particular product groups. Hufbauer (1966) and Freeman (1963 and 1965) demonstrated that patterns of international trade in synthetic materials and electronic capital goods could be explained on the basis of this type of analysis. This type of work led theorists such as Johnson (1969) to revise the neoclassical comparative advantage theory to take account of investment in research and education as a form of capital-intensity. On this basis the export performance of such countries as the United States and Germany is more readily comprehensible, and some reconciliation with the traditional factor intensity theory is possible. Obviously this has enormous implications for the problems of poor countries on the international export market which it is not possible to pursue here.

In the field of development studies, economists have increasingly recognized that the economic issues of development are bound up with the political, social and historical contexts of underdevelopment (Myrdal, 1968; Seers and Joy, 1971; Goldthorpe, 1975; and Sardar and Rosser-Owen, Chapter 15), and this is indeed the moral which emerges throughout this survey. Whether we are concerned with project evaluation, technology assessment, sources of technical change, research creativity or the relationship between science and technology, it is apparent that although economics in the narrow sense has much to contribute, the older tradition of political economy has far greater potential. In all the important fields of research, economic, sociological, psychological and political issues are so intertwined that they cry out for an integrated social science approach. If social scientists fail to cooperate with each other and with technologists in developing this integrated approach, there is a serious danger of naive, technique-based approaches, such as systems research, being substituted. These dangers are already apparent both in capitalist and in socialist countries (Hoos, 1969; Maestre and Pavitt, 1972).

Economists above all should be capable of initiating the return to the classical integrative tradition. Adam Smith, John Stuart Mill and Karl Marx all made outstanding contributions to sociology, philosophy, ethics and political theory as well as to economics. None of them would have accepted the limitations of the modern fragmented social science disciplines. There are many signs in the economics profession of a desire to return to the classical political economy tradition (Rothschild, 1971). Simultaneously there is a swing back to the concept of economics itself as a policy science, not a positive science (Blaug, 1975). Nowhere would these trends be more welcome and more fruitful than in the area of science policy studies.

BIBLIOGRAPHY

Abramowtiz, 1956   Abramowitz, M., 'Resource and Output Trends in the United States Since 1870', *American Economic Association Papers* 46, No. 2, May 1956, pp. 5-23.

Allan, 1966   Allan, T. J., 'The Performance of Information Channels in the Transfer of Technology', *Industrial Management Review* 8, No. 1, 1966, pp. 87-98.

Allen, 1967   Allen, J. A., *Studies in Innovation in the Steel and Chemical Industries,* Manchester University Press, 1967.

Amann *et al.,* 1969   Amann, R., Berry, R., Davies, R. W., Kozlowski, J. P. and Zaleski, E., *Science Policy in the USSR,* Paris, OECD, 1969.

Ames, 1961   Ames, E., 'Research, Invention, Development and Innovation', *American Economic Review* 51, June 1961, pp. 370-381.

Arrow, 1962   Arrow, K., 'The Economic Implications of Learning by Doing', *Review of Economic Studies* 29, June 1962, pp. 155-173.

Baker and Pound, 1964   Baker, N. R. and Pound, W. H., 'R and D Project Selection: Where We Stand', *IEEE Management Transactions* 11, No. 4, 1964, p. 124.

Baran, 1957   Baran, P. A., *The Political Economy of Growth,* New York, Monthly Review Press, 1957.

Bell and Hill, 1977   Bell, R. M. N. and Hill, S. C., 'Paradigm and Practice: Innovation and Technology Transfer Models – Their Unexamined Assumptions and Inapplicability Outside Developed Countries' (mimeo), to be published in Cooper, C. M. (Ed.), *SPRU Papers on Technology and Development* (working title), Wiley, 1977.

Bell *et al.,* 1976   Bell, R. M. N., Cooper, C. M., Kaplinsky, R. M., and Wit Sakyarakwit, *Industrial Technology and Employment Opportunity: A Study of Technical Alternatives for Can Manufacture in Developing Countries,* International Labour Organisation, Geneva, 1976.

Bernal, 1939   Bernal, J. D., *The Social Function of Science,* London, Routledge, 1939.

Blaug, 1963   Blaug, M., 'A Survey of the Theory of Process Innovations', *Economica* 30, No. 17, 1963, pp. 13-32.

Blaug, 1975   Blaug, M., *Kuhn versus Lakatos or Paradigms versus Research Programmes in the History of Economics* (mimeo), London, 1975.

Burns and Stalker, 1961   Burns, T. and Stalker, G. M., *The Management of Innovation,* London, Tavistock Publications, 1961.

Byatt and Cohen, 1969   Byatt, I. and Cohen, A., *An Attempt to Quantify the Economic Benefits of Scientific Research,* London, Department of Education and Science, Science Policy Studies No. 4, 1969.

Cairncross, 1972   Cairncross, A., 'Reflections on Technological Change', *Scottish Journal of Political Economy* 19, No. 2, June 1972, pp. 107-114.

Carter and Williams, 1957	Carter, C. F. and Williams, B. R., *Industry and Technical Progress,* London, Oxford University Press, 1957.
Carter and Williams, 1958	Carter, C. F. and Williams, B. R., *Investment in Innovation,* London, Oxford University Press, 1958.
Carter and Williams, 1959	Carter, C. F. and Williams, B. R., *Science and Industry,* London, Oxford University Press, 1959.
Charpie, 1967	Charpie, R. (Ed.), *Technological Innovation: Its Environment and Management,* Washington, D.C., United States Department of Commerce, 1967.
Clarke, 1974	Clarke, T., 'Decision-Making in Technologically Based Organizations: A Literature Survey Based on Present Practice', *IEEE Transactions on Engineering Management* EM-21, No. 1, February 1974.
Cole *et al.,* 1973	Cole, H. S. D., Freeman, C., Jahoda, M., Pavitt, K. L. R. (Eds.), *Thinking About the Future,* London, Chatto and Windus, and *Models of Doom,* New York, Universe Books, 1973.
Cooper, 1972	Cooper, C. M., 'Science, Technology and Development', *Journal of Development Studies* 9, No. 1, October, 1972.
Cooper, 1973	Cooper, C. M., 'Choice of Techniques and Technological Change as Problems in Political Economy', *International Social Science Journal* 25, No. 3, 1973, pp. 322-336.
Cooper, 1977	Cooper, C. M., *SPRU Papers on Technology and Development* (working title), to be published by Wiley.
Cooper and Sercovich, 1971	Cooper, C. M., and Sercovich, F., *The Channels and Mechanisms for the Transfer of Technology from Developed to Developing Countries,* UNCTAD, Geneva (mimeo), 1971.
Cooper *et al.,* 1971	Cooper, C. M., Freeman, C., Oldham, C. H. G., Sinclair, C. and Achilladelis, B. A., 'Goals of R and D in the 1970's', *Science Studies* 1, 1971, No. 3, pp. 357-406.
Cyert and March, 1963	Cyert, R. M. and March, J. G., *A Behavioral Theory of the Firm,* Prentice Hall, 1963.
Denison, 1962	Denison, E. F., *The Sources of Economic Growth in the United States and the Alternatives Before Us,* Committee for Economic Development, New York, 1962.
Denison, 1967	Denison, E. F., *Why Growth Rates Differ: Post-War Experiences in Nine Western Countries,* Brookings Institution, 1967.
Domar, 1961	Domar, E. D., 'On the Measurement of Technological Change', *Economic Journal* 71 No. 284, December 1961, pp. 709-729.
Dörfer, 1973	Dörfer, I., *System 37 Viggen: Arms, Technology and Domestication of Glory,* Scandinavian University Books, 1973.
Downie, 1958	Downie, J., *The Competitive Process,* London, Duckworth, 1958.
Eads and Nelson, 1971	Eads, G. and Nelson, R., 'Governmental Support of Advanced Technology: Power Reactors and Supersonic Transport', *Public Policy* 19, No. 3, 1971, pp. 405-428.

Enos, 1962a	Enos, J. L., *Petroleum Progress and Profits*, Cambridge, Mass., MIT Press, 1962.
Enos, 1962b	Enos, J. L., 'Invention and Innovation in the Petroleum Refining Industry', in National Bureau of Economic Research, *The Rate and Direction of Inventive Activity*, 1962.
Federation of British Industries, 1961	Federation of British Industries, *Industrial Research in British Manufacturing Industry in 1960*, London. FBI, 1961.
Fellner, 1961	Fellner, W. J., 'Two Propositions in the Theory of Induced Innovations', *Economic Journal* 71, No. 282, June 1961, pp. 305-308.
Fellner, 1962	Fellner, W. J., 'Does the Market Direct the Relative Factor Saving Effects of Technological Progress?' in NBER, *The Rate and Direction of Inventive Activity*, Princeton University Press, 1962.
Fisher, 1973	Fisher, L. A., *The Diffusion of Technological Innovation: A Study of the Adoption of the Electronic Digital Computer in Process Control*, Ph.D. Thesis, Polytechnic of Central London, October, 1973.
Freeman, 1962	Freeman, C., 'Research and Development: A Comparison Between British and American Industry', *National Institute Economic Review*, No. 20, 1962, pp. 21-39.
Freeman, 1967	Freeman, C., 'Science and Economy at the National Level', in OECD, *Problems of Science Policy*, Paris, OECD, 1967.
Freeman, 1972	Freeman, C., *The Role of Small Firms in Innovation in the United Kingdom since 1945*, Bolton Committee of Inquiry Research, Report No. 6, London, Her Majesty's Stationary Office, 1972.
Freeman, 1974	Freeman, C., *The Economics of Industrial Innovation*, London, Penguin Books, 1974.
Freeman and Young, 1965	Freeman, C. and Young, A. J., *The Research and Development Effort in Western Europe, North America and the Soviet Union*, Paris, OECD, 1965.
Freeman, *et al.*, 1963	Freeman, C., Fuller, J. K. and Young, A. J., 'The Plastics Industry: A Comparative Study of Research and Innovation', *National Institute Economic Review*, No. 26, 1963, pp. 22-62.
Freeman, *et al.*, 1965	Freeman, C., Harlow, C. J. E., and Fuller, J. K., 'Research and Development in Electronic Capital Goods', *National Institute Economic Review*, No. 34, 1965, pp. 40-97.
Galbraith, 1952	Galbraith, J. K., *American Capitalism*, Houghton Mifflin, 1952.
Galbraith, 1968	Galbraith, J. K., *The New Industrial State*, Hamish Hamilton, 1968.
Gibbons and Johnston, 1974	Gibbons, M. and Johnston, R., 'The Role of Science in Technological Innovation', *Research Policy* 3, No. 4, 1974, pp. 220-242.
Gilfillan, 1935	Gilfillan, S. C., *The Sociology of Invention*, Chicago, Follet Publishing Company, 1935.
Gilpin, 1968	Gilpin, R., *France in the Age of the Scientific State*, Princeton University Press, 1968.

Gilpin, 1970

Gilpin, R., 'Technological Strategies and National Purpose', *Science* 169, 1970, pp. 441-448.

Gilpin, 1975

Gilpin, R., *Technology, Economic Growth and International Competitiveness,* Report of the Joint Economic Committee of the Congress, U.S. Government Printing Office, 1975.

Gold, 1971

Gold, B., *Explorations in Managerial Economics,* New York, Basic Books, 1971.

Golding, 1972

Golding, A. M., *The Semi-Conductor Industry in Britain and the USA: A Case Study in Innovation, Growth and the Diffusion of Technology,* D.Phil. Thesis, University of Sussex, 1972.

Goldthorpe, 1975

Goldthorpe, J. E., *The Sociology of the Third World,* Cambridge University Press, 1975.

Greenberg, 1969

Greenberg, D., *The Politics of American Science,* Penguin, 1969.

Griliches, 1958

Griliches, Z., 'Research Costs and Social Returns: Hybrid Corn and Related Innovations', *Journal of Political Economy* 66, No. 5, pp. 419-431.

Griliches and Jorgensen, 1966

Griliches, Z. and Jorgensen, D. W., 'Sources of Measured Productivity Change: Capital Input', *American Economic Association* 56, No. 2, 1966, pp. 50-61.

Hahn, 1973

Hahn, F. H., *On the Notion of Equilibrium in Economics,* Cambridge University Press, 1973.

Hamberg, 1964

Hamberg, D., 'Size of Firm, Oligopoly and Research: The Evidence', *Canadian Journal of Economic and Political Science* 30, No. 1, 1964, pp. 62-75.

Hamberg, 1966

Hamberg, D., *Essays on the Economics of Research and Development,* New York, Random House, 1966.

Hirschleifer, 1971

Hirschleifer, J., 'The Private and Social Value of Information and the Reward to Inventive Activity', *American Economic Review* 61, 1971, pp. 561-574.

Hirschman and Lindblom, 1962

Hirschman, O. A. and Lindblom, C. E., 'Economic Development, R and D Policy Making: Some Converging Views', *Behavioral Science* 7, 1962, pp. 211-222.

Hollander, 1965

Hollander, S., *The Sources of Increased Efficiency: A Study of DuPont Rayon Plants,* Cambridge, Mass., MIT Press, 1965.

Hoos, 1969

Hoos, I., *Systems Analysis and Social Policy,* Institute for Economic Affairs, London, 1969.

Hufbauer, 1966

Hufbauer, G. C., *Synthetic Materials and the Theory of International Trade,* London, Duckworth, 1966.

Jewkes, 1972

Jewkes, J., *Government and High Technology,* Institute of Economic Affairs, Occasional Paper No. 37, London, 1972.

Jewkes *et al.,* 1958

Jewkes, J., Sawers, D. and Stillerman, R., *The Sources of Invention,* London and New York, Macmillan, Revised Edition, 1969.

Johnson, 1969

Johnson, H., 'Comparative Cost and Commercial Policy Theory for a Developing World Economy', Wicksell Lecture for 1968.

Jorgensen and Griliches, 1967 Jorgensen, D. W. and Griliches, Z., 'The Explanation of Productivity Change', *Review of Economic Studies* 34, 1967, pp. 249-283.

Kaldor, 1961 Kaldor, N., 'Capital Accumulation and Economic Growth', in Lutz, F. and Hague, D. (Eds.), *The Theory of Capital,* London, International Economic Association, 1961.

Kaldor, 1972 Kaldor, N., 'The Irrelevance of Equilibrium Economics', *Economic Journal* 82, 1972, pp. 1237-1255.

Kamien and Schwartz, 1974 Kamien, M. I. and Schwartz, N. L., 'Market Structure and Innovation: A Survey Supplement' (mimeo), Northwestern University, Illinois, 1974.

Katz, 1972 Katz, J., *Importacion de Tecnologia, Auredizaje Local e Industrializacion Dependiente,* Buenos Aires, Instituto Torcuato di Tella, Centre de Investigaciones Economicas Superie 1502, 1972.

Kennedy and Thirlwall, 1972 Kennedy, C. and Thirlwall, A. P., 'Technical Progress', in *Surveys of Applied Economics,* The Royal Economic Society and the Social Science Research Council, London, Macmillan, 1972.

Kornai, 1972 Kornai, J., *Anti-Equilibrium,* Elsevier-North Holland, Amsterdam, 1972.

Lamberton, 1965 Lamberton, D. M., *The Theory of Profit,* Oxford, Blackwell, 1965.

Lamberton, 1971 Lamberton, D. M. (Ed.), *Economics of Information and Knowledge,* Penguin, 1971.

Langrish, 1974 Langrish, J., 'The Changing Relationship Between Science and Technology', *Nature* 250, 1974, p. 614.

Langrish *et al.,* 1972 Langrish, J. *et al., Wealth from Knowledge,* London, Macmillan, 1972.

Lave, 1966 Lave, L. B., *Technological Change: Its Conception and Measurement,* Englewood Cliffs, New Jersey, Prentice-Hall, 1966.

Lenin, 1915 Lenin, V. I., *Imperialism: The Highest Stage of Capitalism* (English Edition), Martin Lawrence, 1930.

Leontief, 1956 Leontief, W., 'Factor Proportions and the Structure of American Trade: Further Theoretical and Empirical Analysis', *Review of Economics and Statistics* 38, 1956, pp. 386-407.

Lindblom, 1959 Lindblom, C. A., 'The Science of Muddling Through', *Public Administration Review* 19, 1959, pp. 79-88.

Lithwick, 1969 Lithwick, N. H., *Canada's Science Policy and the Economy,* Methuen, Toronto, 1969.

Little, 1963 Little, A. D., *Patterns and Problems of Technical Innovation in American Industry,* Washington, D.C., 1963.

Machlin, 1973 Machlin, D. J., *The Economics of Technical Change in the Pottery Industry,* M.A. dissertation, University of Keele, 1973.

Machlup, 1962 Machlup, F., *The Production and Distribution of Knowledge in the United States,* Princeton University Press, 1962.

Maclaurin, 1953 Maclaurin, W. R., 'The Sequence from Invention to Innovation', *Quarterly Journal of Economics* 67, No. 1, 1953, pp. 97-111.

Maestre and Pavitt, 1972	Maestre, C. and Pavitt, K., *Analytical Methods in Government Science Policy,* Paris, OECD, 1972.
Malthus, 1798	Malthus, T., *Essay on Population,* London, 1798.
Mansfield, 1961	Mansfield, E., 'Technical Change and the Rate of Imitation', *Econometrica,* 29, No. 4, 1961, pp. 741-766.
Mansfield, 1963	Mansfield, E., 'Size of Firm, Market Structure and Innovation', *Journal of Political Economy* 7, No. 61, 1963, pp. 556-576.
Mansfield, 1968	Mansfield, E., *Economics of Technological Change,* New York, 1968.
Mansfield, *et al.,* 1971	Mansfield, E. *et al., Research and Innovation in the Modern Corporation,* New York, Norton and London, Macmillan, 1971.
Marris, 1964	Marris, R., *The Economic Theory of Managerial Capitalism,* Macmillan, 1964.
Marshall and Meckling, 1962	Marshall, A. W. and Meckling, W. H., 'Predictability of the Costs, Time and Success of Development', in National Bureau of Economic Research, *The Rate and Direction of Inventive Activity,* Princeton, 1962.
Marx, 1867	Marx, K., *Capital,* Allan and Unwin Edition, 1938.
Marx and Engels, 1848	Marx, K. and Engels, F., *Communist Manifesto,* London, 1848.
Matthews, 1970	Matthews, R. C. O., 'The Contribution of Science and Technology to Economic Development' in Williams, B. R. (Ed.), *Science and Technology in Economic Growth,* Macmillan, London, 1970.
Meadows *et al.,* 1972	Meadows, D. L. *et al., The Limits to Growth,* New York, Universe Books, and London, Earth Island, 1972.
Meek, 1953	Meek, R. L. (Ed.), *Marx and Engels on Malthus,* London, Lawrence and Wishart, and Second Edition, *Marx and Engels on the Population Bomb,* Berkeley, California, Ramparts Press, 1953.
Metcalfe, 1970	Metcalfe, J. S., 'Diffusion of Innovation in the Lancashire Textile Industry', *Manchester School,* June 1970, pp. 145-162.
Minasian, 1962	Minasian, J. R., 'The Economics of R and D', in *The Rate and Direction of Inventive Activity,* Princeton University Press, 1962.
Monopolies Commission, 1973	Monopolies Commission, *A Report on the Supply of Chlordiazepoxide and Diazepam,* London, Her Majesty's Stationary Office, 1973.
Morand, 1968	Morand, J. C., 'La Recherche et la dévelopement selon la dimension des entreprises', *Le Progrès scientifique,* No. 122.
Morand, 1970	Morand, J. C., 'Recherche et dimension des entreprises dans la communauté economique européenne', Nancy.
Muller, 1962	Muller, W. F., 'The Origins of the Basic Inventions Underlying DuPont's Major Product and Process Innovations', in National Bureau of Economic Research, *The Rate and Direction of Inventive Activity,* Princeton University Press, 1962.

Myrdal, 1968   Myrdal, G., *Asian Drama: An Inquiry into the Poverty of Nations*, 3 Vols., Harmondsworth, Middlesex, Penguin Books, 1968.

Näslund and Sellstedt, 1973   Näslund, B. and Sellstedt, B., 'A Note on the Implementation and Use of Models for R and D Planning', *Research Policy* 2, No. 1, 1973, pp. 72-84.

National Science Foundation, 1969   National Science Foundation, Illinois Institute of Technology Research Institute, *Technology in Retrospect and Critical Events in Science* (TRACES), Washington, D. C., NSF-C535, 1969.

National Science Foundation, 1971   National Science Foundation, *Research and Development and Economic Growth*, Washington, D.C., NSF 72-303, 1971.

National Science Foundation, 1973   National Science Foundation, *Interactions of Science and Technology in the Innovative Process*, Final Report from the Battelle Columbus Laboratory, Washington, D.C., NSF-667, 1973.

Nelson, 1959   Nelson, R. R., 'The Simple Economics of Basic Scientific Research', *Journal of Political Economy* 67, No. 3, 1959, pp. 297-306.

Nelson, 1959   Nelson, R. R., 'The Economics of Invention: A Survey of the Literature', *Journal of Business* 32, No. 2, 1959, pp. 101-127.

Nelson, 1962   Nelson, R. R., 'The Link Between Science and Invention: The Case of the Transistor', in NBER, *The Rate and Direction of Inventive Activity*, Princeton University Press, 1962.

Nelson, 1971   Nelson, R. R., *Issues and Suggestions for the Study of Industrial Organisation in a Regime of Rapid Technical Change*, Yale University Economic Growth Center, Discussion Paper No. 103, 1971.

Nelson and Winter, 1973   Nelson, R. R. and Winter, S., 'Neoclassical versus Evolutionary Theories of Economic Growth: Critique and Prospectus' (mimeo), Yale University, 1973.

Nelson *et al.*, 1967   Nelson, R. R., Peck, M. J., and Kalachek, E. D., *Technology, Economic Growth and Public Policy*, London, Allen and Unwin, 1967.

Nordhaus, 1969   Nordhaus, W. D., *Invention, Growth and Welfare: A Theoretical Treatment of Technological Change*, Cambridge, Mass., MIT Press, 1969.

OECD, 1963, 1970 and 1976   OECD, *The Measurement of Scientific and Technical Activities*, Directorate for Scientific Affairs, Paris, Revised, 1963, 1970 and 1976.

OECD, 1964   OECD, *The Residual Factor and Economic Growth*, OECD, Paris, 1964.

OECD, 1967   OECD, *The Overall Level and Structure of R and D Efforts in OECD-Member Countries*, OECD, Paris, 1967.

OECD, 1971, 1974   OECD, *R and D in OECD-Member Countries: Trends and Objectives*, OECD, Paris, 1971, 1974.

Olin, 1972   Olin, J., *R and D Management Practices: Chemical Industry in Europe*, Stanford Research Institute, Zurich, 1972.

Page, 1975	Page, R. W. in Encel, S., Marstrand, P. K. and Page, R. W., *The Art of Anticipation,* Martin Robertson, 1975.
Pavitt, 1971	Pavitt, K., *The Conditions for Success in Technological Innovation,* OECD, Paris, 1971.
Pavitt, 1972	Pavitt, K., 'Technology in Europe's Future', *Research Review,* 1, No. 3, 1972, pp. 210-273.
Pavitt, 1975	Pavitt, K., *A Survey of the Literature on Government Policy Toward Innovation,* Royal Economic Society Conference, Cambridge, to be published in July 1976.
Pavitt and Walker, 1976	Pavitt, K. and Walker, W., 'Four Country Project: Report of the Feasibility Study', *Research Policy* 5, No. 1, 1976, pp. 1-96.
Pavitt and Worboys, 1974	Pavitt, K. and Worboys, M., *Science, Technology and the Modern Industrial State,* Unit Two, SISCON, University of Leeds, 1974.
Peck, 1968	Peck, M. in Caves, R. (Ed.), *Britain's Economic Prospects,* Allen and Unwin, 1968.
Perroux, 1971	Perroux, F., 'The Domination Effect and Modern Economic Theory', in Rothschild, K. W. (Ed.), *Power in Economics,* London, Penguin Modern Economics, 1971.
Posner, 1961	Posner, M., 'International Trade and Technical Change', *Oxford Economic Papers* 13, No. 3, October 1961, pp. 323-341.
Prest and Turvey, 1967	Prest, A. R. and Turvey, R., 'Cost-Benefit Analysis: A Survey', in *A Survey of Economic Theory* Vol. 3, MacMillan, London, 1967.
Derek Price, 1965	Price, Derek de Solla, 'Is Technology Historically Independent of Science?' *Technology and Culture* 6, No. 4, 1965, pp. 553-568.
Quinn, 1968	Quinn, J. B., *Scientific and Technical Strategy at the National and Major Enterprise Level,* Paris, UNESCO, 1968.
Ray and Nabseth, 1974	Ray, G. F. and Nabseth, L. (Eds.), *The Diffusion of New Industrial Processes,* Cambridge University Press, 1974.
Reekie, 1973	Reekie, W. D., 'Patent Data as a Guide to Industrial Activity', *Research Policy* 2, No. 3, October 1973, pp. 246-266.
Ricardo, 1817	Ricardo, D., *The Principles of Political Economy and Taxation,* London, 1817.
Roberts, 1968	Roberts, E. B., 'The Myths of Research Management', *Science and Technology,* No. 80, 1968, pp. 40-46.
Robinson, 1934	Robinson, J., *Economics of Imperfect Competition,* London, Macmillan, 1934.
Robinson, 1974	Robinson, J., *History versus Equilibrium,* Thames Papers in Political Economy, London, 1974.
Robinson and Eatwell, 1973	Robinson, J. and Eatwell, J., *An Introduction to Modern Economics,* McGraw Hill, 1973.
Rogers, 1962	Rogers, E. M., *Diffusion of Innovations,* New York, Free Press of Glencoe, 1962.
Roll, 1934	Roll, E., *History of Economic Thought,* London, Faber, 1934.

Rosenberg, 1971   Rosenberg, N. (Ed.), *The Economics of Technical Change,* London, Penguin, 1971.

Rosenberg, 1975   Rosenberg, N., 'Factors Affecting the Pay-Off to Technological Innovation' (mimeo), National Science Foundation, 1975.

Rothschild, 1971   Rothschild, K. W. (Ed.), *Power in Economics,* London, Penguin Modern Economics Readings, 1971.

The Rothschild Report, 1971   The Rothschild Report, *A Framework for Government Research and Development,* Cmnd. 4814, Her Majesty's Stationary Office, London, 1971.

Rothwell and Townsend, 1973   Rothwell, R. and Townsend, J., 'The Communication Problem of Small Firms', *R and D Management* 3, No. 3, June 1973, pp. 151-153.

Rothwell *et al.,* 1974   Rothwell, R. *et al.,* 'Sappho Updated', *Research Policy* 3, No. 3, November 1974, pp. 258-292.

Rubenstein, 1966   Rubenstein, A., 'Economic Evaluation of R and D: A Brief Survey of Theory and Practice', *Journal of Industrial Engineering* 17, No. 11, 1966, pp. 615-620.

Salter, 1966   Salter, W. E. G., *Productivity and Technical Change,* Cambridge University Press, 1966.

Sapolsky, 1972   Sapolsky, H., *The Polaris System Development: Bureaucratic and Programmatic Success in Government,* Harvard University Press, 1972.

Scherer, 1965   Scherer, F. M., 'Firm Size, Market Structure, Opportunity and the Output of Patented Inventions', *American Economic Review* 55, No. 5, 1965, pp. 1097-1123.

Scherer, 1973   Scherer, F., *Industrial Market Structure and Economic Performance,* Rand McNally, 1973.

Schmookler, 1966   Schmookler, J., *Invention and Economic Growth,* Harvard University Press, 1966.

Schott, 1975   Schott, K., *The Determinants of Industrial R and D Expenditures,* D.Phil. thesis, Oxford, 1975.

Schumpeter, 1928   Schumpeter, J. A., 'The Instability of Capitalism', *Economic Journal* 38, 1928, pp. 361-386.

Schumpeter, 1934   Schumpeter, J. A., *The Theory of Economic Development,* Harvard University Press, 1934.

Schumpeter, 1939   Schumpeter, J. A., *Business Cycles,* New York, McGraw Hill, 1939.

Schumpeter, 1942   Schumpeter, J. A., *Capitalism, Socialism and Democracy,* New York, Harper and Row, 1942.

Sciberras, 1976   Sciberras, E., *Multinational Electronics Companies and National Economic Policies,* D.Phil. thesis, University of Sussex, to be published in New York, 1976.

Science Policy Research Unit, 1972   Science Policy Research Unit, *Success and Failure in Industrial Innovation,* London Center for the Study of Industrial Innovation, 1972.

Scott, 1975   Scott, T. W. K., *Diffusion of New Technology in the British and West German Manufacturing Industries: The Case of the Tufting Process,* D.Phil. thesis, University of Sussex, 1975.

Seers and Joy, 1971   Seers, D. and Joy, L. (Eds.), *Development in a Divided World,* Harmondsworth, Penguin, 1971.

Sherwin and Isensen, 1966	Sherwin, C. and Isensen, R., *First Interim Report on Project Hindsight,* Washington, D.C., Office of the Director of Defense Research and Engineering, 1966.
Shimshoni, 1970	Shimshoni, D., 'The Mobile Scientist in the American Instrument Industry', *Minerva* 8, No. 1, 1970, pp. 59-89.
Smith, 1776	Smith, A., *The Wealth of Nations,* London, Dent, 1910.
Solo, 1951	Solo, C. S., 'Innovation in the Capitalist Process: A Critique of the Schumpeterian Theory', *Quarterly Journal of Economics* 65, 1951, pp. 417-428.
Solow, 1957	Solow, R. M., 'Technical Change and the Aggregate Production Function', *Review of Economics and Statistics* 39, 1957, pp. 312-320.
Stead, 1974	Stead, H., *Statistics of Technological Innovation in Industry,* Cat. No. 13-555, Statistics Canada, 1974.
Sturmey, 1964	Sturmey, S. G., 'Cost Curves and Pricing in Aircraft Production', *Economic Journal,* December 1964, pp. 954-982.
Thomas, 1971	Thomas, H., 'Some Evidence on the Accuracy of Forecasts in R and D Projects', *R and D Management* 1, No. 2, February 1971, pp. 55-71.
Tilton, 1971	Tilton, J., *International Diffusion of Technology: The Case of Semi-Conductors,* Brookings Institution, 1971.
Turner and Williamson, 1969	Turner, D. F. and Williamson, O. E., 'Market Structure in Relation to Technical and Organisational Innovation', in Heath, J. B. (Ed.), *International Conference on Monopolies, Mergers and Restrictive Practices,* Board of Trade, London, 1969.
UNESCO, 1969	UNESCO, *The Measurement of Scientific and Technological Activities,* Paris, 1969.
Usher, 1955	Usher, A., 'Technical Change and Capital Formation', in *Capital Formation and Economic Growth,* National Bureau of Economic Research, reprinted Rosenberg, N. (Ed.), *The Economics of Technological Change,* Penguin, 1971.
Varga, 1935	Varga, E., *The Great Crisis and its Consequences,* English Edition, London, Modern Books, 1935.
Varga, 1947	Varga, E., *Changes in the Economy of Capitalism Resulting from the Second World War, Moscow, and Soviet Views on the Post-War World Economy,* English translation, Public Affairs Press, Washington, D.C., 1948.
Vernon, 1966	Vernon, R., 'International Investment and International Trade in the Product Cycle', *Quarterly Journal of Economics* 80, 1966, pp. 190-207.
Williams, 1967	Williams, B. R., *Technology, Investment and Growth,* London, Chapman and Hall, 1967.
Wise, 1975	Wise, W. S., 'The Role of Cost-Benefit Analysis in Planning Agricultural R and D Programmes', *Research Policy* 4, No. 3, 1975, pp. 246-262.

Chapter 8

PSYCHOLOGY OF SCIENCE

R. Fisch

University of Konstanz

INTRODUCTION

The investigation of the psychological attributes of scientists and of the scientific process is in a considerably less advanced state than other social studies of science. There has not hitherto been any general systematic review, although there is a relatively comprehensive bibliography (Spiegel-Rösing, 1973, 173-183 continued; Spiegel-Rösing, 1974-1975) and an anthology of journal articles (Eiduson and Beckman, 1973). Lacking integration, sub-ʌtantive research in the field has been spasmodic, discontinuous and frag-.nentary, largely bereft of any cohesive concepts or systematic pursuit of questions and methodologies. Only studies of scientific creativity and productivity thus far show signs of sustained effort, no doubt because for several years the national administrations of the United States, the USSR and perhaps other countries invested heavily in the chance that there might be found some neat process of discovering or manufacturing embryonic Newtons and Lomonosovs.

The psychology of science has two main focuses: 1) the investigation of specific aspects of scientific activity, including output assessment and output evaluation, that is to say the processes of discovery, creativity, productivity, communication, application of scientific knowledge, management of scientific work; and 2) person-oriented studies, treating such topics as the person-

I want to thank Monika Bullinger, Barbara Bonfig, Margrete O'Brian, Akelei Fischer, Annette Gültig, Ulrike Löffelbein, Sylvia Schaller and Siegfried Bettighofer for their assistance in preparing this chapter.

ality of scientists, scientist roles or science as an occupation, scientists in organizations, scientists as producers of science. Both aspects may be dealt with in a single article or book. Studies which take into account the effects of culture and social conditions on the psychological make-up of scientists are conspicuous by their absence because of a dereliction of interdisciplinary interaction in this field between psychologists, sociologists, social anthropologists and social historians.

The methods of investigation in this field are quite diverse in their approach. There are phenomenological descriptions and analyses of scientific work and its conditions, including critical analyses of tasks, roles of scientists and their relationships to scientific and other institutions. There are analyses of personal experience in science drawn from diaries and autobiographies; there are biographical analyses, historiographical analyses, case studies of genius, of highly gifted and eminent scientists and their work.[1] There are psychometric methods ('tests') and efforts of survey research involving questionnaires and objective data.

Taken as a whole, descriptive approaches prevail over the study of functional relationships. Analyses of functional relationships would be of greater interest for science studies since they would allow discussion in terms of cause-and-effect relations, such as changes with aging in scientific activity and productivity (Lehman, 1960; Roe, 1965) or interaction of personal with organizational variables as determinants of scientific or technological output (Pelz and Andrews, 1966).

At this point we should mention some general methodological problems. Many investigations describe features of scientists without comparing them with corresponding features for non-scientists. This problem becomes most urgent in biographical and case studies where no equivalent comparison to non-scientists may be possible. Another problem is the preference for geniuses as subjects of study, with special attention to such eminent, highly creative scientists as Nobel Prize winners (e.g. Zuckerman, 1967). For the investigation of top scientific performance this strategy is legitimate and useful, but from the viewpoint of science studies the 'normal' scientist is evidently also of interest. 'Normal' scientists do the work which sustains to a great extent the system of science, and they display those actions and reactions that are generally attributed to members of the scientific research community.

A preliminary concern must be the sundry definitions of 'scientist'. It seems fruitless at this stage to do more than mention the several types of distinction which must be involved, such as those of pure versus applied

---

[1] It is not possible to report on the numerous biographical and psychobiographical studies in this context. The interested reader might refer to the comprehensive *Dictionary of Scientific Biography* (Gillispie, 1970), which contains about five thousand articles on natural scientists of all nationalities from both the past and present.

science (See Mulkay, Chapter 4), natural versus social and other sciences, hard versus soft sciences (See Sayre, 1961; Derek Price, 1974), science versus engineering and technology (See Layton, Chapter 6). There are also the distinctions involved in the stratification of the scientific community by status and reward (again, see Mulkay, Chapter 4) and by organizational and institutional contexts such as academia, industry and government. For formal purposes definitions by academic degree and professional license also occur, and frequently sociologists and others define a scientist by output, as for example the authorship of research papers, patents, etc. Unless otherwise stated we shall here use the general term 'scientist' without disaggregation.

It is precisely this ambiguity of definition that produces so many variant estimates for the size of the world and national scientific communities. According to the *Statistical Yearbook 1972* edited by UNESCO (1973), the total number of scientists and technologists all over the world comes to more than fifteen million people. In the area of 'research and experimental development' there are much fewer, about 2.4 million in eighty five countries. These figures have been in part calculated on the basis of estimated data (UNESCO, 1973, 589). The number of scientists and technologists who make substantial contributions to knowledge is, however, about a quarter of a million distributed over the entire world (*Annual Directory of Publishing Scientists*, edited by the Institute for Scientific Information; see Derek Price, 1975; Spiegel-Rösing, 1972). The United States lead in the total number of scientists. According to estimates, from one fourth to one third of all scientists in the world live in the United States. The NCR Commission on Human Resources (1974) has located through its doctorate records a population of 272,200 scientists and engineers with a Ph.D. in the United States; this constitutes about 0.1% of the total population.

These figures should serve to illustrate the order of magnitude with which one is dealing when one speaks about scientists and technologists. The popular, subjective impression that being a scientist is something unique, that scientists even belong to a special species, can be taken relative either to the large number of individuals in this field or to the small fraction which they constitute of the general population.

Almost simultaneously with the first dicussions about the establishment of a science of science (Ossowska and Ossowski, 1936), a number of articles appeared which advocated the analysis of the personal and social premises of scientific cognition and insight, the originating of hypotheses, the deriving of scientific laws, etc. This discussion still continues (see for example Müller-Freienfels, 1936; Polanyi, 1958, 1967, 1968; Scriven, 1962; Turner, 1967; Singer, 1971; Brandstätter and Reinert, 1973; Weimer, 1974). The view that personal factors such as individual preferences for certain themes or methods of working may also genuinely influence the process of science is by no means generally accepted. This is understandable, since the philosophy of science and the methodology of science both stress the necessity of excluding personal influences in the discovery and dissemination of scientific results. But a series of thorough, logical (Polanyi, 1968) and empirical research studies (Rosenthal, 1966; Rosenthal and Rosnow, 1969; Mitroff, 1974b) have demonstrated the remarkable influence of person-bound factors throughout the production, interpretation and evaluation of scientific results, even where all efforts were introduced to exclude such factors. In these studies an epistemological point of view predominates.

Other studies are more pragmatically oriented. For example, Mikulinsky and Yaroshewsky (1970) and Gvishiani, Mikulinsky and Yaroshewsky (1973) emphasize the necessity of both a psychology and a sociology of science because of the great number and importance of science policy problems, and the acute necessity of solving them in order to stimulate scientific and technological activity and enhance the efficiency of research institutions. They see a means of solving these problems through the investigation of personal characteristics of the individual scientists, especially their creative power and motivation. They feel that the dynamics of scientific activity — that is, the relationship between the individual researcher and the other members of his research team — will determine the extent of scientific accomplishment (See also Wolkow, 1969). The object of analysis is to obtain psychological determinants of the science process, especially the idea-getting process as well as the personal and social psychological determinants of science development. Rational analyses and descriptions outweigh empirical investigations.[2] There are in addition treatments of such special aspects as: fashion in science (Crane, 1969); factors in the innovation process (Globe *et al.*, 1973), production of hypotheses (Haig, 1975), psychology of research (Kuhn, 1970), scientists' perceptions of the relationship between scientific theory and data (Mitroff, 1975), models of production of knowledge (Nowotny, 1975), emotions and passions in science (Polanyi, 1957), cognitive dissonances as a starting point for scientific analyses (Traxel, 1969), strategies in the research process (Lemaine, 1975), and research behavior (Amelang and Aevermann, 1976).

A systematic collection of articles on the psychology of science was initiated by Ammons and Ammons (1962). Since that time, thirty three articles have been published in the journals *Perceptual and Motor Skills* and *Psychological Reports.* Table 1 is an attempt to give a condensed account of the themes discussed in these articles. Among the approaches which the authors chose we note both the analysis of scientific activity and the person-oriented treatment. The topics which have received the most attention from a

---

[2] See Autorenkollektiv (1974), Bernstein (1966), Dalenius *et al.* (1970), Holton (1973), Jevons (1973), Landfield (1961), Maslow (1966), Naess (1965), Perry (1966), Radnitzky (1974), Ravetz (1971), Simon (1966), Taton (1957), Whitley (1974), Ziman (1968), Zinberg (1974). The bibliography on 'knowledge utilization and dissemination' by Havelock (1972) might also be helpful.

psychological standpoint are the process of discovery and theory development. Both topics should be seen as closely associated with the problems of creativity and productivity. Necessary attempts to analyze systematically the discovery process in the various scientific disciplines as a function of diverse institutional and material (also ecological) conditions are virtually lacking. This is due in part to the fact that each research question provokes a multitude of problems that may not be resolved by concentrating on a single issue nor on the methods of any single discipline. However, the subject matter itself does not present any recognizable obstacles to research, so we seem to have what many authors deem to be a much lamented desideratum.

Table 1: List of thirty three articles on 'Psychology of the Scientist', published as a series in the journals *Perceptual and Motor Skills* and *Psychological Reports* during the years 1963 to 1975

Topics and Authors	Number of Articles
Critical remarks and experiments on: influence of experimenter on outcomes of experiments and interpretation of scientific results Authors: Rosenthal and Fode, 1963; Cordaro and Ison, 1963, Brody, 1965; Rosenthal *et al.*, 1965; Ingraham and Harrington, 1966; Ryder, 1966; Glixman, 1967; Rosenthal, 1967a, 1967b; Harrington and Ingraham, 1967, Harrington, 1967; Goodstein and Brazis, 1970.	12
Task analyses, job analyses and job satisfaction Authors: Lawler, 1963; Platz, 1965; Baker, 1966; Strauss, 1966a, 1966b, 1967.	6
Personal documents of scientists Authors: Ammons, 1962; Hays, 1962; Hull, 1962; Shelly, 1963a; Meltzer, 1966.	5
Creativity and productivity Authors: Shelly, 1963b; Cline *et al.*, 1966; Anderson, 1968; Lacey and Erickson, 1974; Pasewark *et al.*, 1975.	5
Critical remarks on neglect of certain research areas Authors: Ammons and Ammons, 1962; Margoshes and Litt, 1965; Smith *et al.*, 1971.	3
Psycholiterary studies of works of scientists Author: Kirchner, 1970.	1
Technology of scientific work Author: Anonymous, 1963.	1

GENERAL STUDIES ON SCIENTISTS
AND TECHNOLOGISTS

Some of the earlier studies on scientists and technologists were prompted by the question of heredity of high intelligence in man (Galton, 1869; Cattell, 1903; Ostwald, 1909). This is a question which has persisted until today (Bridges and Tiltman, 1931; Cane and Nisenson, 1959; Holton, 1972; Albert, 1975). This question is now most often discussed in terms of creativity.

The more general studies in this area are concerned with science as a profession; with general personality traits, typologies of scientists, scientific styles of thinking and working, self-images of scientists; the relationship between life history, intellectual functions or personality characteristics and the selection and pursuit of a particular science as a profession.[3] A fascinating and comprehensive presentation of ideas and issues concerning science as a profession is given in a still topical essay by Weber, 1919. Blume's book (1974) introduces a 'new look' at the topic; in some parts of it he analyzes the roles and tasks of scientists in terms of a political sociology. This point of view could be seen as a necessary complement to present approaches since it offers new and wider frames of reference in productive critical evaluations of the behavior of scientists. There is, however, no experience in the use of such standards of judgment as of yet.

A second type of general study concentrates on the specific situation of scientists in certain countries, or scientists who belong to certain ethnic groups, for example the scientists of India (Chandra, 1970), Poland (Dobrowolski, 1960), Sweden (Boalt *et al.*, 1973), Russia (Parry, 1973) the United States (Hylander, 1968) and the Baltic (Anderson, 1967).

A third type of study deals with scientists or certain characteristics of scientists in a particular field, for example, economists (Johansson and Rossmann, 1971), social scientists (Bennis, 1955), psychologists (Wispé, 1963), mathematicians (Fisher, 1973), and engineers (Clemens *et al.*, 1970). In this context we should also mention the continuous analyses which Roe puts forth on the eminent representatives of various disciplines (1949a, 1949b, 1950, 1951a, 1951b, 1951c, 1952a, 1952b, 1953). Several of these articles are abridged and annotated in the already mentioned anthology by Eiduson and Beckman (1973).

---

[3] Studies which fall in this general category are: Cattell, 1954; Cattell and Drevdahl, 1955; Eiduson, 1962 and follow-up study in 1974; Feuer, 1963; Hagstrom, 1968; Krohn, 1971; Merton, 1969; Roe, 1953a, 1953b; Williamson, 1953; Znaniecki, 1965; Barber and Hirsch, 1962; Hirsch, 1968; Goldsmith and MacKay, 1964; Ramul, 1966.

MOTIVES, NORMS AND VALUES,
POLITICAL ATTITUDES

In addition to intelligence and creativity, a number of other personal characteristics have received special attention in studies about scientists: motives, norms and values, political attitudes. Common to all these characteristics is the fact that they represent central concepts in the short-term and long-term understanding of behavior.

Motives Most of the previously mentioned monographs and readers on scientists have discussed the motives of scientists in terms of ambition and consciously or unconsciously apprehended ends or goals. The more speculative (including psychoanalytical) approaches can be found among the general studies cited, while the predominantly empirical approaches have been treated in the context of creativity and productivity (see below). The work motivation of scientists in industry and administration has received special attention because of its assumed relationship to scientific output. Four main focuses of research interest, derived from studies on work motivation in general, can be identified (See Mulkay, Chapter 4): direction of motivational orientation, source of motivational stimulation (such as incentives), job dedication, and expectancies about performance and/or outcome of ones work (such as Chalupsky, 1964; Pelz and Andrews, 1966, Chapter 6; Wainer and Rubin, 1969; Goodman, Rose and Furcon, 1970; Gomersall, 1971; Lyon, Ivancevich and Donnelly, 1971). Analogous problems of motivation in scientists in the university setting have been analyzed by Matussek (1967) Oromaner (1969) and Hollon (1975). Gantz, Erickson and Stephenson (1971) tried by psychological tests to assess the motivation of scientists in a research and development population toward management. The motivation to manage apparently is not inherent among scientists, because 'most, though not all, persons choosing science as a career reject power over people, dislike the necessary details of administration inherent in the managerial role, and are thing- rather than person-oriented'. Unfortunately, the authors do not consider the consequences of their descriptions for systematic leadership-training of scientists, which is often suggested as a desideratum in the education of future scientists.

Norms and values Since the question of norms in science has been discussed in detail by Mulkay in Chapter 4, only a few of the more basic problem areas in this field will be dealt with here. In the voluminous literature dealing with norms we find at least three main topics of discussion. First there is the question of norms which guide the process of science. Second there is the discrepancy experienced between norms which determine the science process and those which determine everyday life. These last imply completely different values and goals than does the scientific ethos (a term which is used in this respect in a very broad sense). Frequently mentioned in this context is the existence of two worlds or two realities (Modlin, 1973; Pruyser, 1973; Russett, 1975; Wojick, 1974). Finally, almost inseparably connected with these two topics is a third aspect: the special responsibility of scientists, for example, in the application of their results. The study of norms is complicated by the relationship between institutional and personal norms, by the relationship between norms and behavior, and by the relationship between situational and normative determinants of behavior.

This type of approach to the question of norms in science has received widespread attention as a result of Merton's classic description of ideal types of norms and values in science (1942). Merton described four sets of institutional imperatives for the fulfillment of the primary goal of science, 'the extension of certified knowledge': universalism, communality, disinterestedness, and organized skepticism (See Mulkay, Chapter 4). The existence of these institutional imperatives and their relevance for the process of science have often been doubted or not accepted as sufficient. At the same time many researchers have tested the positive capacity of these imperatives as explicative concepts. The reader can find examples of the actual debate centering on Merton's scientific imperatives in the analyses of Hagstrom (1965), Mitroff (1972, 1973, 1974a), Rothman (1972) and Wunderlich (1974).

The distinction between 'local' and 'cosmopolitan' scientists (Gouldner, 1957; Kornhauser and Hagstrom, 1962; based on Merton's 1942 studies) provides still another value orientation and refers to different attachments, loyalties and reference groups. Local scientists are seen as being interested primarily in the scientific organization in which they work, in its management and reward system and their advancement within it. Cosmopolitan scientists are perceived as highly committed to specialized skills and research achievements, to professional recognition from what is from an organizational standpoint an external reference group. In an empirical test of this approach, Friedlander (1971) assessed behavioral orientations of research scientists in six disciplines: engineering, mathematics, physics, chemistry, physiology and psychology. He found three independent factors; these were research, professional and local orientations. Among scientists in different disciplines there were significant differences on the research and professional levels but none on the local-cosmopolitan dimension. His results indicate that the bipolar dimension of local versus cosmopolitan might be better replaced by a multidimensional concept which, avoiding typologies, would make possible a description of scientists according to their relative position on the abovementioned dimensions.

There is further evidence for the need of a pluralistic view and some new perspectives concerning scientific values, at least for applied science. In a most detailed and competent study Hill (1974) explored different but overlapping classes of scientific values ('ethos of science') as they were perceived by a number of applied scientists. He compared these perceptions with the ideal stereotype presented by the classic literature and related these perceptions to the effectiveness, as perceived by colleagues, of the scientists within the local institution. He found that:

> the ethos of science is composed of, not one, but several classes of virtues: in applied research institutions only those classes are relevant for which some reinforcement exists. Involvement in research (with intrinsic rewards from seeing oneself solving problems, being creative, etc.) provided reinforcement for research process values . . . Behavior regarded by colleagues as successful was associated with an ethos which stressed creativity, flexibility and compromise, and devalued objectivity; less successful researchers emphasized greater persistence and objectivity, but placed less importance on creativity (158-159).

Another approach to the study of values has been chosen by Tagiuri (1965). He obtained data on value orientations from research managers, executives and scientists in industry, using a typology proposed by the philosopher Spranger (1950), who distinguished six varieties of value orientations. He described hypothetical types in these terms: the theoretical, the economic, the aesthetic, the social, the political and the religious. The value orientations of the three industrial classes were not found to be as different as the members of the groups thought. In all groups the type most preferred was the theoretical person and the type least preferred, the social person. Attributions of exaggerated value orientations to the members of the other groups indicate, however, distorted group perceptions, and this could be dysfunctional for collaboration between research managers, executives and scientists.

A further point to be mentioned is that stability and change of values depend on different sources of influence. Barnes (1971) investigated the change of values when first degree graduates, trained to identify with the scientific research community and its values, go into industry and there are confronted with incompatible values. Especially incompatible is the utilitarian expectations of industrial management, which is interested in directing research to practical ends and in concealing results from competitors. Barnes' results show 'complete instability of academic values, once situations become unfavorable to them' (See also Brown and Brown, 1972, on the delineation of scientific values possessed by professors of science and the humanities, and Shils, 1975, on conditions and factors leading to a weakening of university scientists' adherence to the ethos of academic life).

Political attitudes   Three main aspects of political attitudes have been investigated. First among these are attitudes concerning the politics of the local institution. Atwood and Crain (1973), for example, assessed attitudes toward the university role and administrative power and found substantial change in attitudes after a two-year period of confrontation and reorganization on the campus. Lammers (1974) has carried out a case study on determinants of participation in policy making and progressive/conservative stance with respect to issues concerning student and staff power. A relatively new development has also been investigated by Ladd and Lipset (1973b); this concerns attitudes toward unionism held by scientists and faculty members (See also Manley and McNichols, 1975). Second are attitudes toward politics in science. Here we find reference to the analysis of the social dimension of science mentioned earlier. The interview and questionnaire study of Blisset (1972) on 'hidden systems of influence and persuasion' which shape processes in science might serve as an example of this. Third are attitudes toward governmental politics in general and individual political orientation (Schooler, 1971; Blankenship, 1973; FAIA, 1974; Ladd and Lipset, 1973a; Lipset and Ladd, 1974).

Using a subsample of 26,000 natural scientists and engineers from a sample of over 60,000 American scientists of nearly all academic fields, Ladd and Lipset (1972) systematically investigated political opinions and commitments. There were three major focuses of interest: first, political commitments of scientists and engineers on a variety of national issues; second, 'the politics of the most highly achieving and influential scientists and engineers in relation to the orientations and concerns of the rank and file of the academic scientific-engineering community'; and third, evaluations of the scientific enterprise itself. The authors drew four general conclusions:

> First, there is a firm and consistent rank ordering of the professions, in terms of the
> general ideological orientations of their members. Scientists in colleges of liberal arts
> and science are to the left of their colleagues in the business-related applied fields of
> engineering, but at the same time are significantly more conservative than social
> scientists and humanists. . . . Second, the 'establishment', understood as the most
> successful and influential practitioner, is more liberal and change-oriented than the
> rank and file of academic scientists and engineers. . . . The scientific 'establishment' is
> by no means radical, and is doubtless much less socially critical than radical scientists
> would like it to be, but it is to the left of the general membership of the scientific
> professions. Third, if significant changes are occuring in the orientation of scientists
> to their professional roles and activities as they affect the policy, this is not the result
> of the large influx of young academics. . . . Fourth, within academic science, now so
> profoundly politicized, there is considerable dissent on all manner of political and
> professional issues (1099).

Using the same data pool for an approach to analyzing disciplinary problems and issues the authors have also published a study on the politics of American sociologists (Lipset and Ladd, 1972).

PSYCHOLOGICAL ASPECTS IN THE DEVELOPMENT OF SCIENTISTS

The development process which scientists go through to enter the profession is relatively long compared with that of other professions, and continues through adult life. In the following section we will consider three aspects of this developmental process: a) socialization processes, b) career and c) mobility. We should note that all three aspects have in addition some influence on the development of the type and scope of scientific work dealt with. For a comprehensive presentation of problems and results from this research area see also Eiduson, 1973.

Research dealing with the socialization processes which scientists undergo in joining their profession has centered on two approaches: a) case studies that consider the possible important influencing factors in early childhood and youth, and b) studies of the effects of socializing institutions like colleges, universities and organizations which employ scientists and technologists.

Socialization processes Birth order has always received special recognition and was mentioned already by Galton (1874) in his book *English Men of Science* (See also Bliss, 1970, and Datta, 1968, for a relationship of birth order and creativity). It has generally been found that scientists are predominantly firstborns or only children (Faris, 1940; Roe, 1953b; Eiduson, 1962; Cotgrove and Box, 1970), and this is further supported by the fact that university students are to a significant extent firstborns or only children (Schachter, 1963; Capra and Dittes, 1962). There is some research evidence from developmental and social psychology that firstborns and only children are reared in a social climate quite different from that of later-borns; for example, they receive special attention from parents (McDavid and Harari, 1968, 61 and 81).

Similarly, some authors have also considered the death of a parent or both parents during the childhood of a scientist to be an important factor (Roe, 1953b, 84; Eiduson, 1962, 67; Derek Price, 1963, 109; Silverman, 1974). However, Woodward (1974) in a methodically careful and extensive comparative study has shown that the loss of a parent is not significantly more frequent for scientists than for the general population. Nevertheless, the contradictory results suggest that further investigation of this quite common event and its influence on the personal development of scientists is justified. Another point concerning this unique child-environment interaction has been reported by McClelland (1962) and Cotgrove and Box (1970). They have found that natural scientists tend to avoid close personal contacts, and that they began to do so early in childhood. This in turn may be related to the findings of Faris (1940) and Eiduson (1962) concerning social isolation in the early years of these individuals; and also, to Roe (1953a) who reports on an early independence in her sample of eminent scientists.

A special attribute of future scientists appears to be a rather typical early interest shown in the analysis and structure of things. Terman (1954) in his longitudinal study on gifted persons found that they showed a relatively high interest in sciences by the early age of ten. Roe (1951a) reports in a study on eminent biologists that half of the sample mentioned had been fascinated by biology or other natural sciences very early in life. On the whole it is somewhat difficult, though admittedly fascinating, to identify more or less direct relationships between child-rearing practices and/or early childhood experiences and later scientific interests or vocational choice.

The instigation, unfolding and realization of scientific interests depends on a fostering environment. Part of this environment naturally involves the parental influences as described above, while other parts have been identified as concerning social class (Roe, 1951a; West, 1961), ethnic and religious origins (Greeley, 1971) and regional grouping. Concerning social class, Roe (1951a) in her study on eminent biologists revealed that the occupational and educational levels of the subjects' parents were generally upper-middle-class homes, where learning and education were highly valued. With regard to the last two factors Knapp and Goodrich (1952) did an extensive study on those characteristics of American colleges which might be associated with high production of scientists. One of the most striking findings was a geographical-cultural variation in the production of scientists. The most productive schools were to a significant degree the Protestant-related liberal arts colleges of the midwest and west. These results suggest, however, that religious/geographical variables are conflated. This was confirmed by the follow-up study of Astin (1962), who perceived, for example, that the four New York schools had a high Jewish enrollment and, similarly, that the three Utah schools had a high Mormon enrollment. This is in accordance with the study of McClelland (1962), who based his work in turn on that of Weber (1904, 1905) and Merton (1957, 574-606), both of whom stressed the importance of a radical Protestant parental background. Astin found also that not only can institutional conditions be made responsible for high output, but that the output of a school can be largely predicted from the characteristics, that is, academic aptitude, of the entering students. This is in accordance with the fact that students at the university level can at a very early stage be differentiated into those with a main interest in science and those favoring fields of occupational practice (Becker and Carper, 1956; Cooley, 1964; Nichols, 1964; Butler, 1968; Fisch *et al.*, 1970; Orlik *et al.*, 1971; Zinberg, 1971, 1972; Goldman *et al.*, 1973; Goldstein, 1974; Smithers and Dann, 1974; Dawes, 1975).

Hardy (1974), stimulated by the work of Astin, studied the question of whether 'scientists and scholars are recruited equally from all parts of the USA population or [whether] they come disproportionately from selected segments of the citizenry'. Changes over time were also taken into account. The reported data revealed first of all that the Northern states of the United States, in general, are much more 'scholar productive' than the Southern states. Second, they revealed that Utah has been, up until now, the most productive state and, third, that the greatest change in regional productivity over time was the rise in productivity of the Middle Atlantic states from seventh to second place.

In line with Astin (1962), Hardy explains the phenomenon of Utah with reference to the influence of Mormon values, and he explains the phenomenon of the Middle Atlantic states in terms of impact of the Jewish second generation youth. He also stresses the importance of value systems of such 'high producers':

> emphasis on human dignity, goodness and competence; a life pathway of serious dedication, of service to humanity, of continual striving; . . . a pragmatic search for better ways of doing things unfettered by traditional restraints; and a focus on the relatively immediate, foreseeable future which can be affected by personal effort. . . . Given a certain level of intellectual talent and cultural support in educational, scientific and scholarly institutions, youth will frequently choose careers in scientific and scholarly professions. This same cultural milieu apparently also produces disproportionate numbers of inventors and entrepreneurs. . . .

It must be added that this list of values is not only a result of Hardy's empirical study but, also, a result of the author's analysis of available literature.

Further information has also been supplied by Elliot (1975) who in his historiographic study on 503 men of science in Nineteenth-Century American society showed that '. . . both scientists and literary figures came from more or less the same general social and economic sector of the Nineteenth-Century American society'; that 'it was of some importance [for the individual] whether he was born in a 'scientific' or a 'literary' family'; and further, that 'these tendencies are in strong contrast with the biographical profile of inventors'.

Scientific career Becoming a scientist involves not only an educational process[4] and an accumulation of knowledge and skills but also in part a filtering process through which one goes in the course of professional development. The general idealistic expectation is that those scholars who contribute to the development of science and technology within the particular fields of their discipline will pass through the filtering process (c.f. Znaniecki, 1965, 133-134).

Conceptualization of the scientific career as a mere sequence of professional roles is, however, too simplistic. It entails crises of personal development, changes of habit, interest and orientation, and coping with trauma (Kubie, 1953, 1954; Roe, 1963; Ziman, 1970). There is, for example,

---

[4] In the literature some concern for 'educating scientists' can be identified (Kuczynski, 1963; Tilson, 1965; Davies, 1968; McCarthy, 1968; White, 1968; Jaroschewski and Mirski, 1974).

empirical evidence that middle-aged scientists suffer from special problems which can partly be explained by alterations over time to their aim and orientation within both career and personal life (Cotgrove and Box, 1970; Fisch, in press).

The more constant personal and nonpersonal factors (Hudson, 1968; Ferdinand, 1969) must also be considered. Generally one can say that the more important personal factors are a sense of curiosity, combined with ability and high interest and commitment to task, asceticism, and last but not least, fulfillment of the necessary requirements for membership in the local scientific community. These factors form the basis of scientific recognition (Crane, 1965; Cole and Cole, 1967, 1968) in that they appear to be central prerequisites for scientific productivity and quality work.

Nonpersonal factors, on the other hand, are to a large extent concerned with material conditions such as the availability of scientific equipment, funds and personal assistance. They cover also the influencing aspects of the organizational setting, such as the effect of the reputation of the scientific institution and the value and reward system it offers (Glaser, 1963; Rowe, 1973; Zuckerman and Merton, 1971).

Similarities are evident between the concepts of career and social stratification, especially if one remembers the formal definition (succession of different positions in the organizational hierarchy), and as such are of interest for discussion (See Mulkay, Chapter 4).

In most investigations of scientific career, the Ph.D. is taken as a criterion for having attained the status of scientist. This choice is sometimes justified by the statement that the preparation of the doctoral thesis is, above other things, a process of scientific self-determination and self-programming. However, this may be true only for scientists in universities or institutions of basic research. Pelz and Andrews (1966) found that in industrial and governmental R & D laboratories, valuable scientific work is often accomplished by non-Ph.D.'s, especially in technological and engineering research and development (See also Perucci and Gerstl, 1969).

In an attempt to develop measurable aspects, Nowakowska (1975) interprets the concept of scientific career as an interplay between the functions of scientific authority and social recognition, the explanation of which is not necessarily bound to organizational position.

An important stage for any scientist is the termination or the change of his career as a result of being placed in a different organizational context. Middle-aged scientists who make the change from a scientific to an administrative position are typical of this. This seems to happen more in government and industry than in the university. Marcson (1968) and Cotgrove and Box (1970) report that few scientists and engineers ultimately resist a management career, especially in federal laboratories. Hutchinson (1970) explains this by mentioning the low perceived status of scientists compared with administrators in government establishments. Cotgrove and Box (1970) and Bahrdt (1971, 216) interpret the change to management position as a constructive solution of career problems arising from the reduced productivity of some older scientists. Kaplan (1965), on the other hand, describes the conflicting role strains placed on such science administrators, for while most scientists are convinced that science management should best be done by scientists, they find fault in scientists who are satisfied with such positions, since they have renounced research activities.

In this context we must also mention the change to politics as a possible career alternative for scientists, since it is evident that they sometimes use their high prestige as a basis for a political career even though the evidence suggests that the two roles conflict and cannot be easily discharged simultaneously (Gilpin and Wright, 1964; Hagstrom, 1965; Lübbe, 1972). Shils (1968) suggests a fairly good compromise: the 'scientific adviser' should accept some additional functions without leaving the base of his primary role (Primack and von Hippel, 1974; Gianos, 1975; see also Lakoff, Chapter 10, and Nelkin, Chapter 11).

Special career problems can arise if an individual has undergone development and socialization for both the role of researcher and that of practitioner, as it means that two sets of norms and values must be internalized, and that in the end the person is linked to two sometimes conflicting systems of professional communication. Aran and Ben-David (1968) investigated researchers in internal medicine who worked in clinics and found 'in all the cases an element of institutionally generated conflict through turning them to work in research'.

From the perspective of the organization and development of science it is worthwhile to consider the individual differences in career orientations (Hall and Mansfield, 1975). The long-term expectations associated with particular careers, along with information on the effect of situational factors such as organizational goal setting, group climate, research facilities, etc., might help one to understand phenomena like the rise and fall of academic departments of research groups, high fluctuations in research personnel, and remarkable differences in scientific output and the processes involved in effective long-term science management. McCarrey and Edwards (1972) analyzed questionnaire data on professional goals relevant to the job satisfaction of seventy two Ph.D. research biologists. Two groups of scientists were identified. Being inner-directed and primarily task-oriented, the majority of scientists accepted for themselves the values of pure science as characterized by Weber (1919) and Merton (1942), while the other, smaller group held value systems consistent with more outer-directed characteristics, and to this extent were susceptible to the impact of monetary and career rewards. Position and recognition, too, were positively related to quantity rather than quality of published output. This study partially demonstrates the existence of an interplay of value systems and career orientations, an interplay which influences quality and quantity of scientific output and in this way possibly contributes to the extent of scientific development in a research field.

Women, because of their minority status in science, are particularly disadvantaged in scientific careers (Perrucci, 1970; Ferber and Loeb, 1973; Bachtold, 1975; Zuckerman and Cole, 1975). Studies by Motz (1961), Gysbers and Johnston (1968), Elton and Rose (1967), Rand (1968), Watley (1971), Patterson (1973), Graham (1974), Mozans (1974) and Feldman (1975) indicate among other things that acceptance of a masculine role concept as constituted by such factors as achievement orientation, independence, endurance, intellectual self-confidence, research competence and strong goal orientation within task performance furthers a scientific career. Acceptance of such a role, however, by women evokes role conflicts and balance difficulties, because in our culture intellectual competence and achievement, independence and readiness for competition are judged as masculine. Unfortunately, even if these difficulties are overcome, the emotional acceptance of the scientist role is not sufficient for the realization of a scientific career. There seems to be a certain reluctance on the part of the institution to trust such roles to women (Masterman, 1974). Added to this problem is that of the dual-career conflict. A married and family-oriented female scientist will be dependent on her husband's mobility. Taken all together then, possible (but not necessary) outcomes include an inhibition of performance and lowering of levels of aspiration.

Mobility   Academic mobility, as a change of working place, is an important determinant and stimulant of the scientific career. Some of the above-mentioned difficulties in the analysis of scientific career result from mobility, for with mobility socialization processes take place that cannot be easily controlled. These are further conflated with the internal changes in scientists that come from maturity.

For science organizations such as universities, R & D laboratories, etc., mobility is an important stimulus to innovation, since the movement of a knowledgeable individual from one organization to another is perhaps the most efficient way of transferring knowledge. Shimshoni (1970), for example, has shown that in the instrument industry a very large proportion of innovations were associated with the mobility of technical leaders. The same is possibly true for science development in other fields. For more detailed information the interested reader is invited to turn to literature on mobility and career of Ph.D.'s (National Academy of Science, National Research Council, 1968, 1971), on profiles of Ph.D.'s in the sciences (Harmon, 1965), on patterns of mobility of new Ph.D.'s (Hargens, 1969), on age at doctorate and prestige of subsequent academic affiliation (Clemente, 1973a), and on mobility dependent on conditions of the academic labor market (Caplan and McGee, 1958).

Creativity and productivity   The importance of creativity and productivity as a subject of scientific debate and research is indicated by the
relatively high number of publications appearing on these topics. The sheer
quantity forbids a detailed account of these papers, and it is recommended
that interested readers consult the following selection of references (monographs, readers and some general works) for further information: Barron
(1968, 1969), Guilford (1968), Gregory (1967), Gruber (1974), Gruber,
Terrel and Wertheimer (1962), Hadamard (1945), Jaques (1970, Chapters 3,
4 and 5), Koestler (1964; see also Mays, 1973), Kröber and Lorf (1972),
Kubie (1961, 1965), Maier (1970), Mooney and Razik (1967), Osborn
(1963), Pelz and Andrews (1966), Rossman (1964), Stein (1974, 1975), Stein
and Heinze (1960), Storr (1972), Taylor (1964, 1972), Taylor and Barron
(1963). Some general articles on scientific productivity are Allison and
Stewart (1974), Bergum (1974), Garvey and Tomita (1972), Lotka (1926),
Derek Price (1974), Roe (1972), Vlachy (1972), Zener (1968). A most
valuable bibliography of books on creativity from 1950-1970 has been
prepared by Stievater (1971); this bibliography is continuously updated
(Stievater, 1973a, 1973b, 1975a, 1975b).

Creativity, productivity and its criteria   Two explicit aims by which
research on scientific creativity has been guided can clearly be identified: the
construction of tests for the assessment of creativity in the recruitment and
selection of research personnel;[5] and the search for a means to identify and
foster creative talent in grade schools, high schools and universities.[6] Work in
both directions has been hampered by the lack of objective criteria for the
definition of creativity. The first goal should be essentially quality-oriented,
while the second carries dominant overtones of quantity.

Two questions arise at this point. Is the scientist who produces more
quantity to be considered uncreative? Is the scientist who produces a very
small work output of high originality to be considered unproductive? In fact
there is a substantial correlation between creativity and productivity found in
scientists but, as is understood by the concept of correlation, this does not
necessarily mean a logical relationship between the two.

For Mednick (1962) the most essential feature of creativity is the ability
to combine remote associations. The richness of associative bonds is measured

---

[5] E.g. Buel (1965), Buel, Albright and Glennon (1966), Chambers (1964), Cattell
and Butcher (1968), Clemente (1973b), Cline, Tucker and Anderson (1966), Gough
(1961), Hutchings (1967), Lacey and Erickson (1974), MacKinnon (1972), Mullins
(1963), Parloff and Datta (1965), Smith, Albright and Glennon (1961), Shapiro (1966),
Taylor and Ellison (1972), Torrance, Bruch and Morse (1973), Tucker, Cline and
Schmitt (1967), Whiting (1972) and the above-mentioned monographs and readers.

[6] These aspects are comprehensively discussed in the above-mentioned monographs
and readers; see also Edgerton (1959), Hlavsa (1972), Illingworth and Illingworth
(1966), Kubie (1962), Piryov (1972).

by the number of associations a given stimulus item evokes, and the quality of such bonds by the remoteness of the elements associated in a new and useful way by the absence of stereotyped responses. Wertheimer (1954) stresses the recognition of a given problem, achieved through a process of insight, the most important and concluding part of which is closure. This last term refers to some sort of active properties of the psychological problem field itself which create a tendency in the individual to furnish missing links or to eliminate incongruities. Maier (1970) postulates a mechanism which selects parts of past experience and combines them into a new and meaningful pattern. Guilford (1966) establishes a factor-analytical structure-of-intellect model. In this mode, creativity is mainly explained by processes of divergent thinking. In order for such processes to take place, some basic abilities must exist among which ideational fluency, flexibility of set and evaluated ability are regarded as most important factors (for extensions and applications of this view see Hudson, 1963, 1967). According to Getzels and Jackson (1962), creative behavior, as opposed to merely intelligent behavior, represents a socially useful form of curiosity and exploration. Intelligent behavior reflects the ability to solve problems, whereas creative behavior reflects the ability to formulate or pose problems as well as to solve them.

Two categories of criteria can be distinguished. The first of these categories involves the quasi-objective measure of products and personality traits like publication rate (e.g. Lotka, 1926; Derek Price, 1963), number of citations (*Citation Index;* e.g. Derek Price, 1970; Lightfield, 1971; Klingemann, 1974; Spiegel-Rösing *et al.*, 1975), number of patents, awards, scores on creativity tests. The second category involves subjective estimations such as ratings by colleagues or supervisors (e.g. Parmeter and Garber, 1971; James and Ellison, 1973). Sometimes combined measures of both types are used as an overall criterion.

In order to find explanations for the origin of creativity or productivity in science, these indicators are put into relation with personal factors such as intelligence, motives and orientations, and organizational factors such as leadership style, management control, incentives, patterns of communication and form of scientific teamwork. Brogden and Sprecher (1964, 159) point to the necessity of considering control variables in the evaluation of a subject's creativity. They list the following variables: time dimensions such as age or time needed to settle into a job; type of employing organization, such as university, government, industry, etc.; scientific or technological fields; and finally, opportunity variables such as material resources, conditions of social environment, and difficulty or potential of problem area (See Helson and Crutchfield, 1970; Vlachý, 1971a).

Unfortunately, because of the lack of unequivocal criteria, 'creative' remains a subjective value judgment even in such apparently objective measures as creativity tests.

Creative scientists   As already mentioned, most characteristics of creativity have been identified in scientists labeled eminent because of their outstanding scientific contributions. McClelland (1962) has summarized the main results thus far of empirical investigations on the characteristics of creative physical scientists and offers the following distillation. Men are more likely to be creative than women; creative scientists have been educated in a background of radical Protestantism more often than could be expected by chance (See also Datta, 1967) but are themselves not religious; they have few interpersonal contacts, feel easily disturbed by complex emotions and try to avoid them, and are unusually hardworking. Physical scientists like music, dislike art and poetry, and are intensely masculine; they develop a strong interest in the structure of things and in analysis very early in life.

Barron (1969, 101) presents another synthesis of features emerging from empirical studies. Here is a reformulation of his list of personality traits:

Motivation: high ego strength, emotional stability (this is in part contradictory to McClelland's finding), high degree of control of impulses, strong need for independence, self-direction, autonomy, self-sufficiency.

Intelligence: superior general intelligence with emphasis on abstract thinking; preference for comprehensiveness and elegance in explanation.

Cognitive style to be viewed in close connection with intelligence and vice versa: need for orderliness, exactness and methodical thinking, 'together with an excited interest in the challenge presented by contradictions, exceptions, and apparent disorder', and an interest 'in what may appear as . . . imbalance, or very complex balance whose ordering principle is not immediately apparent'; independence in thinking 'although not necessarily in social behaviour'; a special interest in the kind of 'wagering' which involves 'pitting oneself against the unknown, so long as ones own efforts can be the deciding factor'.

Social behavior: high need for influence and power (dominance) including 'forcefulness of opinion, but a dislike of personally toned controversy'; a low interest and 'a somewhat distant or detached attitude in interpersonal relations, though not without sensitivity or insight; a preference for dealing with things or abstractions rather than with people'.

The above-mentioned features characterize speculations on a model creative personality in the scientific field. Assessment techniques are, however, available which allow for more precise definition.

Sex differences   The research findings on sex differences in creativity and productivity present no uniform picture. Marital status can reduce the chance of being fully engaged in scientific work, and this obvious fact is not always taken into account in investigations dealing with the subject.

With respect to publication rate, Astin's data (1973) reveal that on the average women publish less than men, with the publication rate fluctuating from field to field of specialization. According to Groth (1975) the difference may be due partially to values stemming from socio-economic status, patterns of success and societal rewards. Simon and his colleagues (Simon *et al.*, 1967-1968), however, find no differences in publication rate between full-time employed women and men. Married female Ph.D.'s tend to have an even higher output than their male colleagues, according to their results. Ferber and Loeb (1973) have also obtained data indicating no negative influence of marital status on the scientific productivity of women.

Sexist prejudice insists on different thinking styles for men and women. Helson (1967b) examines this problem to his own satisfaction and succeeds in identifying a dimension of 'active organizing control' which is different for males and females. Men are on the average characterized by a high control pattern and women by a low one. Characteristics of the high control pattern are a strong, active direction of cognitive processes and orientation toward integrative mastery and organization of the field. Characteristics of the low control pattern are a low level of active direction, emotional involvement, awareness of participation of the unconscious, and consequently less flexibility and confidence in dealings with the outside world. Helson (1967a) has also investigated the question of which personality traits differentiate creative and noncreative women. Her results indicate that these traits are similar to those of their creative male colleagues: autonomy, high level of aspiration and strong motivation to engage in creative activity. Apart from this, creative women show a personal history in which more weight has accrued to the development of independence and personality than to the fulfillment of female role expectancies (See also Joesting, 1975).

Seen together, most empirical investigations indicate that there are more similarities than differences between male and female scientists with respect to intellectual and personality traits in scientific work. There is little evidence that women's scientific contributions are of a quality different from that of their male colleagues. From the point of view of furthering creative talent in science, men and women are equals.

Environmental conditions   For creativity and productivity the physical and organizational environment must be favorable in various ways. Kaplan (1960) in a theoretical analysis lists five groups of environmental factors which influence creativity: 1) receptivity of or resistance to new ideas; 2) internal and external pressure to produce; 3) toleration of 'oddballs'; 4) freedom to choose problems and change directions; and 5) incentives for creativity. The first of Kaplan's factors, receptivity or resistance to new ideas, seems to be crucial also for the development of science as a whole as described by Kuhn (1961). For although the general expectation is that new and even revolutionary ideas or methods are welcomed in science, Barber (1961) has found evidence of resistance to scientific discovery in scientists themselves. His examples not only indicate active resistance by the scientific community in the field concerned, but also a disregard for or overlooking of innovations because of lack of information. The question then arises as to which specific factors account for the occurrence of innovations, and by which strategies scientists, acting as judges, single out the valid and creative discoveries and theories from among the variety of scientific results offered.

Research on creativity links into history, philosophy, the sociology of science, and research on science development. Creativity has to be confirmed by the judgment of other scientists in order that the products of such creativity reach the innovative stage and in turn are able to influence a wider part of the scientific community. Generally, receptivity or resistance to new scientific ideas is a problem which cannot be discussed exclusively in psychological or sociological terms, since it is influenced also by the properties of the idea in question: for example, its degree of abstractness and formalization, its communicability, its relationship to the existing body of knowledge, its consistency or inconsistency with present cognitive standards and values, and so on.

Among organizational conditions the factors of opportunity, research climate, cooperation and leadership behavior have been of special interest in empirical investigations, as these factors may be influenced or changed by an effective research management, through training programs for research and administration personnel or through suitable provision or restriction of research funds.[7]

Pelz and Andrews (1966) have conducted extensive studies on productive research climates, investigating the effects of personal and organizational factors on different groups of scientists. These factors, identified by way of questionnaire and assessment of objective data, are: coordination and freedom in work performance, communication patterns and communication frequency, diversity of activities, dedication to task, job-relevant motivations, job satisfaction, similarities among researchers in a group, creativity at different stages of project performance, age of scientists, interaction of age of scientists with perceived research climate, and group age (the time for which a team has been working together). The results of this study being very detailed, only some overall impressions can be given as they have been summarized by the authors themselves:

> Effective scientists [as compared to less effective scientists] were self-directed by their own ideas, and valued freedom. But at the same time they allowed several other people a voice in shaping their directions; they interacted vigorously with colleagues.
>
> Effective scientists did not limit their activities either to the world of 'application' or to the world of 'pure science' but maintained an interest in both; their work was diversified.
>
> Effective scientists were not fully in agreement with their organization in terms of

---

[7] For some specific aspects of these topics see Andrews (1967), Cummings, Hinton and Gobdell (1975), Gantz, Stephenson and Erickson (1969), Meltzer (1956), Pelz (1967) and Rodnyi (1972).

their interests; what they personally enjoyed did not necessarily help them advance in the structure.

Effective scientists tended to be motivated by the same kinds of things as their colleagues. At the same time, however, they differed from their colleagues in the styles and strategies with which they approached their work.

In effective older groups, the members interacted vigorously and preferred each other as collaborators, yet they held each other at an emotional distance and felt free to disagree on technical strategies.

Thus in numerous ways, the scientists and engineers whom we studied did effective work under conditions that were not completely comfortable, but contained creative tensions among forces pulling in different directions (Pelz and Andrews, 1966, 7).

Their results show a wide variety of factors which influence research climate and scientific performance. Although a wide range of positive and negative relationships has been identified, the question of their balance remains open. One is able to derive some agreement on the general classes of factors which contribute to productivity and creativity. Much less agreement can be found with regard to the interaction of these factors and their relative importance; hence most conclusions regarding this matter remain rather vague.

Finally, there is some dispute on age and decrement of scientific productivity (Arasteh and Arasteh, 1968; Dennis, 1956, 1958; Lehman, 1953, 1962, 1966; Roe, 1965; Derek Price, 1974). Research evidence is far from being clear cut. Scientists appear to differ in productivity over time, some showing a decrement with increasing age while others do not (See also Lotka's Law: Lotka, 1926). It is questionable how far these phenomena are attributable to aging and career forces. In a state of rapid exponential growth, most scientists at any given time will be recent entries into research. If, therefore, productivity and creativity were constant against time one would find nevertheless the optical illusion that most contributions, large and small, were made by the young.

CONCLUSION

Having now reviewed the field, it is lamentably clear that basic concepts are diffuse and contradictory, and rarely become common to several investigations. For this and other reasons, results cannot really be compared, and little scholarly cumulation has resulted. Much of this may be a product of two forces that arise from the positivist habit of thought that permeates the scientific community and those who choose to investigate it. Natural scientists, at least, often act as if the universe they study were entirely exterior to themselves and all their human and social qualities. The investigators of science, themselves no strangers to this pattern of thought, thus find little intrinsic place for psychology and social study. This is reinforced also in a similar general social attitude that has until recently downgraded all emotional subjectivity and spontaneity. There is today a new receptiveness to social and psychological forces in human affairs, a receptiveness clearly reflected in the new criticism of science (See Ravetz, Chapter 3), in the new priorities in science policy (See Salomon, Chapter 2), and in the new directions in the social studies of science (See Mulkay, Chapter 4). It may now be possible, therefore, to bring together the cross-disciplinary studies in order to integrate the psychology of science with its sociological, historical and philosophical counterparts.

BIBLIOGRAPHY

Albert, 1975

Albert, R. S., 'Toward a Behavioral Definition of Genius', *American Psychologist* 30, 1975, pp. 140-151.

Allison and Stewart, 1974

Allison, P. D. and Stewart, J. A., 'Productivity Differences Among Scientists: Evidence for Accumulative Advantage', *American Sociological Review* 39, 1974, pp. 596-606.

Amelang and Aevermann, 1976

Amelang, M. and Aevermann, D., 'Forschungsbezogene Verhaltensweisen und Einstellungen von Wissenschaftlern', in *Psychologische Rundschau* 27, 1976, pp. 71-94.

Ammons, 1962

Ammons, R. B., 'Psychology of the Scientist II: Clark Hull and his Idea Books', *Perceptual and Motor Skills* 15, 1962, pp. 800-802.

Ammons and Ammons, 1962

Ammons, R. B. and Ammons, C. H., 'Psychology of the Scientist I: Introduction', *Perceptual and Motor Skills* 15, 1962, pp. 748-750.

Anderson, 1967

Anderson, H., 'Baltische Wissenschaftler an der Königsberger Universität', *Baltische Hefte* 13, 1967, pp. 304-310.

Anderson, 1968

Anderson, C. C., 'Psychology of the Scientist XXVIII: Speculations on Nonverbal Creativity', *Perceptual and Motor Skills* 27, 1968, pp. 883-889.

Andrews, 1967

Andrews, F. M., 'Creative Ability, the Laboratory Environment, and Scientific Performance', *IEEE Transactions on Engineering Management* 14, 1967, pp. 76-83.

Anonymous, 1963

Anonymous, J. D., 'Pschology of the Scientist VIII: Seven Rules for Producing Barely Intelligible Prose in Scientific Writing', *Psychological Reports* 13, 1963, pp. 313-314.

Aran and Ben-David, 1968

Aran, L. and Ben-David, J., 'Socialization and Career

Patterns as Determinants of Productivity of Medical Researchers', *Journal of Health and Social Behavior* 9, 1968, pp. 3-15.

Arasteh and Arasteh, 1968   Arasteh, R. and Arasteh, J., *Creativity in the Life Cycle,* Vols. 1 and 2, Leiden, Brill, 1968.

Astin, 1962   Astin, A. W., ' 'Productivity' of Undergraduate Institutions', *Science* 136, 1962, pp. 129-135.

Astin, 1973   Astin, H. S., 'Career Profiles of Women Doctorates', in Rossi, A. S. and Calderwood, A. (Eds.), *Academic Women on the Move,* New York, Russell Sage Foundation, 1973, pp. 139-161.

Atwood and Crain, 1973   Atwood, E. and Crain, S., 'Changes in Faculty Attitudes Toward University Role and Governance', *Journal of Experimental Education* 41, 1973, pp. 1-9.

Autorenkolletiv, 1974   Autorenkollektiv, *Wissenschaftliche Entdeckungen: Probleme ihrer Aufnahme und Wertung,* Berlin (East), Akademie Verlag, 1974.

Bachtold, 1975   Bachtold, L. M., 'Women, Eminence and Career-Value Relationships', *Journal of Social Psychology* 95, 1975, pp. 187-192.

Bahrdt, 1971   Bahrdt, H. P., *Wissenschatfssoziologie – ad hoc,* Düsseldorf, Bertelsmann Universitätsverlag, 1971.

Baker, 1966   Baker, S. R., 'Psychology of the Scientist XV: Level of Research Interest, Status, and Organizational Factors in the Academic Environment: Preliminary Study', *Perceptual and Motor Skills* 23, 1966, pp. 73-74.

Barber, 1961   Barber, B., 'Resistance by Scientists to Scientific Discovery', *Science* 134, 1961, pp. 596-602.

Barber and Hirsch, 1962   Barber, B. and Hirsch, W. (Eds.), *The Sociology of Science,* New York, The Free Press, 1962.

Barnes, 1971   Barnes, S. B., 'Making Out in Industrial Research', *Science Studies* 1, 1971, pp. 157-175.

Barron, 1968   Barron, F., 'The Dream of Art and Poetry', *Psychology Today* 2, 1968, pp. 18-23.

Barron, 1969   Barron, F., *Creative Person and Creative Process,* New York, Holt, Rinehart and Winston, 1969.

Becker and Carper, 1956   Becker, H. S. and Carper, J., 'The Elements of Identification with an Occupation', *American Sociological Review* 21, 1956, pp. 341-348.

Bennis, 1955   Bennis, W. G., 'The Social Scientist as a Research Entrepreneur: A Case Study', Social Problems 3, 1955, pp. 44-49.

Bergum, 1974   Bergum, B. O., 'Self-Perceptions of Members of a Graduate Faculty Whose Publication Rates are High or Low', *Psychological Reports* 35, 1974, pp. 857-858.

Bernstein, 1966   Bernstein, M. S., 'Die Psychologie der wissenschaftlichen Arbeit', *Sowjetwissenschaft-Gesellschaftswissenschaftliche Beiträge* 1, Halbjahr, 1966, pp. 610-621.

Blankenship, 1973   Blankenship, L. V., 'The Scientist as 'Apolitical' Man', *British Journal of Sociology* 24, 1973, pp. 269-287.

Bliss, 1970   Bliss, W. D., 'Birth Order of Creative Writers', *Journal of Individual Psychology* 26, 1970, pp. 200-202.

Blisset, 1972   Blisset, M., *Politics in Science,* Boston, Little, Brown and Co., 1972.

Blume, 1974

Boalt, Lantz and
Herlin, 1973

Brandstätter and Reinert,
1973

Bridges and Tiltman, 1931

Brody, 1965

Brown and Brown, 1972

Buel, 1965

Buel, Albright and
Glennon, 1966

Butler, 1968

Cane and Nisenson, 1959

Caplan and McGee, 1958

Capra and Dittes, 1962

Cattell, 1953

Cattell, 1954

Cattell and Butcher, 1968

Cattell and Drevdahl, 1955

Blume, S. S., *Toward a Political Sociology of Sciences,*
New York, The Free Press, 1974.

Boalt, G., Lantz, H. and Herlin, H., *The Academic
Pattern: A Comparison Between Researchers and Non-
Researchers, Men and Women,* Stockholm, Almqvist
and Wiksell, 1973.

Brandstätter, J. and Reinert, C., 'Wissenschaft als Ge-
genstand der Wissenschaft vom menschlichen Erleben
und Verhalten: Uberlegungen zur Konzeption einer
Wissenschaftspsychologie', *Zeitschrift für allgemeine
Wissenschaftstheorie* 2, 1973, pp. 368-379.

Bridges, T. C. and Tiltman, H. H., *Master Minds of
Modern Science,* Freeport, New York, Books for
Libraries, 1931.

Brody, N., 'Psychology of the Scientist XIII: Scientific
and Religious Experiences Distinguished by their 'Affect' ', *Psychological Reports* 16, 1965, pp. 737-744.

Brown, S. B. and Brown, L. B., 'A Semantic Differential Approach to the Delineation of Scientific Values
Possessed by Professors of Science and Humanities',
Journal of Research in Science Teaching 9, 1972, pp.
345-351.

Buel, W. D., 'Biographical Data and the Identification
of Creative Research Personnel', *Journal of Applied
Psychology* 49, 1965, pp. 318-321.

Buel, W. D., Albright, L. E. and Glennon, J. R., 'A
Note on the Generality and Cross-Validity of Personal
History for Identifying Creative Research Scientists',
Journal of Applied Psychology 50, 1966, pp. 217-219.

Butler, J. R., *Occupational Choice: A Review of the
Literature with Special Reference to Science and
Technology,* Science Policy Studies 2, London, Her
Majesty's Stationary Office, 1968.

Cane, P. and Nisenson, S., *Giants of Science,* New
York, Grosset and Dunlap, 1959.

Caplan, T. and McGee, R. J., *The Academic Market-
place,* New York, Basic Books, 1958.

Capra, P. C. and Dittes, J. E., 'Birth Order as a Selective Factor among Volunteer Subjects', *Journal of
Abnormal and Social Psychology* 64, 1962, p. 302.

Cattell, J. McK., 'A Statistical Study of Eminent Men',
Popular Science Monthly, February 1953, pp.
359-377.

Cattell, R. B., *The Personality and Motivation of the
Research Scientist,* New York, Academy of Sciences,
1954.

Cattell, R. B. and Butcher, H. J., *The Prediction of
Achievement and Creativity,* New York, Bobbs Merrill
Co., 1968.

Cattell, R. B. and Drevdahl, I. E., 'Comparison of the
Personality Profiles of Eminent Researchers with
Those of Eminent Teachers and Administrators and
the General Population', *British Journal of Psychology*
46, 1955, pp. 248-261.

Chalupsky, 1964   Chalupsky, A. B., 'Incentive Practice as Viewed by
                           Scientists and Managers of Pharmaceutical Labora-
                           tories', *Personnel Psychology* 17, 1964, pp. 385-401.
Chambers, 1964   Chambers, J. A., 'Relating Personality and Biograph-
                           ical Factors to Scientific Creativity', *Psychological
                           Monographs* 78, No. 7, 1964, pp. 1-20.
Chandra, 1970   Chandra, S., *Scientists: A Social-Psychological Study,*
                           New Delhi, Bombay, Calcutta, Oxford and Ibh, 1970.
Clemens, Linden and   Clemens, B., Linden, J. and Shertzer, B., 'Engineers'
Schertzer, 1970   Interest Patterns: Then and Now', *Educational and
                           Psychological Measurement* 30, 1970, pp. 675-685.
Clemente, 1973a   Clemente, F., 'Age and Academic Mobility', *Geronto-
                           logist* 13, 1973, pp. 180-185.
Clemente, 1973b   Clemente, F., 'Early Career Determinants of Research
                           Productivity', *American Journal of Sociology* 79,
                           1973, pp. 409-419.
Cline, Tucker and   Cline, V. B., Tucker, M. F. and Anderson, D. R.,
Anderson, 1966   'Psychology of the Scientist XX: Cross-Validation of
                           Biographical Information Predictor Keys across Di-
                           verse Samples of Scientists', *Psychological Reports* 19,
                           1966, pp. 951-954.
Cole and Cole, 1973   Cole, J. R. and Cole, S., *Social Stratification in
                           Science,* Chicago, University of Chicago Press, 1973.
Cole and Cole, 1967   Cole, S. and Cole, J. R., 'Scientific Output and Recog-
                           nition: A Study in the Operation of the Reward
                           System in Science', *American Sociological Review* 32,
                           1967, pp. 377-390.
Cole and Cole, 1968   Cole, S. and Cole. J. R., 'Visibility and the Structural
                           Bases of Awareness of Scientific Research', *American
                           Sociological Review* 33, 1968, pp. 397-413.
Cooley, 1964   Cooley, W. W., 'Current Research on the Career De-
                           velopment of Scientists', *Journal of Counselling
                           Psychology* 11, 1964, pp. 88-93.
Cordaro and Ison, 1963   Cordaro, L. and Ison, J. R., 'Psychology of the Scien-
                           tist X: Observer Bias in Classical Conditioning of the
                           Planarian', *Psychological Reports* 13, 1963, pp.
                           787-789.
Cotgrove and Box, 1970   Cotgrove, S. and Box, S., *Science, Industry and So-
                           ciety,* London, Allen and Unwin, 1970.
Crane, 1965   Crane, D., 'Scientists at Major and Minor Universities:
                           A Study of Productivity and Recognition', *American
                           Sociological Review* 30, 1965, pp. 699-714.
Crane, 1967   Crane, D., 'The Gatekeepers of Science: Some Factors
                           Affecting the Selection of Articles for Scientific
                           Journals', *American Sociologist* 2, 1967, pp. 195-201.
Crane, 1969   Crane, D., 'Fashion in Science: Does It Exist? ' *Social
                           Problems* 16, 1969, pp. 433-441.
Cummings, Hinton and   Cummings, L. L., Hinton, B. L. and Gobdel, B. C.,
Gobdel, 1975   'Creative Behavior as a Function of Task Environ-
                           ment: Impact of Objectives, Procedures and Controls',
                           Academy of Management Journal 18, 1975, pp.
                           489-499.
Dalenius, Karlsson and   Dalenius, T., Karlsson, G. and Malmquist, S. (Eds.),
Malmquist, 1970   *Scientists at Work,* Stockholm, Almqvist and Wiksell,
                           1970.

Datta, 1967	Datta, L. E., 'Family Religious Background and Early Scientific Creativity', *American Sociological Review* 32, 1967, pp. 626-635.
Datta, 1968	Datta, L. E., 'Birth Order and Potential Scientific Creativity', *Sociometry* 31, 1968, pp. 76-88.
Davies, 1968	Davies, D. S., 'Education for a Restless Society: 3. 'Club Sandwiches' for Scientists', *New Scientist* 40, 1968, pp. 31-33.
Dawes, 1975	Dawes, R. M., 'Graduate Admission Variables and Future Success', *Science* 187, 1975, pp. 721-723.
Dennis, 1956	Dennis, W., 'Age and Productivity among Scientists', *Science* 123, 1956, pp. 724-725.
Dennis, 1958	Dennis, W., 'The Age Decrement in Outstanding Scientific Contributions: Fact or Artifact', *American Psychologist* 13, 1958, pp. 457-460.
Dobrowolski, 1960	Dobrowolski, M., *Polnische Gelehrte und ihr Beitrag zur Weltwissenschaft,* Warsaw, Poland, 1960.
Edgerton, 1959	Edgerton, H. A., 'Two Tests for Early Identification of Scientific Ability', *Educational and Psychological Measurement* 19, 1959, pp. 299-304.
Eiduson, 1962	Eiduson, B. T., *Scientists: Their Psychological World,* New York, Basic Books, 1962.
Eiduson, 1973	Eiduson, B. T., 'Psychological Aspects of Career Choice and Development in the Research Scientist', in Eiduson, B., Beckman, L. (Eds.), *Science as a Career Choice,* New York, Russell Sage Foundation, 1973, pp. 3-33.
Eiduson, 1974	Eiduson, B. T., 'Ten-Year Longitudinal Rorschachs on Research Scientists', *Journal of Personality Assessment* 38, 1974, pp. 405-410.
Eiduson and Beckman, 1973	Eiduson, B. T. and Beckman, L., *Science as a Career Choice,* New York, Russell Sage Foundation, 1973.
Elliott, 1975	Elliott, C. A., 'The American Scientist in Antebellum Society: A Quantitative View', *Social Studies of Science* 5, 1975, pp. 93-108.
Elton and Rose, 1967	Elton, C. F. and Rose, H. A., 'Significance of Personality in the Vocational Choice of College Women', *Journal of Counselling Psychology* 13, 1967, pp. 293-298.
Faia, 1974	Faia, M. A., 'The Myth of the Liberal Professor', *Sociology of Education* 47, 1974, pp. 171-202.
Faris, 1940	Faris, R. E. L., 'Sociological Causes of Genius', *American Sociological Review* 5, 1940, pp. 689-699.
Feldman, 1975	Feldman, J., 'Obstacles to Women in Science', *Impact of Science on Society* 25, 1975, pp. 115-124.
Ferber and Loeb, 1973	Ferber, M. A. and Loeb, J. W., 'Performance, Rewards and Perceptions of Sex Discrimination Among Male and Female Faculty', *American Journal of Sociology* 78, 1973, pp. 995-1001.
Ferdinand, 1969	Ferdinand, T. N., 'Personality and Career Aspirations Among Young Technologists', *Human Relations* 22, 1969, pp. 121-135.
Feuer, 1963	Feuer, L. S., *The Scientific Intellectual,* London, New York, Basic Books, 1963.

Fisch, in press — Fisch, R., 'Aspekte Sozialer Orientierung bei Wissenschaftlern, untersucht am Beispiel des Fachs Psychologie', *Kölner Zeitschrift für Soziologie und Sozialpsychologie*, in press.

Fisch, Orlik and Saterdag, 1970 — Fisch, R., Orlik, P. and Saterdag, H., 'Warum studiert man Psychologie?' *Psychologische Rundschau* 21, 1970, pp. 239-256.

Fisher, 1973 — Fisher, C. S., 'Some Social Characteristics of Mathematicians and their Work', *American Journal of Sociology* 78, 1973, pp. 1094-1118.

Friedlander, 1971 — Friedlander, F., 'Performance and Orientation Structures of Research Scientists', *Organizational Behavior and Human Performance* 6, 1971, pp. 169-183.

Galton, 1869 — Galton, F., *Hereditary Genius*, Gloucester, Mass., Smith, 1972 (1869).

Galton, 1874 — Galton, F., *English Men of Science: Their Nature and Nurture*, London, Macmillan, 1874.

Gantz, Erickson and Stephenson, 1971 — Gantz, B. S., Erickson, C. and Stephenson, R. W., 'Measuring the Motivation to Manage in a Research and Development Population', *Proceedings of the Annual Convention of the American Psychological Association* 6, 1971, pp. 129-130.

Gantz, Stephenson and Erickson, 1969 — Gantz, B. S., Stephenson, R. W. and Erickson, C. O., 'Ideal Research and Development Climate as Seen by More Creative and by Less Creative Research Scientists', *Proceedings of the 77th Annual Convention of the American Psychological Association* 4, 1969, pp. 605-606.

Garvey and Tomita, 1972 — Garvey, W. D. and Tomita, K., 'Continuity of Productivity by Scientists in the Years 1968-1971', *Science Studies* 2, 1972, pp. 379-383.

Getzels and Jackson, 1962 — Getzels, J. W. and Jackson, P. W., *Creativity and Intelligence*, New York, Wiley, 1962.

Gianos, 1975 — Gianos, P. L., 'Scientists as Policy Advisers: The Context of Influence', *Western Political Quarterly* 27, 1975, pp. 429-456.

Gillispie, 1970 — Gillispie, C. C. (Ed.), *Dictionary of Scientific Biography*, Vols. 1-11, New York, Charles Schribner's Sons, 1970-1974.

Gilpin and Wright, 1964 — Gilpin, R. and Wright, C. (Eds.), *Scientists and National Policy Making*, New York, Columbia University Press, 1964.

Glaser, 1963 — Glaser, B. G., 'Variations in the Importance of Recognition in Scientists' Careers', *Social Problems* 10, 1963, pp. 268-276.

Glixman, 1967 — Glixman, A. F., 'Psychology of the Scientist XXII: Effects of Examiner, Examiner-Sex and Subject-Sex upon Categorizing Behavior', *Perceptual and Motor Skills* 27, 1967, pp. 107-117.

Globe *et al.*, 1973 — Globe, S., Levy, G. W. and Schwartz, C. M., 'Key Factors and Events in the Innovation Process', *Research Management* 16, 1973, pp. 8-15.

Goldman *et al.*, 1973 — Goldman, R. D., Platt, B. B. and Kaplan, R. B., 'Dimensions of Attitudes toward Technology', *Journal of Applied Psychology* 57, 1973, pp. 184-187.

Goldsmith and Mackay, 1964 — Goldsmith, M. and Mackay, A., *The Science of Science,* London, Souvenir Press, 1964.

Goldstein, 1974 — Goldstein, M. S., 'Academic Careers and Vocational Choices of Elite and Non-Elite Students at an Elite College', *Sociology of Education* 47, 1974, pp. 491-510.

Gomersall, 1971 — Gomersall, E. R., 'Current and Future Factors Affecting the Motivation of Scientists, Engineers and Technicians', *Research Management* 14, 1971, pp. 43-50.

Goodman, Rose and Furcon, 1970 — Goodman, P. S., Rose, J. H. and Furcon, J. E., 'Comparison of Motivational Antecedents of the Work Performance of Scientists and Engineers', *Journal of Applied Psychology* 54, 1970, pp. 491-495.

Goodstein and Brazis, 1970 — Goodstein, L., and Brazis, K. L., 'Psychology of the Scientist XXX: Credibility of Psychologists, An Empirical Study', *Psychological Reports* 26, 1970, pp. 835-838.

Gough, 1961 — Gough, H., 'Techniques for Identifying the Creative Research Scientist', in MacKinnon, D. W. (Ed.), *The Creative Person,* Berkeley, University of California Extension, 1961, pp. 13-17.

Gouldner, 1957 — Gouldner, A. W., 'Cosmopolitans and Locals: Toward an Analysis of Latent Social Roles', *Administrative Science Quarterly* 2, 1957, pp. 281-306.

Graham, 1974 — Graham, P. A., 'Woman in Academic Life', in Kundsin, R. B. (Ed.), *Women and Success: The Anatomy of Achievement,* New York, Morrow, 1974, pp. 238-247.

Greeley, 1971 — Greeley, A. M., 'The Ethnic and Religious Origins of Young American Scientists and Engineers: A Research Note', *International Migration Review* 6, 1971, pp. 282-288.

Gregory, 1967 — Gregory, C. E., *The Mangement of Intelligence,* New York, McGraw Hill, 1967.

Groth, 1975 — Groth, N. J., 'Success and Creativity in Male and Female Professors', *Gifted Child Quarterly* 19, 1975, pp. 328-335.

Gruber, 1974 — Gruber, H. E., *Darwin on Man: A Psychological Study of Scientific Creativity,* New York, Dutton, 1974.

Gruber, Terrel and Wertheimer, 1962 — Gruber, H., Terrel, G. and Wertheimer, M. (Eds.), *Contemporary Approaches to Creative Thinking,* New York, Atherton, 1962.

Guilford, 1966 — Guilford, J. P., 'Intelligence – 1965 Model', *American Psychologist* 21, 1966, pp. 20-26.

Guilford, 1968 — Guilford, J. P., *Intelligence, Creativity and Their Educational Implications,* San Diego, California, Knapp, 1968.

Gvishiani, Mikulinsky and Yaroshevsky, 1973 — Gvishiani, D. M., Mikulinsky, S. R. and Yaroshevsky, M. G., 'The Sociological and Psychological Study of Scientific Activity', *Minerva* 11, 1973, pp. 121-129.

Gysbers, Johnston and Gust, 1968 — Gysbers, N. C., Johnston, J. A. and Gust, T., 'Characteristics of Home-Maker and Career-Oriented Women',

Journal of Counselling Psychology 15, 1968, pp. 541-546.

Hadamard, 1945

Hadamard, J. S., *An Essay on the Psychology of Invention in the Mathematical Field*, Princeton, Princeton University Press, 1945.

Hagstrom, 1965

Hagstrom, W. O., *The Scientific Community*, New York, Basic Books, 1965.

Hagstrom, 1968

Hagstrom, W. O., 'Scientists', in Sills, D. L. (Ed.), *International Encyclopedia of the Social Sciences*, Vol. 14, New York, Macmillan and Free Press, 1968, pp. 107-111.

Haig, 1975

Haig, B. D., 'Can Behavioral Scientists Produce Hypothetical Constructs?' *Psychological Record* 25, 1975, pp. 433-436.

Hall and Mansfield, 1975

Hall, D. T. and Mansfield, R., 'Relationships of Age and Seniority with Career Variables of Engineers and Scientists', *Journal of Applied Psychology* 60, 1975, pp. 201-210.

Hardy, 1974

Hardy, K. R., 'Social Origins of American Scientists and Scholars', *Science* 185, 1974, pp. 497-506.

Hargens, 1969

Hargens, L., 'Patterns of Mobility of New Ph.D.'s among American Academic Institutions'', *Sociology of Education* 42, 1969, pp. 18-37.

Harmon, 1965

Harmon, L. R., *Profiles of Ph.D.'s in the Sciences: Summary Report of a Followup of Doctorate Cohorts 1935-1960*, Washington, D.C., National Academy of Sciences 1293, 1965.

Harrington, 1967

Harrington, G. M., 'Psychology of the Scientist XXIV' Experimenter Bias: Occam's Razor Versus Pascal's Wager', *Psychological Reports* 21, 1967, pp. 527-528.

Harrington and Ingraham, 1967

Harrington, G. M. and Ingraham, L. H., 'Psychology of the Scientist XXV: Experimenter Bias and Tails of Pascal', *Psychological Reports* 21, 1967, pp. 513-516.

Havelock, 1972

Havelock, R. G., *Bibliography on Knowledge, Utilization and Dissemination*, Michigan, Institute for Social Research, 1972.

Hays, 1962

Hays, R., 'Psychology of the Scientist II: Introduction to Passages from the 'Idea Books' of Clark Hull', *Perceptual and Motor Skills* 15, 1962, pp. 803-806.

Helson, 1967a

Helson, R., 'Personality Characteristics and Developmental History of Creative College Women', *Genetic Psychology Monographs* 76, 1967, pp. 205-256.

Helson, 1967b

Helson, R., 'Sex Differences in Creative Style', *Journal of Personality* 35, 1967, pp. 214-233.

Helson and Crutchfield, 1970

Helson, R. and Crutchfield, R. S., 'Mathematicians: The Creative Researcher and the average Ph.D.'', *Journal of Consulting and Clinical Psychology* 34, 1970, pp. 250-257.

Hill, 1974

Hill, S. C., 'Questioning the Influence of a 'Social System of Science': A Study of Australian Scientists', *Social Studies of Science* 4, 1974, pp. 135-163.

Hirsch, 1968

Hirsch, W., *Scientists in American Society*, New York, Random House, 1968.

Hlavsa, 1972

Hlavsa, J., 'The Components of the Creative Intellect and Their Cultivation', in Piret, R. (Ed.), *XIIe Congrès International de Psychologie Appliquée,* Vol. 1, Brussels, EDITEST, 1972, pp. 533-537.

Hollon, 1975

Hollon, C., 'Professorial Machiavellian Orientation, Academic Rank and Tenure', *Psychological Reports* 36, 1975, pp. 222-223.

Holton, 1972

Holton, G., 'On Trying to Understand the Scientific Genius', *American Scholar* 41, 1972, pp. 95-110.

Holton, 1973

Holton, G., *Thematic Origins of Scientific Thought,* Cambridge, Harvard University Press, 1973.

Hudson, 1963

Hudson, L., 'Personality and Scientific Aptitude', *Nature* 198, 1963, pp. 913-914.

Hudson, 1967

Hudson, L., *Contrary Imaginations,* Harmondworth, Middlesex, Penguin, 1967.

Hudson, 1968

Hudson, L., *Frames of Mind: Ability, Perception and Self-Perception in the Arts and Sciences,* New York, Norton, 1968.

Hull, 1962

Hull, C. L., 'Psychology of the Scientist IV: Passages from the 'Idea Books' of Clark Hull', *Perceptual and Motor Skills* 15, 1962, pp. 807-882.

Hutchings, 1967

Hutchings, D., 'Seeking Creativity in Science', *New Scientist* 33, 1967, pp. 416-417.

Hutchinson, 1970

Hutchinson, E., 'Scientists as an Inferior Class: The Early Years of the DSIR', *Minerva* 8, 1970, pp. 396-411.

Hylander, 1968

Hylander, C. J., *American Scientists,* New York, Macmillan, 1968.

Illingworth and Illingworth, 1966

Illingworth, R. S. and Illingworth, C. M., *Lessons from Childhood: Some Aspects of the Early Life of Unusual Men and Women,* Baltimore, Maryland, Williams and Wrekins, 1966.

Ingraham and Harrington, 1966

Ingraham, L. H. and Harrington, C. M., 'Psychology of the Scientist XVI: Experience of E as a Variable in Reducing Experimenter Bias', *Psychological Reports* 19, 1966, pp. 455-461.

Jaques, 1970

Jaques, E., *Work, Creativity and Social Justice,* London, Heinemann, 1970.

Jaroschewski and Mirski, 1974

Jaroschewski, M. G. and Mirski, E. M., 'Einige Überlegungen zur Adaption junger Wissenschaftler', *Spektrum* 5, 1974, pp. 10-11.

Jevons, 1973

Jevons, F. R., *Science Observed: Science as a Social and Intellectual Activity,* London, Georg Allen and Unwin, 1973.

Joesting, 1975

Joesting, J., 'The Influence of Sex Roles on Creativity in Women', *Gifted Child Quarterly* 19, 1975, pp. 336-339.

Johansson and Rossmann, 1971

Johansson, C. B. and Rossmann, J. E., 'Interest Patterns Among Economists', *Journal of Counseling Psychology* 18, 1971, pp. 255-261.

Kaplan, 1960

Kaplan, N., 'Some Organizational Factors Affecting Creativity', *Ire Transactions on Engineering Management* EM-7, 1, 1960, pp. 24-30.

Kaplan, 1965   Kaplan, N., *Science and Society*, Chicago, Rand McNally, 1965.

Kirchner, 1970   Kirchner, J. H., 'Psychology of the Scientist XXIX: Consider This: A Psycholiterary Study of Walden Two', *Psychological Reports* 26, 1970, pp. 403-412.

Knapp and Goodrich, 1952   Knapp, R. H. and Goodrich, H. B., *Origins of American Scientists*, Chicago, University of Chicago Press, 1952.

Koestler, 1964   Koestler, A., *The Act of Creation*, London, Hutchinson, 1964.

Kornhauser and Hagstrom,   Kornhauser, W. and Hagstrom, W., *Scientists in In-*
1962   *dustry: Conflict and Accommodation*, Berkeley, University of California Press, 1962.

Kröber and Lorf, 1972   Kröber, G. and Lorf, M. (Eds.), *Wissenschaftliches Schöpfertum*, Berlin (East), Akademie Verlag, 1972.

Krohn, 1971   Krohn, R. G., *The Social Shaping of Science: Institutions, Ideology and Careers in Science*, London, Greenwood, 1971.

Kubie, 1953   Kubie, L. S., 'Some Unsolved Problems of the Scientific Career', *American Scientist* 41, 1953, pp. 596-613.

Kubie, 1954   Kubie, L. S., 'Some Unsolved Problems of the Scientific Career, II', *American Scientist* 42, 1954, pp. 104-112.

Kubie, 1962   Kubie, L. S., 'The Fostering of Creative Scientific Productivity', *Daedalus* 91, 1962, pp. 294-309.

Kubie, 1965   Kubie, L. S., 'Blocks to Creativity', *International Science and Technology* 42, 1965, pp. 69-78.

Kubie, 1965   Kubie, L. S., *Neurotic Distortions of the Creative Process*, New York, Noonday, 1961.

Kuczynski, 1963   Kuczynski, J., *Über einige Probleme der Ausbildung und Bildung des Wissenschaftlers*, Berlin (East), Akademie Verlag, 1963.

Kuhn, 1961   Kuhn, T. S., *The Structure of Scientific Revolutions*, Chicago, University of Chicago Press, 1961.

Kuhn, 1970   Kuhn, T. S., 'Logic of Discovery or Psychology of Research?' in Lakatos, I., and Musgrave, A. (Eds.), *Criticism and the Growth of Knowledge*, New York, Cambridge University Press, 1970, pp. 1-23.

Lacey and Erickson, 1974   Lacey, L. A. and Erickson, C. E., 'Psychology of the Scientist XXXI: Discriminability of a Creativity Scale for the Adjective Check List Among Scientists and Engineers', *Psychological Reports* 34, 1974, pp. 755-758.

Ladd and Lipset, 1972   Ladd, E. C. Jr, and Lipset, S. M., 'Politics of Academic Natural Scientists and Engineers', *Science* 176, 1972, pp. 1091-1100.

Ladd and Lipset, 1973a   Ladd, E. C. Jr, and Lipset, S. M., *Academics, Politics, and the 1972 Election*, Washington, D.C., American Enterprise Institute, 1973.

Ladd and Lipset, 1973b   Ladd, E. C. Jr. and Lipset, S. M., *Professors, Unions and American Higher Education*, Berkeley, California, The Carnegie Commission on Higher Education, 1973.

Lammers, 1974 — Lammers, C. J., 'Localism, Cosmopolitanism and Faculty Response', *Sociology of Education* 41, 1974, pp. 129-158.

Landfield, 1961 — Landfield, A. W., 'The Science of Psychology and the Psychology of Science', *Perceptual and Motor Skills* 13, 1961, pp. 319-325.

Lawler, 1963 — Lawler, E. E., 'Psychology of the Scientist IX: Age and Authorship of Citations in Selected Psychological Journals', *Psychological Reports* 13, 1963, p. 537.

Lehman, 1953 — Lehman, H. C., *Age and Achievement*, Princeton, Princeton University Press, 1953.

Lehman, 1960 — Lehman, H. C., 'The Age Decrement in Outstanding Scientific Creativity', *American Psychologist* 15, 1960, pp. 129-134.

Lehman, 1962 — Lehman, H. C., 'More About Age and Achievement', *Gerontologist* 2, 1962, pp. 141-148.

Lehman, 1966 — Lehman, H. C., 'The Psychologist's Most Creative Years', *American Psychologist* 21, 1966, pp. 363-369.

Lemaine, 1975 — Lemaine, G., *Stratégies et choix dans la recherche*, Paris, Groupe d'Etudes et de Recherche sur la Science, 1975.

Lipset and Ladd, 1974 — Lipset, S. M. and Ladd, C. L., 'The Myth of the 'Conservative' Professor: A Reply to Michael Faia', *Sociology of Education* 47, 1974, pp. 203-213.

Lipset and Ladd, 1972 — Lipset, S. M. and Ladd, E. C. Jr., 'The Politics of American Sociologists', *American Journal of Sociology* 78, 1972, pp. 67-104.

Lotka, 1926 — Lotka, A. J., 'The Frequency Distribution of Scientific Productivity', *Journal of the Washington Academy of Sciences* 16, 1926, pp. 317-323.

Lübbe, 1972 — Lübbe, H., *Hochschulreform und Gegenaufklärung*, Freiburg, Herder, 1972.

Lyon, Ivancevich and Donnelly, 1971 — Lyon, H. L., Ivancevich, J. M. and Donnelly, J. H., 'A Motivational Profile of Management Scientists', *Operations Research* 19, 1971, pp. 1282-1299.

MacKinnon, 1972 — MacKinnon, D. W., 'The Role of Personality Traits in the Development of Scientific Abilities', in Piret, R. (Ed.), *XIIe Congrès International de Psychologie Appliquée* (Vol. 1), Brussels, EDITEST, 1972, pp. 515-518.

Maier, 1970 — Maier, N. R. F., *Problem Solving and Creativity in Individuals and Groups*, Belmont, California, Brooks/Cole, 1970.

Manley and McNichols, 1975 — Manley, R. R. and McNichols, C. W., 'Attitudes of Federal Scientists and Engineers toward Unions', *Monthly Labor Review* 98, 1975, pp. 57-60.

Marcson, 1968 — Marcson, S., 'Technical Men in Government', *International Science and Technology* 73, 1968, pp. 63-68.

Margoshes and Litt, 1965 — Margoshes, A. and Litt, S., 'Psychology of the Scientist XII: Neglect of Revolutionary Ideas in Psychology', *Psychological Reports* 16, 1965, pp. 621-624.

Maslow, 1966 — Maslow, A. H., *The Psychology of Science*, London, Harper and Row, 1966.

Masterman, 1974   Masterman, M., 'Falling through the Grid, or What Has
                           Happened to the Scarce Women Academics?' *Journal
                           for the Theory of Social Behavior* 4, 1974, pp. 97-107.
Matussek, 1967-68   Matussek, P., 'Der Ehrgeiz in der Wissenschaft', *Hoch-
                           land* 60, 1967-1968, pp. 478-481.
Mays, 1973   Mays, W., 'Koestler and the Nature of Scientific Crea-
                           tivity', *Journal of the British Society for Phenomeno-
                           logy* 4, No. 3, 1973, pp. 248-255.
McCarrey and Edwards, 1972 McCarrey, M. W. and Edwards, S. A., 'Hierarchies of
                           Scientist Goal Objects: Individual Characteristics and
                           Performance Correlates', *Journal of Applied Psycho-
                           logy* 56, 1972, pp. 271-272.
McCarthy, 1968   McCarthy, M. C., 'Education for a Restless Society –
                           The Scourge of Specialisation', *New Scientist* 40,
                           1968, pp. 88-90.
McClelland, 1962   McClelland, D. C., 'On the Psychodynamics of Crea-
                           tive Physical Scientists', in Gruber, H., Terrel, G. and
                           Wertheimer, M. (Eds.), *Contemporary Approaches to
                           Creative Thinking*, New York, Atherton, 1962, pp.
                           141-174.
McDavid and Harari, 1968   McDavid, J. W. and Harari, H., *Social Psychology*, New
                           York, Harper and Row, 1968.
Mednick, 1962   Mednick, S. A., 'The Associative Basis of the Creative
                           Process', *Psychological Review* 69, 1962, pp. 220-232.
Meltzer, 1966   Meltzer, H., 'Psychology of the Scientist XVII: Re-
                           search Has a Place in Private Practice', *Psychological
                           Reports* 19, 1966, pp. 463-472.
Meltzer, 1956   Meltzer, L., 'Scientific Productivity in Organizational
                           Settings', *Journal of Social Issues* 12, 1956, pp. 32-40.
Merton, 1942   Merton, R. K., 'Science and Technology in a Democra-
                           tic Order', *Journal of Legal and Political Sociology* 1,.
                           1942, pp. 115-126 (Also in Merton, 1973, pp.
                           267-278).
Merton, 1957   Merton, R. K., *Social Theory and Social Structure*,
                           Glencoe, Illinois, The Free Press, 1957.
Merton, 1969   Merton, R. K., 'Behavior Patterns of Scientists',
                           American Scholar 38, 1969, pp. 197-225.
Mikulinski and   Mikulinski, S. R. and Jaroshevski, M., 'Psychologie des
Jaroshevski, 1970   wissenschaftlichen Schaffens und der Wissenschafts-
                           lehre', *Zeitschrift für allgemeine Wissenschaftstheorie*
                           1, 1970, pp. 83-103.
Mitroff, 1972   Mitroff, I. I., 'The Myth of Objectivity or Why Science
                           Needs a New Psychology of Science', *Management
                           Science* 18, 1972, pp. 613-618.
Mitroff, 1973   Mitroff, I. I., 'The Disinterested Scientist: Fact or
                           Fiction?' *Social Education* 37, 1973, pp. 761-765.
Mitroff, 1974a   Mitroff, I. I., 'Norms and Counter-Norms in a Select
                           Group of the Apollo Moon Scientists: A Case Study of
                           the Ambivalence of Scientists', *American Sociological
                           Review* 39, 1974, pp. 579-595.
Mitroff, 1974b   Mitroff, I. I., *The Subjective Side of Science*, Amster-
                           dam, Elsevier, 1974.
Mitroff, 1975   Mitroff, I. I., *A Social Psychological Study of Some*

Key Issues in the Philosophy of Science: A Comparison of Eminent Scientists, Unpublished Report, University of Pittsburgh Graduate School of Library and Information Sciences, 1975.

Modlin, 1973 — Modlin, H. C., 'Science and Technology Versus Ethics and Morals', *Bulletin of the Menninger Clinic* 37, 1973, pp. 149-168.

Mooney and Razik, 1967 — Mooney, R. L. and Razik, T. A. (Eds.), *Explorations in Creativity,* New York, Harper and Row, 1967.

Motz, 1961 — Motz, A. B., 'The Roles of Married Women in Science', *Marriage and Family Living* 23, 1961, pp. 374-376.

Mozans, 1974 — Mozans, H. J., *Woman in Science,* Cambridge, MIT Press, 1974.

Müller-Freienfels, 1936 — Müller-Freienfels, R., *Psychologie der Wissenschaft,* Leipzig, Barth, 1936.

Mullins, 1963 — Mullins, C. J., 'Prediction of Creativity in a Sample of Research Scientists', *IEEE Transactions on Engineering Management* 10, 1963, pp. 52-57.

Naess, 1965 — Naess, A., 'Science as Behavior', in Wolman, B. B. and Nagel, E. (Eds.), *Scientific Psychology,* New York, Basic Books, 1965, pp. 50-67.

National Academy of Sciences, 1968 — National Academy of Sciences, National Research Council, *Careers of Ph.D.'s,* Washington, D.C., National Academy of Sciences, National Research Council, 1968.

National Academy of Sciences, 1971 — National Academy of Sciences, National Research Council, *Mobility of Ph.D.'s,* Washington, D.C., National Academy of Sciences, National Research Council, 1971.

National Research Council, 1974 — National Research Council, National Academy of Science (Eds.), *Doctoral Scientists and Engineers in the United States: 1973 Profile,* Washington, D.C., National Academy of Science, 1974.

Nichols, 1964 — Nichols, R. C., 'Career Decisions of Very Able Students', *Science* 144, 1964, pp. 1315-1319.

Nowakowska, 1975 — Nowakowska, M., 'Measurable Aspects of the Concept of Scientific Career', in Knorr, K., Strasser, H., and Zilian, H. G. (Eds.), *Determinants and Controls of Scientific Development,* Dordrecht, Reidel, 1975.

Nowotny, 1975 — Nowotny, H., 'Controversies in Science: Remarks on the Different Modes of Production of Knowledge and Their Use', *Zeitschrift für Soziologie* 4, 1975, pp. 34-45.

Orlik, Fisch and Saterdag, 1971 — Orlik, P., Fisch, R., and Saterdag, H., 'Fragen der sozialen Orientierung von Studienanfängern des Faches Psychologie', *Psychologische Rundschau* 22, 1971, pp. 17-37.

Oromaner, 1969 — Oromaner, M. J., 'The Audience as a Determinant of the Most Important Sociologists', *American Sociologist* 4, 1969, pp. 332-335.

Osborn, 1963 — Osborn, A. F., *Applied Imagination,* New York, Charles Scribner, 1963.

Ossowska and Ossowski, 1936 — Ossowska, M. and Ossowski, S., 'The Science of

Science', *Organon* 1, 1936, pp. 1-12 (Also in *Minerva* 3, 1964, pp. 72-82).

Ostwald, 1909 — Ostwald, W. V., *Grosse Männer, Studien zur Biologie des Genies,* Leipzig, Akademische Verlagsgesellschaft, 1909.

Parloff and Datta, 1965 — Parloff, M. B. and Datta, L., 'Personality Characteristics of the Potentially Creative Scientist', in Masserman, J. H. (Ed.), *Science and Psychoanalysis* (Vol. 7), New York, Grune and Stratton, 1965, pp. 91-106.

Parry, 1973 — Parry, A., *The Russian Scientist,* New York, London, Macmillan, 1973.

Pasewark, Fitzgerald and Sawyer, 1975 — Pasewark, R. A., Fitzgerald, B. J. and Sawyer, R. N., 'Psychology of the Scientist XXXII: God at the Synapse: Research Activities of Clinical, Experimental, and Physiological Psychologists', *Psychological Reports* 36, 1975, pp. 671-674.

Patterson, 1973 — Patterson, M., 'Sex and Specialization in Academe and the Professions', in Rossi, A. S. and Calderwood, A. (Eds.), *Academic Women on the Move,* New York, Russell Sage Foundation, 1973, pp. 313-332.

Pelz, 1967 — Pelz, D. C., 'Creative Tensions in the Research and Development Climate', *Science* 157, 1967, pp. 160-165.

Pelz and Andrews, 1966 — Pelz, D. C. and Andrews, F. M., *Scientists in Organizations,* New York, Wiley, 1966.

Perrucci, 1970 — Perrucci, C. C., 'Minority Status and the Pursuit of Professional Careers: Women in Science and Engineering', *Social Forces* 49, 1970, pp. 245-259.

Perry, 1966 — Perry, S. E., *The Human Nature of Science,* New York, The Free Press, 1966.

Perucci and Gerstl, 1969 — Perucci, R. and Gerstl, J. E., *The Engineers and the Social System,* New York, Wiley, 1969.

Piryov, 1972 — Piryov, G. D., 'The Role of Higher Education for Detecting and Development of Scientific Abilities', in Piret, R. (Ed.), *XIIe Congrès International de Psychologie Appliquée* (Vol. 1), Brussels, EDITEST 1972, pp. 519-524.

Platz, 1965 — Platz, A., 'Psychology of the Scientist XI: Lotka's Law and Research Visibility', *Psychological Reports* 16, 1965, pp. 566-568.

Polanyi, 1957 — Polanyi, M., 'Passion and Controversy in Science', *Bulletin of the Atomic Scientists* 13, 1957, pp. 114-119.

Polanyi, 1958 — Polanyi, M., *Personal Knowledge,* Chicago University of Chicago Press, 1958.

Polanyi, 1967 — Polanyi, M., *The Tacit Dimension,* London, Routledge and Kegan Paul, 1967.

Polanyi, 1968 — Polanyi, M., 'Logic and Psychology', *American Psychologist* 23, 1968, pp. 27-44.

Derek Price, 1963 — Price, Derek de Solla, *Little Science, Big Science,* New York, Columbia University Press, 1963.

Derek Price, 1974 — Price, Derek de Solla, 'The Productivity of Research Scientists', Yearbook of Science and the Future 1975, *Encyclopedia Britannica,* 1974, pp. 409-421.

Derek Price, 1975	Price, Derek de Solla, 'Some Statistical Results for the Numbers of Authors in the States of the United States and the Nations of the World', Preface to *Who is Publishing in Science* (WIPIS), 1975 annual volume, Institute for Scientific Information, Philadelphia, 1975.
Primack and Hippel, 1974	Primack, J. and Hippel, F. von, *Advice and Dissent, Scientists in the Political Arena*, New York, Basic Books, 1974.
Pruyser, 1973	Pruyser, P. W., 'The Practice of Science and Values: A Psychologist's Odyssey', *Bulletin of the Menninger Clinic* 37, 1973, pp. 133-148.
Radnitzky, 1974	Radnitzky, G., 'From Logic of Science to Theory of Research', *Communication and Cognition* 7, 1974, pp. 61-124.
Ramul, 1966	Ramul, K. A., 'Zur Psychologie des Wissenschaftlers', *Sowjetwissenschaft – Gesellschaftswissenschaftliche Beiträge* 1. Halbjahr, 1966, pp. 622-625.
Rand, 1968	Rand, L., 'Masculinity or Feminity? Differentiating Career-Oriented and Homemaking-Oriented College Freshman Women', *Journal of Counseling Psychology* 15, 1968, pp. 444-450.
Ravetz, 1971	Ravetz, J., *Scientific Knowledge and its Social Problems*, Oxford, Clarendon Press, 1971.
Rodnyi, 1972	Rodnyi, N. I., 'Probleme des wissenschaftlichen Schöpfertums und der Organisation der Wissenschaft in den Arbeiten von Naturwissenschaftlern', in Kröber, G. and Steiner, H. (Eds.), *Wissenschaft: Studien zu ihrer Geschichte, Theorie und Organisation*, Berlin (East), Akademie-Verlag, 1972, pp. 96-151.
Roe, 1949a	Roe, A., 'Analysis of Group Rorschachs of Biologists', *Rorschach Research Exchange* 13, 1949, pp. 25-43.
Roe, 1949b	Roe, A., 'Psychological Examinations of Eminent Biologists', *Journal of Counseling Psychology* 13, 1949, pp. 225-246.
Roe, 1950	Roe, A., 'Analysis of Group Rorschachs of Physical Scientists', *Journal of Projective Techniques* 14, 1950, pp. 385-398.
Roe, 1951a	Roe, A., 'A Psychological Study of Eminent Biologists', *Psychological Monographs* 65, 1951, pp. 1-68.
Roe, 1951b	Roe, A., 'A Psychological Study of Physical Scientists', *Psychological Monographs* 43, 1951, pp. 121-239.
Roe, 1951c	Roe, A., 'Psychological Tests of Research Scientists', *Journal of Consulting Psychology* 15, 1951, pp. 492-495.
Roe, 1952a	Roe, A., 'Analysis of Group Rorschachs of Biologists', *Journal of Projective Techniques* 16, 1952, pp. 25-43.
Roe, 1952b	Roe, A., 'Analysis of Group Rorschachs of Psychologists and Anthropologists', *Journal of Projective Techniques* 16, 1952, pp. 212-224.
Roe, 1953a	Roe, A., 'A Psychological Study of Eminent Psychologists and Anthropologists, and A Comparison with

Biologists and Physical Scientists', *Psychological Monographs* 67, 1953, whole No. 2.

Roe, 1953b — Roe, A., *The Making of a Scientist,* New York, Dodd, Mead, 1953.

Roe, 1963 — Roe, A., 'Personal Problems and Science', in Taylor, C. W. and Barron, F. (Eds.), *Scientific Creativity: Its Recognition and Development,* New York, Wiley, 1963, pp. 132-138.

Roe, 1965 — Roe, A., 'Changes in Scientific Activities with Age', *Science* 150, 1965, pp. 313-318.

Roe, 1972 — Roe, A., 'Patterns in Productivity of Scientists', *Science* 176, 1972, pp. 940-941.

Rosenthal, 1966 — Rosenthal, R., *Experimenter Effects in Behavioral Research,* New York, Appleton-Century-Crofts, 1966.

Rosenthal, 1967a — Rosenthal, R., 'Psychology of the Scientist XXIII: Experimenter Expectancy, Experimenter Experience, and Pascal's Wager", *Psychological Reports* 20, 1967, pp. 619-622.

Rosenthal, 1967b — Rosenthal, R., 'Psychology of the Scientist XXVI: Experimenter Expectancy, One Tale of Pascal, and the Distribution of Three Tails', *Psychological Reports* 21, 1967, pp. 517-522.

Rosenthal and Fode, 1963 — Rosenthal, R. and Fode, K. I., 'Psychology of the Scientist V: Three Experiments in Experimenter Bias', *Psychological Reports* 12, 1963, pp. 491-511.

Rosenthal *et al.,* 1965 — Rosenthal, R., Kohn, P., Greenfield, P. M., and Carota, N., 'Psychology of the Scientist XIV: Experimenters' Hypothesis-Confirmation and Mood as Determinants of Experimental Results', *Perceptual and Motor Skills* 20, 1965, pp. 1237-1252.

Rosenthal and Rosnow, 1969 — Rosenthal, R. and Rosnow, R. (Eds.), *Artifact in Behavioral Research,* New York, Academic Press, 1969.

Rossman, 1964 — Rossman, J., *Industrial Creativity,* New York, University Books, 1964.

Rothman, 1972 — Rothman, R. A., 'A Dissenting View on Scientific Ethos', *British Journal of Sociology* 23, 1972, pp. 102-108.

Rowe, 1973 — Rowe, A. R., 'The 'Attraction Value' for a Scientific Career in Industry', *Psychology* 10, 1973, pp. 44-49.

Russett, 1975 — Russett, B. M., 'The Social Scientist as Political Activist: The Ethical Dilemmas', *Worldview* 18, 1975, pp. 45-49.

Ryder, 1966 — Ryder, R. G., 'Psychology of the Scientist XVIII: The Factualizing Game: A Sickness of Psychological Research', *Psychological Reports* 19, 1966, pp. 563-570.

Sayre, 1961 — Sayre, W. S., 'Scientists and American Science Policy', *Science* 133, 1961, pp. 859-864.

Schachter, 1963 — Schachter, S., 'Birth Order, Eminence and Higher Education, *American Sociological Review* 28, 1963, pp. 757-768.

Schooler, 1971 — Schooler, D., *Science, Scientists and Public Policy,* New York, The Free Press, 1971.

Scriven, 1962 — Scriven, M., 'Explanations, Predictions and Laws', in

Feigl, H. and Maxwell, G. (Eds.), *Minnesota Studies in the Philosophy of Science* (Vol. 3), Minneapolis, University of Minnesota Press, 1962, pp. 170-230.

Shapiro, 1966   Shapiro, R. J., 'The Identification of Creative Research Scientsts', *Psychologia Africana* 11, No. 2, 1966, pp. 99-132.

Shelly, 1963a   Shelly, M. W., 'Psychology of the Scientist VI: Scientist as Artist', *Perceptual and Motor Skills* 16, 1963, pp. 635-636.

Shelly, 1963b   Shelly, M. W., 'Psychology of the Scientist VII: The Scientist and the Mortality of Science', *Perceptual and Motor Skills* 16, 1963, pp. 885-886.

Shils, 1968   Shils, E., 'The Profession of Science', *Advancement of Science* 6, 1968, pp. 469-480.

Shils, 1975   Shils, E., 'The Academic Ethos Under Strain', *Minerva* 13, 1975, pp. 1-37.

Shimshoni, 1970   Shimshoni, D., 'The Mobile Scientist in the American Instrument Industry', *Minerva* 8, 1970, pp. 59-89.

Silverman, 1974   Silverman, S. M., 'Parental Loss and Scientists', *Science Studies* 4, 1974, pp. 259-264.

Simon, 1966   Simon, H. A., 'Scientific Discovery and the Psychology of Problem Solving', in Colodny, R. G. (Ed.), *Mind and Cosmos, Essays in Contemporary Science and Philosophy,* Vol. 3 of the University of Pittsburgh Series in the Philosophy of Science, Pittsburgh, University of Pittsburgh Press, 1966, pp. 22-39.

Simon, Clark and Galway, 1967-1968   Simon, R. J., Clark, S. M. and Galway, K., 'The Woman Ph.D.: A Recent Profile', *Social Problems* 15, 1967-1968, pp. 221-230.

Singer, 1971   Singer, B. F., 'Towards a Psychology of Science', *American Psychologist* 26, 1971, pp. 1010-1016.

Smith, Albright and Glennon, 1961   Smith, W. J., Albright, L. E. and Glennon, J. R., 'The Prediction of Research Competence and Creativity from Personal History', *Journal of Applied Psychology* 45, 1961, pp. 59-62.

Smith *et al.*, 1971   Smith, O. W., Smith, P. C., Baumgart, R., Gliner, J. and Goodale, J., 'Psychology of the Scientist XXX: Replication: What Is It?' *Perceptual and Motor Skills* 33, 1971, pp. 691-697.

Smithers and Dann, 1974   Smithers, A. G. and Dann, S., 'Success and Failure Among Engineers, Psychological Scientists and Linguists at a Technological University', *British Journal of Educational Psychology* 44, 1974, pp. 241-247.

Spiegel-Rösing, 1972   Spiegel-Rösing, I., 'Journal Authors as an Indicator of Scientific Manpower: A Methodological Study Using Data for the Two Germanies and Europe', *Science Studies* 2, 1972, pp. 337-359.

Spiegel-Rösing, 1973   Spiegel-Rösing, I., *Wissenschaftsentwicklung und Wissenschaftssteuerung,* Frankfurt am Main, Athenaum, 1973.

Spiegel-Rösing *et al.*, 1975   Spiegel-Rösing, I., Fauser, P. and Baitsch, H., *Beiträge zur Messung von Forschungsleistung: Institutionen, Gruppen, Einzelpersonen,* Bonn, Bundesministerium

	für Bildung und Wissenschaft, 1975.
Spranger, 1950	Spranger, E., *Lebensformen,* Tübingen, Niemeyer, 1950.
Stein, 1974	Stein, M., *Stimulating Creativity: Individual Procedures* (Vol. 1), New York, Academic Press, 1974.
Stein, 1975	Stein, M., *Stimulating Creativity: Group Procedures* (Vol. 2), New York, Academic Press, 1975.
Stein and Heinze, 1960	Stein, M. I. and Heinze, S. J., *Creativity and the Individual,* New York, The Free Press, 1960.
Stievater, 1971	Stievater, S. M., 'A Comprehensive Bibliography of Books on Creativity and Problem Solving: I. From 1950 to 1970', *Journal of Creative Behavior* 5, 1971, pp. 140-151.
Stievater, 1973a	Stievater, S. M., 'Bibliography of Recent Theses on Creativity and Problem Solving: Supplement II', *Journal of Creative Behavior* 7, 1973, pp. 214-222.
Stievater, 1973b	Stievater, S. M., 'Bibliography of Recent Books on Creativity and Problem Solving: Supplement IV', *Journal of Creative Behavior* 7, 1973, pp. 208-213.
Stievater, 1975a	Stievater, S. M., 'Bibliography of Recent Doctoral Dissertations on Creativity and Problem Solving: Supplement VI', *Journal of Creative Behavior* 9, 1975, pp. 217-222.
Stievater, 1975b	Stievater, S. M., 'Bibliography of Recent Books on Creativity and Problem Solving: Supplement VII', *Journal of Creative Behavior* 9, 1975, pp. 211-216.
Storr, 1972	Storr, A., *The Dynamic of Creation,* London, Secker and Warburg, 1972.
Strauss, 1966a	Strauss, P. S., 'Psychology of the Scientist XIX: Satisfaction and Productivity of Engineers and Scientists', *Perceptual and Motor Skills,* 23, 1966, pp. 471-476.
Strauss, 1966b	Strauss, P. S., 'Psychology of the Scientist XXI: Growth and Belonging Perceptions as Factors in the Behavior of Engineers and Scientists', *Perceptual and Motor Skills* 23, 1966, pp. 883-894.
Strauss, 1967	Strauss, P. S., 'Psychology of the Scientist XXIV: Perceptual Distortion of Job Activities Among Engineers and Scientists', *Perceptual and Motor Skills* 25, 1967, pp. 79-80.
Tagiuri, 1965	Tagiuri, R., 'Value Orientation and the Relationship of Managers and Scientists', *Administrative Science Quarterly* 10, 1965, pp. 39-51.
Taton, 1957	Taton, R., *Reason and Change in Scientific Discovery,* New York, Philosophical Library, 1957.
Taylor, 1964	Taylor, C. W., *Creativity: Progress and Potential,* New York, McGraw-Hill, 1964.
Taylor, 1972	Taylor, C. W. (Ed.), *Climate for Creativity,* New York, Pergamon, 1972.
Taylor and Barron, 1963	Taylor, C. W. and Barron, F. (Eds.), *Scientific Creativity: Its Recognition and Development,* New York, Wiley, 1963.
Taylor and Ellison, 1972	Taylor, C. W. and Ellison, R. L., 'Selection of Scientists Who Will Be Productive in Their Careers', in Piret, R. (Ed.), *XIIe Congrès International de Psycho-*

logie Appliquée (Vol. 1), Brussels, EDITEST, 1972, pp. 525-532.

Terman, 1954   Terman, L. M., 'Scientists and Nonscientists in a Group of 800 Gifted Men', *Psychological Monographs* 68, 1954, Whole No. 7.

Terman, 1955   Terman, L. M., 'Are Scientists Different?' *Scientific American* 192, 1955, pp. 25-29.

Tilson, 1965   Tilson, S., 'Educating the Scientist', *International Science and Technology* 39, 1965, pp. 46-53.

Torrance, Bruch and Morse, 1973   Torrance, E. P., Bruch, C. B. and Morse, J. A., 'Improving Predictions of the Adult Creative Achievement of Gifted Girls by Using Autobiographical Information', *Gifted Child Quarterly* 17, No. 2, 1973, pp. 91-95.

Traxel, 1969   Traxel, W., 'Diskrepante Erfahrungen als Ursprünge psychologischer Forschung', *Archiv für die gesammte Psychologie* 121, 1969, pp. 285-293.

Tucker, Cline and Schmitt, 1967   Tucker, M. F., Cline, V. B. and Schmitt, J. R., 'Prediction of Creativity and Other Performance Measures from Biographical Information Among Pharmaceutical Scientists', *Journal of Applied Psychology* 51, No. 2, 1967, pp. 131-138.

Turner, 1967   Turner, M. B., *Philosophy and the Science of Behavior*, New York, Appleton-Century-Crofts, 1967.

UNESCO, 1973   UNESCO, *Statistical Yearbook, 1972*, Paris United Nations Educational, Scientific and Cultural Organization, 1973.

Vlachý, 1971a   Vlachý, J., 'Some Creativity Patterns in Physical Sciences', *Teorie a Metoda* 3, 1971, pp. 83-96.

Vlachý, 1971b   Vlachý, J., 'The Measures of Creativity or Productivity', *Teorie a Metoda* 3, 1971, pp. 127-130.

Vlachý, 1972   Vlachý, J., 'Variable Factors in Scientific Communities (Observations on Lotka's Law)', *Teorie a Metoda* 4, 1972, pp. 91-120.

Wainer and Rubin, 1969   Wainer, H. A. and Rubin, I. M., 'Motivation of Research and Development Entrepreneurs: Determinants of Company Success', *Journal of Applied Psychology* 53, 1969, pp. 178-184.

Watley, 1971   Watley, D. J., 'Career or Marriage? a Longitudinal Study of Able Young Women', in Theodore, A. (Ed.), *The Professional Woman,* Cambridge, Mass., Schenkman, 1971, pp. 260-274.

Weber, 1904, 1905   Weber, M., 'Die protestantische Ethik und der Geist des Kapitalismus', *Archiv für Sozialwissenschaft und Sozialpolitik* 20, 1904, pp. 1-54; 21, 1905, pp. 1-110.

Weber, 1919   Weber, M., 'Science as a Vocation', in Weber, M., *Essays in Sociology* (Gerth, H. H. and Mills, C. W., Eds. and Transl.), New York, Oxford University Press, 1946, pp. 134-156.

Weimer, 1974   Weimer, W. B., 'The History of Psychology and Its Retrieval from Historiography', *Science Studies* 4, 1974, pp. 367-396.

Wertheimer, 1954   Wertheimer, M., *Productive Thinking,* New York, Harper and Row, 1954.

West, 1961   West, S. S., 'Class Origin of Scientists', *Sociometry* 24, 1961, pp. 251-269.

White, 1968   White, S., 'Educating Scientists in the USSR', *New Scientist* 40, 1968, pp. 33-34.

Whiting, 1972   Whiting, B. G., 'How to Predict Creativity from Biological Data', *Research Management* 15, 1972, pp. 28-34.

Whitley, 1974   Whitley, R. (Ed.), *Social Processes of Scientific Development*, London, Routledge and Kegan Paul, 1974.

Williamson, 1953   Williamson, E. G., 'A Program of Research on Characteristics of Scientists', in Hogan, R. M. (Chm.), *Proceedings of the Second Conference on Scientific Manpower 1952*, Washington, D. C., National Science Foundation 1953, pp. 6-14.

Wispé, 1963   Wispé, L. G., 'Traits of Eminent American Psychologists', *Science* 141, 1963, pp. 1256-1261.

Wojick, 1974   Wojick, D., 'The Norm of Rationality or the Rationality of Norms', *Science Studies* 4, 1974, pp. 193-195.

Wolkow, 1969   Wolkow, G. N., 'Probleme der Leitung der Wissenschaft', *Sowjetwissenschaft — Gesellschaftswissenschaftliche Beiträge* 1. Halbjahr, 1969, pp. 303-315.

Woodward, 1974   Woodward, W. R., 'Scientific Genius and Loss of a Parent', *Science Studies* 4, 1974, pp. 265-277.

Wunderlich, 1974   Wunderlich, R., 'The Scientific Ethos: A Clarification', *British Journal of Sociology* 25, 1974, pp. 373-377.

Zener, 1968   Zener, C., 'An Analysis of Scientific Productivity', *Proceedings of the National Academy of Sciences* 59, 1968, pp. 1078-1081.

Ziman, 1968   Ziman, J. M., *Public Knowledge*, Cambridge, University Press, 1968.

Ziman, 1970   Ziman, J. M., 'Some Pathologies of the Scientific Life', *Advancement of Science* 27, 1970-1971, pp. 1-10.

Zinberg, 1971   Zinberg, D. S., 'The Widening Gap: Attitudes of First Year Students and Staff towards Chemistry, Science, Careers and Commitment', *Science Studies* 1, 1971, pp. 287-313.

Zinberg, 1974   Zinberg, D. S., 'Science is a Social-Psychological Activity — Even for Science Students', in Whitley, R. (Ed.), *Social Processes of Scientific Development*, London, Routledge and Kegan Paul, 1974, pp. 242-253.

Znaniecki, 1965   Znaniecki, F., *The Social Role of the Man of Knowledge*, New York, Octagon, 1965.

Zuckerman, 1967   Zuckerman, H., 'Nobel Laureates in Science: Patterns of Productivity, Collaboration and Authorship', *American Sociological Review* 32, 1967, pp. 391-403.

Zuckerman and Cole, 1975   Zuckerman, H. and Cole, J. R., 'Women in American Science', *Minerva* 13, 1975, pp. 82-102.

Zuckerman and Merton, 1971 Zuckerman, H. and Merton, R. K., 'Patterns of Evaluation in Science: Institutionalisation, Structure and Functions of the Referee System', *Minerva* 9, 1971, pp. 66-100.

Chapter 9

MODELS FOR THE DEVELOPMENT OF SCIENCE

Gernot Böhme

Max-Planck-Institut, Starnberg

INTRODUCTION

'Science policy' is generally understood to mean the strategic behavior of politicians in relation to science. But the term 'policy' need not be used so restrictively. Decisions regarding the formulation and execution of science policy are by no means the exclusive purview of the agencies of government. They are also made by scientific organizations, by research managements, and above all by scientists themselves, and not just by their choice of research themes. In point of fact, most of science policy making is performed by the scientists themselves via the activities of advisory boards, of funding organizations, and in the ongoing decision making processes of research centers.

The usual conception of science policy as dealing with the external direction of science leads to scholarly research on such topics as the relation of science to politics, and its finance and organization. Many science policy decisions, however, are in fact strategies concerning the content of science. Such issues as the 'maturity' of a problem, its scientific interest and its relevance condition decisions that are made on particular scientific research problems. All attempts at external control of science must reckon with several features of each particular area, such as its general state, the maturity of its theories or experimental techniques, its potential for development, applicability of basic knowledge, and so on. External policy makers normally seek this information from those with experience in the appropriate fields.

This article was translated by Suzanna Libich, Max-Planck Institute, Starnberg, Federal Republic of Germany.

But their knowledge is personal and informal. There is a need for a reflective knowledge of this aspect of science, of the forms of development of science.

The present chapter sets out to delineate a framework for such reflections upon science. I believe that knowledge of the general structures of the development of science is a prerequisite to rational science policy. Many of the contributions on this subject come from philosophers of science; and philosophy, therefore, will be the dominant theme of this chapter. Within the philosophy of science, a distinction can be drawn between work which is concerned with the problem of validation of scientific theories, and work which is chiefly concerned with the explanation of scientific change. This chapter will confine itself to the latter aspect; that is, it will be concerned with explanations of change, rather than with discussion of the nature of scientific knowledge and demarcation between knowledge and belief – questions which remain of central importance to the mainstream of traditional and critical work in the philosophy of science.

The thesis that a theory of the development of science is relevant to science policy is likely to be received with some skepticism. This skepticism, however, is diffuse. One argument holds that conceptualizations of the development of science have so far contributed little to science policy; another holds that a theory of scientific development is not possible at all. This chapter argues for an instrumentalist strategy: one must know the 'laws' of a field before one can reasonably attempt to plan its development. The trouble is that the theoretical approaches developed thus far have failed to satisfy these basic instrumental requirements. It has not proved possible, through knowledge of the structure of science, to apply to the development of science the strategies implicit among science policies, nor has theory produced the means and methods for evaluating policies subsequently adopted.

It should be pointed out, however, that hitherto the function of theories of scientific development has not generally been to assist policy making for science,[1] but to do something entirely different. Theories have provided a critique of ideology. In resisting planning, the scientific research community has rationalized its position by the thesis that scientific development is autonomous, determined by internal laws. The argument is that since the direction of the development of a science is determined by the inner logic of a set of scientific problems, and since the element of creativity makes the dynamics of this process unpredictable, what can be the sense of trying to influence it by planning? The fact that this thesis, while not refuted, has by now become a theme of scholarly research, may be seen as the result of a continuing debate about theories of scientific development. 'Internalism' and

---

[1] There have been, of course, a few exceptions. Thus the development of the Dutch universities in the Nineteenth Century bore the imprint of Comte's classification of the sciences; similarly, the policy of the BAAS followed Herschel's inductivism.

'externalism' continue to constitute the main dividing line along which the main positions in this area can be ordered,[2] and the unification of these two terms remains a main problem confronting scholars in the field of science policy studies.

Pending such a unification of positions, science policy scholars can now formulate the questions which a theory of scientific development may be expected to answer: In what phase of its development is a science open to external influences? Under what conditions can social problems take the form of scientific problems? At what point in its internal development may a science be expected to resist external influences?[3] When is a discipline to be called 'mature', in the sense that it can act as a subsidiary to problem-solving strategies? When — again in the sense of at what stage in the development of its content — can problem solving in a particular field be organized by a division of labor and by a systematic breakdown into partial problems? What is a 'research front' and what are the mechanisms which generate problems within it? What are the determinants of diversification, and, on the other hand, what are the cognitive conditions under which interdisciplinary work will be successful?

More than anything else these questions point to the direction that research should take. No one will claim that on the basis of the concepts developed thus far, answers can be found. Nonetheless, it should become evident that a discussion initially determined by contradictory images of science (autonomous or controlled) has now reached a point where participants are compelled to seek answers to these pragmatic questions. But as the practical issue is not how science policy decisions are made, but rather how science policy can be devised rationally, no easy answers may be expected.

MODELS FOR THE DEVELOPMENT OF SCIENCE

The practical need of science policy to conceive of science as a well-defined domain of actions has coincided with a substantial interest among historians, philosophers and sociologists in treating science as an isolated object. This conception of science is not necessarily valid, as we know from the history of the rise of modern science as well as from the current tendency of science to diffuse itself into other spheres of human activity. Most of the theoretical

---

[2] See the most recent 'handbook' review of the discussion, Kuhn's contribution on 'The History of Science' in the *International Encyclopedia of the Social Sciences,* Volume XIV.

[3] A systematic approach to the latter two questions has been undertaken in van den Daele and Weingart, 1975.

approaches discussed in this section treat science as an isolated system whose states evolve internally, but which are also exposed to external influences from a changing environment. This mode of treatment seems justifiable at any rate for academic science in the Nineteenth Century, particularly in Europe. Moreover, the tendencies by which this isolation may be altered (through the fusion of science and technology, the dissolution of isolated scientific communities, and by linkages between scientific and social problems) can be described, provided one has given a definition of science as an isolated object. In what follows, all theories of development of science will assume an 'object/environment' schemata, except for those which from the outset approach science within a Marxist framework of theories related to the development of productive forces. In general, the distinction between external and internal factors of development is fundamental. Once this distinction has been established the question arises as to how such external factors influence the development of the content of science. If their significance is but a contingent one, it may be expected that it will prove possible to trace out a developmental logic within the development of science, that is, to give a rational reconstruction of this process. If we then ask what the rationale of the history of science is, the global properties of this history become relevant: Can continuity be demonstrated in the history of science, and if so, what assures it? Is the history of science genuinely cumulative or does it also exhibit losses? Has the history of science tended in a certain direction, toward a goal such as, for instance, 'the approximation of truth' or has it rather tended to follow a natural and unplanned process of development? And last of all, does not reflection upon science and the intention to develop it in a specific manner create conditions for converting the development of science from a 'natural' into a goal-directed process?

These questions, which assume the possibility of a developmental logic of science, lead towards more general questions about the transformation, through different epochs, of accepted models of science. From this vantage point we can consider the Marxist theories, which establish the 'external' links between the development of science and the forces of production. Early theories of the development of science can be categorized either within a theory of cultural evolution (as in Comte), or within the context of theories which establish a linkage between the development of science, the development of technology, and the processes of production.

The models discussed in the following section are important examples of current attempts to 'make sense' of scientific development from epistemological viewpoints. In most cases, their relevance, intended or otherwise, becomes clear in explication. All these models differ in various important respects, however, particularly in the weight given to external and internal factors and in their assumption of continuity or discontinuity as a governing principle of scientific development.

PHASES OF THE DEVELOPMENT OF SCIENCE: KUHN'S THEORY OF NORMAL AND REVOLUTIONARY SCIENCE

Kuhn's theory of the development of science, as elaborated mainly in *The Structure of Scientific Revolutions* (1962, 1970), is characterized by his conception of different phases of scientific development, which emerge not globally for science as a whole but in particular branches or disciplines. Two important elements are at the basis of Kuhn's theory – first, his belief in the existence of crisis-provoking anomalies and in the significance of discontinuities in the history of science, and second, his view of the impossibility of giving empirical and historical meaning to the logic of justification. Kuhn sought to account for the first belief by the use of 'scientific revolutions' and his concept of 'revolutionary science'; the second belief led him to introduce the concept of 'paradigm', a concept which has enabled him to reconstitute the meaning of such phenomena as 'authority', 'tradition' and 'dogma' in modern science (Kuhn, 1961).

In the development of particular sciences, Kuhn distinguishes three stages: 1) the 'pre-paradigm' stage, 2) the 'paradigm' stage of 'normal science', and 3) the stage of revolutionary science. In essence, the pre-paradigm stage is characterized by procedures of trial and error. In a particular research field delimited by its subject matter, facts and experience are collected, explanations and generalizations are sought, often in the absence of any assured results. Rather, the scientist is each time compelled to redefine the foundations of his field. This stage comes to an end with the emergence of a universally recognized scientific achievement that becomes exemplary for further practice. It must be an achievement in theory articulation, as is made evident by the function Kuhn assigns to it. For if scientific achievement is to assume the function of a paradigm, it must enable a scientist to take the foundations of his field for granted; it must also provide a criterion for choosing problems and, in part, provide tools for problem solving.

It is this function of the paradigm which allows Kuhn to designate scientific work in the paradigm phase as 'normal science'. In everyday practice the scientist stands on solid ground and is concerned with problems that can be assumed to have solutions; his activity is puzzle solving. In this 'normal science' there exist but three classes of problem: the determination of significant facts, the matching of facts with theory, and the articulation of theory (Kuhn, 1970, 96).

In the course of his education a paradigm is transmitted to the young scientist as a dogma. It might be argued that this socialization supplies the scientist with rules according to which he can plan his scientific work. Kuhn also refers to such rules (1970, 102), but adds that this is a considerably broadened sense of the term by which 'rule' can be equated with 'established viewpoint' or with 'preconception' (1970, 101). Kuhn's point in making this reservation about the traditional concept of rule is that the paradigm is grasped quasi-intuitively as an orientation, and that work in the style of the paradigm is learned by training and by imitation. Here Kuhn acquiesces to Polanyi's thesis regarding the effectiveness of 'tacit knowledge' in science (1969, 1962).

The vagueness of Kuhn's concept of 'paradigm', evident in this short summary, has been criticized by many, in particular by Masterman (1972). In his 'postscript' of 1969 (Kuhn, 1970), Kuhn reacted to this criticism by distinguishing two different senses in which the term paradigm can be used: in a sociological sense, and in the sense of an exemplary past achievement. In its sociological usage a paradigm stands for the constellation of shared group commitments, the so-called 'disciplinary matrix' of a field. The disciplinary matrix consists of four main components: 1) symbolic generalizations, 2) heuristics, 3) values, and 4) exemplars or paradigms in the narrower sense of the term. Symbolic generalizations denote both simple symbols as well as formulas. Heuristics are preferred permissible analogies and metaphors, which enable problem solving to occur routinely. Values pertain to the quality of predictions and theories. Predictions should have quantitative precision; theories should be simple, self-consistent and integrative.

With the fourth element of the disciplinary matrix, Kuhn reverts to the use of the term paradigm to mean 'exemplars', or particular achievements within a discipline which serve to orient scientists in their practice of problem solving. This fourth shared commitment is that which closely defines communities of specialists, or better, scientific specialties. 'More than other sorts of components of the disciplinary matrix, differences between sets of exemplars provide the community fine-structure of science' (Kuhn, 1970, 249).

For Kuhn, revolutionary phases in science occur when a paradigm can no longer fulfill its function of guiding research. There may be a variety of reasons for this, the most interesting being perhaps the failure of a paradigm in its problem-generating power, exhibiting what Lakatos (1972) describes as a degenerating problem shift. Kuhn himself gives more emphasis to the significance of anomalies (that is, of facts which stubbornly resist being subsumed under a dominant theory). In this phase, however, the revolutionary nature of scientific practice is characterized not only by a high degree of insecurity – there exist no reliable evaluative standards – but also by the impossibility of reaching a rational decision between alternative paradigms. The transition to a new paradigm itself constitutes a discontinuity in scientific development. The reason for this, Kuhn argues, resides in the fact that there exists no commensurability between theories which generate research in a specific field. In the first place, competing theories may entail different standards and definitions of science. Second, while competing theories may nominally incorporate similar or identical concepts, their meaning changes according to changed theoretical relationships (For a radicalization of this thesis, see Feyerabend, 1962). Third, the proponents of competing theories, employing different conceptual and manipulative apparatus, and having different approaches to the object and different theoretical expectations relative to empirical reality, 'practice in different worlds' (Kuhn, 1970, 212). It follows, according to Kuhn, that a decision between competing paradigm candidates is not possible. Conversions to a new paradigm are in part decided 'factually', when sooner or later a community forms as a single group around a theory and thereby gains dominance in the field, and in part by 'persuasive arguments', of which those of a strategic kind are the most important. In this case 'a decision between alternate ways of practicing science is called for, and in circumstance that decision must be based less on past achievement than on future promise' (Kuhn, 1970, 219). Let us briefly summarize the leading features of Kuhn's thesis:

A) First Kuhn's concept of the development of science has given the history and philosophy of science a sociological dimension. In Kuhn's perspective, the validity of a theory is a sociological phenomenon; decisive instances of scientific development, namely the transition from one paradigm to another, have as their corollary reorganizations within the scientific community or formulation of new communities (See Kuhn, 1970, 230). In this sense Kuhn's theses have had an extraordinarily stimulating effect on the sociology of science.

B) The second outcome of Kuhn's model is that scientific development can no longer be simply designated as 'progress'. That is, we may call it 'progress' in that it is a departure from a beginning, but it is not progress proceeding in the direction of any goal. Kuhn describes scientific development as a 'natural' process, and emphasizes the point by occasional comparisons with Darwinian evolutionary theory. According to Kuhn, 'progress' no longer appears in the form of an approximation to truth, but in an accumulation of technical experimental results and of solutions to problems within particular paradigms.

C) This view of progress underlines a third feature of Kuhn's model: the role played by external factors in scientific development. External influences may come into effect in trial and error procedures, which are closely related to craftsmanship and technological devices as well as to the problems posed by social and economic situations. Model and theory building are determined by scientists' experience and by metaphysical preconceptions. In the 'revolutionary stage', external influences affect scientific development in two ways. First, the crisis-inducing factors are themselves often external to science. Anomalies as such do not destabilize an existing paradigm; in fact, discrepancies may be set aside. But particular events may lend weight to particular anomalies. These may, as was the case with astronomy, include social pressures for a calendar reform, and thus be wholly external to science. Second, the factors which may prove decisive in a paradigm debate are in many cases extra-scientific and rooted in metaphysical principles.

Kuhn's model of scientific development has been criticized from many viewpoints. It has been argued, for instance, that available sociological evidence does not support his claims of a connection between paradigms and scientific communities (Ben-David, 1975; for a summary of these claims, see Griffith and Mullins, 1972). Epistemological disagreements have been developed in Lakatos and Musgrave (1972), and the notion of a paradigm has itself been the subject of special criticism of different kinds (Masterman, 1972; Shapere, 1972; Shapere, 1964; Toulmin, 1972). And it has been argued that Kuhn fails to explicate the actual progress of scientific development (King, 1970). Finally, Kuhn's critics have challenged his distinction between 'normal' and 'revolutionary' science (Feyerabend, 1972; Popper, 1972; Toulmin, 1972b). However, these criticisms have all had in common one factor: they have taken weak points in Kuhn's theory as points of departure for several extremely interesting theories of scientific development.[4] This is true particularly in respect to Kuhn's critics who have aimed to establish the continuity of scientific development.

CONTINUITY IN THE DEVELOPMENT OF SCIENCE

Lakatos' methodology of scientific research programs (1972) emerged directly from his confrontation with Kuhn's theory. Departing from Popper, Lakatos initially elaborated a sophisticated falsificationism, within which scientists live with anomalies which in the strict sense falsify established theories. According to Lakatos, a theory is rejected only when there is a rival theory to replace it – a point already made by Popper (1971, 52-55, 83). Lakatos, however, has introduced a new criterion for judging the superiority of a theory: It must provide a 'progressive problem shift'; that is, it must not only resolve problems but extend the 'problem horizon'.

More important, Lakatos claims that a succession of theories can be logically reconstructed. According to Lakatos, a series of theories becomes connected in a research program which develops internally, or, as he has occasionally put it, dialectically. A research program involves a 'hard core' of fundamental ideas about the world, or more particularly about a sphere of reality, and a 'protective belt' of theories which provides a conceptual framework consistent with the hard core by which reality is grasped. In the logic of discovery, the hard core provides a negative heuristic – that is, a set of interdictions which indicate what conceptual tools are not admissible in explicating the subject matter. The function of the protective belt is to provide a positive heuristic, which sets out which theoretical tools are to be

---

[4] For a general survey of the discussion, see also Kisiel and Johnson, 1974, and Weimer, 1974. Kisiel and Johnson contains a Kuhn bibliography.

employed within a given sphere of reality. Lakatos claims, and in several instances he has persuasively demonstrated (e.g. the development of the Bohr model of the atom) that a series of theories may emerge totally within this protective belt, that is, in each case from a process of working out the difficulties and inconsistencies of a theory, something which does not even require an empirical challenge (1972, 149). These conclusions have led Lakatos to the thesis that the history of science can be rationally reconstructed, hence that external influences can at most generate contingent deviations from its internal history.

The major difficulty encountered in the rational reconstruction of the history of science is that of defining what standards of rationality can and should be applied. Lakatos and Krüger, the protagonists of the thesis of 'reconstructability', have taken the 'natural' standpoint, according to which the state of contemporary science provides an adequate standard of rationality. Leaving aside the obvious fact that earlier historical figures did not have this particular standard at their disposal, and recognizing that many of the problems raised by Kuhn cannot be settled in this manner, there is a danger that the history of science will be reconstructed from the vantage point of a history of 'victories'. True enough, Lakatos has recognized that such reconstruction can be effected only with hindsight. Nevertheless, the systematic problems entailed by a rational reconstruction of the history of science are far greater than the methodological ones already indicated. In fact, they entail a large-scale research program into inter-theory relations. A successful logical reconstruction above all requires a clear statement of the logical relations obtaining between succeeding theories.

In recent years, the philosophy of 'inter-theory relations' (Strauss, 1972; Bunge, 1970; Scheibe and Krüger, 1972) has come to have a direct bearing upon theories of scientific development. Progress within the frame of this program may be described as follows: the historical successions of two theories, T_1 and T_2, may under certain circumstances be justified by the statement that T_1 is the prerequisite condition for the articulation of T_2, in the sense that T_1 connects T_2 with empirical facts (the relation of classical physics and quantum mechanics), or in the sense that the conceptual articulation of T_2 is only possible if it is within the perspective of the already existing theory T_1 (the relation of statistical mechanics and thermodynamics: Krüger, 1974a). It might also be the case, by a rough analogy with the first possibility, that theory T_1 assumes for theory T_2 the role of a measurement theory for an object theory and that T_2 is thus not empirically testable without T_2. Another presumably historically frequent version could be that T_2 is an explanatory theory of T_1. In that event T_1 would obviously have to precede T_2 historically and there would also have to be some reason for wanting an explanation (e.g. the relation between Kepler's and Newton's theories of the planetary system; Scheibe, 1972). The last instance constitutes an example of T_1 being sublated into T_2.

To make this explanation comprehensible within a wider context, part of the literature of 'inter-theory relations' speaks of a 'developmental dialectic' (Strauss, 1972, 105-115). Perhaps the concept 'uplation' (Aufhebung) can be used to characterize the position.[5] This concept expresses the denial of discontinuity in the history of science, as well as a denial of the thesis that a theory can be 'displaced' and thus refuted by a succeeding theory. On the contrary, it argues that older theories are integrated with new theories into developing theory-constellations, so that

> it is still possible to determine within the respective state of a science specific fundamental features of its preceding development and this precisely with the help of the inter-theoretical relations it contains (Scheibe and Krüger, 1972, 5).

Accordingly, 'the continuing theoretical acknowledgement of an older theory simultaneously ensures the permanence of the data associated with it' (Krüger, 1974a). However, given that a later theory does not wholly replace an earlier one, this position implicitly rejects both Kuhn's claims as to discontinuity of theory development and discontinuity at the level of data.

Although the investigation of inter-theory relations may eventually lead to an understanding of logical interrelations within science, nothing so far indicates what contribution it can bring to an understanding of the 'dynamics' of this development. This holds also for the concepts created explicitly to grasp 'theory dynamics', concepts generated in the model theory of Sneed (1971) and Stegmüller (1973, 1974). These are attempts to elaborate the concept of physical theories in such a way that their identity becomes conceivable through a process of historical development and theory change.

What is at issue is the logical possibility of theory development, not its explication. The central point made by Sneed and Stegmüller is the so-called 'non-statement view' of theory. In this view, a theory in itself does not state anything but is merely the formulation of a complex structure, or in traditional terms, of a conceptual instrumentarium. Statements can be derived from theories only as statements of the existence of partial models of the theory — that is, of the existence of a sphere of reality which can be grasped with the conceptual tools of the theory in question. Departures in this direction are discernible in Lakatos' distinction between the 'hard core' and the 'protective belt'; they are also visible in the work of Strauss, who draws distinctions in physical theory between the mathematical substructure, the mathematical superstructure and physical interpretation. According to Sneed and Stegmüller, we must distinguish in a theory between the mathematical structures and the intended applications. The intended applications of a theory consist in the mapping of mathematical structures into partial models.

---

[5] Translator's Note: The traditional German philosophical concept 'Aufhebung', usually translated as 'sublation', is given as 'uplation' in M. Strauss (1972). See Chapter 1 of this work, 'Concentration and Uplation in the Evolution of Physics'.

These partial models may include functions which quite possibly belong to a different theory, and in any particular case ensure data generation independent of a given body of theory.

The decisive contribution of this concept to a theory of scientific development is, according to Stegmüller, that it explains the supposed fact that theories remain while scientists' convictions change. The reason for this is that the range of validity of a theory is not essentially a part of the theory itself. Rather, it is built up step by step in the course of the process of research by experimental applications, expansions and restrictions. What Stegmüller does, in order to come closer to Kuhn's concept, is to include the primary applications of a theory in a conceptual 'paradigm' (as a case in point, the application of classical Newtonian particle mechanics to the planetary system), so that each primary application becomes an essential component of the theory. 'Theory dynamics' also stresses the use of structural components which enable theories to maintain their structural identity throughout history.

The approach of Sneed and Stegmüller has a bearing on the research process of normal science, but this is within a perspective in which normal science (or more accurately, a Lakatosian research program) is conceived of as an interesting process in itself. While the conceptual instrumentalistic view of theories does not as yet provide a conceptual schema for the process of scientific revolutions, it at least enables us to understand why, under the particular circumstances, the transition from one theory to another occurs without logical justification. It in fact involves taking hold of a new instrument of knowledge when the old one has failed (Stegmüller, 1973, 246). For this there exist in principle only pragmatic justifications.

The main difficulty encountered by all theories which intend to present the development of science as a continuous process is indubitably that of bridging the hiatus caused by 'scientific revolutions'. It has been pointed out that in such revolutions, so-called superparadigmatic values and norms outlive the shock (Toulmin, 1972b; Radnitzky, 1971). One possibility, therefore, is to extend Lakatos' concept of the research program to embrace the development of modern natural science as a whole, in terms by which it would embody the emergence and realization of such characteristic values and norms as experimentalism, quantification, objectivization, and so on. Presumably this type of approach might make it possible to study certain global properties of the process.

Attempts to conceptualize at least one of these global aspects have been made, in relation to the progressive integration of scientific theories of various sciences. One of these concepts is von Weizsäcker's notion of a 'unified physics'.[6] Von Weizsäcker starts from the observation that physics

---

[6] This quest for a unity of science proceeded in an entirely different manner within the 'unity of science movement'. The expectations of this movement, finding expression

reveals 'an historical development . . . towards unity' (1971, 208). Here von Weizsäcker has in mind Newton's integration of terrestrial and celestial mechanics, the unification of mechanics and thermodynamics in statistical mechanics, and the integration of mechanics and electrodynamics within the special theory of relativity. According to von Weizsäcker, a principle of development underlies this integrative process. In this process, physics, and in a wider sense all of natural science, works out the conditions of its own possibility. The keystone of this development will be a theory which will be built upon concepts which are, in principle, necessary to grasp an object developing over time.

EVOLUTIONARY DEVELOPMENT MODELS

Philosophers who wish to see the continuity of scientific development vindicated are, as a rule, 'internalists'. That is, they are determined to account for the scientific process on those grounds that can be derived from the rationality of the process itself. Discontinuities in the development of science are held to be 'rationality gaps' by which extra scientific factors penetrate into the cognitive process and determine the further development of science. For the same reason scholars who construct the development of science according to a Darwinian model tend to emphasize the discontinuities, arguing that there are points where external factors come into play which make the development of science a natural process. Yet even among the protagonists of evolutionary development there are internalists. For them the process of selection of theories takes place in a domain screened off from others, that is within the scientific community, the community of those competent.

Among this range of models one may place Popper's (1972) theory of the progress of knowledge. According to Popper, theories are attempts to produce solutions to a problem. And it is the rational criticism of scientists which determines the outcome of the struggle for existence in which hypotheses must show their fitness for survival (Popper, 1972, 261). Certainly Popper's model is ambiguous. The question one must ask is whether the conditions of survival are set by the objective problem or by scientific criticism. The emphasis which Popper gives to an 'adequacy of truth' makes one assume the former. In terms of Popper's perspective, the fittest theory

---

in the project of an *Encyclopedia of Unified Science* (See Neurath, Carnap and Morris, 1971) were not directed as in the case of von Weizsäcker to a fundamental theory, but to the realization of a unifield scientific method. Neurath (1970) believed that from the elaboration of logical empiricism and empirical rationalism would emerge a consensus as to scientific method. Thus the form of science unified on the basis of its methods would be diversity in unity – the Encyclopedia.

for survival is not a theory which answers some purpose, but a theory which is nearest to the 'truth'.[7]

> For I did not state that the fittest thesis is always the one which helps our own survival. I said rather, that the fittest hypothesis is the one which best solves the *problem* it was designed to solve, and which resists criticism better than competing hypotheses (Popper, 1972, 264).

In this juxtaposition of solution and criticism as the conditions for survival, Popper's ambiguity again comes to the fore. It becomes comprehensible, however, when one makes explicit the logic, or better, the strategy of theory construction. Thus, theories shall not only solve predefined problems. Rather, by having an excess of empirical content, they should lead to the discovery of new problems. They can, therefore, never be judged merely in terms of their truth content; rather, this requires the pragmatic evaluation of the scientific community competent in the particular field (Böhme, 1974b). For the process of criticism the truth is but a 'regulative idea' (Popper, 1972, 264).

A more elaborate model, although in principle not fundamentally different from Popper's, is the internalistic evolutionary model of Toulmin (1967, 1972a). Mutation and variations in the Darwinian evolutionary schema are in science matched by innovation and the production of ideas. This domain is open to all external influences; psychological and sociological factors can play a role here. Indeed, economic conditions are decisive for the quantity of mutants. From the population of ideas generated in this manner, those fittest for survival are selected. Survival conditions are set by disciplinary standards and explanatory ideals.

Obviously this process of selection loses any similarity to a process in nature in that it ultimately entails a reasoned selection. Toulmin encounters difficulties in those cases in which disciplinary standards and explanatory ideals, that is to say research strategies (1972a, 246), are up for reappraisal (1972a, 232). According to Toulmin, such cases cannot be dealt with by Darwinian concepts but rather according to the model of English common law, where a competent judge does not base his judgment on codified law but tries to dispense justice by taking into account the continuity of history: 'The choice between disciplinary goals or strategies is a matter for the judgment of authoritative and experienced individuals' (Toulmin, 1972a, 242). If Toulmin also is talking about 'populations' of strategies and explanatory ideals, the criterion he asserts is the increase in explanatory power and the deepening of explanations.

As far as the evolution of scientific ideas is concerned, Toulmin does, to be sure, assign a major role to the scientific community. Nonetheless, the

---

[7] Such an incremental form becomes intelligible in terms of Popper's (1972) concept of verisimilitude.

scientific community is in these terms always characterized by specific competences; and ultimately selection proves to be an objective process:

> The ultimate verdict . . . remains an objective, and even a factual matter. For the ways in which Nature will actually respond to our attempts at understanding her is something that goes beyond all human tasks and all human power to alter (Toulmin, 1972a, 245).

In this Toulmin shares Popper's realism.

In a certain sense Toulmin's and Popper's conception of evolutionary scientific development is paradoxical. Or to put it more precisely, it presents a paradox insofar as the Darwinian conception of evolution sees the process of evolution as one which cannot be comprehended by reason, but which can only be explained by causes. For Popper and Toulmin the process of the selection of scientific theories is a rational choice, not a 'natural' process. In this respect the evolutionary model described by Böhme, van den Daele and Krohn (1972) comes closer to Darwinian theory. In this model, external factors do not, as with Popper, have significance only for the rate of scientific development, for problem selection and for the number of innovations; they have relevance also for the selection of theories themselves. Hence this model describes not only the 'intellectual' survival capacity of theories but also their social survival capacity. Since the 'life' of a theory is determined by the existence of a scientific community working on it, its survival will also depend on whether the corresponding scientific community has any real opportunity to establish itself. This possibility in turn is very strongly affected by external conditions, e.g. by whether society shows any need for cultivating such problem-solving capacities. According to Böhme, van den Daele and Krohn, Darwinism acts on the history of science not solely by means of the social selection of alternatives generated within the science. Rather, there is active adaptation to the social and economic survival conditions of science.[8] This adaptation takes place through the operation of 'regulatives' which ensure that results satisfy determinate norms. The authors distinguish between 'internal' and 'external' regulatives. Among the former they class logical-transcendental, logical-strategic and methodological factors; among the latter, social, socio-economic, cultural and religious ones.

According to Böhme and his colleagues, factors external to the development of science have a bearing upon not only the contingent traits but also upon the content of this development itself. If the question is how far external factors act directly upon the determination of the content, then the answer would be that a distinction must be made between social externalism and cognitive externalism; social externalism relates to all situations in which power structures or social and economic needs act as the selective mechanism for internally generated alternatives in science. Cognitive externalism refers to

---

[8] A Lamarckian variant of Darwinism which was contained in Darwin's theory.

the external determination of what is accepted internally in science, in part through the process of justification (explanatory ideals, legitimacy and relevance criteria: see Böhme, 1974b), and in part through the technical-experimental constitution of the objects of a study (Böhme, 1974a).

Historical change of developmental models All the models discussed so far have one characteristic in common: their validity is not limited to particular historical epochs. Yet it is implausible that science has always developed in the same way. The inference may well be that the develop mental model *per se* is subject to historical change and that in each epoch the whole of science exhibits a different form. In this section, therefore, we will discuss concepts which are premised on such radical transformations in the progress of science. We shall deal first with the concept of 'finalization'.

Böhme, van den Daele and Krohn, in characterizing the history of science, use the Darwinian evolutionary concept to emphasize the natural character of this process. But this concept becomes meaningful only when it is viewed against the background of the possible purposiveness of scientific development. Their model, therefore, has qualified Darwinism in the history of science as merely contingent, and does not claim that scientific development can be explained by this concept on a global scale and in all epochs. The model assumes, rather, that changes in the developmental pattern occur in the development of science as a whole, as well as in the development of particular fields. The decisive transformation of the natural process of scientific development into an intended, that is conscious, mission-oriented and planned development is designated as 'finalization'. The notion of 'finalization' in no way signifies any termination of the scientific process but, appealing to the Aristotelian *causa finalis,* denotes a purposive development. Hence 'finalization' as a characteristic of the global process of science marks out the transition between two developmental phases in which scientific development must be understood on the basis of diverse theoretical concepts.

Finalization in any particular discipline is described by a 'phase model' which expands the one formulated by Kuhn. Böhme and his colleagues (Böhme *et al.,* 1976) do not believe that once it has reached the paradigm stage, scientific progress proceeds through the steady succession of paradigms. Rather, with Heisenberg (1971), they state that for determined object areas, there exists something in the order of 'closed theories'. Used strictly in the sense of Heisenberg's terminology this term designates theories which can no longer be improved by minor modifications. Using the term in a somewhat weaker sense, one can speak also of 'completed theories' as referring to theories by which an object of study is comprehended. When a science has achieved a 'complete' theory for any particular field, it is labelled a 'mature discipline'. Once it has reached 'maturity', a discipline can be guided by external purposes in its theoretical development. In a way it is even compelled toward 'maturity' because the internally generated criteria of relevance are no longer adequate to select possible scientific tasks. Research fronts are no longer defined by the problems internal to theory development.

A closer definition of the process of finalization can be seen in four historical dimensions. First, the objects of science itself (e.g. laboratory phenomena) become scientific products. Second, goal orientation implicates not only application of theory but also the development of theory. Third, fundamental theory must have reached a certain degree of maturity. Fourth, science itself starts producing techniques (Böhme et al., 1976, 308f). However, conversion of the pattern of development to a pattern of intentional development cannot be demarcated by these criteria alone. This is the reason why the authors speak not only of finalization but also of its variant 'functionalization'. Functionalization refers to the situation in which, without interposition of the phase of 'complete theory', a short circuit occurs between a science and external goal orientations by input-output models. On the other hand, the authors consider an even more intense version of finalization in which scientific development may not only be guided by external goals, but that the forming of concepts in science will acquire normative dimensions (which will at first seem wholly objectionable to natural scientists) relating it to the social sphere. This prognosis becomes more plausible if we look to human efforts to transform nature, which become ever more salient within science and also ever more politically contentious. Thus the first case study completed on the concept of finalization is concerned with the development of agricultural chemistry (Krohn, Schäfer, 1976).

The finalization concept conjoins three factors which since the latter half of the Nineteenth Century have been decisive for the development of science. First, science is incorporated into the production sphere. This moment is treated by Marxist theoreticians under the rubric 'transformation of science into a direct productive force'. Second, the internal development of science in various disciplines and in various areas has resulted in a certain completion. Third, science is involved in a process which in the transition from traditional to modern society results in the differentiation, planning and administration of particular sections of life. This process has been labelled also as 'the scientification' of the world, and particularly as 'rationalization' (Weber). In recent years science has become reflective during this process and is now increasingly subjected to goal-directed planning.

To date, the concept of finalization has not been tested against a large body of empirical evidence. Moreover, it entails systematic problems, including the definition of 'theoretical maturity', demarcations between 'finalized' and applied science, and the description of the relationship between mature 'fundamental theory' and theoretical special developments. Finally it is, of course, questionable whether a theoretical model can in principle yield the central variable which explains the striking phenomena of scientific development in the Twentieth Century, or whether the most useful frame of reference is not more likely to be found in, for instance, models of the socialization of science (Prüss, 1974).

The concept of finalization is ostensibly externalist. Nonetheless, it has some internalist facets. The emergence of a new developmental type, in the final analysis, is assigned to internal factors ('theoretical maturity'). The reverse holds true in the French epistemological tradition. With the emphasis on internalism (Bachelard in particular), it views fundamental revolutions in science as a part of the general process of historical and cultural developments. The intellectual father of this tradition is no doubt Auguste Comte (1830-1842). In Comte's view, the progress of science must be seen within a sequence of cultural epochs, from 'theological' to 'metaphysical' to 'positive'. Only with the advent of the 'positive' epoch in the Nineteenth Century does science become adequate to its essence. Science only becomes effective when the vain search for 'first causes' and 'forces' is abandoned and the object of man's research becomes purely phenomenological and nomological. Each field of science also goes through three phases which correspond to the major epochs of cultural development, but which exhibit phase lags in relation to each other. The advance of each science depends on the previous advances of other sciences. An inquiry into more concrete, or more complex, subjects can only enter the phase of 'effective' science after the more abstract and elementary sciences have reached it. Thus a succession occurs from arithmetic through geometry, mechanics, chemistry and biology, up to sociology.

A similar concept of major epochs of scientific development was developed by Gaston Bachelard (1972). For Bachelard as for Comte, the prescientific epoch reaches into the Eighteenth Century. It is the Nineteenth Century that marks the beginning of the 'scientific age'. In it the systematization of knowledge in geometrical form penetrates all fields of science. But it is not until Einstein's work (1905) that Bachelard describes the rise of a new epoch in which the spirit of science has definitively divorced itself from all intuitive notions and images.

According to Bachelard, one can distinguish particular epochs by levels of abstraction, and particular developments within each of these epochs by epistemological obstacles which the scientific spirit must surmount. Bachelard's concept is informed by the thesis that there exists no continuity between prescientific knowledge and science. Rather, the transition from the former to the latter is made difficult by the obstacles which must be overcome each time. Hence Bachelard views all prescientific conceptions not as a foundation of science but more as something contrary to science – as an error.

The scientific optimism underlying this standpoint is hardly likely to be shared by many today. Thus Bachelard's disciple, Michel Foucault, propounds an epochal theory from which any idea of progress has been carefully eliminated. To be sure, Foucault's inquiry – dealing with the emergence of clinical medicine (1973), of political economy, of philology and biology (1971) – is mainly centered around the 'epochal threshold' (1775-1825).

Foucault has sought to show that a science concerned with a particular object area has no continuity extending beyond culturally and politically determined thresholds. Rather, within an epoch there exists a close affinity, in terms of their subject matter, between entirely disparate sciences; this affinity is rooted in their epistemic structure. The epistemological 'coupure' which occurs in each of them has greater significance for the development of any particular field than does its intrinsic continuity. Thus, Foucault argues, in the classical age in France, universal grammar, natural history and the analysis of wealth, together conceived their subject matter in terms of the schema of representation and the represented. Science thereby became the 'representation of representation'. After the 'epochal threshold', these respective fields reconceptualized in the light of principles which organized them internally. Thus economics was understood and developed from the perspective of labor, linguistics from that of inflection, the realm of living from that of life. The object areas in question thereby assumed a life of their own; the fields of study assumed a dynamic, and they became 'historicized'.[9]

The studies referred to in this section are rich in historical data and materials. But what is more important is that they may act as a necessary corrective of assumptions made only too rashly in the generation of philosophical models. Another historical dimension of the development of science, in particular its relation to technology, has been investigated on so many levels and in such detail that it is necessary to discuss it separately. To be sure, this is not as yet a field in which scholars have generally accepted explanatory models. There exist only global models describing the connection of science with technology, and on the other hand there are special hypotheses regarding their interaction in particular periods of time.

THE INTERACTION BETWEEN SCIENTIFIC DEVELOPMENT AND TECHNICAL DEVELOPMENT

Bernal (1957), who pursued the relationship of science and technology for the development of science since antiquity, advanced the thesis that science has shown substantial progress only when there had been a relation to practice: in Ionia of ancient times; in the Renaissance with contact between

---

[9] Arguably, these models have little relevance to science policy. Their significance lies primarily in the field of education, which was always at the center of Bachelard's concern. In general, these studies do not question the causal factors in scientific development. However, to this general rule Foucault's *The Birth of the Clinic*, which assesses the impact of the institutional changes brought about by the French Revolution on the development of medicine, is an important exception.

craftspersons and scholars; in the Seventeenth Century within the Royal Society; in the Eighteenth Century in the Lunar society; in the Nineteenth in the Royal Institution; and later, as repeatedly in history scientists contributed to war efforts, an effort which in the Twentieth Century contributed to organized and planned science.

Of particular concern is the relationship of science and technology at the time of the rise of modern natural science. Zilsel developed the thesis, derived from Olschki (1919), that modern science is in essence rooted in the artisanal crafts of the early Renaissance. Zilsel (1942a) traced the emergence of a modern natural science back to the social conjunction of two previously noncommunicating strata: the artisans and the scholars. He believed that through this combination the crafts gave rise to some major characteristics of modern natural science. Thus the concept of scientific progress and of the 'contribution' of technology to science goes back to the tradition of technical improvement (Zilsel, 1945); and by the same token, important elements of the concept of law of natural science are, according to Zilsel, traceable to the craft rules (1942b). This thesis has been criticized by Hall (1959). According to Hall, technology has been significant for science in offering impulses and problems. This explanation has been shared by Hessen (1931), Merton (1970) and also by Bernal (1970). However, Koyré (1948) and later also Hall (1961) tried to show that precisely in its decisive achievement, modern science does not depend on technology but rather has enabled technology to reach a new level of development: to grasp the sensible world with exact concepts. In contrast to this, technology moved in a world of the *à peu près* far into the Eighteenth Century. Calculations were neither customary nor in many cases possible; often no instruments were available for exact measurements. Instruments, in turn, originated from the requirements of science, and they imported the idea of exactness into the domain of technology. With the scientific instrument came the idea of exactness, the 'réalisation consciente de la théorie' (Koyré, 1948, 819).[10]

Depending on the perspective adopted, the direction of this influence will differ, and for each epoch different theses may be advanced. On the whole the following approaches to the relationship between science and technology can be distinguished:

A) One view holds that science and technology develop autonomously and independently of one another. Some support for this position comes from attempts to distinguish science and technology on the basis of their different intentions and of the behavior of those engaged in them (Derek Price, 1965). The question of how these two developments relate to one another is then solved: either in the form of a 'dialectical arrangement'

---

[10] This idea has recently been made the primary interpretative principle of Galilean physics; see Mittelstrass, 1970. Mittelstrass (1974) has also given some outlines for a 'constructive theory of science history'.

(Kranzberg, 1967, 1968) in the sense that at certain stages of its development science uses technology instrumentally for its own ends (or vice versa); or in the form of an evolutionary model (Toulmin, 1969) in which technology sets the conditions for the selection of scientific variants (or vice versa).

B) A second view argues that science has developed by orienting itself to technical apparatus and instruments. In these terms, science consists largely of theoretical attempts to grasp and systematize the manner in which instruments function. Cases in point are the emergence of Gilbert's theory of magnetism (which was based on the existing use of the compass) and the emergence of thermodynamics on the basis of the technical development of the steam engine.

C) A third view, attributable to Koyré, militates against this thesis and claims that the scientific instrument is the decisive connection which links science with technology, and that the technology of science (measurement and experiment) at all times outruns the technology of everyday life.

D) A fourth view holds that not until the late Nineteenth Century was there a possibility of converting scientific knowledge into technology (Hall, 1961). It is further assumed that during the Nineteenth Century the relation of science to technology was reversed partly in conjunction with the 'scientification' of technology. This transition to a scientific technology or, as Koyré put it, to a 'néotechnique', is determined by forms of energy and materials which are man-made, and not supplied by nature. However, opposing this assumption of a unidirectional transformation of technology by science, Moscovici (1968) speaks of reciprocal modification: within the 'division naturelle' both partners assume new roles. From being a mechanistic philosophy where metaphysics conditions experiments, the sciences are transformed into positive sciences; and craft technique is superseded by applied science. This development makes technology receptive to offers from science; natural science, having lost its function of creating world views, itself tends to become merely technical science (Technikwissenschaft).[11]

MARXIST CONCEPTS OF THE
DEVELOPMENT OF SCIENCE

It was said earlier in this chapter that most of the theories to be discussed conceive of scientific development in terms of 'internal' and 'external' factors. This does not hold for Marxist theories, which do not conceive of science as an autonomous complex but rather as one aspect of the process of

---

[11] See Janich, 1973. Regarding the tendency of science and technology to fuse in the Twentieth Century, see also the finalization thesis and the section on 'Marxist Concepts of the Development of Science' which follows directly.

social development. Within this frame of reference two main concerns may be distinguished. One point of interest for Marxist scholars is the social constitution of scientific concepts, the other the functioning of science as a productive force.

This difference in the focus of interest may be given in regional terms; for example, it seems that for Eastern European Marxists, consideration of constitution theory is barred by 'copy theory'. The various Marxist approaches to constitution theory can be classified in terms of the basic concepts of Marxist theory. For example, the constitution of the object of science is grounded in labor (Moscovici, 1968), in the relations of production (Borkenau, 1971), in productive forces (Grossman, 1935), in forms of social intercourse and association (Sohn-Rethel, 1972) and in the value form (Bahr, 1973). According to Moscovici, the dominant form of labor at each stage constitutes a different concept of nature: thus artisanal craft connects with organic nature, the engineer's activity with mechanic nature, and the regulative and inventive labor characterizing our time with cybernetic and synthetic nature. In postulating an epochal change of the forms taken by labor and nature, Moscovici's theory is also a theory of the development of science. Borkenau in 1934 (1971) attempted to derive the rise of modern natural science from the relations of production from the Seventeenth Century onwards. He believed that the compulsion to rationalize had given rise to the downgrading and dehumanizing of human labor, an attitude which was duplicated by the mechanistic view of nature. Grossman (1935) opposed this theory on the basis of economic and historical arguments, and himself formulated the theory that 'mechanics itself had actually acquired its basic concepts from observation of the mechanisms of the machine' (Grossman, 1935, 166).

Sohn-Rethel's 'constitution theory' (1972) also centers on the 'dequalification' or downgrading of nature. Sohn-Rethel holds that in a society in which commodity exchange is the dominant form of social intercourse, the 'real abstraction' from the qualities that exchange entails engenders a conceptual competence which is then sedimented into the modern concepts of nature with their dequalifying impact. With this method, Sohn-Rethel derives such concepts as substance, causality and interaction. Bahr, proceeding along similar lines (1973) has grounded his argument on the form of value which products must assume to act as values in market exchanges. In this way Bahr derives such concepts as weight, number and length.

Notwithstanding their diversity of approach, these attempts to construct a Marxist constitution theory fall short of expectations and intentions. Very rarely does any one of them produce concepts actually employed by natural science; and those concepts which do results are not, as a rule, concepts of the scientific object but meta-concepts, that is to say concepts of the theory of knowledge and philosophy of science, as for instance in the case of Sohn-Rethel, those of Kantian philosophy. And even in those instances, as with Bahr, where the concepts used are those of natural science, no effort is made to show in what way they contribute to the development of natural science. Another criticism is that scarcely any connection is made between these considerations and the actual developmental process of science. Social constitution theories must be derived empirically, with reference to particular historical cases or particular periods and contexts. Only in this way can they become an essential component of a general theory of scientific development.

Given that from the Marxist point of view science is primarily an aspect of social development, profound changes in the developmental pattern of science are by the same token revealed at times of social upheaval, and certain scientific developments can be related to specific changing social functions. Wolkow has distinguished three major epochs of scientific development: 1) orientation to man, in which the main social function of science is the generation of world views; 2) orientation to technology, in which the main social function of science is the development of material wealth; and 3) orientation to man, in which the social function of science is to perfect man's biological and social environment (Wolkow, 1969, 720).[12] From this viewpoint it is a revolution in tools which provides the determining impulse to change and which ushers in the transition from one epoch to the next. Thus the Industrial Revolution and the scientific-technical revolution can be said to represent the two epochal thresholds of scientific development in modern Europe. In the first revolution, the function of science resides primarily in generating world views and thus its main function is explanation and enlightenment. Theoretically it is therefore held to be a form of social consciousness and subsumed in the superstructure. In the second revolution, science is determined by the industrial revolution which in the essence consists of the mechanization of labor. From then onwards science can no longer be assigned to the superstructure but itself becomes a productive force (Kosing, 1964).

Evidently science in the industrial phase is at first a productive force only in the objectified form of machinery. Science still depends upon living labor and merely raises its productivity. By functioning indirectly as a productive force, science at the same time can become independent of the sphere of production. Since it enters production only in the objectified form of the work tool, it can progress outside the sphere of production. The separation of applied from pure science and the autonomy gained by science in the Nineteenth Century both appear as particular expressions of the split between intellectual and physical work (Wolkow, 1969).

The industrial revolution also marks the beginning of the socialization of science: that is, science becomes social labor. It is not as yet productive

---

[12] It is a particular weakness of Wolkow's concept that he lets the second period start with the rise of natural science (712). To locate the actual turning point in the period of the 'young Marx', that is in the industrialization period (715), will more readily meet with a consensus of opinion.

independently, but constitutes general labor[13] whose purely ideal product, in order to be realized, must rely upon living labor.[14] The second epoch of scientific development is thus characterized by antagonistic tendencies. Science becomes a productive force, but as pure science it is ranged against the sphere of production; scientific activity has become social labor, but at the same time as professional intellectual labor it comes into antagonistic social conflict with the working class (Wolkow, 1969).

The third epoch of scientific development, the so-called scientific and technical revolution,[15] also begins with a revolution in the tools of labor. In its effects the scientific-technical revolution 'replaces the logical functions of the producer by machines'. It thereby reinforces the basic law of the development of productive forces, that is, 'the gradual transference of the work functions of the producer to technical instruments' (Autorenkollektiv, 1972, 133, 136). Unlike the industrial revolution, however, the scientific-technical revolution is not merely a technical revolution but is from the very start determined partly by science. This is due on the one side to sciences like cybernetics being a factor in automation and on the other to the dependency of many major industries on the state of science. The scientific-technical revolution entails a fundamental change in the social function of science and its transformation into a direct productive force (Autorenkollektiv, 1972, 193; Wolkow, 1969, 716; Richta and Kollektiv, 1971, 30; Lassow, 1963, 377; see also Moscovici, 1968).[16]

This line of analysis provides an explanation of the increasing economic importance of science and its convergence with other fields of human work. Even the social sciences must on the basis of growing 'socialization' be conceived of as productive forces (Lassow, 1971; Lades and Burrichter, 1970); leading examples of this are industrial psychology and organization theory. Such processes as are not directly productive become scientific as well, such as 'management' functions.

It must be said that within the frame of the development of productive forces, these Marxist models of the development of science as yet lack a compelling empirical basis, by which it can be shown that the connections stated are in fact causal connections. Moreover, the advantage of these models — i.e. that they do not have to introduce the significance of the social and

---

[13] Regarding the Marxist concept of 'general labor' see Kröber and Laitko, 1972, 52.

[14] As the cooperative character of the labour-process becomes more and more marked, so, as a necessary consequence, does our notion of productive labour, and of its agent the productive labourer, become extended. In order to labour productively, it is no longer necessary for you to do manual work yourself; enough, if you are an organ of the collective labourer, and perform one of its subordinate functions (Marx, 508-509).

[15] See Richta (1971 and 1972) and Autorenkollektiv (1974).

[16] For a discussion of this concept see Autorenkollektiv, 1972; also Kedrov, 1966; Klotz and Rum, 1963; and the volume referred to under Kösing, 1964.

economic development via 'external' factors – is largely counterbalanced by the fact that they almost completely disregard the development of the content of science. Their concern is almost exclusively with such questions as organization, the planning of science and its transfer to production. They pay attention only to the progressive integration of science, apparently because it accommodates the idea of a dialectic synthesis on the basis of materialistic philosophy (Rochhausen, 1970; Malecki and Olszweski, 1965; Autorenkollektiv, 1968, 114, 117; Kedrov, 1973). Nonetheless it seems apparent that precisely this perspective offers some promise of grasping the causal dimension of scientific development.

THE STATE OF THE ART: FUTURE PROSPECTS

Indeed, reviewing the different Marxist and non-Marxist models of scientific development, one has the sense that this is a research field rich in exciting ideas as well as in unsolved problems. This may motivate one eagerly to enter the field; or, conversely, it may cause one to keep away from it. Obviously bright ideas alone will accomplish very little, and at any rate progress will be slow. What is needed is conceptual clarification and integration and collaboration among the philosophers and historians and sociologists of science. Many current conceptual inadequacies result largely from the lack of cooperation among these domains. This itself gives rise to specious controversies in which mutual recriminations and accusations – for example, of 'relativism', 'irrationalism', 'sociologism', 'historicism' – are but symptoms of a deeper malaise and mistrust among what are, in many cases, competing intellectual traditions.

Few philosophical models of scientific development have been developed to the level of historically testable hypotheses, and to be sure, hypothesis building and verification have very little tradition in history. Nonetheless, the use of case studies of scientific development, in the context of scientific disciplines and specialties, may prove to be an excellent point of departure (Mullins, 1972, 1973; Lakatos, 1972).

In looking to the future and in examining the outstanding theoretical difficulties with an open mind, one must ask whether the analyses developed so far have managed to integrate the relevant phenomena; and whether the state of theory development itself can be assessed, and if so, in what way.

First, in devising developmental models, a line must be drawn between recurrent part processes and global trends. Processes of the first kind include, for instance, the formation of disciplines and specialties, the rise of interdisciplinarity and the transformation of disciplines into a propaedeutic. It is here more than anywhere else that it should prove possible to construct empirically verifiable hypotheses. Second, it is evident that model building must be evaluated in the light of the phenomena which characterize science itself. In this sense the most striking phenomena to be considered are: quantitative growth (Derek Price, 1963), cumulativeness,[17] the tendency toward unity (von Weizsäcker, 1971; Neurath, 1971), the survival capacity of outlived theories, the usefulness of a given type of knowledge, and the self-thematization of science for the past century.

An actual evaluation of the various approaches in the light of such phenomena is outside the scope of the present essay, except perhaps for a few general remarks about the difficulty of theory construction in taking account of these phenomena. The quantitative growth of science is regarded by many researchers as a stumbling block. Hitherto no one has managed to link this development with other relevant characteristics of the development of science. If anything, social psychology has made a beginning by studying the motivations of scientists since on this basis, for example, it would prove possible to construct the curve of growth of new specialties (Holton, 1953). In addition, Derek Price's findings, viewed by some as ominous, have given rise to reflection about 'qualitative growth' and about the possibility of new forms of scientific integration.

As in the case of the quantitative phenomena, the recognition of the 'unitary tendency', or reductionism and the symptoms of 'the end of science' (von Weizsäcker, 1971; Stent, 1969) seems to be hampered by emotional resistance. Since the notion of the express rights of the different sciences and the familiar view of science as an unbounded field of the unexplored cannot be reconciled with these phenomena, the latter remain external to most models of scientific development.

The question of how 'external factors' affect scientific development raises very complex conceptual problems which fall within the compass of such concepts as truth and objectivity. Yet what is even more important here is the absence of relevant empirical work within the history of science. Presumably this work will occur when historians become more interested in problems arising from the philosophy and sociology of science. A particular deficiency in this respect is the relative neglect of the history of technology, or better, an account of the history of technology in terms of the history of science.

Similarly, the effects of self-thematization or, more generally, the 'reflexive' quality of science have been grasped only inadequately, if at all. It is possible to observe specific shifts in the reflexive self-consciousness of science, shifts which were provoked by difficulties arising within a given discipline: the historical difficulties of empirical psychology gave rise to reflection on the problems of quantification; and those of sociology have today led to reflection on the process of theory construction.

---

[17] For the classification and critique of the 'cumulation theories of science', see Lejkin, 1972.

More fundamentally, the way in which knowledge of 'how science happens' has affected and continues to affect the development of science is not generally agreed upon. The same question applies, with special force, to the influence of the sociology of science on scientific development. It is widely believed that the conceptual difficulties in which the different lines of inquiry seem to be caught now require: 1) a new cognitive sociology of science (Whitley, 1974; Weingart, 1974; Böhme, 1975); 2) a philosophy of science which takes into account the real situation of research (*Pragmatic Philosophy of Science*, Stegmüller, 1973, Vol. 4, Introduction; Böhme, 1974b); and 3) a theory-oriented history of science (*Theoretical History of Science*, Diederich, 1974). This endeavor may help to give a new and more compelling insight into why science is a social process; why outgrown theories are still being used; how social purposes can be integrated into theory development; what has been the significance of conceptual arguments; and what significance may be ascribed to the role of instruments in the development of science.

It seems that so far particular models designed to encompass global trends are justifiable only partially and in terms of distinct epochs. Hence to arrive at a theory of global scientific development one will probably have to start with a theory relating to specific epochs.

Further, if the result is not to be a new type of 'internal history of science' but an avenue of approach capable of overcoming the 'internal' and 'external' dichotomy, the logic of cognitive development must be seen as parallel to the development of the forces of production. Perhaps this will provide models which in their reciprocal interaction will start off new lines of research and explanation in the social and cognitive organization of science.

BIBLIOGRAPHY

Autorenkollektiv, 1968   Autorenkollektiv, *Die Wissenschaft von der Wissenschaft*, Gemeinschaftsarbeit eines Kollektivs am Institut für Philosophie der Karl-Marx-Universität, Leipzig, Berlin, 1968.

Autorenkollektiv, 1972   Autorenkollektiv, *Die gegenwärtige wissenschaftlich-technische Revolution. Eine historische Untersuchung*, Berlin, Akademie-Verlag, 1972.

Bachelard, 1972   Bachelard, G., *La Formation de l'esprit scientifique – contribution à une psychanalyse de la connaisance objective*, Paris, Vrin, 8e édition, 1972.

Bahr, 1973   Bahr, H.-D., 'Die Klassenstruktur der Maschinerie, Anmerkungen zur Wertform', in Vahrenkamp, R. (Ed.),

Technologie und Kapital, Frankfurt, Suhrkamp, 1973.

Ben-David, 1971   Ben-David, J., *The Scientist's Role in Society: A Co-operative Study,* Englewood Cliffs, New Jersey, Prentice Hall, 1971.

Ben-David, 1975   Ben-David, J., 'Probleme einer soziologischen Theorie der Wissenschaft', in Weingart, P. (Ed.), *Wissenschaftsforschung,* Frankfurt, New York, Campus, 1975, pp. 133-161.

Bernal, 1953   Bernal, J. D., 'Science, Industry and Society in the XIXth Century', in *Centaurus* 3, 1953, pp. 133-165.

Bernal, 1957   Bernal, J. D., *Science in History,* 2nd Edition, London, C. A. Watts, 1957.

Bernal, 1967   Bernal, J. D., *The Social Function of Science,* Cambridge and London, The MIT Press, 1967.

Böhme, 1974a   Böhme, G., 'Die Bedeutung von Experimentalregeln für die Wissenschaft', *Zeitschrift für Soziologie* 3, 1974, pp. 5-7.

Böhme, 1974b   Böhme, G., 'Die Bedeutung praktischer Argumente für die Entwicklung der Wissenschaft', *Philosophia Naturalis* 15, Heft 1, 1974, pp. 133-151.

Böhme, 1975   Böhme, G., 'The Social Function of Cognitive Structures: A Concept of the Scientific Community within a Theory of Action', in Knorr, K. D. *et al.* (Eds.), *Determinants and Controls of Scientific Development,* Dordrecht, Boston, Reidel, 1975, pp. 205-225.

Böhme *et al.,* 1972   Böhme, G., van den Daele, W., Krohn, W., 'Alternativen in der Wissenschaft', *Zeitschrift für Soziologie* 1, 1972, pp. 302-206.

Böhme *et al.,* 1976   Böhme, G., van den Daele, W. and Krohn, W., 'Finalization of Science', in *Social Science Information* XV, 1976, pp. 306-330.

Borkenau, 1971   Borkenau, F., 'Der Übergang vom feudalen zum bürgerlichen Weltbild', in *Studien zur Geschichte der Philosophie der Manufakturperiode,* Darmstadt, 1971.

Bunge, 1970   Bunge, M., 'Problems Concerning Intertheory Relations', in Weingartner, S. and Zecha (Eds.), *Inductions, Physics and Ethics,* Dordrecht, Reidel, 1970, pp. 285-315.

Comte, 1830-1842   Comte, A., *Cours de philosophie positive,* Paris, Bachalier, 1830-1842.

Comte, 1975   Comte, A., *Philosophie des sciences,* Paris, PUF, 1975.

van den Daele and Weingart, 1975   van den Daele, W. and Weingart, P., 'Resistenz und Rezeptivität der Wissenschaft. Zu den Entstehungsbedingungen neuer Disziplinen durch wissenschaftspolitische Steuerung', *Zeitschrift für Soziologie* 4, 1975, pp. 146-164.

Diederich, 1974   Diederich, W. (Ed.), *Theorien der Wissenschaftsgeschichte. Beiträge zur diachronischen Wissenschaftstheorie,* Frankfurt, Suhrkamp, 1974.

Feyerabend, 1962   Feyerabend, P. K., 'Explanation, Reduction and Empiricism', in Feigel, H. and Maxwell, G. (Eds.), *Minnesota Studies in the Philosophy of Science III,* Minneapolis, Minnesota University Press, 1962, pp. 28-97.

Feyerabend, 1972   Feyerabend, P. K., 'Consolations for a Specialist', in
                            Lakatos, I., Musgrave, A. (Eds.), *Criticism and Growth
                            of Knowledge*, New York and London, Cambridge
                            University Press, 1972, pp. 197-230.
Foucault, 1971   Foucault, M., *The Order of Things. An Archeology of
                            the Human Sciences*, New York, Pantheon Books,
                            1971.
Foucault, 1973   Foucault, M., *Birth of the Clinic. An Archeology of
                            Medical Perception*, New York, Pantheon, 1973.
Griffith and Mullins, 1972 Griffith, B. C. and Mullins, N. C., 'Coherent Social
                            Groups in Scientific Change', in *Science 40533*, 1972,
                            pp. 959-964.
Grossman, 1935   Grossmann, H., 'Die gesellschaftlichen Grundlagen der
                            mechanistischen Philosophie und die Manufaktur',
                            Zeitschrift für Sozialforschung IV, No. 2, 1935, pp.
                            161-229.
Hall, 1959   Hall, A. R., 'The Scholar and the Craftsman in the
                            Scientific Revolution', in Clage, H. (Ed.), *Critical
                            Problems in the History of Science*, Madison, Wis-
                            consin, 1959, pp. 3-23.
Hall, 1961   Hall, A. R., 'Engineering and the Scientific Revolu-
                            tion', *Technology and Culture* 2, 1961, pp. 333-341.
Heisenberg, 1971   Heisenberg, W., 'Der Begriff der "abgeschlossenen
                            Theorie" in der modernen Naturwissenschaft', in
                            Schritte über Grenzen, München, Piper, 1971, pp.
                            87-94.
Hessen, 1968   Hessen, B., 'The Social and Economic Roots of New-
                            ton's "Principia" ', in Basalla, G., *The Rise of Modern
                            Science*, Lexington, Mass., 1968.
Holton, 1953   Holton, B., 'On the Duality and Growth of Physical
                            Science', *American Scientist* 41, 1953, pp. 89-99.
Janich, 1973   Janich, P., *Zweck und Methode der Physik aus philo-
                            sophischer Sicht*, Konstanz, Universitätsverlag, 1973.
Kedrov, 1966   Kedrov, B. M., 'Naturwissenschaft und wissenschaft-
                            lich-technische Revolution', *Sowjetwissenschaft, ge-
                            sellschaftswissenschaftliche Beiträge* 10, 1966, pp.
                            1055-1064.
Kedrov, 1973   Kedrov, B. M., 'Sur la synthèse des sciences', in *Pro-
                            ceedings of the XVth World Congress of Philosophy*,
                            Vol. 1, Sofia, 1973.
King, 1971   King, M. O., 'Reason, Tradition and the Progressive-
                            ness of Science', *History and Theory* 10, 1971, pp.
                            3-32.
Kisiel and Johnson, 1974   Kisiel, T. and Johnson, G., 'New Philosophies of
                            Science in the USA: A Selective Survey', *Zeitschrift
                            für allgemeine Wissenschaftstheorie* 5, 1974, pp.
                            138-191.
Klotz and Rum, 1963   Klotz, H. and Rum, K., 'Über die Produktivkraft Wis-
                            senschaft', *Einheit Heft* 2, 1963, p. 28.
Kosing, 1964   Kosing, A., 'Bemerkungen zur Wissenschaftstheorie',
                            in *Die Entwicklung der Wissenschaft zur unmittel-
                            baren Produktivkraft*, Leipzig, Karl-Marx-Universität,
                            1964, pp. 124-139.

Koyré, 1948

Kranzberg, 1967

Kranzberg, 1968

Kröber, 1973a

Kröber and Laitko, 1972

Krohn and Schäfer, 1975

Krüger, 1974a

Krüger, 1974b

Kuhn, 1961

Kuhn, 1970

Lades and Burrichter, 1970

Lakatos, 1972

Lakatos, 1973

Lakatos and Musgrave, 1972

Lassow, 1963

Koyré, A., 'Du monde de l'à peu pres à l'univers de la précision', *Critique* 4, No. 28, 1948, pp. 806-823.

Kranzberg, M., 'The Unity of Science-Technology', *American Scientist* 55, 1967, pp. 48-66.

Kranzberg, M., 'The Disunity of Science-Technology', *American Scientist* 56, 1968, pp. 21-34.

Kröber, G., 'Die wissenschaftlich-technische Revolution und das Problem der Entwicklungsgesetzmässigkeit der Wissenschaft', in *Proceedings of the XVth World Congress of Philosophy* Band 2, Sofia, 1973, pp. 91-94.

Kröber, G. and Laitko, H., *Wissenschaft und Sozialismus*, Berlin, VEB Deutscher Verlag der Wissenschaften, 1972.

Krohn, W. and Schäfer, W., *The Origins and Structure of Agricultural Chemistry*, unpublished manuscript, 1975.

Krüger, L., 'Wissenschaftliche Revolution und Kontinuität der Erfahrung', in Bubner, K., Cramer, R., Wiehl, *Tendenzen der Wissenschaftstheorie*, Göttingen, Vandenhoeck u. Ruprecht, 1974.

Krüger, L., 'Die systematische Bedeutung wissenschaftlicher Revolutionen, Pro und Contra Th. Kuhn', in Diederich, W. (Ed.), *Theorien der Wissenschaftsgeschichte*, Frankfurt, Suhrkamp, 1974.

Kuhn, T. S., 'The Function of Dogma in Scientific Research', in Crombie, A. C. (Ed.), *Scientific Change: Historical Studies in the Intellectual, Social and Technical Conditions for Scientific Discovery and Technical Invention from Antiquity to the Present*, London, Heinemann, 1961, pp. 347-369.

Kuhn, T. S., 'The Structure of Scientific Revolutions', in Neurath, R. and Carnap, T. M. (Eds.), *Foundations of the Unity of Science* Vol. II, Chicago and London, 1970, pp. 53-272.

Lades, H. and Burrichter, C., *Produktivkraft Wissenschaft. Sozialistische Sozialwissenschaften in der DDR*, Hamburg, Drei Mohren Verlag, 1970.

Lakatos, I., 'Falsification and the Methodology of Scientific Research Programmes', in Lakatos and Musgrave (Eds.), *Criticism and the Growth of Knowledge* 2nd edition, New York and London, Cambridge University Press, 1972, pp. 91-196.

Lakatos, I., 'History of Science and Its Rational Reconstructions', in Buck, R. C. and Cohen, R. S. (Eds.), *Boston Studies in the Philosophy of Science* Vol. III, Dordrecht, Reidel, 1973, pp. 91-136.

Lakatos, I. and Musgrave, A. (Eds.), *Criticism and the Growth of Knowledge*, New York and London, Cambridge University Press, 1972.

Lassow, E., 'Probleme der Produktivkrafttheorie in der Periode des umfassenden Aufbau des Sozialismus und der technischwissenschaftlichen Revolution', *Deutsche*

	Zeitschrift für Philosophie 15, 1963, pp. 373-398.
Lassow, 1971	Lassow, E., 'Produktivkräfte und Sozialismus', *Deutsche Zeitschrift für Philosophie* 8, 1971, pp. 1007-1027.
Lejkin, 1972	Lejkin, E. G., 'Zur Kritik der kumulativen Konzeptionen der Wissenschaftsentwicklung', in Kröber and Steiner (Eds.), *Wissenschaft: Studien zu ihrer Geschichte, Theorie und Organisation,* Berlin, Akademie-Verlag, 1972.
Marx, no publication date	Marx, K., *Capital,* translated from the third German edition by S. Moore and E. Aveling, edited by F. Engels, Vol. 1, Moscow, Foreign Languages Publishing House, no publication date.
Masterman, 1972	Masterman, M., 'The Nature of a Paradigm', in Lakatos and Musgrave (Eds.), *Criticism and the Growth of Knowledge* 2nd Edition, New York and London, Cambridge University Press, 1972, pp. 59-89.
Merton, 1970	Merton, R. K., *Science, Technology and Society in Seventeenth-Century England,* New York, Harper and Row, 1970.
Mittelstrass, 1970	Mittelstrass, J., *Neuzeit und Aufklärung,* Berlin, New York, 1970.
Mittelstrass, 1974	Mittelstrass, J., 'Prolegomena zu einer konstruktiven Theorie der Wissenschaftsgeschichte', in Mittelstrass, J., *Die Möglichkeit von Wissenschaft,* Frankfurt, Suhrkamp, 1974, pp. 106-144.
Moscovici, 1968	Moscovici, S., *Essai sur l'histoire humaine de la nature,* Paris, Flammarion, 1968.
Mullins, 1972	Mullins, N. C., 'The Development of a Scientific Specialty: The Phage Group and the Origins of Molecular Biology', *Minerva* 10, 1972, pp. 51-82.
Mullins, 1973	Mullins, N. C., 'The Development of Specialties in Social Science: The Case of Ethnomethodology', *Science Studies* 3, 1973, pp. 245-273.
Neurath, 1971	Neurath, O., 'Unified Science as Encyclopedic Integration', in Neurath, Carnap and Morris (Eds.), *Foundations of the Unity of Science* Vol. 1, 3rd Edition, Chicago and London, Chicago University Press, 1971, pp. 1-27.
Neurath, Carnap and Morris, 1971	Naurath, O., Carnap, R. and Morris, C. (Eds.), *Foundations of the Unity of Science: Toward an International Encyclopedia of Unified Science,* Vol. I, II, 3rd Edition, Chicago and London, Chicago University Press, 1971.
Olschki, 1919	Olschki, L., *Geschichte der neusprachlichen wissenschaftlichen Literatur,* Leipzig, 1919.
Polanyi, 1962	Polanyi, M., *Personal Knowledge,* New York, Harper Torchbooks, 1962.
Polanyi, 1969	Polanyi, M., *Knowing and Being: Essays,* London, Routledge and Kegan Paul, 1969.
Popper, 1971	Popper, K. R., *Logik der Forschung* 4th Edition, Tübingen, Mohr, 1971.
Popper, 1972a	Popper, K. R., *Objective Knowledge: An Evolutionary*

Popper, 1972b

Derek Price, 1963

Derek Price, 1965

Prüss, 1974

Radnitzky, 1971

Richta and Kollektiv, 1971

Richta and Kollektiv, 1972

Rochhausen, 1970

Scheffler, 1972

Scheffler, 1967

Scheibe, 1972

Scheibe and Krüger, 1972

Shapere, 1964

Shapere, 1966

Sohn-Rethel, 1972

Spiegel-Rösing, 1973

Sneed, 1971

Approach, Oxford, Clarendon, 1972.
Popper, K. R., 'Normal Science and its Dangers', in Lakatos and Musgrave (Eds.), *Criticism and the Growth of Knowledge,* New York and London, Cambridge University Press, 1972, pp. 51-53.
Price, Derek de Solla, *Little Science, Big Science,* New York, Columbia University Press, 1963.
Price, Derek de Solla, 'Is Technology Historically Independent of Sciences? A Study in Statistical Historiography', *Technology and Culture* 6, 1965, pp. 553-568.
Prüss, K., *Kernforschungspolitik in der BRD:* Projekt Wissenschaftsplanung III, Frankfurt, Suhrkamp, 1974.
Radnitzky, G., 'Theorienpluralismus – Theorienmonisumus: einer der Faktoren, die den Forschungsprozess beeinflussen und die selbst von Weltbildannahmen abhängig sind', in Diemer (Ed.), *Der Methoden- und Theorienpluralismus in der Wissenschaft,* Meiserhaim am Glan, Verlag Anton Hain, 1971, pp. 134-185.
Richta, R. and Kollektiv, *Politische Ökonomie des 20. Jahrhunderts,* Frankfurt, Makol, 1971.
Richta, R. and Kollektiv, *Technischer Fortschritt und industrielle Gesellschaft,* Frankfurt, Makol, 1972.
Rochhausen, R., 'Differenzierung und Integration im System der Wissenschaften und ihre Folgen für die Wissenschaftsprognostik, Organisation und Klassifizierung sowie für das Bildungssystem', in *Philosophenkongress der DDR 1970,* Teil 4, Berlin, VEB Verlag der Wissenschaften, 1970, pp. 123-131.
Scheffler, I., 'Vision and Revolutions: A Postscript on Kuhn', *Philosophy of Science* 39, 1972, pp. 366-374.
Scheffler, I., *Science and Subjectivity,* New York, Knopf, 1967.
Scheibe, E., 'Die Erklärung der Kepplerschen Gesetze durch Newtons Gravitationsgesetz', in Scheibe, E. and Süssman, G. (Eds.), *Einheit und Vielheit. Festschrift für C. F. von Weizsäcker zum 60. Geburtstag,* Göttingen, Vandenhoeck und Ruprecht, 1972.
Scheibe, E. and Krüger, L., 'Inter-theoretische Relationen in der Naturwissenschaft', DFG-Projektvorschlag, Ms. Göttingen, Philosophy Seminar, 1972.
Shapere, D., 'Discussion on T. S. Kuhn: The Structure of Scientific Revolutions', *Philosophical Review* 73, 1964, pp. 383-394.
Shapere, D., 'Meaning and Scientific Change', in Colodny, R. (Ed.), *Mind and Cosmos,* Pittsburgh, University of Pittsburgh Press, 1966, pp. 41-85.
Sohn-Rethel, A., *Geistige und körperliche Arbeit,* Frankfurt, Suhrkamp, 1972.
Spiegel-Rösing, I., *Wissenschaftsentwicklung und Wissenschaftssteuerung. Einführung und Materiel zur Wissenschaftsforschung,* Frankfurt, Athenäum, 1973.
Sneed, J. D., *The Logical Structure of Mathematical*

	Physics, Dordrecht, Reidel, 1971.
Stegmüller, 1973	Stegmüller, W., _Probleme und Resultate der Wissenschaftstheorie und analytischen Philosophie_ II, 2.Halbband/IV, 1. Halbband, Berlin, Heidelberg and New York, Springer, 1973.
Stegmüller, 1974	Stegmüller, W., 'Theoriendynamik und logisches Verständnis', in Diederich (Ed.), _Theorien der Wissenschaftsgeschichte,_ Frankfurt, Suhrkamp, 1974, pp. 167-209.
Steiner, 1971	Steiner, H., 'Der sozialökonomische Charakter der Vergesellschaftung der Wissenschaft als theoretische und methodologische Grundlage für ihre wissenschaftstheoretische Analyse', _Deutsche Zeitschrift für Philosophie_ 19, 1971, pp. 1471-1489.
Stent, 1969	Stent, G., _The Coming of the Golden Age,_ New York, The Natural History Press, 1969.
Strauss, 1972	Strauss, M., _Modern Physics and Philosophy,_ Dordrecht Reidel, 1972.
Toulmin, 1967	Toulmin, S., 'The Evolutionary Development of Natural Science', _American Scientist_ 55, 1967, pp. 456-471.
Toulmin, 1969	Toulmin, S., 'Innovation and the Problem of Utilization', in Grüber, W. H. and Marquis, D. G. (Eds.), _Factors in the Transfer of Technology,_ Cambridge, MIT Press, 1969, pp. 24-38.
Toulmin, 1972a	Toulmin, S., _Human Understanding_ Vol. 1, Oxford, Clarendon Press, 1972.
Toulmin, 1972b	Toulmin, S., 'Does the Distinction between Normal and Revolutionary Science Hold Water?' in Lakatos and Musgrave (Eds.), _Criticism and the Growth of Knowledge,_ New York and London, Cambridge University Press, 1972, pp. 39-47.
Vlachý, 1972	Vlachý, J., 'Science in Retrospect and Forecast', _Teoria a Methoda_ IV, No. 2, 1972, pp. 105-160.
Weimer, 1974a	Weimer, W. B., 'The History of Psychology and its Retrieval from Historiography: I. The Problematic Nature of History' _Science Studies_ 4, No. 3, July 1974, pp. 235-258.
Weimer, 1974b	Weimer, W. B., 'The History of Psychology and its Retrieval from Historiography: II Some Lessons for the Methodology of Scientific Research', _Science Studies_ 4, No. 4, October 1974, pp. 367-397.
Weinberg, 1970	Weinberg, A. M., _Probleme der Grossforchung,_ Frankfurt, Suhrkamp, 1970.
Weingart, 1972	Weingart, P. (Ed.), _Wissenschaftssoziologie I. Wissenschaftliche Entwicklung als sozialer Prozess,_ Frankfurt, Fischer-Athenäum, 1972.
Weingart, 1974	Weingart, P. (Ed.), _Wissenschaftssoziologie II. Einleitung,_ Frankfurt, Fischer-Athenäum, 1974.
Weizsäcker, 1971	Weizsäcker, C. F. von, _Die Einheit der Natur,_ München, Hanser, 1971.
Whitley, 1974	Whitley, R. D., 'Cognitive and Social Institutionalization of Scientific Specialties and Research Areas', in

Whitley, R. D. (Ed.), *Social Processes of Scientific Development*, London, Routledge and Kegan Paul, 1974.

Wolkow, 1969   Wolkow, G. N., 'Der Wandel in der sozialen Orientierung der Wissenschaft', *Sowjetwissenschaft* 2. Halbjahr, 1969, pp. 709-720.

Yuasa, 1962   Yuasa, M., 'Center of Scientific Activity: Its Shift from the 16th to the 20th Century', *Japanese Studies in the History of Science* 1, 1962, pp. 57-75.

Zilsel, 1942a   Zilsel, E., 'The Sociological Roots of Sciences', *American Journal of Sociology* XLVII, 1942, pp. 544-562.

Zilsel, 1942b   Zilsel, E., 'The Genesis of the Concept of Physical Law', *The Philosophical Review* 3, 1942, p. 245.

Zilsel, 1945   Zilsel, E., 'The Genesis of the Concept of Scientific Progress', *The Journal of the History of Ideas* 6, 1945, p. 325.

Zloczower, 1966   Zloczower, A., *Career Opportunities and the Growth of Scientific Discovery in 19th Century Germany*, Jerusalem, Hebrew University, Eliezer Kaplan School of Economics and Social Sciences, 1966.

3

Science Policy Studies: The Policy Perspective

SANFORD A. LAKOFF
D. NELKIN
HARVEY M. SAPOLSKY
BRIGITTE SCHROEDER-GUDEHUS
EUGENE B. SKOLNIKOFF
ZIAUDDIN SARDAR
AND DAWUD G. ROSSER-OWEN

Chapter 10

SCIENTISTS, TECHNOLOGISTS AND POLITICAL POWER

Sanford A. Lakoff

University of California at San Diego

HISTORICAL EVOLUTION: PAST AND PRESENT

Because science and technology have come to be critical elements of political power only in the modern era, it is only in recent years that the relationship between scientists and technologists and the state has become problematical. In the past, technical advances were sometimes stimulated by military necessity; in even rarer instances, they conferred victory in battle or changed the very nature of warfare. Sulphur gas was used at Delium in 424 BC; in the Third Century BC Archimedes responded to patriotic pleas by designing huge engines of war which enabled his native Syracuse to repel a Roman invasion. Gunpowder and the longbow revolutionized warfare. Combustible mixtures and missiles launched with the aid of such delivery systems as slings, bows and catapults, were used in military operations for many centuries before this one. None of these inventions, however, opened avenues of influence to their developers. Galileo was rewarded with a thousand ducats and a life professorship for providing the Doge of Venice with a militarily useful telescope. Leonardo da Vinci needed no special incentive to turn his fecund imagination to the design of ingenious military machines, though he suppressed a sketch of a submarine 'on account of the evil nature of man' (Morton, 1969). Neither of these Renaissance geniuses of science and technology would have ventured to claim a role in politics by virtue of their talents or accomplishments and if they had done so, their claims would have been met with ridicule. The situation is different now, for at least two fundamental reasons:

1. Never before have the great world powers depended as they do now on

the regular contributions of science and technology to war-making and defensive capacities. Political power is now as much or more a function of superiority in military technology as it is of the size of armies and the economic capacity to sustain total conflict. Scientists and technologists must therefore be relied upon to design improved weapon systems, assess proposed new systems, advise governments with respect to the menace of technical developments elsewhere and estimate the feasibility and likely value of agreements to refrain from certain types of development and to fix force levels in mixed forms of parity (For a fuller discussion of this, see Sapolsky, Chapter 12).

2. Never before have the economic as well as the social and ecological consequences of scientific discovery and technological innovation been so influential upon the fortunes of particular nations and upon the entire world system. Scientists and technologists have therefore become important contributors in the quest for economic growth and security, and for the alleviation of disease, poverty and overpopulation.

These changing conditions inevitably entail alterations in the relationship of scientists and technologists to political power, which may be summarized in three related and easily confirmed observations:

1. Scientists and technologists, especially those most prominent in their disciplines and professions, have acquired an unprecedented degree of access to the councils of the decision makers in every advanced society. In open societies, they also enjoy an ability to address the general public on matters related to their special competence and they can expect that their views will be taken seriously.

2. Because the progress of science and the achievement of new technological objectives depend heavily on public subvention, governments in advanced societies have acquired a reciprocal influence upon the purveyors of knowledge. To a considerable extent, they can direct research towards socially designated priorities and prevent it from moving, or at least from moving quickly, in other directions. Technology is even more subject to such manipulations.

3. Because of the increasing social bearing of their work, many scientists and technologists have come to feel that they have both a personal responsibility for the uses to which their work is put and a right as well as a duty to participate actively in the political processes by which these uses are determined.

As all these related changes have occured they have attracted considerable attention, not only from scholars, social critics, theorizers and moralists, but even from novelists and playwrights.[1] Underlying much of this work is an

---

[1] Among the modern writers of fiction who have treated the social role of scientists and technologists are H. G. Wells, Aldous Huxley, Robert Musil, C. P. Snow, and Friedrich Dürrenmatt.

awareness of the changing social image of science and technology (See Salomon, Chapter 2 and Ravetz, Chapter 3). In the not too distant past, this image was of a benevolent if indirect and slow moving 'servant of man' (Cohen, 1948). Indeed, from at least the latter half of the Eighteenth Century and continuing into the present, the progress of science and technology has been seen as the basis of all social progress and of the faith of rational humanists in the indefinite perfectibility of the human species (Manuel, 1962; Lakoff, 1966). Nowadays, however, science and technology are sometimes vilified as causes of real or impending catastrophes and scientists and technologists are regarded with suspicion, not only because they are capable of producing great harm, but because they are thought to be guided by a desire to enhance the instruments of power, and possibly to acquire power themselves, without having a sense of purpose to guide their efforts (Mumford, 1967; Ellul, 1954; Roszak, 1970). And even those who do not join in the vilification are apt to be apprehensive about the ability of fragile modern societies to absorb all the unsettling changes that science and technology now produce in such relentless profusion.

In a more academic perspective, social scientists have tried to illumine the actual changes in the political role of scientists and technologists, changes which are reflected, sometimes faithfully, sometimes in exaggerated and distorted form, in the changing image. It is with these efforts that we shall be concerned here.

THE TRADITION THAT SCIENCE IS POLITICALLY NEUTRAL

In the earliest period of the development of modern science, it was not expected, even by the champions of the new science, that its practitioners would wish to claim power − except over nature and even then on behalf of humanity in general, and not on behalf of some particular state or creed. Francis Bacon insisted that, contrary to the suspicions of some hostile critics, science was merely a 'new instrument' with which to pursue established ends. Men of science would have no reason whatever to rebel against secular authority or to undermine religious faith, according to Bacon. He reserved for an unfinished and unpublished manuscript the more radical vision of the 'new Atlantis', a scientific utopia in which real authority was exercised by the fathers of 'Solomon's House' and traditional religious and secular authorities were apparently reduced to mere figureheads (Lakoff, 1966; Haberer, 1969). In practice, those scientists who acted upon Bacon's vision by forming the Royal Society of London were adjured in 1663 by the distinguished chemist Robert Hooke to bear in mind that their business was 'to improve the knowledge of natural things, not meddling with Divinity, Metaphysics,

Moralls, Politicks, Grammar Rhetorick or Logic ' (Weld, 1848).

Political neutrality became one of the implicit norms of science and it was one that was respected by the authorities, on the whole (For a fuller discussion of this, see de Beer, 1960). Thus during the Napoleonic Wars, Sir Humphrey Davy was allowed to travel to Paris to receive an award from the Institute of Science, and a French scientist, the Chevalier de Rossal, was invited to dine with the Royal Society, at the suggestion of a member of the society who was a hydrographer with the Admiralty (Rose and Rose, 1970, 180). The same British Admiralty was to instruct the captains of its man-o-wars not to molest the enemy's scientific expeditions in time of war (See also Woolf, 1959). It is undoubtedly true that these courtesies were not extended out of any reverential attitude toward science but in disdain for its impracticality (Salomon, 1970, 213); but the fact remains that for many years scientists fell under no great compulsion to respect political boundaries or to choose between their devotion to cosmopolitan science and their loyalty to the nation. There were isolated episodes which might have served as portents of unhappy changes to come. The chemist Joseph Priestley was forced to flee his home in Birmingham by mobs angered by his support for the French revolutionaries, and possibly even more by his Unitarian faith. Another equally celebrated chemist, Lavoisier, was executed by French revolutionaries 'at least as much because he represented "Aristocratic science" as because he exploited the people as a "taxfarmer" ' (Rose and Rose, 1970, 20). These were very exceptional events, however; in quieter times, scientists were left alone and a tradition was established, rooted in the necessity of the very communication which was so essential to researchers, that science was an international affair: 'The invisible college of scientists, tied by their letters, their visits and their publications, was committed almost by sheer scarcity of numbers, to be international in character in the early days, and the personal visit or private letter remained an important mode of contact' (Rose and Rose, 1970, 180).

THE END OF NEUTRALITY AND INTERNATIONALISM

The tradition of scientists' neutrality and internationalism was rudely shaken, if not totally destroyed, by the outbreak of World War I. Scientists and technologists in all the combatant countries responded to nationalistic propaganda and their own patriotic promptings by enlisting their talents in the service of the nation-state (Meynaud and Schroeder, 1962; Schroeder-Gudehus, 1973 and Chapter 13). In a dramatic gesture, a large number of leading German scientists and other intellectuals issued a manifesto to the world in which they identified the cause of their homeland with that of civilization itself. On both sides there was great effort to make up for the losses, in raw materials and access to technology, which the war had caused, and there was apparently little thought among scientists of the setback which the cause of scientific neutrality or internationalism had suffered. In relatively short order many technologists and a significant number of scientists were caught up in the fever of war work. So valuable were the contributions of chemists that World War I is sometimes referred to as the 'chemist's war'. In particular, they were responsible for increasing the lethal effect of explosives and for making possible the use of harmful gases — a development which did not prove decisive, but which did provide a frightening foretaste of the ways in which scientific contributions were to make warfare even more terrible.

With the end of the war, nationalistic fever subsided for a time, and scientists readily reverted to more accustomed practices. Students from all countries mingled at the great universities and laboratories of Europe. While there was keen competition for priority in discovery, there was also widespread recognition of the interdependence and fellowship of researchers everywhere and a belief in the benefits that all humanity would derive from the work of science. Before very long, however, this effort to return to the golden age of international collaboration was gravely undermined as a result of the intensification of nationalism in two of the defeated countries, Germany and Russia, and the rise in these countries of political ideologies which denied the autonomy of science and made it all but impossible for scientists to be neutral in politics. As Salomon has observed, it was 'under the totalitarian regimes, that politics laid its hands on science from the outset, and on two planes, ideology and the realities of action' (Salomon, 1970, 32).

In post-revolutionary Russia, pledges of a new internationalism were soon succeeded by an insular defensiveness, coupled with suspicion of all 'bourgeois' influences. Scientists were made to understand that they were not to behave like the intelligentsia of Czarist days, whose critical independence had helped to make the revolution possible. Many who were presumed to be unable to meet this test became victims of the purges conducted by the new regime in order to weed out potential enemies. For scientists, loyalty to the new society was interpreted to require a much more guarded approach to contacts with foreigners, and in some cases a rejection of Western or bourgeois science, as it was called, in favor of the promotion of indigenous notions whose philosophic foundations or practical tendencies seemed more in keeping with the character and needs of Soviet society (Joravsky, 1961). In certain disciplines, among them mathematics and physics, scientists discovered that so long as they paid lip service to the philosophy of dialectical materialism and were circumspect in their dealings with the outside world, they could get on with their work and even became privileged members of the new society. Social scientists, including psychologists, could only continue their work under much more severe constraints.

The single most notorious instance of the interference of the political authorities with the work of scientists arose in the case of genetics. In the hope of increasing agricultural productivity, the Stalin regime gave credence and support to the agronomist T. D. Lysenko, who claimed to be a disciple of the Russian plant breeder I. V. Michurin. With help and encouragement from Stalin and the Politburo, Lysenko wrested control over the research facilities from 'orthodox' geneticists, notably N. I. Vavilov, who was ousted from the presidency of the Lenin Academy of Agricultural Sciences and later arrested. Only after the death of Stalin and the repeated failure of efforts to adapt his claims of experimental success to actual conditions was Lysenko exposed as a charlatan (Joravsky, 1970; Medvedev, 1969; Zirkle, 1959).

When the Nazis attained power in Germany, they too instituted a purge of scientists who were deemed unfit to serve the 'new order', either because they were of 'non-Aryan' ancestry or because they held left-wing political views. In Germany, too, certain scientific work was denounced as invalid because those who had contributed significantly to it were stigmatized as racial inferiors or ideological enemies. The most notrious case was that of the theory of relativity, which, because it had been developed by Albert Einstein, was denounced as mere 'Jewish physics' at a meeting of German physicists convened with the encouragement of the Nazi authorities. The purge of the universities and independent laboratories met with no significant resistance in part because certain of the leading scientists took the view that such extreme measures would be forsworn once the regime had cleaned house and gotten the country back to its old, well-ordered condition. They reasoned that by staying at the helm they would be in a position to exert influence with the new regime for the sake of science and the universities (Heisenberg, 1971, 173). It has also been observed, however, that such acquiescence was the result of a traditional definition of the scientific vocation which had no place for a strong belief in social responsibility (Haberer, 1969).

In response to these developments and the increasing threat of another world war, scientists in Britain and America reacted by closing their laboratories to students from the totalitarian countries and, in the case of nuclear physicists, by adopting self-censorship. In England the attitudes of scientists went through an abrupt change. At first, many associated themselves with the pacifist position of the Cambridge Scientists Anti-War Movement or with the Oxford Oath, whose adherents pledged not to take part in any future war, whatever its justification. In 1939 scientists were urged by J. D. Bernal in particular and by many other leading scientists to abandon their tradition of political neutrality and their professions of pacifism in order to defend democracy against fascism. Bernal argued that it was the very responsibility of scientists to science itself that demanded the rejection of their traditional neutrality. Fascism, he pointed out, posed such a threat to the freedom of inquiry and therefore to science as to be incompatible with the survival of science. This threat, he declared, had compelled the realization that 'the work of science does not end in the laboratory; that the scientist needs to be concerned immediately with the conditions under which he and his fellow scientists are working and ultimately with the state of society which will permit science to continue to exist' (Bernal, 1939, 397). The outbreak of war stilled the controversy over such assertions, but the fact that they could be made and accepted widely indicated that even before the democratic state was to turn to them for help, many scientists were coming to the view that their commitment to science was inseparable from a commitment to political systems that respected the liberty of inquiry. In itself, this was a significant change from the previous view of science as a politically neutral activity.

WORLD WAR II AND THE
DEVELOPMENT OF THE ATOMIC
BOMB

During World War II, scientific research and technological development both played important roles in the military and non-military aspects of the conflict. Synthetics were developed to substitute for raw materials in short supply. New drugs, notably penicillin, were developed which greatly improved medical treatment of war injuries (Handler, 1970, 637). In the military area, the most intense pressure from governments was for improvements in existing techniques of offense and defense and for new devices which would be of immediate utility on the field of battle. Most wartime research was therefore concentrated on such areas as gunnery, explosives, targeting devices, aeronautical engineering and telecommunications.

In the early stages of the war, scientists and engineers made a vital contribution to the winning of the 'Battle of Britain' through the invention of radar. Radar enabled the outnumbered Royal Air Force to inflict heavy losses on the attacking German Luftwaffe. When the German scientists also developed radar, the Allied scientists countered by introducing techniques capable of 'confusing' the enemy's radar. Especially in the early stages of the air war, the use of radar made a decisive difference in the ability of Britain to defend itself.

Later in the war, German engineers succeeded in developing pilotless missiles, first unguided and then guided, by which the war could be carried to Britain even after the Luftwaffe was forced to concentrate its diminishing resources on the defense of Germany from air attack. Too late to affect the outcome of the war, the Germans also developed the jet-powered aircraft, an invention which was to revolutionize civil and military aeronautics soon afterward.

Almost making one forget the other major accomplishments, the most consequential research project of the war period was the successful effort to develop a nuclear fission or atomic bomb, undertaken by Britain and the United States with the valuable assistance of refugee scientists from Germany and other areas conquered by Germany. The German research made little progress, partly as a result of research errors and partly because of lack of encouragement or pressure from government officials[2] (Irving, 1967). Well after the war had ended with the dropping of the atomic bomb on Hiroshima and Nagasaki, a group of German physicists put out the claim that they had deliberately refrained from providing Hitler with such a destructive weapon in the hope that Allied scientists would exercise a similar restraint (Jungk, 1956). The most prominent of this group, Werner Heisenberg, claimed that early in the war he had travelled to occupied Copenhagen with the intention of broaching an informal moratorium to another distinguished physicist, Niels Bohr, in the hope that Bohr would win the agreement of scientists working for the Allied side (Heisenberg, 1971). Whether because he was too circum-spect in advancing the proposal, or because he may at the time have advanced it merely as one possibility, he succeeded only in intensifying Bohr's fear that German scientists might provide the Nazis with an atomic weapon which would enable them to complete their conquest of the world. Bohr soon escaped to England, where he sounded the alarm among other physicists and helped stimulate the effort to persuade the Allied governments to pursue the atomic weapon, lest Germany achieve it first.

At the urging of a group of refugee scientists, of whom the most famous was Einstein, the American government gave limited encouragement to the scientists involved in the preliminary research. Thanks to significant accom-plishments in Britain and to the success of Enrico Fermi in demonstrating the first atomic chain reaction, this limited support was greatly expanded in the creation of the code-named Manhattan Project. The project eventually cost two billion dollars, an enormous amount, considering that the last peacetime budget called for a total government expenditure of under 1.5 billion dollars for all research and development. Although the project was under military control and the research was 'compartmentalized' to maximize security, the scientists and engineers who worked on it entered into a relationship with the government which in effect subsidized a research effort in which, perforce, only they could determine the pace and the priorities, and which, although it could not be guaranteed to succeed, held out the promise of a quantum jump in weaponry. The pattern set in the Manhattan Project (termed by Nelkin the 'Manhattan Syndrome' in Chapter 11) was to become the basis for the vast growth in support for research and development activities, especially in pursuit of military objectives, which occurred after the war.

The Manhattan Project was also unique in that it was a military project

---

[2] In Japan on the other hand a major effort to develop an atomic bomb seems to have been made but abandoned when the pilot plant was destroyed by an accidental firebomb. See Yagi and Price, 1962 and Weiner, 1977.

designed to be of immediate practical utility but which required scientific as well as technological advances. Many of the scientists who had participated in the project came to feel that inasmuch as the bomb could not have been produced without their cooperation, they had both a special responsibility for what was done with it and the right to a voice in political decisions affecting atomic energy. Some were uneasy because it appeared that the bomb would be used against Japan, now that the war in Europe was virtually over. Having devoted themselves to the production of the weapon in fear that Germany would achieve it first, they felt it was unnecessary to use it against Japan and that to do so could make it impossible to achieve international agreement against the spread of nuclear weapons after the war. These thoughts were summed up in a far-sighted document urging the American government to consider the post-war situation as well as immediate military needs before deciding to use the atomic bomb against Japan (Jungk, 1956, Appendix B).

Efforts to persuade government officials to refrain from using the bomb, except in a technical demonstration, proved fruitless, partly because the scientists appointed to advise the decision makers confessed that they could see no effective alternative to military use. Unknown to the scientists, a secret agreement had been entered into by President Franklin D. Roosevelt and Prime Minister Winston Churchill calling for the use of the weapon against Japan. President Truman, with support of high level advisers, saw no reason to refrain from using it as planned, in view of the casualties which were anticipated in the event an invasion of the Japanese home islands proved necessary to end the war (Dupré and Lakoff, 1962; Hewlett and Anderson, 1962; Sherwin, 1975).

In retrospect, those who made this decision have been criticized for making a momentous decision with unnecessary haste and for taking too narrow a view of the alternatives which might have led just as quickly to a Japanese surrender. The charge has also been made that the decision was made to forestall possible criticism of the government for having spent so much to develop a weapon that was not to be used. It has also been alleged that the bomb was used primarily to preclude the entry of the Soviet Union into the Pacific War and to assert American military power as a warning against efforts to expand communism to Western Europe (Alperovitz, 1965). For the scientists who had acted out of a mixture of scientific challenge and social responsibility in working to produce the bomb, the actual use of the bomb aroused mixed emotions. It had succeeded in ending the war but it had also caused immense human suffering. They now recognized that they had loosed upon the world a weapon of unparalleled destructiveness. Having been frustrated in their attempt to influence the decision to use the bomb, many of the American scientists determined to try to influence the future path of policy with respect to the development of atomic energy.

THE ATOMIC ARMS RACE AND
THE 'SCIENTISTS' MOVEMENT'

With the war over but the atomic bomb a dramatic new reality in the international balance of power, the Societ Union moved to end the Anglo-American monopoly by developing its own atomic weapons. Little is known about the history of this effort, but it can safely be assumed that it was made a matter of high priority, in view of the fact that success was achieved by 1949. Even in France, where the primary concern was reconstruction and recovery, the eventual achievement of atomic weapons was seriously considered. Frédéric Joliot-Curie, Director of the new National Center for Scientific Research, and Raoul Dautry, Minister of Reconstruction in the Provisional Government, tried to persuade the cabinet to underwrite an atomic energy program without delay because of its potential military and economic significance. Minimal support was provided, but it was not until 1958 that a French government finally decided to produce an atomic bomb, in order to achieve a French nuclear strike force that would be free of foreign control (Scheinman, 1965, 5, 212). After France, the People's Republic of China also entered the nuclear club and fears of a virtually uncontrollable spread of nuclear weapons came to seem all too well founded.

Scientists in all the major powers found themselves called upon to assist in programs of nuclear weapons development, and for the most part they responded to such appeals without great objection. At the same time, however, some became actively involved in campaigns to promote international control of dangerous atomic weapons. In the United States, an 'Atomic Scientists' Movement' sprang up shortly after World War II; it was aimed at making the public aware of the great dangers posed by the introduction of nuclear weapons (Alice K. Smith, 1965; Strickland, 1968). The scientists active in this movement argued that the destructiveness of the new weapons was by no means fully appreciated by the military officers and politicians who seemed to think they could continue to pursue policies based on national self-interest and military strength, even though nuclear weapons made war unthinkable and international agreement was an imperative need. During the decade of the 1950's, similar movements appeared in other countries, such as the Committee for Nuclear Disarmament (CND) in Britain, but these European efforts were generally broader in membership than the American movement, which was centered around activistic scientists, and more uniformly committed to the sole objective of unilateral disarmament, a cause in which only a small number of American scientists believed.

Although such movements succeeded in forcing public attention to the issue of nuclear weapons and disarmament, they were greatly overshadowed by the intensification of the Cold War between the communist and non-communist nations of Europe and North America. As a result of this antagonism, atomic arsenals were greatly expanded and the arms race transformed into a race to perfect ever more 'sophisticated' weapons and delivery systems. In 1949, stunned by the loss of the atomic monopoly (which had been accurately predicted by scientists) and fearful that the Soviet Union would now press on to develop a thermonuclear or hydrogen bomb, the American government ordered a 'crash' program to develop the new weapon. The order was given against the advice of a committee of scientific advisers appointed to counsel the Atomic Energy Commission. The committee, headed by J. Robert Oppenheimer, wartime director of the Los Alamos Laboratory where the atomic bomb had been produced, advised against the crash program for technical as well as moral and political reasons. A few years later, the AEC responded to criticisms of Oppenheimer's 'lack of enthusiasm' for the development of a thermonuclear weapon by lifting his security clearance – a move which precipitated a special hearing and a venting of the policy disagreements which had developed within the American scientific community. (Stern, 1969). As these events took place in the United States, with considerable publicity, in the Soviet Union there were similar efforts which came to light only later. Peter Kapitsa refused Premier Stalin's order to work on the atomic bomb and was therefore placed under house arrest. Andrei Sakharov, the prime developer of the Soviet thermonuclear bomb, tried from 1958 to 1962 to persuade the authorities to forego atomospheric nuclear testing, but was rebuffed by Khruschev (Salisbury, 1974, 9-12).

THE EXPANDING SOCIAL ROLE OF
THE SCIENTIST AND TECHNOLOGIST

While military research and development underwent steady expansion by all the major powers, other aspects of science and technology also came to have greater social importance. Some of this was an indirect result of expenditures for military objectives. In the United States and the Soviet Union, which were making the heaviest investments in military research and development, whole industries, especially in such economically important areas as aerospace, atomic energy, communications, and in the case of the United States, com puters, were benefitting considerably. In addition, a significant share of this expenditure has supported the education and training of scientists and engineers. The result was that already by 1962, there were approximately 436,000 scientists and engineers in the United States, 415,000 in the USSR, and only 148,000 in all of Western Europe, which had approximately the same population as the United States (Gilpin, 1968, 27).

These developments convinced politicians in many countries that investments in science and technology, whether military in character or designed to promote economic growth, were indispensable instruments of national security and power. Leading politicians took it as an axiom that 'a nation's power to prosper in peace, survive in war, and command the respect of its neighbors, depends very largely on its degree of scientific and technological advance' (Hogg, 1964, 11-12). The American expenditure of three per cent of Gross National Product for research and development was taken as a target of emulation, on the theory that only by reaching such a level of expenditure could a sustained high rate of economic growth be assured, at a time when such growth required innovation and technologically qualified labor.

This conviction led to a widespread effort, in country after country, to formulate a national science policy and to create a government mechanism, whether through the creation of a minister of state, a ministry, or simply a coordinating or advisory mechanism, which would, in theory, enable the government to make social objectives the basis of allocations for science and technology (See Salomon, Chapter 2). By developing and implementing a national science policy, it was felt, a government would be able to assign priorities to different areas of research and to allocate scarce resources in accordance with national needs.

The discussion of science policy revived an older debate over the merits and demerits of planning in science. The cause of planning had been advocated by Bernal in 1939 on the Marxist ground that science ought to be an instrument of society. In opposition to this view, Michael Polanyi argued that external political interference with the self-determining 'republic of science' would only retard research and infringe upon the freedom of inquiry – a freedom necessary to the success of the effort. A Society for Freedom in Science was created to express the viewpoint stated by Polanyi, but the coming of war mooted the controversy. In recent times, the debate has been renewed as, on the one side, efforts to formulate criteria for the public support of science and to promote a more significant role for government as the coordinator of research activities have gone forward (Shils, 1968); and, on the other, some voices have been raised in criticism of the distortion of research priorities due to governmental support (Nieburg, 1966), and in favor of the 'disestablishment' of science.

This issue has also become entangled with another – the controversy over the assumption that the continuous development of science and technology for the sake of national power and economic growth was to be taken for granted as a necessary and desirable objective. Opposition to the nuclear arms race and the proliferation of nuclear weapons became the focus of one set of objections; concern for the depletion of natural resources and the impact of unlimited technological and economic growth on the finite resources of the earth, as well as in producing over-population, was another (Meadows, 1972; Commoner, 1971). As a result, the concern for the social relationship of science and technology has come to have several different facets. Some of this concern is aimed at promoting a better integration of the two, some at dissolving the partnership or at raising questions about the potential for good or evil inherent in such a partnership.

One certain result of these developments has been the expansion of the role of scientists and technologists in relation to social decision making. Whether as individuals, as members of professional associations, or through their institutional associations, scientists and technologists have come to play — and to be expected to play — a vital role in the identification, discussion and resolution of major social issues in which science and technology are critical components. The nature of the relationship of scientists and technologists to political power has therefore come in for intense scrutiny; some people predict the eventual rule of a scientific elite, others argue that scientists and technologists can have no independent political influence of any significance, but are instead merely agents, witting or otherwise, for other elites or social forces which determine the course of history.

THE SPECTER OF TECHNOCRACY

The most radical hypothesis offered in favor of the view that the growing importance of science and technology must enhance the power of those who pursue and apply knowledge, is embodied in the concept of technocracy. While this hypothesis has by no means won wide endorsement, it has attracted a great deal of popular as well as academic interest. An American physicist turned publicist, Ralph Lipp, has warned that unless the subject is carefully discussed 'we face the real danger of a layered society in which a scientist elite faction floats on top and dominates our policy making. The danger is that a new priesthood of scientists may usurp the traditional roles of democratic decision making' (Lipp, 1965, 3). An American senator has issued a similar warning: 'Faceless technocrats in long, white coats are making decisions today which rightfully and by law should be made by the Congress' (Quoted by Don K. Price, 1964, 57).

However exaggerated such statements may seem, in view of the actual role generally played by scientists and technologists in government today, the argument which lies behind them cannot be entirely dismissed *a priori*. Given a proper statement, the technocracy hypothesis rests on the perception of a tendency, at work in all governments, for those who possess knowledge also to acquire power, as this knowledge becomes the source of power. As a prediction, this hypothesis holds that political functions increasingly tend to devolve upon non-political authorities or, alternatively, that positions of political authority are filled by those with the requisite technical qualifications. Formal systems of authority thus become either facades behind which power is exercised by technocrats, or they become structures which merely serve as legitimate platforms for the exercise of such authority. In effect authority is transferred from those traditionally or nominally vested with it, whether they be appointed or elected, to those capable of exercising it.

Sometimes it is also implied that a technocratic set of values or attitudes accompanies this transformation of real power, which expresses itself in an elevation of technical rationality above all other considerations.

This hypothesis was first advanced in the Nineteenth Century by a number of speculative writers, including especially the French 'prophets of progress' (Manuel, 1962), notably Henri de Saint-Simon and Auguste Comte, his disciple and the founder of sociological positivism. Saint-Simon and Comte held that earlier forms of social and political organization would in time be superseded by a 'positive' or 'scientific' stage of social evolution in which authority would be conferred upon a class of benign public servants, chosen for their superior achievements in pure and applied research; and that these *savants* would supervise the applications of scientific findings to the needs of society. With this transfer of authority from the traditional monarchs and from the more recent folly, as they thought it, of elective parliaments (producing government by collectivities of incompetents), erroneous social policy would be swept away, and human misery with it. Under the aegis of this new public directorate of the enlightened, all sciences including the highest and last to mature, the social sciences (or as Comte preferred, 'social physics') would be brought to fruition and accorded the respect and support due to them as the very foundation of the new and final stage of social history.

The same hypothesis — but this time removed from the larger historical setting into which it had been embedded — was given an indirect restatement by the elite theorists of the early Twentieth Century, notably Gaetano Mosca. Mosca was primarily concerned to show that despite the illusions fostered by a naive acceptance of democratic beliefs, ruling elites were an inevitable feature of every social system. In each recorded instance, he contended, a ruling class has arisen composed of those in whom some particularly valued characteristic had been perfected. This class used its superior ability to dominate the rest of society and then sought to maintain its grip even after the characteristic that had enabled it to attain power ceased to be so highly valued. In modern times, Mosca suggested, technical competence was such a characteristic. 'Specialized knowledge and really scientific culture . . .' he observed, 'become important political forces only in a highly advanced stage of civilization, and only then do they give access to membership in the ruling class to those who possess them' (Mosca, 1939, 59). In Europe and North America, this advanced stage had begun to be reached, and Mosca therefore considered the scientists and engineers whose work was becoming socially important in warfare and in the provision of public services as having already become 'fairly important . . . both socially and politically' (Mosca, 1939, 60).

Mosca's theory depicted the purveyors of knowledge as one set of recruits to the ruling class, but by no means as a group likely to attain decisive control over other elements of the political elite. Like his contemporary, Vilfredo Pareto, Mosca had a conception of a 'circulation of elites', as Pareto called it, whereby changing social needs would render an older group obsolete and raise up a new one – unless the older group were wise enough to 'coopt' the newer one. The American theorist Thorstein Veblen raised the possibility that a conflict might arise between the 'pecuniary' or capitalist class and those he labeled 'the engineers' – a term by which he meant all those who contributed to industry by their work rather than their ownership of wealth (Veblen, 1921). Like Mosca, however, Veblen stopped well short of prophesying a successful revolt of the engineers and their replacement of the property owners; his point was simply that a tension-existed between the two groups which would express itself in a struggle for control.

Others intrigued by the same notion have expressed it in modified form James Burnham, in a book which acquired a certain vogue, suggested that a 'managerial revolution' accompanying the separation of ownership from control would become increasingly intolerable until it led eventually to the rule of the managers, in the corporate economy as well as in government, where the bureaucracy would become the locus of power (Burnham, 1941). More recently, John Kenneth Galbraith has called attention to the existence of 'technostructure' which, he contends, includes the corporate managers who wield effective control over the American economy – a control largely unrestrained by market forces since the corporations manipulate the markets – and their bureaucratic counterparts in government, especially the regulatory commissions, who are in effect allies of the corporate managers. Galbraith does not go so far as to suggest that the power of the technostructure is absolute, but he argues that unless the political system is used to curb the power of the corporate sector, this relatively effective administrative control will be used to promote the interest of privately owned corporations to the detriment of the public interest (Galbraith, 1967).

In these usages, the concept of technocracy has been broadened from its original narrow focus on scientific and technological competence to include administrative ability and position in organizational hierarchies. The same definitional stretching is evident in the most explicit and most extensive effort to formulate and test the hypothesis, the work of Jean Meynaud, which is primarily directed to French experience (Meynaud, 1960). Meynaud came to the conclusion that while technician-administrators were indeed achieving such prominence in government as to make the use of the term technocracy a realistic description, evidence was lacking as yet to support a claim that technocrats were about to 'dethrone' politicians. Because technical specialists lack both the legitimacy and the political resources available to politicians, they are, Meynaud argued, unable fully to supplant them. To this judgment may be added the consideration that technocrats achieved an extraordinary degree of power during the period in which Meynaud did his research because of the 'immobilisme' that paralyzed French politics and created the vacuum into which the technocrats, as the only lasting and stable element in government, inevitably moved. French scientists, moreover, differ from their colleagues in other countries inasmuch as they tend to 'remain aloof from society and its problems' or, if they have political interests, to express these interests by identifying with an ideological tradition rather than by forming political action groups (Gilpin, 1968, 368-370). The French technocrats – like those *anciens polytechniciens* who played an important role in persuading the government to develop nuclear weapons (Scheinman, 1965, 212) – are apt to be technologists rather than scientists and they draw on a correspondingly narrower base of support and prestige.

Meynaud's conclusions concerning the unlikely prospects for 'pure' technocracy were reenforced by another theoretical effort by Don K. Price (1964), based primarily upon American experience and to a lesser extent upon a comparison of the American and British civil services. Price concluded that under modern conditions power is effectively shared by four 'estates'; these are comprised of politicians, administrators, scientists and professionals. Each of the estates is likely to have some influence over the outcome of any particular policy decision, depending upon where it falls along a spectrum running from the pure pursuit of truth at one extreme to the play of political will at the other.

With Meynaud, however, Price concluded that scientists lack the political resources to exercise determining influence whenever the issue turns on political choices rather than technical considerations alone. Unlike Meynaud, however, he also pointed out that in order to deal with conditions of technical complexity, it was inevitable that all governments, whatever their traditional penchant for humanistic amateurism (as in the case of Britain), would be compelled to integrate technical capacity into the political process, with results that would be beneficial, on the whole, from the standpoint of efficient and responsible government. He also pointed out that the fusion of economic and political power brought about by the concern of modern governments for innovation had actually been accompanied by a considerable diffusion of previously centralized authority; the idea that growth in governmental authority necessarily required the growth of a vast, centralized bureaucracy had therefore 'effectively been destroyed' (Don K. Price, 1964, 75).

Other social theorists more concerned with the general structure of authority and with the role of all intellectuals, including scientists, have come to similar conclusions. Thus Talcott Parsons suggests that those who possess the knowledge vital to society become claimants for political power, but he adds that while it is understandable that they should feel a growing concern for social policy and should want a 'right to be heard' in order to exercise influence, it is not at all likely that they will acquire significant control, because their authority arises in a context limited by their special role, and those who enjoy such social authority to do so solely by virtue of their performance in this role. 'In their own right', he suggests, however, 'intellectuals, the more so the "pure" in our sense their cultural specialization, are necessarily *not* among the primary holders of political power or controllers of economic resources' (Parsons, 1969, 19). Similarly, Suzanne Keller, after describing members of the technical professions as belonging to a new 'strategic elite', concluded that this elite was not so indispensable as to be able to claim political power (Keller, 1963).

A recent sociological reconsideration of the technocracy hypothesis has led to a somewhat different conclusion. Daniel Bell suggests (1974) that in the 'post-industrial' stage of social history — a stage defined above all by application of theoretical knowledge to social affairs — the technically competent (above all the theoreticians) can be expected to achieve greater social prominence than ever before. Bell suggests that they will also play an important role in decision making, often in conflict with politicians, and that they will have a special importance because of their command of a new 'intellectual technology' (including the use of computers, simulation techniques, etc.) which is vital to the management of complex organizations. Bell too, however, stops well short of proposing that scientists and technologists are likely to acquire a decisive share of political authority, as have others who have also considered the issue (Brzezinski, 1970; Lane, 1966).

Among theorizers who have been intrigued by the technocracy hypothesis, then, there is certainly no strong consensus in favor of its actual or even potential validity. On the contrary, the general conclusion they draw is that while specialized knowledge is becoming increasingly indispensable in government, scientific or technological expertise is not likely to win for its possessors a decisive share in political power. At most it gives them access to the councils of the decision makers and the opportunity to use this access to exert influence. In no actual society is scientific or technological knowledge considered to be a sufficient source of moral or legal authority, and since the exercise of power entails considerations of group and national interest, as well as representation and legitimacy, there is little reason to expect the rise of outright technocracy. It is another and more open question whether a technocratic attitude may come to prevail which does not imply the rule of experts so much as it does a penchant for technological solutions to social problems (Ferkiss, 1969 and 1974; Habermas, 1969; Marcuse, 1964).

Since the political role of scientists and technologists is not adequately accounted for by the technocracy hypothesis, most empirical investigators tend to shun it and instead concentrate on the political characteristics and functions peculiar to scientists and technologists, as these are demonstrated either in actual experience or in interviews and surveys.

POLITICAL DIMENSIONS:
THE POLITICAL CHARACTERISTICS
OF SCIENTISTS AND TECHNOLOGISTS

It has sometimes been suggested, on occasion by scientists themselves, that the entry of scientists and technologists into the political arena would change the character of politics for the better. Scientists, so it is said, develop certain habits of mind which are all too rarely found in politicians, and which give them a keen concern with facts, objectivity and a logical approach to problem-solving. Presumably, they have little taste for the sort of rhetorical exaggeration that clouds the perception of politicians. Because scientists are trained in the scientific method, it is argued, they are likely to approach all questions, including political ones, with a concern for rigorous definition, for the acquisition of relevant information, and for the development of a course of action (or of alternatives) which will be usable in real-world conditions. Unlike the diplomat, who tends to think there are no solutions but only steps toward a resolution of conflict, a scientist is apt to believe that by the use of reason solutions can be identified, whether or not the parties to a particular conflict will accept them (Schilling, 1964, 154).

Sometimes scientists have described their capacities in terms which make such descriptions seem to be plausible accounts of their own self-estimations. Thus, a scientist employed in the American Manhattan Project observed that 'after the war there will undoubtedly be pressure from political and commercial interests. The only group with real information and no direct bias will be the scientists' (Quoted by Alice K. Smith, 1965, 20). A somewhat more restricted claim, but one which also passes over the possibility of irrationality or bias among scientists, is contained in the statement issued in the Vienna Declaration of the Pugwash Movement: 'Scientists are, because of their special knowledge, well equipped for an early awareness of the danger and promise arising from scientific discoveries. Hence they have a special competence and a special responsibility in relation to the most pressing problems of our times' (Quoted by Salomon, 1970, 158).

Others have sought to explain why this attitude should appear plausible to scientists: 'Among all forms of expertise, that of the scientist seems best equipped to neutralize the element of passion in social debates and to propose purely technical solutions; the scientific method, not the scientific spirit, should be able to reduce the equivocal terms of action involved in conflicts of values to the objective findings of unprejudiced judgment' (Quoted by Salomon, 1970, 161).

Skolnikoff, reflecting on the actual experience of scientists active in government, has described the attitudes which many bring with them and the frustrations they encounter. Often a scientist enters government service 'with a strong sense of optimism that any problem once adequately defined can be solved. At the same time, he may underrate the complexity of the problems and choices facing the government and the difficulty of obtaining solid information on which to base decisions'. He may therefore come to appear naive. He is apt to be annoyed by 'fuzzy and imprecise political constraints' since he is used to examining a problem 'on its merits'. The same 'desire for objectivity and simple rationality carried over from science also tends to lead to impatience with the delays of political in-fighting' and a reluctance to compromise. The scientist will tend to want to comprehend an entire problem and not be satisfied with a narrow technical issue; he will emphasize quantifiable techniques in describing and resolving a problem — for better or for worse (Skolnikoff, 1967, 241-243).

These characteristics may well predispose all scientists to exhibit certain tendencies in their political behavior, but they are by no means the only determining characteristics. Whenever technical considerations merge with political considerations, the values and biases of scientists will come into play as much as they will in the case of politicians. Studies of the political attitudes of scientists and technologists have shown a considerable variation. One study showed a significant distribution along a liberal-conservative axis which correlates with intellectual orientation and disciplinary affiliation. Theorizers tend to be more liberal, possibly because they are intellectually disposed to favor innovation and reform, while applied researchers and engineers, who rely in their work on the exploitation of the tried and true, tend to be conservative in their political views. Another possible explanation which seems to fit the data is that the more academic the scientific work, the less its practitioners are apt to be committed to the preservation of the status quo; and conversely, the more practical the work, the more its practitioners come to feel they depend upon the maintenance of an existing social system (Ladd and Lipset, 1972; for other studies and more detail see Fisch, Chapter 8).

Another important source of bias is institutional and vocational affiliation. A researcher employed by a company producing chemical pesticides is apt to share the perspective of his employer in controversies involving the safety of such pesticides. A researcher working for a government regulatory agency is likely to take the view that a new drug must first be proved safe before it is authorized for use, whereas a doctor anxious to be able to prescribe a drug which may help a patient will probably be more concerned with the efficacy of the drug against a disease than with unknown and long-range dangerous side-effects.

For such reasons, although for some purposes it is useful to think of scientists as sharers in a common culture (Snow, 1964), or as members of a single community (Haberer, 1969), or as adherents to a set of norms (Storer, 1966), for political purposes it is well to bear in mind the cross pressures that operate when scientists and technologists must function as experts involved with the resolution of policy questions.

THE POLITICAL FUNCTIONS OF
SCIENTISTS AND TECHNOLOGISTS

Scientists and technologists become involved in policy questions in three principal modes: as advocates of support for research and higher education, as advisers to government agencies, and as adversaries debating public questions in which technical issues are critical components. Each of these modes poses a different set of opportunities and constraints.

A. As Advocates of Support   As public funds become the single largest source of support not only for pure and applied research but in many cases also for industrial development, scientists and technologists inevitably are enlisted in the effort to seek such support. They become advocates on behalf of their particular research or on behalf of research and education generally. Professional organizations formed to serve the interests of scientists in particular disciplines generally resist 'politicization' except in connection with activities aimed at enhancing the position of their members as professionals. In this limited sense, they too perform an advocacy function (Nichols, 1974; Rich, 1974).

An interesting case in point is provided by the pioneering efforts to organize scientists in Britain. Early in 1917, a small group of politically committed scientists formed the National Union of Scientific Workers, aiming to radicalize the scientific profession. As the group's manifesto observed: 'One of the main reasons why Science does not occupy its proper place in the national life is that scientific workers do not exercise in the political and industrial world an influence commensurate with their importance'. But the union developed a classic problem that often affects organizations of workers, especially professional workers. Some members wanted it to serve strictly as a professional association, whereas others envisioned it as a platform for addressing larger social and political issues in which the membership had only an indirect and remote interest, indeed, many leaders who have since become well known were inspired by this opportunity. In 1927 the organization was renamed the Association of Scientific Workers and the constitution was changed so as to distinguish it from a trade union and to state its purpose to be the improvement of working conditions and relations between workers and employers. Just before World War II it was the focus for the great 'Planning of Science' debates in which Bernal and others first promoted the new science policy views. By 1942, however, the organization became a trade union and, abandoning radical policies, merged into a much larger Association of Scientific, Technical and Managerial Staffs (Rose and Rose, 1970, 52).

The self-interested role of scientists and technologists becomes perhaps most evident in the case of activities aimed at achieving public support for research which they themselves would like to carry out. When private industry is to carry out such research, the same self-interest may well be intense. Some who have sought such support have been criticized as 'hard sell technologists' who have persuaded legislators that they can purchase national security by supporting the development of more advanced weapon systems (York, 1970, 11). Such scientists and technologists may readily be classified by lobbyists, especially when they make common cause with labor unions and localities in order to bring pressure to bear to provide such support as a way of providing employment and other economic benefits for a region.

But the same classification can also be made, in some instances, with respect to 'pure' researchers (Weingart, 1970). In discussing the campaign by scientists to win public support for an expensive particle accelerator, a high energy physicist remarked that it was commonly observed among scientists that 'scientific research is the only pork barrel [an American term for the distribution of political patronage] for which the pigs determine who gets the pork' (Quoted by Greenberg, 1967, 151). Scientists have made plausible arguments with respect to the need for the support of basic research, but one sympathetic critic has observed of this discussion: 'Too much of what scientists have said comes down to sophisticated special pleading for university-based research, or for special disciplines' (Reagan, 1969, 70). He points out that the scientific community has been very reluctant to make interfield comparisons so as to face up to the priority problem in the allocation of research funds. It is arguable, to cite another example, that the preference of scientists for institutional support rather than project support is, in part at least, an effort to wrest control of those funds from the granting agencies. When scientists argue the merits of institutional and project support, they are usually well aware that one type of support is probably more beneficial to researchers at the leading institutions, while the other is more distributive. For such reasons, even such a presumably disinterested organization as the American National Academy of Sciences has been described as a 'self-serving advocate' (Boffey, 1975, 83).

Although research expenditures are not likely to be determined by arguments offered by scientists in support of research subsidies, a realistic and candid appraisal of the lobbying role of scientists must also take into account their inclination to support or tolerate programs which may confer indirect benefits upon science. Two cases in point are the American space program and the Anglo-French Concorde project. If scientists and engineers were inclined to avoid political entanglements and to concentrate on attaining direct support of science and engineering, they might have taken very different public positions on these projects. Many American scientists and engineers did not criticize the manned lunar landing project, even though at least some of them opposed the project as wasteful. Many were inhibited from campaigning against the project by the belief that the support generated by the space program would be beneficial to science. It was also argued that such programs, by dramatizing the social value of science, would serve to generate a climate in which other projects would be supported.

The SST project was in fact actively opposed by many American scientists, who feared not only that it would have adverse effects on the environment but that if the government were to support this 'big science' project, it would be unable and unwilling to support others. In Britain and France, on the other hand, scientists and engineers who had complained about the low level of research funding, were apparently prepared to accept funding for the SST on the ground that without such a pretext it would not be forthcoming. Scientists and technologists, in other words, have learned the political lesson that to secure public support they must be able to persuade the politicians and the public that there are direct and immediate benefits attached to the support; and they have been willing to act on this maxim.

B. As Advisers When scientists and technologists become advisers to government agencies, the conflict becomes obvious between their perception of themselves as objective analysts, engaged in transferring the scientific method to the political realm, and the nature of their other political characteristics. In every modern state, the giving of advice by scientists and technologists is now routine in virtually every aspect of governmental activity. In the United States fifteen hundred scientists serve on tens of committees and panels (National Academy of Sciences, 1972). Formally such committees are appointed to provide administrators, policy makers and legislators with the technical counsel that the experts alone can provide. In reality, the line between the technical judgment and the policy judgment of such advisers may be difficult if not impossible to draw. 'The tendency to expand their role beyond that of purely technical advice into political, financial and organizational spheres' has been criticized, 'but this tendency is inherent in the nature of scientific advising' (Brooks, 1964, 84).

Scientists and technologists who have served as advisers on matters of defense policy in the United States have often found it impossible to separate the technical from the political aspects of the problems with which they were asked to deal, and as a result they have been compelled to make judgments that extend well beyond mere technical competence. 'Most often, they were dealing not with hard technical facts, but with expectations, judgments and uncertainties about science and technology, all of which could alter significantly the nature of a political action' (Skolnikoff, 1967, 231).

Similarly, studies of the role of American scientists in the nuclear test ban negotiations have found that while scientists may assume that they are strictly objective and dispassionate (Gilpin, 1964, 4), in reality their attitudes and behavior reflected 'differing views over the questions of Western military strategy, the motivation of the Soviet Union, and the political desirability of a nuclear test ban' (Gilpin, 1962, 279). Others who have examined similar negotiations have come to the same conclusion (Uyehara, 1966; Jacobson and Stein, 1966).

Well aware of the pitfalls of seeking advice from those they cannot directly control, politicians are apt to make appointments to committees with the inclinations of the members in mind. Indeed, the reason for the appointment of scientific advisory committees is not always simply to acquire information. A committee may be appointed essentially to provide legitimacy for a decision which has all but finally been reached in advance (Reiser, 1966, 295). The authority of scientific advisers 'can be used by policy makers in order to depersonalize and relinquish responsibility for unpopular decisions' or to manipulate the timing of promulgation of a decision (Ezrahi, 1974).

Politicians anxious to avoid such accusations, make a special effort to appoint committees whose membership reflects a balance of viewpoints, whether in terms of political ideology or perspective on a particular issue. Such an effort, however, runs counter to the normal tendency of politicians to attempt to build support for the position that they have chosen in advance. Another way of avoiding the accusation is to delegate the power to appoint an advisory committee to a scientific institution, which is presumably unbiased and not beholden to the particular politician requesting the assistance. Even in such cases, however, the evidence suggests that a tacit coherence may develop between the bias of the politician (or of an agency) and that of the leadership of the institution, particularly when the institution comes to depend upon a continuing relationship with the politician or agency.

Scientists who take positions, whether as members of such committees or in direct public expressions which run counter to the wishes of politicians, may risk certain effective forms of retaliation. They may be blacklisted by government agencies and refused further appointments; in some cases, they or their institutions may be denied public support because of the outspoken views they have expressed. When, in other words, the scientific process is not insulated against the full force of political controversy and its normal outcomes, the involvement of scientists in decision making can have harmful repercussions on the research process, and it may at times compromise the scientists who enter it.

C. As Adversaries   Controversy among scientists over scientific questions is hardly new, and it may be said to be a necessity for progress, when what is at stake is the validity of a theory or a particular finding. While a discipline is still not mature or when there are 'major unresolved uncertainties' (Ezrahi, 1974, 222), controversies will be difficult to resolve, since standards are not well established and authorities do not command the respect of the qualified. A case in point is the controversy generated by the cosmological theories of Immanuel Velikovsky, which, while they are held to be unscientific by the great majority of astronomers, nevertheless have defenders among qualified scientists. In more recent times, however, scientists have become adversaries not only over scientific questions but over scientific questions which have a bearing on social policy, and this is a relatively new phenomenon. Many examples come to mind, including the controversy over the effects of tobacco smoking upon health, the effects of pesticides, the safety of nuclear power, and the link between genetics and intelligence (For further instances and general discussion, see Nelkin, Chapter 11).

In controversies of this kind, scientists inevitably enter the political arena, since the positions they take are intended to influence public opinion and governmental policy. In the United States, adversarial politics involving scientists and technologists have found a particularly hospitable environment. One important reason for this is the separation of powers that characterizes the American system of government. Since the legislature is independent of the executive and jealous of its powers, it often functions as a watchdog and critic of the executive. This is especially pronounced when the executive and the legislature are controlled by different political parties. Because of this inherent conflict between the two branches, scientists and technologists denied a hearing in the executive are often welcome to take their grievance to the legislature. Congressional committees anxious to catch the executive in mistakes will readily provide a platform from which dissenters can address the public and seek redress from Congress.

In one important instance, however, the American system has not functioned in this way, because a deliberate effort was made to abridge the principle of the separation of powers. In the single case of atomic energy, the Congress decided to create a Joint Committee which would have close ties to the Atomic Energy Commission, the executive agency charged with administering both civil and military activities in this field (Green and Rosenthal, 1963). Because the relationship of the committee and the commission did in fact become extremely intimate, critics charged that the committee was incapable of performing the Congressional oversight function. As Ralph Nadar put it, rather than a watchdog the committee had become the Siamese twin of the AEC (Lakoff, 1974, 594). As a result, this particular committee was not as hospitable to scientists critical of AEC policy as it might have been if it had functioned more in accordance with the principle of the separation of powers.

In more general terms, it would seem highly likely that scientists and technologists will become active in the adversary mode in all parliamentary systems of government, for the reason that more and more controversial issues of public concern are coming to involve technical questions. In principle, however, there would seem to be a serious conflict between the scientific mode of establishing truth and the adversarial mode. The adversarial mode originates in judicial proceedings, where the aim is to adjudicate claims rather than to establish truth by the method of logical deduction and experimental validation. An adversarial system 'is directed primarily toward power, i.e. the assertion of claims and the influencing of decision outcomes' (Mayo, 1969, 20). The result is that the style of the lawyer differs considerably from that of the scientist: 'Scientific truth is established by objective demonstration and confirmed by replication; political truth is established by consensual agreement, usually after an "adversary contest" ' (Quoted by Mayo, 1969, 23).

In some cases, the adversarial contest takes place in courtrooms where procedures are strictly defined. Even in such relatively ideal settings, however, it will be no easy matter for laymen to decide between scientists and technologists whose expert testimony produces contradictory estimates. Still more difficult for laymen to judge are controversies which take place, so to speak, in the court of public opinion, where there are no rules regarding the validity of evidence or permitting cross-examination; where only the professional responsibility of the expert serves as a restraint upon misrepresentations. A case in point, which has been well analyzed in these terms, is the debate which took place in the United States during the late 1960's over the installation of anti-ballistic missiles (ORSA, 1971; Cahn, 1971).

While the inquiry generated in this case was in no way definitive of the issues at stake, it points up a number of the problems associated with the role of scientists as adversaries in matters where technical and political controversies are intertwined. When the adversary process is carried from the courtroom, where it is bound by strict rules of procedure designed to protect the integrity of the process, to the court of public opinion, substitute rules need to be developed if the result is to meet a standard of fairness and adequacy. Otherwise, the side of the debate which is best able to manipulate opinion will carry the contest, regardless of the soundness of its viewpoint. In non-judicial proceedings, special efforts must be made to assure that both sides have the same access to public opinion and that neither can make misstatements of facts and judgments of possibilities which are not subject to rebuttal. In legislative hearings, it may be advisable to change the ordinary techniques for taking testimony to assure that expert witnesses in conflict confront each other directly and are made subject to a modified form of cross-examination (Mazur, 1973).

The role of scientists and technologists as adversaries also raises the larger question of the moral and social responsibilities which must weigh upon them as their work becomes consequential in virtually every area of social concern, from matters of defense policy to the applications of biomedical research.

SCIENTISTS, TECHNOLOGISTS AND SOCIAL RESPONSIBILITY

While some scientists and technologists may consider that they are discharging their social responsibilities by providing society with the fruits of their labor, or with their service as advisers to government agencies and their participation in the debate of public issues, it has lately been argued that the social responsibility of the pursuer of knowledge extends further than these activities alone. Since the character of research is bound to be influenced by the aims of its supporters, much science and technology will be devoted to the purposes of government and industry, at times to the detriment of society. Since governments are likely to have a short-sighted interest in the expansion of power and prosperity, and industry in the increase of profits, simply to do research for such sponsors and to respond to problems they raise is not to behave in a socially responsible way. Instead, it is argued, scientists must devote themselves to 'critical science' (Ravetz, 1971, 424, and Chapter 3) or to 'science in the public interest' (Primack and von Hippel, 1974, Nelkin, Chapter 11).

A good example of what those who take this point of view have in mind is the problem of protecting the environment from the harmful effects of new technologies. Since governments and industries are anxious to develop and exploit new technologies, they tend to be neglectful of the environmental impact of these technologies. Only if scientists initiate research on such matters and bring the results to public attention will the potential dangers of new technologies become so evident as to compel regulation and control. Rachel Carson's lonely crusade against the indiscriminate use of chemical pesticides met at first with indifference and hostility from the only government agencies concerned, whose primary responsibility was the promotion of agricultural productivity; and it met with powerfully financed opposition from the large corporations which profited from the manufacture of the chemicals. Only as she was able, with the help of other researchers and environmentalist groups, to challenge the existing regulations in the courts and to arouse public opinion did she eventually succeed.

Proponents of the need for critical science argue plausibly that to depend upon such lonely crusades is to depend upon the unlikely chance that in every case likely to result in social injury, a scientist will have the insight, the gifts and the persistance of a Rachel Carson — as well as the good fortune she had in raising the pesticide issue just as concern for the environment was becoming widespread. It would be better, they suggest, to institutionalize the critical review of new technologies, a process now underway in certain places. 'Instead of isolated individuals sacrificing their leisure and interrupting their regular research for engagement in practical problems, we now see the emergence of scientific schools of a new sort. In them, collaborative research of the highest quality is done, as part of practical projects involving the discovery, analysis and criticism of the different sorts of damage inflicted on man and nature by runaway technology, followed by their public exposure and campaigns for their abolition'. Cited as examples are the research undertaken on the environment at Washington University in Saint Louis, and that undertaken by scientists associated both with the American and British Society for Social Responsibility in Science (Ravetz, 1971, 424).

The proponents of critical science tend to assume that the socially responsible tactic for scientists concerned with the public interest is to attempt to appraise proposals of new technology in order to generate resistance against those which threaten harm. Such an approach, however, is apt to be regarded as entirely negativistic, unless it is supplemented by an effort of 'positive science' in the public interest – research, in other words, which aims at proposing feasible alternatives (such as the substitution of biological and species-specific pesticides for the indiscriminate use of highly toxic chemicals).

The approach may also err in assuming that governments and industry are inherently anxious to develop all new technologies, regardless of their ultimate social harm, and that no reliance can be placed upon measures they might take to weigh potential benefit and harm. In fact, however, governments have responded to precisely the sort of criticism that is behind the campaign for critical science, or for science in the public interest, by strengthening the agencies charged with the regulation of new drugs and other medical technologies, by creating new agencies responsible for promoting arms control (so as to remove the subject from the control of the defense agencies), and by supporting environmental protection. These measures may indicate that the objective of protecting the public interest may also be served by integrating balancing agencies into the structure of government itself.

A still more general effort of this kind is involved in the movement for 'technological assessment', or the effort to forecast the likely social consequences of new technologies (See Nelkin, Chapter 11). As governments institute procedures for attaining such assessments, a source of support becomes available for research on such topics. Provided that the solicitation of the research and the presentation of the results are insulated from political interference, the procedure could have far-reaching effects in assuring a balanced approach. The trouble with it, of course, is that because the support for such an approach must come from the government itself, and because the administrators of the process are responsible to the government, they may be reluctant to sponsor studies which could prove embarrassing to the government. For this reason, independent sources of such research will remain important, even if governments do commit themselves to serious efforts in technology assessment. Intermediate institutions, notably the universities, standing between government and private industry, could have a major role to play in this regard. In the international context, organizations like the Stockholm Institute for International Peace Research and the Pugwash Conferences have a similar value.

Organizations which are formally independent of government agencies but dependent upon them for research support are inevitably in a difficult position. Non-profit advisory organizations like the Rand Corporation in the United States are bound to be torn between a desire to maintain their critical independence of governmental agencies and at the same time to continue to receive support from those agencies and remain in a position to influence policy (B. L. R. Smith, 1966). Diversification of support is essential for such independence to be maintained. Different measures have been found necessary by the United States National Academy of Sciences – National Research Council, which has instituted a system to review committee reports, and which has taken other steps to assure that these reports are drawn up by scientists either not directly interested in the outcome or whose potential conflicts of interest are made known (Boffey, 1975, 251).

Another problem that arises when scientists leave the laboratory for the public arena is that they are tempted to trade upon their scientific reputations in order to pronounce on subjects for which they may have little or no technical qualification. No law can or should prevent a Nobel laureate in biology from denouncing his country's foreign policy as sheer madness or another Nobel laureate in physics from insisting that the white race is inherently more intelligent than the black, yet the fact is that their status in science gives the views of such figures a prominence that they would not otherwise deserve on grounds of scholarly competence. Scientists who claim a special authority to pronounce on public matters related to their technical field of specialization have a corresponding obligation not to abuse the privilege they claim by extending it beyond the proper limit. As Derek Price has observed, 'Hurt as it might, one must admit some truth to the platitude that the scientist outside his chosen discipline reverts to the status of laymen' (1966, 247). He is of course not only a layman but also a citizen – and it is this last fact which may well create difficulties, for if he is overly inhibited, he will invite the criticism that he is morally indifferent or politically irresponsible.

It is certainly understandable that scientists should feel a special responsibility to bring public attention to the moral and social consequences they see flowing from their work. They may even have an obligation to desist from a line of inquiry, as Julius Stone suggests, 'as soon as it becomes clear that it is likely to bring about a mankind-endangering situation which no one has any foreseeable capacity to handle' (1974). Even excellent scientists have human failings, however. They may not be able to foresee the dangers that may conceivably flow from their work, or they may not be able to weigh the benefits of it against the dangers. A nuclear physicist who has himself warned of the dangers of atomic radiation notes tartly that 'among scientists and technologists there are many who are enthusiastic environmentalists and ecologists for all technologies but their own' (Gofman, 1971, 30). A leading scientific administrator has challenged the contention that a scientist's technical expertise gives him any extraordinary insight into political questions: 'Those scientists who feel that they shoulder a special social responsibility, because scientific knowledge is the root of the technological changes which transform the social and political environment, have to decide themselves how to deal with their sense of moral obligation. But they enjoy no special franchise in the public world. Because they are trained, or assumed to be trained, to search for objective truth, they are not necessarily better able to define the best ways to reach the goals of social justice than are other men' (Zuckerman, 1971, 2). The claim that because scientists have 'the future in their bones' they and they alone must make the 'cardinal decisions' (Snow, 1962) has been derided by at least one professional strategist, who contends that almost no scientist 'has been regularly successful at foreseeing future technologies' and that the specialized knowledge of scientists does not extend to the comprehensive approach necessary in the formulation of policies (Wohlstetter, 1964, 228).

The actual experience of scientists and technologists in politics, then, although it is fraught with problems for conscientious scientists and for laymen as well (who must often decide upon the basis of contradictory expert testimony), does not suggest that in an era in which science and technology are critical social concerns, politics can be expected to undergo a radical transformation. There is as yet no evidence that technocracy is the 'wave of the future', even if there is ample evidence of occasional conflict between technical experts and responsible politicians. In democratic systems of government, public decisions are influenced by a variety of factors. Among these are public opinion, the will of significant interest groups, and the judgment of elected officials, administrators and entire branches of government. Scientists and technologists are likely to have a significant impact in shaping the views of those who make decisions; but except in rare cases, where the matter at issue is entirely or almost entirely a matter of scientific judgment, the views of scientists are not likely to determine the outcome exclusively. The diversity of opinions and interests among scientists makes it all but impossible for them to constitute a coherent pressure group for any policy other than the support of science, and even on this score they are apt to have divided counsel. If there is somewhat less diversity among the leading members of the scientific and technological professions, the diversity is still great enough to assure the failure of any attempt to construe them as an actually or potentially homogenous political movement.

Insofar as most political decisions, especially those having domestic applications, reflect the interplay of interested groups, scientists and technologists can serve a particularly useful social role in articulating policy alternatives and contributing to public debate. Even when they identify themselves with interested groups, but especially when they speak out independently, they contribute to the strengthening of the adversary process which lies at the heart of the parliamentary system of government. There can be no guarantee that even informed and enlightened political leaders will make wise decisions, but it is surely better for society to have the best and fullest advice from experts in all fields, even if the advice is rife with contradiction, than for scientists and technologists to be treated as mere instruments for the carrying out of political decisions. Such a policy has a double default: political leaders may make costly mistakes, out of ignorance of technical possibilities and limitations; and scientists and technologists may refuse to render their best services to society, out of a sense of alienation. Since conscience cannot be institutionalized, the best hope for social responsibility in science and technology rests with the practitioners themselves. The individual scientist and technologist has been well described symbolically as 'the Prometheus of the modern world', of whom it can be said that 'whether he likes it or not, his vocation hurls him into the political arena; the pure sky of theory, indifferent to the contingencies of history, belongs in an age of science which has been swept away by its own operational inefficiency' (Salomon, 1970, 227).

EPILOGUE: KNOWLEDGE AND POWER IN SCHOLARLY PERSPECTIVE

In this chapter, as in the others in this volume, an effort has been made to review both what is known and thought about the political experience of scientists and the literature in which this knowledge is recorded. In reviewing this literature, it is hard not to be struck by its diversity. It includes speculation about the changing structural trends in society and politics which result from the growing importance of science and technology as forces in history; studies of the actual role of scientists and technologists in particular decisions; examination of the advisory mechanisms used in various governments; surveys of the political attitudes of scientists and technologists, and examinations of the problems of conscience, both in principle and in practice, which arise for scientists and technologists. It is of course also striking that so much of the literature concerns American experience — though the predominance of this material in the chapter no doubt also reflects the author's greater familiarity with this experience.

The diversity is probably inevitable and enriching; the preponderance of American material registers the intensity of the American involvement with science and technology and also the character of American politics, in which, as de Tocqueville was the first to note, voluntary associations of all sorts play an important role. Scientists and technologists have become involved in politics in America to a degree and in a variety of ways that may be unique, or perhaps an indication of what is to happen elsewhere in the near future. In any case, the literature would be richer, and the opportunities for comparative study much improved, if more of the investigations were made with respect to other political systems and with the native's appreciation for their nuances. Case studies of conflicts among scientists or between scientists and government agencies would be particularly helpful.

Although this literature is already so sizable as to warrant the conclusion that the field of study, although comparatively new, is well established, there is still reason for caution on this score. It is difficult to know with certainty whether the problems posed by advances in science and technology will compel significant and long lasting changes in domestic and international political systems, or whether any changes will prove to be temporary; and whether, even if such changes do take place, they will be reflected in the particular roles of scientists and technologists or in much broader effects, such as in growing international interdependence (See Skolnikoff, Chapter 14) or the increasing importance of bureaucratic organization. It is essential for future research in this area to emphasize this broader perspective. There is urgent need to integrate the diverse approaches to the study of scientists, technologists and power.

BIBLIOGRAPHY

Alperovitz, 1965 — Alperovitz, G., *Atomic Diplomacy,* New York, Simon and Schuster, 1965.

Bell, 1973 — Bell, D., *The Coming of Post-Industrial Society: A Venture in Social Forecasting,* New York, Basic Books, 1973.

Benveniste, 1972 — Benveniste, G., *The Politics of Expertise,* Berkeley, California, Glendessary Press, 1972.

Bernal, 1967 — Bernal, J. D., *The Social Function of Science,* London, Routledge and Kegan Paul, 1939. Reissued by MIT Press, Cambridge, Mass., in 1967.

Birkenhead, 1962 — Birkenhead, The Earl of, *The Professor and the Prime Minister: The Official Life of Professor F. A. Lindemann, Viscount Cherwell,* Boston, Houghton Mifflin, 1962.

Blissett, 1972 — Blissett, M., *Politics in Science,* Boston, Little Brown, 1972.

Boffey, 1975 — Boffey, P. M., *The Brain Bank of America: An Inquiry into the Politics of Science,* New York, McGraw Hill Book Company, 1975.

Brooks, 1964 — Brooks, H., 'The Scientific Adviser', in Gilpin, R. and Wright, C. (Eds.), *Scientists and National Policy Making,* New York, Columbia University Press, 1964, pp. 73-76.

Brooks, 1968 — Brooks, H., *The Government of Science,* Cambridge, Mass., MIT Press, 1968.

Brown, 1971 — Brown, M. (Ed.), *The Social Responsibility of the Scientist,* New York, The Free Press, 1971.

Brzezinski, 1970 — Brzezinski, Z. K., *Between Two Ages: America's Role in the Technetronic Era,* New York, Viking Press, 1970.

Burnham, 1941 — Burnham, J., *The Managerial Revolution,* New York, Day, 1941.

Cahn, 1971   Cahn, A. H., *Eggheads and Warheads: Scientists and the ABM,* Cambridge, Mass., Science and Public Policy Program, MIT, 1971.

Caldwell, 1968   Caldwell, L. K., *Science, Technology and Public Policy: A Selected and Annotated Bibliography,* 3 Vols., Bloomington, Indiana, Indiana University, 1968.

Clark, 1965   Clark, R. W., *Tizard,* Cambridge, Mass., MIT Press, 1965.

Cohen, 1948   Cohen, I. B., *Science: Servant of Man,* Boston, Little Brown, 1948.

Commoner, 1971   Commoner, B., *The Closing Circle: Nature, Man and Technology,* New York, Knopf, 1971.

DeBeer, 1960   DeBeer, G., *The Sciences Were Never At War,* London, Thomas Nelson and Sons, 1960.

Doern, 1972   Doern, G. B., *Science and Politics in Canada,* Montreal, McGill and Queen's University Press, 1972.

Dupré and Lakoff, 1962   Dupré, J. S. and Lakoff, S. A., *Science and the Nation: Policy and Politics,* Englewood Cliffs, New Jersey, Prentice Hall, 1962.

Eitzen and Maravell, 1968   Eitzen, S. and Maravell, G., 'The Political Party Affiliations of College Professors', *Social Forces* 47, December 1968, pp. 145-153.

Ellul, 1964   Ellul, J., *La Téchnique ou l'enjeu du siècle,* Paris, Librairie Armand Colin, 1954. Translated as *The Technological Society,* New York, Knopf, 1964.

Ezrahi, 1971   Ezrahi, Y., 'The Political Resources of American Science', *Science Studies,* April 1971, pp. 1, 2, 117-133.

Ezrahi, 1974   Ezrahi, Y., 'The Authority of Science in Politics', in Thackray, A. and Mendelsohn, E. (Eds.), *Science and Values,* New York, Humanities Press, 1974.

Ferkiss, 1969   Ferkiss, V., *Technological Man: The Myth and the Reality,* New York, Braziller, 1969.

Ferkiss, 1974   Ferkiss, V., *The Future of Technological Civilization,* New York, Braziller, 1974.

Frutkin, 1965   Frutkin, A. W., *International Cooperation in Space,* Englewood Cliffs, New Jersey, Prentice Hall, 1965.

Galbraith, 1967   Galbraith, J. K., *The New Industrial State,* Boston, Houghton Mifflin, 1967.

Gilpin, 1962   Gilpin, R., *American Scientists and Nuclear Weapons Policy,* Princeton, New Jersey, Princeton University Press, 1962.

Gilpin, 1968   Gilpin, R., *France in the Age of the Scientific State,* Princeton, New Jersey, Princeton University Press, 1968.

Gofman, 1971   Gofman, J., 'Nuclear Power and Ecocide: An Adversary View of New Technology', *Bulletin of the Atomic Scientist* 27, 1971, pp. 28-32.

Gofman and Tamplin, 1971   Gofman, J. W. and Tamplin, A. R., Toward an Adversary System of Scientific Inquiry, in *Poisoned Power: The Case Against Nuclear Power Plants,* Emmaeus, Pennsylvania, Rodale Press, 1971, Chapter 12.

Goldsmith and MacKay, 1966   Goldsmith, M. and MacKay, A. (Eds.), *The Science of Science,* Harmondsworth, England, Pelican, 1966.

Green and Rosenthal, 1963   Green, H. P. and Rosenthal, A., *Government of the Atom,* New York, Atherton Press, 1963.

Greenberg, 1967   Greenberg, D. S., *The Politics of Pure Science,* New York, New American Library, 1967.

Haberer, 1969   Haberer, J., *Politics and the Community of Science,* New York, Van Nostrand Reinhold, 1969.

Habermas, 1969   Habermas, J., *Technik und Wissenschaft als "Ideologie",* Frankfurt am Main, Suhrkamp, 1969.

Handler, 1970   Handler, P. (Ed.), *Biology and the Future of Man,* New York, Oxford University Press, 1970.

Heisenberg, 1971   Heisenberg, W., *Physics and Beyond: Encounters and Conversations,* tr. by Pomerans, A. J., New York, Harper and Row, 1971.

Hewlett and Anderson, 1962   Hewlett, R. G. and Anderson, O. E. Jr., *The New World, 1939-1946,* University Park, The Pennsylvania State University Press, 1962.

Hogg, 1964   Hogg, Q. M., *Science and Politics,* Chicago, Encyclopedia Britannica Press, 1964.

Huxley, 1958   Huxley, A., *Brave New World Revisited,* New York, Harper and Row, 1958.

Irving, 1967   Irving, D., *The German Atomic Bomb: The History of Nuclear Research in Nazi Germany,* New York, Simon and Schuster, 1967.

Jacobson and Stein, 1966   Jacobson, H. K. and Stein, E., *Diplomats, Scientists and Politicians,* Ann Arbor, University of Michigan Press, 1966.

Jones, 1966   Jones, R. V., 'Scientists and Statesmen: The Example of Henry Tizard', *Minerva* 4, 1966.

Joravsky, 1961   Joravsky, D., *Soviet Marxism and Natural Science 1917-1932,* New York, Columbia University Press, 1961.

Joravsky, 1970   Joravsky, D., *The Lysenko Affair,* Cambridge, Mass., Harvard University Press, 1970.

Jungk, 1956   Jungk, R., *Heller aus tausend Sonnen,* Bern, Alfred Scherz Verlag, 1956, tr. by Cleugh, J. as *Brighter than a Thousand Suns.*

Keller, 1963   Keller, S., *Beyond the Ruling Class: Strategic Elites in Modern Society,* New York, Random House, 1963.

King and Melanson, 1972   King, L. R. and Melanson, P., 'Knowledge and Politics', *Public Policy* 20, Winter 1972, pp. 82-101.

Ladd and Lipset, 1972   Ladd, E. C. and Lipset, M. S., 'Politics of Academic Natural Scientists and Engineers', *Science* 176, 9 June 1972, pp. 1091-1100.

Lakoff, 1966   Lakoff, S. A., 'The Third Culture: Scientists in Social Thought', in Lakoff, S. A. (Ed.), *Knowledge and Power,* New York, The Free Press, 1966.

Lakoff, 1974   Lakoff, S. A., 'Congress and National Science Policy', *Political Science Quarterly* 89, Fall 1974, pp. 589-611.

Lane, 1966   Lane, R. E., 'The Decline of Politics and Ideology in a Knowledgeable Society', *American Sociological Review* 31, 1966, pp. 649-662.

Lapp, 1965	Lapp, R., *The New Priesthood: The Scientific Elite and Uses of Power,* New York, Harper and Row, 1965.
Leiserson, 1965	Leiserson, A., 'Scientists and the Policy Process', *American Political Science Review* 59, 1965, pp. 408, 418.
Marcuse, 1964	Marcuse, H., *One-Dimensional Man: Studies in the Ideology of Advanced Industrial Society,* Boston, Beacon Press, 1964.
Mayo, 1969	Mayo, L. H., 'Scientific Method, Adversarial System and Technology Assessment', Monograph No. 5, Washington, D. C., Program of Policy Studies in Science and Technology, 1969.
Mazur, 1973	Mazur, A., 'Disputes Between Experts', *Minerva* 11, April 1973.
Meadows *et al.,* 1972	Meadows, D. H., Meadows, D. L., Randers, J. and Behrens, W. W. III, *The Limits to Growth,* New York, Universe Books, 1972.
Medvedev, 1969	Medvedev, Z. A., *The Rise and Fall of T. D. Lysenko,* New York, Columbia University Press, 1969.
Meynaud, 1968	Meynaud, J., *Technocratie et politique,* Bellanger, La Ferbe-Bernard, 1960, tr. as *Technocracy,* New York, The Free Press, 1968.
Meynaud and Schroeder, 1962	Meynaud, J. and Schroeder, B., *Les Savants et la vie internationale,* Lausanne, Etudes de Science politique, 1962.
Morton, 1969	Morton, L., 'War and Social Change', in Silvert, K. H., *The Social Reality of the Scientific Truth,* Hanover, N. H., American University Field Staff, Inc., 1969.
Mosca, 1923	Mosca, G., *The Ruling Class,* New York, McGraw Hill, 1939. Translation and revision of *Elementi di Scienza Politica,* 1923.
Mumford, 1967	Mumford, L., *The Myth of the Machine,* New York, Harcourt, Brace, 1967.
National Academy of Sciences, 1972	National Academy of Sciences, *The Science Committee,* Washington, D. C., National Academy of Sciences, 1972, 2.
Nelkin, 1972	Nelkin, D., *The University and Military Research: Moral Politics at MIT,* Ithaca, New York, Cornell University Press, 1972.
Nelkin, 1975	Nelkin, D., 'The Political Impact of Technical Expertise', *Social Studies of Science* 5, January 1975, 1.
Nichols, 1968	Nichols, D., *Political Attitudes of a Scientific Elite,* unpublished dissertation, Department of Political Science, MIT, 1968.
Nichols, 1974	Nichols, D., 'The Associational Interest Groups of American Science', in Teich, A. (Ed.), *Scientists and Public Affairs,* Cambridge, Mass., MIT Press, 1974, pp. 123-170.
Nieburg, 1966	Nieburg, H. L., *In the Name of Science,* Chicago, Quadrangle Press, 1966.
ORSA, 1971	Operations Research Society of America, *Operations Research,* issue on Guidelines for the Practice of Operations Research 19, No. 5, September 1971, pp. 1123-1258.

Paloczi-Horvath, 1964 — Paloczi-Horvath, G., *The Facts Rebel*, London, Secker and Warburg, 1964.

Parsons, 1969 — Parsons, T., 'The Intellectuals: A Social Role Category', in Rieff, P. (Ed.), *On Intellectuals*, Garden City, New York, Doubleday, 1969.

Polanyi, 1962 — Polanyi, M., *The Republic of Science: Its Political and Economic Theory*, Chicago, Roosevelt University, 1962.

Derek Price, 1966 — Price, Derek de Solla, 'The Science of Science', in Goldsmith, M. and MacKay, A. (Eds.), *The Science of Science*, Harmondsworth, England, Pelican, 1966, pp. 244-261.

Price and Yagi, 1962 — Price, Derek de Solla and Yagi, S., 'Japanese Bomb', Letters to the Editor, *Bulletin of the Atomic Scientist* XVIII, 1962, p. 29.

Don K. Price, 1965 — Price, Don K., *The Scientific Estate*, Cambridge Mass., Harvard University Press, 1965.

Primack and von Hippel, 1974 — Primack, J. and von Hippel, F., *Advice and Dissent: Scientists in the Political Arena*, New York, Basic Books, 1974.

Ravetz, 1971 — Ravetz, J. R., *Scientific Knowledge and its Social Problems*, London, Oxford University Press, 1971.

Reagan, 1969 — Reagan, M. D., *Science and the Federal Patron*, New York, Oxford University Press, 1969.

Reid, 1969 — Reid, R. W., *Tongues of Conscience: Weapons Research and the Scientists' Dilemma*, New York, Walker and Co., 1969.

Reiser, 1966 — Reiser, S. J., 'Smoking and Health: The Congress and Causality', in Lakoff, S. A. (Ed.), *Knowledge and Power: Essays on Science and Government*, New York, The Free Press, 1966, pp. 293-311.

Rich, 1974 — Rich, D., 'Private Government and Professional Science', in Teich, A. H. (Ed.), *Scientists and Public Affairs*, Cambridge, Mass., MIT Press, 1974, pp. 3-37.

Rose and Rose, 1970 — Rose, H. and Rose, S., *Science and Society*, Harmondsworth, England, Pelican Books, 1970.

Roszak, 1970 — Roszak, T., *The Making of a Counter Culture*, Garden City, New York, Doubleday, 1970.

Rotblat, 1972 — Rotblat, J., *Scientists in the Quest for Peace: A History of the Pugwash Conferences*, Cambridge, Mass., MIT Press, 1972.

Sakharov, 1974 — Sakharov, A., *Sakharov Speaks*, New York, Knopf, 1974.

Salisbury, 1974 — Salisbury, H. E., Foreword, in Sakharov, A., *Sakharov Speaks*, New York, Knopf, 1974.

Salomon, 1971 — Salomon, J.-J., 'The Internationale of Science', *Science Studies* 1, 1971, pp. 23-42.

Salomon, 1973 — Salomon, J.-J., *Science et Politique*, Paris, Editions du Seuil, 1970. Translated as *Science and Politics*, Cambridge, Mass., MIT Press, 1973.

Scheinman, 1965 — Scheinman, L., *Atomic Energy Policy in France Under the Fourth Republic*, Princeton, New Jersey, Princeton University Press, 1965.

Schilling, 1964

Schilling, W. R., 'Scientists, Foreign Policy and Politics', in Gilpin, R. F. and Wright, C. (Eds.), *Scientists and National Policy Making,* New York, Columbia University Press, 1964.

Schooler, 1971

Schooler, D. Jr., *Science, Scientists and Public Policy,* New York, The Free Press, 1971.

Schroeder-Gudehus, 1973

Schroeder-Gudehus, B., 'Challenges to Transnational Loyalties: International Organizations after the First World War', *Science Studies* 3, 1973, pp. 93-119.

Sherwin, 1975

Sherwin, H. J., *A World Destroyed: The Atomic Bomb and the Grand Alliance,* New York, Knopf, 1975.

Shils, 1968

Shils, E. (Ed)., *Criteria for Scientific Development: Public Policy and National Goals,* Cambridge, Mass., MIT Press, 1968.

Skolnikoff, 1967

Skolnikoff, E. B., *Science, Technology and American Foreign Policy,* Cambridge, Mass., MIT Press, 1967.

Smith, 1965

Smith, A. K., *A Peril and a Hope: The Scientists' Movement in America, 1945-47,* Chicago, University of Chicago Press, 1965.

Smith, 1966

Smith, B. L. R., *The RAND Corporation: Case Study of a Nonprofit Advisory Corporation,* Cambridge, Mass., Harvard University Press, 1966.

Snow, 1961

Snow, C. P., *Science and Government,* Cambridge, Mass., Harvard University Press, 1961.

Snow, 1964

Snow, C. P., *Two Cultures: And a Second Look,* New York, Mentor Books, 1964.

Stern, 1969

Stern, P. M., with Green, H. P., *The Oppenheimer Case: Security on Trial,* New York, Harper and Row, 1969.

Stone, 1973

Stone, J., 'Knowledge, Survival and the Duties of Science', *American University Law Review* 23, 1973, pp. 231-61.

Storer, 1966

Storer, N. W., *The Social System of Science,* New York, Holt, Rinehart and Winston, 1966.

Strickland, 1968

Strickland, D. A., *Scientists in Politics,* Lafayette, Indiana, Purdue University Studies, 1968.

Teich, 1974

Teich, A. H., 'Political and International Laboratories: A Study of Scientists' Attitudes', in Teich, A. (Ed.), *Scientists and Public Affairs,* Cambridge, Mass., MIT Press, 1974, pp. 171-235.

Turner and Spaulding, 1969

Turner, H. A. and Spaulding, C., Political Attitudes and Behavior of Selected Academically Affiliated Professional Groups', *Polity* 1, Spring, 1969, pp. 309-336.

Uyehara, 1966

Uyehara, H., 'Scientific Advice and the Nuclear Test Ban Treaty', in Lakoff, S. A. (Ed.), *Knowledge and Power: Essays on Science and Government,* New York, The Free Press, 1966, pp. 112-161.

Veblen, 1921

Veblen, T., *The Engineers and the Price System,* New York, Huebsch, 1921.

Vig, 1968

Vig, N. J., *Science and Technology in British Politics,* Oxford, Pergamon Press, 1968.

Weingart, 1970

Weingart, P., *Die amerikanische Wissenschaftslobby,*

Dusseldorf, Bertelsmann, Universitatsverlag, 1970.

Weld, 1848   Weld, C. R., *A History of the Royal Society with Memoirs of the Presidents,* London, John Parker, 1848, Vol. 1, p. 146.

Wohlstetter, 1964   Wohlstetter, A., 'Strategy and the Natural Scientists', in Gilpin, R. and Wright, C. (Eds.), *Scientists and National Policy Making,* New York, Columbia University Press, 1964, pp. 174-239.

York, 1970   York, H. F., *Race to Oblivion: A Participant's View of the Arms Race,* New York, Simon and Schister, 1970.

York, 1976   York, H. F., *The Advisers: Oppenheimer, Teller and the Super Bomb,* San Francisco, W. H. Freeman, 1976.

Zirkle, 1959   Zirkle, C., *Evolution, Marxian Biology and the Social Scene,* Philadelphia, University of Pennsylvania Press, 1959.

Zuckerman, 1971   Zuckerman, Sir S., *Beyond the Ivory Tower: The Frontiers of Public and Private Science,* New York, Taplinger, 1971.

Chapter 11

TECHNOLOGY AND PUBLIC POLICY

D. Nelkin

Cornell University

INTRODUCTION

'Science Finds – Industry Applies – Man Conforms'. This was the theme of the Chicago World's Fair in 1933 which was celebrating 'a century of progress'. But if a world's fair in the 1970's were to focus on technology, it might rather adopt the theme, 'Science Finds – Industry Applies – Man Controls'; for concern with the undesirable impacts of science and technology has dampened the celebration of progress, and the central issue in the field of science, technology and public policy has shifted from support to direction and control.

The emphasis on science and technology as a means of achieving social goals developed during the years following World War II (See Salomon, Chapter 2). The importance of science to national wartime policy led to increased federal funding of basic scientific research and greater involvement of scientists in government (See Lakoff, Chapter 10, and Sapolsky, Chapter 12). These changing political relationships gave rise to a prolific literature on science policy and its implications both for science and for government.[1]

The field of science, technology and public policy flourished. But with no conceptual framework to provide shape and direction, it was described in

---

[1] Don K. Price's *Government and Science* (1954) was a key book in generating interest in the field of science, technology and public policy. See also Gilpin (1962) and Wohlstetter (1964). Much of the early literature in this field focused on the use of science and technology and the role of scientists in the military. Denny (1965) and Rettig (1969) have reviewed some of this literature.

1965 as 'a literature in search of a field' (Denny, 1965). Ten years later, science, technology and public policy might better be called 'a field in search of definition'; for although the subject has gradually become a distinct field of inquiry, its scope and limits remain poorly defined.[2]

Much of the literature until the late 1960s conveyed a pervasive optimism based on faith in progress and the assumption that science brings order and rationality to public policy. Prophets of 'post-industrial society' predicted the decline of politics as scientific rationality and objective standards of truth became the basis of public decisions (Lane, 1966; Bell, 1960; Brzezinski, 1970). In a 'technotronic age', logical, precise and instrumental approaches to decision making would replace intuition and politics, contributing to the resolution of difficult social problems (Weinberg, 1966).

This optimistic faith in science followed from a period of unprecedented economic growth; and it was therefore likely to recede at a time of social crisis (Brooks, 1965, 68). Indeed, events of the mid-1960's — especially the Vietnam War and the environmental movement — brought a transformation in public attitudes toward science and technology in the United States, and generated compelling pressures for more deliberate policies regarding their use and control.[3] These demands for increased social direction of both science and technology have begun to give shape to the recent policy literature in this area. The emphasis is increasingly on how science and technology can be channelled for social purposes.

> It is modern science that has made the relationship between knowledge and social action a radical problem. . . . Conscious calculation of social direction must therefore replace the automatic and semi-spontaneous adjustment of society to new knowledge that generally sufficed in the past (Dror, 1968, 3-4).

In this chapter I shall organize the rapidly expanding literature on the relationship of science and technology to public policy in terms of three related issues: the use of science and technology to meet public needs, the unintended and undesirable consequences of science and technology; and the control and regulation of technological change.[4] These three issues — the use,

---

[2] In organizing a massive bibliography of the field, Caldwell (1968 and 1972) claims that he could not define a coherent area of study. He includes categories on the philosophy and history of science and technology; their nature and impact; governmental, legal and organizational relationships; personnel and education; and the relationship of science to culture, the humanities and religion.

[3] Don K. Price (1974) contends that the support of fundamental research after World War II, on the basis of scientific merit without reference to any applied purpose, had been a radical departure from the traditional view that science should be directed to pragmatic ends. Demands for utility are merely a reassertion of this traditional view.

[4] In discussing science, technology and public policy, it is often difficult to distinguish science from technology, for science is increasingly perceived in terms of its utility; and concerns with the impact of technology, as the public face of science, reflect back upon basic science. In order to set some limits to this chapter, I shall not discuss

impact and control of science and technology — form the framework of an analysis emphasizing the political dimensions of science policy decisions. First, I shall outline the general forces that determine the use of science and technology: the bases for allocating resources, the strategies for research and the problems of utilization. Second, I shall review the growing concern with the negative impacts of science and technology, and how these impacts emerge on the policy agenda. Finally, I shall analyze efforts to regulate, assess and control technological change drawing examples mainly from the American context.

Reviewing the field in this framework will highlight the political forces — conflicting values, ambivalent attitudes and diverse interests — that influence the relationship of science and technology to public policy. Despite the rationality basic to the scientific endeavor, the process of decision making in this area is highly political, directed and constrained by the needs and conflicting demands of established organizations and political groups. Thus, the central questions I shall raise throughout this chapter are those basic to politics: 'questions relating to power and justice and freedom — about the purposes and the limits of the new power that science and scientific institutions may exercise in [a] constitutional system' (Don K. Price, 1969).

THE USE OF SCIENCE AND TECHNOLOGY

When Gulliver visited the mythical science-oriented society of Laputa, he found scientists to be of no use at all in public matters. They were involved in only the most useless and even counterproductive activities: softening marble for pillows or inventing ways to prevent the growth of wool on lambs in order to propagate naked sheep. Swift might have been satirizing today's tendency to scrutinize science in terms of its direct utility; for a key policy issue remains how to direct science and technology to the resolution of pressing social problems.

The space program demonstrated the dramatic accomplishments that could be achieved by linking organized scientific research to technological development. Nelson (1974) describes the 'moon-ghetto syndrome' — the belief that an allocation of resources to technological development would assure limitless control over social and urban problems. A similar optimism underlies the concept of the 'technological fix' (Weinberg, 1966; Etzioni and

---

policies for basic research (See Salomon, Chapter 2), nor for the military (See Sapolsky, Chapter 12). I shall focus rather on technology and science only as they are perceived to have policy application in meeting civilian goals. There are, however, considerable areas of overlap since discussions of the use of science deal invariably with policies to stimulate research.

Remp, 1973)[5] — the search for quick technological solutions for profound
social problems. The application of science and technology, however, has
proven far more difficult than anticipated. We often lack a comprehensive
understanding of social problems and therefore of appropriate ways to
contain them, but even when such knowledge exists, political and social
factors severely constrain the use of science and technology. Landing a lunar
module was complex, but it did not involve assessments of 'the relative
political strengths of the inhabitants of the Sea of Tranquillity and the Ocean
of Storm' (Yarmolinsky, 1970, 32). In contrast, the use of science and
technology for social purposes is constrained by political conflict that complicates the allocation of resources for research and development, by the
difficulty of breaking down problems into parts which can be approached
scientifically; and by the inability to define social objectives or to determine
the relevance of given technologies to specific social problems.

In this section I shall address three sets of questions: First, what are the
forces which determine the allocation of resources for research and development? Second, how does one design strategies for the effective development
of science and technology? That is to say, what is the appropriate balance of
basic and mission-oriented research? Of professional versus public control?
Finally, what are the political and organizational problems of utilizing technology to fulfill social objectives while diverse groups, defining these objectives in different ways, battle over the distribution of technical resources?

Allocation of Resources   Public policies are established in a context of
political and cultural expectations, intense competition, and often the personal biases of policy makers themselves (Schoettle, 1968). Setting priorities
for non-defense R & D requires large public investment and therefore considerable political support. Yet political support is complicated by often
vague policy objectives that are subject to the diverse preferences of various
socio-economic groups. What, for example, are the goals of transportation
policy? Should priority be given to highways or subways? Should a program
be designed to benefit the suburbs or the inner city? What will be the effect

---

[5] Both the 'technological fix' and the 'moon-ghetto syndrome' are based upon
assumptions about the origin of social problems and also about the source of the
difficulties of resolving them. Difficulties, for example, can be attributed to weakness in
leadership, organizational problems, insufficient resources, or an inadequate state of
knowledge or technology. Etzioni and Remp (1973) categorize various approaches to
resolving social problems: the 'liberal reformist approach' (increasing resources and
strengthening existing programs); the 'psychotherapeutic approach' (providing remedial
social service programs based on the concept of human malleability); the 'rationalistic
social planning approach' (fostering major social reorganization according to a given
plan); and the 'technological approach'. This last approach assumes that given a better
state of knowledge and appropriate technology, social problems are amenable to resolution.

of new transportation systems on neighborhoods (Schneider, 1968)? Even when objectives are widely accepted, R & D strategies involve a spectrum of non-technical decisions. There is certainly consensus on the value of improved medical services, but should research priorities be directed to easing the problems of the aged, or to curing diseases of the young? How can one choose between the development of high technology medical facilities and centers for the delivery of routine health services? These are political choices involving allocation of resources among often conflicting interests.[6]

What, then, are the forces that influence the allocation of resources for R & D? The largest single determinant is, of course, existing budget priorities, but within this context three factors are of critical importance: a) national objectives, b) the perceived urgency of specific problems, and c) the convergence of political will with technological opportunity.

a) National political objectives. National political goals clearly influence priorities for technological development, and often these goals develop more in response to external challenges than to internal needs. The desire for international prestige, the need to maintain a competitive edge in the world market, and the cold war all affect national research policies (OECD, 1971). Even large allocations of resources to internal needs often appear as a response to external challenge. The energy program developed in response to the oil embargo (and significantly, was called Project Independence). The imagery of 'war' (war on pollution – on cancer – on poverty) as an approach to social problems is a way of translating internal needs into external challenges.

External objectives may, however, prevail against the development of technology for social purposes. Small European countries (Sweden and the Netherlands) specialize in particular technologies in order to capture the export market in a limited area (Gilpin, 1970). Other countries (the United States, the Soviet Union and France) try to maintain a broad base of development in advanced science and technology. United States policy has been influenced mainly by the cold war; thus most government R & D expenditure – nearly ninety per cent of it in the 1960's – has been in space, defense and atomic energy. Private industry has followed, concentrating – with government dollars – on activities related to these three sectors (Nelson *et al.*, 1967; Mansfield, 1968). In France and England, the desire to maintain autonomy in most areas of advanced technology is a major policy consideration. There has been a heavy investment in such diverse fields as computers, reactor development and aviation, often with insufficient consideration of marketing possibilities or the adequacy of industrial structures. Too small to

---

[6] For example, to transplant a kidney costs at least $5,000, while it costs $130 per year to provide one person with routine health care. One million dollars can buy kidney dialysis centers to service 25,000 patients. Or it can buy comprehensive ambulatory health care for 1,250,000 (Harvard, 1968, 3).

maintain a comprehensive development program, France and England have had to limit their R & D activities in some areas, importing technologies such as computers and nuclear reactors.[7] But national technological autonomy remains an important influence on R & D, often overriding internal priorities. It has also complicated efforts to direct science and technology to problems with international dimensions. Advanced technologies in the nuclear and aviation sectors, programs to resolve environmental problems or to exploit ocean resources require increased international cooperation, yet commitment to such programs is heavily influenced by calculations of national objectives (Williams, 1973; Skolnikoff, 1970 and Chapter 13).

National practices with respect to the balance of public and private responsibility also affect the allocation of resources. The United States has tended to leave to the private sector technological development for internal, non-defense purposes.[8] Market demands were expected to yield an appropriate level of technological development to meet needs in such areas as housing and health care delivery (Nelson, 1968). Market mechanisms, however, were generally perceived to be inadequate, failing to generate an optimal allocation of R & D resources, and since the mid-1960's there has been expanding government activity in these areas. The situation has been quite different in European countries where political conventions, combined with the urgency of public needs following World War II, created a much more central policy role for national government in domestic issues.[9]

b) Perceived urgency. A second and related set of forces shaping priorities for the use of science and technology is the perceived urgency of public sector problems and the pressure for their immediate resolution.[10] The

---

[7] In both France and England, the development of both computers and nuclear reactors was highly controversial. France had to choose between American and German technologies. Interestingly, American expertise was chosen during the Gaullist period despite antagonistic political attitudes toward the United States at the time.

[8] One exception is the area of agricultural technology which has received extensive government sponsorship. The space program is also clearly an exception.

[9] In France, however, 'La Défense Nationale' was top priority during the Gaullist period, justifying massive national economic efforts to maintain economy in this sector. One may recall the famous saying attributed to Charles de Gaulle about domestic issues: 'L'intendance suivra'.

[10] Perceptions of urgency tend to shift although the original problems may not be solved (Schon, 1971). For example, an urgent priority in the United States in the 1950's was to create efficient metropolitan governments. In the 1960's interest shifted to the social problems arising from poverty, and in the 1970's energy and natural resources are urgent priorities. One finds a similar pattern in France. In the 1950's the prime concern was reconstruction, which entailed the economic support of R & D in the heavy industry sector. In the 1960's the focus was on prestigious technological projects (i.e. the 'Plan Calcul' for the development of computers, the Concorde, or the plan to develop, on a national basis, a civil fission reactor program). In the 1970's the stress is on economic efficiency. Public policies launched by the French President give little doubt about the desire to achieve such an objective (e.g. the recent financial cutbacks in the urban highway program to benefit mass transit systems, or the elimination of the French space program to maintain the development of the European one).

importance of these pressures is evident in the allocation of funds in the United States for biomedical research. From 1948-1968, Congressional appropriations for biomedical research have increased at a significantly greater rate than in other areas. Specifically, 'dread diseases' such as cancer have had top priority (Strickland, 1972). There is more research on diseases which affect primarily the aged than there is on childhood ailments.[11] And while cardiovascular disease kills three times as many people as cancer, it is the latter, with its emotional impact, that attracts the greater attention.

Drug addiction was a long-neglected problem until drug-related crime began to affect middle-class communities. This chronic social problem was then quickly identified as urgent and became the focus of increased research in the hopes of protecting public safety. As we shall discuss later, problems related to public health and safety have a sense of urgency which places them high on the policy agenda.

Perceptions of urgency are influenced by special interests. Often scientists themselves serve as an interest group, using their expertise to promote their own projects as urgent priorities (King and Melanson, 1972). But more often it is the needs of large, formal organizations that dominate policy decisions. Public needs often become equated with organizational imperatives that follow from existing investments (See Layton, Chapter 6); thus 'big science', a massive and costly enterprise, tends to be self-perpetuating (Weinberg, 1966a). For example, the maintenance of NASA (National Aeronautics and Space Agency) as a viable organization was a major imperative behind United States efforts to develop a solar energy program and the space shuttle. Similarly, the European space project 'Ariane' was kept alive by the French government – despite the stringent budget policy for fiscal year 1975 – in order to maintain the employment level at the SNIAS (Société Nationale des Industries Aeronautiques et Spaciales) following the decline of the 'Concorde' and 'Airbus' programs.

c. *Political will and technological opportunity.* The third and perhaps overriding factor shaping priorities for science and technology is the convergence of technological opportunity; that is the availability of an appropriate technology, with political readiness to accept technological change. 'It takes both the perception of a need and the "ripeness" of a scientific field . . . to produce the rapid take-off [of R & D]" (Brooks, 1974, 503). Wallace Sayre and Bruce Smith (1969) evaluate the extent to which specific problems are both politically and technically 'ready' for solution. For example, the technology to improve the safety of automobiles existed when the issue became politically attractive to Congress. Thus the activities of consumer advocate Ralph Nader rapidly led to the introduction of safety

---

[11] The NIH Institute of Child Health and Human Development received only $106 million in the 1974 budget as compared to a combined total of $765 million for research on cancer and heart disease.

features such as seat belts and collapsible steering columns. On the other hand, we are 'politically ready' for a cure for cancer, but an adequate technology does not yet exist. Conversely, while the technology does exist for solid waste disposal programs, the political will in this area is still weak. And problems such as low-cost housing or mass production of artificial organs are neither politically nor technically ready for solutions.

The relationship of 'political will' to the use of science is further developed in Dean Schooler's analysis (1971) of the factors influencing the policy role of scientists. Schooler defines nine policy arenas in which governmental activity has a varying impact on the distribution of wealth, status and power within a society.[12] In some arenas, government activity is intended to produce common benefits for society. Government entrepreneurial activities such as the space program, for example, are perceived as distributive; that is to say, not directed to benefit some particular groups more than others.[13] At the other extreme, policies for municipal services or housing are redistributive, a term implying readjustments of wealth, status and power; and in these arenas conflict is inevitable. Schooler argues that scientists are most active in those policy arenas which involve minimal conflict. This suggests that the use of science and technology is influenced largely by the degree of political consensus about specific problems.

Strategies[14]   Even if there is considerable agreement about an appropriate allocation of resources, conflict remains concerning R & D strategies. There are several unresolved questions: a) What are the relative advantages of centralized versus pluralist planning, and of public versus private development? b) What is an appropriate balance between large-scale, mission-directed programs and basic research? c) Who should decide such questions of strategy — the public which provides the funds or the professionals involved in research?

a) Centralization versus pluralism. In all countries governments stimulate innovation, especially in sectors where firms are too small to afford independent research. Government efforts may take several forms: grants and

---

[12] This model uses Lowi's (1964) concept of arenas. Lowi's policy arenas are defined in terms of the impacts or expected impacts of certain government policies on society. Each policy arena is characterized by a particular set of political relationships. Policies are either distributive, redistributive, regulative or self-regulative in terms of the impact of government activity.

[13] Even in a government entrepreneurial area such as space, however, there are considerable distributional effects. Specific cities like Los Angeles thrived from the aerospace industry. Also, engineers gained enormously from the space program, for example, while poor and less educated people did not.

[14] Brooks (1973b) has reviewed the arguments concerning research strategies, dealing with the questions of how best to organize the search for knowledge and how to couple knowledge with existing needs.

contracts to support research in private industry or non-profit institutions, special purchasing procedures, or measures to disseminate technical information. The organization of government activities differs in various countries, and this, of course, affects the development of science and technology within these countries (See Salomon, Chapter 2).

In 1945, the Vannevar Bush report supplied the premises underlying the United States government support of scientific research through a contract system, but Bush's recommendations for a monolithic funding organization were largely bypassed in favor of a commitment to pluralism. A sectoral system subsequently developed in which resources were made available to autonomous sectors such as defense, health or agriculture. Each sector, under this system, makes independent decisions about R & D relevant to its own mission through a specialized agency. Central surveillance or coordination is limited; the justification is that decentralization stimulates competition, creating 'a dynamic market-place of ideas', and facilitating the direct application of research to policy.

The sectoral approach in the United States was effective in a situation of expanding resources. However, by the late 1960's, the scarcity of funds and the growing concern with the social utility of research called for more thoughtful decisions about R & D strategy.[15] The pluralist system limited comparisons of the relative utility of various projects. Moreover, the coupling of science and technology to agencies favored specific and often narrowly defined programs that often resulted in the neglect of important but more vaguely defined social problem areas. Thus, concerns both with the efficiency of scientific research and with its relationship to social goals have brought arguments for a more centralized organization of research.[16]

---

[15] A major turning point in the realization that the prolonged period of generous federal research expansion was over was marked by the Mansfield Amendment of 1969. This amendment to a Department of Defense authorization bill precluded DOD sponsorship of any research not having a direct relationship to military functions. It was intended to force the transfer of major R & D funds to civilian agencies, and to encourage reexamination of national science policy towards a more carefully planned and centrally controlled system. The Mansfield Amendment caused agencies to reevaluate research contracts according to their relationship to specific agency functions. The trend toward 'direct social utility' has also been reflected in experiments with new programs such as Research Applied to National Needs (RANN) within the National Science Foundation. Similarly, in Great Britain the Rothschild Report (1971) emphasized the utility of science and technology, giving ministries increased financial control over Research Councils, and advocating a 'customer contract' principle as the basis for applied R & D.

[16] Actually, the tendency to create new organizations may be as flourishing an activity in centralized systems as in the more decentralized sectoral approach. Over the past ten years, France has given life to new institutions, 'Missions', 'Délégations', 'Centres Nationaux', all of which reflect technological development in new fields (nuclear energy, ocean exploitation, space, computer science).

European countries have had more centralized structures. In France, the DGRST, a central administrative body, advises the government on science policy decisions and fosters and controls large-scale R & D programs. Research funding, however, is channelled through different departments which monitor the design and performance of specific R & D programs (Aigrain, 1974). In the United Kingdom, at one time, the Department of Scientific and Industrial Research had wide responsibilities for industrial research as well as for much academic research. In contrast to the United States, however, the British look to decentralization, and since the Rothschild Report (1971) a more decentralized structure has been adopted, based on departmental responsibility for government-supported applied research and development (Brooks, 1973b; OECD, 1972-74).

The main differences between European and American strategies lie in the role of private enterprise. In the United States, control of technology development has been left largely to private enterprise except in areas relating to military or space programs; the federal government serves as referee rather than as initiator of new technology. Government has intervened only when the level of investment is too large for private industry or when there is little profit incentive for private industry innovation (Nelkin, 1970). But even when government does intervene, private enterprise remains the principal performer. While the government finances about two thirds of national R & D efforts, R & D is primarily executed in the private sector.

European countries rely more on government research units than on contracts with private firms. Only the multinational corporations have sufficient size and financial strength to absorb the risks of technological development. They have been an important instrument for developing and diffusing technology, but the corporations are perceived as reflecting a trend towards external control that sharply conflicts with the preference for national control of technology.[17]

b) Basic research versus the Manhattan project syndrome. The Manhattan project and the Apollo program demonstrated the ability of large-scale coordinated scientific efforts to fulfill difficult objectives. Subsequently these programs have served as models for what are euphemistically labelled as 'wars' on various social or medical problems. The question is whether, in specific problem areas, a massive, highly directed approach is more effective than a more dispersed and loosely organized system of research. There are conflicting opinions; the availability of extensive funds allows an R & D capacity of critical size and concentration to acquire the necessary equipment and scientific skills. But mission-directed programs at too early a stage in scientific

---

[17] Drucker (1974) takes issue with this perception in respect to developing countries. He argues that a policy for self-sufficiency is not realistic, and that the integration of productive capacities into the world economy through multinationals is the most promising means of leverage for developing countries.

understanding can be wasteful; they are likely to concentrate on non-productive directions determined more by the needs of large organizations than by research realities (McElroy, 1973).

When is the state of knowledge in a field sufficient to warrant a massive development program? This is a difficult question contingent upon the 'ripeness' of a science, the funding available, the distribution of scientists and other factors. It poses particular problems in the biomedical area where there are often extraordinary pressures to move quickly from basic research to development programs.[18] Cooper (1971) provides examples of premature transfer in the field of medicine where urgency may prevail over caution. Many biomedical researchers are concerned that the cancer program will inevitably be organized around a few dominant scientists and proceed within a narrow intellectual framework based on existing ideas. This is a time, they argue, for wide ranging support of basic research in which directions are independently determined by many different scientific laboratories. Money, manpower and organizational management − characteristic of a crash program − can resolve a problem when the basic principles are understood. Biological research, however, has no general theory on which to mount a massive assault on specific diseases. According to James Shannon, the capacity to diagnose, cure or prevent disease will depend on 'empirical approaches, serendipity and the brilliance of too few gifted individuals' (Strickland, 1972, 189).[19]

c) Public versus professional influence. The allocation of public funds to specific areas of science and technology has raised the issue of public versus professional influence on technical decisions. Who is to establish priorities for expenditures of funds − lay policy makers who represent the public in the allocation of funds, or professional scientists who understand the nature of the scientific and technical process? Science is a self-regulating profession, accustomed to internal control through collegial review. Engineers, too, despite their client orientation, rely heavily on professional norms to guide the quality and direction of their work.

The conflict between government responsibility and scientific autonomy was an issue in the early 1960's; at this time increased funds for basic research brought realization that the government was in fact setting priorities for science. While availability of public funds created new opportunities, increased governmental direction also threatened loss of freedom (Gilpin and

---

[18] Premature response to research results is also an increasing problem in developing programs to regulate science and technology. Improved capacity to detect carcinogenic effects, for example, has led to controversial regulations by the United States Food and Drug Administration (as in the cyclamate ban).

[19] A similar debate is taking place concerning the International Biology Program (a large scale program of ecosystems modelling). It is far too early to judge its effectiveness. In each case much of the criticism reflects irritation with the concentration of resources that inevitably leaves some scholars without support.

Wright, 1964). Professionals have usually been able successfully to subvert efforts of laymen to control the strategies of scientific research as is evident in the evolution of the national cancer program. This continued autonomy has rested on assumptions about the value-free nature of scientific work and has been considerably less effective in social sciences to the extent that they are perceived as linked to political viewpoints (Brooks, 1976).

The perception of science as a useful public resource has added new dimensions to the conflict between autonomy and control. The power of the scientist is enhanced by the utility of his work, but his autonomy in regulating the direction of this work can be significantly undermined by demands for social utility as external criteria of social merit compete with internal criteria of scientific quality (Weinberg, 1966). As science has become increasingly involved in public issues, the scientific community appears ill-equipped to deal with the implications of its interdependent relationship with the government (See Lakoff, Chapter 10). Joseph Haberer (1969) points out the absence of an institutional ethic governing the relationships between science and its external environment, arguing that such an ethic is necessary if scientists are to maintain an appropriate balance between their professional autonomy and their public role.

Problems of Utilization   A new technological development is a major resource. It may infringe on the interest of existing industries or benefit some groups more than others; the awarding of a major contract, for example, can effect the basic economic situation of a region (Lowi, 1975). Policies for the use of technology may succeed or fail on the basis of how affected interests respond. Political obstacles to the utilization of technology have been especially evident in efforts to transfer technology from space and defense to the public sector.[20] Lobbyists for massive public expenditure on military and space R & D argued that technology could be transferred to the civilian sector to help resolve such problems as transportation and housing. This never really materialized; 'spinoffs' were few in number and the technical competence developed in specialized areas was not easily adapted to other problems. Bureaucratic concerns with this situation stimulated technical dissemination programs within NASA and other government agencies. But these efforts encountered considerable difficulties and many programs collapsed (Doctors, 1969; Nelkin, 1971). Innovation of service sector technology has been obstructed by the uncertainties of the potential market (See Freeman, Chapter 5).[21]

---

[20] Extended discussion of the problems of technology transfer can be found in Furash (1968), Berkowitz (1970) and Gruber and Marquis (1969).

[21] For a discussion of innovation and its relationship to market demands, see Nelson (1959, 1968), Schmookler (1966) and Mansfield (1968). Note, however, that if a problem is perceived as urgent, this may stimulate innovation and even lead to accept-

But even when appropriate technologies exist, there are further obstacles to their acceptance. Studies of innovation suggest that the political acceptability of a new technology depends both on the character of the technology itself and on the norms and expectations of those who are likely to be affected. Everett Rogers (1962) lists five characteristics of an innovation that affect its adoption: its relative advantage over other ideas, its compatibility with existing values and practices, its complexity, its divisibility (the ability to use the innovation on a limited basis) and its communicability. If an innovation introduces a tangible improvement over an existing system without upsetting organizational structures and practices, it is likely to be accepted. The New York City Fire Department, for example, welcomed the introduction of 'slippery water' (the addition of long-chained polymers to water in order to reduce turbulence and friction and to increase the rate of flow). This technology permits the use of a smaller hose with no loss of efficiency. Its benefits in improving the convenience and safety of fire fighting are substantial, immediately visible and, most important, require no change in the organization of the fire department. On the other hand, innovations that call for major changes confront the 'dynamic conservatism' of organization — the remarkable tendency to fight to remain the same (Schon, 1967).

Many service sector innovations imply organizational change in precisely those areas where specific objectives and valid measures of the effectiveness of innovations are most difficult to conceptualize. What does a better education look like? What are the criteria for evaluating a new educational technique? Innovation may threaten traditional practices and familiar relationships. Thus school systems, beset with an oversold educational technology, greet programs of computer-based instruction with skepticism if not open hostility; teachers fear that technically trained personnel will displace existing staff or threaten teacher-student relationships; and parents fear that experiments or even new science curricula might affect the academic success of their children or infringe on their traditional values (Oettinger, 1969; Nelkin, 1977).[22]

Utilization of technology is sensitive to given political concentrations of power. A National Academy of Sciences panel (1969) observes that:

> When a new and less costly building technique would disrupt the construction industry, one can rely on the opposition of those building interests that would be

---

ance of otherwise controversial technologies. For example, at the height of the heroin scare in the late 1960's the public was willing to accept the controversial use of an addictive drug, methadone, to treat heroin addicts (Nelkin, 1973).

　[22] Similar concerns have confronted efforts to introduce multiphasic screening as a means of efficient medical diagnosis. A highly effective but impersonal procedure, this technology has been criticized as threatening to the human aspects of the doctor-patient relationship.

disadvantaged, but not unorganized advocacy by the residents of the ghetto, who might benefit from cheaper housing . . . . A thorough consideration of the relative merits of alternative technologies is rendered difficult if not impossible by the presence of powerful spokesmen for the old technologies and the absence of effective spokesmen for the new.

The housing industry, for example, includes a network of government and private institutions (contractors, architects, unions, suppliers, brokers and realtors) oriented around the development of individualized housing. This highly fragmented industry is largely dependent on traditional methods and tends to resist many kinds of technological change. Similarly, the Federal Bureau of Public Roads and the government agencies and interest groups organized around the private automobile long resisted mass transportation technologies. And in France, an identical pattern occurs as 'Le Grand Corps des Ponts et Chaussées' has opposed mass transit outside the Paris region (Thoenig, 1973).

In sum, there is no single set of values to guide the allocation of resources for science and technology, and even the existence of appropriate technologies to meet public needs does not guarantee that they will be utilized. The use of science and technology may depend on the crisis of the moment, the biases of political authorities, or the interests and activities of groups concerned with their own perpetuation. Bargaining and compromise are at the heart of public policy, and science policy is no exception to this (Bauer, 1968). And the bargaining process is likely to be of increasing importance as belief in the usefulness of science and technology is matched by concern with their troublesome social impacts.

IMPACT OF SCIENCE AND TECHNOLOGY

Science and technology have a significant capacity to shape nearly every aspect of human experience — from industrial development and work to religious beliefs. We live in a 'technological society' in which all activities are touched with the effects of science and technology so much so that we are often unaware of the permeation of scientific values into the fabric of modern life (Ellul, 1964). Advances in science and technology underly the development of modern industry and agriculture, shaping the physical structure of cities and influencing the social structure within modern societies and the relationships between nations. Technological changes increasingly affect patterns of resource use and population growth, forcing attention to the global impacts of science and technology.

The implications of science and technology have been of recurrent concern. Science once threatened the feudal system, undermining the religious beliefs and fundamental assumptions about man's place in nature. Technology was long associated with social disruption and urban blight – Blake's 'dark Satanic mills'. By the Twentieth Century, however, technology became associated with the positive consequences of economic progress and accepted if it fulfilled its primary purpose. Unintended and negative effects of technological change, difficult to anticipate or to conceptualize, were likely to be ignored (Bauer, 1969). There has developed, however, a growing literature on these second-order consequences of science and technology. It emphasizes that progress contains many contradictions, and that useful industrial technologies may lead to disastrous environmental and social problems. It notes that humane advances in medical science may threaten basic values and that techniques of efficient decision making may challenge democratic principles (Brooks, 1973a).

This literature on the impact of science and technology is largely descriptive and pragmatic, intended to generate policies of control or to encourage appropriate caution in specific areas of scientific or technical advance. It focuses largely on the impact of technology, but criticism reflects back on science as the source of technological advance. This section briefly focuses on these concerns with the negative aspects of technology, first exploring specific areas that are threatened by technological change.

Four areas of technological impact have assumed special importance as policy issues: the environment, work, civil liberties and democratic values. Technologies affecting these areas are controversial and the subject of high-level policy consideration. We will analyze how these problems appear on the policy agenda. What brings specific issues to public attention? Problems caused by technological change become 'front burner' issues in some places, but are ignored in others. Certain impacts of technology are of concern primarily to scholars; others are actively debated in public forums and generate specific policies of control. Why do some of the negative effects of technology become political issues, while others fail to arouse public interest? Two variables appear to effect the policy importance of technological impacts: the degree to which they provoke a public response. and their relationship to organized political and economic interests.

Areas of Impact

a) On the environment.[23] The 'environment' became a major political issue in the mid-1960's. The problems, however, were not new. Scholars have argued that the lead painting which decorated the pottery of upper-class Roman homes weakened the population and contributed to the decline of the Roman Empire (Gilfillan, 1965). In the United States, the conservation movement grew in the late Nineteenth Century; naturalists and foresters such as Charles Sargent, Bernhard Fernow and John Muir were concerned with

---

[23] For a bibliography of the social science literature on the environment, see Morrison (1973) and Caldwell and Siddigui (1974).

destructive farming and timber practices. But conservation and wildlife management soon became specialized and official activities – the responsibility of government bureaucracies – and the movement declined in political significance after World War I (Fleming, 1972; Nash, 1973; Passmore, 1974). Moreover, during this period technological development was increasingly valued as important to progress and the health of the national economy.

The renewal of public concern about environmental problems is often identified with the publication of Rachel Carson's *Silent Spring* (1962) which introduced millions of people to the systemic effects of pesticides. The testing of nuclear devices and the fear of radioactive fallout stimulated sensitivity to the environmental impacts of technology. And a continuing flow of news about environmental insults – some dramatic crises, others less visible but still ubiquitous problems – sustained public interest in the issue.

Sills (1975) suggests the vast scope of issues that have become part of the environmental movement: pollution, diminishing natural resources, inadequacy of world food supplies, and population growth. In 1972 some three hundred books on the environment were published in the United States; they ranged from popular descriptions to technical studies; they dealt with air, water and noise pollution, the potential radiological effects of civilian nuclear power programs, the impact of pesticides and the general problem of industrial wastes (Caldwell and Siddigui, 1974). Interest in these issues has been expressed in the proliferation of voluntary associations, in the protests confronting nearly every technological development that threatens the environment, and in governmental committees, conferences and legislation. The United Nations Conference on Human Environment in Stockholm in June 1972 brought together representatives of one hundred thirteen nations and led to the establishment of a world environmental secretariat, the United Nations Environmental Program (UNEP). Policies to ameliorate the environmental impact of technology are on the agenda of all national governments. They include programs for pollution abatement, population control and natural resources preservation; but actual activities depend on the extent to which they conflict with economic goals.

The United States Congress, through the National Environmental Policy Act (NEPA) of 1969 and the Environmental Quality Improvement Act of 1970, established environmental protection as national policy and set up procedures to improve environmental quality. These precedures require developers to present environmental impact statements for public review. This has given the environmental movement a sense of political efficacy; and the activity of citizens' groups, combined with the active role of the courts in the implementation of NEPA, has effectively kept the environmental impact of technology on the policy agenda. Nevertheless, as the environmental movement begins to impinge on other goals (e.g. the need for new sources of energy or concern for local employment), enthusiasm wanes and its goals are seriously compromised.

b) On the workplace.[24] The impact of technology on work has been a policy issue since the early days of industrial automation. Early concerns, often associated with the Luddites, focused on the fear of unemployment due to automation and technological change. Industrial expansion helped to avoid the anticipated problems, and concern shifted to indirect impacts of technology – problems of boredom and alienation caused by the routine and fragmented character of assembly-line work, and disruptions due to geographic mobility and skill obsolescence. Technological change in the work place produced several discomforting paradoxes. While technology has created new, higher-level jobs, requirements for specialized skills have blocked occupational mobility for many people. While educational changes have led to higher employment expectations, many monotonous jobs require submissive and dependent behavior. The specialization that follows from technological development tends to foster rigid hierarchical arrangements calling for patterns of coordination in industry that are implemented through tight supervision. Such organizational features have converged with the rigors of the assembly line to alienate the industrial worker, and this is reflected in industrial protest, absenteeism and general dissatisfaction with work (HEW, 1973).

The changing demands for labor that follow from technological change have also required relocating workers in new industries, upgrading their skills and training them for new careers (National Commission, 1966; Faunce, 1968; Nelson *et al.,* 1967). These needs are reinforced by the vulnerability of high-technology labor to economic fluctuations, a fact which became evident in the United States with the layoff of thousands of specialized engineers from the aerospace industry in the late 1960's.

Some high-technology professions have special problems of occupational safety, such as the radiation exposure from working on the development of electronic products, and the biological hazards of working with toxic substances in the chemical industry (Epstein and Grundy, 1974). The health hazards of polyvinyl chlorides, a class of chemicals used as the basis of many plastics, potentially endangers 1.5 million workers. One of the most serious safety problems is that of radiation exposure among plutonium workers. In the United States about seven to eight thousand people work in plutonium operations, and about seventeen thousand have worked in such employment since World War II. In 1969, a large fire at an Atomic Energy Commission plant which produced radioactive plutonium called attention to the special occupational hazards of the nuclear industry. Problems of protecting nuclear workers are further complicated by the employment of transient workers. Outside crews are often hired for work in nuclear fuel reprocessing plants for a short period until they reach the legal limit of radiation exposure; they have

---

[24] For an annotated bibliography and discussion of the central issues of technology and work, see Harvard (1969b).

limited instruction in safety procedures and are often unaware of the hazards of their job. The actual effect of exposure to small doses of plutonium, a potent carcinogen, is uncertain. It is, however, a major occupational hazard that will increase in importance as the nuclear fuel industry develops. Thus there are efforts in the United States to develop a registry of nuclear workers and to reevaluate the adequacy of occupational standards that were set in 1949.

The general malaise in the work place reflected in loss of production and absenteeism has generated interest in industrial democracy and worker control (Pateman, 1970; Vanek, 1971). There are many experiments with co-determination and decentralized arrangements of production. Yugoslav and Swedish industry have reorganized assembly lines to give workers more contact with the entire process of production, and they have established a system of participation in the management of firms. Experiments in democratization of industry have four objectives of equal importance: productivity, job satisfaction, improved working environments and security of employment. While reportedly successful in Sweden and in other isolated experiments which are watched with increasing interest, labor policy tends to concentrate on manpower programs that better adjust the working population to the exigencies of technological production (HEW, 1973).

c) On individual rights and civil liberties.[25] The early 1960's saw the burgeoning of electronic technology. The ability to create national computerized data banks with vast information storage capacity was first welcomed as a way to improve the efficiency of government and to provide an adequate and timely data base to assist the development of workable public policies. But technological opportunity also opened up new possibilities for the misuse of information.

Westin (1967) and Shils (1967) raise key issues of abuse of privacy and potential social control. Should some kinds of information be excluded from government files because they are too sensitive? What kinds of safeguards and laws should be developed? Should individuals have the right to check their own files? How can individuals be protected from harrassment on the basis of computerized information? For example, the 'cyclade' project in France, a plan for an integrated data bank for scientific information, is a source of controversy because it is a potential basis for an automated information system that can be misused by the police. Cases of computer crime have illustrated the vulnerability of data bank systems despite elaborate safeguards. Concern with the potential threats of these new technologies to civil liberties has been nourished by an occasional extreme proposal; for

---

[25] For an annotated bibliography and review of the civil liberties issues involved in biomedical research, see Harvard (1968). See also the monthly *Hastings Center Report* published by the Institute of Society, Ethics and Life Sciences (Hastings Institute). On data bank systems, see Westin and Baker (1972) and Hunt and Turn (1974).

example, a federal security agency proposed a surveillance scheme in which miniature electronic devices would be attached to criminals or suspect citizens, to be monitored by computers as 'an electronic substitute to social conditioning, group pressure, and individual motivation' (Mason, 1973). However, most scholarly analyses suggest that systematic electronic surveillance is a remote and unlikely possibility (Westin, 1970).

Scientific advances in the biomedical area raise similar questions. Techniques of genetic control (by chemical or surgical intervention) evoke images of the excesses of the eugenics movement (Bergsma, 1974; Hilton, 1972). And behavior control, such as electronical stimulation of the brain or the use of psychological or chemical manipulation, raises spectors of mass government control of behavior. Assessments of techniques of behavior control suggest that such fears are often exaggerated (Valenstein, 1973; Roslansky, 1966; Ulrich, 1966). But several pernicious proposals suggest how technologies, intented to resolve social problems, may be easily abused. In 1965 studies suggested that males with a high delinquency rate have a higher than expected incidence of the XYY genotype. This tenuous observation led to speculation about the relationship between violence and this genetic abberation, and stimulated a controversial discussion about preventive incarceration and other means to control XYY males in order to protect the public. Concerned with the implications of XYY research, a group of scientists at Harvard University proposed in 1974 that such research be forbidden at the institution, but such restrictions were voted down by the Harvard Medical School Faculty.

Similar issues were raised when a White House adviser proposed that all six to eight year old children take psychological tests to predict their criminal potential, and that those who failed be sent to a rehabilitation center. And in 1971, in a controversial speech to the American Psychological Association, its president, Kenneth B. Clark, suggested that, given the barbaric propensities of men, a requirement be imposed on all political leaders 'that they accept and use the earliest perfected form of psychotechnological, biochemical intervention which would . . . reduce or block the possibility of using power destructively' (See Valenstein, 1973). A more realistic danger is presented by the methadone maintenance program for heroin addicts. For those who control an addict's access to drugs have enormous power, and the social goal of reducing crime may easily lead to a disregard of the dignity and rights of the individual (Gerwitz, 1969, 1210; Nelkin, 1973).

d) On democracy.[26] The implications of technological change for political choice is a persistent theme in the literature on science and public policy. Many of the impacts of technology on the vaguely defined set of

---

[26] For an annotated bibliography and review of the impact of technology in the polity, see Harvard (1969a).

values known collectively as 'democracy' are subtle and indirect. Several tendencies in a technological society threaten democratic principles. First of these is the blurring of distinctions between public and private interests. Government is intended to be an independent and representative force, serving to balance and control vested interests. But through its system of contracts, government agencies may develop a stake in industrial development, reducing their capacity to exercise independent control.[27]

A second characteristic of a technological society is the power afforded to those who control technical information. Analyses of post-industrial society point to the increasing importance of scientific knowledge as an 'apolitical' basis of policy formation (Bell, 1960 and 1973; Lane, 1966; see also Lakoff, Chapter 10).

> Much of the history of social progress in the Twentieth Century can be described in terms of the transfer of wider and wider areas of public policy from politics to expertise . . . . often the problems of political choice have become buried in debates among experts over highly technical alternatives (Brooks, 1965, 68).

Expertise, if accessible, is a useful resource – a source of informed choice that can create many possibilities for increased democratization. But it may also serve as a weapon for social manipulation in the name of rationality (Benveniste, 1972; Melanson, 1973). It may be a window dressing or public relations device to justify policies already determined, or a 'paprika' which adds color but little substance to given perspectives (Martin, 1973; Wilensky, 1956). The increasing requirements for technical expertise as a basis for public decisions have also created a sense of political alienation – a loss of personal efficacy. Thus, the role of expertise has revived the old debate on 'technocracy'; that is to say, the argument over the extent to which government is controlled by experts. Meynaud (1968) observes a shift of political power from elected representatives to technocrats who are not directly accountable to the public. Marcuse (1964), on the other hand, argues that technology is an instrument that reinforces the political status quo:

> Today political power asserts itself through its power over the machine process and over the technical organization . . . . Validated by the accomplishments of science and technology, justified by its growing productivity, the status quo defies all transcendence.

Scientists themselves are seldom in positions of power, but they enhance the power of those who dispose of technical resources (Ealau, 1973). This may lead to a more rational and efficient society, but it also undermines the legitimacy of elected political leaders. Government can be reduced to a position of legitimacy that is based less on its representative nature than on

---

[27] The best examples of this can be seen by tracing the history of regulatory agencies and their gradual assimilation of the goals of the industries they regulate.

its ability to manipulate and control the context of facts and values in which policies are shaped (Lowi, 1972).[28]

Finally, the use of sophisticated decision-making techniques also threatens to undermine democratic principles. Quantification, it is feared, can create a false sense of confidence in the understanding of complex problems, confusing efficiency with the moral and political ends of social policy (Myrdal, 1969).[29] Computer simulations, for example, used as a basis for decision making:

> lend an aura of rigor and infallibility not justified by the hardness of the data or the validity of the assumptions on which they are based. They may thus come to be relied on disproportionately, especially in decision-making situations in which the issues are large and the uncertainty great (Harvard, 1972).

Policy Importance Whether or not the impacts of science and technology appear on the policy agenda depends on a number of factors including the extent of public response to particular problems and the relationship of the particular issue to organized political and economic interests.

a) Public response. Some problems become salient policy issues when dedicated individuals – Rachel Carson, Ralph Nader, Linus Pauling – mobilize public concern through writing or persistent political activity. The influence of individuals, however, depends on a responsive public. Hirschman (1970) provides a model that helps to explain the increasing political response to the problems of technological change. If there are many opportunities to 'exit' from a system, there is wide latitude for its deterioration. But when options to exit decline, that is when there are decreasing opportunities to escape from the impact of technological change, and when affected groups are more likely to voice their concern, to make demands on the political system.

Political demands tend to focus on issues that are highly visible or dramatic, especially if they relate to public safety. In March 1967 the Torrey Canyon, a huge oil tanker, spilled more than 100,000 tons of crude oil into the ocean off the southwest coast of Britain, causing extensive damage to marine life and to the beaches in both England and France. A similar problem occured in January 1969 with a massive oil leak from an offshore drilling operation near Santa Barbara, California. Millions of gallons of oil were lost, despoiling thirty miles of beach. The media dramatized the incident with

---

[28] Interestingly, it was a technology – the invention of printing and the subsequent extension of literacy – that reduced the power of the church to manipulate and control information and thereby contributed significantly to democratization.

[29] The literature on the limits of rationalistic models of decision making is extensive. See, for example, Arrow (1964), Boguslaw (1965), Hoos (1974), and Lindblom (1965).

vivid photographs of oil-coated birds. These dramatic and costly accidents had a profound impact on the environmental movement, mobilizing many people who previously had little concern with such issues. They campaigned for more stringent regulation of offshore drilling and shipment of oil, and generated increased federal interest in environmental legislation (Steinhart, 1972).

A similar public response has occured in visible cases of industrial pollution. A smoker in the Soviet Union threw a cigarette in the Iset River and it caught fire, dramatizing the problems caused by industrial wastes in all societies (Goldman, 1970). When cities were small and industries dispersed, waste disposal problems were of little interest. Mercury discharge from industry, for example, was long accepted as a reasonable cost of industrial activity. However, a series of incidents led to the realization that the expansion of industry and the quantity of waste were exceeding the capacity of the natural environment to absorb damage, and that this was harmful to human health. A discovery that pickerel in a lake on the United States-Canadian border contained excessive mercury resulted in a ban on commercial fishing. Soon afterwards, a chemist discovered a high mercury level in canned tuna fish and it was recalled from grocery shelves. These discoveries coincided with a widely publicized tragedy in Minamata City, Japan, where forty eight people died from eating fish contaminated by mercury discharge from a local chemical plant.

Tragedies have also provoked public concern with industrial safety practices. An explosion in the Flicksborough chemical factory in Ireland which killed thirty workers and leveled part of a town became a symbol of technological disaster. Subsequently, the siting of chemical plants has been a controversial political issue in Great Britain. Similarly, a large fire at an AEC plutonium process plant called public attention to the occupational hazards in the nuclear industry.

Dramatic events have brought the problem of drug regulation to the level of major policy concern. The thalidomide tragedy raised questions about a number of technical issues: appropriate testing procedures for new drugs, the kinds of data necessary to permit the sale of drugs, the certainty with which one must be able to predict a clinical response before marketing a product, and the kinds of animals that are appropriate test subjects (Lasagna, 1969). Once the thalidomide problem was discovered, a once reluctant United States Congress quickly passed legislation which gave greatly increased regulatory control to the Food and Drug Administration.

Acceptance of new technologies may be strongly influenced by their potential impacts on public health or physical safety (MRI, 1973). It is relatively easy to provoke public opposition to technological change if there is a possible hazard to health involved; for laymen who are unable to evaluate the details of technical arguments tend to choose those options with the least apparent risk. The arguement that fluoridation is slow poisoning was more persuasive to the public than the promise of reduced tooth decay, and fluoridation was generally rejected by those communities where the question was voted in referendum (Crain *et al.,* 1969). Similarly, the potential health risks of nuclear accidents have spurred citizen opposition to nuclear power plants (Nelkin, 1971). Indeed, many aspects of the civil nuclear energy program, from the transport of radioactive material to the storage of nuclear wastes, have become political issues because of their bearing on public safety (Willrich, 1973).

The visible and dramatic impacts of certain technologies and their effect on health and safety have brought public concern, but the policy response also depends on many political and economic factors. The socio-economic status of groups affected by a technology, or the ability of organizations responsible for technological development to divert attention away from negative consequences, may have a significant bearing on the political salience of a problem.

b) Political and economic interests. The Alaska pipeline was long delayed by environmental concerns that were aroused by the oil spills. However, the pipeline was eventually approved in the face of opposition as the energy crisis created new priorities. Similarly, given the economic problems and energy needs of Great Britain, the environmental hazards involved in drilling for North Sea oil have provoked little discussion. The decision to develop a nuclear power program in England was far less controversial than similar plans in the United States. To some extent historical factors affect the perceptions of a problem. In the United States nuclear power tends to remain associated with wartime uses. The debates following World War II left a fear of radiation that is still evident in discussions about civilian nuclear power. But in England, coal mining has bitter associations, and nuclear power appears to be relatively advantageous. Construction of nuclear power plants in France was at first accepted as a source of local employment. The French-made nuclear power facilities on the banks of the Loire received a larger number of visitors than the Renaissance Chateaux situated nearby. The acceptance of nuclear power plants also reflected a confidence that government and the EDF (Electricité de France) would protect local communities against industrial hazards. However, when the French government announced the plan for a very large expansion of the nuclear program, opposition developed; this was in part due to fear of radiation, but was also provoked by resentment of a nuclear program based on the purchase of American reactors.

The magnitude of a potential hazard may have less to do with its salience as a policy issue than political factors. Legislators will often ignore warnings by technical advisers if they contradict existing policies or would expose an administration to political difficulties. Recommendations to limit the use of DDT were ignored for eight years until protest and litigation indicated the strength of public concern. Similarly, the administration continued to support the SST (supersonic transport) for years despite warnings by United

States Presidential science adviser Lee Dubridge:

> Granted that this is an exciting technological development, it still seems best to me to avoid the serious environmental and nuisance problems, and the government should not be subsidizing a device which has neither commercial attractiveness nor public acceptance (U.S. Congressional Record, 1969).

The importance of politics becomes apparent when one compares diverse policy responses to similar problems. Why is it, for example, that a 'dead' lake may provoke public action in one location, but be totally ignored in another? Why are there active efforts to control air pollution in some cities while in others similar problems fail to become policy issues?

Crenson (1971) attempts to explain how seemingly important problems fail to become policy issues; he compares the response to pollution incidents in contiguous cities with similar air quality problems. In one of the cities, air pollution had long been an active political issue. In the other, the problem was outside the limits of political debate, because United States Steel, the company at the source of the pollution, controlled the power structure and local employment. Thus the company could limit the scope of policy concerns and air quality was not on the policy agenda until federal regulations intervened.

Many economic and political factors enter the definition of policy problems. For example, the public was led to support environmental protection policies by arguments that environmental quality was an issue of human survival. These policies, however, quickly became controversial when it became evident that they would have significant economic implications (Morrison, 1972). Sills (1975) describes the growing body of literature that attacks the environmental movement as a middle class social activity that ignores the needs of the less affluent. Indeed, environmentalists tend to be educated, middle-class citizens with the resources to engage in citizen group protest. Their efforts to limit technological development have been criticized as 'elitist', 'a racist shuck', 'a threat to social justice', and 'the rich man's politics of choice versus the poor man's politics of necessity' (See Neuhaus, 1971). Regulations to minimize pollution may also put the factory worker out of his job; zoning to preserve environmental quality may preclude low-cost housing; and limiting technological development may directly conflict with job mobility and other needs of low-income people (Babcock and Callies, 1973). Similarly, poor nations have viewed the environmental movement as a threat to development.

There are, of course, responses to this criticism of the environmental movement. Environmentalists argue that the negative impacts of technology also affect poor and working-class populations. As the wealthy move to suburban areas, it is the poor, remaining in the inner cities, who suffer the worst insults of technological change. Studies of air pollution in United States cities, for example, suggest that the most polluted areas coincide with inner-city housing for low-income groups (Zupan, 1973). In any case, the problems of how low-income groups must be handled are a separate issue, because technological progress in the past has not by itself led to more equitable income distribution.

Criticism of the environmental movement raises the important question of how various groups can translate their concerns with technological change into public policy. Developers often justify the burdens of technology imposed on a local area by claiming that their project is 'in the public interest' or that it serves 'the greatest good for the greatest number'. However, communities that bear the burdens of technology are more and more often refusing to sacrifice their local interests. The difficulties in balancing local costs with regional or national benefits suggest the broader problem underlying most efforts to evaluate the impacts of technology: the difficulty of measuring and incorporating the intensity of localized negative impacts into calculations of 'the greatest good' (Nelkin, 1975).

Concern with the impacts of science and technology has proven to be not only costly but politically problematic, involving choices that threaten various groups within the political system. The rapid rate of development of science and technology has upset established relationships and threatened accepted values and expectations. Efforts to deal with these problems raise new and difficult policy dilemmas of regulation and control.

CONTROL

The development of science and technology is normally controlled by budget allocations, tax policies and the general process of government standard-setting. Federal governments, heavily subsidizing R & D and controlling tariffs, have an automatic leverage over technological change.[30] Concern with the destructive potential of science and technology, however, has generated various special strategies of regulation and control. Some of these may be called *participatory* controls, involving efforts by citizen groups and scientists to obstruct special technological developments; to 'blow the whistle' on research that has potentially destructive applications; and to encourage increased participation by affected interests in decision making. Others of these are strategies that develop as a *reaction* to the impact of existing technologies. Regulatory agencies and the courts are reactive institutions. Although they may set standards regulating future scientific and technological activities, they act in response to technologies that are sufficiently well-advanced that

---

[30] Note, for example, that the United States Congressional vote which blocked the SST was not a ban on its development but simply a decision to withdraw public monies; this in itself was an effective means of control.

their impacts are evident. Given the momentum of technological change, there are also efforts to develop systematic *anticipatory* controls – that is, procedures to predict the social, political and economic impacts of new scientific and technological developments.

Controls may require social trade-offs, pitting economic growth against environmental reform or considerations of efficiency against equity. And they may involve coercive constraints on freedom and autonomy in areas of private and public decision making. This section discusses strategies of participatory, reactive and anticipatory controls and their controversial implications.

Participatory Controls   Everywhere, scientific and technological projects are obstructed or delayed as various groups try to bring community values to bear on technological decisions. Heightened sensitivity to the environmental and social impacts of modern technology is reflected in disillusionment with the specialized institutions of a technological society, and in increased demands for local control as a means to generate desirable policies. In the United States there has been marked proliferation of voluntary associations – of citizens and of scientists – concerned with controlling technological change. White and Sjoberg (1972) have labelled this tendency 'mobilization politics' – political action in which groups mobilize to oppose specific decisions and demand a voice in technical issues that are normally handled at the agency level. Carroll (1971) coined the term 'participatory technology' which he defined as 'the inclusion of people in the social and technical processes of developing, implementing and regulating a technology'.

a) Citizen group involvement. Citizen groups in the United States have proliferated in response to technological change.[31] Some are temporary coalitions formed to protect local interests by opposing projects such as power plants or airports. Other groups are organized on a more permanent basis, often as branches of a national organization such as the Sierra Club or Friends of the Earth. Such organizations often form on the basis of shared ideological perspectives. They have means to acquire needed expertise, a stable budget, and direct channels to the media and to political authorities.

Citizen group activity at the local level generally begins as a reaction against plans to introduce a specific technology. Demands, however, often escalate from these specific concerns to questions of responsibility and local control (Morrison, 1972). For example, a community organization demanding specific changes in airport operating procedures in order to reduce noise

---

[31] This movement toward increased citizen participation is primarily an American phenomenon. Traditional relationships between citizens and government, and problems of access to information about government decision making, have limited similar activities in most European countries.

soon begins to question the adequacy of the decision-making process, and to search for ways to influence airport decisions, such as a long-range master plan to be approved in public forum (Nelkin, 1974).[32]

The cumbersome nature of citizen participation is extraordinarily threatening to organizations responsible for technical planning. They predict polarization and political paralysis, and anticipate costly delays that will seriously obstruct technological progress (Gakenheimer, 1975). Emphasizing the technical competence required to make efficient decisions, these organizations seek decision-making autonomy while those who demand greater public involvement argue that technical competence and efficiency are not a sufficient basis for authority.

Robert Dahl (1970), concerned with the bases of authority in a democratic society, argues that 'personal choice' must prevail as a criterion for accepting authority as legitimate, except in situations where either special competence or the need for efficiency is clearly of overriding importance. A surgeon's competence, for example, must prevail over personal choice on the operating table but not in the decision of whether or not to undergo surgery. In situations of crisis, participation based on 'personal choice' must necessarily give way to efficiency. Military organizations, hospitals or other institutions with urgent and explicit objectives tend to be authoritarian, for efficiency and competence prevail as a legitimate basis for their authority.

The usual context of technological decision making, however, is not one of crisis, and objectives are often complex and controversial, perceived by diverse groups in quite different ways. Citizen participation is cumbersome and subject to demographic manipulation, but it potentially allows the expression of existing diversity. This can lead to more rational choice; for adversary procedure and the anticipation of challenge may improve the quality of input into decision (Coser, 1956). Thus, the policy literature reflects the considerable interest in finding practical and reasonable ways to engage citizens at an early stage of technical decision making before plans are crystallized and options limited.[33]

Public participation in decisions involving science and technology poses

---

[32] A similar evolution from specific demands to a concern with the decision-making process has been evident in other areas as well: note the concern with patients' rights in critiques of medical practice, with local control in urban planning, and with corporate accountability in the consumer movement. See Nelkin (1975) for a review of the similarities among these various movements with respect to their concerns with expert decision making.

[33] Increasing demands for direct participation in planning are discussed in Thompson (1970) and Alford (1969). Proposals for various mechanisms of participation include electronic referenda (Calder, 1971); lay representation on the boards of management of research institutes, universities and other organizations engaged in research (Rose and Rose, 1969); and increased development of locally based citizen pressure groups (Commoner, 1966).

special difficulties for the nonexpert. Complex data supporting a particular development cannot be challenged without counterexpertise (Benveniste, 1972; Mazur, 1973; Nelkin, 1975). Inequities in the distribution of technical knowledge have stimulated 'public interest science', a movement among scientists to engage in political activity which they deem to be in the public interest.

b) Public interest science. The involvement of scientists in political activity has long been a sensitive and divisive issue within the scientific community (See Lakoff, Chapter 10). Scientists approach political issues with ambivalence and find it difficult to reconcile the ideal of scientific autonomy and objectivity with demands for public responsibility.[34] Issues concerning the impact of technology, charged with conflicting public values and uncertain technical dimensions, pose particular problems (Nelkin, 1971). Since World War II, scientists have served as expert advisers, but they often experience considerable ambivalence as formal advisory mechanisms are manipulated to suit the political needs of public officials. Those who speak up against administration policies are not likely to remain in advisory positions (Don K. Price, 1974). Generally the close relationship between consultants and the agencies they advise tends to foster uncritical evaluation of new technologies. 'On the whole, the greatest occupational hazard of advisory committees is not conflict, but platitudinous consensus', claims Brooks (1964). And Haberer (1969) describes the relationship of scientists to government as 'prudential acquiescence'. In this light, many scientific activists do not try to influence agencies directly, but take questionable issues to the public, using the media or dramatic devices to turn problems of science and technology into policy issues.

A striking period of political activism among scientists developed with the concern about the dangers of nuclear testing during the 1950's (Gilpin, 1962; Wittner, 1969). Later, during the Vietnam War, the energies of scientific activists focused on anti-war activities and the issue of military-related research in universities (Nelkin, 1972). More recently, the environment, natural resources and energy are prevailing concerns. Several major scientific societies

---

[34] The literature reflects the ambivalence of scientists about their political relationships. Is science an autonomous, self-regulating activity concerned only with discovery and diffusion of knowledge? Or a resource dedicated to the promotion of knowledge to improve the condition of man? Are scientists a 'new priesthood' displacing the political elite? Or are they 'handmaidens' to established political authorities? Should scientists remain neutral and apolitical? Or should they take adversary positions in public affairs relating to the application of science and technology? These diverse images are described and analyzed in Chapters 10 and 13 of this volume, and in Blume (1974), Gilpin and Wright (1964), Haberer (1969), Merton (1973), Don K. Price (1965, 1969a), Primack and von Hippel (1974) and Teich (1974). Note that the concept of the public interest itself is sufficiently vague as to exacerbate the problems of scientists' involvement.

have formed committees to conduct technical studies of policy problems such as chemistry and the environment, herbicides in Vietnam, or the impact of weather modification (Rich, 1974). Independent groups of scientists have developed technical critiques of government policies. Some, like the Federation of American Scientists, work through conventional political channels to influence national policy. Others become embroiled in local controversies. Organizations such as the Center for Science in the Public Interest, the Center for Concerned Engineers and the Union of Concerned Scientists devote their attention to providing technical information to citizens (Nichols, 1974). In these ways, public-interest scientists seek to provoke administrative and legal reaction to the problems posed by scientific and technological change.[35]

Reactive Controls   Regulatory agencies and the courts are continually faced with many new and difficult problems posed by science and technology. They are primarily reactive institutions; they do not seek out potential hazards of new technologies but deal with existing problems that threaten particular interests. They register complaints, but do not try to discern future impacts of nascent technologies. Administrative and legal controls are used to influence scientific and technological development in several ways. They can modify the structure of economic incentives to discourage harmful practices, issue directives to regulate or prohibit private activity or change decision-making structures by creating the apparatus to monitor technology.

a) Regulatory agencies. Regulatory agencies are traditionally expert and non-political bodies with both judicial and legislative responsibilities. They were created as independent commissions to regulate industry when private enterprise provided inadequate public protection. They regulate industrial practices by setting rates and safety standards and issuing permits, and they influence the development of technology by controlling prices, profits and entry into the market (Noll, 1971; Mainzer, 1973).

The Interstate Commerce Commission (ICC) was the first of these agencies, created in 1887 and given considerable power to control industrial practice. Then in 1920, during a period of concern with rapid industrial development, new legislation gave the Commission the additional responsibility of fostering industrial growth and insuring fair profit for private owners of regulated industries. These new responsibilities clearly conflicted with the regulatory function. Subsequently, the conflicting responsibilities of many

---

[35] Some scientists have responded to the problems of technology by questioning its intrinsic form and experimenting with alternate or soft technologies. They argue that the principle problems of modern technology can be avoided by designing technologies that are non-polluting and use only renewable resources. Alternate technologies (electric-generating windmills, devices to convert wastes into fertilizer, systems of biological pest control) are designed for production and use on a local level. Most proponents of alternate technology are not seeking to jettison scientific knowledge but to use it in new ways (Clark, 1973).

commissions – to promote as well as to regulate industry – have created many problems which are exacerbated as the impacts of technology assume increasing importance.

The efficacy of agency control has also been limited by the hazy distinction between public and private sectors of the economy. Government involvement in supporting scientific and technological advance in areas such as domestic nuclear power and aviation creates problems of regulation.

> When government makes a decision to develop a technology on a more or less predetermined time scale, there is a natural tendency for those who have a vested interest in the program . . . to become obsessed with their programmatic objectives and to minimize the social hazards or problems which may be inherent in the practice of the technology after it has been developed (Green, 1968).

Given such biases, the political autonomy of commissions often fails to serve its intended purpose. Commissions were organized to be independent of partisan politics; they were intended as a means to protect weak as well as powerful political interests. However, the concept of political autonomy was based on the association of politics with party affiliation; it neglected the role of special interests as a political force. Yet commissions, especially those that deal with a single industry like the Federal Communications Commission, are often co-opted by these interests. As isolation from politics weakens their response to current political concerns, they tend to adapt more to the interests of the industries they regulate than to public demands.

The complexity of technology and its systemic character creates special problems of regulation. Specialized commissions responsible for regulating specific industrial activities are often unsuited to cope with systemic problems. Proposed reforms include greater centralization and coordination of regulatory activities through a single administrative official, and a system of expanded representation that would formally recognize the reality of interest group pressure on regulatory agencies. There has been some actual reorganization in crucial areas. The establishment in the United States of the Environmental Protection Agency and the Council for Environmental Quality in 1970 centralized control of projects likely to have adverse environmental impacts. The Energy Reorganization Act of 1974 abolished the Atomic Energy Commission and set up separate agencies, one responsible for R & D and domestic uses of atomic energy, another for the regulation of nuclear facilities.

Improvements in the technology of detection, for example the increasing ability to detect toxic substances likely to be carcinogenic, continuously create new problems for regulatory agencies. In addition, new problems caused by technological advance tend to generate proposals for new regulatory bodies – special review boards in hospitals, new environmental monitoring agencies or ombudsmen-type organizations to audit new technology programs. These often incorporate increased lay participation. But for the aggrieved citizen, the courts are the primary means of access to a responsive decision-making forum.

b) The courts. The courts are one of the few formal decision-making mechanisms that can be used by private citizens who have a grievance. Citizen-initiated lawsuits have increased in response to problems associated with technology, and litigation has been a major means to restrict and direct technological change (Bereano, 1974). The role of the courts in this area has expanded with the extension of the legal doctrine of standing which determines who has a right to be heard in court. The extension allows a private citizen to present a grievance as an advocate of the public interest without an alleged personal economic injury.[36]

The courts function in several ways with respect to science and technology. First, they define responsibility for damages caused by technology. Judgments based on tort law have tended to impose damages, thus internalizing the costs of technology within the enterprise generating them. Some scholars argue that such incentives are the appropriate means to foster technological responsibility (Katz, 1969). Others feel that economic pressures are generally ineffective; enterprises are often willing to pay damages rather than change their practices. Moreover, the courts are intrinsically hampered in such decisions by the difficult problem of establishing proof of harm (Tribe, 1971).

The courts, however, can also respond to complaints by imposing injunctions against proposed technologies that may be harmful. This function has expanded in the United States where the courts have become the institutions responsible for evaluating controversial environmental impact statements and for overseeing the implementation of the National Environmental Policy Act (NEPA). The Alaska pipeline, for example, was delayed by court injunction when the oil companies failed to demonstrate acceptable design criteria for the pipeline and to give adequate consideration to alternate routes (Sax, 1971). Through such decisions the burden of responsibility for environmental damage has shifted to developers, and the threat of injunction has become a major means to encourage thorough investigation of the impacts of technology in order to meet statutory requirements.

A third role of the courts is to galvanize administrative agencies and regulatory commissions into more effective action by reaffirming standards. In an important case testing the implementation of NEPA, *Calvert Cliffs vs.*

---

[36] The new concept of 'standing' was developed in a United States Supreme Court decision (*Sierra Club vs. Morton,* 19 April 1972). It held that direct *individual* interests (which need not be economic) were sufficient to present a grievance, and that an *organization* could not merely allege non-economic injury. In a charming extension of the rules of standing, Stone (1974) proposes that 'we give legal rights to forests, oceans, rivers and so-called other natural objects in the environment'; that 'trees have standing', that is, the right to seek redress on their own behalf.

AEC (1971), a United States court of appeals forced the AEC to take into account general environmental as well as radiological hazards in licensing power plants.

The courts have thus played a major role in policy issues concerning science and technology. Yet they are not primarily policy-making bodies. Despite a well-developed system of using 'expert witnesses', the courts cannot deal with esoteric scientific information that necessarily involves many uncertainties. Many of the problems of technology require evaluation of potential risks at some future date. Judgments must be based on statistical evidence; cancer risk, for example, requires statistical evaluation. Yet judges are accustomed to ruling on the basis of dramatic past events; they expect to 'see' the injured person. Moreover, the courts are constrained to make yes-or-no rulings in highly specific situations. Operating in a context of accepted norms and values, they avoid general rulings that would set new precedents.

Developments in science and technology continually raise problems that require reanalysis of legal principles. What, for example, is the appropriate role of law in controlling fetal research or genetic experimentation? When medical researchers studying aborted fetuses were tried for 'grave robbing' in Boston, this intimidated other researchers. How can the courts deal with such new questions that arise in the wake of expanded clinical research without stifling scientific progress? How can they deal with questions of fairness when technological changes justified by 'public interest' infringe on local community interests? In response to such issues, scholars search for ways to extend legal concepts and to establish a basis for judicial decisions in areas of new scientific and technological development.[37]

c) Regulation and the dilemmas of government control. Government efforts at regulation and control have focused both on questionable research practices and on the undesirable social applications of R & D. The ethical problems of human experimentation have been widely analyzed (Barber, 1973; Katz, 1972). In the United States, practices of human experimentation are regulated by guidelines from the Surgeon General's Office, and these are based on the Nuremburg codes requiring voluntary and informed consent as a means to protect research subjects. However, the general expansion of clinical research plus several scandals involving the abuse of experimental subjects in federally funded research programs have stimulated efforts to strengthen regulations. These would impose strict controls on research using prisoners, children, the mentally ill and others in constraining situations which limit the 'voluntary' nature of research participation.

---

[37] Carroll (1971) describes the difficulties of finding conceptual correspondence between scientific and technological developments and legal concepts. Scientific systems may further different values than do legal systems. The problems of the courts in dealing with policy questions of fairness are analyzed by Tribe (1972) and Michelman (1967).

Administration controls over application of R & D operate mainly through market incentives: taxation procedures to reduce the sale of harmful products, effluent fees and penalties to discourage practices that cause pollution, or rate schedules adjusted to provide incentives for safeguards. But controls may also emphasize direct government power to set standards and to prohibit harmful practices. This power is exercised through the granting of permits for the construction and operation of large-scale facilities such as airports and power plants, or through the requiring of specific protections such as automobile seat belts, or safeguards to prevent illegal access to national data banks. Control is exercised through direct prohibition of certain products such as cyclamates, pesticides or drugs that are felt to be inadequately tested.

As agencies impose restrictions and controls, they are compelled to make their decisions on the basis of uncertain knowledge and the inherent difficulties in establishing cause and effect relationships between a new technology and its risks. To approve a drug for marketing, the Food and Drug Administration (FDA) must judge its safety and efficacy, but there is little agreement about how much knowledge is in fact adequate to evaluate the safety of a drug or new drug treatment program (Lasagna, 1969). There are many cases of over-hasty implementation as new detection skills and diagnostic techniques are developed. The discovery of a technique to diagnose phenylketonuria (PKU), a genetic defect associated with mental retardation, was followed immediately by legislation requiring compulsory screening programs. Positive diagnosis calls for a drastic deprivation diet. A number of deaths were caused by this diet before it was discovered that the testing procedures were yielding false positives (Anderson, 1967). Yet the screening programs clearly had benefits that would be lost by delay.[38]

Direct government controls over both research methodologies and applications raise difficult policy problems. Compulsory controls elicit accusations of government paternalism and overprotection. Should there be compulsory controls when risks are primarily assumed by individuals?[39] How can individual risks be balanced against social benefits? These questions assume their most dramatic form in efforts to control biomedical research practices. The literature on human experimentation illustrates several general questions bearing on the control of research methods. Should a system of ethics be codified into law? And if so, can general ethical criteria be translated into workable guidelines in specific situations? Scientists strongly resist external controls as obstructing useful scientific and technical progress (Lederberg, 1971). They argue that traditional means of self-regulation through the

---

[38] A similar problem in assessing the appropriate extent of knowledge necessary before policy implementation has occurred in policies concerning auto emissions. Note, for example, the discovery of sulfur after catalysts were installed.

[39] This issue is especially controversial in cases of government regulations concerning smoking and automobile safety.

collegial review system, or in the case of doctors, their responsibility to patients, are adequate safeguards — that autonomy is necessary to maintain the effectiveness of the scientific endeavor. Thus, professional societies and research establishments often try to set their own codes of ethics to regulate the work of their constituents and to avoid direct controls from outside the profession.

Controls over the applications of technology also present difficult choices. Restrictions on the use of pesticides, for example, can limit necessary food production, a choice pejoratively labelled 'cancer versus corn'. There are special problems of regulating products with a small but important market such as life-saving drugs for rare but extremely serious diseases. Is it reasonable that such products must meet the same criteria as products serving a broad market? And will such hurdles discourage vitally needed innovation in areas such as drugs and specific pesticides for insect control (Djerassi *et al.*, 1974)? In these areas, increased prices caused by regulatory pressures on industry can discourage the development of new and beneficial technologies.

In the development of biomedical technologies, there are efforts to exercise direct professional controls through bans on certain kinds of research (e.g. genetic research) that may lead to destructive applications. The controversial work linking race and IQ brought about discussions of 'forbidden knowledge' (Wartofsky, 1974). And just as some scientists have boycotted defense work, individuals have also refused to work in questionable areas of biomedical research.

Both regulation and litigation remain passive controls. The courts and regulatory agencies neither promote change nor anticipate future problems, they merely react to outside initiatives. They may have an impact on future planning, but only through their response to the problems of existing technologies. Thus the rapid pace of change has prompted a search for ways to anticipate new technologies and their consequences, and to exercise control through prevention.

Anticipatory Controls   New technologies become integrated into society before their impact is fully realized and, once woven into the economic, political and cultural system, change is difficult. The commitment to the private automobile, for example, has complicated the development of mass transit systems. To avoid such situations, techniques of forecasting and assessment have been developed to anticipate prospective technologies and to predict their potential consequences. Computer-based information systems, social indicators, Planning-Programming-Budgeting Systems (PPBS), modeling, gaming and simulation, future-conjecture methods, Delphi, program evaluation and technology assessment: these are all elaborate techniques to reduce uncertainty and to allow rational direction of technological change before there are major and irreversible commitments.

a) Forecasting and futures research. Some forecasting techniques are simply extrapolations from past trends, such as efforts to predict the short-term effect of investment practices. Others are conditional statements based on a defined set of assumptions such as the demographic projections that follow from interpretation of fertility and mortality trends (Ayres, 1969; Bright and Schoeman, 1973). These techniques, though often considering many variables, are ultimately based on extrapolations that imply a continuity between the past and the future. This is often empirically difficult to justify (Milch, 1975).

Other techniques minimize references to the past, projecting the future in terms of desirable objectives (Salomon, 1973 and Chapter 2; Jantsch, 1967). Delphi, for example, was a controversial technique developed by the Rand Corporation to obtain systematically the judgments of experts about anticipated change. Experts were polled anonymously in a set of sequential interrogations designed to bring together diverse points of view concerning the likely consequences of future technologies. Such definitions of the future are intended to serve as a guide to present planning and research, but the technique, poorly validated, has had little influence.

'Think-tanks' such as the Hudson Institute in New York and the Maison de Futuribles (SEDEIS) in Paris specialize in evaluating the future for policy purposes by generating 'scenarios' of long-term possible events and by assigning probabilities to various outcomes. Their efforts are constrained by methodological difficulties. Prediction implies a sophisticated understanding of functional relationships, and it assumes order and rationality in systems likely to be influenced by chance. Technological forecasting, claims Salomon (1973), 'defies chance as if it were dealing with a reality independent of man'. Prediction is based on the profoundly optimistic expectation that: 'Provided techniques are perfected and applied systematically to government decisions affecting science, rationality will soon make a mockery of history by mastering all chance events'. However, like the Roman techniques of interpreting omens, predictions themselves may create the future, 'substituting the art of forecasting for the art of decisions and transferring technical trends into social objectives' (Salomon, 1973, 106-7).

Michael (1973) also emphasizes the 'unpredictability of the future, the limited rationality of men, the logical and operational dilemmas of setting goals and priorities, the pragmatic and expedient conduct of politics' (Michael, 1973, 4). But he argues that the resulting lack of planning – the policy of 'disjointed incrementation' based on negotiation by competing interest groups – is inadequate in a technological society. He advocates a system of 'long-range societal planning' that incorporates techniques of future studies in a spirit that emphasizes 'learning how to act in light of continuously revised anticipation of the future'.

b) Technology assessment. The term technology assessment was coined

by a subcommittee of the United States Congress, and defined by Congress-
man Emilio Q. Daddario as 'a method of analysis that systematically appraises
the nature, significance, status and merit of a technological process' (Hetman,
1973, 55). It is essentially an extended version of cost-benefit analysis — a
technique to evaluate the full range of possible effects of technology in order
to guide public policy and to make anticipatory social decisions that would
minimize undesirable side effects. Assessments are in principle carried out
before a new technology is applied; thus it is an anticipatory control — an
early warning system to minimize risk and maximize public advantage.
Assessments are also called for as new scientific results change our understanding of existing well-established technologies, as in the case of the effect
of freon, released by aerosol spray cans, on the ozone layer.

Technology assessments are intended to be comprehensive. One of the
more elaborate approaches lays out seven steps to an assessment: defining a
task, describing relevant technologies, developing the nontechnological factors influencing applications of the technology, identifying areas that would
be most influenced by application, tracing the process by which the technology influences a society, identifying alternate programs for obtaining
maximum public advantage from the technology and finally analyzing the
social consequences of each option.[40]

Most studies fall far short of this comprehensive ideal. They range from
simple analyses of the direct technical performance of proposed technologies
to comprehensive economic and environmental evaluations. Some focus narrowly on a specific technology to assess its potential consequences. Partial
assessments often select specific categories of technological impacts (such as
environment) to explore in depth. There are experiments with multidisciplinary analyses of selected aspects of technological development —
exhaustive evaluations of projects such as the expansion and siting of airports.[41] Another type of assessment, called a 'multi-impact evaluation', is an
open-ended analysis of a single technology that attempts to explore as many
broad aspects of the problem as possible. For example, a National Academy
of Engineering assessment of subsonic aircraft noise (1969) considered technological possibilities of noise reduction, economic effects on local and
regional areas, social factors relating to individual rights, safety and recrea-
tion, and the political feasibility of implementing change.

These assessments are based on complex predictive techniques: 'relevance

---

[40] This type of approach was developed by MITRE Corporation for the United
States Office of Science and Technology. Hetman (1973) thoroughly reviews and
documents the various approaches to technology assessment. There is also increasing
interest in this approach in Europe (Derian and Staropoli, 1975).

[41] Good examples of such assessments were the evaluation of sites for the Third
London Airport and the study of the impact of the expansion of New York's Kennedy
Airport. See Commission on Third London Airport, 1970; and National Academy of
Sciences and Engineering, 1971.

trees' to trace chains of technical activities, 'mapping' and 'matrices' to lay out various responses to technological development, 'cross-impact analyses' to evaluate probabilities that certain future events will occur.

There is considerable debate about the appropriate institutions that should be responsible for technology assessment. The National Academy of Sciences Panel (1969) recommended a constellation of organizations adopting 'as neutral a stance as possible' and located strategically in both the executive and legislative branches of government. In the United States, the Office of Technology Assessment is actually located within Congress in order to provide the legislative branch with independent analysis of technical matters and to assist in decisions about technological priorities. This location reflects efforts by Congress to increase legislative control over the execution and implementation of technology. It suggests the feeling that decisions concerning science and technology are too vital to be left to private enterprise or to administrative agencies responsible only to the Presidency (Lakoff, 1974).

Technology assessments are based on the assumption that 'objective' identifications of the impacts of technology will help yield rational solutions. But assessment itself is a political process involving evaluation of the social desirability or undesirability of specific technologies. If technology assessment becomes a major tool for policy makers, it will be subject to considerable political discussion despite efforts to maintain objectivity. Recognizing this, some of the literature suggests that useful technology assessment mechanisms require decentralized and adversary structures. Folk (1972) argues that simply introducing greater quantities of information will not solve a problem when it is difficult to separate assessment from the interests served by technology. He rejects the idea of value-free assessment, proposing the establishment of opposition groups to perform 'counterassessments' and to shape the policy process through adversary proceedings. Green (1972) similarly argues that any new governmental institution for technology assessment is bound to be influenced by vested interests. He proposes an agency that would act as 'devil's advocate' or 'technological ombudsman', focusing on the negative consequences of new technologies and playing the role of adversary in the Congressional and public forum. Mayo (1972) argues for decentralized assessment centers intended to anticipate emerging problem areas. A decentralized structure, he claims, would be more flexible and effective than a centralized system and more accountable to the potentially affected public.

The search for controls brings us full circle to the forces affecting the use of science and technology. Brooks (1974) expects that the direction of future R & D will be influenced by the regulations and controls placed on industrial technology. Enforcement of pollution controls will require the development of new technological capabilities. The screening of chemicals and drugs will require 'defensive' research directed to establishing criteria of acceptability. And the general trend toward setting performance rather than design standards — as in the case of air pollution controls — may encourage innovation to meet required specifications.

CONCLUSION

This chapter has focused on the political forces that determine priorities for the use of science and technology; that shape perceptions of their impacts and direct the means of control. It has emphasized the ambivalent attitudes, conflicting interests, and diverse values that complicate decisions concerning both the application of science and technology and efforts to control negative impacts. It has suggested that choices in this area are no more rational than policies in other fields which are less dominated by expectations of rational progress and technical neutrality; for decisions concerning the use and control of science and technology involve difficult political judgments bearing on social values and future goals.

We tend to search for useful technologies with little systematic under- standing of social values and how they are affected by new developments in science and technology. Thus, efforts both to stimulate innovation appro- priate to civilian sector problems and to develop effective controls proceed with somewhat random success. Many expectations such as the anticipated 'spin-offs' from military technology have failed to materialize. And 'rational' decisions about technology often fail to consider values such as neighborhood integrity — values that may be emotional and intangible, yet are greatly affected by technological change (Nelkin, 1974; Tribe, 1971). Very basic questions concerning the effect of science and technology remain to be explored. How can 'qualitative' social impacts be compared to measurable economic advantages? How can individual costs be weighed against wider social values? We have described the contradictions inherent in several areas of scientific and technical development: national data banks are useful because of the value of improved governmental efficiency, but they can result in a drastic loss of individual freedom. Similarly, human experimentation makes a necessary and valuable contribution to improved medical knowledge, but these benefits must be balanced against the risks to the subjects of experimentation. The central problem in both controlling technological change and in setting priorities for the future development of science and technology is choosing between such conflicting and incommensurate values.

This perspective suggests some research directions for the study of science and technology policy. First, we need to examine and compare systematically efforts to direct science and technology to constructive social purposes, and to monitor the effect of increased control on scientific scholarship and technological innovation.

Second, given the political dimensions of science policy, the evaluation of decisions concerning science and technology will require better measures of 'welfare' and 'illfare' (Olson, 1973). Technologies affect different socio-economic groups in quite different ways (LaPorte, 1974). How does the use and regulation of specific technologies reflect diverse interests? Are the costs and benefits of technological decisions distributed in a reasonably equitable fashion? Measures of the consequences of science and technology must be based on understanding the concerns of those who are affected by technological change. This suggests the need of field studies to explore the diverse perceptions of affected groups, including those whose perceptions may be perceived as 'irrational'.[42]

Third, we need policy research directed less toward the legitimizing of established practices than toward critical social analysis of the institutions — public and private — whose activities bear on the development of science and technology policy. Boffey's study of the National Academy of Sciences (1975) is a useful example. But other organizations, less obviously concerned with policy, are also important in determining the use of science and technology. Public authorities and large industries as well as federal agencies should be studied to understand the balance between organizational imperatives and social goals as they influence the development and implementation of technology.

Fourth, a political perspective requires greater attention to the interaction of fact and value that enters policy decisions in a 'consultative commonwealth' in which professional expertise plays an increasingly significant political role (Eulau, 1973). Harvey Brooks (1976) describes the tendency to convert political questions into technical questions, to refer sensitive political questions to 'apolitical' experts. This is reflected in the proliferation of commissions, and in the increasingly important role of consultants. The nature of consulting relationships — the ways in which governments and corporations responsible for technological development use consultants, commissions, scientific advisers and their in-house technical staffs — is an important area for policy research. Case studies could usefully be developed to evaluate critically the assumptions that underly technical reports and especially the projections and models used as a basis for technical planning.

A related set of studies should explore how scientists and engineers can assume increased responsibility concerning dangerous industrial practices or potential misuse of their work without fear of reprisal. This will require monitoring the personal experiences of scientists who have attempted to raise such questions and evaluating such measures as the recent provisions in the coal mine safety act which prohibit discrimination against coal miners who report unsafe conditions. Related research could focus on the role of pro-

---

[42] The importance of understanding such perceptions has become evident with the expanding political power of fundamentalist groups bent on influencing science teaching (Nelkin, 1976, 1977).

fessional societies in establishing ethical standards for their members.

Questions of the liability of technical administrators and personnel also require further analysis (Brooks, 1975). What would be the implications of a system of 'engineering malpractice'? Useful models for the technology sector may develop as solutions to the problems of medical malpractice are further explored. Similarly, rapidly developing changes in the legal doctrines concerning product liability may yield models for establishing liability for the use and development of technology (Weinstein *et al.*, 1974).

Efforts to direct and control science and technology systematically are bound to encourage divisiveness and conflict. To ask 'what ought to be' implies defining future needs and long-term social goals. To develop policies prescribing future directions for science and technology implies challenging the validity of present commitments. Studies of social and political conflict can clarify the implications of policies for science and technology by identifying the diverse values and needs of those affected by technological change. Conflict concentrates vague social tensions into focused demands, defining articulate positions if not clear priorities. It challenges practices that are accepted from habit rather than from clear understanding of desired social objectives, and it prevents the ossification of social systems, exerting pressure for innovation and useful change. Thus, understanding the conflicts that develop over technological change can help to define appropriate policies concerning future directions for science and technology.

BIBLIOGRAPHY

Aigrain, 1974	Aigrain, P., 'Trends in Research Funding', *Physics Today*, November 1974, pp. 32-37.
Alford, 1969	Alford, R., *Bureaucracy and Participation*, Chicago, Rand McNally, 1969.
Anderson and Swaiman, 1967	Anderson, J. A. and Swaiman, K. F. (Eds.), *Phenylketonuria and Allied Metabolic Diseases*, Conference Procedures, U.S. Department of Health, Education and Welfare, Washington, D.C., April 1966.
Arrow, 1964	Arrow, K. J., 'A Strategy of Decision', *Political Science Quarterly* 79, 1964, pp. 585ff.
Ayres, 1969	Ayres, R., *Technological Forecasting and Long Range Planning*, New York, McGraw Hill, 1969.
Babcock and Callies, 1973	Babcock, R. and Callies, D., 'Ecology and Housing: Virtues in Conflict', in Clawson, M. (Ed.), *Modernizing Urban Land Policy*, Baltimore, Johns Hopkins Press, pp. 205-220.
Barber *et al.*, 1973	Barber, B. *et al.*, Research on Human Subjects: Prob-

lems of Social Control in Medical Experimentation, New York, Russell Sage, 1973.

Bauer, 1968 — Bauer, R. A., 'Introduction', in Bauer, R. and Gergen, K. (Eds.), *The Study of Policy Formation,* New York, The Free Press, 1968.

Bauer, 1969 — Bauer, R. A., *Second Order Consequences: A Methodological Essay on the Impact of Technology,* Cambridge, Harvard University Press, 1969.

Bell, 1960 — Bell, D., *The End of Ideology,* Glencoe, Illinois, The Free Press, 1960.

Bell, 1973 — Bell, D., *The Coming of Post Industrial Society,* New York, Basic Books, 1973.

Benveniste, 1972 — Benveniste, G., *The Politics of Expertise,* Berkeley, The Glendessary Press, 1972.

Bereano, 1974 — Bereano, P., 'Courts as Institutions for Assessing Technology', in Thomas, W. (Ed.), *Scientists in the Legal System: Tolerated Meddlers or Essential Contributors?* Ann Arbor, Michigan, Ann Arbor Science Publishers, Inc., 1974, pp. 73-96.

Bergsma, 1974 — Bergsma, D. (Ed.), *Ethical Social and Legal Dimensions of Screening for Human Genetic Diseases,* Miami, Symposia Specialists, 1974.

Berkowitz, 1970 — Berkowitz, M., *The Conversion of Military Oriented Research and Development to Civilian Uses,* New York, Praeger, 1970.

Blume, 1974 — Blume, S., *Toward a Political Sociology of Science,* New York, The Free Press, 1974.

Boffey, 1975 — Boffey, P., *The Brain Bank of America,* New York, McGraw Hill, 1975.

Boguslaw, 1965 — Boguslaw, R., *The New Utopians: A Study of System Design and Social Change,* Englewood Cliffs, New Jersey, Prentice Hall, 1965.

Bright and Schoeman, 1973 — Bright, J. and Schoeman, M. (Eds.), *A Guide to Practical Technological Forecasting,* Englewood Cliffs, New Jersey, Prentice Hall, 1973.

Brooks, 1964 — Brooks, H., 'The Scientific Adviser', in Gilpin, R. and Wright, C. (Eds.), *Scientists and National Policy Making,* New York, Columbia University Press, 1964, pp. 73-96.

Brooks, 1965 — Brooks, H., 'Scientific Concepts and Cultural Change', *Daedalus* 94, Winter 1965, pp. 66-83.

Brooks, 1973 — Brooks, H. 'The Physical Sciences: Bellweather of Science Policy', in Shannon, J. A. (Ed.), *Science and the Evolution of Public Policy,* New York, The Rockefeller University Press, 1973, pp. 105-134.

Brooks, 1973a — Brooks, H., 'Technology and Values: New Ethical Issues Raised by Technological Progress', *Zygon* 8, 1 March 1973, pp. 17-35.

Brooks, 1973b — Brooks, H., 'Knowledge and Action: The Dilemma of Science Policy in the 1970's', *Daedalus,* Spring 1973, pp. 125-144.

Brooks, 1974 — Brooks, H., 'Are Scientists Obsolete?' *Science* 186, 8 November 1974, pp. 501-508.

Brooks, 1975   Brooks, H., 'Scope of Business Responsibility in the
                                Assessment of Technology', Business and Society
                                Workshop, 24-25 March 1975 (mimeo).

Brooks, 1976   Brooks, H., 'The Federal Government and the Auto-
                                nomy of Scholarship', in Frankel, C. (Ed.), *Contro-
                                versies and Decisions,* New York, Russell Sage Founda-
                                tion, 1976, pp. 235-258.

Brzezinski, 1970   Brzezinski, Z., *Between Two Ages,* New York, Viking,
                                1970.

Bush, 1945   Bush, V., *Science, the Endless Frontier,* Washington,
                                D.C., U.S. Government Printing Office, July 1945.

Calder, 1971   Calder, N., *Technopolis,* New York, Clarion Books,
                                1971.

Caldwell, 1968-72   Caldwell, L. K., *Science, Technology and Public
                                Policy: A Selected and Annotated Bibliography,* 3
                                Vols., Bloomington, Indiana, Indiana University,
                                1968, 1969, 1972.

Caldwell and Siddigui, 1974   Caldwell, L. K. and Siddigui, *Environmental Policy,
                                Law and Administration: A Guide to Advanced Study,*
                                Environmental Studies Program, Indiana University,
                                Bloomington, Indiana, June 1974.

Carroll, 1971   Carroll, J. 'Participatory Technology', *Science* 171, 19
                                February 1971, pp. 647-653.

Carson, 1962   Carson, R., *Silent Spring,* Boston, Houghton Mifflin,
                                1962.

Clark, 1973   Clark, R., 'The Pressing Need for Alternate Tech-
                                nology', *Impact of Science on Society* 23, No. 4,
                                1973, pp. 257-272.

Commission on Third London   Commission on Third London Airport, *Papers and
Airport, 1970   Procedures,* London, Her Majesty's Stationary Office,
                                1970.

Commoner, 1966   Commoner, B., *Science and Survival,* London, Gol-
                                lancz, 1966.

Cooper, 1971   Cooper, J., *The Quality of Advice: Philosophy and
                                Technology of Drug Assessment* 2, The Smithsonian
                                Institution, Washington, D.C., 1971.

Coser, 1956   Coser, L. A., *The Functions of Social Conflict,* Glen-
                                coe, Illinois, The Free Press, 1956.

Crain *et al.,* 1969   Crain, R., *The Politics of Community Conflict,* New
                                York, Bobbs Merrill, 1969.

Crenson, 1971   Crenson, M., *The Unpolitics of Pollution,* Johns
                                Hopkins Press, 1971.

Dahl, 1970   Dahl, R., *After the Revolution,* New Haven, Yale
                                University Press, 1970.

Denny, 1965   Denny, B. C., 'Science and Public Policy: A Literature
                                in Search of a Field', *Public Administration Review*
                                XXV, September 1965, pp. 239-248.

Derian and Staropoli, 1975   Derian, J. C. and Staropoli, A., *La Technologie Incon-
                                trolee,* Paris, Presse Universitaire de France, 1975.

Djerassi *et al.,* 1974   Djerassi, C. *et al.,* 'Insect Control of the Future: Op-
                                erational and Policy Aspects', *Science* 186, 15 Novem-
                                ber 1974, pp. 596-607.

Doctors, 1969   Doctors, *The Role of Federal Agencies in Technology*

Transfer, Cambridge, Mass., MIT Press, 1969.

Dror, 1968 — Dror, Y., *Public Policy Reexamined,* Scranton, Pennsylvania, Chandler Publishing Company, 1968.

Drucker, 1974 — Drucker, P., 'Multinational, Myths and Realities', *Foreign Affairs* 53, 1 October 1974, pp. 121-134.

Ellul, 1964 — Ellul, J., *The Technological Society,* New York, Knopf, 1964.

Epstein and Grundy, 1974 — Epstein, S. S. and Grundy, R. D. (Eds.), *Consumer Health and Product Hazards,* Cambridge, Mass., MIT Press, 1974.

Etzioni and Remp, 1973 — Etzioni and Remp, *Technological Shortcuts to Social Change,* Russell Sage Foundation, 1973.

Eulau, 1973 — Eulau, H., 'Social Revolution and the Consultative Commonwealth', *American Political Science Review* 67, March 1973, pp. 169-191.

Faunce, 1968 — Faunce, W. A., *Problems of an Industrial Society,* New York, McGraw Hill, 1968.

Fleming, 1972 — Fleming, D., 'Roots of the New Conservation Movement', *Perspectives in American History* 6, 1972, pp. 1ff.

Folk, 1972 — Folk, H., 'The Role of Technology Assessment in Public Policy', in Teich, A. (Ed.), *Technology and Man's Future,* New York, St. Martin's Press, 1972, pp. 246-254.

Furash, 1968 — Furash, E. E., 'The Problem of Technology Transfer', in Bauer, R. A. and Gergen, K. J., *The Study of Policy Formation,* New York, The Free Press, 1968, Chapter 8.

Gakenheimer, 1975 — Gakenheimer, R., Technics and Conflict: *The Open Study in Urban Transportation,* Cambridge, Mass., MIT Press, 1975.

Gewirtz, 1969 — Gewirtz, P., 'Methadone Maintenance for Heroin Addicts', *Yale Law Review* 78, June 1969, pp. 1210ff.

Gilfillan, 1965 — Gilfillan, S. C., 'Lead Poisoning and the Fall of Rome', *Journal of Occupational Medicine* 7, 1965, pp. 53-60.

Gilpin, 1962 — Gilpin, R., *American Scientists and Nuclear Weapons Policy,* Princeton, Princeton University Press, 1962.

Gilpin, 1970 — Gilpin, R., 'Technological Strategies and National Purpose', *Science* 169, 31 July 1970.

Gilpin and Wright, 1964 — Gilpin, R. and Wright, C. (Eds.), *Scientists and National Policy Making,* New York, Columbia University Press, 1964, pp. 41-53.

Goldman, 1970 — Goldman, M., 'The Convergence of Environmental Disruption', *Science* 170, 1970, pp. 37-42.

Green, 1968 — Green, H., 'Technology Assessment and the Law: Introduction and Perspectives', *The George Washington Law Review* 36, July 1968, pp. 1033-1043.

Green, 1972 — Green, H., 'The Adversary Process in Technology Assessment', in Kasper, R. (Ed.), *Technology Assessment,* New York, Praeger, 1972, pp. 45-59.

Greenberg, 1966 — Greenberg, D., 'Mohole: The Project that Went Awry', in Lakoff, S. (Ed.), *Knowledge and Power,* New York, The Free Press, 1966, pp. 89-90.

Haberer, 1969   Haberer, J., *Politics and the Community of Science,*
                                 New York, Van Nostrand Reinhold, 1969.

Harvard University, 1968   Harvard University, *Implications of Biomedical Tech-
                                 nology,* Program on Technology and Society, Research
                                 Review 1, Cambridge, Mass., 1968.

Harvard University, 1969a   Harvard University, *Technology and the Polity,* Pro-
                                 gram on Technology and Society, Research Review 4,
                                 Cambridge, Mass., 1969.

Harvard University, 1969b   Harvard University, *Technology and Work,* Program
                                 on Technology and Society, Research Review 2, Cam-
                                 bridge, Mass., 1969.

Harvard University, 1969c   Harvard University, *Technology and Values,* Program
                                 on Technology and Society, Research Review 3, Cam-
                                 bridge, Mass., 1969.

Harvard University, 1972   Harvard University, *A Final Review,* Program on Tech-
                                 nology and Society, Cambridge, Mass., 1972.

Hastings Institute   Hastings Institute of Society, Ethics and the Life
                                 Sciences, *The Hastings Center Report* (monthly),
                                 Hastings-on-Hudson, New York.

Hetman, 1973   Hetman, F., *Society and the Assessment of Tech-
                                 nology,* Paris, OECD, 1973.

HEW, 1973   HEW, *Work in America,* Cambridge, Mass., MIT Press,
                                 1973.

Hilton *et al.,* 1972   Hilton, B. *et al., Ethical Issues in Human Genetics,*
                                 New York, Plenum Press, 1972.

Hirschman, 1970   Hirschman, A., *Exit, Voice and Loyalty,* Cambridge,
                                 Mass., Harvard University Press, 1970.

Hoos, 1972   Hoos, I. R., *Systems Analysis in Public Policy: A
                                 Critique,* Berkeley, University of California Press,
                                 1972.

Hunt, 1974   Hunt, M. K., *Privacy and Security in Data Bank
                                 Systems: An Annotated Bibliography,* Rand Corpora-
                                 tion, Santa Monica, California, 1974.

Jantsch, 1967   Jantsch, E., *Technology Forecasting in Perspective,*
                                 Paris, OECD, 1967.

Katz, 1972   Katz, J., *Experimentation with Human Beings,* New
                                 York, Russell Sage, 1972.

King and Melanson, 1972   King, L. and Melanson, P., 'Knowledge and Politics',
                                 Public Policy 20, Winter 1972, pp. 83-101.

Lakoff, 1974   Lakoff, S., 'Congress and National Science Policy',
                                 Political Science Quarterly 89, No. 3, 1974, pp.
                                 589-611.

Lane, 1966   Lane, R., 'The Decline of Politics and Ideology in a
                                 Knowledgeable Society', *American Sociological Re-
                                 view,* October 1966, pp. 649-662.

LaPorte, 1974   LaPorte, T., *Beyond Machines and Structures: Bases
                                 for Political Criticism of Technology,* Working Paper
                                 10, Institute of Governmental Studies, Berkeley, Cali-
                                 fornia, June 1974.

Lasagna, 1969   Lasagna, L., 'The Pharmaceutical Revolution: Its Im-
                                 pact on Science and Society', *Science* 166, 4 Decem-
                                 ber 1969, pp. 1227-1233.

Lederburg, 1971   Lederburg, J., 'Human Values in a Technological Society', *Dimensions Symposium,* Winter 1971, pp. 2-8.

Lindblom, 1965 — Lindblom, C. E., *The Intelligence of Democracy,* New York, The Free Press, 1965.

Lowi, 1964 — Lowi, T. J., 'American Business, Public Policy, Case Studies and Political Theory', *World Politics* 16, July 1964, pp. 677-715.

Lowi, 1972 — Lowi, T. J., 'Blurring of Sector Lines: Rise of New Elites from One Vantage Point, The Conference Road, *Information Technology,* New York, 1972, pp. 131-148.

Lowi *et al.,* 1975 — Lowi, T. J. *et al., Policide: Politics and the Building of the Metropolis,* New York, MacMillan, 1975.

Mainzer, 1973 — Mainzer, L., *Political Bureaucracy,* Glenview, Illinois, Scott, Foresman and Company, 1973.

Mansfield, 1968 — Mansfield, E., *The Economics of Technological Change,* New York, W. H. Norton, 1968.

Marcuse, 1964 — Marcuse, H., *One Dimensional Man,* Boston, Beacon Press, 1964.

Martin, 1973 — Martin, B. L., 'Experts in Policy Processes', *Polity,* 1973, pp. 149-173.

Mason, 1973 — Mason, G. L., 'The Future of Repression', in Wolff, R. P. (Ed.), *1984 Revisited,* New York, Knopf, 1973, pp. 41-74.

Mayo, 1972 — Mayo, L. H., 'The Management of Technology Assessment', in Kaspar, R. (Ed.), *Technology Assessment,* New York, Praeger, 1972, pp. 71-116.

Mazur, 1973 — Mazur, A., 'Disputes Between Experts', *Minerva* 11, No. 2, April 1973, pp. 243-262.

McElroy, 1973 — McElroy, W. D., 'The Utility of Science' in Shannon, J. A. (Ed.), *Science and the Evolution of Public Policy,* New York, The Rockefeller University Press, 1973, pp. 19-29.

Meek and Straayer, 1971 — Meek, R. and Straayer, J. (Eds.), *The Politics of Neglect: The Environmental Crisis,* Boston, Houghton Mifflin Company, 1971.

Melanson, 1973 — Melanson, P. (Ed.), *Knowledge, Politics and Public Policy,* Cambridge, Winthrop Publishers, Inc., 1973.

Merton, 1973 — Merton, R., *The Sociology of Science,* Chicago, University of Chicago Press, 1973.

Meynaud, 1968 — Meynaud, J., *Technocracy,* London, Faber and Faber, 1968.

Michael, 1973 — Michael, D., *On Learning to Plan and Planning to Learn,* San Francisco, Jossey Bass, 1973.

Michelman, 1967 — Michelman, F., 'Property, Utility and Fairness: Comments on the Ethical Foundations of Just Compensation Law', *Harvard Law Review* 80, April 1967, pp. 1226ff.

Midwest Research Institute, 1973 — Midwest Research Institute, *Public Concern Over Technology — Case Histories of Unstructured Technology Assessments,* Washington, D.C., National Science Foundation, RANN Program, 1973.

Milch, 1975 — Milch, J., 'Inverted Pyramids: The Use and Misuse of Aviation Forecasting', *Social Studies of Science* 6, February 1976, pp. 5-31.

Morrison *et al.*, 1972	Morrison, D. E. *et al.*, 'The Environmental Movement', in Burch, W. Jr., Cheek, N. Jr., Taylor, L. (Eds.), *Social Behavior, Natural Resources and the Environment*, New York, Harper and Row, 1972.
Morrison *et al.*, 1973	Morrison, D. *et al.*, *Environment: A Bibliography of the Social Science Literature*, Environmental Protection Agency, 1973.
Myrdal, 1969	Myrdal, G., *Objectivity in Social Research*, New York, Pantheon Books, 1969.
Nash, 1973	Nash, R., *Wilderness and the American Mind*, Revised Edition, New Haven, Yale University Press, First Edition, 1967.
National Academy of Engineering, 1969	National Academy of Engineering, *A Study of Technology Assessment*, Washington, D.C., U.S. Government Printing Office, 1969.
National Academy of Sciences, 1969	National Academy of Sciences, *Technology: Process of Assessment and Choice*, Washington, D.C., U.S. Government Printing Office, 1969.
National Academy of Sciences and Engineering, 1971	National Academy of Sciences and Engineering, *Jamaica Bay and Kennedy Airport: A Multidisciplinary Study*, Washington, D.C., 1971.
National Commission on Technology, Automation and Economic Progress, 1966	National Commission on Technology, Automation and Economic Progress, *Technology and the American Economy*, Washington, D.C., U.S. Government Printing Office, 1966.
Nelkin, 1971a	Nelkin, D., *The Politics of Housing Innovation: The Fate of the Civilian Industrial Technology Program*, Ithaca, Cornell University Press, 1971.
Nelkin, 1971b	Nelkin, D., *Nuclear Power and Its Critics*, Ithaca, Cornell University Press, 1971.
Nelkin, 1972	Nelkin, D., *The University and Military Research*, Ithaca, Cornell University Press, 1972.
Nelkin, 1973	Nelkin, D., *Methadone Maintenance – A Technological Fix*, New York, Braziller, 1973.
Nelkin, 1974	Nelkin, D., *Jetport, The Boston Airport Controversy*, New Brunswick, New Jersey, Transaction Books, 1974.
Nelkin, 1975	Nelkin, D., 'The Political Impact of Technical Expertise', *Social Studies of Science* 5, February 1975, pp. 35-54.
Nelkin, 1976	Nelkin, D., 'Science or Scripture', in Holton, G. and Blanpied, W. (Eds.), *Science and its Public*, Dordrecht, Holland, D. Reidel, 1976, pp. 209-227.
Nelkin, 1977	Nelkin, D., *Science Textbook Controversies and the Politics of Equal Time*, Cambridge, Mass., MIT Press, 1977.
Nelson, 1959	Nelson, R. R., 'The Economics of Invention: A Survey of the Literature', *The Journal of Business*, April 1959, pp. 101-127.
Nelson, 1968	Nelson, R. R., 'Technological Advance, Economic Growth and Public Policy', in Heller, W. (Ed.), *Perspectives on Economic Growth*, New York, Random House, 1968, pp. 187-202.

Nelson, 1974 — Nelson, R. R., 'Intellectualizing About the Moon-Ghetto Metaphor: A Study of the Current Malaise of Rational Analysis of Social Problems', *Policy Sciences* 5, December 1974, pp. 375-414.

Nelson *et al.*, 1968 — Nelson, R., Peck, M., Kalachek, E., *Technology, Economic Growth and Public Policy*, Washington, D.C., Brookings Institute, 1967.

Neuhaus, 1971 — Neuhaus, R., *In Defense of People*, New York, MacMillan, 1971.

Nichols, 1974 — Nichols, D., 'The Associated Interest Groups of American Science', in Teich, A. (Ed.), *Scientists and Public Affairs*, Cambridge, Mass., MIT Press, pp. 123-170.

Noll, 1971 — Noll, R., *Reforming Regulation: An Evaluation of the Ash Council Proposals*, Washington, D.C., The Brookings Institution, 1971.

OECD, 1971 — OECD, *Science Growth and Society: A New Perspective*, Paris, 1971.

OECD, 1972-74 — OECD, *The Research System*, Vols. 1, 2, 3, Paris, 1972, 1973, 1974.

Oettinger, 1969 — Oettinger, A. G., *Run Computer Run*, Cambridge, Harvard University Press, 1969.

Olson, 1973 — Olson, M., *The Logic of Collective Action*, Cambridge, Harvard University Press, 1973, Appendix (original edition, 1965).

Passmore, 1974 — Passmore, J., *Man's Responsibility for Nature: Ecological Problems and Western Tradition*, New York, Scribners, 1974.

Pateman, 1970 — Pateman, C., *Participation and Democratic Theory*, Cambridge, The University Press, 1970.

Don K. Price, 1954 — Price, Don K., *Government and Science*, New York, New York University Press, 1954.

Don K. Price, 1965 — Price, Don K., *The Scientific Estate*, Cambridge, Harvard University Press, 1965.

Don K. Price, 1969 — Price, Don K., 'Science and Technology in a Democratic Society', in *Educating for the 21st Century*, Urbana, University of Illinois Press, 1969.

Don K. Price, 1969a — Price, Don K., 'Purists and Politicians', *Science* 163, 3 January 1969, pp. 25-31.

Don K. Price, 1974 — Price, Don K., 'Money and Influence: The Links of Science to Public Policy', *Daedelus* 103, Summer 1974, pp. 97-114.

Primack and von Hippel, 1974 — Primack, J. and von Hippel, F., *Advice and Dissent: Scientists in the Political Arena*, New York, Basic Books, 1974.

Rettig, 1969 — Rettig, R., 'Science, Technology and Public Policy', *World Politics*, 1969, pp. 273-293.

Rich, 1974 — Rich, D., 'Private Government and Professional Science', in Teich, A. (Ed.), *Scientists and Public Affairs*, Cambridge, Mass., MIT Press, 1974, pp. 3-38.

Rogers, 1962 — Rogers, E., *Diffusion of Innovation*, New York, The Free Press, 1962.

Rose and Rose, 1969 — Rose, N. and Rose, S., *Science and Society*, Harmondsworth, England, Penguin Books, 1969.

Roslansky, 1966 Roslansky, J. D. (Ed.), *Genetics and the Future of Man,* New York, Appleton-Century Crofts, 1966.

Rothschild, 1971 Rothschild, L., *A Framework for Government Research and Development,* London, Her Majesty's Stationary Office, Command 4714, 1971.

Salomon, 1973 Salomon, J.-J., *Science and Politics,* Cambridge, Mass., MIT Press, 1973.

Sax, 1971 Sax, J., *Defending the Environment,* New York, Knopf, 1971.

Sayre *et al.,* 1969 Sayre, W., Smith and Bruce, L. R., *Government, Technology and Social Problems,* New York, The Institute for the Study of Science in Human Affairs, 1969.

Schmookler, 1966 Schmookler, J., *Invention and Economic Growth,* Cambridge, Harvard University Press, 1966.

Schneider, 1968 Schneider, L. M., 'Urban Mass Transportation: A Survey of the Decision-Making Process', in Bauer, R. and Gergen, K. (Eds.), *The Study of Policy Formation,* New York, The Free Press, 1968, pp. 239-280.

Schoettle, 1968 Schoettle, E. C. B., 'The State of the Art in Policy Studies', in Bauer, R. and Gergen, K. (Eds.), *The Study of Policy Formation,* New York, The Free Press, 1968, pp. 149-180.

Schon, 1967 Schon, D. A., *Technology and Change,* New York, Dell, 1967.

Schon, 1971 Schon, D., *Beyond the Stable State,* New York, Random House, 1971.

Schooler, 1971 Schooler, D. Jr., *Science, Scientists and Public Policy,* New York, Random House, 1971.

Shils, 1967 Shils, E., 'Privacy and Power', in de Sola Pool, I. (Ed.), *Contemporary Political Science,* New York, McGraw Hill, 1967.

Sills, 1975 Sills, D., 'The Environmental Movement and Its Critics', *Human Ecology,* 3, No. 1, 1975, pp. 1-41.

Skolnikoff, 1970 Skolnikoff, E. B., *The International Imperatives of Technology,* Geneva, Carnegie Endowment for International Peace, March 1970.

Steinhart and Steinhart, 1972 Steinhart, C. and Steinhart, J., *Blowout: The Santa Barbara Oil Spill,* Belmont, California, Duxbury Press, 1972.

Stone, 1974 Stone, C. D., *Should Trees Have Standing?* Los Altos, California, William Kaufman, 1974.

Strickland, 1972 Strickland, S., *Politics, Science and Dread Disease,* Cambridge, Harvard University Press, 1972.

Teich, 1974 Teich, A. (Ed.), *Scientists and Public Affairs,* Cambridge, Mass., MIT Press, 1974.

Thoenig, 1973 Thoenig, J. C., *L'Ere des technocrates,* Paris, Editions d'Organisation, 1973.

Thompson, 1970 Thompson, D. F., *The Democratic Citizen,* Cambridge, Cambridge University Press, 1970.

Tribe, 1971a Tribe, L., 'Legal Frameworks for the Assessment and Control of Technology', *Minerva* 9, No. 2, 1971, pp. 243-255.

Tribe, 1971b Tribe, L., 'Towards a New Technological Ethic: The

	Role of Legal Liability', *Impact of Science on Society* 21, July 1971, pp. 215-222.
Tribe, 1972	Tribe, L., 'Policy Science: Analysis or Ideology', *Philosophy and Public Affairs* 2, Fall 1972, pp. 66-110.
Ulrich *et al.*, 1966	Ulrich, R. *et al.* (Ed.). *Control of Human Behavior*, Glenview, Illinois, Scott Foresman, 1966.
Valenstein, 1973	Valenstein, E., *Brain Control*, New York, John Wiley and Sons, 1973.
Vanek, 1971	Vanek, J., *The Participatory Economy*, Ithaca, Cornell University Press, 1971.
Wartofsky, 19/4	Wartofsky, M. W., 'Social and Epistemological Constraints on Science', AAAS, 140th Meeting, February 1974.
Weinberg, 1966	Weinberg, A., 'Can Technology Replace Social Engineering?', *University of Chicago Magazine* 59, October 1966, pp. 6-7.
Weinberg, 1966a	Weinberg, A., *Reflections on Big Science*, Cambridge, MIT Press, 1966.
Weinstein *et al.*, 1974	Weinstein, A. S. *et al.*, 'Product Liability: An Interaction of Law and Technology', *Duquesne Law Review*, 12, No. 3, Spring 1974, pp. 425-550.
Westin, 1967	Westin, A. F., *Privacy and Freedom*, New York, Athenaum, 1967.
Westin, 1970	Westin, A. F., *Information Technology in a Democracy*, Cambridge, Harvard University Press, 1970.
Westin and Baker, 1972	Westin, A. and Baker, M., *Databanks in a Free Society*, New York, Quadrangle Books, 1972.
White and Sjoberg, 1972	White, O. and Sjoberg, G., 'The Emerging New Politics in America', in Hancock, M. D., and Sjoberg, G. (Eds.), *Politics in the Post-Welfare State: Responses to the New Individualism*, New York, Columbia University Press, 1972, pp. 11-35.
Wilensky, 1956	Wilensky, H., *Intellectuals in Labor Unions*, Glencoe, The Free Press, 1956.
Williams, 1973	Williams, R., *European Technology*, London, Croom Helm, 1973.
Willrich and Taylor, 1973	Willrich, M. and Taylor, T., *Nuclear Theft: Risks and Safeguards*, Cambridge, Mass., Ballinger, 1973.
Wittner, 1969	Wittner, L. S., *Rebels Against War*, New York, Columbia University Press, 1969.
Wohlstetter, 1964	Wohlstetter, A., 'Strategy and the Natural Scientists', in Gilpin, R. and Wright, C. (Eds.), *Scientists and National Policy Making*, London, Columbia University Press, 1964, pp. 174-239.
Yarmolinski, 1970	Yarmolinski, A., 'New Structures for Federal, State and Local Government Cooperation', Eastern Regional Conference on Science and Technology for Public Programs, Cambridge, Mass., 1970.
Zupan, 1973	Zupan, J. M., *Distribution of Air Quality in the New York Region*, Washington, D.C., Resources for the Future, 1973.

Chapter 12

SCIENCE, TECHNOLOGY AND MILITARY POLICY

Harvey M. Sapolsky

Massachusetts Institute of Technology

INTRODUCTION

Today, as has been the case for more than three decades, the search for new and more fearsome weapons holds the first priority for the world's scientists and engineers. By the same token, research on military R & D policy must have a high place in science policy studies. No other activity absorbs a greater share of the total investment in research than does the effort to advance the science and technology of warfare. A plausible, if not precise, estimate is that military research and development accounts for about one third of the world's research and development expenditures (Forsberg, 1972). Perhaps as many as one million scientists and engineers are currently at work on military projects. In policy studies much work has been engendered by analysts for the military establishments on the one side and by peace research and citizens' advocates on the other.

The prime cause of this preoccupation with weapons is obvious. The world's superpowers, the United States and the Soviet Union, have been since World War II in a continuous competition for military supremacy that has been manifested mainly in the development of technologically sophisticated weapons. As the leading nations in terms of scientific and technological capabilities, their research priorities, heavily skewed toward the instruments of war, greatly influence world R & D statistics.

I would like to acknowledge the assistance I have received in preparing this paper from Ted Greenwood, Eugene Skolnikoff, Randall Forsberg, Dorothy Nelkin, Judith Reppy, Milton Leitenburg, Jean-Jacques Salomon, Sanford Lakoff, Ina Spiegel-Rösing, Derek de Solla Price and Karen Stenbo Sapolsky.

Nations seeking major-power standing in the world have to pursue technological objectives selected by the two superpowers (Gilpin, 1968; Dorfer, 1973). Either through research or purchase they must match American and Russian ballistic missiles, fighter bombers, attack submarines, and main battle tanks, or be subject to them.

Even when nations lack such ambitions, they apparently cannot afford to ignore the technological priorities of the superpowers, especially those of the United States, because of the commercial and organizational by-products that are associated with military research (Servan-Schreiber, 1967; Layton, 1969). A substantial investment in weapons-related research may not by any means guarantee current economic prosperity (Holloman and Harger, 1971; Thurow, 1971), but it does entail an ability to produce supersonic aircraft, large computers, nuclear reactors, deep ocean drilling equipment and the like which in the minds of many are the technological harbingers of future prosperity (e.g. Bell, 1973).

Nevertheless, only a few nations are seriously involved in the effort to develop technologically advanced weapons, and their lot is not an enviable one. Great technological and political uncertainties beset weapon projects. The difficulty in predicting the actions of one's potential adversaries and the direction of technologies is a substantial barrier to success in the development of weapons. Attempts to improve the internal efficiency of the enterprise have been continually frustrated by these uncertainties (Holley, 1964; Perry, 1970; Sapolsky, 1973).

Ironically, additional investments in military R & D do not always increase national security, and may at times decrease it. Advances in weapon technology, by enhancing the real or apparent military might of one adversary over another, can produce further uncertainty about intentions and increased opportunities for miscalculations. Because of the continuing threat of weapon improvements, the balance of terror may be much more precarious than it need be (York, 1969 and 1971; Feld *et al.,* 1971; Brooks, 1975).

Of increasing interest to many are schemes to curtail or perhaps even eliminate military-related research. In the West, at least, there is, according to opinion surveys, a growing weariness with the burdens of maintaining a large military establishment (Russett, 1974). There is a gradual erosion of military expenditures relative to non-military expenditures associated with shifting budget priorities of governments (Forsberg, 1972). Beyond this, however, the obstacles to substantial reductions are significant. International tensions persist, and with them the risks of falling behind in the development of weapons. Among those who are ready to articulate these risks are scientists and engineers who have become dependent upon military justifications for their research support (Cahn, 1972; but note also Wolf, 1972).

We must, therefore, review the magnitude, directions and priorities of the undertaking, the technical substance and consequences of the weaponry with all that these imply for policy direction and control.

SCIENCE, TECHNOLOGY AND WAR

Governments have long acted as patrons of science in the hope of gaining improvements in the instruments and techniques of war; what is new in our time is the scale of the patronage offered and the impact which science has had on warfare. Until recently, the technology of weapons changed only gradually, often with centuries passing between major shifts (Hall, 1970; McElwee, 1974). And more frequently than not it was the artisan or the inventor instead of the scientist or the military engineer who first perceived the opportunities for change (Brodie and Brodie, 1962; Wolf, 1970; Derek Price, 1973).

Science has come to the forefront in warfare only as the instruments and techniques of war have been linked together in a systematic fashion. Thus World War I, despite the introduction of such innovations as aircraft and tanks and the use of poison gas and submarines, remained essentially a clash of massed armies because this linkage was not made. Scientists and engineers, though mobilized for the conflict, contributed little to its outcome (Scott, 1920; Kevles, 1969).

The glacial pace of weapon innovations has led commentators to characterize military bureaucracies as being highly resistant to technological change (e.g. Morrison, 1966; DeGregori and Pi-Sunyer, 1966; note also Zuckerman, 1966). Until recently, at least, this seemed to be an accurate description. The horse, for example, appeared in military maneuvers and manuals as late as the 1940's despite the fact that decades earlier the machine gun had eliminated it from combat and the internal combustion engine had eliminated it from support missions (Katzenback, 1968; Morrison, 1966). Today, however, the military, perhaps to a greater extent than any other bureaucratic institution, has internalized the maxim that there is a continuous need to promote and to adjust to technological change.

World War II marked the crucial turning point in the relationship between science and war, as indeed it did in the evolution of science policy (See Salomon, Chapter 2, and Lakoff, Chapter 10). It is not just that at this moment in history war suddenly became scientific. On the contrary, as Brodie (1973) and Vietnam reminded us, war continues to be an unpredictable political undertaking. Rather, it is that during World War II weapons and their use in military operations came to be analyzed scientifically for the first time. Scientists and engineers not only worked on the development of weapons, but also advised on the tactical deployment of weapons. The practical experience which weapon researchers gained from an exposure to operational issues increased both the pace of weapon innovation and the operational effectiveness of the equipment that was developed (Baxter, 1946; Holley, 1970).

The atomic bomb, of course, has been the weapon development most identified with World War II. In terms of providing a symbol of the destructive capability generated by military research it was clearly unmatched. But in terms of influencing the actual course of the fighting, dozens of other developments such as radar, sonar, the submarine snorkel, the proximity fuse, and, as we have recently learned, advances in cryptography (Winterbotham, 1974) probably were of equal or greater importance in that conflict (Baxter, 1946). Taken together, these weapon developments convinced political, military and scientific leaders of the value of a continuing effort to spur weapon research (Bush, 1945, 1949; Smith, 1966). The organizational arrangements that were established there to promote military research and development activities during the war were not fully dismantled at its conclusion; instead they were retained and expanded. The victors competitively sought as war booty the weapon research resources of Germany, including its leading military scientists and engineers (Lasby, 1971). Their own growing antagonism set the stage for the technological competition that largely continues today unabated, detente and arms limitation treaties notwithstanding.

Previously confined to the periphery of power, scientists and engineers came in the years immediately following World War II to enter the highest councils of government in both the East and the West (See Lakoff, Chapter 10). Their advice was sought on weapon procurements and on the resources being allocated to R & D activities, the scale of which grew rapidly during this period. Whether the actual scope of the influence of scientists and engineers, now obviously diminished, ever extended to the pivotal policy decisions of government is a subject of debate. For some they, and especially the scientists among them, constituted a self-conscious elite that displaced other contenders for influence, contenders who were less conversant with the technical issues facing government (e.g. Snow, 1961; Wood, 1964; Smith, 1966). For others, their influence was always illusionary as it was dependent upon the acceptance of narrow decisional premises which were then and still are being determined by the dominant political forces (e.g. von Hippel and Primack, 1972; Boffey, 1975). In this view they were and remain as Baritz (1961) described: social scientists in American industry, the servants of power. The truth, however, most likely lies somewhere in between these two characterizations, with the influence of scientists and engineers on government policy, initially quite large in the immediate post war years, diminishing as the traditional political elites grew more confident in their own abilities to deal with the technical issues brought about by the revolution in military technology, and as they became less tolerant of the claims of scientists and engineers for political and bureaucratic autonomy in government. But no matter what view prevails in the debate, it is clear that scientists and engineers, by their involvement in post war weapon research and policy making, obtained a political visibility for themselves and an affluence and status for science that stands unmatched in history.

MILITARY R & D AS A
NATIONAL PRIORITY

Though the genesis of the issue is clear, at least in bold outline, it is, not surprisingly, impossible to gain a precise assessment of the present position of the various nations in regard to that share of the world's scientific resources they devote to military R & D activities. Some nations, among them the Soviet Union, find it in their interest to report essentially nothing about the level or composition of the military research work they undertake; military research figures for these nations must necessarily be estimates constructed from information reported for other purposes. Even when data on this topic are available, however, it is difficult to be certain of their comparability due to the inevitable national variations in accounting procedures and definitions (Brooks, 1975). Accounting, never included among the exact sciences, always has its political purposes. The United States government, for example, broadened its definition of military research to include equipment, test and evaluation expenses at the time of the launching of the first Sputnik in order to increase quickly the size of the military research budget, and thus allay domestic political concerns about the adequacy of its weapon research effort.

In addition, there is the problem of knowing what to include as militarily relevant research. Nations do not conveniently place all of what they intend to be weapon-related research in a single ministry labeled defense. Much of the research effort conducted or supported by nuclear development, space, and even academic science agencies can be of military value. In the United States it is known that about half the research of the organization that was until recently titled the Atomic Energy Commission is work related to nuclear munitions or reactors for naval vessels. But how much of the Indian, Israeli or South African nuclear research efforts is weapon-related is less certain.

Finally, there is the problem of selecting appropriate currency conversion rates for cross-national comparisons of military research and development expenditures. There are, alas, similar problems which attend comparability for estimates of R & D manpower and for equivalence rates between one weapon system and another. Given the variability that exists among nations in capital investments and levels of scientific training and efficiency of research personnel employed on military projects, it is difficult to establish conversion rates that are persuasive. Do you equalize the value of a dollar spent on military research in Sunnyvale, California, or in Lexington, Massachusetts, with the value of a ruble spent on military research in Kuybyshev or Novosibirsk by recording its productivity as being 2.0, 1.0, 0.5 or 0.25 that of the ruble? Though many have been attracted by the conversion problem, the differences in their choice of rates and the ease with which such choices can be used for political purposes do not generate much confidence in the accuracy of the resulting comparisons (Brunner, 1965; U.S. General Accounting Office, 1971; Bazell, 1971; Forsberg, 1972).

Nevertheless, one is not at a complete loss when one is seeking to assess the role which military research plays as a national priority. The United States and the Soviet Union, by their own admissions, outspend every other nation in the world in the search for new and improved weapons, though each disputes their relative ranking and neither is willing to claim the lead. In terms of the size of their military research programs, they are only each other's rival (See Table 1), and if all the billions invested in space research by the United States and the Soviet Union were considered military research, as many observers believe should be the case, the dominance of the two rivals would only be more dramatic.

Military R & D activities are highly concentrated, greatly exceeding the concentration of R & D activities in general (Forsberg, 1972). The complexity and cost of modern weapons have caused most nations to import a substantial portion of their armaments. Only a few nations attempt to maintain a comprehensive weapon development program that includes a full range of conventional and strategic systems. It is said, for example, that there are but six or seven nations – the United States, the Soviet Union, China, the United Kingdom, France, Sweden and perhaps Israel – currently capable of independently developing combat-competitive fighter aircraft and even some of them are not likely to continue to maintain such a capability (Dorfer, 1973). Similar small numbers are involved in the development of nuclear-powered submarines, long range missiles, tanks of advanced design and helicopter gun platforms. Yet, the urge to have large production runs and thus reduce the cost of one's own weapon development and procurement activities (Kaldor, 1972), as well as the political advantages of acting as a supplier nation, keeps the flow of technologically advanced weapons open to nations that do not set aside a significant share of their defense expenditures for military research (Stockholm International Peace Research Institute, 1971 and 1974). There appears to be no shortage of modern weapons even in a world where only a relatively few nations are involved in their design and development.

The vast bulk of military R & D funds is spent on the development of weapon systems and on their test and evaluation (or as it is called in the Soviet Union, their assimilation into production). In the United States, for example, approximately eighty per cent of the Department of Defense's R & D obligations in 1975 were for weapon development activities including test and evaluation. Work directed toward the development of new missiles and aircraft accounted for well over half of this effort. The military's support of basic research activities, though less than three per cent of the total Department of Defense R & D obligations and less than ten per cent of the total United States investment in basic research that year, still amounted to several hundred million dollars. In this category, work is concentrated in the engineering disciplines and the physical sciences, but involves, if only in small

Table 1. Military R & D: Average Annual Expenditures,
1967-1970* (in Millions of U.S. Dollars)

United States	$8,708.9
Soviet Union**	5,692.0-8,250.0
United Kingdom	859.6
France	770.8
FR Germany	352.3
Sweden	106.4
Canada	89.0
India	62.0
Japan	52.8
Netherlands	17.1

* Appropriate R & D exchange rate as explained in Appendix A of Forsberg (1972).
** 1968. Calculated using estimates of expenditures Soviet defense/space (Nimitz, 1974) minus space percentage of United States for the same year times the Forsberg (1972) mid-range Soviet R & D exchange rate.

Sources: Forsberg, 1972, Table A; Nimitz, 1974.

ways, nearly every field of investigation (National Science Foundation, 1975).

As Chart 1 describes, many Western and non-aligned nations have recently reduced the military proportion of their total R & D activities (See Freeman, Chapter 7). The trend of Soviet military R & D expenditures, the subject of much speculation, is less clear as is the future direction of the United States effort. The pressure of domestic concerns such as the protection of environmental quality, the desire for a broadening of social welfare, and the quest for improvements in health status apparently have led to a shift in relative research priorities in many nations. Nevertheless, as the absolute level of spending for weapon research has not been reduced, military R & D remains a source of national and international concern (e.g. York, 1971; Report of the Secretary General, 1971).

THE NATURE OF MODERN WEAPONS

National military policies depend not only on the national will and on international forces, but also on the changing nature of the available military technologies. The atomic bomb used against Hiroshima can be said to have been both the first modern weapon and the last of the old. The bomb was new in the sense that it demonstrated in a single, horrible moment the devastating and destructive power of sophisticated technology. The bomb was less than modern, however, in the sense that ancillary equipment upon which

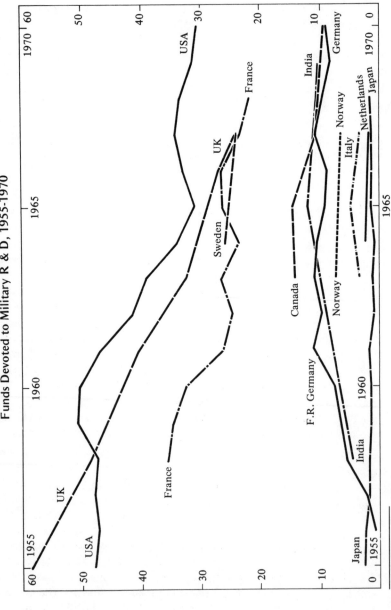

Chart 1. Long Term Trends in the Proportion of National R & D
Funds Devoted to Military R & D, 1955-1970

Source: Forsberg, 1972, Chart 8

its effectiveness depended was developed independently. The physical size of the bomb, for instance, was determined by the dimensions of the bomb bay doors of the B-29, an aircraft that had been designed years before without any consideration for its eventual nuclear delivery mission (Brown, 1963).

A first major change since World War II is that weapons have been increasingly developed as integrated systems. That is, it has been recognized that if weapon designs are to be optimal in terms of their military purpose, the definition of a weapon and its development has to include the weapon's delivery mechanism, its logistics support, its crew training facilities and its deployment tactics. Thus, the development of the Fleet Ballistic Missile System by the United States Navy included not just the development of the Polaris weapon system, (i.e. the missile subsystem, the navigation subsystem, the fire control subsystem, and the missile launcher subsystem), but also the development of the nuclear submarines, the logistic support ships, the forward bases, the repair facilities, the training schools, the communications stations and the research laboratories that are needed to keep the missiles at sea and ready to fire (Sapolsky, 1972).

A second characteristic of modern weapons is that they are designed to meet a variety of potential and real threats. For example, the Armored Personnel Carrier (APC) was initially conceived as a lightly armored troop transporter which would provide tanks with an infantry screen in order to protect the tanks from enemy infantry infiltration and attack. However, because the APC was expected to operate in the same battlefield environment as the tank, it soon acquired a large caliber gun to protect itself from enemy tanks, an antiaircraft gun, extra armor, protective equipment for nuclear and chemical warfare, and elaborate target acquisition and communications equipment. It now looks much like a tank and is thought to be vulnerable to infantry infiltration and attack (*International Defense Review*, 1971).

A third characteristic of modern weapons is that they are designed to operate in or to have effects upon environments not previously thought to be part of warfare (Leitenberg, 1973; see also Calder, 1968). Nuclear submarines patrol under the polar icecap. Submarine detection devices are implanted in the ocean's floor. Satellites provide global surveillance, navigation and communications capabilities. Chemical herbicides have been used to destroy the vegetation of large tracts of land, and weather modification techniques, such as those that would increase rainfall in designated areas, have been tested.

These design characteristics often result in the development of costly and complex weapons. Compared with the situation during World War II, relatively few weapons are produced, but their rate of obsolescence is higher. It is not rust or combat as much as the imaginations of the weapons designers that converts modern weapons into scrap. Development costs for modern weapons can approach production costs, and their combined operations and maintenance costs often exceed their combined development and production costs (Peck and Scherer, 1962; Facer, 1975).

The weapons acquisition process, as a consequence, is pervaded by two kinds of uncertainty. One is technological uncertainty and the other is political uncertainty. Technological uncertainty is exemplified by the question: Can a specific item be developed in a specified time for a specified price? In a complex weapon system, the failure to develop one item can cause the entire system to be essentially worthless. If the guidance mechanism of a ballistic missile does not work, it matters little how excellent are its rocket motors or crew training facilities. Political uncertainity is exemplified by the question: Will the item proposed be considered valuable when it is finally developed? Perceived threats and national strategies can change rapidly. The C5A's potential ability to ferry several hundred combat-equipped troops to distant trouble spots, for example, was admired by policy makers in the United States a lot more in 1965 when the aircraft was designed than it was in 1971 when the aircraft was ready for deployment. Weapons projects take years to complete and, with rare exception, are buffeted by both kinds of uncertainty throughout their history.

Competing for scarce resources, proponents of particular weapon systems, including scientists and engineers who are often the initiators of new weapon projects, tend to exaggerate the military benefits that are likely to accrue from the developments they propose and to depreciate the technological and political risks that are likely to be involved in such developments. The outcomes, however, frequently do not match the initial promises; vast sums may be expended for what are at best only marginal or questionable security gains. Studies of United States weapon developments, for example, show a persistent pattern of cost overruns, schedule slippages, and performance defects despite a declining index of technological advancement for at least certain types of weapons and much effort at managerial improvements (Peck and Scherer, 1962; Harman, 1970; Perry, 1970). The experience of other nations, Eastern and Western, though less accessible, appears to be similar (Kaldor, 1972; Leitenberg, 1973; Holloway, 1974).

Some commentators on military research appear susceptible to classification as technological determinists, a common assumption among them being that what is feasible in weapon technology will be produced (e.g. York, 1971; Lapp, 1971; Schwartz, 1971; note also Ellul, 1965 and Yanarella, 1975). The willingness of governments to pursue the slightest technological opportunity in weapons and the range of weapon technologies currently at their command lends support to this assumption. Nevertheless, weapon developments are not infrequently terminated and not only because their technological infeasibility has been convincingly demonstrated. Considerations of costs relative to expected military benefits and of the availability of alternative weapons are necessarily also components of termination decisions; or else such aborted but surely feasible systems as the XB-70 manned bomber, or the SNARK cruise missile would have been completed (Ruina, 1971; Wohlstetter, 1974).

The number and cost of weapon developments cancelled for some reason or other are staggering and give another indication of the scale at which scientific and technological resources are being absorbed by the military research effort. The United States alone during the 1960's terminated thirty seven major systems, writing off investments of over $6.7 billion (U.S. Senate Committee on Appropriations, 1973; see also Weidenbaum, 1975). It is important to note, however, that it is specific projects rather than entire programs that are more likely to be cancelled. Thus, despite the demise of the XB-70 and despite the demise of the SNARK, the quest for advanced manned bombers and long range cruise missiles continues (Lambright and Sapolsky, 1976). Apparently governments, or at least those subdivisions of governments charged with the task of developing weapons, are unwilling or unable to forego the exploration of weapon technologies even in the face of obvious failure, disappointment or political defeat stemming from competition with other national priorities and advocacies. New weapons, it would seem, are less the product of technological forces than they are of institutional and socio-political factors.

THE ORGANIZATION OF MILITARY R & D EFFORTS

Nations utilize a variety of structural arrangements to develop weapons. In the United States, though there are government-managed weapon laboratories and arsenals, the private sector is a significant participant in the weapon acquisition process. Universities are actively involved in the conduct of military research. Non-profit corporations advise on design and management questions. And business firms perform research, development, test, evaluation and management functions as well as manufacture weapons. In the development of major weapons the coordination of the disparate organizational elements is a problem; it is not uncommon in these projects for a single firm to be designated by the government as the manager for an entire weapon system and to hold responsibility for direction of a large network of subcontractors in the development and production of the weapon system. Coordination is sought by means of contracts and financial incentives (Peck and Scherer, 1962; Danhof, 1968; Yarmolinsky, 1971; Fox, 1974).

In Europe the private sector's participation in the weapon acquisition process, though substantial, is somewhat less than is the practice in the United States. This is so in part because European governments rely more upon their own facilities for the management of weapon projects and in part because a number of the major armament firms have been nationalized. In order to obtain the industrial scale required to develop modern weapons, the European governments have recently sought both to rationalize their armament industries through merger and nationalization and to establish a multinational consortium (Layton, 1969; Kaldor, 1972; Facer, 1975).

In the Soviet Union interorganizational coordination is said to be a continuing problem in the management of the economy. The performance of armaments industries in this respect, however, is thought to be substantially better than is the case in the consumer-oriented industries, supposedly because of the high priorities placed on their work. Unique features of the Soviet weapon acquisition process include the use of the Soviet Academy of Sciences for the management of a number of military research facilities, the maintenance of competitive design bureaus, and the practice of extensive prototyping (Korol, 1965; Gill, 1968; Alexander, 1970; Cambell, 1974; Judy, 1974).

The high cost and frequent failure of weapon projects has led to a continuous search for efficiency improvements in the weapon acquisition process and much debate. In the United States, for instance, there has been a succession of policy reforms including the use of incentive contracts (Scherer, 1964; Fisher, 1968), the adoption of the planning, programming and budgeting system (Novick, 1965; Wildavsky, 1966; Hitch, 1967), and increased centralization of decision-making authority (Hammond, 1968; Putnam, 1972; Stockfish, 1973; Fox, 1974; Murdock, 1974), each one of which was heralded as a panacea and then severely questioned. Recently, while French and Russian commentators have been admiring the flexibilities of the American development system, American attention has focused on the experience of Avions Marcel Dassault-Brequet and the Soviet Ministry of Aviation and their use of an incremental acquisition strategy (e.g. Perry *et al.*, 1971). Given the uncertainties inherent in the development of advanced weapon technologies, it would seem, however, there is no certain way to avoid expense and error when developing weapons (Note Holley, 1964). Only rarely, as in the case of ballistic missiles, when a technological opportunity and a consensus on weapon strategies converge will the development process seem efficient (Sapolsky, 1972).

Another aspect of the weapon acquisition process that has been the subject of an extended discussion is the relationship of basic research to the development of weapon technologies. The science policy assumption held by governments for much of the period since World War II has been that substantial investments in basic or undirected research are required in order to provide the scientific base for rapid technological progress in fields of interest, including weapons. With the urging of scientists, the military took the lead in supporting basic research on a scale previously not contemplated by government (Bush, 1954; Komos, 1966; Don K. Price, 1965 and 1966; Brooks, 1966; Sturm, 1968).

By the mid 1960's, however, first the military departments and then other agencies of government had begun to question the value of their investments in basic research. Budgetary pressures in the West, at least, forced an examination of the division between support for development projects, work with goals specifically related to agency missions, including in the case of the military, work on the direct advancement of weapon technologies, and support for basic research, work of a more theoretical and long term nature not always clearly linked to agency missions. The United States Department of Defense's Project Hindsight, for example, sought to identify the sources of weapon system improvements by describing the purpose and institutional location of work done up to twenty years earlier that was embodied in a sample of currently deployed weapon systems (Scherwin and Isenson, 1967; Isenson, 1969). The finding that basic research activities in the postwar years contributed little to operational weapon systems, having as it did the perhaps unintended implication that basic research work should not be supported, led to the study being challenged on both methodological and policy grounds (e.g. Brooks, 1968; Krielkamp, 1971). A counterstudy, TRACES, sponsored by the National Science Foundation, an agency specifically charged with the support of academic research, found that important and common technologies had their root in scientific work of the most basic and undirected type, done in some cases centuries earlier; it concluded that such research was indeed useful and worthy of support (Illinois Institute of Technology, 1968). While subsequent discussion failed to resolve conclusively the methodological issues involved in identifying the social and economic utility of research investments, policy did change (Krielkamp, 1971; see also Department of Education and Science, 1969; National Science Foundation, 1972; Kursunogh and Perlmutter, 1973; for further discussion of Project Hindsight and TRACES, see Layton, Chapter 6). Government agencies, and the military in particular, began to reduce their support for undirected research, buttressed by the sentiment that government sponsorship of research should in large measure − if not exclusively − be confined to work that has an obvious link to current operational needs. This sentiment found expression in the United States in the so-called Mansfield Amendment (Nichols, 1971; Maddox, 1972; Organization for Economic Cooperation and Development, 1974) and in Britain in the Rothschild Report (Rothschild, 1971). Where once the military was the prime sponsor for basic research, this is no longer the case in the United States and in at least certain other nations as well.

For many, however, the only truly important issue which relates to the organization of the weapon acquisition process is the pressure that existing institutional arrangements generate for the perpetuation of the competition in arms, or as Kurth (1971) expressed it (See also Kaldor, 1972), whether or not there exists a 'follow-up imperative'. The concern here is with the potential political influence of armament employment and with the probable preferences of organizations involved in the development of weapons, both industrial contractors and the military, for their own institutional maintenance. It is pointed out that in the arms-producing nations the armament industries provide employment that is often geographically concentrated and politically important. The participation of profit-making organizations in the weapons acquisition process adds an obvious financial incentive for the continuous development of new weapons. In the United States a voluminous literature that is highly suspicious of this institutional pattern, or 'Military Industrial Complex' as it is referred to by its critics, has recently appeared (e.g. Neiberg, 1966; Adams, 1968; Lapp, 1969; Barnet, 1969; Proxmire, 1970; Melman, 1970; see also Moskos, 1972; Slater and Nordin, 1972). The suspicions expressed, though contemporary and American, are not entirely without historical antecedents (Engelbrecht and Hanighen, 1934; Mills, 1956; Wiltz, 1963), and they have at least partial applicability to other nations, especially the Soviet Union (Sheren, 1970; McDonnell, 1975).

Given their predilection for conspiratorial theories of politics, critics of the Military Industrial Complex have not stimulated much serious scholarship (Smoke, 1975). Little empirical testing of their concepts has been done and that which has is at best inconclusive. Lieberson (1971), for example, examined the dependency of large American corporations on military expenditures in order to test elitist versus pluralistic descriptions of the economy; he found, not surprisingly, that the impact of such expenditures was highly differentiated, with a few industries and corporations being much more dependent than most (See also Weidenbaum, 1963; Kaysen, 1963; Scherer, 1971; Wolf, 1972; Kaner and Thorson, 1972). Lieberson argues that rather than depict military-industry linkages as collusive and dominating, he would prefer to describe them as one important economic interest among many; this view is much more akin to pluralist perceptions of American society than he seems willing to admit. Attempts to explore the profitability of the armaments industries have been able to demonstrate every conceivable relationship, depending upon the accounting technique they used. The most thorough analysis, that of the United States General Accounting Office (1971), which considered in its calculations the large capital investments made by the military in the plant and equipment of these industries, found that, though there were variations, the overall level of profits for armaments was close to the average experience of American industry as a whole (See also Scherer, 1971; Carroll, 1972; Wolfe, 1972; Rosen, 1973; Weidenbaum, 1975). Russett's analysis of Congressional roll calls (1970) failed to find the expected direct relationship between military spending in Congressional districts and voting on defense-related issues (See also Cobb, 1973). The problem may well be that roll call analysis is too blunt an instrument to capture adequately the Congressional subtleties involved in furthering the interests of constituents. It might be more revealing, for instance, to explore as Leiberson (1971) and Niskanen (1971) have partially done the overrepresentation of Congressmen from affected districts on committees dealing with special interests, whether defense or not, and the biases that this overrepresentation generates in legislative and spending decisions in Congress. As to Kurth's theory of the follow-on imperative in the award of United States weapon contracts, there are apparently too many definitional ambiguities for a sufficient test to be made (Kanter and Thorson, 1972).

Others, less self-consciously antagonistic toward government than are the Military Industrial Complex critics, have also taken an institutional approach to the analysis of the weapon acquisition process. Mostly political scientists, they have tended to concentrate on identifying the factors affecting the introduction of major innovations in weapons and have relied heavily upon case histories of weapon projects for their data. (Among the many case histories that have been prepared are Davis, 1967; Lambright, 1967; Perry, 1967; Art, 1968; Armocost, 1969; Jayne, 1969; Yanarella, 1971; Sapolsky, 1972; Dorfer, 1973; Head, 1973; Greenwood, 1975; Steinbruner and Carter, 1975.) Their work, which has yet to be fully aggregated and summarized (Allison and Morris, 1975; but note Davis, 1967), stresses the dominant role of the military services in determining the rate and direction of weapon innovations. Weapon innovations, in this view, gestate over many years and are often championed by bureaucratic entrepreneurs who rise up from the ranks of weapon designers or the officer corps. As the projects approach the advanced development stage, they are absorbed more fully into the politics of the sponsoring service and their fate is influenced strongly by the service's internal resolution of goals and its bargaining position at the highest levels of government.

The official descriptions of the weapon acquisition process, of course, are devoid of any recognition of institutional influences, either macro-sociological or micro-bureaucratic. Instead, the process is portrayed as a quasi-scientific undertaking involving the weighing at fixed points in a weapon system's development of such factors as the technological opportunities, expected costs, projected enemy capabilities, and strategic doctrine. If only in the aspiration of certain of its participants, it is a process potentially governable by cost/effectiveness studies (Hitch and McKean, 1961; Hitch, 1967; Enthoven and Smith, 1971).

A complete understanding of the weapon acquisition process, it would seem, will require an amalgamation of the various perspectives. An activity as large and long-sustained as the acquiring of new weapons is bound to have developed its own institutional dynamics. But such an activity also would not be continually with us if it systematically ignored technical and strategic realities.

The contribution which the weapon research effort makes to the national security and strategy — whose enhancement is, after all, its ultimate and perhaps only legitimate objective — is increasingly being questioned. For some the fear is that the competition in arms, because of the interaction that occurs between weapon development decisions of the competitors, is slipping into a destabilizing arms race. The uncertainty about intentions and capabilities, it is said, leads to a cycle of apparently prudent steps that leaves everyone worse off than they were before the cycle began (See Garwin and Bethe, 1968; Rathjens, 1969; York, 1969; Cheyes and Wiesner, 1969; Field *et al.*, 1971; Rathjens, 1975). For others the fear is that the weapon acquisition process has become so oriented to serving its own internal needs that it weakens security by generating weapons which are too costly to produce in quanities sufficient for an adequate defense (Niskanen, 1972 and 1973; see also Stockfish, 1973; Art, 1974; Facer, 1975). Until the process which guides the acquisition of weapons is better investigated, we will have difficulty in discerning whether either or both of these fears is justified. Without further evidence we will certainly not know what policy instruments can be used to avoid the dangers to security which are feared.

THE EFFECT ON THE MILITARY: SCIENCE AND WARFARE

The link between science and war, first forged during World War II and since strengthened, has had effects that go beyond the design and procurement of new weapons. Obviously the military's role in society has been altered, as have been the organization of science and the conduct of war. Each of these topics deserves a lengthy analysis; all that can be done here is to highlight the major themes.

The effect on the military of the revolution in weapon technologies, as Janowitz (1960 and 1964) and other students of military organization point out, has been to reduce its societal autonomy (Note also Janowitz and Little, 1965; Coates and Pellegrin, 1965; Biderman and Sharp, 1968; Lang, 1969; Moskos, 1970; Little, 1971). Now permanently mobilized because of the reach of nuclear missiles, the peacetime military must seek more resources from society for its maintenance than it once did. Due to the complexity of weapons and the management problems they create, the skill differential between military and civilian occupations, once great, narrows considerably. New social groups, less willing to be subject to military discipline, and at times, as in the case of the American involvement in Vietnam, even hostile to military policy, must be recruited and/or involved in order for the military to function. The military's task is redefined to include a war-prevention as well as a war-fighting responsibility, but because the society as a whole is as vulnerable to destruction as are military forces, civilian authorities are more prone to intervene in the direction of military activities than they once were. The increased dependence of the military on society creates tensions within the military that have yet to be fully resolved (Janowitz, 1971; Abrahamsson, 1972; Moskos, 1973).

Science too is now permanently mobilized, but not exclusively for war. Weapon projects gave science its first experience with very large-scale undertakings. The successes that were achieved, indeed impressive, led scientists and politicians to believe that the organizational model used to solve defense problems, the large, centrally directed national program, would be effective in solving other public problems (Lessing, 1968; Ramo, 1969; Webb, 1969; Platt, 1969; see also Salomon, Chapter 2, and Nelkin, Chapter 11). Some scientists, at least, wanted alternatives to the military rationale for the support of science. And most politicians were ready to accept the claim that answers existed for the crises of the day. As a result, work toward such objectives as economic development, urban progress, the defeat of cancer, energy independence and technological independence have become part of the justification for the support of science by government (Lakoff, 1973; Smith, 1973; Organization for Economic Cooperation and Development, 1974; Wright and Long, 1975; Lambright, 1975).

The permanent mobilization of science, however, is not without its problems. While science has always made utilitarian claims to gain support (Manning, 1967; Miller, 1970), the visibility and specificity of its current applied objectives make science unusually vulnerable to failures of achievement. In addition, not all of science can be accommodated within the framework of national programs. Some disciplines, quite valuable to the progress of science itself, are certain under these arrangements to be beyond the margin of support. Finally, there is the issue of the legitimacy of the objectives selected. Now public, the goals of science can be – some say must be – contested politically both within and outside science (See Ravetz, 1971; Blume, 1974).

The overall effect on warfare of the military research effort has been to increase the destructive capabilities of the forces employed. To be sure, not all of military research is directed toward that end; work goes on in repairing battle wounds, in making rations more tasty, and in preventing machinery from rusting. Some advances such as that which eliminates noise in the equipment of missile-carrying submarines can even help reduce the danger of war by making the submarines less vulnerable to detection and destruction (Note Brooks, 1975). Nevertheless, the thrust of this effort, and the most used measure of progress in military research, is efficiency in target destruction.

The reason why this is the case, as Davis (1974) suggests, lies in the pressures existing in the technology-producing nations. Advanced industrial nations have, as he notes, a diminishing ability to field mass armies. If judged by the incentives necessary for recruitment, military service, especially in the combat arms, has progressively less attraction to their citizens. The tolerance of these nations for suffering casualties is also declining (Davis, 1974; Brooks, 1975). In World War I fifty thousand deaths in a single battle was for all parties an expected, if undesired, consequence of war. In Vietnam a rate of two hundred combat deaths per week was considered politically unacceptable for American forces.

Technology, in this situation, becomes a necessary substitute for manpower. An important object of research is to automate combat tasks, that is, to field weapons which reduce the exposure to casualty of one's own forces while inflicting as much destruction as possible on the forces of the other side. From this perspective nuclear weapons are ideal, as they have extremely low manning ratios to potential casualties inflicted. The same pressures operate in the design of conventional weapons as well. Witness the work on precision guided munitions and laser targeting devices. The technologically more sophisticated side always is thought to have the advantage; except, of course, that the advantage is always fleeting if one has as an opponent another industrialized nation (Cliffe, 1972; Canby, 1975; Digby, 1975; Foster, 1975). Perhaps when conventional weapons approach the efficiency of strategic weapons, the total stalemate will be upon us. In the meantime the destructiveness of war is certain to grow.

ARMS CONTROL

Individually and collectively, scientists and engineers have been among the strongest advocates for the control of arms (See Lakoff, Chapter 10). At the end of World War II, for instance, Norbert Wiener, the founder of cybernetics, publicly stated that he would not aid the military agencies in the United States in utilizing his work. More recently, Andrei Sakharov, often referred to as the father of the Soviet hydrogen bomb, has at great personal risk spoken out against the continuous accumulation of weapons. For nearly two decades, the Pugwash Conferences have provided a forum at which scientists and engineers from around the world have discussed the opportunities for limiting weapons and for the peaceful application of scientific and technological resources. (For a history of the Pugwash Conferences, see Rotblat, 1972.) Scientists and engineers have played important roles in various arms control efforts such as the debate over the deployment of an antiballistic missile system in the United States, the Nuclear Test Ban Treaty, and the worldwide movement to halt the development of biological weapons (Chayes and Wiesner, 1969; Robinson, 1971; Cahn, 1972). And yet, even the most committed among them would concede that the pace of weapon development has hardly slackened because of their efforts and that there remain substantial obstacles to the control of arms.

These obstacles are different for different types of weapon projects. Large-scale development projects, though technically susceptible to external monitoring, are buttressed by economic and institutional interests. Smaller-scale applied research projects, perhaps less problematic in terms of their supporting interests, are nearly immune to external monitoring.

Unobtrusive verification techniques have been effectively used by the superpowers to monitor each other's force deployments (Greenwood, 1973). Presumably, the same techniques can be used to determine the existence of any major weapon project that they might agree to ban since these projects, if carried out, reveal themselves through such details as the prodigious consumption of energy, large employment concentrations and the construction of specialized facilities. The problem is, of course, gaining agreement to demobilize resources currently utilized in the development of major weapon systems. If the West European experience is a guide, the transferability of these resources can be expected to be low even when they are superfluous militarily (Kaldor, 1972; Vais, 1975). Organizations, perhaps more so than individuals, are reluctant to face the uncertainties of shifting fields (Allison, 1973). In the United States and the Soviet Union, where claims for the potential reemployment of the resources for military purposes can be made, the affected interests are not likely to be any more cooperative. Moreover, restrictions placed on one type of weapon development in themselves create incentives to redeploy the resources freed to other types of weapon developments. When the major naval powers of the world agreed in the 1920's to limit the number of capital ships, work was concentrated on the development of aircraft carriers and submarines, ship types not then classified as capital. Today, in the face of agreements to limit the quantity of strategic missiles, the United States and the Soviet Union are busy exploring qualitative improvements in these missiles (Smoke, 1975; Brooks, 1975).

Applied research projects present other problems. Although scientists and engineers employed on these projects may have grown accustomed to military support, their work most often can easily be shifted to apparently peaceful activities. The resources they absorb are neither large nor politically significant. Work at this level, however, is extremely difficult to monitor and to control. Discoveries in genetics, for example, can have dangerous military as well as beneficial medical applications. The existence and direction of the work can easily be disguised. Even on-site inspections are likely to reveal little about the intent of the research. And since intent is such a crucial element in this type of activity, there is bound to be much uncertainty about the effectiveness of restrictions achieved or asserted.

It is precisely this uncertainty that leads some to argue that it is perhaps best not to attempt to control applied military research (e.g. Ruina, 1971; see also Coffey, 1974). With sure knowledge of what is technologically feasible or infeasible in weapons gained through one's own research, one need not assume a potential adversary possesses the capability to alter dramatically the power balance. Continued military research might well enhance the opportunity for increased mutual trust, the keystone of disarmament.

Ironically though, the superpowers might someday discover that the true danger to peace lies not in a future breakthrough in a weapon technology, but in their own past achievements in weapons. Knowledge once created is indestructable. The diffusion of nuclear power, binary gas or some other awesome weapon technology to nations or political groups not allied with or controlled by one of them could well destroy the balance of mutual terror which they have so carefully constructed and which could well be the final legacy of the billions they have invested in military research in the years since World War II. It is not merely that we have here problems of formidable technical difficulty and the most trying kind of socio-political decision making. We also lack the fundamental knowledge of so much of the process of decision making in this area. Clearly the implications of military research and development run through the very fabric of science policy, and we must therefore claim for research in this area a much higher priority and a more integrative approach than hitherto.

BIBLIOGRAPHY

Abrahamsson, 1972 — Abrahamsson, B., *Military Professionalization and Political Power,* Beverly Hills, California, Sage Publications, 1972.

Adams, 1968 — Adams, W., 'The Military Industrial Complex and the New Industrial State', *American Economic Review* 58, 1968, pp. 652-665.

Alexander, 1970 — Alexander, A. J., *R & D in Soviet Aviation,* Santa Monica, California, RAND, 1970.

Allison, 1973 — Allison, G. T., 'Organizational and Administrative Factors Affecting Shifts in Defense Expenditures', in Udis, B. (Ed.), *The Economic Consequences of Reduced Military Spending,* Lexington, Mass., D. C. Heath, 1973.

Armacost, 1969 — Armacost, M. H., *The Politics of Weapon Innovation,* New York, Columbia University Press, 1969.

Art, 1968 — Art, R. J., *The TFX Decision,* Boston, Little Brown, 1968.

Art, 1974 — Art, R. J., 'Restructuring the Military-Industrial Complex: Arms Control in Institutional Perspective', *Public Policy* 22, No. 4, 1974, pp. 423-460.

Baritz, 1961 — Baritz, L., *The Servants of Power,* Middletown, Conn., Wesleyan University Press, 1961.

Barnet, 1969 — Barnet, R. J., *The Economy of Death,* New York, Athenaum, 1969.

Baxter, 1946 — Baxter, J., *Scientists Against Time,* Boston, Little Brown, 1946.

Bazell, 1971 — Bazell, R., 'Arms Race: Scientists Question Threat from Soviet Military R & D', *Science,* 20 August 1971, pp. 707-709.

Bell, 1973 — Bell, D., *The Coming of Post-Industrial Society,* New York, Basic Books, 1973.

Biderman and Sharp, 1968 — Biderman, A. D. and Sharp, L. M., 'The Convergence of Military and Civilian Occupational Structures', *American Journal of Sociology* 73, 1968, pp. 381-399.

Blume, 1974	Blume, S. S., *Toward a Political Sociology of Science,* New York, Free Press, 1974.
Boffey, 1975	Boffey, P., *The Brain Bank of America,* New York, McGraw-Hill, 1975.
Brodie and Brodie, 1962	Brodie, B. and Brodie, F., *From Crossbow to H-Bomb,* Bloomington, University of Indiana Press, 1962.
Brodie, 1973	Brodie, B., *War and Politics,* New York, The MacMillan Co., 1973.
Brooks, 1966	Brooks, H., 'Basic Science and Agency Missions', in Weyl, J. (Ed.), *Research in the Service of National Purpose,* Washington, U.S. Government Printing Office, 1966.
Brooks, 1968	Brooks, H., *The Government of Science,* Cambridge, Mass., MIT Press, 1968.
Brooks, 1975	Brooks, H., 'The Military Innovation System and the Qualitative Arms Race', *Daedalus* 104, No. 3, 1975, pp. 75-98.
Brown, 1963	Brown, H., 'Management of Defense Research and Development', in Kast, F. E. and Rosenzweig, J. E. (Eds.), *Science, Technology and Management,* New York, McGraw-Hill, 1963.
Brunner, 1966	Brunner, J., *The Cost of Basic Scientific Research in Europe,* Santa Monica, California, RAND, 1965.
Bush, 1949	Bush, V., *Modern Arms and Free Men,* Cambridge, Mass., MIT Press, 1949.
Bush, 1945	Bush, V., *Science, the Endless Frontier,* Washington, U.S. Printing Office, 1945.
Cahn, 1972	Cahn, A., *Eggheads and Warheads,* Cambridge, Mass., MIT, 1972.
Calder, 1968	Calder, N. G., *Unless Peace Comes,* London, Allen Lane, 1968.
Cambell, 1974	Cambell, R. W., 'Problems of Technical Progress in the USSR', in Bornstein, M. and Fusfeld, D. (Eds.), *The Soviet Economy,* 4th Edition.
Canby, 1975	Canby, S. L., 'Regaining a Conventional Military Balance in Europe', *Military Review* 55, No. 6, 1975.
Carroll, 1972	Carroll, S., 'Profits in the Airframe Industry', *Quarterly Journal of Economics,* 1972.
Chayes and Wiesner, 1969	Chayes, A. and Wiesner, J. B., *ABM: An Evaluation of the Decision to Deploy an Anti-Ballistic Missile System,* New York, Signet Books, 1969.
Cliffe, 1972	Cliffe, T., 'Military Technology and the European Balance', *Adelphi Papers,* No. 89, 1972.
Coates and Pellegrin, 1965	Coates, C. H. and Pellegrin, R. J. (Eds.), *Military Sociology,* University Park, Maryland, Social Science Press, 1965.
Cobb, 1973	Cobb, S., 'The United States Senate and the Impact Defense Spending Concentrations' in Rosen, S. (Ed.), *Testing the Theory of the Military-Industrial Complex,* Lexington, Mass., Lexington Press, 1973.
Coffey, 1974	Coffey, J. I., 'New Approaches to Arms Reduction in Europe', *Adelphi Papers,* No. 105, 1974.
Danhof, 1968	Danhof, C. H., *Government Contracting and Technological Change,* Washington, D.C., Brookings, 1968.

Davis, 1967   Davis, V., *The Politics of Innovation: Pattern in Navy Cases*, Denver, University of Denver Press, 1967.

Davis, 1974   Davis, V., 'Levée en Masse, C'est Finie: The Deterioration of Popular Willingness to Serve', in Lovell, J. P. and Kronenberg, P. S. (Eds.), *New Civil-Military Relations*, New Brunswick, New Jersey, Transaction Books, 1974.

DeGregorie and Pi-Sunyer,   DeGregorie, T. and Pi-Sunyer, O., 'Technology, Tradi-
1966   tionalism and Military Establishments', *Technology and Culture* 7, 1966, 4-2-407.

Department of Education   Department of Education and Science, *An Attempt to*
and Science, 1969   *Quantify the Economic Benefits of Scientific Research*, London, HMSO, 1969.

Digby, 1975   Digby, J. F., *Precision-Guided Weapons*, Santa Monica, California, RAND, 1975.

Dorfer, 1973   Dorfer, I., *System 37 Viggen*, Oslo, Universitets-forloget, 1973.

Ellul, 1965   Ellul, J., *The Technological Society*, New York, Vintage Books, 1965.

Engelbrecht and Hanighen,   Engelbrecht, H. C. and Hanighen, F. C., *Merchants of*
1934   *Death*, New York, Dodd Mead, 1934.

Enthoven and Smith, 1971   Enthoven, A. C. and Smith, K. W., *How Much is Enough?*, New York, Harper and Row, 1971.

Facer, 1975   Facer, R., 'The Alliance and Europe, Part III: Weapon Procurement in Europe– Capabilities and Choices', *Adelphi Papers*, No. 108, 1975.

Feld *et al.*, 1971   Feld, B. *et al.*, *Impact of New Technologies on the Arms Race*, Cambridge, Mass., MIT Press, 1971.

Forsberg, 1972   Forsberg, R., *Resources Devoted to Military Research and Development*, Stockholm, Almquist & Wiksell, 1972.

Foster, 1975   Foster, J. L., 'The Future of Conventional Arms Control', a paper prepared for delivery at the 1975 meeting of the American Political Science Association, San Francisco, Sept. 2-5, 1975.

Fisher, 1968   Fisher, I. N., *A Reappraisal of Incentive Contracting Experience*, Santa Monica, California, RAND, 1968.

Fox, 1974   Fox, R. J., *Arming America: How the U.S. Buys Weapons*, Cambridge, Mass., Harvard University Press, 1974.

Freeman, *et al.*, 1971   Freeman, C., Oldham, C. H. G., Cooper, C. M., Sinclair, T. C., Achilladelis, B. G., 'The Goals of R & D in the 1970's', *Science Studies* 1, No. 3-4, pp. 357-406.

Freeman and Young, 1965   Freeman, C. and Young, A., *The Research and Development Effort in Western Europe, North America and the Soviet Union*, Paris, OECD, 1965.

Garwin and Bethe, 1968   Garwin, R. L. and Bethe, H. A., 'Anti-Ballistic Missile Systems', *Scientific American* 218, No. 3, 1968.

Gilpin, 1968   Gilpin, R., *France in the Age of the Scientific State*, Princeton, Princeton University Press, 1968.

Gill, 1968   Gill, R. R., 'Decision Making in Soviet Science Policy', *Bulletin of the Atomic Scientists* 24, No. 4, 1968, pp. 15-19.

Greenwood, 1973	Greenwood, T., 'Reconnaissance and Arms Control', *Scientific American* 228, No. 2, 1973, pp. 14-25.
Greenwood, 1975	Greenwood, T., *Making the MIRV*, Cambridge, Ballenger, 1975.
Hall, 1970	Hall, R., 'Science, Technology and Warfare, 1400-1700', in Wright, M. and Paszek, L. (Eds.), *Science, Technology and Warfare*, Washington, USAF, 1970, pp. 3-24.
Hammond, 1968	Hammond, P. Y., 'A Functional Analysis of Department of Defense Decision-Making in the McNamara Administration', *American Political Science Review* 62, No. 2, 1968, pp. 57-69.
Harmon, 1970	Harmon, A. J., *A Methodology for Cost Factor Comparison and Prediction*, Santa Monica, California, RAND, 1970.
Head, 1973	Head, R. G., 'Doctrinal Innovation and the A-7 Attack Aircraft Program', in Head, R. G. and Rikke, E. J. (Eds.), *American Defense Policy*, 3rd Edition, Baltimore, Johns Hopkins Press, 1973.
Hitch and McKean, 1961	Hitch, C. J. and McKean, R. N., *The Economics of Defense in the Nuclear Age*, Cambridge, Mass., Harvard University Press, 1961.
Hitch, 1967	Hitch, C. J., *Decision Making for Defense*, Berkeley, University of California Press, 1967.
Holley, 1964	Holley, I., *Buying Aircraft: Material Procurement for the Army Air Forces*, Washington, D.C., Department of the Army, 1964.
Holley, 1970	Holley, I., 'The Evolution of Operations Research and Its Impact on the Military Establishment: The Air Force Experience', in Wright, M. and Paszek, L. (Ed.), *Science, Technology and Warfare*, Washington, D.C., USAF, 1970, pp. 89-109.
Holloman and Harger, 1971	Holloman, H. and Harger, 'America's Technological Dilemma', *Technology Review* 73, 1971, pp. 30-40.
Holloway, 1974	Holloway, D., 'Technology and Political Decision in Soviet Armament Policy', *Journal of Peace Research* 4, 1974.
Illinois Institute of Technology, 1968	Illinois Institute of Technology, *Technology in Retrospect and Critical Events in Science* (TRACES), Washington, D.C., National Science Foundation, 1968.
International Defense Review, 1969	*International Defense Review*, 'The Tracked APC — Some New and Existing Types Reviewed', 1971.
Isenson, 1969	Isenson, R., 'Project Hindsight: An Empirical Study of the Sources of Ideas Utilized in Operational Weapon Systems', in Gruber, W. H. and Marquis, D. G. (Eds.), *Factors in the Transfer of Technology*, Cambridge, Mass., MIT Press, 1969.
Janowitz, 1960	Janowitz, M., *The Professional Soldier*, New York, The Free Press, 1960.
Janowitz, 1964	Janowitz, M. (Ed.), *The New Military*, New York, Russell Sage Foundation, 1964.
Janowitz, 1971	Janowitz, M., 'The Emergent Military', in Moskos, C. C. (Ed.), *Public Opinion and Military Establishment*, Beverly Hills, California, Sage, 1971.

Janowitz and Little, 1965   Janowitz, M. and Little, R., *Sociology and the Military Establishment*, New York, Russell Sage Foundation, 1964.

Jayne, 1969   Jayne, E. R., *The ABM Debate: Strategic Defense and National Security*, unpublished PhD dissertation, MIT, 1969.

Judy, 1974   Judy, R. W., 'The Case of Computer Technology', in Bornstein, M. and Fusfeld, D. (Ed.), *The Soviet Economy*, 4th Edition, Irwin.

Kaldor, 1972   Kaldor, M., *European Defense Industries – National and International Implications*, Sussex, Institute of the Study of International Organization, University of Sussex, 1972.

Kanter and Thorson, 1972   Kanter, A. and Thorson, S. J., 'The Weapons Procurement Process: Choosing Among Competing Theories', *Public Policy* 20, No. 4, 1972, pp. 479-524.

Kaysen, 1963   Kaysen, C., 'Improving the Efficiency of Military Research and Development', *Public Policy* 12, 1963, pp. 219-273.

Komos, 1966   Komos, N., *Science and the Air Force*, Arlington, Virginia, Historical Division: Office of Aerospace Research, 1966.

Krielkamp, 1971   Krielkamp, K., 'Hindsight and the Real World of Science Policy', *Science Studies* 1, 1971, pp. 43-66.

Kevles, 1969   Kevles, D., 'Millikan: Spokesman for Science in the Twenties', *Engineering and Science*, 1969, pp. 17-22.

Kursunoglu and Perlmutter,   Kursunoglu, B. and Perlmutter, A., *Impact of Basic*
1973   *Research on Technology*, New York, Plenum Press, 1973.

Kurth, 1971   Kurth, J. R., 'A Widening Gyre: The Logic of American Weapons Procurement', *Public Policy* 19, 1971, pp. 373-404.

Lakoff, 1973   Lakoff, S. A., 'The Vicissitudes of American Science Policy at Home and Abroad', *Minerva* 11, 1973, pp. 175-190.

Lambright, 1967   Lambright, W. H., *Shooting Down the Nuclear Plane*, Indianapolis, Bobbs-Merrill, 1967.

Lambright, 1975   Lambright, W. H., *Governing Science and Technology*, New York, Oxford University Press, 1976.

Lambright and Sapolsky, 1976   Lambright, W. H. and Sapolsky, H., 'Terminating R & D', *Policy Sciences*, Spring, 1976.

Lang, 1969   Lang, K., *Sociology of the Military: A Selected and Annotated Bibliography*, Chicago, Inter-University Seminar on Armed Forces, 1969.

Lapp, 1969   Lapp, R., *The Weapons Culture*, New York, Norton, 1969.

Lapp, 1971   Lapp, R., *Arms Beyond Doubt*, New York, Cowles Publishing Co., 1971.

Lasby, 1971   Lasby, C., *Project Paperclip*, New York, Athenaum, 1971.

Layton, 1969   Layton, C., *European Advanced Technology*, London George Allen and Unwin, 1969.

Leiberson, 1971   Leiberson, S., 'An Empirical Study of Military-

Industrial Linkages', *The American Journal of Sociology* 76, No. 4, 1971, pp. 562-584.

Leitenberg, 1973   Leitenberg, M., 'The Dynamics of Military Technology Today', *International Social Science Journal* 25, No. 3, 1973, pp. 336-357.

Lessing, 1968   Lessing, L., 'Systems Engineering Invades the City', *Fortune* 77, 1968, pp. 154-156, 217-221.

Little, 1971   Little, R. W. (Ed.), *Handbook of Military Instructions,* Beverly Hills, California, Sage, 1971.

Maddox, 1972   Maddox, J., 'American Science: The Endless Search for Objectives', *Minerva,* 1972, pp. 129-140.

Manning, 1967   Manning, T. G., *Government in Science,* Lexington, Kentucky, University of Kentucky Press, 1967.

McDonnell, 1975   McDonnell, J., 'The Soviet Defense Industry as a Pressure Group', in MacGuire, M., Booth, K. and McDonnell, J. (Eds.), *Soviet Naval Policy: Objectives and Constraints,* New York, Praeger, 1975.

McElwee, 1974   McElwee, W., *The Art of War,* Bloomington, Indiana, University of Indiana, 1974.

Melman, 1970   Melman, S., *Pentagon Capitalism,* New York, McGraw-Hill, 1970.

Mikulak, 1971   Mikulak, R., *A Second Look at U.S. and Soviet Research and Development,* Cambridge, Mass., Center for International Studies, MIT, 1971.

Miller, 1970   Miller, H. S., *Dollars for Research: Science and Its Patrons in Nineteenth Century America,* Seattle, University of Washington Press, 1970.

Mills, 1956   Mills, C. W., *The Power Elite,* New York, Oxford University Press, 1956.

Morrison, 1966   Morrison, E., *Men, Machines and Modern Times,* Cambridge, Mass., MIT Press, 1966.

Moskos, 1972   Moskos, C. C. Jr., 'The Military-Industrial Complex: Theoretical Antecedents and Conceptual Contradictions', in Sarkesian, S. (Ed.), *The Military-Industrial Complex: A Reassessment,* Beverly Hills, California, Sage, 1972.

Moskos, 1973   Moskos, C. C. Jr., 'The Emergent Military: Civil, Traditional or Plural? ', *Pacific Sociological Review* 16, 1973, pp. 255-279.

Murdock, 1974   Murdock, C. A., *Defense Policy Formation,* Albany, New York, University of New York Press, 1974.

National Academy of Sciences, 1965   National Academy of Sciences, *Basic Research and National Goals,* Washington, D.C., U.S. Government Printing Office, 1965.

National Science Foundation, 1972   National Science Foundation, *Research and Development and Economic Growth/Productivity,* Washington, D.C., National Science Foundation, 1972.

Neiberg, 1966   Neiberg, H. L., *In the Name of Science,* Chicago, Quadrangle, 1966.

Nichols, 1971   Nichols, R. W., article in *Science* 172, 1971, p. 29.

Nimitz, 1974   Nimitz, N., *The Structure of Soviet Outlays on R & D in 1960 and 1968,* Santa Monica, California, RAND, 1974.

Niskanen, 1971   Niskanen, W. A., *Bureaucracy and Representative Government*, Chicago, Aldine Atherton, 1971.

Niskanen, 1972   Niskanen, W. A., 'Coherent Decentralization of U.S. Defense Force Planning', in Tuite *et al.* (Eds.), *Interorganizational Decision Making*, Chicago, Aldine, 1972, pp. 277-286.

Niskanen, 1973   Niskanen, W. A., 'The Problems of Resource Allocation', in Kinter, W. and Foster, R. (Eds.), *National Strategy in a Decade of Change*, Lexington, Mass., D.C. Heath and Co., 1973, pp. 145-157.

Novick, 1965   Novick, D., *Program Budgeting: Program Analysis and the Federal Budget*, Cambridge, Mass., Harvard University Press, 1965.

OECD, 1974   OECD, *The Research System, Vol. III* (Canada and the United States, General Conclusions), Paris, OECD, 1974.

Peck and Scherer, 1962   Peck, M. J. and Scherer, F. M., *The Weapons Acquisition Process: An Economic Analysis*, Boston, Graduate School of Business Administration, Harvard University, 1962.

Perry, 1970   Perry, R. L., *A Review of System Acquisition Experience*, Santa Monica, California, RAND, 1971.

Perry *et al.*, 1967   Perry, R. L., *The Ballistic Missile Decisions*, Santa Monica, California, RAND, 1967.

Perry *et al.*, 1971   Perry, R. L. *et al.*, *System Acquisition Strategies*, Santa Monica, California, RAND, 1971.

Platt, 1969   Platt, J., 'What We Must Do', *Science*, 1969, pp. 285-290.

Derek Price, 1973   Price, Derek de Solla, 'The Relationship Between Science and Technology and Their Implications for Policy Formation', in Strasser, G. and Simons, E. M. (Eds.), *Science and Technology Policies*, Cambridge, Mass., Ballinger, 1973.

Don K. Price, 1965   Price, Don K., *The Scientific Estate*, Cambridge, Mass., Harvard University Press, 1965.

Don K. Price, 1966   Price, Don K., 'Federal Money and University Research', *Science* 151, 1966, pp. 285-290.

Proxmire, 1970   Proxmire, W., *Report from the Wasteland*, New York, Praeger, 1970.

Putnam, 1972   Putnam, W. D., *The Evolution of Air Force System Acquisition Management*, Santa Monica, California, RAND, 1972.

Ramo, 1969   Ramo, S., *Cure for Chaos*, New York, David McKay, 1969.

Rathjens, 1969   Rathjens, G. W., 'The Dynamics of the Arms Race', *Scientific American* 220, No. 4, 1969.

Rathjens, 1975   Rathjens, G. W., 'Changing Perspectives on Arms Control', *Daedelus* 104, No. 3, 1975, pp. 201-214.

Ravetz, 1971   Ravetz, J. R., *Scientific Knowledge and its Social Problems*, London, Oxford, 1971.

Report of the Secretary   Report of the Secretary General, *Economic and Social*
General, 1971   *Consequences of the Armaments Race and its Extremely Harmful Effects on World Peace and Security,*

	New York, United Nations General Assembly, 1971.
Robinson, 1971	Robinson, J. P., *The Problem of Chemical and Biological Warfare,* Vol IV (CB Disarmament Negotiations), Stockholm, Almquist & W, 1971.
Rosen, 1973	Rosen, S., 'Testing the Theory of the Military-Industrial Complex', in Rosen, S. (Ed.), *Testing the Theory of the Military-Industrial Complex,* Lexington, Mass., Lexington, 1973.
Rothschild, 1971	Rothschild, L., *The Organization and Management of Government R & D,* London, Her Majesty's Stationary Office, 1971.
Ruina, 1971	Ruina, J. P., 'Aborted Military Systems', in Field, B. T. *et al.* (Eds.), *Impact of New Technologies on the Arms Race,* Cambridge, Mass., MIT Press, 1971.
Russett, 1970	Russett, B. M., *What Price Vigilence,* New Haven, Yale University Press, 1970.
Russett, 1974	Russett, B. M., 'The Revolt of the Masses: Public Opinion on Military Expenditures', in Lovell, J. P. and Kronenberg, P. S. (Eds.), *New Civil-Military Relations,* New Brunswick, New Jersey, Transaction Books, 1974.
Sapolsky, 1972	Sapolsky, H., *The Polaris System Development,* Cambridge, Mass., Harvard University Press, 1972.
Sapolsky, 1973	Sapolsky, H., 'The Military Industrial State in Comparative Perspective', a paper prepared for the Conference on Comparative Defense Policy, U.S. Air Force Academy, Colorado Springs, 1973.
Scherer, 1964	Scherer, F. M., *The Weapons Acquisition Process: Economic Incentives,* Boston, Graduate School of Business Administration, Harvard University, 1964.
Scherer, 1971	Scherer, F. M., 'The Aerospace Industry', in Adams, W. (Ed.), *The Structure of American Industry,* New York, MacMillan, 1971.
Scherwin and Isenson, 1967	Scherwin, C. W. and Isenson, R. S., 'Project Hindsight', *Science* 156, 1967, pp. 1571-1577.
Schwartz, 1971	Schwartz, E. S., *Overkill,* New York, Ballantine Books, 1971.
Scott, 1920	Scott, L. N., *Naval Consulting Board of the United States,* Washington, D.C., U.S. Government Printing Office, 1920.
Servain-Schreiber, 1967	Servain-Schreiber, J.-J., *Le Défi Américain,* Paris, DeNoel, 1967.
Sheren, 1970	Sheren, A., 'Structure and Organization of Defense-Related Industry', in U.S. Congress, Joint Economic Committee, *Economic Performance and the Military Burden in the Soviet Union,* Washington, D.C., U.S. Government Printing Office, 1970.
Slater and Nardin, 1972	Slater, J. and Nardin, T., 'The Concept of a Military-Industrial Complex', in Rosen, S. (Ed.), *Testing the Theory of the Military-Industrial Complex,* Lexington, Mass., Lexington Books, 1972.
Smith, 1966	Smith, B., *The RAND Corporation,* Cambridge, Harvard University Press, 1966.

Smith, 1973   Smith, B. L., 'A New Science Policy in the United
                                       States', *Minerva* XI, 1973, pp. 162-174.
Smoke, 1975   Smoke, R., 'National Security Affairs', in Greenstein,
                                       F. I. and Polsby, N. W. (Eds.), *International Politics,*
                                       Vol. 6 of *The Handbook of Political Science,* Reading,
                                       Mass., Addison-Wesley, 1975.
Snow, 1961   Snow, C. P., *Science and Government,* Cambridge,
                                       Harvard University Press, 1961.
Steinbruner and Carter, 1975   Steinbruner, J. and Carter, B., 'Organizational and
                                       Political Dimensions of the Strategic Posture: The
                                       Problem of Reform', *Daedelus* 104, No. 3, 1975, pp.
                                       131-154.
Stockfish, 1973   Stockfish, J. A., *Plowshares into Swords,* New York,
                                       Mason and Lipscomb, 1973.
Stockholm International   Stockholm International Peace Research Institute, *The*
Peace Research Institute,   *Arms Trade with the Third World,* Stockholm,
1971   Almquist & Seksell, 1971.
Stockholm International   Stockholm International Peace Research Institute,
Peace Research Institute,   *World Armaments and Disarmaments: SIPRI Year-*
1974   *book 1974,* Stockholm, Almquist & Seksell, 1974.
Sturm, 1968   Sturm, T. A., *The USAF Scientific Advisory Board –*
                                       Its First Twenty Years, Washington, D.C., U.S. Gov-
                                       ernment Printing Office, 1968.
Thurow, 1971   Thurow, L., 'Research, Technological Progress and
                                       Economics', *Technology Review* 73, 1971, pp. 45-51.
Udis, 1975   Udis, B., *Adjustment of High Technology Organiza-*
                                       tions to Reduced Military Spending: The European
                                       Experience, Washington, D.C., U.S. National Science
                                       Foundation, 1975.
U.S. General Accounting   U.S. General Accounting Office, *Comparison of Mili-*
Office, 1971a   *tary Research and Development Expenditures of the*
                                       United States and the Soviet Union, Washington, D.C.,
                                       U.S. Government Printing Office, 1971.
U.S. General Accounting   U.S. General Accounting Office, *Defense Industry*
Office, 1971b   *Profit Study,* Washington, D.C., U.S. Government
                                       Printing Office, 1971.
U.S. National Science   U.S. National Science Foundation, *Federal Funds for*
Foundation, 1975   *Research Development and Other Scientific Activities,*
                                       Fiscal Years 1974, 1975 and 1976.
U.S. Senate Committee on   U.S. Senate Committee on Appropriations, *Depart-*
Appropriations, 1973   *ment of Defense, Appropriations for the Year 1973,*
                                       52nd Congress, 2nd Session Washington, D.C., U.S.
                                       Government Printing Office, 1973.
von Hippel and Primack, 1974   von Hippel, F. and Primack, J., *Advice and Dissent,*
                                       New York, Basic Books, 1974.
Webb, 1969   Webb, J. E., *Space Age Management: The Large Scale*
                                       Approach, New York, McGraw-Hill, 1969.
Weidenbaum 1965   Weidenbaum, M. L., 'Defense – Space Business', in
                                       Reagan, M. D. (Ed.), *Politics, Economics and the*
                                       General Welfare, Chicago, 1965.
Weidenbaum, 1975   Weidenbaum, M. L., *The Economics of Peacetime De-*
                                       fense, New York, Praeger, 1975.
Wildavsky, 1966   Wildavsky, A., 'The Political Economy of Efficiency',

	Public Administration Review 26, 1966, pp. 7-14.
Wiltz, 1963	Wiltz, J. E., *In Search of Peace*, Baton Rouge, Louisiana, State University Press, 1963.
Wohlstetter, 1974	Wohlstetter, A., 'Rivals, but no Race', *Foreign Policy*, No. 16, 1974, pp. 48-81.
Winterbotham, 1974	Winterbotham, F., *The Ultra Secret*, New York, Harper and Row, 1974.
Wolf, 1972	Wolf, C. Jr., 'Military-Industrial Simplicities, Complexities and Realities', in Sarkesian, S. (Ed.), *The Military-Industrial Complex: A Reassessment*, Beverly Hills, California, Sage, 1972.
Wolf, 1970	Wolf, J. B., 'Commentary on Hall's Science, Technology and Warfare, 1400-1700', in Wright, M. and Paszek, L. (Eds.), *Science, Technology and Warfare*, Washington, D.C., USAF, 1970, pp. 33-43.
Wood, 1964	Wood, R. C. 'Scientists and Politics: The Rise of an Apolitical Elite', in Gilpin, R. and Wright, C. (Eds.), *Scientists and National Policy Making*, New York, Columbia University Press, 1964.
Wright and Long, 1975	Wright, C. and Long, D. (Eds.), *Science Policy of Industrial Nations*, New York, Praeger, 1975.
Yanarella, 1971	Yanarella, E. J., *Pentagon Decision Making and Bureaucratic Politics in the ABM Controversy, 1955-1967*, unpublished PhD dissertation, University of North Carolina, 1971.
Yanarella, 1975	Yanarella, E. J., 'The Technological Imperative and the Strategic Arms Race', *Peace & Change* 3, No. 1, 1975, pp. 3-16.
Yarmolinsky, 1971	Yarmolinsky, A., *The Military Establishment*, New York, Harper and Row, 1971.
York, 1969	York, H., 'Military Technology and National Security', *Scientific American* 221, No. 2, 1969.
York, 1971	York, H., *Race to Oblivion*, New York, Simon & Schuster, 1971.
Zuckerman, 1966	Zuckerman, S., *Scientists and War: The Impact of Science on Military and Civil Affairs*, London, International Publications Service, 1966.
Zaleski *et al.*, 1969	Zaleski, E. *et al.*, *Science Policy in the USSR*, Paris, OECD, 1969.

Chapter 13

SCIENCE, TECHNOLOGY AND FOREIGN POLICY

Brigitte Schroeder-Gudehus

University of Montreal

INTRODUCTION: HISTORICAL PERSPECTIVE

For a long time science and technology have developed at a considerable distance from foreign policy and international politics, although this distance began to narrow earlier for technology than it did for science. International relations in science, building on a long tradition, were originally of an essentially private character, involving individual scholars, academic institutions or learned societies. The objectives of these international scientific relations were obvious and noncontroversial: study and training, exchange of information, collaboration and debate.

Throughout the Nineteenth Century, however, despite the intrinsic universality of basic research, scientific activities did not exclude political overtones. The self-esteem of the great savant reflected back on his nation, and consequently, governments and the public vicariously basked in the fame and glory of the scientists. There was in fact a growing tendency to evaluate and to compare the different nations' contribution to the advancement of scientific knowledge in terms of preeminence and inferiority, ascent and decline. From at least the time of Francis Bacon onwards, scientists had presented a country's leadership in the world of science as a political asset. Now a gloomy future was predicted for the nation which would allow itself to be outdistanced by its competitors (Paul, 1972; Cardwell, 1957, 59-65, Ashby and Anderson, 1974; Ben-David, 1970, 1971). Although most of the time this concern with scientific preeminence and decline hardly spread beyond academic circles and the educated public, it became an important ingredient of national intellectual self-perception. The importance of a nation's scientific achievements and international status was widely used moreover as a tactical argument in domestic politics. Governments were thereby urged to support more generously the institutions of higher learning and research in order to provide the national scientific community with the appropriate means to serve the country and to assure its work the necessary international aura.

Government involvement, however, was slight. Science became relevant to foreign policy only to the extent that it developed into a factor of national wealth and security. In the late Nineteenth Century, the close connection between scientific preeminence and industrial power was particularly striking in the case of the German Empire (Gilpin, 1968, 22-23; Landes, 1969, 175-176; Henderson, 1975). The determining influence of high scientific capabilities on a country's economic position was most conspicuous in the chemical industries (Haber, 1958; Beer, 1959; Hohenberg, 1967). Indeed, German expansion on the world market went far from unnoticed. Towards the end of the century and throughout the decades preceeding World War I, an increasing number of publications mirrored concern over the economic aspects of German *Weltpolitik,* at the same time rarely failing to mention, with either admiration or bitter resentment, the contribution of German science and scientists to their nation's power and drive.[1] Although these contemporary observers seldom bothered to explore in any detail the complex relationship between science and technology, between research, application and production, or to substantiate further the usual allegation that German science was particularly well supported by a farsighted government, scientific potential began gradually to be recognized as a prerequisite for technical excellence and industrial success. In short, it began to be recognized as a national resource. Quantitative indicators were developed to compare different countries' scientific capabilities: annual output of trained scientists, research personnel in industry, papers published and, after the turn of the century, national shares of Nobel Prizes (e.g. Richet, 1915). Governments were urged, more than ever, to mobilize more efficiently the available potential, or to emulate foreign examples,[2] and foreign policy was called upon to protect, to further and to use this potential as much as any other factor of national strength.

It must be noted, however, that the belief in the importance of science and

---

[1] Among the abundant contemporary literature, see for instance Hauser (1915), Howard (1907), Cambon (1909, 1914), Usher (1913). The economic and political contribution of science to German imperialism became one of the most salient themes of the polemical war literature (e.g. Leudet and Petit, 1916).

[2] One of the arguments supporting the creation of the *Kaiser-Wilhelm-Gesellschaft,* founded in 1911, was the need to follow the American example of non-university related research institutions, such as the Rockefeller Institute or the Carnegie Institution (M-P-G, 1961, 80-94; Wendel, 1975; Burchardt, 1975). See also Paul (1972), Cardwell (1957), Ashby and Anderson (1974), Kevles (1968), Graham (1975).

research for national strength tended again to be shared more readily by the different national research communities and industrial leaders than by the politicians, statesmen or diplomats (Pfetsch, 1974, 103-128). The latter group by the end of the century had certainly accepted technology among the array of foreign policy concerns, as is demonstrated, for instance, by the great powers' interest in and support of international fairs and universal exhibitions (Poidevin, 1969, 340-349). It seemed reluctant, however, to devote equal attention to foreign or international scientific affairs.[3] Public support for the international movement of science and scientists was limited to what would be called today 'cultural foreign policy', that is, some concern for scientific prestige abroad. On the whole, governments left to their departments of education or to private initiative and munificence the task of supporting science and research, and continued to apply a policy of *laissez-faire* to their research communities' international involvement.[4] At the same time, however, governments became increasingly concerned with scientific and technical matters specifically linked to public services (i.e. meteorology, epidemiology, seismology, etc.). Indeed, a considerable amount of intergovernmental cooperation developed in functional areas where the availability of new knowledge, techniques and instruments required collaboration: coordination of activities, exchange of information, standardization of measurements, etc.[5]

[3] There were some exceptions, such as Japan, which systematically imported foreign experts or sent students abroad to be trained in order to build up a scientific and technical capability of its own (Nakayama, Swain and Yagi, 1974; Koizumi, 1976).

[4] During the Nineteenth Century the international network of scholarly collaboration had expanded steadily; from the 1850's onward, while individual contacts were maintained and developed along traditional lines, new forms of collaboration emerged. Transnational scientific organizations appeared first, of course, in those disciplines which depended for their advance on simultaneous observations or on a permament coordination of activities (L'Heritier, 1938; Cox, 1966; Mieghem, 1968; Daniel, 1973, Howard-Jones, 1975), but gradually scientists in practically all disciplines, and engineers too, began to meet more often and more regularly to discuss current experiences and the state of the art, and to organize their various disciplines.

The number of international scientific congresses increased substantially: from one or two meetings a year between 1850 and 1860, the annual average rose to about thirty before the turn of the century. International organizations multiplied at the same rate: twenty five were founded between 1870 and 1880, and almost three hundred between 1900 and 1914. The phenomenon is not surprising, for during the second half of the Nineteenth Century international collaboration in meetings and associations developed practically in all areas of human interest and activity (UAI, 1957 and 1960; T. Ruyssen, 1961; Lyons, 1963).

[5] The meteorologists met in 1853 and the telegraphists in 1864; in the same year, the European Association of Geodesy was founded; the First International Polar Year was organized in 1882-1883; an International Latitude Service was established in 1875; international sanitary conferences, 'primarily scientific in their aims' (Reinsch, 1916, 57; Howard-Jones, 1975) began to meet in 1851. These are but a few examples (UAI, 1957) Among the most important intergovernmental functional organizations founded during this period are the International Bureau of Weights and Measures (1875) and the former International Institute of Agriculture (1905).

International committees or central bureaus were set up in many instances. These bodies were usually linked to the corresponding technical departments or agencies of the member states, departments which also appointed and instructed the delegates. With a few exceptions, such as the Meter Conference of 1875, this cooperation scarcely caught the attention of high level diplomats. The ministries of foreign affairs were involved generally in only the formal aspects: drafting of agreements, signatures, annual payment of membership fees, etc.

World War I confirmed the strategic importance of science and technology, although neither of them was to be decisive for the final outcome of the confrontation. Aside from the development of poison gas, which was the most conspicuous contribution of science to warfare (Brown, 1968; Whittemore, 1975, with many bibliographical references), advanced scientific and technical capabilities had proven their value in many other sectors of the war effort, both military and civilian (MacLeod and MacLeod, 1970, 1971, 1975; Dupree, 1964, 192-216; Kevles, 1968; Varcoe, 1970; Cardwell, 1957, 220-225; La France, 1959; Yerkes, 1920). The peace treaty with Germany, by the way, showed the evidence that the lesson had not been lost this time on the diplomats. For the first time, a peace treaty carried detailed provisions concerning a country's technical capabilities, trying to curtail and control certain sectors of German industrial production and research. During the interwar years, this awareness of science and technology as essential factors in the build-up of a nation's economic power and military strength became widely generalized, although public support remained relatively low and the organization of research in most countries did not develop beyond halfhearted efforts.

At the turn of the century, foreign policy was interested in matters of science and technology only so far as they were related to international trade and military preparedness; in the years 1918-1919 it seemed opportune and probably sufficient to change the balance of power by acquiring industrial secrets and patents.[6] Another decade or two had yet to elapse before a decisive change occured in the perception of science and technology as prominent factors of international politics in the wake of World War II. Indeed, a significant item was added, in 1945, to the list of strategically important material: the appropriation of brainpower itself became an object of international contention. The transfer of German scientists to the United States and the Soviet Union (Lasby, 1971; Goudsmit, 1947; Bar-Zohar, 1965) very well illustrates, among history's miscellanea, the dramatic changes in facts and perceptions.[7] It should be kept in mind, however, that science and

---

[6] See, for instance, Brown (1968) on the attitudes of the United States' chemical industries toward the problem of German patents.

[7] High geographical mobility of scientists – scholars and students – is in itself not new. However, intellectual migration had hardly been considered in former centuries in terms of transfer of brainpower, in terms of brain drain. The massive emigration of

technology had already emerged as factors of international politics during the preceding decades. Industrialized countries had already acquired some experience with international cooperation in functional areas. Foreign policy had already used scientific and technological excellence as an instrument of cultural expansion. The question should at least therefore be raised whether the difference over time lies in scale rather than in substance.

There is presumably no need to delineate the events and phases since 1945 of both world politics and scientific and technical progress. They were the environment to which foreign policies had to adapt and of which, at the same time, they were an essential part. At practically every level of the political process science and technology seem to constitute a constant factor of change, affecting established parameters of decision making and transforming traditional patterns of interaction, tying together more and more tightly the interlocking systems of international and domestic politics. Since science and technology affect almost to the same extent theory and practice, content and method of foreign policy, the most significant issues arising from their complex interaction will be organized accordingly in this chapter.

The first part of this chapter deals with the fact that science and technology have become important power factors; it highlights in its first section the prominent position of matters related to science and technology among the priorities of foreign policies, among their objectives and their instruments. The second section discusses the role which science and technology play in the expanding network of intergovernmental cooperation and in the emergence of new actors on the international scene.[8] The second part of this chapter deals with the consequences for the process of foreign policy making of the growing presence of scientific and technical matters in national and international affairs. Finally, the third part of the chapter analyzes the existence and the political aspects of a transnational scientific community, a community which to a certain extent is parallel to the political community of nations.

SCIENCE AND TECHNOLOGY AS POWER FACTORS

Goals and instruments of foreign policy   The post-war development of

academics from Nazi Germany has certainly changed the patterns of distribution of top-level scientists among the world's advanced nations; it has been argued, however, that the impact of this transfer on the development of American science, physics in particular, should not be exaggerated (Weiner, 1969).

[8] The impact of scientific and technical developments on international organization and the international system as a whole is one of the essential questions to be raised in this context. This is dealt with by Skolnikoff in Chapter 14.

modern weaponry, unprecedented in its sophistication and destructive power, and the equally unprecedented development of civilian technologies, have firmly established the protection and advancement of scientific and technological capabilities among the objectives of foreign policy. Scientific discoveries of new technologies have now become factors most likely to upset the balance of power. The capacity of deterrence is dependent on science and technology, and so are the prospects for arms control and disarmament (See Sapolsky, Chapter 12). Wealth and prosperity have become dependent on the production of and international trade in high technology goods. Scientific and technical matters have invaded traditional areas of foreign policy. In fact, transfer or sharing of scientific capabilities has become an important aspect, motive and element in the cohesion of international alliances. This is as much for the dependence they may entail or the will of independence they may reflect, when small or middle-sized countries through cooperation with the dominant power try to join the front of technology and know-how. It occurs also when they pool their resources and capabilities to fight the dominant influence of a superpower within their own boundaries or on the world market.

Because of the wide disparities in the distribution of scientific and technical capability among the nations of the world, the increasing permeation of science and technology into national and international politics has a different meaning for different countries, generating opportunities and constraints for foreign policies which are far from equal from one government to the other (See Sardar and Rosser-Owen, Chapter 15). Even in situations of less dramatic inequality, scientific and technical superiority usually enables a dominant nation further to consolidate and extend its already powerful position, be it only by setting the standards of international competition in military and civilian technology. This superiority tends, in fact, to influence the priorities of science policies within those countries which participate by choice or by necessity in this competition. Advanced nations, however, by the very role which high technology holds in their economic prosperity, have not escaped the drawbacks of growing interdependence. The more their economies are built on international trade with high technology products and the more they are based on foreign supplies of raw materials, the more they have become vulnerable to disruptive events beyond their control.

There is, however, no doubt that science and technology have contributed to change the pattern of the geopolitical constraints which for centuries influenced the calculations of foreign policies. Science and technology have therefore created new assets and new liabilities to be reckoned into the nations' bargaining power. They have added new dimensions to the rationales of conflict and collaboration, and they have certainly complicated in many instances the already intricate chessboard of political choice. Indeed, though national security and economic prosperity rank high among foreign policy objectives, the prominent role that science and technology hold in both military preparedness and economic power makes competition and conflict between priorities more likely to occur and more difficult to arbitrate. This is particularly true in areas such as space, nuclear or ocean technologies which have civilian as well as military uses. It is argued, for example, that the commercial advantages of selling atomic reactors and fuel processing equipment to Third World countries may not compensate for the risk of enabling such nations to develop nuclear weapons. The imperatives of national security and competitive industrial advantage may conflict with the desire to intensify commercial relations and exchange in technological sectors of industry with a potentially hostile nation, in order to improve the political atmosphere and chances for detente. This is reflected, for example, in the debate on American policy toward the Soviet Union in the mid-1970's.

Where foreign policy tries to influence perceptions as in the example just mentioned, science and technology have continued to broaden considerably the range of available instruments. Scientific and technical achievements become more than ever highly valued assets in the competition for international prestige. Considerations of international prestige are also a factor in the choice of particular priorities in national science policies. Putting a man on the moon was, above all, to benefit the United States' foreign policy (Van Dyke, 1964; Logsdon, 1970).

A reputation for scientific and technical excellence is assumed to do more than enhance a country's status as a whole. Scientific prestige usually generates flows of information and stimulates collaboration. These are factors which are certainly among the most unobtrusive ways of 'opening doors' and are, as such, greatly appreciated from time to time by governments. Again and again, scientific relations have served as a substitute for otherwise unachievable political contacts (Barghoorn, 1960). Thanks to its distinctive flavor of human progress, apolitical universalism and disinterestedness, scientific collaboration functions much better than ballets, orchestras, ping pong players or hockey teams as a carrier of potential influence and a signal of international good will. (Consider, for example, the place given to cooperation in the fundamental sciences in the 'Third Basket' of the Helsinki Conference on European Cooperation and Security.)

In the arsenal of foreign policy, science and technology thus dominate the whole range of instruments from coercion to peaceful penetration, from domination to persuasion, from intimidation to elusive gestures of rapproachement and conciliation.

It is surprising that, for many years, the role of science and technology as decisive elements in the international balance of power did not elicit much noticeable attention from the group of scholars who usually deal with the systematic study of international relations and foreign policy. With a few exceptions, for instance Wright (1968, 79-106), the broader literature such as treatises, textbooks and monographs still has a tendency to consider science and technology only at the periphery, and even then in very general terms.

Only in very recent works do 'science' and 'technology' begin to show up as substantive entries in the indexes. Of course, in the post-World War II studies on strategic problems the role of scientific and technical capabilities was implicit (e.g. Kissinger, 1957). Of the early studies dealing directly with the question of science, technology and their impact on foreign policy, some still provide interesting reading, such as the report on *Science and Foreign Relations*, prepared by L. V. Berkner for the State Department in 1950. It is deeply steeped in the atmosphere of the cold war, reflecting much of the ideological climate of that period.

With the advent of the 1960's and 1970's, while studies on international relations and foreign policy continued to recognize in general terms the value of scientific and technical capabilities in the 'calculus of power' (e.g. Morgenthau, 1964, 223; Aron, 1962; Sprout and Sprout, 1967), authors also began to deal in more detail with the role of science and technology in international relations and foreign policy. The first studies to appear in these years focused directly on the impact of science and technology on the political situation of particular countries (on American foreign policy, Skolnikoff, 1967; on France, Gilpin, 1968) or dealt specifically with these questions in the framework of more general works (Rosecrance, 1973; Kolodziej, 1974).

To a large extent, however, the literature shows a tendency to be issue-oriented, giving much attention to the description of objectives, international implications and decision-making processes in areas such as space policy (Van Dyke, 1964; Frutkin, 1965; Logsdon, 1970; US House of Representatives, 1971a); nuclear policy (Kramish, 1963; Scheinman, 1965; McBride, 1969; Willrich, 1971; US House of Representatives, 1974a); or ocean policy (Basiuk, 1968; US House of Representatives, 1971a, 1971b; Wenk, 1972; English, 1973; Hollick, 1973; Hollick and Osgood, 1974; Osgood, Hollick, Pearson and Orr, 1976). Debates and research were stimulated considerably by the work done within international organizations, particularly OECD and UNESCO. The series on national science policies, for instance, published by these agencies, gave significant attention to international aspects. To a certain extent this set the standards for the analytical approach to these matters.

International events such as the Nonproliferation Treaty and the problems arising from its implementation, the Law of the Sea Conferences, the worldwide problems of energy and food supply and of the environment (See Skolnikoff, Chapter 14) have influenced considerably the orientation of research. The impact of science and technology on foreign policy is hardly analyzed any more without giving detailed consideration to the problems of international interdependence and cooperation.

International cooperation and transnational actors   Science and, even more, technology have indeed not only affected the strategic conditions of conflict and accommodation for the nation-state considered individually.

Their impact on military and economic rivalries is almost matched by the influence they have exerted on the development of international cooperation, its substance, its scope, its organization. The emergence of global problems generated by the prodigious advances of science and technology, and the need for collective responses, have been defined as the most salient features of post-war politics (Skolnikoff, 1972). The consequences are obvious: growing interdependence, considerable change in the patterns of interaction between sovereign states, and a steady expansion, in number and size, of international organizations. How far the international system as a whole is bound to be affected, is still under discussion. Certain scholars consider science and technology as prime agents of international change and, as a consequence, they characterize traditional concepts and practices of state sovereignty as moving relentlessly toward obsolescence. Other scholars regard with skepticism this theory of the 'international imperatives of technology'. They maintain, on the contrary, that the behavior of states, even in areas heavily related to technology, is basically dependent on political choice (Ruggie, 1972, 1975) and can still be 'explained in terms of the conventional focus of the territorial nation-state' (Nau, 1974, 1).

Besides increasing technological interdependence, another phenomenon is constantly blurring traditional patterns of state interaction; this is the appearance of powerful transnational actors. The existence of transnational relations is not new. International pressure groups have existed and transnational forces have built up thanks to the power of common interests and beliefs, and to the porosity of national boundaries (Meynaud, 1961). History offers famous examples of big enterprises bypassing governments and interfering with official foreign policies. Only the recent technical developments, however, could produce transnational concentrations of power as they are constituted at present by the multinational corporations. The benefits of new technologies, especially in the domaines of transportation and communication, accrue also to other transnational forces. In consequence, from revolutionary movements to multinational firms, governments have to face transnational actors which do not fit into the traditional framework of international relations.

Seen from the vantage point of the acting state, the present situation implies, at first sight, a considerable reduction of the margin of political choice and a significant limitation of domestic control. Governments must cooperate to solve certain transnational problems. Responsibilities have to be delegated to an increasing number of international organizations which, however officially instructed and subject to consent by the member states, tend to develop a momentum of their own. Transnational actors such as the multinational corporations, operating from a domestic base and linked to the national economy, may engage in parallel or contrasting 'foreign policies' of their own.

Even though the autonomy of governments in foreign policy decisions has generally narrowed, the residual margin of choice certainly varies with the content matter — and with the technical and economic capabilities which cooperating states can muster. This is easily illustrated by the case of multilateral organizations which are by and large considered to dilute or to neutralize the overwhelming presence of powerful states and to offer to weaker nations better political leverage. It seems, however, that within organizations strongly involved in scientific or technical matters advanced member countries tend to establish their influence by the sheer weight of their expertise and technical capabilities (Cox and Jacobson, 1973, 371-436). The growing international interdependence which the increasing web of organizational links between states seems so convincingly to reflect, is not therefore greeted with unanimous enthusiasm. It has been argued, for instance (Nau, 1974, 3, 21), that regardless of the flavor of world solidarity they convey, globalism and technological interdependence are giving advanced countries new opportunities to exploit these advantages and may thus contribute to 'a more subtle and total form of imperialism than was possible in any previous period of history'.

In matters of world-wide urgency, little choice may be left to governments but to cooperate (See Skolnikoff, Chapter 14). However, options remain usually more flexible when international cooperation is regarded as a means of rationalizing production and commercialization or of sharing exorbitant costs. In some fields of basic research, and in many sectors of technology such as nuclear energy or space applications, costs run so high that the pursuit of research, development and production on a strictly national basis would be beyond the possibilities of small or middle-sized countries. Alternatively, it would require, on their part, drastic reallocations of domestic resources. Experience has shown so far that the success of cooperative arrangements tends to vary with the distances separating their objectives from industrial application (Touscoz, 1973; Williams, 1973; Nau, 1974). R & D costs are easier to spread than commercial advantages. International collaboration in basic research, remote from industrial application and originating in most cases from concern with sharing talent and cost, faces less difficulties (Crane, 1971). A notable instance of this is CERN, the European nuclear research facility in Geneva. Tensions over the problem of 'just return' tend, however, to beset even those organizations and programs which have no direct link with marketable products or services.

The type of organization is generally determined by the nature of the problem which collaboration is intended to solve, and institutional arrangements for international cooperation show great diversity.[9] There are intergovernmental organizations such as the specialized agencies of the United

---

[9] See, for instance, Touscoz (1973) for a typology of international scientific and technical organizations according to their function; and Skolnikoff (1972) on bilateral institutional links; see UNESCO (1969).

Nations or, within the European community, EURATOM; there are inter-agency arrangements such as the agreements between NASA and its European counterparts; and there are government-sponsored cooperative ventures or consortia of private industry such as the Anglo-French Concorde program or the elusive agreements and rapproachements in the European computer and reactor industries (Williams, 1973; Nau, 1974, 1975).

Because of the importance of and interest in European cooperation, this sector of the literature tends to accentuate somewhat less the relative im-balance toward United States problems (Foch, 1970; Standtke, 1970; Project Perseus, 1971; Courteix, 1972; Touscoz, 1973; Williams, 1973; Nau, 1974, 1975). In general the problems of international cooperation in areas related to science and technology have attracted relatively strong scholarly interest, although the approaches chosen for the individual studies vary widely; some authors emphasize the transnational character of the issues involved (Keohane and Nye, 1971); others concentrate on the institutional framework of inter-national cooperation (Touscoz, 1973; Courteix, 1972; Communautés européennes, 1970; White, 1970) or deal mainly with the interplay of national interests within international organizations (Cox and Jacobson, 1974). All these studies, of course, give consideration to the problems of comparative motivation, effort and effectiveness of cooperative endeavors; it can be anticipated, however, that future research on the impact of science and technology on foreign policy will focus increasingly on questions of transnational relations and the emergence of global or sectorial international regimes (Ruggie and Haas, 1975).

In fields where, at least for the larger developed countries, it is not absolutely impossible to 'go it alone', the tendencies of policies in matters of international cooperation are far from clear. It seems that international collaboration, which was long considered to be a good thing in itself, tends to undergo more and more scrutiny with respect to its comparative efficiency. There is some evidence for the hypothesis that the relative disillusionment with international cooperation which made itself felt in the late 1960's (Project Perseus, 1971) has not completely vanished from the minds of the decision makers.[10] The advantages of the sharing of talent, costs and markets have to be balanced in every case against the sacrifices in autonomy and

---

[10] This tendency is clearly reflected in many of the discussions surrounding the elaboration and implementation of national budgets of R & D in industrialized countries, and in the debate on questions such as the availability of 'extra money' for international undertakings. Although some more systematic information can already be found in the literature (Project Perseus, 1971; Williams, 1973; Science Council, 1973; Nau, 1974), one has to rely mainly on the editorial pages and comments on current events in the press, the major scientific journals (such as *Nature, Science, La Recherche, New Scientist, Physics Today,* etc.) and the usual government sources such as official docu-ments, parliamentary debates, etc. See, for instance, US State Department (1974), which is revealing in its defensive overtones.

flexibility which necessarily go with cooperative agreements. Further, the advantages of capability sharing and the sacrifices of autonomy both have to be balanced against the political purpose which might be involved.

In fact, technological developments sometimes force cooperative behavior upon governments, but they also give them new opportunities to use cooperation as a political tool. For instance, they enable them to control and to watch potential competitors, as was partly the case for early EURATOM; to enhance technological prestige, as was the case for the Concorde; to support the credibility of Britain's European commitment, as was partly the case for Britain's decision in the early 1970's to contribute to the 300 GeV accelerator of CERN (Flowers, 1973). Indeed, political purpose, in these cases namely the intention to influence perceptions, accounts for a great deal of the considerable increase in the number and scope of bilateral agreements on international scientific cooperation. The Soviet-American collaboration in space, culminating in the 1975 'handshake in space', is certainly one of the most spectacular examples. Governments have been accused of resorting too easily to this particular method of improving the national image and showing friendly intentions (*Nature*, 1973, 548, and 1975, 669; Science Council, 1973; Schroeder-Gudehus, 1974).[11] Criticism has particularly focused on the so-called 'umbrella agreements' of scientific cooperation and exchange, which are innocuous and well-suited to protect politicians from returning empty-handed when negotiations have not yielded possibilities of agreement in any other domain. Many of the recent comments on American foreign policy, where science and technology are usually described as the 'handiest instruments of detente' (*Science*, 1974, 237), have somewhat cynical overtones.

This criticism is voiced mainly within administrations such as the general accounting offices, treasury boards or ministries of finance, but also by representatives of the scientific communities who may discover little concern with national research priorities in the choice of contracting parties and the content of the agreements. The appropriate integration of priorities of domestic and foreign policy gives rise to disagreements which are not particular, though, to matters of research policy and international scientific cooperation. The extension, in general, of international cooperation into an unprecedented number of social, economic, scientific and technological domains has been a major factor in the transformations which the process of foreign policy making has undergone in recent decades.

---

[11] US House of Representatives (1975) summarizes a certain number of criticisms as well as arguments in defense of bilateral agreements (75-83); see also US State Department (1974). For further information one has to rely on sources such as those mentioned *supra*.

THE PROCESS OF FOREIGN POLICY MAKING:
ADJUSTMENTS, GAPS AND BARRIERS

Scientific and technical developments have affected the conduct of foreign policy in various ways. The working conditions of diplomacy itself have been drastically transformed, as has been the management of many social functions in modern society. Because of the facilities and speed of transportation and telecommunication, responsibilities of embassies and missions abroad have very much decreased. Ministries are closely linked to observation and negotiation in foreign countries. Through the influence of scientific and technical developments, the acceleration of communication has been extraordinary, but so has the acceleration of events, of actions and of responses. Decision making in foreign policy tends therefore to concentrate on the highest level of government, a tendency that, like summit diplomacy, is taking away from the ministerial level much of its initiative and authority. The conduct of foreign policy also shares with society at large the burden of the information explosion and the need to devise appropriate methods of processing a constant oversupply of reports and documents, etc.

Among the more specific consequences of science and technology for the process of foreign policy making, the most striking may be summarized as follows: the difficulty of integrating political and technical objectives; the difficulty of overcoming the obstacles of institutional fragmentation by adequate consultation, coordination and arbitration, and the challenge of 'parallel foreign policies' coming from public and private sectors; and the difficulty of mobilizing the necessary expertise to deal adequately with matters related to science and technology.

Because the fundamental authority over foreign policy is held at the highest level of government, ministries of foreign affairs have been accustomed throughout history to face contention from other agencies of the executive branch, and especially from the military. The risk that ministries of defense might hold and impose divergent viewpoints was already a common phenomenon when these branches of the government were still called ministries of war. Since then, mainly because of technological advances in warfare, the consequences of their options have become more widespread and more complex. The choice of certain types of armament or of certain strategic concepts (how to secure resources and mobility, for instance) have a much wider and more immediate impact than ever before on broader segments of society and on the conditions of foreign policy. Because domestic interests are so heavily involved, foreign ministries increasingly face powerful coalitions within or outside the executive branch.

In addition to traditional contenders, almost entirely new challenges have emerged. Ministries of foreign affairs in virtually all countries for decades took little notice of the greater and greater degree to which science and technology pervaded international politics. Not enough importance was attached to the phenomenon to entrust a particular administrative unit with the responsibility for international scientific and technical affairs. Almost without exception, such units were not created until the 1960's (Skolnikoff, 1967; US House of Representatives, 1965). Geographical, not functional, divisions characterized the organizational setup of ministries of foreign affairs. International scientific and technical matters had not, however, entirely escaped government attention in the past. Other departments or agencies had taken care of them as part of their missions. By the time the role of science and technology in central political issues had become obvious and ministries of foreign affairs tried to secure more significant participation and control over national involvements and commitments, other bureaucracies had built a tradition of international responsibilities in the field which they were quite unwilling to yield. These agencies are usually able to mobilize the indispensable scientific and technical skills, and they also possess equally valuable experience and connections with their counterparts abroad or within the relevant international organizations. Mission-oriented departments therefore tend to question the wisdom of turning over scientific and technical matters from the hand of the expert to the judgment of the generalist, and they are also apprehensive of the interference of foreign policy goals with the rationality of their missions. They usually show little understanding for the argument that only ministries of foreign affairs have the necessary overview to evaluate properly the respective merits of competing priorities. This is precisely the reasoning which motivates the determination in other parts of the executive branch not to abandon the responsibilities they hold. They have misgivings that their interests and those of the segments of society related to their mission might be used by the diplomats as trade-offs in the international bargaining process.

However, the more technical the issue, the greater the power of the specialized bureaucracies and expert groups. They may use their technical understanding to eliminate from the array of available options those which they consider inappropriate with respect to their agency's point of view. Options may also be preempted before the matters reach the attention of those responsible for foreign policy. Delegations of experts may hammer out bilateral or multilateral agreements which policy makers will find difficult to endorse in broader foreign policy terms. Governments may discover themselves speaking with more than one voice at international conferences.

However frustrating this fragmentation of initiative and responsibility might be, ministries of foreign affairs have little choice in many instances but to share with others the conducting of international affairs. The mere volume of transnational and transgovernmental relations seems to defy any attempt at detailed monitoring. It is also obvious that these ministries cannot muster all the necessary skills. They depend for the elaboration and the implementation of science-and-technology-related policies on the advice and the collaboration of those who are in command of the relevant expertise. Even before corporations grew into world-wide empires, industries and commercial enterprises had developed networks of international relations and devised strategies to improve or to protect their competitive position. Now, with the economies of developed countries being so heavily dependent on international trade with high technology goods and services, competitiveness has become a prime concern of national governments. Measures are taken to protect markets, and also to encourage rationalization and to stimulate innovation. Interest has grown considerably in other countries' innovative capabilities and their in dustrial strategies. Their science policies are watched closely for their organization, their content — and their results.

Foreign ministries were originally hardly prepared to serve as a relay for technical information of this type. The interested agencies and segments of the private economy had largely developed their own channels of information and influence instead. It became obvious, however, that the process of foreign policy making required a better understanding of scientific and technical matters. The apparatus of diplomacy needed to develop a new blend of expertise. New efforts were made by creating in the ministries, alongside the traditional geographical divisions, other divisions which were entrusted with functional areas of foreign policy. In presidential systems, such as that of the United States, institutionalization of the new interest and competence was not limited to the State Department. Policy making in this area shifted at times to the White House, with the President's Scientific Adviser and the Office of Science and Technology considering foreign policy matters to be entirely within their concern and authority (Skolnikoff, 1967). In the French Fifth Republic the establishment of various *délégations* is another response to the need for new competence and efficiency (Gilpin, 1968; Courteix, 1972; Kolodziej, 1974), the *Quai* gradually losing control and authority over significant subject matters of foreign policy, just as did its counterparts in other countries.

Shifts in the organizational structure did not and do not solve, however, the difficult problem of integrating scientific expertise into the political process, although in various instances scientists have been associated as experts with international negotiations (Gilpin, 1962; Jacobson and Stein, 1966). Bridging the gap between scientific rationality and political understanding, between scientific possibilities and diplomatic constraints, has been recognized as a major challenge to modern diplomacy (Berkner, 1950; Science Council, 1973; US House of Representatives, 1975). The imperatives of belligerence had produced as early as World War I the institution of 'scientific attachés', liaison officers in charge of channelling relevant technical information between Washington and the capitals of the Entente. In the wake of World War II, the institution was again considered (Needham, 1945; Berkner, 1950). In the following years an increasing number of developed countries tried to create, by appointing 'scientific attachés' to some of their major embassies, a judicious blend of 'science and diplomacy'. The organizational integration of the scientific attachés and their specific functions vary, of course, from one foreign policy system to the other, and as far as their functions are concerned from one host country to the other. They tend to encompass essentially the gathering and dissemination of relevant information on scientific and technical developments, on science policy measures and their results. Scientific attachés assist also in the negotiation of international agreements, the establishment of contacts between the respective countries' scientific and industrial milieux; here and there they enter the territory of the commercial attachés to promote their country's high technology products. No country, however, seems to have achieved the symbiotic expertise which would be ideally required. The current practice appears to be to throw the scientist (or the engineer) and the diplomat together and to hope that some kind of interdisciplinary wisdom will flow from this collaboration. Nevertheless, and in spite of the fact that the institution of the scientific attaché did not become a cornerstone of an organizational structure allowing for greater scientific influence on the process of foreign policy making, it has been given considerable attention (Skolnikoff, 1967; Greenwood, 1971a, 1971b; Derek Price, 1971; US House of Representatives, 1975). Furthermore technology, not science (in the sense of basic science), emerges more and more as the major concern of foreign policy; consequently scientific attachés are increasingly recruited among engineers rather than among scientists.

The recourse to outside scientific and technical advice always raises the question of expertise versus advocacy, of objectivity versus political bias. Expertise in any field constitutes a potential road to political influence. These problems, inherent in the advisory system, are discussed elsewhere in this volume (See Lakoff, Chapter 10), but it deserves to be mentioned here that, in matters of foreign policy too, scientific expertise can usually be mobilized to support divergent policies.

It would be misleading in any case to minimize the burden of political choice and to consider the intricacies of foreign policy making in science-and-technology-related areas mainly as a question of available expertise and appropriate mechanisms of coordination. There is, of course, widespread agreement with the statement that objectives of domestic policies and objectives of foreign policy have to be coordinated. In the case of science policy, for instance, national priorities and scientific and technical activities extending beyond national boundaries should be consistent with the goals and constraints of foreign policy, and vice versa. However, this has become increasingly difficult to achieve: the broadening scope of the subject matter involved in international issues has correspondingly widened the diversity of interests concerned. Broader foreign policy goals, objectives of mission-oriented agencies and their clienteles, parochial concerns of bureaucracies, interests of powerful agents of the country's economy, socio-professional sectors or private citizens' groups tend to come into play. What case studies reveal about the interplay of the interests of subnational groups in the process of policy making (e.g. Logsdon, 1970; Van Dyke, 1964; US House of Representatives, 1974a; Hollick, 1973; Hollick and Osgood, 1974) seems to confirm to a large extent the bureaucratic interpretation of foreign policy, especially with regard to issues relatively remote from 'high' diplomacy, such as many scientific and technical affairs. Much of the work done on multi-bureaucratic decision making in general is therefore useful in this context (Allison, 1971; Allison and Halperin, 1972; critical: Krasner, 1972). The more global the issue, the more likely is the presence of conflicting interests,[12] the more narrow the latitude of maneuver in international nego-tiation, the more limited the possibility for the negotiators to sacrifice some interests as trade-offs in the bargaining process. Those limits are all the more narrow as the increasing interpenetration of the public and the private sector, and the necessity of securing all available expertise and, at a later stage, indispensable support for implementation, have brought the representatives of many organized interests very close to the various levels of the decision-making process.

To integrate the various national policies and domestic concerns on which foreign policy decisions and international commitments might impinge there-fore requires usually more than procedures of mere 'coordination'. National positions put forward in international negotiations are often tenuous com-promises between basically incompatible interests, more or less consistent programs of negotiated objectives; they are very remote from the model of rational, centralized decision making. The concept of coordination necessarily implies recourse to negotiation and, if disagreement persists, to arbitration by the next higher level of authority. Negotiation reflects distribution of power. Arbitration discriminates, carrying conscious risks of domestic or foreign discontent. However prominent the science-and-technology-related content of the issue, the definition of national objectives remains therefore basically a matter of political choice. Scientific and technical expertise – however successfully integrated into the mechanisms of foreign policy making – cannot, in this sense, 'depolitise' the solution of domestic and international conflict.

Among the domestic groups involved at various levels and degrees in the

---

[12] Commitments to the principle that the 'polluter must pay' may suit foreign policy goals and satisfy the environmentalists, but they hurt the competitive position of national industries. Agreements to reduce catches may produce unemployment in the fisheries as well as a food shortage. Deep sea mining companies may press for a *laissez-faire* regime of the oceans that would be highly unpopular with developing countries and harmful to a developed nation's image abroad. Marine scientists may share the military's concern for unimpaired mobility and access to coastal waters, against the petroleum companies' desire to extend coastal states' exclusive jurisdiction. The negotia-tions surrounding the establishment of a new regime for the oceans disclose within foreign policy particularly impressive crosscurrents of interests, domestic and trans-national coalitions (See Hollick and Osgood, 1974).

process of foreign policy making, scientists represent a very particular case of political ambivalence. They are nurtured and celebrated as a national resource; they can be seen lobbying for specific policies when their socio-professional interests are at stake;[13] they are, in many instances of international scientific collaboration, closely dependent on government support and associated with government policies (See, for example, the history of the International Geophysical Year, US House of Representatives, 1973b). They are called upon as experts to enhance their government's bargaining skills, and they are credited at the same time with the aura of a powerful transnational force, invested with the mission to promote international understanding and peace. The connection is obvious between these expectations and the specificity of the scientific enterprise. It has become commonplace to credit scientists with the capacity of untangling the web of international conflict, that is, of carrying their habit of dispassionate problem solving beyond scientific and technical matters into the area of international politics and using the solidarity which bestows on scientists all over the world the common norms and language of science to bridge the depths of political and ideological antagonism (Rotblat, 1967, 7). What emerges from the intricate mixture of motives, hopes and merits is the unsurprising fact that the transnational community of scientists has *sui generis* become an actor on the scene. It deserves, as such, some special consideration.

POLITICAL DIMENSIONS OF THE INTERNATIONAL SCIENTIFIC COMMUNITY

Basic research, at least in the 'hard' sciences, is certainly the most impressive example of cooperative effort across national boundaries. Knowledge accumulated through individual contributions is in principle transmissible and bears no trace of the language, the culture, the nationality or the ideological allegiance of the contributor, because the scientists act as if there were only one universe to discover. The unifying element of this international community is, indeed, the ideal observance of the norms, universal and identical, which govern scientific activity in all nations and give validation and evaluation without which the act of scientific creativity is incomplete (See Mulkay, Chapter 4).[14] It appears from this characterization that the solidarity among

---

[13] The research community of oceanographers, for instance, makes considerable efforts within the current law of the sea negotiations to avoid restrictions being imposed on marine research (e.g. Hollick and Osgood, 1974).

[14] The ideology of scientific internationalism has been defined as 'the propositions and rhetoric asserting the reality and necessity of supranational agreement on scientific doctrine, of transnational scientific intercourse among scientists, and of international collaboration in scientific work' (Forman, 1973, 155).

scientists applies only to a highly specific area, and that their disregard of national boundaries applies *a priori* to a very specific level of human activity. The relevance of this specific internationality to international politics and foreign policy is not immediately obvious and should be examined more closely. Two aspects elicit particular attention. There is in the first place the contention that the internationality of science and the practice of scientific research shape the political attitudes of scientists, giving them a particular bias toward international understanding and peace. There is in the second place the possibility that scientists use their privileged access to the international level to the benefit of their socio-professional interests; that, in other words, scientists from different countries constitute potential or actual international pressure groups.

It could be argued indeed that scientists, by virtue of their activity in collaboration with foreign colleagues, may well take for granted the existence of an apolitical 'parallel' community, structured without regard to political boundaries, nation-states and ideological camps. They may even consider the functioning of the international scientific community as a model, as a 'working utopia', and carry the principles of scientific internationalism into the sphere of political choice; these principles would necessarily contribute to shape their opinions on matters of foreign policy. There might be a risk then that the international scientific community, by the solidarity it commands, could create conflicts of loyalty among its members and generate 'parallel foreign policies' in contradiction to the objectives of the nation-states.

There is little evidence in practice, however, for scientists' loyalty to science being stronger than their loyalty to their homeland. Despite the well-known array of venerable anecdotes from the times when political considerations did not yet interfere with the Republic of Science, even history does not confirm the cliches of the sciences never having been at war (DeBeer, 1960) or of a scientific community being beyond and above politics — notwithstanding such instances as Sir Humphrey Davy travelling to Paris in the midst of an Anglo-French war, or the French granting a safe-conduct to Captain Cook in the South Sea (critical: Dupree, 1964a; Salomon, 1970). Besides the fact that governments did indeed not interfere with international activities of their scientists as long as they did not perceive these activities as yielding tangible benefits for the state, the concepts of loyalty and allegiance were also not the same from one century to the next.[15] The considerable increase of international scientific organizations and conferences during the Nineteenth Century — important elements of the functionalist promise (Baldwin, 1907; Eijkman, 1911; Woolf, 1916, 213-226; Reinsch, 1916, Mitrany, 1943) — had little to do with internationalistic attitudes of the scientists

---

[15] It is true that scientists changed easily from country to country — but so did the generals (L'Héritier, 1939, 638). Benjamin Thompson, Count Rumford, constitutes a case in both categories!

involved. The emergence of these organizations was to a great extent the international dimension of the process of organization and professionalization which characterizes the development of Nineteenth Century science. Scientists as a socioprofessional group showed no distinctive tendency to share in the burgeoning movements of internationalism and pacifism (see footnote 15, p. 491). The much celebrated foundation in 1899 of the International Association of Academies was based, to a great extent, on domestic considerations. The academies wanted to prevent government interest and support being diverted from their established institutions to the benefit of the international activities of learned societies and scientific unions mushrooming outside their authority. The 'Internationale of Science' broke down in 1914, and the International Association of Academies did not survive the war. Although the Manifesto of the Ninety Three German Intellectuals of October 1914 became a symbol of science capitulating to political power (See Lakoff, Chapter 10), there was little difference between the scientific elites of the Central Powers and those of the Entente in their outbursts of rabid nationalism (See Leudet et Petit, 1916). Vindictiveness and resentment kept scientific communities apart even after the war was over (Schroeder-Gudehus, 1973), although there were, of course, examples of personal contacts across the lines, proving that political motivation did not automatically command individual behavior in the practice of science (Forman, 1973).[16]

History does not in general offer evidence that the benefits of the international scientific community's experience of collaboration and rational problem solving extend beyond the boundaries of their science. Scientific universalism did not breed political internationalism or attitudes able to withstand the pressure of national allegiances. The possibility of multiple loyalties, of identification with goals and norms other than those of the nation-state, ceased to exist when conflict arose. It evaporated when the objects of these dual loyalties were no longer furnishing 'compatible solutions to different needs' (Guetzkow, 1955).

The decades following World War II produced, however, a phenomenon in the Pugwash Movement which comes closer than ever to the idea of the international scientific community taking initiatives of political rapprochement. Named after the Canadian village where the first meeting took place, this movement assembled leading scholars from both the socialist and the capitalist countries at regular intervals, thus providing the possibility of informal contacts between outstanding scientists of either side who were concerned with the military consequences of scientific discoveries in a highly antagonistic international system (Rotblat, 1972). In a largely exhortatory declaration in 1958 the third Pugwash Conference stated that the ability of

---

[16] The International Research Council, founded in 1919 and excluding German and Austrian scientists until 1926, became in 1931 the International Council of Scientific Unions.

scientists all over the world to work together was an excellent instrument 'for bridging the gap between nations and for uniting them around common aims'; for developing 'a climate of mutual trust, which is necessary for the resolution of political conflicts'. Although taking up familiar cliches the declaration remained remarkably cautious (Rotblat, 1972, 154). There is no doubt that the Pugwash meetings stimulated the discussion on arms control and helped to bring to a successful outcome negotiations on the test ban treaty of 1963 (Jacobson and Stein, 1966; Gilpin, 1962). Whether atomic test bans or arms limitations necessarily led to a 'more unified world', as has been stated years later (Weisskopf, 1972) is not, however, immediately obvious. Nor does it seem justified to relate the Pugwash scientists' concern and action primarily to internationalistic attitudes. They are much more closely linked to and part of the new sense of social and political responsibility which the development and the eventual use and availability of the atomic bomb triggered in the mind of the scientists. The participants of the first Pugwash meetings were mainly physicists.

The strong sense of responsibility and mission which pervaded a considerable fraction of the American scientific community during the post-war years (Gilpin, 1962; Kimball-Smith, 1965) deserves to be mentioned here because it left its imprint on the literature.[17] The *Bulletin of the Atomic Scientists,* for instance, is a typical product of this moral concern, a journal which made an important contribution to the public debate on problems of disarmament, international conflict resolution and rapprochement. Whereas with the exception of a few individuals and periods of great patriotic fervor natural scientists had not usually felt compelled to engage in writing on current events and especially not on foreign policy issues, now, in the aftermath of the bomb, they became rather prolific writers. This massive participation of scientists as authors of political analysis is an innovation of the post-war years and continues to characterize the current literature.

Only relatively recently have the political implications of scientific internationalism attracted scholarly interest among sociologists, political scientists and historians. Historians of science, traditionally interested in conceptual developments, have only recently begun to pay attention to the sociopolitical context of research and the role of international influence and migrations. Political scientists seldom feel equipped to look into problems of scientific or technical substance, nor are they often inclined to look beyond the borders of their countries or back to the evidence accumulated during past centuries. They have contributed significantly, however, together with the sociologists, to a better understanding of scientists as citizens, destroying largely the myth

---

[17] In spite of the obvious implications for foreign policy, the opposition of American scientists to the bomb or scientists' opposition to military research in general (Nelkin, 1972) is more organically linked to the question of the scholar's relationship with the state (See Lakoff, Chapter 10).

of the scientists as an apolitical person (e.g. Ladd and Lipset, 1972; Blankenship, 1973).

In the field of science policy studies, the international dimension of political attitudes among scientists has been examined (Salomon, 1970, 1971; Haberer, 1972; Schroeder-Gudehus, 1966, 1973; Teich, 1974). Confirming evidence can be gathered from historical studies about the receptiveness of scientific elites to ideologies of nationalistic or internationalistic taint (Ringer, 1969; Paul, 1972a; Schwabe, 1969; Forman, 1973). A host of widely scattered documents, archival material and secondary literature remains to be examined and integrated; but so far the image of an apolitical harmony within the Republic of Science has not survived critical analysis.[18]

Although scientists as a socioprofessional group are obviously far from sharing identical views on the political bearing of scientific universalism, their spokesmen usually do not hesitate to pick up such themes when they appear in official statements or comments on official government policies. Scientists also do so when high prominence is given to science and technology in the conduct of foreign policy, and science and technology are declared to be practically the most significant ingredients of a 'new diplomacy'. Scientists tend to applaud when the traditional camaraderie among scientists is extolled as an inspiring example for international political discussion and problem solving.[19] They applaud also when because of the transfer of scientific and technical capabilities science and technology are seen as instrumental in gradually defusing the tensions arising from the increasing North-South contrast of living standards (Jones, 1971; Moravcsik, 1975a, 1975b; critically, Wade, 1975). The rhetoric of the international scientific community conveniently coincides in these cases with official government policies.[20]

There is no doubt, however, that, with or without genuine commitments to the ideology of political internationalism, scientists have taken an essential

---

[18] Nor has the rhetoric of the brotherhood among equals. Transfer of scientific and technical capabilities, within the international scientific community, relations between 'center' and 'periphery' are not viewed anymore as manifestations essentially of solidarity, but analyzed in terms of domination and dependence (Leite-Lopez, 1966; Rossi, 1973; Wade, 1975). The wisdom of the transfer is questioned or basically accepted (Jones, 1971; Moravcsik and Ziman, 1975; Moravcsik, 1975), but discussion tends to focus on the problems of inequality (See Sardar and Rosser-Owen, Chapter 14).

[19] See, for example, David (1972a, 357, and 1972b, 1106), and as an illustration of the whole discussion Abelson (1972, 701; 1973, 233; Wade, 1974, 780, 781).

[20] There seems surprisingly little reaction on the part of the scientists against a growing official tendency to place science at the beginning of a continuum which goes to technology, industry and international trade; that is, a tendency to see scientific cooperation as a way to help 'speed new technologies out of the R & D stage and into commercial markets'. See, for instance, David, (1972b, 1106), Scott (1975, 70), Sullivan (1975, 70). Interpretations of this kind are, of course, incompatible with the whole argument of disinterestedness, neutrality and apoliticism as the basis of the scientists' international mission.

part in the extraordinary expansion of international, governmental and non-governmental organizations and networks of cooperation which characterizes the post-war period (OECD, 1965; Crane, 1971; US House of Representatives, 1973b; International Yearbook of International Organization, current issue). Technical developments having increased the speed of communication and the possibilities of collecting, storing and retrieving the world's output of scientific literature, the international scientific community has begun to interact at an impressive scale; and scientists as a socioprofessional group may not always find it easy to avoid developing entrepreneurial tendencies. For years they derived considerable encouragement from the political context. It may be naive to assume that the governments were always completely convinced of the merits of international scientific activities, but due to the general historical environment of the 1950's and early 1960's, the 'spirit of collaboration' had become a powerful norm of behavior. Widely read publications such as the Brooks Report (OECD, 1971, 48) have expressed sobering views on the proliferation of organizations or projects of scientific collaboration. The Brooks Report, in particular, mentions the fact that international cooperative research 'has often been initiated by successful pressure groups of specialists in particular disciplines ... rather than for reasons of overall policy, involving more systematic review of alternatives'. Indeed, one aspect of the political dimension of the international scientific community is the possibility of it acting as an international pressure group, initiating or inspiring programs of international governmental or nongovernmental organizations.[21] Since state participation in international projects is usually translated into support for the participating national scientists, the program ultimately benefits its initiators. It has obviously not been an iron rule in many countries to discuss the international commitments of the national scientific community and to decide about them in the light of national priorities. Perhaps this is because the structures of science policy did not provide in all cases the necessary mechanisms for coordination (King, 1974, 82-83). In recent years budgetary constraints and especially the drying up of 'extra money' for international endeavors seem to have muted somewhat the former enthusiasm for international projects.[22]

---

[21] One has also to take into account the symbiosis of interest which may link international organizations to clienteles within national boundaries, in academic institutions or mission-oriented agencies. International organizations, like states, have to prove their legitimacy. Concern for recognized crucial issues helps demonstrate usefulness, and segments of national scientific communities are in many cases readily mobilized as legitimizing reference groups. Legitimization is reciprocal, since endorsement of a research orientation or a specific program by an international organization tends to be a powerful asset in the competition for recognition and for funds on the national level.

[22] See for instance the difficulty of financing high energy physics research in Europe on a cooperative basis (New Scientist, 1975, 132) and the hesitant beginnings of the European Science Foundation (Sherwood, 1975).

Among the concerns of foreign policy and of governments in general, cooperation in the basic sciences seems to fade again into the background among the tools of 'cultural foreign policy' (e.g. US House of Representatives, 1975). Priority is given to scientific sectors with prospects for practical application, and to technology. It is highly probable therefore that the community of basic science will lose power and influence before having been able to demonstrate that the international imperatives of scientific enterprise constitute a factor of political cohesion. No doubt exists, however, that the inherent requirements of scientific activity include the free and worldwide circulation of information and transnational collaboration. The international scientific community derives its cohesion from this need to communicate for the purposes of legitimation, validation and evaluation, and from its willingness to discard political barriers which would prevent this communication. Significant spill-over from the recognition of scientific needs to political options, from scientific universalism to political internationalism, has not been demonstrated. International scientific cooperation – from the point of view of foreign policy – remains above all a way of sharing scarce resources and a privileged tool of unobstrusive communication.

BIBLIOGRAPHY

Since politics are the main fabric of this particular subject matter within the field of science policy studies, a great part of the reading has to be done right across the editorial pages, current events sections and topical articles of the major scientific journals which address a broad audience. These include *Science, Nature, La Recherche, New Scientist, Bild der Wissenschaft, Scientific American, Science Forum, Physics Today*, etc. This means that a great deal of the available literature is fragmentary, biased and subject to rapid decay. After this necessary *caveat* it is easy to see that the purpose of the following bibliography is essentially illustrative. The titles are presented alphabetically because the work relevant to the field would not split up naturally to fit the integrative approach which I had chosen to delineate the most salient features of the subject matter. Many of the studies mentioned have been undertaken within the framework of other disciplines and from the vantage point of other interests. The link between the various aspects of the relationship between science, technology and foreign policy is certainly not explicit in all of them. This of course is the major problem of the field of science policy studies. There seem to exist only a few possibilities, however, to improve the situation. One of these would be the addition to the traditional standards of scholarship of some interdisciplinary competence. If this cannot always be expected from the individual scholar, it should become a rule of conduct to secure, for a given research at least, the proper collaboration.

Abelson, 1972   Abelson, P., 'Science, Technology and Diplomacy',
                                 Science 178, 1972, p. 701.

Abelson, 1973 — Abelson, P., 'Departure of the President's Science Adviser', *Science* 179, 1973, p. 233.

Allison, 1971 — Allison, G. T., *Essence of Decision*, Boston, Little, Brown and Co., 1971.

Allison and Halperin, 1972 — Allison, G. T. and Halperin, M. H., *World Politics* 24, 1972 (supplement, pp. 40-79).

Ashby and Anderson, 1974 — Ashby, E. and Anderson, M., *Portrait of Haldane at Work*, London, MacMillan, 1974.

Baldwin, 1907 — Baldwin, S. E., 'The International Congresses and Conferences of the Last Century as Forces Working Toward the Solidarity of the World', *American Journal of International Law* 1, 1907, pp. 565-578.

Barghoorn, 1960 — Barghoorn, F. C., *The Soviet Cultural Offensive: The Role of Cultural Diplomacy in Soviet Foreign Policy*, Princeton, Princeton University Press, 1960.

Bar-Zohar, 1965 — Bar-Zohar, M., *La chasse aux savants allemands, 1944-1960*, Paris, Fayard, 1965.

Basiuk, 1968 — Basiuk, V., 'Marine Resources Development, Foreign Policy and the Spectrum of Choice', *Orbis* 12, Spring 1968, pp. 39-72.

Beer, 1959 — Beer, J. D., *The Emergence of the German Dye Industry*, Urbana, University of Illinois Press, 1959.

Ben-David, 1962 — Ben-David, J., 'Scientific Endeavour in Israel and the United States', *The American Behavioural Scientist* 6, No. 4, 1962, pp. 12-18.

Ben-David, 1970 — Ben-David, J., 'The Rise and Decline of France as a Scientific Centre', *Minerva* 8, No. 2, 1970, pp. 160-179.

Ben-David, 1971 — Ben-David, J., *The Scientist's Role in Society: A Comparative Study*, Englewood Cliffs, New Jersey, Prentice Hall, 1971.

Berkner, 1950 — Berkner, L. V., *Science and Foreign Relations: Report to the State Department*, Washington, D.C., 1950.

Berkner, 1958 — Berkner, L. V., 'Earth Satellites and Foreign Policy', *Foreign Affairs* 36, No. 2, 1958, pp. 221-231.

Blankenship, 1973 — Blankenship, L. V., 'The Scientist as an Apolitical Man', *The British Journal of Sociology* 24, No. 3, 1973, pp. 269-287.

Brodie and Brodie, 1962 — Brodie, B. and Brodie, F., *From Crossbow to H-Bomb*, Dell, 1962.

Brown, 1968 — Brown, F. J., *Chemical Warfare: A Study in Restraints*, Princeton, Princeton University Press, 1968.

Cambon, 1909 — Cambon, V., *L'Allemagne au travail*, Paris, Roger, 1909.

Cambon, 1914 — Cambon, V., *Les derniers progrès de l'Allemagne*, Paris, Roger, 1914.

Cardwell, 1957 — Cardwell, D. S. L., *The Organisation of Science in England*, London, Heinemann, 1957.

Communautés Européennes, 1970 — Communautés Européennes, *Les cadres juridiques de la coopération internationale en matière scientifique*, Brussels, Commission des Communautés Européennes, 1970.

Cordell, 1971 — Cordell, A. J., *The Multinational Firm, Foreign Invest-*

ment and Canadian Science Policy, Ottawa, Science Council of Canada, 1971.

Coulomb, 1969 — Coulomb, J., 'Le Passé et l'avenir de la coopération scientifique internationale', *ICSU Bulletin* 1969, No. 19, 1969, pp. 4-18.

Courteix, 1972 — Courteix, S., *Recherche scientifique et relations internationales: la pratique française*, Paris, Librairie Générale de Jurisprudence, 1972.

Cox, 1966 — Cox, J. F., 'Adophe Quetelet et son action en faveur de la collaboration internationale au XIXe siècle', *Cahiers d'histoire mondiale* x, No. 1, 1966, pp. 125-136.

Cox and Jacobson, 1973 — Cox, R. W. and Jacobson, H. K. (Eds.), *The Anatomy of Decision: Decision Making in International Organization*, New Haven, Yale University Press, 1973.

Crane, 1971 — Crane, D., 'Transnational Networks in Basic Science', *International Organization* 25, No. 3, 1971, pp. 585-601.

Daniel, 1973 — Daniel, H., *One Hundred Years of International Cooperation in Meteorology,, 1873-1973*, Geneva, WMO, 1973.

David, 1972a — David, E. E., 'The President's Message on Science and Technology', *Science* 176, 1972, p. 357.

David, 1972b — David, E. E., 'Soviet-US Summit: Science Accords Open the Way to Joint Projects', *Science* 176, 1972, p. 1106.

DeBeer, 1960 — DeBeer, G., *The Sciences Were Never at War*, London, Nelson, 1960.

Dupree, 1964a — Dupree, H. A., *Science in the Federal Government: A History of Policies and Activities to 1940*, New York, Harper and Row, 1964.

Dupree, 1964b — Dupree, H. A., 'Nationalism and Science – Sir Joseph Banks and the Wars With France', in *Festschrift for Frederick B. Artz*, Durham, North Carolina, Duke University Press, 1964, pp. 37-51.

Eijkman, 1911 — Eijkman, P. H., *L'Internationalisme scientifique (sciences pures et lettres)*, La Haye, Bureaux Préliminaires de la Fondation pour l'Internationalisme, 1911.

English, 1973 — English, T. S. (Ed.), *Ocean Resources and Public Policy*, Seattle, University of Washington Press, 1973.

Flowers, 1973 — Flowers, B., 'SCR and 3000 GeV', *New Scientist* 57, 29 March 1973, pp. 715-716.

Foch, 1970 — Foch, R., *Europe and Technology: A Political View*, New York, International Publication Service, 1970.

Forman, 1973 — Forman, P., 'Scientific Internationalism and the Weimar Physicists: The Ideology and Its Manipulation', *Isis* 64, 1973, pp. 150-180.

La France devant la recherche scientifique, 1959 — *La France devant la recherche scientifique*, Paris, La Documentation Française, Notes et Études Documentaires, No. 2580, 1959.

Frutkin, 1965 — Frutkin, A., *International Cooperation in Space*, Englewood Cliffs, New Jersey, Prentice Hall, 1965.

Gilpin, 1962	Gilpin, R., *American Scientists and Nuclear Weapons Policy*, Princeton, Princeton University Press, 1962.
Gilpin, 1968	Gilpin, R., *France in the Age of the Scientific State*, Princeton, Princeton University Press, 1968.
Goudsmit, 1947	Goudsmit, S. A., *Alsos: The Failure of German Science*, New York, Henry Schuman, 1947.
Graham, 1975	Graham, L., 'The Formation of Soviet Research Institutes', *Social Studies of Science* 5, No. 2, 1975, pp. 303-329.
Greenwood, 1971a	Greenwood, J. W., 'The Scientist-Diplomat: A New Hybrid Role in Foreign Affairs', *Science Forum* 4, No. 1, 1971, pp. 14-18.
Greenwood, 1971b	Greenwood, J. W., 'The Science Attaché: Who He Is and What He Does', *Science Forum* 4, No. 2, 1971, pp. 21-25.
Guetzkow, 1955	Guetzkow, H., *Multiple Loyalties: Theoretical Approach to a Problem in International Organization*, Princeton, Woodrow Wilson School of Public and International Affairs, 1955.
Haber, 1958	Haber, L. F., *The Chemical Industry During the Nineteenth Century: A Study of the Economic Aspects of Applied Chemistry in Europe and North America*, London, Oxford University Press, 1958.
Haberer, 1972	Haberer, J., 'Politicalization of Science', *Science* 178, 1972, pp. 713-724.
Hauser, 1915	Hauser, H., *Les méthodes allemandes d'expansion économique*, Paris, Armand Colin, 1915.
Henderson, 1975	Henderson, W. O., *The Rise of German Industrial Power, 1834-1914*, Berkeley, University of California Press, 1975.
Hohenberg, 1967	Hohenberg, P., *Chemicals in Western Europe,, 1850-1914*, Chicago, University of Chicago Press, 1967.
Hollick, 1972	Hollick, A. L., 'Seabeds Make Strange Politics', *Foreign Policy* 9, 1972, pp. 148-170.
Hollick and Osgood, 1974	Hollick, A. L. and Osgood, R. E., *New Era of Ocean Politics*, Baltimore, The Johns Hopkins University Press, 1974.
Howard, 1907	Howard, E. D., *The Cause and Extent of the Recent Industrial Progress of Germany*, New York, Houghton Mifflin, 1907.
Howard-Jones, 1975	Howard-Jones, N., The Scientific Background of the International Sanitary Conferences, 1851-1938, Geneva, W.H.O., 1975.
Jacobson, and Stein, 1966	Jacobson, H. K. and Stein, E., *Diplomats, Scientists and Politicians: The United States and the Nuclear Test Ban Negotiations*, Ann Arbor, The University of Michigan Press, 1966.
Jones, 1971	Jones, G., *The Role of Science and Technology in Developing Countries*, New York, Oxford University Press, 1971.
Keohane and Nye, 1971	Keohane, R. O. and Nye, J. S. (Eds.), *Transnational Relations and World Politics*, International Organiza-

tion 25, No. 3, 1971, Special issue.

Keohane and Nye, 1974 — Keohane, R. O. and Nye, J. S., 'Transgovernmental Relations and International Organizations', *World Politics* 27, 1974, pp. 39-62.

Kevles, 1968 — Kevles, D. J., 'George Ellery Hale, the First World War and the Advancement of Science in America', *Isis* 59, No. 4, 1968, pp. 427-437.

Kimball-Smith, 1965 — Kimball-Smith, A., *A Peril and a Hope: The Scientists' Movement in America, 1945-47*, Chicago, Chicago University Press, 1965.

King, 1974 — King, A., *Science and Policy: The International Stimulus*, London, Oxford University Press, 1974.

Kissinger, 1957 — Kissinger, H. A., *Nuclear Weapons and Foreign Policy*, New York, Harper and Brothers for the Council on Foreign Relations, 1957.

Kolodziej, 1974 — Kolodziej, E. A., *French International Policy Under De Gaulle and Pompidou: The Politics of Grandeur*, Ithaca, Cornell University Press, 1974.

Koizumi, 1976 — Koizumi, K., 'The Emergence of Japan's First Physicists, 1868-1900', *Historical Studies in the Physical Sciences* 6, 1976, pp. 3-108.

Kramish, 1967 — Kramish, A., *The Watched and the Unwatched: Inspection in the Non-Proliferation Treaty*, London, Institute for Strategic Studies, 1967.

Krasner, 1972 — Krasner, S. D., 'Are Bureaucracies Important (Or Allison Wonderland)?' *Foreign Policy* 7, 1972, pp. 159-179.

Ladd and Lipset, 1972 — Ladd, E. C. and Lipset, M. S., 'Politics of Academic Natural Scientists and Engineers', *Science* 176, 1972, pp. 1091-1100.

Landes, 1969 — Landes, D. S., *The Unbound Prometheus: Technological Change and Industrial Development in Western Europe from 1750 to the Present*, London, Cambridge University Press, 1969.

Lasby, 1969 — Lasby, C., *Project Paperclip: German Scientists and the Cold War*, New York, Athenaum, 1971.

Layton, 1969 — Layton, C., *European Advanced Technology: A Program for Integration*, New York, Fernhill House, 1969.

Leite-Lopes, 1966 — Leite-Lopes, J., 'Science for Development: A View from Latin America', *Bulletin of the Atomic Scientists* 22, September 1966, pp. 7-14.

Leudet and Petit, 1916 — Leudet, M. and Petit, G. (Eds.), *Les Allemands et la science*, Paris, Alcan, 1916.

L'Héritier, 1938 — L'Héritier, M., 'La Coopération intellectuelle avant le siècle des nationalités', in *Wirtschaft und Kultur: Festschrift zum 70. Geburtstag von Alphons Dopsch*, Baden-Leipzig, Rohrer, 1938.

Logsdon, 1970 — Logsdon, J. M., *The Decision to Go to the Moon: Project Apollo and the National Interest*, Cambridge, MIT Press, 1970.

Lyons, 1963 — Lyons, F. S. L., *Internationalism in Europe, 1815-1914*, Leydon, A. E. Sijthoff, 1963.

MacLeod and Andrews, 1970   MacLeod, R. M. and Andrews, E. K., 'The Origins of the DSIR: Reflection on Ideas and Men, 1915-1916', *Public Administration*, 1970, pp. 23-48.

MacLeod and Andrews, 1971   MacLeod, R. M. and Andrews, E. K., 'Scientific Advice in the War at Sea, 1915-1917: The Board of Invention and Research', *Journal of Contemporary History* 6, No. 2, 1971, pp. 3-40.

MacLeod and MacLeod, 1975   MacLeod, R. M. and MacLeod, E. K., 'War and Economic Development: Government and the Optical Industry in Britain, 1914-1918', in Winter, J. (Ed.), *War and Economic Development*, London, Cambridge University Press, 1975.

Mann-Borgese, 1971   Mann-Borgese, E., 'The World Communities', *The Center Magazine* 4, No. 5, 1971, pp. 10-18.

Margolis, 1973   Margolis, H., *Technical Advice on Policy Issues*, London, Sage Publications, 1973.

Max-Planck-Gesellschaft, 1961   Max-Planck-Gesellschaft z.F.d.W., *Fünfzig Jahre Kaiser-Wilhelm-Gesellschaft und Max-Planck-Gesellschaft zur Förderung der Wissenschaften*, Göttingen, MPG, 1961.

Meynaud, 1961   Meynaud, J., *Les Groupes de pression internationaux*, Lausanne, Etudes de Science Politique, 1961.

Meynaud and Schroeder, 1962   Meynaud, J. and Schroeder, B., *Les savants dans la vie internationale*, Lausanne, Etudes de Science Politique, 1962.

Mieghem, 1968   Mieghem, J. van, 'International Cooperation in Meteorology', in International Union of Geodesy and Geophysics, XIVth General Assembly, *Reports of Proceedings*, Toronto, 1968, pp. 110-128.

Mitrany, 1943   Mitrany, D., *A Working Peace System*, London, Royal Institute of International Affairs, 1943.

Moravcsik, 1973   Moravcsik, M. J., 'The Transmission of a Scientific Civilization', *Bulletin of the Atomic Scientists* 29, No. 3, 1973, pp. 25-28.

Moravcsik, 1975   Moravcsik, M. J., *Science Development: The Building of Science in Less Developed Countries*, Bloomington, Indiana, International Development Center, 1975.

Moravcsik and Ziman, 1975   Moravcsik, M. J. and Ziman, J., 'Paradisia and Dominatia: Science and the Developing World', *Foreign Affairs* 53, No. 4, July 1975, pp. 699-724.

Morgenthau, 1970   Morgenthau, H. J., 'Modern Science and Political Power', in *Truth and Power: Essays of a Decade*, New York, Praeger, 1970.

Mylonas, 1976   Mylonas, D., *La genèse de l'UNESCO: la conférence des ministres alliés de l'éducation, 1942-1945*, Brussels, Bruylant, 1976.

Nakayama, Swain and Yagi, 1974   Nakayama, S., Swain, D. L. and Yagi (Eds.), *Science and Society in Modern Japan: Selected Historical Sources*, Tokyo, University of Tokyo Press, Cambridge, MIT Press, 1974.

Nathan and Norden, 1968   Nathan, O. and Norden, H. (Eds.), *Einstein on Peace*, New York, Schocken Books, 1968.

Nature, 1973   'Anglo-Soviet Science: Hopes for the Future?' *Nature* 242, 1973, p. 548.

Nature, 1975	'Are Summit Agreements of Much Use? ' *Nature* 253, 1975, p. 669.
Nau, 1974	Nau, H. R., *National Politics and International Technology: Nuclear Reactor Development in Western Europe*, Baltimore, The Johns Hopkins University Press, 1974.
Nau, 1975	Nau, H. R., 'Collective Responses to R & D Problems in Western Europe, 1955-1958 and 1968-1973', *International Organization* 29, No. 3, Summer 1975, pp. 617-653.
Needham, 1945	Needham, J., *The Place of Science and International Scientific Cooperation in Post-War World Organisation*, Chungking, British Scientific Mission in China, 1945.
Nelkin, 1972	Nelkin, D., *The University and Military Research: Moral Politics at MIT*, Ithaca, Cornell University Press, 1972.
New Scientist, 1975	'So Much for European Collaboration', *New Scientist* 68, October 1975, p. 132.
Noyes, 1958	Noyes, W. A., 'Science and Foreign Policy', in *Science and Diplomacy, Headline Series*, No. 130, 1958, pp. 19-28.
OECD, 1965	OECD, *Organisations scientifiques internationales*, Paris, OECD, 1965.
OECD, 1971	OECD, *Science, Growth and Society: A New Perspective*, Paris, OECD, 1971.
Paul, 1972	Paul, H. W., *The Sorcerer's Apprentice: The French Scientist's Image of German Science, 1840-1919*, Gainesville, University of Florida Press, 1972.
Pfetsch, 1974	Pfetsch, F., *Zur Entwicklung der Wissenschaftspolitik in Deutschland*, Berlin, Duncker & Humblot, 1974.
Poidenin, 1969	Poidenin, R., *Les Relations economiques et financières entre la France et L'Allemagne de 1898-1914*, Paris, A. Colin, 1969.
Derek Price, 1971	Price, Derek de Solla, 'The World Network of Scientific Attachés', *Science Forum* 4, 1971, pp. 34-35.
Project Perseus, 1971	*Project Perseus*, A Preliminary Examination of Intergovernmental Cooperation in Science and Technology Affecting Western Europe, Report to the Council of Europe, University of Sussex, Science Policy Research Unit, 1971.
Reform des Auswärtigen Dienstes, 1971	*Reform des Auswärtigen Dienstes*, Bericht der Kommission für die Reform des Auswärtigen Dienstes, Bonn, Bundesministerium des Auswärtigen, 1971.
Reinsch, 1916	Reinsch, P. S., *Public International Unions: Their Work and Organization*, Boston, World Peace Foundation, 1916.
Richet, 1916	Richet, C., 'Science française et science allemande', in Leudet, M. et Petit, G. (Eds.), *Les Allemands et la science*, Paris, Alcan, 1916, pp. 345-363.
Rosecrance, 1973	Rosecrance, R., *International Relations: Peace or War?* New York, McGraw-Hill Book Co., 1973.
Rossi, 1973	Rossi, G., 'La Science des pauvres', *La Recherche*, No.

	30, January 1973, pp. 7-14.
Rotblat, 1967	Rotblat, J., *Pugwash: A History of the Conferences of Science and World Affairs*, Prague, Academy of Sciences of the CSR, 1967.
Rotblat, 1972	Rotblat, J., *Scientists in the Quest for Peace, A History of the Pugwash Conferences*, Cambridge, MIT Press, 1972.
Rothstein, 1972	Rothstein, R. L., *Planning, Prediction and Policy Making in Foreign Affairs*, Boston, Little, Brown and Co., 1972.
Ruggie, 1972	Ruggie, J. G., 'Collective Goods and Future International Collaboration', *American Political Science Review* 66, 1972, pp. 874-893.
Ruggie and Haas, 1975	Ruggie, J. G. and Haas, E. B. (Eds.), *International Responses to Technology: International Organization* 29, 1975, N. 3, pp. 557-920, special issue.
Ruyssen, 1961	Ruyssen, T., *Les Sources doctrinales de l'internationalisme*, Paris, Presses Universitaires de France, 1961.
Salomon, 1970	Salomon, J.-J., *Science et politique*, Paris, Seuil, 1970 (English: *Science and Politics*, London and New York, 1973).
Salomon, 1971	Salomon, J.-J., 'The "Internationale" of Science', *Science Studies* 1, No. 1, 1971, pp. 23-42.
Scheinman, 1965	Scheinman, L., *Atomic Energy Policy in France Under the Fourth Republic*, Princeton, Princeton University Press, 1965.
Schilling, 1959	Schilling, W. R., 'Science, Technology and Foreign Policy', *Journal of International Affairs* 13, No. 1, 1959, pp. 7-18.
Schilling, 1964	Schilling, W. R., 'Scientists, Foreign Policy and Politics', in Gilpin, R. and Wright, C. (Eds.), *Scientists and National Policy Making*, New York, Columbia University Press, 1964, pp. 144-173.
Schroeder-Gudehus, 1966	Schroeder-Gudehus, B., *Deutsche Wissenschaft und internationale Zusammenarbeit 1914-1928*, Carouge-Genève, Dumaret et Golay, 1966.
Schroeder-Gudehus, 1973	Schroeder-Gudehus, B., 'Challenge to Transnational Loyalties: International Scientific Organizations after the First World War', *Science Studies* 3, No. 2, 1973, pp. 93-118.
Schwabe, 1969	Schwabe, K., *Wissenschaft und Kriegsmoral: Die deutschen Hochschullehrer und die politischen Grundfragen des Weltkrieges*, Göttingen, Musterschmidt, 1969.
Science, 1974	'US-Soviet Summit: Make Science not War', *Science* 185, 1974, p. 237.
Science Council of Canada, 1973	Science Council of Canada, *Canada, Science and International Affairs*, Ottawa, Information Canada, 1973.
Scott, 1975	Scott, J. T., 'International Cooperation in Physics', *Physics Today* 28, 1975, p. 70.
Sewell, 1975	Sewell, J. P., *UNESCO and World Politics*, Princeton, Princeton University Press, 1975.

Sherwood, 1975   Sherwood, M., 'Building a Little Part of Europe', *New Scientist* 68, 16 October 1975, pp. 151-152.

Sherwin, 1975   Sherwin, M. J., *A World Destroyed: The Atomic Bomb and the Grand Alliance,* New York, Knopf, 1975.

Shils, 1961   Shils, E., 'Metropolis and Province in the Intellectual Community', in Dandekar, V. M. and Sovani (Eds.), *Changing India,* Bombay, 1961, pp. 275-294.

Skolnikoff, 1967   Skolnikoff, E. B., *Science, Technology and American Foreign Policy,* Cambridge, MIT Press, 1967.

Skolnikoff, 1972   Skolnikoff, E. B., *The International Imperatives of Technology,* Berkeley, Institute of International Studies, University of California, 1972.

Sprout and Sprout, 1962   Sprout, H. and Sprout, M., *Foundations of International Politics,* Princeton, New Jersey, D. van Nostrand Co., 1962.

Standtke, 1970   Standtke, K. H., *Europäische Forschungspolitik im Wettbewerb,* Baden-Baden, Nomos, 1970.

Sullivan, 1975   Sullivan, W., 'US-Soviet Program Lags, Scientist Says', *New York Times,* 30 January 1975, p. 20.

Teich, 1974   Teich, A. H., 'Politics and International Laboratories: A Study of Scientists' Attitudes', in Teich, A. H. (Ed.), *Scientists and Public Affairs,* Cambridge, MIT Press, 1974, pp. 173-235.

Touscoz, 1973   Touscoz, J., *La Coopération scientifique internationale,* Paris, Editions techniques et économiques, 1973.

UAI, 1957   UAI, *Les 1.976 organisations internationales fondées depuis le Congrès de Vienne: liste chronologique,* Brussels, Union des Associations Internationales, 1957.

UAI, 1960   UAI, *Les Congrès internationaux de 1681 à 1899: liste complète,* Union des Associations Internationales, 1960.

UNESCO, 1969   UNESCO, *Bilateral Institutional Links in Science and Technology,* Paris, UNESCO, 1969.

UNESCO, 1971   UNESCO, *Scientists Abroad,* A Study of the International Movement of Persons in Science and Technology, Paris, UNESCO, 1971.

US Department of State, 1974   US Department of State, *International Scientific Cooperation: A Summary of Tangible Benefits,* Washington, D.C., US Government Printing Office, 1974.

US House of Representatives, 1971a   US House of Representatives, Committee on Science and Astronautics. *A General Review of International Cooperation in Science and Space,* Hearings before the Subcommittee on International Cooperation in Science and Space, Washington, D.C., US Government Printing Office, 1971.

US House of Representatives, 1971b   US House of Representatives, Committee on Foreign Affairs, *Exploiting the Resources of the Seabed,* Washington, D.C., US Government Printing Office, 1971 *(Science, Technology and American Diplomacy).*

US House of Representatives, 1972a

US House of Representatives, Committee on Foreign Affairs, *The Baruch Plan: US Diplomacy Enters the Nuclear Age,* Washington, D.C., US Government Printing Office, 1972 *(Science, Technology and American Diplomacy).*

US House of Representatives, 1972b

US House of Representatives, Committee on Foreign Affairs, *Commercial Nuclear Power in Europe; The Interaction of American Diplomacy with a New Technology,* Washington, D.C. US Government Printing Office, 1972. *(Science, Technology and American Diplomacy).*

US House of Representatives, 1973a

US House of Representatives, Committee on Foreign Affairs, *US-Soviet Commercial Relations: The Interplay of Economics, Technology Transfer and Diplomacy,* Washington, D.C., US Government Printing Office, 1973 *(Science, Technology and American Diplomacy).*

US House of Representatives, 1973b

US House of Representatives, Committee on Foreign Affairs, *The Political Legacy of the International Geophysical Year, An Analysis of Attitudes, Behavior Patterns and Procedures Followed in the IGY as a Step Toward Detente,* Washington, D.C., US Government Printing Office, 1973 *(Science, Technology and American Diplomacy).*

US House of Representatives, 1974a

US House of Representatives, Committee on Foreign Affairs, *US Scientists Abroad: An Examination of Major Programs for Nongovernmental Scientific Exchange,* Washington, D.C., US Government Printing Office, 1974 *(Science, Technology and American Diplomacy).*

US House of Representatives, 1974b

US House of Representatives, Committee on Foreign Affairs, *US Foreign Policy and the Export of Nuclear Technology to the Middle East,* Hearings Washington, D.C., US Government Printing Office, 1974.

US House of Representatives, 1974c

US House of Representatives, Committee on Foreign Affairs, *Brain Drain: A Study of the Persistent Issues of International Scientific Mobility,* Washington, D.C., US Government Printing Office, 1974, *(Science, Technology and American Diplomacy).*

US House of Representatives, 1975

US House of Representatives,, Committee on International Relations, *Science and Technology in the Department of State: Bringing Technical Content into Diplomatic Policy and Operations,* Washington, D.C., US Government Printing Office, 1975 *(Science, Technology and American Diplomacy).*

Usher, 1913

Usher, R. G., *Pangermanism,* New York, Houghton-Mifflin, 1913.

Van Dyke, 1964

Van Dyke, V., *Pride and Power: The Rationale of the Space Program,* Urbana, University of Illinois Press, 1964.

Varcoe, 1970

Varcoe, I., 'Scientists, Government and Organized Research in Britain, 1914-1916', *Minerva* 8, No. 2, 1970, pp. 192-216.

Varcoe, 1974   Varcoe, I., *Organizing for Science in Britain: A Case Study,* London, Oxford University Press, 1974.

Wade, 1973   Wade, N., 'Nixon-Brezhnev Summit: A New Clutch of Compacts', *Science* 181, 1973, pp. 39-40.

Wade, 1974   Wade, N., 'Kissinger on Science: Making the Linkage with Diplomacy', *Science* 184, 1974, pp. 780, 781.

Wade, 1975   Wade, N., 'Third World: Science and Technology Contribute Feebly to Development', *Science* 189, 1975, pp. 770-776.

Weiner, 1969   Weiner, C., 'A New Site for the Seminar: The Refugees and American Physics in the Thirties', in Fleming, D. and Bailyn, B. (Eds.), *The Intellectual Migration, Europe and America, 1930-1960,* Cambridge, Harvard University Press, 1969.

Weisskopf, 1972   Weisskopf, V., 'The Significance of Science', *Science* 178, 1972, p. 14.

Wendel, 1975   Wendel, G., *Die Kaiser-Wilhelm-Gesellschaft, 1911-1914: Zur Anatomie einer imperialistischen Forschungsgesellschaft,* Berlin, Akademie-Verlag, 1975.

Wenk, 1972   Wenk, E. Jr., *The Politics of the Oceans,* Seattle, University of Washington Press, 1972.

White, 1970   White, I. L., *Decision Making for Space: Law and Politics in Air, Sea and Outer Space,* Lafayette, Indiana, Prudue University Press, 1970.

Whittemore, 1975   Whittemore, G. F., 'World War I, Poison Gas Research and the Ideals of American Chemists', *Social Studies of Science* 5, 1975, No. 2, pp. 135-163.

Williams, 1973   Williams, R., *European Technology: The Politics of Collaboration,* London, Croom Helm, 1973.

Woolf, 1916   Woolf, L. S., *International Government,* London, Allen and Unwin, 1916.

Wooster, 1973   Wooster, W. S., 'Interactions Between Intergovernmental and Scientific Organizations in Marine Affairs', *International Organization* 27, 1973, pp. 103-113.

Wright, 1968   Wright, G., *The Ordeal of Total War, 1939-1945,* New York, Evanston, London, Harper and Row, 1968.

Yerkes, 1920   Yerkes, R. M. (Ed.), *The New World of Science: Its Development During the War,* New York, Freeport, 1920.

Chapter 14

SCIENCE, TECHNOLOGY AND THE
INTERNATIONAL SYSTEM

Eugene B. Skolnikoff

Massachusetts Institute of Technology

GENERAL EFFECTS OF SCIENTIFIC AND
TECHNOLOGICAL DEVELOPMENT:
INTRODUCTION

Just as the advances and applications of science and technology have changed social structures within nations, they have also changed the international scene in a way that is substantial and accelerating. Many of the changes closely linked to developments in science and technology are immediately obvious: massive increases in destructiveness of weapons, growing inter-dependencies among nations, new patterns of resource use, burgeoning population, and the development of technologies that are global in nature. Some of the developments in science and technology which affect international relations are rather more subtle: blurring of domestic and international affairs within nations, increased pressure to establish rules and capabilities for dealing with the growing requirements of international decision making and management, substantial changes in the foreign policy making processes of national governments, feedback from the international scene to national science policies, and the growth of what has come to be called transnational relationships (international relationships outside of governments; for more on this see also Schroeder-Gudehus, Chapter 13).

The international significance of developments in science and technology could make this one of the central organizing themes of science policy studies. But actual research in the science policy field has followed a different path. Studies that have dealt with the international dimension of science and technology have produced, with few exceptions, issue-oriented reports concerning such objects as oceans, arms control or energy, or highly nation-centered reports which examine the domestic impact of science and technology (the role of scientists in policy making, discussions on export policy, etc.).

The reasons for this are logical, and stem from several factors. Historically science and technology have been seen by governments as a means of serving national interests. They developed from within particular social and political settings, and there are inherently greater opportunities for productive research within a national setting or within particular issue-areas. Unfortunately, this basically national research orientation has some very undesirable effects: lack of anticipation and understanding of the international changes wrought by science and technology, poor ability to cope with issues as they impinge on international affairs, little understanding of how science and technology might be directed to avoid or ameliorate issues, and enormous surprise and fear when the overall magnitude of the changes which science and technology have worked on the international scene begin to be realized.

There have been a few attempts to examine the overall impact of science and technology on international affairs, but very few. Given the momentum of the existing organization of the science policy field, such overall studies for the most part are rather general, with limited objectives for any specific policy issue or research interest. Instead, the objectives are likely to be to show the interactions among different areas, to point up the implications that arise when the whole is greater than the sum of the parts, and to highlight relatively neglected areas for research that may not seem relevant when the subject is viewed piecemeal.

All of the major studies that have attempted this general overview to date have focused heavily on the international political impacts of science and technology and the policy responses of nation-states and international organizations; and only incidentally on the social, economic or legal implications, or on the implications for the conduct of research and development themselves. The key works by Haskins (1964), Fox (1968), Brzezinski (1971), Sprout and Sprout (1971), Skolnikoff (1972), Ruggie and Haas (1975) and a forthcoming study by Brown and Fabian all have that character. The discussion that follows will present essentially this view, including as well the main work in allied fields, partial though it may be.

An overview of the effects on the international system of advancing science and technology cannot inherently be very precise. There are several reasons for this, the most important being that science and technology alone are not the causes of change. Rather it is the interaction in myriads of ways of the scientific and technological enterprises with social, economic and political aspects of human affairs that brings about change. The many inventions and developments that went into, for example, the creation of television did not have international affairs in mind, nor did the industrial and commercial exploitation of the technology, nor did the kind of programming created for it. The steps beyond the laboratory were all heavily conditioned by economic and other social motives, rather than simply by the existence of the technology. Its adoption was by a series of diffuse individual decisions. Yet, because of its eventual widespread distribution, and the messages transmitted on it, TV has become a powerful source of changing expectations of poor countries; a purveyor of information that modifies the character of foreign policy debates; a conscious or inadvertent means of altering images of foreign societies; and an economic factor in its own right. The same arguments apply, for example, to many other communications developments, such as the impact of low-cost transistor radios throughout the world.

In a similar vein, developments in medical and sanitary science and technology were undertaken usually in response to local social needs. The developments were spread widely through political and economic mechanisms; they were often the sum of many private decisions, and they provided an essential ingredient to the population explosion so significant to political and economic affairs on a global basis. Science and technology, in turn, provided the technical tools to make birth control possible, but the actual use of those tools was determined by other, nontechnical factors.

The resource interdependencies that loom so large in the international context of the 1970's also have roots in nationally oriented, market-oriented developments in science and technology. It is the appetite of and for technological artifacts — the automobile and its derivative technologies, the intensive reliance on energy in industrial societies, the technological basis of high-productivity farming — that has been a major factor in calling forth contemporary trading patterns in raw materials and finished products. In turn, these new trading patterns are major ingredients in the 'dependency relationships' that have become such a striking characteristic of international affairs. The link to technological development is broad rather than direct.

The very development of technology can be, and usually is, governed by the social, political and economic setting (See Layton, Chapter 6). This is most obvious with respect to military technology, in which the objectives set at a political/strategic level have considerable bearing on the resulting technology (See Sapolsky, Chapter 12). But it is at least equally true with regard to most commercially exploitable technologies in market economies, where the prospects of economic gain, the control of R & D resources by particular segments of the society, the structure of relevant industrial sectors, the extent and character of government regulation, and similar factors, all conspire to influence the technology that the system produces. Similarly, in socialist economies the structure of the government, the pattern of economic incentives, and the determinants of allocation of R & D resources, mean that the technology that emerges and is exploited is in an important sense a derivative of the system.

Economic considerations, in particular, are a fundamental factor internationally as well as nationally in determining the progress of science and technology, the policies that govern resource allocations to science and technology, and the resulting effects (See Freeman, Chapter 7). The threshold costs of investment in R & D are a major element in separating the poor and small countries from the richer, industrialized ones. Much of the economic viability and strength of many multinational corporations arises from their ability to spread the costs of R & D across world markets (which is also, in turn, a basis for the incentives for corporations to seek world instead of solely national markets). The significance of world trade in high-technology products to national economies has also stimulated national R & D, and given substantial advantage to those countries with the resources to engage in costly scientific and technological development. In many respects, economic motives have been the driving force, along with military competition, behind public and private investment in science and technology.

In addition to the diffuseness of the links between scientific and technological development and change in international affairs, there is the difficulty of being precise about what change has taken place. How can interdependence be measured? There has been an attempt to provide a framework for precise analysis of interdependence (Alker *et al.*, 1974). Simple comparisons of trade statistics are not enough for they say nothing about absolute dependence, potential substitutes, availability of capital or relative national wealth. Similarly, the appearance on the international scene of new issues which stem directly or indirectly from science and technology – e.g. nuclear power, space, ocean and mineral exploitation – cannot be measured in meaning or importance solely by quantitative statistics.

Thus, a discussion of the overall effect of science and technology on international affairs must necessarily be imprecise, and to some degree, arbitrary. But, it is important to achieve some kind of overview, for clearly developments in science and technology are among the root generators of change in the international system and, as such, they are important aspects of science policy studies. What follows is an analysis that highlights major areas of evolution in international affairs in which science and technology have figured prominently. Some of the important problems that this relationship poses will be discussed with some speculation about the future. It must also be recognized that the relationship is necessarily reciprocal: the international objectives of nations have also had a profound effect on the direction of development of science and technology. A large portion of the governmental R & D budget in the United States, for example, can be considered to be motivated by foreign policy objectives (defense, space, atomic weapons), or by developments in other nations.

It must be observed that with few exceptions it is technology rather than science that has significant effects on international affairs. Occasionally, as in the case of nuclear research during World War II, or oceanographic research that opens up new fishing grounds, or atmospheric research that will in time make possible improved weather forecasting and weather control, scientific research is closely involved. Even then, however, it is the technological application of research that has the actual impact on the international scene rather than the scientific research itself. In this chapter, it is technology that will be primarily discussed, with science mentioned only when directly relevant.

FIVE GENERAL INTERNATIONAL EFFECTS OF TECHNOLOGY

1. **Interdependence**   There are many ways of summarizing the impact of technology on the international system of nations. The most useful for purposes of this essay is to single out five quite general categories of impact that represent the thrust of the writings mentioned earlier, in particular Haskins (1964), Skolnikoff (1972), and Ruggie and Haas (1975).

Perhaps the most striking nonmilitary change in international affairs since World War II has been the gradual, but in cumulative terms overwhelming, growth of interdependence among nations. By almost every measure the degree of global interdependence is unprecedented (Alker *et al.*, 1974). Only the Soviet Union and China still attempt to maintain a substantial degree of autarchy, though their policies are of necessity now being modified; all other industrialized countries have long since recognized that they are inextricably tied to the policies and economies of others.

The growth of interdependence cannot, of course, simply be traced to science and technology. It is instead a product of many developments: rapid industrialization, reduction of trade barriers, population growth, increased specialization or division of labor among nations, and others. Yet it is a fact that, increasingly, progress in science and technology has required new resources not available domestically, and that it has created an unprecedented dependence on resources for the production of energy. It has provided the essential ingredients for population growth and has made possible increases in food production to meet demands created by population growth and increased affluence. It has provided the knowledge base for the production and marketing of new products, and it has made possible the transportation advances required for the increases in trade, the rapid communications capability that must accompany it, and the capacity to find and exploit needed resources.

Interdependence goes well beyond these obvious characteristics. The development of what can be called global technologies — technological systems that are global in operation or application, such as space technologies, transportation, communications — necessarily requires collaboration in order to operate and exploit the technologies. And, the ease with which information and ideas are communicated across borders with modern technology has created its own interdependencies for audiences and for information. The capability for multi-national corporations to flourish as they have is dependent on rapid transportation and communications technology.

The importance of technology for economic growth has made technology itself a focus of international transfer and thus interdependence. Tech nological information and education, and technologists themselves, are increasingly important elements of international relationships.

Lastly, a concomitant of the growth in scale of modern societies, and of the increased physical power that technology places in human hands, involves global effects that stem from actions within individual nations. Gradual environmental degradation, often on an international or even global level, emphasizes the interdependence of nations. And, the use of modern technological power to make major alterations in national topography that could affect global climate, or the large-scale application of nuclear technology for energy production with the danger of diversion of nuclear material suitable for weapons use, equally demonstrates the degree of now unavoidable interaction. The recently publicized danger of inadvertent laboratory production, as a side effect of genetic research, of entirely new pathogens that could have catastrophic global epidemic results, serves to exaggerate the point (Wade, 1974).

Clearly, traditional concepts of national sovereignty, of the complete national control of domestic affairs, have greatly altered significance in reality, if not in rhetoric. Interdependence, inextricably bound up with advances and applications of science and technology, has become a major attribute of international affairs today with far-reaching consequences on national and international behavior. Yet, the relationship is such a general and overarching one that it is difficult to deal with in detail in a single framework. A spate of studies, usually of the doomsday variety, has emerged that attempts to show some of the global implications (Falk, 1971; Meadows *et al.*, 1972; Brown, 1972). However, these studies are not strictly speaking part of the science policy studies literature since they make little attempt to tie either the analysis or the recommendations to a professional appreciation or interest in science and technology.

2. The Meaning of Warfare   Another of the obvious and dramatic changes in international affairs related to advances in science and technology is in the field of armaments. Weapons systems changes over centuries have had major effect on the organization of society and on the importance of geopolitical factors in the relations among nations (Brodie and Brodie, 1962). The developments since World War II have greatly accelerated the process, and have introduced wholly new elements in international affairs. Much of this is discussed by Sapolsky in Chapter 12, but a few observations are particularly relevant to the subject of this chapter.

There are four major characteristics of modern weapons systems that have had the greatest impact on international affairs; a fifth is becoming more important and may loom as large as the others in the future.

The four currently most important characteristics are destructive power, range, speed of delivery, and weapons complexity and cost (in dollars and technological talent). The new characteristic of potential importance is accuracy of delivery.

The effects of these characteristics are evident. The fantastic increase in destructive capability of nuclear weapons has drastically altered the meaning of strategic warfare, and has thus significantly changed the ability of the major powers to consider war as a viable policy option. A resort to massive strategic warfare between superpowers is an irrational policy in the present condition of stalemate, in that it is almost certain to bring about the destruction of the national interests it would be designed to serve. Strategic weapons development and acquisition, then, are for the purpose of ensuring a balance of weapons capabilities so that no side has a possible advantage that could overturn the stalemate.

In effect, the destructive power of nuclear weapons has meant in practice that they cannot be used against major powers similarly armed; this fact has greatly reduced the willingness of the superpowers to face a military confrontation at any level of armaments, for fear of uncontrollable escalation.

The expansion of the effective range of strategic weapons to essentially global dimensions has had several significant geopolitical consequences. Ocean areas anywhere in the world have become important for freedom of deployment of military vessels. Forward bases have lost most of their value for strategic warfare purposes, though they are still relevant for so-called limited war or for more traditional political purposes. And, the significance of geographical terrain and proximity of position loses much of its meaning with respect to strategic confrontations between superpowers. Nations act as though little has changed in this regard, however.

Speed of delivery has its major implications on the policy process within nations and on the relative power of different actors in that process. Reaction times for life and death decisions for a whole nation are now determined by the delivery time of a nuclear missile – on the order of thirty minutes. Inevitably, the power of decision must be lodged in a very few hands, whatever the constitutional or traditional assumptions. The effects are felt not only in time of war, but in time of peace when the power of the chief of state is thereby greatly enhanced in the conduct of foreign policy. Moreover, many other aspects of the character of the policy process are greatly altered by the time-demands of nuclear weapons decision making: the information available for decisions, the ability to allow public or legislative debate, the complexity of the weapons control technology, and the linking of power from a chief of state directly to lower levels of command because of extreme time requirements.

Weapons complexity and cost add new elements in geopolitical relations and reduce the meaning of others. The quality, size and health of a nation's R & D resources become major factors in a power equation, while the meaning of geography, of size of population, and of other traditional factors is devalued. Nations are now dependent on their R & D communities in unprecedented ways, including a new dependence on technologists in decision making as a result of the complexity of the choices to be made.

The cost of modern weapons systems has served to separate the rich from the very rich. In effect, only two nations are so far able to maintain full arsenals of modern weapons. Whatever their previous position, all the others are thus of lesser power and influence, at least in that area derived from military capabilities. The new class of superpowers, able to destroy each other but only to face unavoidable destruction in return, and with no present consequent rivals, is a new phenomenon in international affairs.

The development of phenomenal accuracy of delivery of weapons could change this situation, and could have substantial effects on other aspects of warfare as well. At the strategic level, when coupled with multiple warhead missiles, the danger that one superpower could obtain a credible first-strike capability to initiate nuclear war without danger of substantial retaliation from the other becomes more serious. Thus, greater accuracy could upset the standoff just described. The effects of this possibility on the political behavior of nuclear states could obviously be substantial. Short of a meaningful arms control agreement, the results will be evident in a few years.

At the level of limited or conventional warfare, great accuracy of delivery could enormously increase the effectiveness of conventional weapons: aircraft bombing, anti-aircraft, anti-tank and others. It is conceivable that a substantial revolution in the effectiveness of low-level combat could occur with substantial, though presently uncertain, implications for the meaning and frequency of conventional warfare.

In fact, in general, technology has had much less substantial effects on conventional warfare since World War II than it has had on strategic war. Strategic weapons have received primary R & D emphasis. Under the constraints on the use of nuclear power, conventional war has even flourished, often with the nuclear powers hobbled and unable to exert their full influence because of the fear of escalation. It is quite likely that technology will increasingly find its way to the conventional war arena, through developments in accuracy, electronic warfare (use of technology for battlefield surveillance and control; Gillette, 1973), more 'efficient' explosives, anti-aicraft weapons and hand-held weapons. The effects may be very substantial within a very few years.

And, these weapons may increasingly be used for another recent phenomenon: small terrorist groups disrupting complex society in order to influence international political decisions. The growing ability to put powerful force in small packages, to provide highly destructive, accurate weapons in easily managed sizes, and the decreasing barriers to nuclear proliferation, make diffusion of significant weapons all but certain to more nations or to subnational groups. The international effects are likely to be profound.

3. **New Patterns of Interactions and New Actors** Related to the interdependence theme, but deserving separate mention, is the growth of new patterns of linkages and interactions among nations, often outside the full or even partial ken of governments (Keohane and Nye, 1971). Developments in science and technology have contributed to, or made possible, these new patterns by forming the base for new high-technology industries with worldwide markets; by making possible easy and profitable production of consumer products divided among many countries; by undergirding the high-technology, energy-intensive economies that require organization on an international scale; and by providing the necessary capability, through high-speed transportation and communication, for these interactions to take place and grow.

As a result, transnational relationships involving international companies, international organizations of all kinds, cross-national interest groups, and individuals, have flourished. The immediate effect is not only greater interdependence, but also an intensification of a new degree of interaction among nations, with governments only in partial control and involvement, and often with only partial knowledge of what is taking place (See Schroeder-Gudehus. Chapter 13).

Even formal intergovernmental relationships have grown at an explosive rate, with many more international organizations having substantial political functions to perform on the international scene (Singer and Wallace, 1970; Skolnikoff, 1972). No international organization is without a substantial role in science and technology; many have been formed entirely around new technologies (e.g. International Atomic Energy Agency, International Civil Aeronautics Organization, Intelsat). The impact on international organizations is discussed in greater detail below.

In effect, there are now many more actors in international affairs that have an effect, and must be taken account of, in policy: multinational corporations, private and governmental international organizations, international labor unions, and interest groups cutting across national borders. The traditional focus of public attention remains on governments, but, largely outside of public view, governments must share the actual conduct of international affairs with many others.

4. **Rich and Poor** Technology has made possible quite directly the rapid industrialization of what has come to be called the 'developed' countries of the world. But it has also prompted dramatic changes in the poorer, less developed nations (See Sardar and Rosser-Owen, Chapter 15).

The introduction of public health technologies has contributed to a population explosion with massive global and national implications. With a population size which reached two billion in 1940, three billion in 1960, over four billion by 1975 and which is expected to exceed six billion by the end of the century, there are obvious and critical questions about mankind's ability to support such a growing population, and about the effect on the quality of life in doing so (Gardner, 1973; Frejka, 1973; Gordon, 1974). Within nations, especially the poorer nations, population growth has meant that per capita economic growth has been excruciatingly slow, and that a host of other problems has arisen, notably large-scale migration to urban areas, difficulties in food distribution, and basic problems of governance.

At the same time, technology in the form of expanded and cheaper communication and transportation has made evident even to isolated populations long imbued with the idea of the unchanging continuity of their lives, how others live and by implication what could be possible for them. Popularly called the 'revolution of rising expectations', this has had a profound effect on the social and political structure of the developing countries, and on their international policies (Lerner, 1958). It has also contributed to the proliferation of the idea of nationhood, and thus to the growth in numbers of independent countries.

Increasingly, these countries are asserting themselves in international affairs, often in concert, confronting the richer countries with demands for 'their share' of prosperity, resources, or political power. Their influence in international organizations has grown, to the point of domination as a group in some bodies.

Technology itself has become an issue in this process, as the developing countries become convinced that technology is the essential base for economic development (Schiavo-Campo *et al.*, 1970; Jones, 1971; Singer, 1973) The existence of technological gaps – different levels of technological competence in different countries – has become an important political issue, not only for economic reasons, but also because the specter looms of continuing dependency relations between technologically advanced and backward countries, a form of neo-colonialism that could reestablish the hegemony of the colonial powers in new, more subtle ways.

A concomitant of technological gaps is the movement of scientists and engineers from developing countries to positions in more advanced technological nations (US Congress, 1974). This migration, commonly called a brain-drain, has been a serious political and economic issue for many years, and is likely to continue to be a problem until the countries suffering from it reach the state of development that provides attractive positions for trained personnel at home. The economic effects of the brain-drain are not easily measured, but the phenomenon supports the concern which developing countries show about the future pattern of their relations with the industrialized world.

5. Domestic Policy Processes: Foreign Policy and Feedback to Science

Policy Science and technology have also contributed directly and massively to the changes in the policy processes by which foreign policy is formulated and carried out in all countries, especially the more developed nations of the world; and international developments have in turn been important factors in national science policies. (This is discussed in detail by Schroeder-Gudehus in Chapter 13 but deserves mention here.)

One implication for domestic policy making has earlier been pointed out: the tendency for power to gravitate to the chief of state in response to the compressed decision-making time required by modern strategic weapons systems, and the greater consequences that flow from their use.

There are other implications. Many more parts of government have a say in and affect foreign policy than used to be the case. A direct result of interdependence, essentially every agency of national governments has foreign programs or contacts, and often has a major effect in practice on a nation's international position. Thus, in the formulation of foreign policy, the previously dominant position of a foreign minister has been heavily eroded on many issues on which he must share responsibility with others.

Moreover, on those issues with important technological aspects, he may be at a substantial disadvantage because of the superior technical knowledge of other ministries of government.

The revolutions in communication and transportation have also had direct effects in reducing the independence or authority of ambassadors in favor of ministers who are now in a position to communicate instructions quickly, or travel themselves to deal with issues on the spot. Rapid communications have also added enormously to the paper flow, since it now becomes so easy to require frequent reporting and to question instructions, or to negotiate matters that formerly were left to those in the field. It also has meant that all foreign ministers must be more concerned with a set of relationships — numerous and broader, global in fact — that makes it impossible to concentrate on any one relationship for any length of time.

Science and technology have themselves become the necessary concern of foreign ministries, though this is rarely carried out to appreciable extent in practice. Science and technology are supported by governments for national purposes, whatever the commonly-held assumptions. But, a large proportion of the R & D budget of any nation, and particularly of those of the advanced countries, is in fact motivated by foreign policy concerns: in the United States this proportion is well over half, including military R & D, and some proportion of the Atomic Energy Commission and Space Agency budgets. Other R & D objectives, thought of primarily as domestic, can also have important international implications — research in agriculture, health, alternative energy sources, technologies related to trade, nutrition, communications and others.

Yet it is a rare foreign ministry that has any say at all in the allocation of R & D resources. Most foreign offices have very little influence on national science policy, even though the results of R & D are likely to have significant impact on international relations, and the results foregone by R & D not performed might equally have altered a nation's international position.

Nations are responsive to science policies of other countries, however, especially in those areas likely to affect military and economic relationships. Foreign offices are not usually the vehicle for bringing these external influences to bear; rather military and industrial ministries or private industry, even though they have more limited mission responsibilities, are more directly involved. In one period in the United States — during the 1950's and early 1960's — the President and his staff tended to become the primary focus through which foreign science policies influenced United States science policy (Skolnikoff, 1967).

In the armaments area, the military technological capabilities and future potential of possible adversaries have a direct motivating effect on the allocation of R & D resources. Whether research and development is the cause of the arms race or the result of it is a question which remains in contention (York, 1970; Wohlstetter, 1974; Nacht, 1975), but there is no question that most of the industrialized nations allocate a good proportion of their national R & D expenditures on the basis of their presumed international military position (See Sapolsky, Chapter 12).

In the economic sphere, the importance of high-technology products in overall foreign trade has made technologically advanced nations particularly conscious of the need to maintain their position vis-a-vis other nations (Gilpin, 1975; Vernon, 1970). In Western countries this has resulted in a variety of different science policies and institutional developments designed to stimulate industry to innovate, to be able to compete effectively at home and abroad with foreign based corporations (Gilpin, 1968; OECD, 1972, 1973, 1974).

And scientific prowess itself has become a general indicator of a nation's status and prestige, or at least has been assumed to be so. Particularly during the 1950's and 1960's, funding levels for science and technology in the United States, and presumably in the Soviet Union, were heavily influenced by the implicit and often explicit competition between the two nations (Skolnikoff, 1967; Van Dyke, 1964). Competition in high-energy physics, in oceanography, in space exploration, and in many other fields, was a major factor in determining national science policies, at least of the major technological countries.

Even for the developing countries, however, the international nature of the scientific community and the general aura of technological success of the United States and the USSR led them to follow the general pattern of science policies of the superpowers. Only in recent years has there been much attention to alternative paths of scientific and technological development and that has had but marginal impact so far (Schumacher, 1973; see also Sardar and Rosser-Owen, Chapter 15).

These five categories of impact of technology on the international system show well how much the pattern of international affairs has altered in terms of numbers of actors, dependency relations, military power, relevance of scientific and technological capability, and other significant attributes. But, it is much less clear how the underlying assumptions with which governments approach international affairs have altered, if at all (Skolnikoff, 1971). Governments still approach the international system as an arena in which their sovereignty and freedom of action are sacred and untouchable, in which they are competing for power and advantage with relatively short time horizons, and with concepts of the national interest defined in a quite traditional zero-sum calculus. In the face of a greatly altered international scene, the evidence of fundamentally altered political behavior – or even tendencies in that direction – is hard to find.

SEVEN SPECIFIC ISSUE-AREAS

1. **Food and Population**   National policies for science and technology are primarily seen from a national perspective, even when the issues are largely or inherently international. This is not surprising, given both the nation-state orientation of the international system and the relative weakness of foreign offices in dealing with R & D allocations, both of which tend to give dominance to primarily domestically oriented, technical agencies of government. Thus, science policy issues stemming from the international scene are largely dealt with, at least initially, within governments, and only later through international action and negotiation. Many issues, however, increasing in number and importance, can only be described and considered in international terms, whatever final form the determination of policy will take.

Science policy studies in the field of science, technology and international affairs, are concerned with the analysis of existing issues, with new issues arising from technology, and with understanding the alternative policies and their implications. A few of the more important technology-related international issues are singled out here for brief schematic attention, to show the nature of the science and technology policy issues involved. These illustrate well the range of issues, and the varied relationship of science and technology to them.

The dimensions of the population explosion have already been described. The impact has of course many parts, but one of the most critical and immediate questions is the availability of food to feed that population. The issues are exceedingly complicated, but a few major considerations stand out.

Essentially, only three countries in the world are able now to produce food substantially in excess of their own needs: the United States, Canada and Australia. The productivity of agriculture in those countries, as everywhere, is heavily dependent on continuing technological advance, though the rate of return of technological innovation is likely to be higher in countries that have farther to go in applying new technology to their agriculture. The actual product of the major food-exporting countries is also dependent on other factors, notably the weather, the price structure, and the rising cost of inputs for an energy-intensive agriculture. Weather is a critical factor, and there is considerable concern that weather patterns have been more favorable in recent years than is likely to be the case in the future (SMIC Report, 1971).

The cost of necessary inputs, and of the food itself, becomes a more serious factor for poor, food-deficit countries. A fall in production internally or in the granary countries will raise the price of food, making it even more difficult to obtain the food, or to distribute it to those with the least ability to pay.

There are disagreements about the seriousness of the aggregate food situation in the mid-1970's and for the medium-term future, though it seems likely that food production during that period can meet overall requirements (Brown and Eckholm, 1974; Schertz, 1974; *Science,* 1975). Whether the food can reach those who most need it is another question very much dependent on distribution networks, ability to pay, institutional capabilities in food-deficit countries and other factors.

For the longer term, the prognosis is much more pessimistic, because of the momentum of population growth and the slow-moving ability to bring about social change and economic development. An increase in agricultural productivity in the food-deficit countries themselves is essential, and possible with the application of improved agricultural practices based heavily on the results of past R & D. But, until recently, most agricultural R & D was devoted to improving productivity in the richer countries; in the past several years a network of international agricultural research institutes has been founded that focuses on the particular needs of the poorer countries. Still, the bulk of the agriculture R & D resources of the United States, for example, continues to be focused on the United States and not on the developing countries.

Improved agricultural technology alone will not solve the overall food/population needs. The technologies must be used; this requires political, economic, institutional and social changes in the countries themselves and internationally. Moreover, if population continues to grow at rates between two and three per cent per year, it will be increasingly difficult for food production to keep pace.

Social science research now points to the close interaction between, on the one hand, economic growth, availability of food, infant mortality, the role of women and similar factors; and on the other, motivation for limiting family size. Much remains to be learned about these relationships and about the ways to influence them (Scrimshaw, 1974). It is a critical inquiry for the global future.

Voices have already been raised advocating a policy that would ignore the plight of the developing countries on the grounds that they will not take the internal measures required and in the long run will bring the developed countries down with them (Paddock and Paddock, 1967; Greene, 1975; Berg, 1975). In the future, if population growth continues unabated, we can only pose the issue with more insistence.

2. Energy It is now abundantly clear to everyone what degree of importance energy issues have assumed on the international agenda. Oil imports account roughly for seventy per cent of the energy needs of Japan, fifty per cent for Western Europe, and ten per cent for the United States (UN, 1974; Winger, 1972). The 1973 embargo by the major oil-producing countries in the Middle East resulted in major upheavals in industrialized countries, upheavals that demonstrated their vulnerability, added enormously to world-wide inflation, and disrupted the international monetary system.

The dependence on oil of the industrialized countries, in fact of all countries, is a product of growing industrialization based on the availability of cheap and abundant energy. It is a contentious issue just how much oil is still in the ground, but it is clear that a major part of known supplies resides under the control of a very small number of countries. It is also clear that existing oil dependence relations cannot be substantially or quickly altered; rather the focus has to be on how future energy demands will be met.

Thus in the short term little can be done except in the realms of political action and perhaps conservation measures. But modifying the longer-term relationship is a technology-intensive problem that requires present action. Alternative energy technologies, especially nuclear power, more intensive oil exploration and exploitation techniques, technology for deeper ocean drilling, environmentally safe coal mining techniques, improved and safer transport technology, more efficient technologies for energy consumption, are all relevant objectives that require R & D investments well in advance of their realization. More difficult than the problems themselves is the analysis of the wisest R & D resource allocation among these objectives, since they cannot all be given the same priority. Such analysis necessarily requires broad studies that involve the interaction of scientific and technological with political and economic factors (MIT Energy Laboratory Policy Study Group, 1974).

3. Atomic Energy Though atomic energy is obviously part of the energy equation, it deserves separate mention because of the particular global issues it poses. Here is an example of an international subject that came into existence directly as a result of science and technology. Its potential for beneficial use is great — but so is its actual and potential misuse.

Several factors make this an area of international concern: the possibility of diverting nuclear fuel from peaceful to military or terroristic uses, the problems of safety and waste disposal involved in the peaceful uses of nuclear technology, and the importance of this technology in meeting the future energy needs of many countries.

It is expected that reactors will number in the thousands, each one producing waste fuel capable of being processed to produce atomic weapons, and that breeder reactors will be developed and installed that can produce weapons-grade material directly, with concomitant fuel transport and disposal requirements. We are just beginning to see some of the dimensions of the issues (Willrich, 1971a; Willrich and Taylor, 1974). The explosion of a nuclear device in India, one of the world's poorest although scientifically advanced countries, emphasizes the danger.

Political efforts to bring this issue under control make little progress in spite of the nuclear nonproliferation treaty, yet the policies which advance the nuclear technologies and promote their use move ahead rapidly. The implications of these technologies, and what can be done to make their application safe and useful, must be the focus of more – and more intensive – national and international study than they have received to date (Willrich, 1971b).

4. Environment   Since the start of the 1970's the international community has come to recognize in substantial ways the fact that the global environment is threatened with serious deterioration because of acts and activities previously thought of as national or domestic in nature. The issues involved vary from cosmic concerns about overheating or cooling the earth's atmosphere as a result of waste products of civilization, to the problems of accidental oil spills or the use of insecticides or fertilizers as necessary adjuncts of intensive agriculture. They can be two-country issues such as Great Lakes pollution, or limited multinational issues such as Rhine river pollution or deterioration of the Baltic and Mediterranean Seas, or global issues such as alteration of the earth's heat balance or spread of DDT.

A perfect symbolic (and actual) issue of a global nature has arisen because of scientific evidence that fluorocarbons from aerosol cans and refrigerator coolants may be building up in the upper atmosphere with serious adverse effects on the earth's ozone layer (Hammond and Maugh, 1974). The issue illustrates many points: the global nature of man's ability to tamper with the environment; the diffuse decision making that led to the problem (involving production – largely in the United States so far – of billions of aerosol cans for individual sale, and the worldwide production of refrigerators); the time lag between the recognition of the problem and the ability to reverse the effect; the importance of scientific understanding of the atmosphere; the urgent need for global monitoring systems; and the difficult regulatory and R & D measures that will be required to deal with it.

Once again, the issues are substantially rooted in science and technology for an understanding of the present situation, for the means to monitor the pollution and its effects, and for ways to ameliorate or avoid undesirable effects. The issues, however, cannot be studied in technological isolation; in fact, technology is only one facet of the issues and of their resolution. They involve a multitude of factors which must be analyzed within a common framework if effective policy agreements are to be reached (See also Nelkin, Chapter 11).

5. Oceans   Ocean policy issues are among the oldest facing the inter national community, and those for which there is the longest experience of international policies. Yet, technology has transformed this traditional area so that it raises quite new questions that are of great political and economic sensitivity to nations.

Advances in the technology of fishing – larger ships, longer range, refrigeration, new gear – have revolutionized that industry to the point where there is now serious concern about overfishing and substantial depletion of many fish species, and related concern over the large fishing fleets now ranging far from home waters (Gullion, 1968).

Technological advances with regard to the exploration of mineral and organic resources on and under the seabed have opened an entirely new area of enormous economic importance, especially in relation to energy and resource issues (McKelvey *et al.*, 1969).

The use of the seas as the unique base of invulnerable deterrent force adds an entirely new military dimension to the importance of the oceans for national purposes (Tsipis *et al.*, 1973).

These three factors, in particular, are the focus of international deliberations and negotiations, with quite far-reaching political significance. Broad-based analyses relating the technical facts and uncertainties to the policy issues, are required as essential inputs to the policy process within nations and internationally that will deal with these issues.

If successful, the law-of-the-sea conference that began in 1973 will set the stage for quite new international ocean relationships with new definitions of national jurisdiction, new codification of international rights and responsibilities, and possibly even international jurisdiction and control of the resources of at least the deep sea portion of the oceans (Bouchez and Kaijen, 1973).

6. Outer Space   Outer space is another example of an issue-area that is entirely the product of advances and applications of science and technology. Unknown in these terms until 1957, there are now extensive nonmilitary technologies in place, some even of a privately owned commercial nature, including communications, meteorology, navigation and most recently remote sensing for earth resource surveys.

All of these technologies raise obvious questions about control of space rights of overflight and observation, sharing of benefits, transfer of technology, appropriate international political machinery for control, and related issues. They also raise the more traditional issues of how nations can maximize their political and economic interests in this new area; what political benefits cooperation might bring; and how the technology might be 'misused' for hostile purposes. And they raise questions about future R & D objectives, and what resources should be allocated for them.

Space-related issues are by now a 'traditional' science policy subject among some science policy analysts (Van Dyke, 1964; Kash, 1967; Bloomfield, 1968). As in other issue-areas, we can only see these problems clearly when the interface between technology and policy issues is fully realized.

7. **Technology and Trade, Multinationals, Transfer of Technology** A phalanx of economically oriented international issues centering around technology has emerged and has increasingly important overtones (See Freeman, Chapter 7). All of these issues touch on extremely sensitive areas of national interest, although information and understanding about them is often inadequate. All of them have to do with the movement and significance of technology in international transactions.

International trade in technology has become an important factor for advanced industrial nations as well as for developing countries. The United States in the 1960's maintained a favorable trade balance through its lead in high-technology products in conjunction with its more stable agricultural exports (International Economic Report, 1973). The Europeans at that time were worried about their 'technology gap' (Gilpin, 1968; Spencer, 1970; Kaufman, 1970). In a few years the situation changed and, as the favorable high-technology balance of the United States shrank, many people advocated export controls on technology to prevent the 'undervalued' export of the country's chief commodity. The Nixon Administration attempted to launch a major program of new technological initiatives to 'regain' the international lead (Shapley, 1971).

National science policy clearly has a great deal to do with the competitive position of a nation in its technology products, though the ability of a nation effectively to develop new high-technology industries through government stimulation is not yet proven. The United Kingdom, France, the United States have all tried, with mixed success at best (Gilpin, 1968; Williams, 1973; Zysman, 1974). The comparative lessons, an excellent objective of science policy studies, have yet to be adequately developed.

For developing countries, international trade in technology is one way to bring in the technology they need (See Sardar and Rosser-Owen, Chapter 15). But, that raises many of the questions associated with the uncertainties of the transfer of technology (Little *et al.,* 1970; Jones, 1971; Poats, 1972; Stewart, 1973). The difficulties of technology transfer are manifold. They have to do with the adequacy of scientific and technology infrastructure in the recipient countries, the lack of knowledge applicable in the setting of the less-developed countries, the need for adaptation and innovation of technical knowledge if it is to be useful, the relevance of the social and political setting the lack of adequate resources devoted to R & D for problems of the developing countries rather than for those of the industrialized countries, and others.

Observers agree, however, that perhaps the most important carriers of technology across borders are the multinational enterprises. Their role, and their significance as extra-governmental institutions, are just beginning to be studied in the depth and with the competence required (Vernon, 1971, 1974). Multinationals clearly have great importance for both developing and industrialized countries, and constitute centers of financial and technological power that can shape or frustrate policies of some nations to an uncertain degree. High technology is the base of many of the corporations, and the currency of others; the study of multinationals *must* include science policy aspects.

APPROACHES TO INTEGRATION ACROSS ISSUE-AREAS

As noted earlier, most studies of the interaction of science and technology with the international system deal with specific issue-areas as have been outlined in the previous section. A few studies attempt to integrate across issue-areas to point out more general lessons for science policy and/or for international affairs. One such analysis (Skolnikoff, 1972) focuses on the implications for international political machinery and the necessary international operations of an international system. Another (Ruggie and Haas, 1975) develops a more general discussion of the implications for the international political system.

All of the issues discussed, and others not mentioned, require that they be dealt with by nations in an international environment. All require some form of international negotiation and agreement, and many require the agreement and cooperation of two or more nations. Some lead to consortia of two or a few countries pooling their efforts to deal with a problem. Some issues call for full-scale organizations with operating and other responsibilities. Some may not require such referral to an organization, but may be amenable to such an approach.

In fact, these technology-related issues are forcing an increasing number of subjects into a framework that requires global international organizations to deal with them. Moreover, to deal adequately with these questions requires that the organizations perform functions that are governmental in nature: regulation, control, inspection, allocation of resources, operation and adjudication. For the oceans, fisheries commissions attempt to regulate ocean fishing areas or specific species; the Intergovernmental Maritime Consultative Organization regulates shipping and oil pollution; a new body may well be established for control of deep sea resources. For health matters, the World Health Organization operates several world-wide disease eradication programs and attempts to regulate health matters. For space, various applications of technology have resulted in new operating organizations such as Intelsat, or new broad management responsibilities conferred on existing global organizations such as the World Meteorological Organization. For atomic energy, the International Atomic Energy Agency has been created to attempt to regulate the flow of fissionable material. For energy broadly, there is no global organization, nor is there one for population. Multinational corporations, presenting a new and powerful political and economic force on the international scene, many based on technological developments have no international supervision through formal intergovernmental mechanisms. And they benefit substantially thereby (Vernon, 1971; Barnet and Müller, 1974). All international organizations today are seized to some extent with science and technology; all are seized with the implications of science and technology. In fact, science and technology are major causes of the growth and proliferation of international organizations since World War II.

The need to create or turn to international machinery for these issues raises obvious questions about the ability of existing or potential machinery to carry out the responsibilities indicated. In turn, those questions raise others about the attitudes of governments toward international organizations and about the willingness of nations to delegate responsibility to organizations over which they have only limited influence.

The record to date is not an encouraging one. International governmental organizations carry out many functions satisfactorily, some superbly, but most of their responsibilities are limited to those functions that do not carry substantial economic or political risk for nations. When organizations are entrusted with such responsibilities (for example, in some fisheries commissions), it is usually the case that the organizations are very limited in membership or scope, or are dominated by the countries with the largest stake in the issue. Governments remain reluctant to delegate what they see as important matters of national sovereignty. At the same time, limitations in the effectiveness of operation of international bodies due to political and bureaucratic causes create doubts as to the ability of these bodies to carry out sensitive responsibilities, thereby reinforcing the reluctance of governments to invest them with important tasks. Moreover, the organization of the international system into issue-specific organizations gives little ability to deal with the more common phenomenon: problems that cross many issue areas (for example, energy/food/resources problems).

However, the pressing nature of many issues, the need to deal with them in an international environment, the results of advancing technology and burgeoning population, and the growing pressure from developing countries to force more issues into a multilateral framework (where they have more influence) rather than a bilateral one, leads inexorably to expansion of the international agenda. In the past few years there has been a spate of large-scale conferences dealing with the environment, oceans, food and population, each one occasioning some steps forward in institutional, legal or policy terms.

Ruggie (1972) combines a neo-functionalist approach, one that relates cooperation in the performance of tasks to growing political cooperation, with a public good theory to attempt to derive a more flexible analytical tool for predicting the responsibilities that will fall to international machinery. He shows how problems dealing with collective decision making within nations have quite similar analogs internationally, and concludes, however, along with the neo-functionalist approach, that organizational patterns and cooperation that result will be issue-specific or actor-specific rather than universal or superstate in character.

Ruggie and Haas, in a major new study (1975) of international response to technology, focus on the relation of scientific and technological knowledge to political choice with regard to international regimes. Using case studies in fields as diverse as oceans, communications, R & D cooperation in Western Europe, weather modification and others, they develop a pattern of inter-actions that crosses issue areas. They also seek an effective relation between knowledge and politics to assist in the design of politically realizable and useful international regimes.

Another integrative approach characterizes the few legal scholars who have attempted to look in detail at the effects of science and technology on the international system (Henken, 1969; Black and Falk, 1972). Not surprisingly, these scholars focus on the legal structure that is and will be required to deal with the implications of science and technology. Notwithstanding a certain rigidity in the definition of international law, the conclusions again are quite similar to the more political approach in illustrating the new requirements that will have to be met by international mechanisms of some kind to deal with the problems posed by the effects of science and technology.

A quite different approach by the 'Systems Dynamicists' must briefly be mentioned here, though as noted earlier it should not be thought of as part of the science policy studies literature. Meadows, in *Limits to Growth* (Meadows *et al.*, 1972), is among the most widely known practitioners, under the tutelage of Jay Forrester (Forrester, 1971). A more advanced effort of the same genre has now appeared (Messarovic and Pestel, 1975). The approach is an attempt to create a dynamic model of all significant physical relationships (resources, energy, pollution, population, etc.) which with the use of computer runs of the model can help to anticipate the results of current global trends under a variety of possible developments.

This is obviously an ambitious exercise but the *Limits to Growth*, which has had worldwide public attention, has come under much criticism because of the simplistic nature of many of the relationships, the wide uncertainty of many assumed parameters, the lack of integration of relevant social aspects, the neglect of some obviously important factors (technological innovation, price effects, and political variables), and the widespread publicity given to a necessarily tentative first attempt. The highly pessimistic conclusion of almost unavoidable catastrophe within one hundred years, coupled with the mystique of its sponsor (The Club of Rome), its MIT base, and its computer aura have given the study unparalleled notoriety and impact. A study at the University of Sussex, among other studies, sharply challenges its methodology and conclusions (Cole *et al.*, 1973).

CONCLUDING REMARKS

Whether or not such prophets of doom are right, it is clear that it will be exceedingly difficult, at best, to meet the manifold problems raised by population growth, economic development, unequal distribution of wealth, scarce resources, environmental degradation, and diffusion of power. Science and technology are part of the cause of all those problems, and also part of the solution.

In fact, the political problems of governance of complex societies are likely to overwhelm, or at least to precede, any actual physical limitations on social development (Skolnikoff, 1974; Brunner and Brewer, 1971). Policies for the international implications of science and technology are among those problems of governance that will be most difficult, and most important. They are thus a critical portion of science policy studies.

BIBLIOGRAPHY

Alker *et al.*, 1974   Alker, Jr., H. R., Bloomfield, L. P. and Choucri, N., *Analyzing Global Interdependence*, Cambridge, Mass., MIT, Center for International Studies, 1974.

Barnet and Müller, 1974   Barnet, R. J. and Müller, R. E., *Global Reach: The Power of Multinational Corporations*, New York, Simon and Schuster, 1974.

Berg, 1975   Berg, A., 'The Trouble with Triage', *The New York Times*, 15 June 1975, pp. 26-28.

Black and Falk, 1972   Black, C. E. and Falk, R. A., *The Structure of the International Environment* Vol. IV, Princeton, New Jersey, Princeton University Press, 1972.

Bloomfield, 1968	Bloomfield, L. P. (Ed.), *Outer Space: Prospects for Man and Society*, for the American Assembly, revised edition, New York and Washington, D.C., Praeger, 1968.
Bouchez and Kaijen, 1973	Bouchez, L. J. and Kaijen, L. (Eds.), *The Future of the Law of the Sea*, The Hague, Nijhoff, 1973.
Brodie and Brodie, 1962	Brodie, B. and Brodie, F., *From Crossbow to H-Bomb*, New York, Dell, 1962.
Brown, 1972	Brown, L. R., *World Without Borders*, New York, Random House, 1972.
Brown and Eckholm, 1974	Brown, L. R. and Eckholm, E. P., *By Bread Alone*, Washington, D.C., Overseas Development Institute, 1974.
Brown and Fabian, 1975	Brown, S. and Fabian, L., 'Toward Mutual Accountability in the Nonterrestrial Realms', *International Organization* 29, No. 3, 1975.
Brunner and Brewer, 1971	Brunner, R. D. and Brewer, G. P., *Organized Complexity: Empirical Theories of Political Development*, New York, The Free Press, 1971.
Brzezinski, 1970	Brzezinski, Z., *Between Two Ages: America's Role in the Technocratic Era*, New York, Viking Press, 1970 (also as a Viking Compass Book, 1971).
Cole *et al.*, 1973	Cole, H. S., Freeman, C., Jahoda, M. and Pavitt, K. L. R. (Eds.), *Thinking About the Future: A Critique of the Limits to Growth* (for the Science Policy Research Institute, University of Sussex), London, Chatto and Windus, 1973 (U.S. title: *Models of Doom*).
Falk, 1971	Falk, R. A., *This Endangered Planet*, New York, Random House, 1971.
Forrester, 1971	Forrester, J. W., *World Dynamics*, Cambridge, Mass., Wright-Allen, 1971.
Fox, 1968	Fox, W. T. R., 'Science, Technology and International Politics', *International Studies Quarterly* 12, No. 1, 1968, pp. 1-15.
Frejka, 1973	Frejka, T., *The Future of Population Growth: Alternative Paths to Equilibrium*, New York, Wiley-Interscience for the Population Council, 1973.
Gardner, 1973	Gardner, R. N., Report of the Seminar, *The United Nations and the Population Problem*, Aspen, Colorado, Aspen Institute for Humanistic Studies and the Institute of Man and Science, 1973.
Gillette, 1973	Gillette, R., 'Military R & D: Hard Lessons of an Electronic War', *Science* 182, No. 4112, 1973, pp. 559-561.
Gilpin, 1968	Gilpin, R., *France in the Age of the Scientific State*, Princeton, New Jersey, Princeton University Press, 1968.
Gilpin, 1975	Gilpin, R., *Technology, Economic Growth and International Competitiveness* (A report prepared for the use of the Subcommittee on Economic Growth of the Joint Economic Committee, Congress of the United States, 94th Congress, 1st Session, Joint Committee Print), Washington, D.C., U.S. Government Printing Office, 9 July 1975.

Gordon, 1974   Gordon, L., 'Population Trends and Prospects', in
                                Wilson Jr., T. W. (Ed.), *World Population and a Global
                                Emergency,* Aspen, Colorado, Aspen Institute for
                                Humanistic Studies, 1974, Appendix A, pp. 33-43.
Greene, 1975   Greene, W., 'Triage: Who Shall be Fed? Who Shall
                                Starve? ', *The New York Times* 5 January 1975, pp.
                                9-11, 44-45, 51.
Gullion, 1968   Gullion, E. A. (Ed.), *Uses of the Seas* (for the Ameri-
                                can Assembly), New York, Prentice Hall, 1968.
Hammond and Maugh, 1974   Hammond, A. L. and Maugh, T. H., II, 'Stratospheric
                                Pollution: Multiple Threats to the Earth's Ozone',
                                Science 186, No. 4161, 1974, pp. 335-338.
Haskins, 1964   Haskins, C. P., *The Scientific Revolution and World
                                Politics* (for the Council on Foreign Relations), New
                                York, Harper and Row, 1964.
Henkin, 1968   Henkin, L., *How Nations Behave,* New York, Praeger,
                                1968.
International Economic Report *International Economic Report of the President,*
of the President, 1973   Washington, D.C., United States Government Printing
                                Office, 1973.
Jones, 1971   Jones, G., *The Role of Science and Technology in
                                Developing Countries* (for the International Council of
                                Scientific Unions), London, New York and Toronto,
                                Oxford University Press, 1971.
Kash, 1967   Kash, D. E., *The Politics of Space Cooperation,* La-
                                fayette, Indiana, Purdue University Studies, 1967.
Kaufman, 1970   Kaufman, R. H., *The Technology Gap: United States
                                and Europe,* prepared by the Atlantic Institute
                                (Special Series in International Economics and De-
                                velopment), New York, Praeger, 1970.
Keohane and Nye, 1971   Keohane, R. O. and Nye Jr., J. S. (Eds.), *Transnational
                                Relations and World Politics,* Cambridge, Mass., Har-
                                vard University Press, 1971 (also in *International Or-
                                ganization* XXV, No. 3, 1971).
Lerner, 1958   Lerner, D., *The Passing of Traditional Society:
                                Modernizing the Middle East,* New York, The Free
                                Press, 1958.
Little, *et al.,* 1970   Little, I., Scitovsky, T., and Scott, M., *Industry and
                                Trade in Some Developed Countries: A Comparative
                                Study,* New York, Oxford University Press, 1970.
McKelvey *et al.,* 1969   McKelvey, V. E., Tracey, J. I., Jr., Stoertz, G. E. and
                                Vedder, J. G., *Subsea Mineral Resources and Problems
                                Related to their Development,* Geological Survey Cir-
                                cular 619, Washington, D.C., U.S. Geological Survey,
                                1969.
Meadows *et al.,* 1972   Meadows, D., Meadows, D. L., Randers, J. and
                                Behrens, W. W., III, *The Limits to Growth: A Report
                                for the Club of Rome's Project on the Predicament of
                                Mankind,* New York, Universe Books, 1972.
Mesarovic and Pestel, 1974   Mesarovic, M. and Pestel, E., *Mankind at the Turning
                                Point: The Second Report to the Club of Rome,* New
                                York, Dutton, 1974.

MIT Energy Laboratory Policy Study Group, 1974
MIT Energy Laboratory Policy Study Group, 'Energy Self-Sufficiency: An Economic Evaluation', *Technological Review* 76, No. 6, 1974, pp. 22-58.

Nacht, 1975
Nacht, M., 'The Delicate Balance of Error', *Foreign Policy* 19, Summer 1975.

OECD, 1972
OECD, *The Research System: Comparative Survey of the Organization and Financing of Fundamental Research* Vol. 1 (France, Germany, United Kingdom), Paris, OECD, 1972.

OECD, 1973
OECD, *The Research System: Comparative Survey of the Organization and Financing of Fundamental Research* Vol. II (Belgium, Netherlands, Norway, Sweden, Switzerland), Paris, OECD, 1973.

OECD, 1974
OECD, *The Research System: Comparative Survey of the Organization and Financing of Fundamental Research* Vol. III (Canada, United States, General Conclusions), Paris, OECD, 1974.

Paddock and Paddock, 1967
Paddock, P. and Paddock, W., *Famine 1975,* Boston, Mass., Little, Brown and Co., 1967.

Poats, 1972
Poats, R. M., *Technology for Developing Nations: New Directions for U.S. Technical Assistance,* Washington, D.C., Brookings Institution, 1972.

Ruggie, 1972
Ruggie, J. G., 'Collective Goods and Future International Collaboration', *American Political Science Review* LXVI, No. 3, 1972, pp. 874-893.

Ruggie and Haas, 1975
Ruggie, J. G. and Haas, E. B. (Eds.), 'International Responses to Technology', *International Organization* 29, No. 3, Summer 1975.

Schertz, 1974
Schertz, L., 'World Food: Prices and the Poor', *Foreign Affairs* 52, No. 3, 1974.

Schiavo-Campo and Singer, 1970
Schiavo-Campo, S. and Singer, H. W., *Perspectives of Economic Development,* Boston, Houghton-Mifflin, 1970.

Schumacher, 1973
Schumacher, E. F., *Small is Beautiful: A Study of Economics as if People Mattered,* London, Blond and Brigs, Ltd., 1973.

Science, 1975
Science, 'Food', 188, No. 4188, 1975.

Scrimshaw, 1974
Scrimshaw, N. S., 'The World-Wide Confrontation of Population and Food Supply', *Technology Review* 77, No. 2, 1974, pp. 12-19.

Shapley, 1971
Shapley, D., 'Magruder in White House: SST Man Plans New Technology Take-Off', *Science* 174, No. 4007, 1971, pp. 386-388.

Singer, 1973
Singer, H. W., 'The Development Outlook for Poor Countries: Technology is the Key', *Challenge,* May-June 1973, pp. 42-47.

Singer and Wallace, 1970
Singer, J. D. and Wallace, M. C., 'Intergovernmental Organization in the Global System, 1815-1964: A Quantitative Description', *International Organization* XXIV, No. 2, 1970, pp. 238-287.

Skolnikoff, 1967
Skolnikoff, E. B., *Science Technology and American Foreign Policy,* Cambridge, Mass., MIT Press, 1967.

Skolnikoff, 1971
Skolnikoff, E. B., 'Science and Technology: The Im-

plications for International Institutions', *International Organization* XXV, No. 4, 1971, pp. 759-775.

Skolnikoff, 1972   Skolnikoff, E. B., *The International Imperatives of Technology: Technological Development and the International System* (Research Series No. 16), Berkeley, California, Institute of International Studies, University of California, 1972.

Skolnikoff, 1974   Skolnikoff, E. B., *The Governability of Complexity*, Cambridge, Mass., Center for International Studies, MIT, 1974.

SMIC, 1971   SMIC, 'Report of the Study of Man's Impact on Climate', *Inadvertent Climate Modification*, Cambridge, Mass., MIT Press, 1971.

Spencer, 1970   Spencer, D. L., *Technology Gap in Perspective: Strategy of International Technology Transfer*, New York, Spartan Books, 1970.

Sprout and Sprout, 1971 Sprout, H. H. and Sprout, M., *Toward a Politics of the Planet Earth, New York*, Van Nostrand Reinhold Co., 1971.

Stewart, 1973   Stewart, F., 'Trade and Technology', in Streeter, P. (Ed.), *Trade Strategies for Development*, New York, Wiley, 1973.

Tsipis *et al.*, 1973   Tsipis, K., Cahn, A. H., and Feld, B. T., *The Future of the Sea-Based Deterrent*, Cambridge, Mass. and London, MIT Press, 1973.

UN, 1974   United Nations, Department of Economic and Social Affairs, Statistical Office, World Energy Supplies, 1969-1972, *Statistical Papers*, Series J, No. 17, New York, United Nations, 1974.

US Congress, 1974   United States Congress, House, Committee on Foreign Affairs, *Brain Drain: A Study of the Persistent Issue of International Scientific Mobility*, prepared for the Subcommittee on National Security Policy and Scientific Developments, Committee Print, Washington, D.C., U.S. Government Printing Office, 1974.

Van Dyke, 1964   Van Dyke, V., *Pride and Power: The Rationale of the Space Program*, Urbana, Illinois, University of Illinois Press, 1964.

Vernon, 1970   Vernon, R. (Ed.), *The Technology Factor in International Trade*, National Bureau of Economic Research Conference Series, No. 22, New York, Columbia University Press, 1970).

Vernon, 1971   Vernon, R., *Sovereignty at Bay: The Multinational Spread of U.S. Enterprises*, New York, Basic Books, 1971.

Vernon, 1974   Vernon, R., 'Multinational Enterprises in Developing Countries: An Analysis of National Goals and National Policies', prepared for UNIDO (mimeo, draft 7 June 1974), New York, UNIDO.

Wade, 1974   Wade, N., 'Genetic Manipulation: Temporary Embargo Proposed on Research', *Science* 185, No. 4148, 1974, pp. 332-334.

Williams, 1973   Williams, R., *European Technology: The Politics of*

Willrich, 1971a

Willrich, 1971b

Willrich, and Taylor, 1974

Winger, 1972

Wohlstetter, 1974

York, 1970

Zysman, 1974

Collaboration, New York, Halstead (Wiley), 1973. Willrich, M. (Ed.), *Civil Nuclear Power and International Security* (Praeger Special Studies in International Politics and Public Affairs), New York, Praeger, 1971. Published in cooperation with the Center for the Study of Science, Technology and Public Policy, University of Virginia.

Willrich, M., *Global Politics of Nuclear Energy* (Praeger Special Studies in International Politics and Public Affairs), New York, Washington, D.C., and London, Praeger, 1971.

Willrich, M. and Taylor, T. B., *Nuclear Theft: Risks and Safeguardss (A Report to the Energy Policy Project of the Ford Foundation)*, Cambridge, Mass., Ballinger (J. B. Lippincott), 1974.

Winger, J. G., *Foreign Policy Implications of the Energy Crisis*, statement before the U.S. Congress, House Committee on Foreign Affairs, Hearings before the Subcommittee on Foreign Economic Policy, 92nd Congress, 2nd Session, Washington, D.C., U.S. Government Printing Office, 1972.

Wohlstetter, A., 'Is There a Strategic Arms Race? ', *Foreign Policy* 15, 1974, pp. 3-20.

York, H., *Race to Oblivion*, New York, Simon and Schuster, 1970.

Zysman, J., *French Industry Between the Market and the State*, unpublished Ph.D. dissertation, Cambridge, Mass., MIT, 1974.

Chapter 15

SCIENCE POLICY
AND DEVELOPING COUNTRIES

Ziauddin Sardar and Dawud G. Rosser-Owen

Muslim Institute, London

SCOPE AND TERMINOLOGY

Introduction: a three faction world? It is almost a truism to state that the world is divided into two great blocs, the Communist and the Capitalist, confronting one another. In addition to these two blocs, we have in recent years acquired another concept, that of the Third World. This concept is based upon the assertion that the two-bloc theory has been an oversimplification of things and needs some modification (Fanon, 1965; Sartre, 1967; Jenkins, 1971; Rhodes, 1970). Despite the widely differing states existing in the world today, the countries of the Third World appear, at first glance, to have problems similar to those of countries within the Communist and Capitalist Blocs; they often propose similar solutions to them, as can be seen by examining their planning proposals. Within these proposals five objectives are typically advanced, with economic growth, measured by change in national income, as the prime goal. These five goals are: 1) increase in the growth rate (net national income), 2) industrialization, 3) full employment without inflation, 4) a more equal distribution of income, and 5) a balance of international payments. The last four objectives are presented in varying

The authors would like to express their acknowledgement of the valuable assistance which the Muslim Institute gave to them in allowing their time to be engaged in other things. They would also like to thank Dr. J. R. Ravetz and Mr. J. A. MacKelvie, who read parts of the manuscript and gave much helpful advice. Finally, Dawud Rosser-Owen wishes to express his appreciation to his wife and daughter for the sympathy and support which they gave him during the writing of this.

orders of importance in various plans. We have considered below how the relevant bits of these relate to science policy.

The concept of the Occident   It is not uncommon to find that the Capitalist Bloc is referred to widely by the term 'The West'. An unfortunate duality of meanings creeps into the use of its logical counterpart, 'The East' (i.e. the Communist Bloc or the Orient); it may be that its users intend this duality of meanings. It seems to us, however, that there is little basic difference in the cultural and territorial origins of the Capitalist West and the Communist East. In our framework we shall refer to them as the Occident.

This Occident is no longer restricted to Europe and Outremer but has its 'outremers' all over the place. Anything therefore which belongs to the Occident, whether found in Europe or in Asia, is occidental. Any 'Oriental' who aspires to what is occidental or who has achieved his aspirations is thus either occidentalizing or has been occidentalized. It should be stated that, although we have often considered that which is occidental to be undesirable, inappropriate or out-and-out bad, we do not mean the term to be inherently pejorative; we are willing to see good occidental things and bad oriental things. We are not Tagorists. We use the term, to sum up, as a means of embracing Europe and its offshoots (both physical and emotional, capitalist and communist). Thus to us the EEC, Comecon (or NATO and the Warsaw Pact), the United States, the USSR, Australia, China, Japan, India, Venezuela, etc., are all part of the Occident. All of these are countries governed by occidentalized elites.

The development continuum   When 'development' first achieved notability as a concept in comparative politics, or as a dynamic in international relations, the basic assumptions were those of a linear teleology vis-à-vis the industrialized countries of the Occident. These countries were considered to be 'developed', industrially, economically, technologically, institutionally and often culturally; others were considered to be progressing along a continuum toward the goal which was development on the occidental model. We could consider this an ethnocentric view of the world or, with Panekkar, a specifically Europe-centric view. It seems to be a late manifestation of the Social Darwinist ideas of the Victorian era, ideas such as 'The White Man's Burden', 'Manifest Destiny', pressures for 'Reforms' in the Ottoman Grand State, and the like. The norm of development was thus the Occident, and in order for countries to develop, they had to occidentalize; implied in this was an abandonment of cultural and other legacies which inhibited progress toward this goal (Almond and Coleman, 1970; Pye and Verba, 1963; Apter, 1964; Rostow, 1963; Kipling, 1974; US Congressional Records, 1898).

It is usual to define a continuum which runs from developed countries down through less-developed and underdeveloped in the developing class and to undeveloped at the lowest possible level. A typical basis for characterization is that given by Scafeti (1969) in terms of: 1) *per capita* income, 2) percentage of labor force in agriculture, 3) per output energy consumption, 4) literacy rate, 5) productivity, and 6) general consumption.

It is highly unlikely that such a place as an 'undeveloped country' could be found, but it is not uncommon to find areas of undeveloped land, as distinct from unused land. Development in some assumed way being connected with the process of industrialization, a place like the Sahara Desert, is, by and large, undeveloped although it is much used by groups of people such as Berbers and Tawariq (Touareg), and therefore is by no means unused.

The inadequacy of the term 'development' has been much written about, and its value-laden nature has been highlighted. This has caused people to be sensitive about the concept and its effects, and to redefine the term to exclude the apparently embarrassing bits. So development becomes identified almost wholly with economics or technology. But no matter how the coy academic redefines the term to placate his own susceptibilities, the old development and its effects go on, because the people operating this development perceive it *à l'Occident* as being what must be aspired to.

The occidentalizing dynamic of development and development policies to date must therefore be stated. Any theory of development seems to imply acculturation as long as the development involved is international or intercultural. If it were possible to have an *intra*cultural theory of development then it would presumably be possible to eliminate acculturation as far as that involves alien cultures; this need not necessarily be a good or desirable thing, as cross-cultural stimuli often produce highly desirable results. But, let it be said, it is not the effect of some such benevolent cross-cultural fertilization that cause concern. It is the cultural depradations and freebooting of occidentalism which have aroused this concern; for no matter how one might conceive of development, it is the changes which it produces in societies that upset people. Lucien Pye (Pye *et al.,* 1966) gave a definition of development as being a multidimensional process of social change, which in fact sums up the problem. It is not enough simply to install a water-desalination plant in Saudi Arabia. One must also deal with many associated problems: finding the manpower fitted to operate it; dealing with the disruption of local economies and habitats unused to abundant water; handling the problem of salt disposal; and so on, down to coping with the changes wrought in the educational system.

As a sort of short-hand definition, Pye's is very useful; indeed we would use it as the synopsis of our own definition of development. We feel that development is a strategic compound of private and collective actions, with their intended and unintended consequences, through which a society moves from one state of organization, one system of ideas, beliefs and traditions, and one stock of equipment, to another. In this definition we have attempted to show that development is far from a simple, anodyne economic process of raising living standards or increasing the rate of growth. Indeed, the economics, science and technology of the process are only parts of the 'state of organization', 'systems of ideas, beliefs and traditions' and 'stock of equipment'; there are other parts also. To judge from the experiences of 'developing' countries, the emphasis should be that development means a definite cultural shift, and that this is sometimes an intended strategic consequence and sometimes – indeed, often – an unintended consequence of some superficially attractive scheme embarked upon lightly, from the point of view of culture.

Conspicuous Technology   One of the more public effects of having an occidentalized elite taking the political decisions involved in science policy, and indeed in having occidentalized scientists and technologists who are themselves willing to participate in such schemes even if they are not actually rooting for their adoption, is conspicuous technology. This is a sort of international 'keeping up with the Joneses' or 'gamesmanship'. It clearly illustrates the problem of who is taking what decisions about science policy, and whether they are really appropriate for the domestic needs of the country. A clear example, in our opinion, of such profligacy is the Indian aerospace program or the atomic energy schemes of many countries. The Indian atomic energy scheme also has the element of conspicuous technology taken to an extreme with its development of an atomic bomb. India's neighbors can only see this move as aggressive and expansionist; thus it can lead to the destabilization of the area of South Asia and add a further element to the already destabilized Southeast Asian and Middle Eastern spheres, with the consequent arms race that this produces. And yet few of these countries have sufficient domestic resources to keep up their current occidentalized development programs without competitive, escalating arms programs being added to the bill. Parallels to this can be found all over the globe (See for example Herrera, 1972; Blackledge, 1972); it is a major problem of developing countries that they embark upon such prestige projects to the neglect of more necessary but less prestigious ones. 'The fault . . . lies not in our stars but in ourselves that we are underlings' (Shakespeare, 1598). The real problem would appear to be not so much inappropriate development programs as inappropriate decision makers.

What is the role of science policy in development? The function of science policy within a developing country is to provide a systematic analysis of its actual domestic development needs. Government and other political institutions within the country then use the criteria provided by this analysis in their effort to allocate the proper resources, scientific knowledge and personnel to these development needs. In this case, what is the necessary sort of development? We have expanded on this below, but in brief it is not a cultural happening, implied or otherwise, but a strategy or strategies to enable the country to use its natural resources to its own best advantage; to improve its trading position in relation to those markets most likely to suit its requirements; to improve the quality of life for its citizens; to improve the governance and economy of the interior; to facilitate effective government of the frontier areas; to improve communications both physical and political; to improve the defense capability; and so on. Native science and technology and their attendant personnel must service these needs, not those of some external reference point, and not in the spirit of international class consciousness or social deprivation (c.f. Rahman, 1972, on the attitudes of the Indian scientific community, which have their widespread analogies around the world, e.g. Sagasti, 1975; Chowdhury, 1973; Zahlan, 1969). As with science and technology so too with education, industrial training programs, communications, defense technology, the production and training of government servants. These and other fields should not be occidentalized but domesticated.

Of course, a factor which figures largely in the process of domestication is the self-confidence of the society. If the society lacks confidence in its own cultural sufficiency, then it will be prepared to allow itself to be changed by the new technology. Lack of self-confidence also leads to a lack of selectivity in importing technologies and an unwillingness to adopt and modify them to meet local needs. This, of course, increases the likelihood of cultural erosion. The subversion of culture is not a necessary outcome of importing technologies, provided the society in question has an awareness of the value systems inherent in the technologies and self-confidence in its own cultural sufficiency; provided it displays selectivity and scrutiny in its imports and in their adaptation and modification; provided it comes to an internal agreement that undesirable changes in the society shall not take place; and provided it monitors the impact of the imports and abandons them if they prove corrosive.

It is not desirable to have an antitechnology movement as a reaction to the disruptiveness of occidentalism. The social damage in many developing countries, it seems to us, is not altogether a product of the event of colonialism but also of a general lack of self-confidence within the traditional societies in the developing countries. This lack of self-confidence has produced the feeling that something else is better; this is an underlying factor even if it is not expressed or admitted. Rahman (1972) observed this phenomenon in the behavior of the Indian scientific community toward British scientific happenings. Perhaps the most coherent statement of technology policy in developing countries is Sagasti's list (1975, 5-9) of seven principles upon which the 'development of sound and coherent technology policies should be based'. Although writing about Latin America and technology policy, his comments are consistent with our own normative position and are equally applicable to science policy in the developing world as a whole:

> On the basis of the knowledge and experience accumulated to date, it is possible to identify several principles on which the development of sound and coherent tech-

nology policies should be based. These principles represent the 'minimum common denominator' on which we have to agree if the subject of technology policy is to be treated seriously.

1. Technological progress, defined as the continuous and cumulative process of creation, diffusion, and utilization of knowledge, is one of the most important factors in the socio-economic development of Latin America. In order to overcome the situation of underdevelopment, Latin American countries must counteract the negative effects of the technological domination exercised by the industrialized nations and their large enterprises. . . . Simultaneously attending to the creation of an indigenous technological capacity, the regulation of the process of importation of foreign technology, and by promoting the demand for local technology..

2. The importance acquired by science and technology in the development process makes it necessary to establish an explicit and coherent technology policy, differentiated from scientific, economic, labour, educational, and industrial policies, although closely related to them. *The technology policy must be subordinated to economic and social development: technological progress cannot be considered an end by itself, but a means towards attaining broader objectives.* . . . (our emphasis).

3. The formulation and implementation of technology policy must have a solid national basis and even more limited geographical basis whenever the territorial extension and diversity require it. Government intervention at the national level is essential and constitutes a pre-requisite for international cooperation in the field. 'Market forces' are not enough to promote by themselves technological development and to insure its correspondence with socio-economic objectives. Government action at the national level and that of regional and international bodies, should be directed towards regulating the importation of technology and reinforcing the bargaining power of technology buyers, promoting interconnections between indigenous technological activities and productive process, stimulating technological research oriented towards socio-economic needs, and fostering the development of a technological capacity in the productive sector.

4. Policies for technological development cannot ignore the world context within which the economies of Latin American countries operate. Given that Latin America imports almost all of its technology from industrialized countries, it becomes imperative to obtain the best possible advantages from technology suppliers by strengthening the bargaining power of buyers, by establishing government controls, and by developing the capacity to identify, select and incorporate technology, without stopping the flow of imported technology. In consequence, the development of an indigenous technological capacity must be guided by a strategy of *selective interdependence,* choosing research fields according to the possibility and convenience of importing technology, the local comparative advantages, the specific needs of the country and the possibility of exporting the technology which might be produced. At the subregional level, this could be complemented by a common strategy for the definition of priority areas, and by a greater interconnection and interdependence of the national systems for the production of technology.

5. When formulating and implementing technology policy it is necessary to act simultaneously over the demand and supply of technology. The traditional viewpoint of science policy, which limits itself to encouraging the generation of knowledge without exploring its possible link with productive activities and development needs, must be overcome. When acting upon the demand for technical knowledge new interlocutors appear for defining and putting into practice a technology policy. These include, for example, ministries of industry, economics, agriculture and mining, industrial credit organisations, business chambers, professional associations and other similar institutions. All of this implies the need to establish a new network of institutional interconnections, clearly differentiated from the organizational struc-

tures for the traditional science policy, which was supported mainly by research centres and educational entities.

6. A technological development policy should take into account the characteristics of the different productive sectors and branches. It is not advisable to establish a 'horizontal' policy common to all of them. On the contrary, it is necessary to design a set of flexible policies according to the types of technology involved, the need for technological activities, the distortions introduced by the ownership structures, the number and size of enterprises, and the characteristics of the technology market. This would lead to a set of 'vertical' policies differentiated according to the branches and sectors of production.

7. Due to the recent origin of the concept of technology policy, and to the changing pace of external and internal factors which condition it, such policy must be kept flexible and should be implemented gradually. It must have a certain degree of independence, so that it will not be unduly affected by changes in other policies. However, it is also necessary to maintain close coordination and linkage with other development policies in order to avoid developing an isolated technology policy that would be rendered useless. Success in this field will depend to a large extent on the manner in which this dilemma between independence and coordination is resolved. . . .

Taking the principles outlined in the preceding section as a base, four main lines of action can be defined for the formulation and implementation of a technology policy: fostering the demand for local technology, increasing the technology absorption capacity, regulating the process of importation of technology, and developing the production of technology.

Action in these four fields must take place simultaneously, interrelating the phases encompassed by each and looking for complementarities.

It should therefore become an axiom that cultural strength must be a factor in a strategy for development. This should be a general rule and not restricted to science policy. Developed countries should view the strengthening of indigenous cultures as a desirable rather than a suspicious phenomenon, for selectivity will produce a more dynamic yet stable country which will be to the long-term — and, of course, short-term — benefit of all.

HISTORICAL PERSPECTIVE

Planning for development: the conventional views   With the exception of oil-rich countries, the developing countries combine a plentiful supply of labor with a serious lack of capital, both plant and available loanable funds. To increase the output of the economy it is necessary to increase the stock of capital; this seems more reasonable than an increase in the already over-abundant labor force. Treating capital as a limiting factor and observing that in general the more capital the greater the level of output, growth in that output is often considered to be dependent on the speed with which new capital is accumulated and upon the ratio of capital to output — that is, the value of capital required for a given annual value of output. We will illustrate this with a numerical example. Suppose that the level of output last year was 100%, and that the capital output ratio remains constant at 3 to 1, and that investment this year constitutes 15%. Clearly, output will be increased by 5% as a result of an increase to the capital stock of 15%.

The theoretical background is from a Harrod-Domar-Lewis-Rostow doctrine of development in which the main driving force is capital accumulation, and the principal problem is raising the proportion of savings in national income (Rostow, 1963; Jolly, 1971). Harrod-Domar's model assumes a 'cumulative self-sustaining growth' if an economy can show a rate of investment of ten to twelve per cent, with a capital output ratio of three to one and a rate of population growth of two per cent per annum. To set an economy along the path of self-sustaining development, Rostow's 'take-off' concept required the fulfillment of the following three related conditions:

1. A rise in the rate of productive investment from, say, five per cent or less to over ten per cent of national income.

2. The development of one or more substantial manufacturing sectors, with a high rate of growth.

3. The existence or quick emergence of a political, social and institutional framework which exploits expansion in the modern sector and the potential external economy effects of the take-off ratio, and thus gives growth (Rostow, 1963).

Most developing countries cannot raise their domestic savings ratios to ten per cent of the national income and are forced to embark upon their development programs with investment levels which fall considerably short of the target. Their first problem is finding pathways for increasing the funds so badly needed for development. Resources for investment come from public and private earnings and from foreign sources. We shall now examine the sources of savings in some detail.

Internal sources of income   In Europe, the Industrial Revolution was financed by private savings. One can thus legitimately assume this source to be of primary importance for development in the Third World. However, the volume of savings needed for industrial development is so vast that in countries with minute income levels this is rarely possible.

The private savings in Europe came from various investments, but generally the system was that British commercial and banking interests invested huge amounts of loanable funds in European and North American enterprises. The British funds came from profits of its own industrial revolution and expansion, which in turn were made possible by the incredibly large profits made from slaves in the Great Trade Triangle. Such vast sums of money were available that the only comparable source of loanable funds today is the oil-rich OPEC Consortium.

Without such funds, the problem of the availability of capital is solved by persuading people to hold their savings in financial forms, such as bank deposits, rather than in unproductive assets such as precious metals and jewelry. Thus branch banking is encouraged and attempts are made to hold inflation in check to ensure that holding bank deposits does not yield negative returns. In this way attempts are made to channel private savings, through the financial system, into productive investment (Fry, 1971).

The other internal source is public savings. This is the difference between revenues raised (from taxation, operations of nationalized industry, etc.) and current public expenditure. There are only two ways of increasing these savings: higher taxation (including corporation taxation on private companies) or increased profits from nationalized industry. Considerable work has been done on preparing new tax structures for developing countries; particular attention has been focused on strategies for taxing land, as land is the chief asset of developing countries. But the populace, usually already burdened by severe taxation, does not welcome such measures and governments are invariable reluctant to introduce them.

Nationalized industries usually run with severe losses (partly because of general inefficiency, both of management and labor, and partly because of political pressures and governmental interference) which force them to maintain levels of prices at which costs only can be recovered and a labor force much larger than the optimum can be employed. Such controls are imposed to meet the objective of full employment without inflation, and in reponse to union pressure.

With internal sources of savings severely stretched, the developing countries, it is said, find themselves inevitably having to turn to foreign aid.

Foreign aid The concept of foreign aid emerged as the European Recovery Program or Marshall Plan, which was designed to help Europe to recover from the damage and destruction the area suffered during World War II. Under the Marshall Plan, each participating country was required to prepare comprehensive four-year and annual plans embracing its resources and the utilization of these resources; these plans then became the basis for government policy and action. During the Marshall Plan period, the United States actively provided aid and supported the formulation of plans in the countries of Western Europe (Waterston, 1966).

Even in the years of the Marshall Plan, the tendency for powerful aid-donor countries to use their position in order to effect changes in the governmental policies of the aid receiver was evident. Britain, which exercised the United Nations Mandate over Palestine, was required to allow an immediate influx of some one hundred thousand European Jews and an increase in the immigration quota. The initial refusal of the British Foreign Secretary, Ernest Bevin, on the grounds that it was likely to produce intercommunal strife in the Mandated territory, was met in effect by the challenge, 'no increase, no Marshall Aid'. He backed down on the grounds that he had to choose between the risk of a possible intercommunal strife in the Mandated

Territory against certain starvation in Britain.

In January 1949, Point Four of President Truman's message to the Congress also proposed aid to the developing countries. Truman thus laid the foundation of a new political, economic and ideological movement which promised a 'revolution of rising expectation' and high hopes were pinned on foreign aid. In the early 1950's economists argued that limited aid over a decade or two would ensure the self-sustaining economic development of the recipient, and thus remove the need for external assistance. This hope was based on the experiences gained from the Marshall Plan. However, the analogy between the aid to Western European countries and the developing countries is a false one. In the case of Western Europe, war-damaged economies had to be restored, while those of the developing countries had to be developed. Western Europe had the expertise and institutions required for recovery from World War II, and the ending of the Marshall Plan after four years contrasts sharply with the never-ending aid plans for the developing countries.

Help to developing countries is given in two general forms: in terms of 'experts' in their capacities as teachers and consultants, and in terms of economic loans. Both of these means of giving aid are frequently used by the aid donors as a means of furthering their global strategies, somewhat along the lines of the choice given to the citizens of Melos as described by Thucydides. Among the 'technicians' sent by the Soviet Union to Chile, Egypt, Turkey and other countries to advise on domestic projects were large numbers of officers active in the KGB and the GRU; the subsequent carrying out of projects in these countries brought noticeable increases in domestic subversion and in subversion in neighboring countries. A similar phenomenon was noted with regard to the Chinese technicians working on the TanZam Railway. The activities of the American CIA are well known in this matter (Moss, 1973-74; Copeland, 1969). In the guise of consultants, experts may, for example, carry out feasibility or preinvestment studies, help to set up laboratories or institutes, take part in surveys of natural resources, advise on programs of work, or introduce new lines of work (the last two cases are little different from the normal activities of a visiting scientist).

To carry out any or all of these activities an expert must exhibit talents considerably wider than the area of his particular expertise. He should have a thorough appreciation of the local cultural values and norms and a knowledge of the resources — human, intellectual, technical, informational, organizational and management — available to him. In a great many cases the consultant is unable to overcome his *déformation professionnelle*. This inability is crucial, because it prevents him from thinking other than as a narrowly trained specialist, that is to say, in terms of occidental values.

Foreign economic aid operates on an even more destructive level. Leaving aside possible political motivation and the consequential use of aid as a lever, the fact is that loans are often tied to imports from the source, thus reducing the development usefulness of the loans. An example of the unfairness that can creep into the system is the barter arrangements which are common between Third World aid receivers and Comecon aid donors. To take a case in point, the Egyptian Arab Republic (then called the United Arab Republic) part-paid the Soviet Union for military equipment in oranges. The Soviet Union resold these oranges for hard foreign currency, thereby gaining financially and strategically (Allen and Smethurst, 1965). In addition to the import-from-the-source string, high shipping charges from certain lenders make the whole exercise futile.

In this form economic aid was poured into the developing countries during the 1950's and 1960's. In 1970 the total burden of indebtedness of the developing countries had soared to sixty six billion US dollars. Consequently, the ratio of debt service payments to foreign exchange earnings reached as high as twenty two per cent in the case of India and Pakistan, and thirty five per cent in the case of Chile. Of the fourteen billion US dollars transferred to developing countries in 1970, no less than 5.9 billion was absorbed by debt servicing. Brazil's debt-servicing payment in 1969 *exceeded* the total assistance flow in the same year by one hundred thirty seven billion dollars, giving rise to the question: *Who is aiding whom?* The total debts of developing countries now stand at about $130,000,000,000 (*New Internationalist*, 1976).

Then there is the problem of trade. To sustain their development efforts, the developing countries need access to the world market; the developed world, however, has not really yet given fair opportunities for trade to the developing countries, and particularly not to the less-developed countries. The rich world appears to pursue a policy of protection against the manufactured goods and even against the agricultural products of developing countries. Consequently, the developing countries' share in world trade has been continuously declining: from thirty per cent in 1950 to 21.3 per cent in 1960 and to 17.3 per cent in 1970. Prices of primary products are falling, resulting in huge losses in export earnings to the less developed countries. Little interest is taken in international schemes for price-support and commodity agreements. In 1968 eleven developed market economy countries extended public subsidies to their agriculture to the tune of fourteen billion US dollars — an amount equivalent to one per cent of their GNP, and more than the total foreign aid that was given to all the developing countries in that year. Over and above this, the growth of trade of the less-developed countries is hampered by quantitative market manipulation.

The above analysis shows not only that injustice and bias are built into the system, but that they are The System. As such, no amount of aid will transform poor countries into highly developed ones. But more than this, aid sets up a whole range and variety of damaging repercussions (See Bauer, 1974).

Foreign loans   An alternative to foreign aid is foreign loans. Indeed, for most practical purposes they are the only alternative. Foreign loans can be obtained by a developing country in one of two ways. It can borrow direct from a country such as Britain, France or the United States. In the cases of Britain and France, such lending is usually to the members of their common-wealths and is given to them on more favorable terms than it would be to nonmembers. The developing country can also borrow from some inter-national finance organization. This could either be a bank or bank con-sortium, or an agency for a particular country (the 'Gnomes of Zurich'), or, more usually, one of the international agencies. There are a number of such agencies; perhaps the most recent is the Islamic Development Bank. The most well-known of such agencies are the International Bank for Reconstruction and Development (the 'World Bank'), the International Monetary Fund (IMF), and the International Finance Corporation (IFC). The essential dif-ference that used to exist between the IMF and the IFC was that the loans of the latter were much cheaper than those of the former (cheaper in terms of interest payments). Projects were put up to the IFC, whose body of experts examined and assessed the proposals. Money was advanced on the basis of viability of the project as assessed. Perhaps such activities could be extended into the realm of cooperative ventures as we suggested above.

However, foreign loans, from whatever source they are obtained, have inherent problems for developing countries:

1. The mounting burden of debt servicing not infrequently culminates in moratoria and severe curtailments of domestic programs.

2. Repayments of loans are often insisted upon in international hard currencies and not in the currency of the borrowing country, or in gold. The effect of this is:

3. Foreign exchange earnings are diverted abroad to debt servicing and loan repayment instead of to domestic investments. Furthermore, there is the attendant depletion of the country's gold reserves. When (or if) the loan is reduced to manageable proportions, there is a further diversion of funds away from investment to rebuild reserve balances.

4. Even 'cheap loans' are often too expensive for developing countries to carry without a struggle.

The result of such a burden not uncommonly is a failure on the part of the government to satisfy the expectations of the electorate or whoever put the government in power — often the joint chiefs of the defense staff. This failure often leads to its replacement by another government. The process inevitably continues, and the only result accruing to the developing country is a certain destabilization of the political system. Stability may return with a regime prepared to go to a Superpower for the desired goodies and become a satellite, a Faust, a latter-day colony.

There have been various efforts to overcome these problems, not least among them a liberalizing of aid-loan policies of the developed countries and of the international financial agencies. Certain innovations, such as Special Drawing Rights, have been introduced to allow countries to pay for things in their own currencies. Conferences have also been held, but more fruitful things have come from the peripatetics of the international bankers. It is quite probable that the changing attitudes stem in large part from the Pearson Report.

Pearson's Report In the closing years of the 1960's, declining foreign aid appropriations indicated a crisis of confidence in the capability of the developing countries to overcome the massive problems confronting them. Responding to the crisis, the World Bank formed a commission to undertake a study of the results of over twenty years of aid, and on the basis of this study to offer proposals for the future.

The commission was headed by the Rt. Hon. Lester B. Pearson, a former Prime Minister of Canada, and the Pearson Report (Pearson, 1969) is considered by many to be a turning point in the relations between the rich and the poor nations. The key concept to emerge from the report was that of partnership: the motives and purpose of aid policies in the past had been many and varied, Pearson stated, but now the primary objective should be the promotion of economic development in cooperative relationships between the rich and the poor. Pearson asserted that increases in foreign aid should be clearly aimed at helping the developing countries to reach a path of self-sustained growth at reasonable levels. The reasonable level of growth in 1970 was considered by the commission to be at least six per cent. This growth rate should raise the rate of capital formation of the developing countries. Combined with adequate attention to the promotion of exports, it should lead the developing countries by the end of the century to take their place as self-reliant partners in the international economy and to finance the investments and imports they need for continued rapid growth without foreign capital on concessional terms.

In addition to introducing the concept of 'partnership' the Pearson Report made many other recommendations. We will outline some of these recommendations which, when considered as a coordinated whole, form a strategy for the strengthening of international cooperation for development.

The commission urged the developing countries to become more outward-looking and competitive in the world trade market. It noted that excessive extensions of export credits to developing countries have in some cases given rise to acute debt crises. The prevention of these crises must primarily be the task of the developing countries themselves, but some restraint on the part of the creditor governments is called for. The commission proposed the development of an 'early warning system' and suggested that several debt rearrangements would be necessary. When such arrangements are required, they should seek to restore a framework for orderly development finance and try to avoid the need for repeated reschedulings. Debt relief should be recognized as a legitimate form of aid. If future debt crises are to be forestalled, sound financial policies must be pursued and the terms of aid must be within the borders of morality.

The tying of aid to purchases in donor countries imposes both direct and indirect costs on aid receivers and distorts the channels of world trade. The commission noted that balance-of-payments problems had been the principal reason for tying policies, and the creation of the new Special Drawing Rights (SDR's) in the International Monetary Fund (IMF) may provide an opportunity for a joint attack on the tying problem.

Food aid represents a special case of tying. Prospects are that an increasing number of developing countries will become independent of food grain imports or become exporters. Gradually, food aid should be subsumed under general aid programs so as to permit recipients to choose aid-financed imports without distortion to their own or to the donor's economy.

Among other things the Pearson Report noted that despite the growth of technical assistance (ten per cent per annum in the 1960's), it failed to adapt to the requirements of the developing countries and it had not been integrated with capital assistance. Similarly, educational help to developing countries only served to buttress traditional methods of teachings, and attempts to search for new methods and for a new education conceived by and for developing countries have been too rare. The Commission also expressed concern for the rapid population growth in the developing countries. It recommended that countries which have not yet recognized the dimensions of their population problems should take cognizance of its impact on their development efforts and take appropriate action.

Although it displays no overt recognition of the undermining of cultures by science and technology, the really important contribution of the Pearson Report is its understanding that development is a value-laden concept. In sum, it tended to recommend more of the traditional remedies but did stress the need for reemphasis and the imbalance in the system. Pearson's idea of 'partnership' was, perhaps, too far ahead in 1969; but today, in the midst of an energy crisis and fast depleting natural resources, when people tend to discover that they are all dwellers on the same planet and thereby compelled to cooperate for the survival of 'Spaceship Earth', the concept of 'partnership' is much more attractive (Sardar, 1976). Perhaps the developed countries will now take Pearson's ideas to heart.

SOME ASPECTS OF DEVELOPMENT

The multidimensional process   Development, as we stated earlier, is not simply an economic process but a strategic blend of private and collective actions, with their intended and unintended consequences, through which society moves from one state of organization, one system of ideas, beliefs and traditions, and one stock of equipment, to another. We propose to consider this concept of development in relation to access to natural resources, education and training, agriculture and industrialization, the attitudes and traditions of societies, and the effects which development projects have produced in the societies of developing countries.

There are in all states areas of 'difficult country'. By and large, however, such country consists of marginal land which may not be essential to the economic well-being of the society. In developing countries such 'difficult country' may in fact occupy most of the land surface of the state and, far from being marginal, may contain valuable natural resources. The extraction of minerals, timber, etc., and the use of such 'difficult country' may well be a major headache for the government. These geographical areas and the resources they contain – fast rivers, hardwood jungle, fertile soils in forested land or great mountain ranges containing ores – may necessitate the marshalling of considerable amounts of capital, both plant and money, and may often be at once great obstacles and great assets. There might be a good market in timber of a certain type, and the country might equally have an abundant supply of it; but it could be located in such a difficult area that the cost of extracting it would be uneconomical. The possession of such a commodity might thus be no better than a lack of it.

It is very important, for any country, that there be an adequate means of extracting and transporting products, whether primary or secondary. This might seem to be stating the obvious; it is not always, however, adequately appreciated. Development requires adequate communications, for without them it is not possible to extract natural resources, or to move secondary products, or even to govern. It is not uncommon to find countries with, for example, good natural harbors becoming effectively two countries (or rather two economies), one developed or developing and the other undeveloped or developing. It is possible to have a developed urban society and an underdeveloped nonurban (not necessarily rural) society, such as in France, Italy, the USSR, and in many other countries.

Social capital   For many developing countries, the colonial inheritance is often vital in this respect. The importance of such social capital as railway networks, ports and harbor facilities, adequate factory buildings and efficient communications technology for government and development cannot be overstated. Investment in the provision of this social capital is a costly business; indeed, its maintenance alone consumes a substantial proportion of GNP. Thus, such developing countries have tended to rely upon the colonial inheritance and content themselves with patching it up, in order to divert scarce investment funds to industrialization programs and the like which are commonly accorded high priority in development plans. Some new investment has indeed taken place, mainly in the provision of better port facilities, new devices in verbal communication such as telex, and airports. The construction of airports has not infrequently verged on conspicuous technology, particularly when the airports are sited near the capital city, such as the Subang airport serving Kuala Lumpur or Yesilköy airport serving Istanbul.

However, the specific items of social capital which are relevant to development are, of course, those which have to do with the transport of raw materials to factories and the transport of manufactures away from both factory and country. Important in science policy are the institutions which train and supply personnel. Mostly these come from a colonial period, with additions in some cases. It is such institutions which draw the attentions of the decision makers, for reasons of occidentalization which we have previously outlined. The question might well be put whether these institutions adequately serve the needs of the society, or whether some changes are necessary; and whether there exists an alternative educational system which might well supply the right sort of personnel and scientific knowledge according to the developing country's principle of domesticity.

The glib assumption is that such institutions do adequately serve the needs of the society and that the society ought to lend support to science policy in order to improve this service. Where institutions such as attitudes and traditions get in the way they ought to be modified. Such an attitude is well exemplified by stating Chowdhury's (1973) enumeration of Basalla's (1967) 'seven tasks to be fulfilled for a successful transition from a dependent scientific culture to an independent one':

1. Resistance to science on the basis of philosophical and religious beliefs must be overcome and replaced by positive encouragement of scientific research.

2. The social role and place of the scientist must be determined to ensure society's approval of his labors.

3. The relationship between science and government should be clarified, so that at most science receives financial support and encouragement and at least government maintains a neutral policy in scientific matters.

4. The teaching of science should be introduced at all levels of the educational system.

5. National scientific organizations should be founded which are specifically devoted to the promotion of science.

6. Channels must be opened to facilitate national and international scientific communication.

7. A proper technology base should be made available for the growth of science.

The conclusion one can reach from these seven tasks is that, although scientific culture may be independent regarding funds and research programs, etc., it is certainly not independent epistemologically; it is still occidental and unmonitored.

We would strongly disagree with certain of these tasks, and we consider others to be simply irrelevant to the real needs of the developing countries. They take no true cognizance of the cultural base of the society; indeed, according to these specifications, when society presents an obstacle to science, it must be replaced. Now, the cultural system which supports such resistances to science and technology has a value of its own, and one should not be so arrogant as to tinker around with it lightly. The result would be to repeat in the developing world the moral and spiritual disasters of the Occident.

The traditional background   We have dwelt much throughout this chapter on the attitudes, traditions, and culture of the developing countries, and upon our view that the preservation of the integrity of these must be one of the criteria of science policy in developing countries. It is part of the outlook of the occidentalized elites that 'West is best', and that what is part of the traditional heritage of these developing countries must either be apologized for, reformed or abandoned. This attitude can only ensure a repeat of what has happened in occidental industrial societies, these same societies which today are turning to the 'Orient' to supply the absent soul to their way of life. This does not make sense.

Social values and norms, patterns, ways of thinking, are all reflections of culture. Culture forms the people. Culture makes a Malay different from a Spaniard, a Japanese different from an American. Culture itself is, in its highest sense, an elaboration of the religion of a given society. It is a means by which values are translated into the whole fabric of day-to-day living. Admixed with it are the local customs and traditions which have been passed down through the centuries; a culture is the history of a people and an expression of its beliefs. It molds the individual and controls him. Culture is the main means of the education of the child and adult; acculturation is the process by which the individual is taught by formal and informal means to accept the values and norms of the parent society. In a very real sense, then, the occidentalizer is an apostate.

The peculiar circumstances of Western Europe caused the mutation of that science which it had obtained from the Muslim world (Mendelsohn, 1973; Nasr, 1976). In the Thirteenth Century, Albertus Magnus, wearing Arab clothes, taught in Arabic at the Sorbonne the sciences of mathematics, astronomy and optics. He had learned these sciences at the University of Cordoba in Muslim Spain. Roger Bacon also studied in Muslim Spain and taught the same subjects at Oxford along with Robert Marsh and Thomas the Welshman (Hunke, 1960). This is the beginning of the story of 'modern Western science'. Why then should the Muslim world produce people who apologize away their Islam for the mutated form of what Albertus Magnus and Roger Bacon taught?

This synopsis of history indicates that there are belief systems which encourage learning and have their own traditions of science. A similar parallel might be sought in Chinese cultural history, for example. It should not be assumed that because there is a resistance to scientific development or to certain technologies that cultures are categorically resistant to change. There are three main reasons for the resistance normally found among non-occidentalized people. First of all, they are inherently conservative and have to be really convinced of the necessity for a particular change. Second, they are basically suspicious of the actions of the occidentalized elite, whom they consider to have turned their backs on non-occidental cultures. Third, they are anxious to ensure that their culture shall not be eroded or undermined. Indeed, as the subversive effects of earlier imports become widely realized, such resistance increases (Sardar, 1977).

These are all very understandable reasons, and they should be respected. One should not straightaway conclude from them that the people in question are reactionary or opposed to change, and that the needs of science policy must impose some occidental value system in order to develop. One should deduce from them that the people are anxious for their cultural survival. Thus, another substantial element in science policy in developing countries must be to assure the people that all due care is being taken to protect their traditional heritage. Assurances alone are no good. If they remain empty words, then resistance might increase and produce its latter-day Luddites. It is necessary that visible, tangible evidence emerge in order for the truth of the claim to be accepted. Most members of the culture will embrace a better quality of life as a desirable goal, but they will in all probability not accept that their culture is a fair price to pay for it.

Educational systems   Such reassurances can best be provided by government policy toward education. It is the educational system which in many countries is a source of daily concern to parents, anxious about the religion and culture of their children. By giving due weight to cultural considerations in the formulation of curricula, some measure of support may well be forthcoming.

In most developing countries it is possible to identify two educational systems which exist side by side (See, for example, Siddiqui, 1974 and 1975). There is the principal educational system, which is the one which receives the most support from the government, enjoys high status and provides the personnel for the better jobs in the country. This system is the occidental one, and it is modelled on similar systems in the Occident. Usually this means that it approximates either the British, French, German or American systems. By and large the assumptions of the educational philosophy of this system are corrosive to traditional values, as they accept the occidental norms and tend to accord the traditional values a lower status. Even where a certain historical or religious element is present in the curriculum, as in Malaysia, Egypt or Pakistan, all too often it is taught with insufficient seriousness or accorded value to the traditional culture. Such attitudes are transmitted to the stock of assumptions of the students, who are progressively socialized to further and further occidental values. It is the products of such a system who graduate to the top jobs and who go to the Occident for higher education and other forms of training.

The students of the traditional system of education, the Alternative Education System, are normally poorly provided with books, teaching aids, buildings and conditions of study. Also the caliber of teachers is frequently too low and the methods of teaching are often antiquated. The curriculum lacks imagination and does not normally include subjects such as are taught in the principal education system, for example, scientific subjects or modern foreign languages. The system tends to produce graduates who are well-equipped, despite the odds, in the traditional knowledge of the culture. However, the status accorded to them and the sort of jobs available for them are considerably inferior to that encountered by the graduates of the principal education system.

There are values and norms in the principal education system which militate against traditional cultures. This is observable even in the Occident. It would seem unlikely that this system could be reformed to take proper care of culture to serve the aim of domesticity in the developing nation. However, with more available funds and material and the opportunity to teach such things as modern languages and scientific subjects, it is quite probable that the new products of the alternative educational system would represent this principle of domesticity in science and technology personnel. There is nothing in the traditional systems of education which militates against the production of scientists and technologists of high caliber. We believe there is more to offer the developing countries in improving the curricula and teaching materials of their alternative educational systems than in giving so much unwarranted attention to the occidentalized principal educational systems.

The money cost of such a policy would be less than the frequently wasteful use of scarce funds in typical current educational investments For example, many students are sent abroad for higher education. This is not merely at the graduate level but quite commonly at the undergraduate level as well. Living in the Occident and in daily intimate contact with it produces in the student, often as a result of the socialization received during his occidentalized education 'at home', a feeling of satisfaction. He enjoys living in the West. Many students fail to return home. Others return home only for a short period, say, to serve out repayment contracts with government departments which have paid their fees while abroad, and then go back to the Occident. This is a chief cause of the 'brain drain'.

Education and training   The great magnitude of the brain drain from India, Pakistan, Egypt and Syria to the West is well known. Not all of these people, however, come to the Occident to settle or to enter employment semipermanently as expatriates. Many do come temporarily as students, both graduate and undergraduate, and in various training capacities. It can be noticed that people from different countries who come to the Occident conform to certain patterns according to their country of origin and the task they have to perform in the Occident (Rahman, 1972; Zahlan, 1969; Moravcsik, 1975). For example, there is a very high percentage of graduate medical students among Syrians and Egyptians in Britain.[1]

The caliber of the students and their attitude toward their tasks in the Occident vary. As most of them are sponsored by their governments, we might conclude that they are the best available products of the domestic educational systems. By and large this is true, but we must note certain distorting factors such as the background of an elite family (and hence unequal access to the wheels of government; Niromand, 1969), and outright bribery (Alatas, 1968; Qurashi, 1975). However, on the whole, they are the best available; this does not necessarily say much for their stock of knowledge and ability as judged by the educational standards and expectations of the host country.

Students from the Middle East and Southeast Asia seem to approximate occidental standards better than do those from South Asia (Zahlan, 1967; Nader and Zahlan, 1965; Scalopino, 1976; Geertz, 1963; Golay, 1961). However, a noticeable feature among them is a lack of that critical, analytical or downright argumentative attitude of the native occidental student, an attitude which we have come to expect as a part of the process of learning in occidental higher educational institutions.

Where training such people in the Occident is carried out by some arrangement with the mother country, for example, by secondment from a university or a research institute or in relation to a specific development project, there is a much better chance that the students will return to deploy their talents where they are most needed. Without such binding return arrangements, there is a high 'failure to return' rate, as expectations and prospects are so much better than 'at home' (Zahlan, 1969).

Anyone who has trained such students knows the problem of the 'guru attitude'. The teacher is always right, even when he may be known to be wrong. This outlook is not only opposed to scientific temper, it prevents the full development of creative talent. This is especially noticeable among the students from South and Southeast Asia. At a later stage, the Guru worshipper returns home and becomes the Master Guru. By no means do all students have this attitude, but for those who do, the difficult process of weaning must be attempted.

Another problem lies in the relevance of the training received in the Occident in relation to the sort of job which the student is to do when he returns, and in relation to the needs of his country. There are certain

---

[1] Muslim Institute files and UNESCO statistics.

considerations regarding such training. There has been much criticism of the products and course contents of the two universities in the Communist Bloc which deal with the developing countries: the Patrice Lumumba University in Moscow and the International University of Prague. There has also been criticism of the more conventional universities in the communist countries, such as Leningrad, Moscow, Karl Marx. The value of teaching and the certificates awarded is considered in many developing countries such as Nigeria, Egypt, Pakistan, to be nearly nil.

There are growing considerations about the need to send people to the Occident for higher degrees or for other training. There is speculation that the higher training might be better or more cheaply provided locally, either in the home or some nearby country, where the cultural needs of the student and his society might at least form a common ideology for the people involved, and where more attention might be paid to the real needs of the country. A natural extension of this consideration is to point out the regrettable fact that occidental degrees, and hence occidentally qualified people, enjoy higher status and obtain better job opportunities than do local ones. Examples of this abound. One could cite the higher status, but low value to the real needs of the country, of a degree in Comparative Laws ('Muhammadan Law') from the University of London (Centre for Advanced Legal Studies/SOAS). Such a degree is valued much more highly in Malaysia, the Sudan or Turkey than a comparable degree in Shari'ah Law from the University of Al Azhar in Cairo, the oldest university in the world, or from the University of the Qarawiyyin in Fez, Morocco, the second oldest university in the world. A reflection of this is even found as indicated earlier, in occidental institutions in the developing countries; thus the same difference in status holds true for a degree in Laws from Ilahiyet Fakultesi of Ankara, Istanbul Universities, the University of Malaya in Kuala Lumpur, or the University of Singapore as compared to a similar degree from Al Azhar or Qarawiyyin.

One must even ask the question whether a higher degree is really needed at all for the task to be done. Often such a high degree is not necessary for the task but is desirable in the society of a developing country for certain other things. The marriage prospects of a PhD from McGill or Cantab are better than those of a PhD from Karachi or Punjab, and any PhD fares better than a mere MA or MSc. Such fringe benefits are, of course, highly desirable to the individuals concerned, and we do not wish to obstruct any person's gateway to matrimonial bliss, but they may not really help national development. As a result of such happenings, one finds in many developing countries people who are overqualified and overtrained for the job they are actually doing. The same job could be done by less well qualified people or by the same people without the three years and thousand currency units in the Occident which it took to acquire their higher academic qualification.

Thus the PhD fetish creates quite a problem. A higher degree, especially from the West, as opposed to the Occident generally, improves the person's chances of a better job. Salary scales in developing countries involve too rigid an equation with levels of qualifications and pay expected in the Occident. This means that the best-qualified people in the developing countries earn salaries which are out of proportion to the local scales; this further enhances the disparities of wealth in the system. There is a further problem in that the unemployed graduates from the blossoming native institutions expect to find jobs and high pay, and they do not get them. Cambodia prior to Sihanouk's downfall is an excellent case study of this. Cambodia has produced a dissident, highly educated, highly articulate 'bourgeois' youth group, which has formed a recruiting ground for various extreme 'revolutionary movements', such as the Tupamaros and the like (Wilkinson, 1976; Fairbairn, 1975; Oppenheimer, 1974; Inter Doc, 1973).

Agriculture and land reform   Many experts sent from developed countries have concluded that most developing countries would achieve faster rates of growth by investing in agriculture, where there is comparative advantage, than by attempting to industrialize. This conclusion is based on the reasoning that the majority of the population in the developing countries still lives in rural areas and will continue to do so for the foreseeable future in spite of the rapid and often chaotic expansion of the urban population. With the rapid increase in overall population it is conceivable that the developing countries would not industrialize fast enough to provide work and adequate living facilities for the increase in population each year. Even if this were achieved, it would do little to reduce unemployment or even underemployment and inadequate conditions of work and housing in both town and country. In these conditions, it would be a great advantage merely to secure reasonable standards of nutrition. This immediately indicates a concentration upon agricultural development in order that the rural population may adequately feed itself as well as provide a surplus of food for the urban areas. To achieve this, new methods of agriculture would be required and this in turn would mean the provision of such things as improved types of seeds and fertilizers, and marketing facilities for the increased output.

The improvement in seeds and fertilizers has taken the form of the so-called 'Green Revolution', and great hopes have been placed on the ability of the Green Revolution to lead the underdeveloped countries toward development (Johnson, 1972).

This strategy for agricultural development entails three major problems. First, increasing productivity in agriculture has usually meant increasing the output *per person* rather than the output *per acre,* which, even when possible, is often uneconomical. Thus, increasing productivity leads to fewer persons working the same area of land. Mechanization and increasing productivity per man usually result in rural depopulation and mass migrations to towns. This happens because fewer people are needed to work the same area of land, and because the land holdings are concentrated to provide larger areas which optimize the use of machinery. More land can be worked with the same amount of machinery, and thus largely the same labor force; this releases further people from the land, and they inevitably drift to the towns looking for work. Such a phenomenon is analogous to the Enclosures of the British Agricultural Revolution (Mingay, 1967). It is an inevitable result of land reform policies, whoever carries them out: a worse result came from the enforced collectivization program followed by Lenin in the Red River Delta in North Vietnam. If jobs are not increasing fast enough in towns, unemployment is created by such strategies. This is counterproductive.

Secondly, for some time world prices of primary products have been decreasing relative to those of manufactured goods. As development along this path will have to aim at increasing export to pay for the imported capital and manufactured goods, the going is uphill. However, as we noted earlier, the position of primary products on the world market is very likely to improve.

Finally, it has almost become a cliche to remind others that agriculture is not only an 'economic activity' but just as much a 'way of social existence'. Agricultural development means introducing new techniques to the villagers and persuading them that it is to their own 'advantage' to use them. Basically, this is asking them to change their life styles and usually their culture as well (See Rao, 1975).

In many cases the Green Revolution increased output per acre and often with unforeseen disastrous side effects (Milton, 1973). However, this is not the main limitation of the Green Revolution. This agricultural revolution cannot be isolated from its general context; it is based on the assumptions and experience of European agrarian reforms, particularly in Britain, which were followed by the Industrial Revolution. But it is taking place in areas of the globe which do not occupy a dominant position in the world economic system. It is, therefore, absurd to reason in analogous terms and to suppose that the present-day Green Revolution in the developing countries can yield the same results as those achieved by the agricultural revolution in Britain, except in parallel terms of human misery. Herein lies the limitation of the Green Revolution.

The limitation of the Green Revolution, that is, of the development of middle-sized farms employing capital-intensive processes, is consequently inherent in the principal contradiction of the system. The domination of the Occident over the developing world makes it impossible to follow the path of the British agricultural revolution.

Among the few countries that have managed to achieve rapid and sustained agricultural development, Mexico is the most oft-quoted example. Venezian and Gamble (1969), for example, give a detailed account of the Mexican success story. The principal factors responsible for the growth of agricultural output in Mexico have been the expansion of cultivated land areas and increase in yields which, in turn, can be traced to large-scale public investments in irrigation work and the adoption by farmers of improved agricultural practices, mainly high-yield seeds and fertilizers. Mechanization and technical improvements have played a less important role in agricultural growth, but improvements in transportation and communication have played a substantial part. However, there is only one catch in the agricultural growth of Mexico:

> The fact is that after so many years of revolution and reform, made by and for the peasants primarily . . . and of sustained government action to promote agriculture, those who have benefited the least are precisely a majority of the farm population. This is becoming a crucial issue in Mexican development today. Repeatedly, there is discontent and unrest in many rural areas where living conditions have remained strikingly low, in spite of the advances achieved on the average (Venezian and Gamble, 1969, 192).

In fact, a basic characteristic of Mexican agriculture has been that after an initial period of intensive land and resource distribution up to 1940, a renewed process of economic concentration has taken place despite the land reform policies. This, while contributing to overall growth rates, has favored mainly the progress of a special band of entrepreneurs at the expense of the majority of the rural population.

Although agricultural growth rates vary from country to country, the results are often similar. It should be pointed out, however, that schemes of land reform to increase agricultural production rarely, if ever, have benefited the agricultural laborer, or even the smallholding farmer. They of necessity involve his dispossession in some way, and should not be viewed as being designed to aid the peasantry or yeoman. The cost in terms of human misery, which is a feature of land reform, is too high to bear in a democratic, open society. Hence, agricultural development programs invariable fail to achieve the ultimate goal, as they are inhibited by the ethical climate from going all out towards it. Land reform can be stated simply as reducing the number of agricultural units by increasing their size to make the use of machinery a viable proposition. This inevitably leads to dispossession and unemployment among the rural population. 'Land to the peasants' movements invariably have disastrous consequences for agricultural production and lead to shortages and starvation in the country as well as in the towns (Moss *et al.*, 1973-74).

Industrialization and manpower problems Such problems are not so great for industrialization. The labor force is composed of town dwellers, many of whom will have moved from the villages and so have already become uprooted and accustomed to change of some sort. Nevertheless, one of the most serious problems of industrialization involves the labor force. Working in industry requires a sense of time which is quite different from that required in agricultural work. Time-keeping and absenteeism are often critical problems in the developing countries for this reason.

Management creates another problem as there is no readily available body of managers to run the factories being built. Academic training, as noted earlier, does not help much, especially in interpersonal relationships in work and home environments, and without these relationships it is difficult to imbue the required entrepreneurial outlook.

Management in developing countries depends, therefore, to a great extent on expatriates. Some are settled (a colonial legacy), but many are recent arrivals, who are there by invitation because of their technological skill. At different hierarchical levels one large organization may have British, Americans, Germans, Russians, Indians and representatives of different national tribes. Though English is often the national language, these people do not find it easy to communicate with one another, to the detriment of efficiency. Instinctively there is a mistrust of other nationalities and the use of a home language to discuss difficulties in front of expatriates is quite common.

There is an unexpectedly large variety of resources available to the developing countries to assist in the development of managers, but these resources are ineffectively used. In view of past experience, it seems that plans to assist the process by which individuals become managers and the process by which they manage successfully would be more valuable than projects which provide only additional resources. Shone (1975) points out that four kinds of 'process aid' could be useful: 1) to overcome obstacles to efficient operation of management development; 2) to make these processes shorter or easier; 3) to help out particularly difficult stages of the process; and 4) to improve the efficiency of the use of existing resources. Of course, the priorities will depend very much on the local situation.

Management aside, the production problems of industrialization are immense. The machinery, spare parts and sometimes even the raw materials have to be imported. If the problems of production are solved, then a market for the product has to be created. This is a decisive factor. The success or failure of industrialization depends on whether or not the developing countries can sell their manufactures. In the end, the developing country is unable to compete against the developed countries which already have well-established markets. It must therefore find alternative markets; these can be either at home or in other developing countries.

There are two distinct types of industrialization programs operating in the developing world. One is designed to substitute domestically produced commodities for imported manufactured goods, while the other concentrates on products for export. The import substitution strategy suffers from the defect that protection from foreign competition has to be provided for the industries which are established. Even if the developed countries accept that the developing country has a point in seeking to protect its nascent industries, and even if they do not reciprocate with a protectionism of their own against other products of the developing country, such products are not likely to be those in which the country has a comparative advantage. However, foreign exchange can be saved. This latter point is not always realized, as witnessed by the establishment of iron and steel plants in India (Khan, 1970). There the indirect foreign exchange cost of producing a ton of steel, in the form of expenditure on plant, certain raw materials, etc., turned out to be greater than the direct foreign exchange cost of importing the finished product. At the same time there were domestic resources used in this production which could otherwise have been used elsewhere. It must always be conceded in such a situation that the country may have a strategic interest in the establishment of such industries.

Concentrating on industries for export earnings might appear to be the best long-term strategy, but in the short run this can lead to serious balance of payments problems. Machinery must be imported and paid for long before receipts start to flow in from these exports. Quality control and marketing are the two critical factors for successful exporting and few developing countries are proficient in either.

Two suggestions might be made to counter these disadvantages. Long-term credit arrangements should be made by international funders to allow the country to carry the cost of capital investment programs. Even better, instead of credit being extended, cooperative ventures could be entered into by banking consortia and the country at low interest, preferably at zero rate but with profit sharing. Secondly, the developing country might establish agency arrangements with some competent marketing firm to take care of its products. Quality control can only really be overcome by having the right personnel: these must either be native, or accepting a transitionary period, expatriate.

Over the past few years, there has been a steady decline in the agricultural population of the developing countries. This has been accompanied by expanding production, which indicates significant increases in labor productivity. Current distributions of the labor force between sectors in developing countries are estimated at: agriculture, 42-57 per cent; industry, 12-19 per cent, tertiary 21-32 per cent. In the most advanced industrial states this distribution was recently estimated at 315 per cent, 33-46 per cent and 48-61 per cent respectively (Lengelle, 1972). Increased productivity in agriculture is linked to development in other sectors. The decline in agricultural population has in fact been accompanied by a substitution of other things for labor. Evidence of this can be found in the international statistics for purchases of fertilizers, tractors and other industrial inputs.

SOME RECENT TRENDS

New theories of underdevelopment   The propagators of the thesis that the social function of science in the Occident as described by Bernal (1970) is quite different from that in developing countries (Furtado, 1964; Subrahmaniam, 1972; Herrera, 1972; Cervantes, 1970; Sunkel and Paz, 1970) consider underdevelopment to be a historically unique form of economic organization. This form cannot be identified in the early period of development in the Occident because it is a product of interaction between 'precapitalistic economic forms' and 'industrial capitalism' itself. The unique economic organization of underdevelopment calls for autonomous theories and the social function of science in the developing countries. These theories are broadly classified as theories of the 'marginalization of science' (Cooper, 1973; Furtado, 1964) and have emerged mainly from Latin America. Basically they rely on Latin American experience with underdevelopment to show how the underdeveloped economy alienates local scientific institutions from production. These arguments for the theory of dependency have arisen mainly because Latin American social scientists found existing theories inadequate for explaining their circumstances.

International trade theory, with its emphasis on mutually advantageous relationships involved in international specialization, failed to explain the main disadvantages of the developing country. On the other hand, the superficially attractive theories of Marxism, even though they emphasized the exploitative nature of the relationship between the developed and the developing countries, nevertheless had as their bases the dynamics of occidental capitalism and communist imperialism, and not the fragmented, capitalistic, aid-dependent development of the developing countries. A new theory was therefore needed to explain underdevelopment. Not surprisingly, such a theory soon postulated the world economy as a system with Latin America as a subsystem.

For a vast proportion of writers, the theory of dependency is a substitute for analysis. Most works on dependency give a descriptive catalog of various aspects of the relationship between the Occident and Latin America. Cervantes (1970), for example, lists six different types of dependence: technological, economic, financial, cultural, structural and politico-military. He gives a brief description of each type (e.g. cultural dependency is the result of Latin Americans studying comics, books, magazines, watching films and TV programs, all of which were produced in the Occident and distributed and broadcast in Latin America); he attributes the various facts of dependency to the basic one of backward dependent capitalism; he assumes that the last is the cause of underdevelopment; and he concludes facilely that the only solution is a socialist revolution. Naive analyses such as this abound in works on dependency.

Some authors do, however, suggest a necessity for a historical, global, structural and total approach. Sunkel and Paz (1970) make a more thorough analysis and come to the conclusion that the laws of motion of underdeveloped countries are a reflection of the laws of motion of the developed countries. This type of analysis is particularly strong in the works of Cardoso (1971), who is probably the most original and stimulating thinker on dependency.

Technology transfer   One of the major components of the dependency argument concerns the concept of technology transfer by which technology is imported from a nation of the Occident to a developing country. This transfer of technology usually takes place directly to a firm in a developing country or indirectly through the subsidiaries of multinational corporations. The technology is introduced either as direct investment, capital goods export or through the licensing of potential technical knowledge to local firms.

The technology sold to the developing countries almost always tends to support the interests of capital and technology suppliers, whether private firms or governments. Furthermore, as transferred technologies are seldom adaptive to the local conditions of the developing countries, they contribute either feebly to development or hinder true progress (Sutton, 1972).

Dickson's analysis (1974) avers that transfer is more than just an articulation of the economic relationships between the industrialized and the developing countries. It is also an important means by which those relationships are maintained and controlled through the constraints imposed on technological choice. Once the disguise of neutrality is stripped away, the political motivations come to the fore and we see technology as a means of social control.

The transfer of technology goes parallel with the transfer of the ideology of industrialization. A transferred technology imposes itself on the cultural patterns of the developing countries. Among others Wells (1972) demonstrated this. His study of technological choice carried out on a sample of fifty industrial plants in Indonesia (covering such industries as soft drinks, cigarettes, plastic sandals and bicycle tires) shows that often the technology selected in any one instant was not the most appropriate for the prevailing conditions of economy, production and organization.[2]

Even if one accepts technology transfer as desirable, it can never be a substitute for local research capability. There are four main reasons for this (Cooper, 1967):

1. The occidental technologies are not designed for the needs and capabilities of the developing countries.

2. The transfer of technology will not deal with: a) the collection of data on all natural resources available; b) the development of means to exploit

---

[2] To safeguard the interests of the developing countries from inappropriate technologies, the Working Party of Experts of the Pugwash Conference on Science and World Affairs has produced a 'Code of Conduct in the Field of Technology Transfer'. See the report of the International Group of Transfer of Technology, UN Trade and Development Board: TD/B/520 of 6 August 1974.

natural resources of the developing countries under their particularly unique conditions; c) the development of processing methods suitable for the particular raw materials available in the developing countries; nor d) further development of modern technologies already installed in the country.

3. In the long run, if indigenous research capabilities are not developed and too much reliance is placed on the imported technology, it will not be possible to use the resources in the developing countries to the full. If we assume that there is a similar proportionate distribution of the intellectual talents required for research work between all human populations, a long-term limitation on the development of science in the developing countries means that their populations are condemned to a level of intellectual activity well below their natural potential.

4. The effective transfer of technology from abroad, under favorable conditions of development, depends partly upon the existence of scientifically and technically qualified personnel. We have already shown that scientific establishments in the developing countries are fragmentary, disorganized, disunited, of limited professional competence and intellectualy isolated.

The Chinese model of development For their own long-term interest, developing countries are compelled to develop indigenous resources and capabilities. In doing so the developing countries might well benefit from a study of the Chinese model of development (Jones, 1971; Klatt, 1965; McFarlane, 1971; Wu and Sheeks, 1970). The Chinese science policy rests on eight assumptions (Ray, 1970): 1) growth of the agriculture sector by relying solely on its own resources; 2) economic decentralization; 3) small-scale rural industries; 4) use of rural underemployed labor; 5) nonmaterial incentives; 6) mass labor mobilization used as a means to increase productivity; 7) capital accumulation sustained at a level sufficient to support continued leaps in production for an indefinite period of time; and 8) political ideology overruling objective economics.

A model of development based on these assumptions attempts to integrate rather than to fragment social, political and economic goals in decision making about scientific and technological developments; and it makes science serve production through a complex series of linkages between industry and agriculture, rural and urban development, and manual and mental labor (Rifkin, 1975).

The 'self-reliance' model seeks to increase agricultural production by developing technologies that best utilize local material and labor resources. This ensures that the urban population is not the only recipient of profits from a peasant revolution.

To achieve these goals the Chinese have developed a dual sector economy which is said to use modern as well as intermediate, in this case traditional, technologies in the heavy industrial as well as the agrarian sectors. As a result, small and medium-sized industries have emerged throughout the nation, while the R & D sector has experienced beneficial growth, so it is claimed.

This policy of 'walking on two legs' might have advantages for a labor-rich but capital-scarce country. Among these advantages are (Rifkin, 1975):

1. Support of the expansion of the modern industrial sector by allowing traditional technologies to handle the less complex, more labor-intensive aspects of these enterprises.

2. Expansion of the agrarian sector with the aid of local industrialization to relieve agricultural bottlenecks in the development process.

3. Alleviation of the employment problem by the absorption of surplus labor into small-scale, labor-intensive enterprises.

4. Contributions to both increased production and national morale by large segments of unskilled or semiskilled population in the rural area.

The Chinese model may or may not have lessons in it, but the concept of 'self-reliance', that is, the ability to manage one's own national resources, is a safe concept for the developing countries to adopt. This is also the message of the advocates of alternative technology. The peculiarities of the Chinese system must be borne in mind, and hedged around with question marks after the failure of the Great Leap Forward.

Alternative technology   Alternative technology is not a coherent philosophy. It is a collection of a large number of ideas and concepts, many of them quite incoherent, almost as diverse as the name of the outlook: intermediate technology, appropriate technology, soft technology, humane technology, new alchemy, peoples' technology, radical hardware, biotechnic, etc. Each of these names emphasizes a different aspect of the new technology: workers' control, demystification of expertise, reform of work rules, low specialization, development under the condition of low capital, local or regional self-sufficiency, balanced economic development, resource conservation, low-energy use, reduced technological risks, and so on. While the outlooks of these alternative technology philosophies are slightly divergent, all have one common denominator: a severe criticism of the nature of modern technology.

Conventional technology is value-laden and destructive; it is capital-intensive, production-oriented and a threat to environmental safety (Dickson, 1974; Clarke, 1973; Schumacher, 1975; Fromm, 1968; North, 1976; Harper *et al.,* 1976). Among its other characteristics we may mention its dependence on centralization, its liability to misuse, its resource exploitative nature and its tendency toward dehumanization (Milton, 1972). At best, as Schumacher (1975) points out, modern technology produces 'know-how'; but know-how is nothing by itself; it is a means without an end, a mere potentiality, an unfinished sentence. In contrast, alternative technologies tend to be small-scale, labor-intensive, participatory, decentralized, understandable and controllable.

At present there are two threads of thought that knit all concepts of alternative technologies together. First, all ideas of alternative technologies reduce productivity to a second order determinant. Obviously, when the productivity is so low that it cannot even meet the bare necessities, increasing production becomes very important. But once the basic necessities are assumed, and a little surplus is produced, the problem ceases to be one of sheer quantity and the emphasis is not placed on quality of productive effort, the distribution of goods and the uses to which the products are put. As long as alternative technologies produce a small surplus, they can claim a rationality for satisfying human needs − a rationality much superior to conventional technology. Second, if production is to be relegated to a second place, modern economics, which sees consumption as the end of activity, must be replaced by an enlightened alternative. As such, alternative technologies are based not on the economic theories of Adam Smith, Malthus and Keynes, but on more liberating economic outlooks. Schumacher's (1975) intermediate technology, for example, calls for Buddhist economics. The difference between Buddhist and Western or occidental economics is that the former tries to maximize human satisfactions by the optimal pattern of consumption, while the latter tries to maximize consumption by optimal pattern of productive effort. All this means that the pressures of living under Buddhist economies are very much less than the stresses and strains of living under the occidental models.

Besides being labor-intensive, alternative technologies aim at being simpler and easier for people with a low level of technological culture to understand and practice. The equipment involved is much cheaper and offers a low scale of production − a distinct advantage for small markets. Often obsolete or secondhand equipment embodying simpler technology is already available. Consider the case of India. Any rational strategy for development, as Reddy (1975) points out, must start from the following set of facts: 1) eighty per cent of India's population lives in the villages; 2) sixty per cent of the population has a per capita expenditure of less than one rupee per day; and 3) about twenty million people are unemployed, while about two hundred million are underemployed. All this demands a strategy based on employment generation in rural areas, a dispersal of mini-production units, and the production of inexpensive goods of the mass consumption variety. Such a strategy demands philosophy as well as techniques of the alternative technologies. The problem is that the developing countries see the whole advocacy of alternative technology as an attempt on the part of the developed world to thwart their efforts at 'modernization'. Advocates are often charged that this is only an attempt on the part of the rich to dump all their obsolete equipment on the poor.

The main factors of resistance to the spread of alternative technologies in the developing countries are their own institutions and interest groups. As we pointed out earlier, in many developing countries there is an apparent alliance between the native, occidentalized ruling elite and certain foreign interests.

This alliance exercises a stranglehold on the spread of alternative technologies. There are five basic arguments against alternative technologies. First, it is argued, if people have to learn new technologies, they might just as well learn the most modern and effective ones, as the intellectual effort involved is essentially the same. Second, the cost of a particular plant installation with alternative technologies may be low, but because of lower productivity the actual capital cost per unit produced will often be higher; hence the final cost per unit produced will also be higher. Third, the maintenance cost of secondhand and obsolete equipment is higher and their operation often needs a higher level of individual skill. Furthermore, spare parts could become unobtainable and would have to be specially made at greater cost. Fourth, only by raising productivity can employment be increased. This will bring cost and prices down and hence promote consumption and the ability to export in competition with similar products. Fifth and finally, development implies social change and dislocations are part of the process of social change. These phenomena can be taken care of by appropriate social policies and programs. Many communities are prepared to pay the price of social disruption, if necessary, to raise their standards of living as soon as possible to approximate those which they already perceive through the modern communication media.

Such criticisms overlook the fundamental basis of alternative technologies: to replace capital-intensive technologies with labor-intensive ones and to replace production-consumption oriented economies with less voracious ones. Furthermore, alternative technologies, even the very simple ones, will be new technologies derived by indigenous research and development. So, simple technologies do not always imply obsolete, imported technologies.

Alternative technologies have emerged from the realization that conventional technologies enforce a bias toward the occidental civilizations. This realization, however, is not new. Some developing countries have been complaining about the inbuilt bias in The System for many years. Their criticisms of The System have been particularly severe during the various meetings of UNCTAD.

The UNCTAD meetings   UNCTAD (United Nations Conference on Trade and Tariffs) was established to find a solution to the problem of inherent injustices in The System. Four UNCTAD conferences have been devoted to this theme. UNCTAD represents one of the efforts of the developing countries to change, by persuasion, negotiation and moral pressure, some of the structural deformities in the world economy. UNCTAD I met in Geneva in 1964. It tried to focus attention on the pricing problem of developing countries' exports in the world market. The 'rich' nations opposed these proposals and even when they were accepted by the conference, their implementation remained optional. UNCTAD II met in Delhi in 1968 and was the scene of a greater degree of confrontation between the developed countries and the developing nations. The latter organized themselves as the 'Group of 77' and prepared the 'Algiers Charter' (1967) to formulate their demands — only to have cold water poured over their efforts by the developed countries. Despite some forty resolutions and declarations at UNCTAD II, the fundamental wrongs remain unredressed and basic attitudes unchanged. UNCTAD III met at Santiago in May 1972 and UNCTAD IV met in Nairobi in March 1976; both suffered a fate similar to that of their predecessors.[3]

However, while it might be fair to say that the developed countries have lacked a readiness to see the developing countries' point of view, it must also be said that the developing countries have manifested an unnecessary spirit of confrontation and an unpreparedness to see the point of view of the developed nations (this can be seen in many of the 'Third World Bloc's' efforts in the UN). Too often such conferences become a forum for the 'international class struggle' and the rhetoric of conflict and confrontation. As such, it is hardly surprising that the four UNCTAD meetings met such an abysmal end.

Let us emphasize what we stated earlier: that time is now ripe for all sides to accept Pearson's concept of 'partnership'. Only partnership and mutual understanding and cooperation can lead the entire development debate to a more fruitful conclusion. One major tenet in all the foregoing is that the integrity of a nation's cultural heritage and institutional structure is of the essence. Development cannot be construed merely in economic terms; it carries inevitable cultural change. A major consideration in science policy for developing nations must therefore be the preservation of cultural assets. It is from such a standpoint that we have reviewed major issues in development such as foreign aid, technology transfer, problems in education and manpower, industrialization, and issues involving agriculture and land reform. Such policy recommendations as we have presumed to make on these points derive, of course, from our own normative positions which had to be added to our reviewing of the state of research. It is unfortunate that we were forced to this, but so much of the scholarly rather than political literature derives only from the narrow economic tradition and omits any systematic study of the cultural issues we have chosen to stress. Clearly we have here a desideratum for future work on developing countries in the fields of science policy studies.

---

[3] The efforts of the developing countries bore fruit, and some of their frustrations were alleviated, at the Sixth Special Session of the UN General Assembly from 9 April to 1 May 1974. This was the first session of the UN in the last twenty nine years which devoted itself exclusively to man's search for a just economic order.

BIBLIOGRAPHY

Abdoulaye, 1956 — Abdoulaye, L. Y., *Les Masses africaines et l'actuelle condition humaine,* Editions Présence Africaine, Paris, 1956.

Alatas, 1968 — Alatas, S. H., *The Sociology of Corruption,* Singapore, Donald Moore, 1968.

Alexander, 1947 — Alexander, R. J., *Labour Movements in Latin America,* London, Fabian Publication, 1947.

Allen and Smethurst, 1965 — Allen, G. R. and Smethurst, R. G., *Impact of Food Aid on Donor and Other Food Exporting Countries,* FAO, Unipub, 1965.

Almond and Coleman, 1970 — Almond, G. A. and Coleman, J. S. (Eds.), *The Politics of Developing Areas,* Princeton, Princeton University Press, 1970.

Almond and Verba, 1963 — Almond, G. A. and Verba, S., *The Civic Culture,* Princeton, Princeton University Press, 1963.

Anderson *et al.,* 1967 — Anderson, C. W. *et al.,* Issues of Political Development, New Jersey, 1967.

Apter, 1964 — Apter, D., *Ideology and Discontent,* Free Press of Glencoe, New York, 1964.

Badion, 1964 — Badion, S., *Les Dirigeants africains face à leur peuple,* Paris, F. Masparo, 1964.

Bailey, 1966 — Bailey, F., *Tribes, Castes and Nations,* Manchester, 1966.

Basalla, 1967 — Basalla, G., 'The Spread of Western Science', *Science* 156, 5 May 1967, pp. 612-621.

Bauer, 1974 — Bauer, P. T., 'Foreign Aid, Forever?' *Encounter* 42, No. 3, March 1974, pp. 15-29.

Bawany, 1970 — Bawany, E. A., *Revolutionary Strategy for National Development,* London, Paperbound Limited, 1970.

Beckerman, 1974 — Beckerman, W., *In Defence of Economic Growth,* London, Cape, 1974.

Bell, 1960 — Bell, D., *The End of Ideology,* New York, The Free Press of Glencoe, 1960.

Benjamin, 1965 — Benjamin, A. C., *Science, Technology and Human Values,* University of Missouri Press, 1965.

Bernal, 1970 — Bernal, J. D., *Science in History,* London, Penguin, 1970.

Bernard and Pelto, 1972 — Bernard, H. R. and Pelto, P. J., *Technology and Cultural Change,* London, MacMillan, 1972.

Bhatt, 1966 — Bhatt, V. V. (Ed.), *Impact of Foreign Aid on Indian Economic Development,* International Publications Service, 1966.

Binder, 1964 — Binder, L., *The Ideological Revolution in the Middle East,* New York, Wiley, 1964.

Binder *et al.,* 1965 — Binder, L. *et al.,* *Crisis and Sequences in Political Development,* Princeton, Princeton University Press, 1965.

Blackledge, 1972 — Blackledge, J. P., *The University as an Adapter of Technology in a Developing Country* (unpublished), Denver, Colorado, Denver Research Institute, University of Denver, 1972.

Bose, 1972

Boulding and Mukerjee, 1972

Braibenti and Spengler, 1961

Cardoso, 1971

Carney, 1961

Cervantes, 1970

Chowdhury, 1973

Clark, 1973

Conflict Study, 1973

Cooper, 1967

Cooper, 1973

Copeland, 1969

Crane, 1974

Davis, 1958

Deutsch, 1953

Deutsch, 1970

Dickson, 1974

Dumont, 1962

Duncanson, 1974

Edwards, 1969
Eiseman, 1974

Epstein, 1958

Ezrachi and Tal, 1973

Fanon, 1965

Bose, T. C., *The Superpowers and the Middle East,* Asia Publishing House, 1972.

Boulding, K. E. and Mukerjee, T. (Eds.), *Economic Imperialism: A Book of Readings,* University of Michigan Press, 1972.

Braibenti, R. and Spengler, J. J. (Eds.), *Traditions, Values and Socio-Economic Development,* Duke University Press, 1961.

Cardoso, F. H., *Ideologias de la Burguesia Industrial et Sociedades Dependientes (Argentina y Brazil),* Mexico, Siglo XXI editores, 1971.

Carney, D., *Government and Economy in British West Africa,* New Haven, Yale University Press, 1972.

Cervantes, J. L. C., *Superexplotacion, Dependencia y Desarrollo,* Editorial Nuestro Tiempo, Mexico, 1970.

Chowdhury, P. N., *Economics of Research and Development,* New Delhi, Peoples' Publishing House, 1973.

Clark, R., 'The Pressing Need for Alternative Technology', *Impact of Science on Society* 23, No. 4, 1973.

Conflict Study, Special Report, 'Security of the Cape Oil Route', Institute for the Study of Conflict, London, 1973.

Cooper, C., 'Science and Underdeveloped Countries', in *Problems of Science Policy,* Paris, OECD, 1967.

Cooper, C. (Ed.), *Science, Technology and Development,* London, Frank Cass, 1973.

Copeland, M., *The Game of Nations,* Allen & Unwin, London, 1969.

Crane, D., 'An Interorganisational Approach to the Development of Indigenous Technological Capabilities: Some Reflections on the Literature', Paris, OECD, Occasional Paper, No. 3, CD/TI(74)31, 1974.

Davis, H. E., *Government and Politics in Latin America,* New York, Ronald Press, 1958.

Deutsch, K. W., *Nationalism and Social Communication,* Cambridge, MIT Press, 1953.

Deutsch, K. W., *Politics and Government,* Boston, Houghton Mifflin, 1970.

Dickson, D., *Alternative Technology and Politics of Technical Change,* London, Fontana/Collins, 1974.

Dumont, R., *L'Afrique Noire est mal partie,* Paris, Edition du Seuil, 1962.

Duncanson, D. J., *Government and Revolution in Vietnam,* OUP, 1974.

Edwards, M., *Raj,* London, Pan Books, 1969.

Eiseman, T., *Impact of Foreign (US) Education on Engineering Families in India,* Bombay, 1974.

Epstein, A. L., *Politics in an Urban African Community,* Manchester University Press, 1958.

Ezrachi, Y. and Tal, E., *Science Policy and Development: The Case of Israel,* London, Gordon, 1973.

Fanon, F., *Wretched of the Earth,* London, 1965.

Fei and Goston, undated	Fei, J. C. H. and Goston, R., *Technology, Transfer, Employment and Development*, New Haven, Yale Economic Growth Center, Discussion Paper No. 71.
Frank, 1969	Frank, A. G., *Capitalism and Underdevelopment in Latin America*, London, 1969.
Frank, 1970	Frank, A. G., *Latin America: Underdevelopment or Revolution?*, London, 1970.
Fromm, 1968	Fromm, E., *The Revolution of Hope: Towards a Humanized Technology*, New York, 1968.
Fry, 1971	Fry, M. J., *Development Planning in Turkey*, Leiden, Brill, 1971.
Fuller, 1961	Fuller, J. F. C., *The Conduct of War*, London, Allen and Unwin, 1961.
Furnivall, 1948	Furnivall, J. S., *Colonial Policy and Practice*, CUP, 1948.
Furtado, 1964	Furtado, C., *Development and Underdevelopment*, University of California Press, 1964.
Geertz, 1963	Geertz, C. C. (Ed.), *Old Societies and New States*, New York, Free Press of Glencoe, 1963.
Gelinier, 1967	Gelinier, O., 'International Relations and the Competitive Economy – The Case of Underdeveloped Countries', in Gelinier, O., *The Enterprise Ethic*, London, 1967.
Gerassi, 1967	Gerassi, J., *The Great Fear in Latin America*, London, 1967.
Ginzberg, 1963	Ginzberg, E. (Ed.), *Technology and Social Change*, New York, Columbia University Press, 1963.
Golay, 1961	Golay, F. H., *The Philippines: Public Policy and National Economic Development*, Ithaca, Cornell University Press, 1961.
Goulet, 1971	Goulet, G., *The Cruel Choice*, New York, 1971.
Halpern, 1963	Halpern, M., *The Politics of Social Change in Middle East and North Africa*, Princeton, Princeton University Press, 1963.
Harper, *et al.*, 1976	Harper, P. *et al.*, *Racial Technology*, Wildwood House, London, 1976.
Harrison, 1960	Harrison, S. S., *India: The Dangerous Decades*, Princeton, Princeton University Press, 1960.
Hayami and Rutton, 1971	Hayami, Y. and Rutton, V. W., *Agriculture Development: An International Perspective*, Baltimore and London, Johns Hopkins Press, 1971.
Hayter, 1971	Hayter, T., *Aid as Imperialism*, London, Penguin, 1971.
Heady, 1966	Heady, F., *Bureaucracies in Developing Countries: Internal Roles and External Assistances*, Bloomington, 1966.
Herrera, 1972	Herrera, A., 'Social Determinants of Science Policy in Latin America', *Journal of Development Studies* 9, October 1972, pp. 19-37.
Hetman, 1973	Hetman, F., *Society and the Assessment of Technology*, Paris, OECD, 1973.
Hetzler, 1969	Hetzler, S., *Technological Growth and Social Change*, New York, Praeger, 1969.

Hunke, 1960	Hunke, S., *Allahs Sonne über dem Abendland: unser arabisches Erbe*, Stuttgart, 1960.
Huntington, 1968	Huntington, S. P., *Political Order in Changing Societies*, New Haven, Yale University Press, 1968.
Interdoc, 1973	Interdoc, *Guerilla Warfare in South East Asia*, Interdoc, 1973.
Janowitz, 1964	Janowitz, M., *The Military in the Political Development of New Nations*, University of Chicago Press, 1964.
Jenkins, 1971	Jenkins, R., *Exploitation*, London, Paladin, 1971.
Johnson, 1962	Johnson, H. G., *The Role of Military in Underdeveloped Countries*, Princeton, Princeton University Press, 1962.
Johnson, 1972	Johnson, S., *The Green Revolution*, London, Hamish Hamilton, 1972.
Johnston, 1970	Johnston, B. F., 'Agriculture and Structural Transformation in Developing Countries: A Survey of Research', *Journal of Economic Literature*, 8, No. 2, 1970, pp. 369-403.
Jolly, 1971	Jolly, R., 'The Aid Relationship; Reflections on the Pearson Report', in Ward, B. *et al.* (Eds), *The Widening Gap: Development in the 1970's*, New York, Columbia University Press, 1971.
Jones, 1971	Jones, G., *Role of Science and Technology in Developing Countries*, OUP, 1971.
Jones *et al.*, 1971	Jones, G. *et al.*, *Planning, Development and Change: A Bibliography of Development and Change*, University of Hawaii Press, 1971.
Khan, 1970	Khan, M. S., *Planning and Economic Development in India*, Asia Publishing Company, 1970.
Kipling, 1974	Kipling, R., *Complete Poetical Works of Rudyard Kipling*, London, 1974.
Kirby, 1967	Kirby, E. S., *Economic Development in East Asia*, London, Allen & Unwin, 1967.
Klatt, 1965	Klatt, W. (Ed.), *The Chinese Model*, Hong Kong, University of Hong Kong Press, 1965.
Leiserson, 1973	Leiserson, A., 'The Politics of Science: Science Politics, Science Policy, Policy Science – The Whole Thing', *Polity* 6, No. 1, Fall 1973.
Lengelle, 1972	Lengelle, M., 'Labour Productivity in Agriculture and the Balance Between the Three Main Sectors of the Economy in Developing Countries', *Revue Européenne des Sciences Sociales* 10, No. 26, 1972, pp. 223-237.
Lerner, 1968	Lerner, D., *The Passing of Traditional Society*, New York, 1968.
Lewis, 1964	Lewis, J. W., *Major Doctrines of Communist China*, New York, W. W. Norton, 1964.
Leys, 1969	Leys, C., *Politics and Change in Developing Countries: Studies in Theory and Practice of Development*, CUP, 1969.
Little, Scitowsky, and Scott, 1970	Little, I., Scitowsky, T. and Scott, M., *Industry and Trade in Some Developing Countries*, OUP, 1970.
von der Mehden, 1963	von der Mehden, F., *Religion and Nationalism in*

	South East Asia, Madison, University of Wisconsin Press, 1963.
MacKelvie, 1975	MacKelvie, J. A., Germany and the Outbreak of World War I (unpublished), 1975.
McFarlane, 1971	MacFarlane, B., 'Mao's Game Plan for China's Industrial Development', Innovation 23, August 1971.
Mendelsohn, 1973	Mendelsohn, E., 'A Human Reconstruction of Science', Boston University Journal, Spring 1973.
Merhav, 1968	Merhav, M., Technological Dependence, Monopoly and Growth, London, Pergamon, 1968.
Milton, 1972	Milton, J., Careless Technology: Ecology and International Development, London, Tom Stacey, 1972.
Mingay, 1967	Mingay, E., The Agricultural Revolution, London, Allen & Unwin, 1967.
Mintz, 1965	Mintz, J. S., Mohammed, Marx and Marhaen, New York, Praeger, 1965.
Miscond, 1964	Miscond, C. A., Tunisia: The Politics of Modernisation, New York, Praeger, 1964.
Mishan, 1970	Mishan, E. J., Technology and Growth: The Price We Pay, London, Praeger, 1970.
Montgomery and Siffin, 1966	Montgomery, J. D. and Siffin, W. J., Approaches to Development: Politics, Administration and Change, New York, 1966.
Moore, 1974	Moore, B., The Social Origin of Dictatorship and Democracy, London, Pelican, 1974.
Moravcsik, 1973	Moravcsik, M. J., 'Science and Technology in National Development Plans: Some Case Studies', US Agency for International Development, Washington, D.C. (unpublished), 1973.
Moravcsik, 1975	Moravcsik, M. J., Science Development: The Building of Science in Less Developed Countries, Indiana, International Development Research Center, Indiana University, 1975.
Morawetz, 1974	Morawetz, D., Economic Integration in Developing Countries: The Andean Group, Cambridge, Mass., MIT Press, 1974.
Moss, 1973	Moss, R., The Santiago Model, London, Institute for the Study of Conflict, Conflict Studies 31 & 32, January 1973.
Moss, 1974	Moss, R., Chile's Marxist Experiment, Halsted Press, 1974.
Mueller and Steffons, 1947	Mueller, H. N. and Steffons, H. J. (Eds.), Science, Technology and Culture, AMS Press, 1947.
Mukerjee, 1968	Mukerjee, P. K., Underdevelopment, Educational Policy and Planning, Asia Publishing House, 1968.
Mukerjee, 1974	Mukerjee, K. (Ed.), Social Sciences and Planning in India, Asia Publishing House, 1968.
Myrdal, 1968	Myrdal, G., Asian Drama: An Enquiry into the Poverty of Nations, New York, 1968.
Nader and Zahlan, 1969	Nader, C. and Zahlan, A. B., Science and Technology in Developing Countries, CUP, 1969.
Nasr, 1976	Nasr, S. H., Islamic Science, World of Islam Festival Publishing Co., London, 1976.

Nasser, 1959	Nasser, G. A., *The Philosophy of the Revolution,* Smith, Keynes and Marshall, New York, 1959.
Nettl, 1969	Nettl, J. P.., 'Strategies in the Study of Political Development', in Leys, C. (Ed.), *Politics and Change in Developing Countries.*
New Internationalist, 1976	*New Internationalist* 35, January 1976.
Niromand, 1969	Niromand, B., *Iran: The New Imperialism in Action,* New York and London, Modern Reader Paperbacks, 1969.
North, 1976	North, M. (Ed.), *Time Running Out? Best of Resurgence,* Prism Press, London, 1976.
Oppenheimer, 1974	Oppenheimer, M., *Urban Guerilla,* London, Pelican Books, 1974.
Organski, 1965	Organski, A. F. K., *Stages of Political Development,* New York, Knopf, 1965.
von Paczensky, 1971	von Paczensky, G., *Die Weissen Kommen: Die Währe Geschichte des Kolonialismus,* Hoffmann u. Campe, Hamburg, 1971.
Paradis, 1963	Paradis, K., *Technological Choice Under Development Planning,* International Publishing Service, 1963.
Pearson, 1969	Pearson, L., *Partners in Development,* New York, Praeger, 1969.
Pennoch, 1964	Pennoch, J. R. (Ed.), *Self-Government in Modernizing Nations,* New Jersey, Prentice-Hall, 1964.
Derek Price, 1970	Price, Derek de Solla, *The Nature of the Scientific Community,* New Haven, Yale University Press, 1970.
Pye and Verba, 1970	Pye, L. W. and Verba, S., *Political Culture and Political Development,* Princeton, Princeton University Press, 1970.
Pye *et al.,* 1966	Pye, L. W. *et al., Aspects of Political Change,* Little Brown, Boston, 1966.
Qubain, 1965	Qubain, F. I., *Education and Science in the Arab World,* Baltimore, Johns Hopkins Press, 1965.
Qurashi, 1975	Qurashi, I. H., *Education in Pakistan,* Royal Book Company, Karachi, 1975.
Rahman, 1972	Rahman, A., *Anatomy of Science,* Delhi, National Publishing House, 1972.
Rahman *et al.,* 1973	Rahman, A. *et al., Science and Technology in India,* Indian Council for Cultural Relations, 1973.
Rao, 1973	Rao, S. R., 'An Example for the Third World', *New Scientist* 59, 23 August, 1973, pp. 451-452.
Ravetz, 1971	Ravetz, J. R., *Scientific Knowledge and its Social Problems,* OUP, 1971.
Ray, 1970	Ray, D. M., 'The Future of Maoist Model of Development', *Asian Forum* 11, No. 2, Washington, D.C., 1970, pp. 123-135.
Reader, 1961	Reader, D. H., *The Black Man's Portion,* Cape Town, OUP, 1961.
Reddy, 1975	Reddy, A. K. N., 'Alternative Technology: A Viewpoint from India', *Social Studies of Science* 5, 1975, pp. 331-342.
Restivo and Venderpool, 1974	Restivo, S. P. and Venderpool, C. K. (Eds.), *Comparative Studies in Science and Society,* Merrill, 1974.

Rhodes, 1970   Rhodes, R. I., *Imperialism and Underdevelopment: A Reader*, New York, Monthly Review Press, 1970.

Rifkin, 1975   Rifkin, S. B., 'The Chinese Model for Science and Technology: Its Relevance for Developing Countries', *Technological Forecasting and Social Change* 7, No. 3, 1975, pp. 233-256.

Rose and Rose, 1976   Rose, H. and Rose, S., 'The Incorporation of Science' in Rose, H. and Rose, S. (Eds.), *The Political Economy of Science: Ideology in/for the Natural Science*, MacMillan, 1976.

Rosenberg, 1960   Rosenberg, N., *Capital Formation in Underdeveloped Countries*, AER, 1960.

Rosser-Owen, 1976   Rosser, Owen, D. C., *Social Change in Islam: The Progressive Dimension*, Slough, Open Press, 1976.

Rostow, 1963   Rostow, W. W., *The Stages of Economic Growth: A Non-Communist Manifesto*, CUP, 1963.

Sagasti, 1975   Sagasti, F. R., 'A Framework for the Formulation and Implementation of Technological Policies: A Case Study of ITINTEC in Peru', International Forum on Technological Development (unpublished), 1975.

Said and Simmons, 1974   Said, A. A. and Simmons, L. (Eds.), *The New Sovereigns: Multinational Corporations as World Powers*, New York, Prentice-Hall, 1974.

Sardar, 1975   Sardar, Z., 'The Quest for a New Science', *Muslim Institute Papers* 1, Slough, Open Press, 1975.

Sardar, 1976   Sardar, Z., 'Where Will We Be in the Year 2000?' *Quest: Journal of the City University*, Summer 1976.

Sardar, 1977   Sardar, Z., *Science, Technology and Development in the Muslim World*, Croom-Helm, London, 1977.

Sartre, 1967   Sartre, J.-P., *Preface to Fanon: The Condemned of the Earth*, London, 1967.

Scafeti, 1969   Scafeti, A. C., *Implications of Agricultural and Industrial Development*, Systems Development Corporation, Santa Monica, California, 1969.

Scalopino, 1976   Scalopino, R., *Asia and the Road Ahead*, University of California Press, 1976.

Schon, 1967   Schon, D., *Technology and Change, The New Heraclitos*, London, 1967.

Schumacher, 1975   Schumacher, E. F., *Small is Beautiful*, London, Abacus, 1975.

Shils, 1955   Shils, E., 'End of Ideology?', *Encounter* 52, No. 8, November 1975.

Shone, 1975   Shone, K. J., 'Management Aid in Developing Countries', *Quest: Journal of the City University*, 29 Spring 1975.

Siddiqui, 1974   Siddiqui, K., *Conflict, Crisis and War in Pakistan*, MacMillan, 1974.

Siddiqui, 1975   Siddiqui, K., *Functions of International Conflict: A Socio-Economic Study of Pakistan*, Royal Book Co., Karachi, 1975.

Stepan, 1976   Stepan, N., *Beginnings of Brazilian Science: Oswaldo Cruz, Medical Research and Policy, 1870-1920*, Science History Publications, 1976.

Subrahmanian, 1972

Sunkel and Paz, 1970

Sussex Group, 1970

Sutton, 1972

Tunaya, 1962

UN, 1963a

UN, 1963b

Venezian and Gamble, 1969

Waterston, 1966

Wellisz, 1971

Wells, 1972

Wilkinson, 1976

Wilson, 1971

Wriggins, 1960

Wu and Sheeks, 1970

Yalcintos, 1973

Zahlan, 1967

Zahlan, 1969

Zimon, 1968
Zimon, 1969

Subrahmanian, K. K., *The Flow of Capital and Technology to India,* New Delhi, Peoples' Publishing House, 1972.

Sunkel, O., and Paz, P., *El Subdesarrollo Latinoamericano y la Teoria de Desarrollo,* Mexico, Siglo XXI editores, 1970.

Sussex Group, 'Draft Introductory Statement for the World Plan of Action for the Application of Science and Technology to Development', Annex II to UN. Science and Technology for Development: Proposals for the Second UN Development Decade, New York, 1970.

Sutton, A. C., *Western Technology and the Soviet Economic Development 1930-1945,* New York, Hoover Institution, 1972.

Tunaya, T. Z., *Islamcilik Cereyani,* Istanbul, Baha Matbaasi, 1962.

UN, Department of Social Affairs, Report of the World Social Situation, New York, 1963.

UN, Science and Technology for Development, Report of the UN Conference on the Application of Science and Technology for the Benefits of the Less Developed Areas, 8 Volumes, New York, 1963.

Venezian and Gamble, *The Agriculture Development of Mexico: Its Structure and Growth Since 1950,* New York, Praeger, 1969.

Waterston, A., *Development Planning: Lessons of Experience,* OUP, 1966.

Wellisz, S., 'Lessons of Twenty Years of Planning in Developing Countries', *Economic Quarterly* 38, No. 128, May 1971.

Wells, L. T., 'Economic Man and Engineering Man: Choice of Technology in Low Wage Country', *Economic Development Report,* Autumn 1972.

Wilkinson, P., *Terrorism versus Liberal Democracy: The Problem of Response,* Institute for the Study of Conflict, London, 1976.

Wilson, G. W., *Technological Development and Economic Growth,* Indiana University Press, 1971.

Wriggins, W. H., *Ceylon: Dilemmas of a New Nation,* Princeton, Princeton University Press, 1960.

Wu, Y. L. and Sheeks, R., *The Organisation and Support of Scientific Research and Development in Mainland China,* New York, Praeger, 1970.

Yalcintos, N., Reports to Governments of FR Germany and Turkish Republic, unpublished.

Zahlan, A. B., 'Science in the Arab Middle East', unpublished.

Zahlan, A. B., 'Migrations of Scientists and the Development of Scientific Communications in the Arab World', unpublished.

Zimon, J., *Public Knowledge,* CUP, 1968.
Zimon, J., Proceedings of the Royal Society. A 311 349-369, 1969.

SUBJECT INDEX

NAME INDEX

Abelson, P., 494n
Abrahamsson, B., 458
Abramovitz, M., 244
Achilladelsis, B. A., 29, 260, 261
Adams, W., 456
Aevermann, D., 280
Agassi, J., 150, 171
Aigrain, P., 402
Alatas, S. H., 554
Albert, R. S., 282
Albertus Magnus, 551
Albright, L. E., 293n
Alexander, A. J., 454
Alford, R., 419n
Alker, Jr., H. R., 510, 511
Allen, G., 169, 178
Allen, G. R., 545
Allen, J. A., 257
Allen, Tom, 212, 226
Allison, G. T., 457, 461, 489
Allison, P. D., 103, 135, 293
Almond, G. A., 536
Altman, I., 114
Altner, P., 12n
Amann, R., 103n, 226, 256
Amelang, M., 280
Ames, E., 232, 234
Ammons, C. H., 280, 281
Ammons, R. B., 280, 281
Anderson, C. C., 281
Anderson, D. R., 281, 293n
Anderson, H., 282
Anderson, J. A., 425
Anderson, M., 473, 474n
Anderson, O. E., 363
Andrews, F. M., 278, 283, 290, 293, 297, 297n
Anthony, L. J., 109
Apter, D., 536
Aran, L., 291
Arasteh, J., 298
Arasteh, R., 298
Aristophanes, 71-72
Armocost, M. H., 457
Arnold, P., 74
Aron, 480
Arrow, K. J., 230, 413n
Art, R. J., 457, 458
Ashby, E., 473, 474n
Astin, A. W., 280, 288, 289

Astin, H. S., 295
Atwood, E., 285
Autorenkollektiv, 280n, 341, 341n, 342
Ayres, R., 427

Babcock, R., 416
Bachelard, Gaston, 152-153, 160-161, 335
Bachtold, L. M., 292
Bacon, Francis, 46, 73-74, 154, 170, 206, 211, 357, 473
Bacon, Roger, 551
Badash, L., 167
Bahr, H. D., 339, 340
Bahrdt, H. P., 291
Bailyn, B., 113
Baitsch, H., 10, 12n, 13n, 14n, 101
Baker, M., 410n
Baker, N., 213
Baker, N. R., 256
Baker, S. R., 281
Baldwin, S. E., 491
Baran, P. A., 248
Barber, B., 51, 94, 97n, 98, 106, 108, 113, 114, 119, 127, 155, 156, 282n, 296, 424
Bardos, J. P., 10, 11
Barghoorn, F. C., 479
Baritz, L., 446
Barnes, B., 22, 79, 97n, 99n, 106, 129, 150, 158, 175, 177
Barnes, S. B., 169, 285
Barnet, R. J., 456, 526
Barnett, H. G., 199
Barron, F., 293, 295
Barthélémy, C., 116, 119
Bar-Zohar, M., 476
Basalla, George, 151, 159, 162, 171, 178, 550
Basiuk, V., 480
Battelle, 203, 207
Bauer, P. T., 545
Bauer, R. A., 406, 407
Bauer, R. E., 217
Baumgart, R., 281
Baxter, J., 445, 446
Bayer, A. E., 101
Bazell, R., 448
Beaver, D., 110, 111, 112
Becker, H. S., 288

587

NOTES ON CONTRIBUTORS

Gernot Böhme was born in Dessau, Germany, in 1937. He studied mathematics, physics and philosophy in Göttingen and Hamburg and received his Ph.D. from Hamburg (1965) and his Habilitation from Munich (1973). He has been Wissenschaftler Assistent at the University of Hamburg (1965-1966) and at the University of Heidelberg (1966-1969), and Wissenschaftlicher Mitarbeiter at the Max-Planck-Institut zur Erforschung der Lebensbedingungen der wissenschaftlich-technischen Welt in Starnberg since 1969. His books include *Über die Zeitmodi* (Vandenhoeck & Ruprecht, 1966), *Zeit und Zahl* (Klostermann, 1974) and (Ed.) *Protophysik* (Suhrkamp, 1976).

Rudolf Fisch was born in 1939 in Hagen, Westphalia, West Germany. After his early studies in physics and psychology in Frankfurt, Münster and Bochum, he received his diploma in psychology from Münster (1964), his Dr.Phil. from Bochum (1967) and his Habilitation from the University of Saarbrücken (1972). He taught at the University of Bochum, the University of Düsseldorf and the University of Saarbrücken, became Professor for Social Psychology at the University of Konstanz in 1974, and is now Dean of the Faculty of Social Sciences at that university. His field of interest includes studies in motivation, conflict and cooperation, social psychological analyses of science organization at the university level, and psychology of the scientist. He has published *Konfliktmotivation und Examen* (Meisenheim, Hain, 1970) and has in press *Motivation und die Arbeit des Wissenschaftlers.*

Christopher Freeman was born in the United Kingdom in 1921 and received his B.Sc. in economics from the London School of Economics with its first class in 1948. He has been a Senior Research Officer at the National Institute of Economic and Social Research, London, and is now Director of the Science Policy Research Unit at the University of Sussex and R. M. Phillips Professor of Science Policy at that institution. Among his many publications is a major book, *The Economics of Industrial Innovation* (Penguin, 1974).

Sanford A. Lakoff was born in 1931 in Bayonne, New Jersey, USA. He received a B.A. (1953) from Brandeis University and an M.A. (1955) and Ph.D. (1959) in political science from Harvard University. He has taught at Harvard, the State University of New York at Stony Brook and the University of Toronto. He is currently professor of political science and chairman of the department at the University of California at San Diego. He is co-author with J. S. Dupré of *Science and the Nation: Policy and Politics* (1962) and author of *Equality in Political Philosophy* (1964) and has served as editor/contributor of *Knowledge and Power: Essays on Science and Government* (1966); in addition he has edited (with M. Cranston) *A Glossary of Political Ideas* (1969), and (with D. Rich) *Private Government: Introductory Readings* (1973). His writings on science policy studies have also appeared in *Minerva, Political Science Quarterly* and *Science.*

Edwin T. Layton, Jr., was born in Los Angeles, California, USA, in 1928. He received his B.A. (1950), M.A. (1953) and Ph.D. (1955) in history from UCLA. He has taught at the University of Wisconsin, Ohio State University, Purdue University and Case Western Reserve University. He is currently professor of the history of technology at the University of Minnesota. He is the author of three books and several journal articles and numerous short articles and reviews. His book, *The Revolt of the Engineers, Social Responsibility and the American Engineering Profession* (Case Western University Press, 1971), won the Dexter Prize of the Society for the History of Technology. The research for this book produced a lasting interest in the policy implications of technology, an interest which found expression in a graduate course at Case Western Reserve University in technology and public policy. He has been active in the Society for the History of Technology, having been on the executive board and the editorial board; since 1972 he has been chairman of the committee on honors for this organization.

Roy MacLeod was born in 1941 in the USA and educated at Harvard (B.A., 1963) and Cambridge (Ph.D., 1967). His undergraduate background was in the biochemical sciences, intellectual history and the history of scientific ideas, while his graduate work was in administrative history, social and economic history and sociology. Following four years as a Research Fellow of Churchill College, Cambridge, and a Research Fellow of the Science Policy Research Unit of the University of Sussex, he was in 1970 appointed to his present position as Reader in the History and Social Studies of Science at the University of Sussex. He has been a visiting professor at Indiana University (1969) at the Ecole Pratique des Hautes Etudes (1970-1971 and 1973) and at the Free University of Amsterdam (1973-1974). His published work has been chiefly in the historical sociology of science and medicine; in the history of science in its relations to economics and government; and in the historical relations of expertise and bureaucracy in modern industrial states.

Michael Mulkay was born in London in 1936. He received his first degree, in sociology, from the London School of Economics in 1965. Since then he has received an M.A. from Simon Fraser University, British Columbia, and a Ph.D. from the University of Aberdeen. He has held lectureships in sociology at both of these universities, as well as the position of Assistant Director of Research at the University of Cambridge from 1970-1973. He is at present

Reader in Sociology at the University of York, England. He has published three books: *Functionalism, Exchange and Theoretical Strategy* (Routledge, 1971), *The Social Process of Innovation* (Macmillan, 1972) and (with D. O. Edge) *Astronomy Transformed* (Wiley Interscience, 1976).

Dorothy Nelkin was born in 1933 in Boston, Massachusetts, USA. She received a B.A. in philosophy from Cornell University in 1954 and worked for many years of the adaptive behavior of marginal groups, focusing on migrant farm workers in the United States. She is associate professor at Cornell University, jointly in the Program on Science, Technology and Society and the Department of City and Regional Planning. Since 1970 she has worked on various social and political dimensions of science and technology. Her books include *Migrant, Nuclear Power and Its Critics, The Politics of Housing Innovation, Methadone Maintenance – A Technological Fix, The University and Military Research, Jetport,* and *Science Textbook Controversies and the Politics of Equal Time.*

Derek de Solla Price was born in London, England, in 1922. He received a B.Sc. from the University of London (1942), a Ph.D. in physics from the University of London (1946), a Ph.D. in history of science from the University of Cambridge (1954) and an honorary M.A. from Yale University (1960). He is Avalon Professor of the History of Science at Yale University. In 1946 he first wrote on the exponential growth of science and has since continued this statistical investigation toward more extensive studies relating to science policy. In 1971 when the International Council for Science Policy Studies was founded he became its first president. He has published about two hundred scientific papers and six books, including *Science Since Babylon* (Yale University Press, 1961, Enlarged Edition, 1975), *Little Science, Big Science* (Columbia University Press, 1963) and *Gears From the Greeks: The Antikythera Mechanism – A Calendar Computer From ca. 80 B.C.* (Science History Publications, 1975; American Philosophical Society Transactions, 1975).

Jerome Raymond Ravetz was born in 1929 in Philadelphia, Pennsylvania, USA. He received his B.A. (1950) from Swarthmore College and his Ph.D. in mathematics from Trinity College, Cambridge (1954). After teaching mathematics at Pennsylvania and at Durham, England, he went on a Leverhulme Research Fellowship in the history and philosophy of science to the University of Leeds in 1957, where he has since been Lecturer, Senior Lecturer and Reader. He has been a visiting professor at Utrecht in the History of the Exact Sciences. Since 1973 he has been part-time Executive Secretary of the Council for Science and Society in London. He has published articles on the history of the exact sciences and on Francis Bacon. In 1965 he published a short monograph on Copernicus and, in 1971, his major book, *Scientific Knowledge and Its Social Problems* (Oxford University Press; Penguin, 1973).

Dawud G. Rosser-Owen, born in 1943 in South Wales, read political science at the University of Kent at Canterbury. A Research Fellow at the Muslim Institute, London, his prime area of research concerns the social implications of science and technology, with special interest in the social and political development of Southeast Asia. He is a Sufi Shaikh of the Naqshbandi *Tariga*.

Jean-Jacques Salomon was born in 1929 in France and has been head of the Science Policy Division of the Organisation for Economic Cooperation and Development since 1966 and professor of science policy at the Conservatoire National des Arts et Métiers, Paris since 1972. He received his Licence ès Lettres in philosophy (1953), a Certificat d'Ethnologies Sciences (1954) and a Doctorat ès Lettres in philosophy (1970) from the Sorbonne, Paris. He has been president of the International Council for Science Policy Studies since 1974. Among his many publications dealing with science policy are *Science and Politics* (Seuil, 1970; Macmillan and MIT Press, 1973); (Ed.) *The Research System,* Vols. I, II and III (OECD, 1972, 1973, 1974); and *International Scientific Organisations* (OECD, 1965).

Harvey M. Sapolsky was born in 1939 in Haverhill, Massachusetts, USA. He received a B.A. in government from Boston University in 1961, an M.P.A. in 1963 and a Ph.D. in political economy and government in 1967, both from Harvard University. He was appointed Assistant Professor of Political Science in 1966 and Associate Professor of Political Science in 1970 at the Massachusetts Institute of Technology. Among his major publications are *The Polaris System Development* (Harvard University Press, 1972) and the 'Science Policy' chapter in *Handbook of Political Science* (F. Greenstein and N. Polsby, Eds., Addison-Wesley, 1975). In addition to science policy his research interests include bureaucratic politics and health policy.

Ziauddin Sardar, born in 1951 in Northern Pakistan, read physics and then information science at the City University, London. A Research Fellow of the Muslim Institute, London, he is the author of *Science, Technology and Development in the Muslim World* (Croom Helm, 1977) and *The Destiny Beyond* (Open Press, 1977). He is at the Hajj Research Centre, King Abdul Aziz University, Jeddah, Saudi Arabia.

Brigitte Schroeder-Gudehus was born in Blankenburg, Germany, in 1931. She received her Licence ès Sciences Politiques at the University of Lausanne (1958) and her Doctorat ès Sciences Politiques from the University of Geneva, Graduate Institute of International Studies (1966). Since 1966 she has been at the University of Montreal, first teaching international relations in the Department of Political Science and, since 1973, as a professor at the Institut d'histoire et de sociopolitique des sciences. From 1971-1972 she was a science adviser of the Science Council of Canada. Her publications include

Les savants dans la vie internationale (in collaboration with Jean Meynaud, Lausanne, 1962), *Deutsche Wissenschaft und internationale Zusammenarbeit 1914-1918* (Geneva, 1966), 'The Argument for the Self-Government and Public Support of Science in Weimar Germany' (*Minerva* 10, 1972) and 'La coopération scientifique bilatérale' (*Etudes internationales* 5, 1974); *Les scientifiques et la paix,* a study on the politics of international scientific cooperation, in press.

Eugene B. Skolnikoff was born in 1928 in Philadelphia, Pennsylvania. He received an S.M. and S.B. (1950) in electrical engineering from MIT, an M.A. and B.A. (1952) in politics, philosophy and economics from Oxford while studying on a Rhodes Scholarship, and a Ph.D. (1965) in political science from MIT. After a variety of posts, including five years on the White House Staff of the President's Special Assistant for Science and Technology, he returned to MIT. Since then, he has served as Chairman of the Department of Political Science from 1970-1974, and became Director of the Center for International Studies at MIT in 1972. He has been a consultant to government departments and international organizations, holds diversified posts in professional societies, and was instrumental in the development of the science and public policy field in universities in the United States and abroad. He has focused his research and teaching interests in the field of science and public policy, especially the interaction of science and technology with international affairs. His research publications include *Science, Technology and American Foreign Policy, The International Imperatives of Technology* and numerous articles.

Ina Spiegel-Rösing, born in Breslau, Poland, in 1942, has been educated at the Free University of Berlin, Harvard University and Duke University. She received her Diploma in psychology at the Free University, Berlin, her Ph.D. in psychology at the Ruhr Universität, Bochum, and her Habilitation in the sociology of science at the University of Konstanz. She is currently professor for Wissenschaftsforschung (social studies of science) at the University of Ulm. Her major book publications include: *Gleichgewichtstendenz und Selbstaufwertungshypothese. Beitrag zur Selbstkritik des sozialpsychologischen Forschungsprozesses (Consistency and Self-Enhancement: Contribution to the Self-Critique of the Social Psychological Research Process,* 1971); *Wissenschaftsentwicklung und Wissenschaftssteuerung. Einführung und Material zur Wissenschaftsforschung (Development and Control of Science,* 1973); *Memorandum zur Förderung der Wissenschaftsforchung (A Memorandum on the Advancement of the Social Studies of Science,* 1973); and *Beiträge zur Messung von Forschungsleistung. Institutionen, Gruppen, Einzelpersonen (Contributions to the Measurement of Research Achievement: Institutions, Groups, Individuals,* with H. Baitsch and P. Fauser, 1975).